The History of
CHARLTON ATHLETIC
Valley of Tears
Valley of Joy

The History of
CHARLTON
ATHLETIC

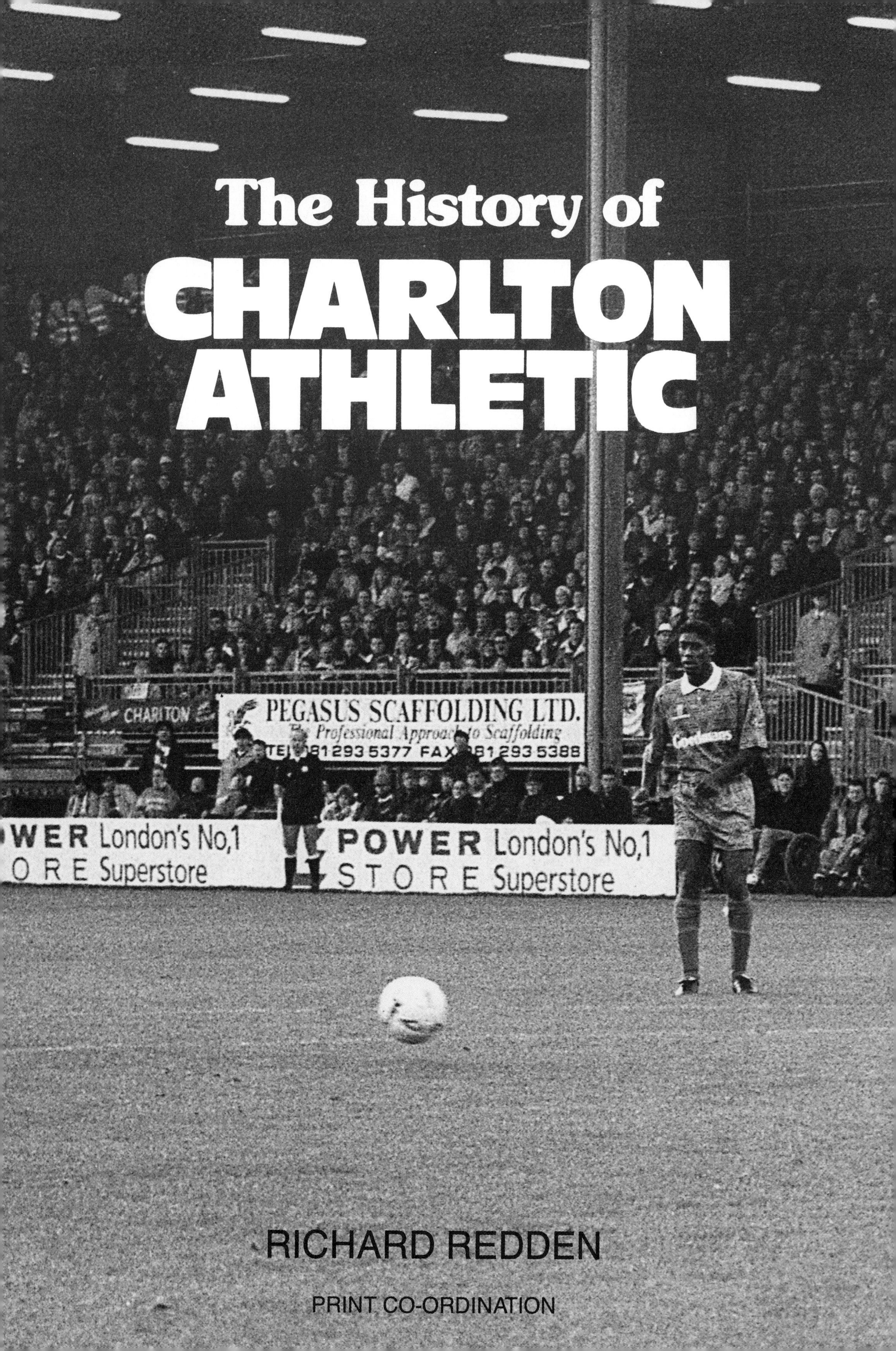

PEGASUS SCAFFOLDING LTD.
The Professional Approach to Scaffolding
TEL 081 293 5377 FAX 081 293 5388

CHARLTON

WER London's No.1
ORE Superstore

POWER London's No,1
STORE Superstore

RICHARD REDDEN

PRINT CO-ORDINATION

Preceding pages:

The Valley in 1974 – aerial picture by Mike Loveridge.

Colin Walsh scores the first goal at The Valley for seven years.

Above: Going home. The scene at Woolwich Town Hall after the club finally won planning permission for the new Valley on April 2, 1991.

First published 1990   Second Edition 1993
Reprinted 1991   © Richard Redden 1993

Contents

ISBN 0 9522652 0 6

Published by Print Co-ordination, London SE1 5TE
Printed by Butler and Tanner Limited, Frome, Somerset

Author's note and acknowledgements

THIS is the revised version of my club history The Story of Charlton Athletic 1905-1990, updated to take in the momentous events leading up to and including the return to The Valley.

The earlier book was published at one of the lowest points in the club's fortunes after its first planning application to return to The Valley had been rejected.

It was a time of deep emotion among the fans and the book seemed to catch and symbolise that emotion. It rapidly sold out two editions, the demand far far exceeding my wildest expectations when I first began to write it.

But I had always intended that book to mark the return to The Valley. So it was a history without an end.

Now I have been able to add that ending – to finish the story as I had longed for it to be finished.

I am only sorry it has taken so long. This was because of severe contractual problems over the previous book that I had not anticipated.

I am grateful to Herbert Snijder of Print Co-ordination for bringing out this book and to Charlton Athletic Football Club for stepping in to resolve those problems on my behalf and so make this book possible.

I likewise want to renew my tributes to all those who helped me in the first edition of the book, to all those who have helped me again in this edition, and to those who have helped me for the first time in this book.

Besides Herbert Snijder, my greatest debt goes to Tom Morris, whose magnificent photographs of modern times made the first edition such a success. Tom has provided many of the new photographs in this edition.

My other huge debt is to the club programme statisticians Michael Whelan and John Farrell for the immense and unselfish help they gave me in compiling statistics and for the way they were always on call to allow me to tap their own vast knowledge of the club.

I would like to thank Samantha Howatson and Brian Aldrich for use too of their fine photographs of The Valley return and to Mike Loveridge for permission to use his superb and wonderful nostalgic photograph of The Valley in 1974, with its magnificent views of the East and South Terraces which are now just a memory.

I would like to thank Don Curnick especially for his careful and conscientious copying of old photographs and to Roger Ford for further photographic advice and help.

I was also delighted when Roy King was appointed to the post of Stadium Manager to the new Valley as he also was immensely helpful in providing detailed historical help.

I would also like to pay tribute to two former players, George Green and Peter Croker, who guided me through the earlier history of the club – and to George's wife Connie for her patience and hospitality.

I must also say a particular thank you for help to that old stalwart of the club John Yarnton, a man held in much affection as the press steward on match days. This 'thank you' is made more poignant by the death of John's wife, Barbara, just two months after The Valley return.

Barbara was the cook at the club's training ground and like John a much loved person around the club.

In revising this book, I have made extensive use not only of club material but also of the Mercury newspaper. Words cannot describe the contribution the Mercury made in keeping the Charlton flag flying in the club's home district during the long years of exile.

Lesser papers might not have bothered with a club that had departed the district. The Mercury not only cared – it campaigned. Without it, Charlton may never have enjoyed the volume of support needed to make the difficult journey of return.

My thanks go to the Sports Editor, Peter Cordwell, and to Mercury reporter Rick Everitt, also a valuable help in his other role as editor of the Voice of The Valley fanzine.

This history has also drawn on heavily for its earlier historical detail on the late and fondly remembered Kentish Independent which so faithfully reported the club's affairs from Charlton's foundation in 1905 until the paper's demise in the 1980s.

I especially acknowledge the excellent reporting of Peter Burrowes, the sports editor of the Independent, particularly on the troubles of 1983 and 1984. His service to the club and deep commitment to it continue in his role of press officer.

Other newspaper sources used were the Kentish Times, Evening Standard, The Guardian, and The Times.

I was delighted that the success of my first book – after a barren Charlton spell of over 30 years without any club literature – led on to the publication of three more books about Charlton which wonderfully compensated for all those barren years.

They were all books which complemented this one by covering different ground. Colin Cameron's two books must be about the most impressive statistical books of any club anywhere in world football.

His Valiant 500 published in 1991 listed the details of every player in Charlton's League history. Colin followed that up in 1992 by a truly monumental work, listing details of every first class game ever played by the club, Home and Away with Charlton Athletic 1920-1992.

Rick Everitt's Battle for The Valley in 1991 looked in expert depth at The Valley itself, its history and the fight to secure Charlton's return.

Before these books and mine, only two books have given any detailed historical account of Charlton – Jimmy Seed's autobiography and a soft-covered booklet written by Anthony Bristowe in 1949.

I drew on them particularly for the earlier part of this work, but was unable to establish whether any copyright still existed as the publishers were defunct, although the Copyright Receipt Office of The British Library were extremely helpful. If that copyright does still exist with any other firms, then I make full acknowledgement of the invaluable use made of these two books.

I am also grateful to other authors and publishing firms for permission to use extracts of their books. I am grateful to Simon Inglis, Bryon Butler and Tony Pawson, not only for granting permission to use material but also for their generosity of response and warm welcome of the fact that a history of Charlton was being written.

I am also grateful for the similar generosity shown by Queen Anne Press, Macdonald, for permission to use material from that excellent and authoritative work on wartime football, Soccer at War by Jack Rollin. I am also grateful to Pelham Books for permission to quote from Alan Mullery's very lively autobiography.

Libraries used were the Greenwich Local History Library, the Lewisham Local History Library, The Guildhall Library and the British Newspaper Library. I am particularly grateful to the staffs of the Greenwich and Lewisham libraries which I used intensively. They were always attentive and helpful. Other photographs were supplied by Hulton Picture Library and Sport & General Ltd.

I would like to thank the many others who helped me at stages in the book: Joe Merryweather, son of an original committee member, who provided valuable information on the pre-World War One period; Andy Solomon for historical help; Charlie Hall, player, trainer and physiotherapist with the club for helping with picture identification; Bill Jenner who did such heroics in fundraising for the club as a supporter and later a director; Steve Sutherland, the club's former commercial manager, and now marketing executive for the Football League; Paul Watts, Paul Cruickshank; John Baxter; Roy Gallagher; Gordon Ducker, Chris Ritchie; Wes Whitehouse; Bob Bridge; John Coxon and Jan Ciolek.

My son, James, and daughter Katherine, both fans themselves, helped greatly with proof-reading the statistics.

But last and by no means least, I would warmly like to thank the club staff and directors for their help in bringing out this new edition, and in particular chairman Roger Alwen and club secretary Chris Parkes for checking vital details.

I would stress, however, that all opinions in the book are mine and not the club's and that I alone am responsible for any errors that may have unwittingly occurred in this revision.

Richard Redden,
West Wickham,
Kent.
October 1993.

Never a More Unusual Club

RARELY can a football club have seen such a day of joy as Charlton's return to The Valley after seven long years of exile.

One of the most famous grounds in the country had lain silent and derelict, its pitch and terraces overgrown with wild grass, trees and bushes, its buildings forlorn and decaying.

Now a bright winter's day cast its sunshine on a new Valley of life and happiness, on a day full of emotion.

It was day of sweet and fond memory of past heroes, of Sam Bartram, surely the most remarkable goalkeeper ever, Don Welsh, captain extraordinary, Johnny Summers, that fearless tank of a forward who died so tragically of cancer while still a player, those two supreme forward talents, Eddie Firmanl and Stuart Leary, that rampaging pirate of a goal scorer, Derek Hales.

It was a day so completely in the tradition of the eventful and bitter sweet history of Charlton Athletic.

There have been more famous clubs than Charlton Athletic and there have been more successful clubs, although Charlton have fleetingly had their share of fame and fortune. But there has never been a more unusual and distinctive club than Charlton Athletic.

They were the first club to rise from the old Third to First Division in successive seasons, finishing runners-up in their first season in the top flight.

They staged the greatest-ever recovery in a game in the history of League football, pulling back from a four-goal deficit – and with only ten men – to record a 7-6 victory over Huddersfield Town in 1957.

They featured in the joint highest scoring draw in League history – 6-6 at home to Middlesbrough in 1960.

They were the first club to use a substitute in League football.

They were the first club in modern times to retain a place in the top flight through play-offs.

They were the first club in peacetime to give up a home and share a ground.

And for a time, Charlton's beloved stadium, The Valley, had the biggest capacity in the League.

But the real tragedy of the club is that Charlton Athletic could have been permanently among the giants of English football. In the boom of post-war soccer, Charlton were amongst the leaders with huge crowds averaging over 40,000.

But the money generated was not reinvested, in either players or stadium, to ensure that the club's greatness of that time became permanent – in the way that Arsenal and Tottenham Hotspur became great clubs.

With the boom of the 1940s over, the decline slowly began and with relegation from the First Division

in 1957, that decline was ultimately to turn into catastrophe.

The trauma of the near-closure of the club and then the loss of their historic home, The Valley, left Charlton with only a core support of fans.

But the years of exile and the depth of the club's troubles had a deeply saving grace. Out of adversity came a new spirit which reinvigorated the club and which bound it together, from fan to director, in a way missing at many bigger and more impersonal clubs.

It was this sense of identity that propelled the fans on, never to give up hope of return to The Valley, while ever the stadium physically remained.

It was a spirit which united fans of all ages. The younger fans cared as much for The Valley as the older fans with their years of memories.

It was the emergence of a new and spirited younger generation to take on The Valley fight that ultimately led to success.

The club was fortunate in its fightback from exile that the campaigning spirit of its fans was matched by the right men appearing on the board who were themselves genuine fans.

It was equally unfortunate in that the present board, or their like, did not appear earlier in its history.

Then their energy and talents would surely have restored Charlton Athletic Football Club to its leading position of old, rather than being spent on a financially exhausting rescue operation which inevitably drained away the strength of the club on the football field itself.

The spiritual home to which the fans returned on December 5, 1992, was a very different physical home – made so by the years of dereliction and the need to fulfill modern safety requirements.

Gone were the vast terraces that made the Valley so memorable and the remains of the old giant East Terrace now stood empty and desolate with a vast metal scaffolding scar across it – a passageway for fire engine access and for fans to the revived Jimmy Seed stand.

No more was The Valley The Valley of The Guardian leader column's fond description at the time of the exile to Selhurst:

'The Valley, for good or ill, is utterly different. A great natural bowl. Stand on the top of the East Terrace and, even if the football gladiators far below are having a bad day, the panorama across dockland is one of the great sights of London. There's a sense of history in the higgledy-piggledy mix of spare acres, 50-year-old stands and the goals that Sam Bartram once defended. When the sun shines, it's one of the most endearing grounds in the country; when a storm crackles over the Thames, you watch the Twilight of the Gods from a natural balcony.'

That Valley had gone for ever.

I dedicate this history to:

To the memory of all those Charlton fans who died in the years of exile and who never lived to see the homecoming, including my late friend, Len Thomas.

To Alice, my granddaughter, born just a month before the homecoming to make 1992 a happy year indeed, in the fond hope that she, like my sons and daughter, will be a Charlton fan.

The Rise of the New Reds

IT is to another club — Arsenal — that Charlton Athletic really owe their existence as a Football League team, for the area in which Charlton were born as an amateur club, at the start of this century, was Arsenal's domain.

Between 1886 and 1913, Arsenal were the Woolwich club and played in the district. They were founded as a team from workers at the famous military workshop, Woolwich Arsenal, and were first known as Dial Square FC, after a landmark within the vast ordnance factory. The name was changed to Royal Arsenal and then to Woolwich Arsenal. Their ground was at Manor Field, Plumstead, two miles to the east of Charlton.

Woolwich Arsenal were the first Southern team to play in the Football League, being elected to the Second Division in 1893. Until the turn of the century, the club was still run by men connected with the arsenal at Woolwich. But then, as financial pressures built up, this strong local link began to weaken. The club fell into the ownership of a wealthy estate agent and property developer, Henry Norris, who, in 1913, uprooted it, lock, stock and barrel, to Islington in faraway North London, a move as traumatic to local fans as Charlton Athletic's modern move in the other direction across London.

Of this distinctive area of Thames-side London, one might paraphrase Oscar Wilde's famous saying: "To lose one football club may be regarded as a misfortune; to lose both looks like carelessness."

Woolwich Arsenal's move left a gaping hole in the South London football scene. The only nearby club was Millwall Athletic — they dropped 'Athletic' in 1925 — of the Southern League, who played at North Greenwich from 1901 before moving to The Den, in New Cross in the Lewisham area, in 1910. Into that gap came Charlton Athletic.

Charlton was a village just south of the river, between the Greenwich and Woolwich areas. Now it is a part of urban London in the London Borough of Greenwich, which incorporates both Greenwich and Woolwich. The area is full of history, nestling along the south shore of the Thames to the east of London, as the great river broadens itself ready for its final march to the sea.

Just a short distance from Charlton, to the west, is the old Greenwich Observatory and park and the Royal Naval College. And Charlton boasts one of the best preserved of Jacobean houses — Charlton House — now used as a community centre by the council. Near the bottom of the hill from Charlton

House sits The Valley, the home of Charlton Athletic from 1919 to 1985 with one short break. And a short walk further and you come to the banks of the Thames, near the Anchor & Hope pub and the modern Thames Barrier.

Cradle of Rugby

IN sporting terms, the area was not just the cradle of the Arsenal and Charlton Athletic. It was also the cradle of Rugby Union. Football in the area, before the barrier between rugby and association codes arose, began with the founding of the Blackheath Club in 1857. Blackheath, along with two other local football clubs, Blackheath School and Perceval House (Blackheath), were three of the 11 London and suburban clubs who met on 26 October 1863, at the Freemason's Tavern in Lincoln's Inn Fields, to found the Football Association.

At that time, football was moving away from the 'catch and run' rugby type of game towards a dribbling game. And of those founding clubs, only Blackheath were committed to the 'catch and run' game. Meetings were held by the founding members to try to amalgamate the best elements of both types of game, but they foundered on irreconcilable differences and things came to a head on 8 December 1863, when Blackheath withdrew from the FA.

Around the Blackheath club and its view of what football should be, there developed the distinctive Rugby Union game, although the RU body itself was not established until 1871. Had Blackheath stayed in the Football Association, perhaps there would have been no need for an Arsenal or a Charlton Athletic to arise in the area. Of such twists of fortune is history formed — sporting as well as otherwise.

The Beginning

CHARLTON Athletic Football Club was founded in 1905, from teenage boys living in Victorian-built streets close to the Thames, centred on West Street, East Street and Harden's Manorway. The boys, tired of street kickabouts, decided at a meeting in West Street one fine summer evening to form an organized team for the following season. The date was 9 June.

The area lies today between the Woolwich Road and the Thames Barrier. Most of the houses have disappeared, to be replaced by industrial and warehouse buildings. East Street has been renamed Eastmoor Street and West Street is now Westmoor Street.

There is some confusion as to the exact origins

of the club. The cause is the handbook published by Charles Cooper in 1946 and erroneously called *History and High Lights of Charlton Athletic FC (1903-1946)*. It states that the club had their origins in a team named Charlton Reds, originally known as East Street Mission and then Blundell Mission.

This is almost certainly an error. Charlton Reds were a separate club and newspaper reports of the period clearly have both Charlton Athletic and Charlton Reds playing as separate teams. Nor is there any reference to Charlton Reds in early pre-World War Two club handbooks.

The name Charlton Athletic appears for the first time in the *Kentish Independent* and the *Woolwich Pioneer* newspapers after the beginning of the 1905-06 season. The first reference to the club in the *Independent* was an appeal for friendly fixtures on 27 October — at that time the newspaper carried lists of appeals by teams for matches. The Charlton Athletic team was described as having an average age of 15½ and being of medium strength.

The address of the secretary was given as J.Mackenzie, of 5 York Street, Charlton. This was Jim Mackenzie.

To make the confusion over the origins worse, another club also started at that time with the name Charlton Athletic but quickly changed its name to Grove Athletic in November 1905. They appear to have had an even younger team.

Because of the name confusion, the first definite account of a Charlton Athletic game can only be ascribed to a *Kentish Independent* report of 22 December 1905, on the game against Silvertown Wesley.

The report read: 'Silvertown Wesley met with yet another reverse on Saturday last, being defeated by Charlton Athletic at Charlton. Wesley were outclassed in every department with the exception of Kersley, the goalkeeper, who played a magnificent match throughout.' Irritatingly, the paper gave no score.

The error over Charlton Reds was cleared up in the club's 1955 jubilee handbook, which reported direct testimony from the original players. But the error irritatingly reappeared in the 1971 handbook, which commemorated 50 years in the Football League. The author had obviously simply reproduced the 1946 account.

In fact, in those Edwardian years there were many teams with the name of Charlton — Charlton Albion, Charlton Villa, Charlton Invicta, Charlton United, Charlton Clarion, Charlton Wesley Guild, Charlton Amateurs, Charlton Victoria, Charlton YMCA, Charlton Clarence, Charlton Argyle and Charlton Reds.

First Home

SIEMEN'S Meadow, where the youngsters played their home games, was at the back of the Derby Arms (now a club called 'Forty's'), a piece of rough ground almost on the banks of the River Thames, next to the Royal Dockyard at Woolwich. Siemens Road still exists, a small road near the Woolwich Road and about half a mile from The Valley.

'Meadow' was something of a misnomer. It was a piece of waste land with hardly a blade of grass, more commonly known as the 'Brickfield' and a spot for dumping rubbish. Today, industrial buildings in Harrington Way cover the 'Meadow'.

The boys' first purchase was a football, raised by each of them contributing threepence. The colours of red and white were chosen and red flannelette shirts were home-made out of material from a drapery store in Hare Street, Woolwich.

The boys were so short of money that at first they bought only goal-posts without the crossbar, putting tapes across the top. The posts were stored at the rear of a shop in East Street.

The first dressing-room was at the rear of a cook-shop in Frances Street — Ogilby Hill as it was called in those days. The first headquarters was The Crown pub in East Street, demolished by a direct hit from a German bomb during World War Two. The licensee, Harry Wells, became the club's first president.

During the first season, the organization of the team advanced so much that it affiliated to the London Football Association. The first captain was goalkeeper W.'Bodger' King and the vice-captain Eddie Marshall, the centre-half. Other personalities of the early team included Arthur Ellis, who took over in goal but who later played frequently at full-back or half-back, Bill 'Porky' Bonner at outside-right, Jimmy Keyes at inside-forward, Jack Sudds at left-half, Albert 'Mosky' Mills at outside-left and Alf Booth at centre-forward.

'Mosky' Mills — first name Albert — was an early addition to the founding team. He joined Charlton after playing against them for Crescent United. Mills was a player who both scored goals and made them for others and he went on to gain representative honours with the London FA in the 1911-12 season, along with full-back Bob Smith. Mills was seriously injured in World War One, but recovered to play for Charlton again and appeared in two games in the club's first season in the Football League.

Eddie Marshall, like Mills, was a major personality in the club and was to continue playing for Charlton after the war. His was to be a leading voice in the fight by some club members against professionalism. His father was a strong supporter of the side and his elder brother, Fred 'Snowy' Marshall, also went on to play in the team at centre-forward.

The last surviving member of the original committee of 1905 was Joe Merryweather, who died in 1977 at the age of 95. His son, also Joe, keeps up the tradition of support and is a match-day steward at Selhurst Park. The last surviving player was Arthur Ellis, who died at Welling on 21 December 1966, at the age of 76.

The season 1906-07 marked the team's entry into league football in the form of the Lewisham League, Third Division. Jim Mackenzie continued as secretary with Harry Hughes as his assistant, W.'Bodger' King remained as captain and Eddie Marshall as vice-captain.

They started the season with friendlies and won their first match, 4-0 against Braby's Ironworks, who protested at the state of the 'Meadow' pitch. On 22 September, the team travelled to Nunhead to play Nunhead Swifts Reserves in their first league match. According to the *Lewisham Borough News*, Charlton were 4-0 up at half-time and won 6-1. It was to prove the forerunner of a highly successful season.

The team for the opening Lewisham League game was: King; Mitchell, Wilson, Silcox, Marshall, Sudds, Bonner, Thomas, Jarvis, Lines, Mills. The scorers were Bonner, Marshall, Mills (two) and Lines (two).

Full-back Johnny Mitchell was, like Mills, to feature in Charlton's opening Football League season. His brother, Albert, a forward who later came into the side, went on to play one game in the first Football League season.

Promotion Decider

THE crucial game in that first Lewisham League season was the penultimate one — on Saturday 2 March 1907 — against promotion rivals Millwall Rangers. Charlton beat Rangers 7-1 to top their division and clinch promotion to the Second Division. The 12 players who were photographed at the end of the season as the title-winning team were: W.Wilson; W.Higgs, W.King (captain), J.Sudds, J.Mitchell, A.Buckenham, W.Bonner, W.Pirie, E.Marshall, C.Broom, A.Mills and A.Thomas.

Charlton finished top with 35 points (17 wins, one draw) from 18 games, with Millwall Rangers runners-up (31 points from 18 games). In fact, Charlton lost their final game, against Fossdene Old Boys Reserves, but the match was awarded to them because the Old Boys had fielded ineligible players.

Other opponents in Charlton's first-ever season of competitive football were St John's Lads Institute, Braby's Reserves, Brockley Invicta, Nunhead Swifts, West Greenwich Lads Institute, Alberton United and Dartmouth Athletic Reserves.

The championship decider against Millwall Rangers was to prove the last match Charlton were to play at Siemen's Meadow. The 'Meadow' was an obviously unsatisfactory ground for an increasingly successful team and to cap the poor conditions endured during the season, the pitch got a covering

Charlton's first-ever team — the youngsters of the 1905-06 season.

just before the last game there — the owners started dumping rubbish in the middle of it.

The players spent an evening moving the rubbish behind the goal-posts. But it happened again the next day and the club had to strike a bargain with the foreman of the gang for the rubbish to be dumped on the non-playing part of the Meadow until after the match.

The following season the club decided to make do with a pitch on Woolwich Common. Later on, when Siemen's factory was built on the Meadow, the dry-cell shop occupied the site of the original pitch.

The club's second home, Woolwich Common, remains an open space today, south-east of The Valley, off the Shooters Hill Road. At the Woolwich Common ground, the players had to cart the goal-posts a mile from East Street to and from the ground for every game — a double burden since, as well as playing in Division Two of the Lewisham League, Charlton also entered Division Two of the Woolwich League. In those days it was not unusual for one team to play in two different leagues.

But as the team prospered, so did facilities for the players and soon, for Saturday away matches, the team

Charlton Athletic's first league-winning team, champions of the Lewisham League Third Division in 1906-07. Back row (left to right): J.Merryweather, H.Hughes, W.Wilson, W.Higgs, W.King (captain), J.Sudds, H.T.Wells (president). Middle: E.Holt (first aid), J.Mitchell, A.Buckenham, W.Bonner, W.Pirie, E.Marshall, J.Mitchell, J.MacKenzie (honorary secretary). Front: C.Broom, A.Mills, A.Thomas.

had the use of a horse-brake which set off from outside The Crown. It was not long before 'away' supporters were following them regularly in two brake-loads.

The club lost their opening Woolwich League game, 2-1 against No.1 Depot Royal Field Artillery, on 28 September 1907, when they had only nine players. But they won their first Lewisham League Division Two match a week later, 4-0 against Paternoster Athletic.

Charlton also entered the Woolwich Challenge Cup, being beaten by Lansdown, later known as Charlton Amateurs, 3-0 at Shooters Hill on 7 October 1907. The defeat was probably partly due to Eddie Marshall fracturing his wrist after ten minutes.

Charlton, though, enjoyed yet another successful season, winning both leagues, but their success in the Lewisham League was somewhat peculiar to say the least. The Second Division was divided into two sections, with each team playing ten games. Charlton won four and lost one, but gained the points for all the other five games because their opponents cried off. With 18 points they finished joint top with North Greenwich Amateurs.

The teams played off on Good Friday to decide who would top the section and meet the winners of the other section, St Joseph's, Rotherhithe. Charlton won with an 87th-minute goal from Bill Pirie. However, St Joseph's failed to turn up for the final play-off and Charlton were declared champions of the division.

Easter Tragedy

BUT on Easter Sunday, tragedy followed the Good Friday game. Like many of the Charlton team and other young men who lived by the Thames, Pirie was a keen oarsman. On the Sunday, he volunteered to fill a vacant place in a crew. They got into difficulties and he was drowned when the boat overturned. Charlton called off their Easter Monday fixture and a benefit game was held on 30 April — a 4-0 victory against Bostall Heath Athletic.

That game was played at a private ground, Pound Park, and soon afterwards the Charlton club negotiated for its use — the first ground that they could really call their own. Pound Park was off Charlton Lane, less than a quarter of a mile away from where The Valley was to be. At the same time, the headquarters of the club was moved from The Crown to a more convenient pub, the Royal Oak, in Charlton Lane. Around the enclosure was a hedge which, whilst not enough of a barrier to charge for admission, nevertheless gave sufficient privacy for a collection box to be taken round.

The first match of that 1908-09 season was a Lewisham League Division One fixture on 5 September 1908, against Wellcome Institute, which Charlton won 3-1. In November 1908, Jim Mackenzie went to sea and was replaced by Harry Hughes as secretary. Mackenzie was later to lose his life at sea in World War One. A second team was formed this season.

The Pound Park pitch was far from level and often brought complaints from opponents. In 1976, memories of it were recalled by an old Charlton supporter, Tom Bates. He was born in 1900 and as a young lad was one of the team's helpers. He recalled riding with the players from their dressing-room to Pound Park in an old van.

The next season the club managed to introduce a 'cash at the gate' system and Tom collected the admission fee when the gatekeeper broke off to have a pint. He also helped with kit in the dressing-room. The price of admission was twopence for adults and a penny for children. The players had to pay a subscription to play for the club. Another memory was of regular fixtures against Charlton Amateurs on Christmas Day and Boxing Day, when the players wore top hats and bonnets. Tom also spent some of his time fishing for tadpoles on the site of what was to become The Valley itself.

The 1908-09 season saw yet more success, the club completing a hat-trick of triumphs in the Lewisham League. They won the First Division, after a play-off with North Greenwich Amateurs, with substantially the same team that had started the club's organized football life in the Third Division.

The club had dropped out of the Woolwich League for this one season, but entered the Blackheath & District League, Division Two, and the Woolwich Cup. The success continued. They won both competitions. The club had tried to play the reserve team in Division Three of the Woolwich League, but resources were not sufficient to maintain two teams.

To gain the Cup, they had to wait until the next season. Two replays in the semi-finals against New Beckton left no time for the Final to be played before the summer break. Their opponents when the tie was finally staged, were the Army Service Corps, Woolwich, who were beaten 3-0. The match was played at Chard's Farm, off Cemetery Lane at Charlton, before a crowd of 2,000.

RASC included several professionals and were the Army Cup winners of that year, so the victory was a notable triumph in the young Charlton's history. Two of the goals were scored by Harry 'Razor' Calcutt, who died, aged 73, around the New Year of 1959-60 and was among several of the original amateur players still living in the Charlton area after World War Two, including Mills. Calcutt, who usually played at inside-right, served on The Valley groundstaff after his retirement from a local engineering firm.

Charlton now left the Lewisham League but the hat-trick of successes was repeated in 1909-10, with the First Divisions of the Woolwich and Blackheath Leagues, and the Woolwich Cup, all being won. The club also lost in the the Charlton Charity Cup Final — on the old Arsenal ground at Plumstead. The result was a 2-1 defeat by Personnal Ordnance College Boys.

In the 1910-11 season, E.Heath, secretary of the Woolwich League, took over as club secretary with Harry Hughes as his assistant. The First Divisions of the Woolwich and Blackheath League were again won. The club won the Woolwich Cup outright because of three successive victories. Later, the Cup was presented to the Woolwich War Memorial Hospital for an annual competition in aid of hospital funds.

A new competition for Charlton was the London Junior Cup, in which they went out in a fourth-round replay to Silvertown Rubber Company.

Every year since they began in league football, Charlton had won trophies and the next season, 1911-12, saw no let-up in this tremendous run of success which had established Charlton as one of the most powerful junior clubs in the area. They resigned from the Blackheath League and entered the First Division (Eastern Section) of the Southern Suburban League, losing only one of the 20 games and scoring 83 goals against only eight conceded. They went into a play-off with the winners of the Western Section, Summerstown, winning 5-1 in a match marred by Bob Smith suffering a serious fracture of the leg which ended his career.

They were runners-up in the Woolwich League and won the Charlton Charity Cup by beating Army Service Corps, Woolwich, 2-0 in the Final at the old Arsenal ground. Charlton went out in the second round of the London Junior Cup and did not play in the Woolwich Cup. That season they lost three players to Catford Southend — Sudds, Wilson and

Calcutt — but the playing strength was more than maintained.

In 1912-13, Charlton again won the Eastern Section of the Southern Suburban League and beat the Western Section winners, Carshalton Athletic, 4-0 in the Final. The Woolwich League title was regained.

Charlton reached the fifth round of the London Junior Cup. They lost 3-1 to Riding Establishment, Royal Artillery, in the Charlton Charity Cup at Arsenal's ground — about to be vacated for the move to Islington. But two days later, they gained revenge by beating the same team 3-0 in the Final of the Woolwich Cup — their last game as a junior side — at the Angerstein Athletic Ground on Horn Lane.

In November 1912, Charlton signed a man who was to become one of the club's most prominent players, outside-right Alf 'Scotty' Kingsley, born in Barbados but Charlton-bred. He became an integral part of the side in the years that saw the surprise rise to Football League status.

At the annual general meeting in May 1913, the first step was taken along that road when the club decided to go for senior amateur status. An initial meeting and then a resumed meeting were held at the Bugle Horn in Charlton Village. The result was that the London League, the London Senior Cup and the Kent Senior Cup were entered in addition to the Southern Suburban League. The change in status coincided with another change of ground, the UGB company buying Pound Park for extracting sand to manufacture glass.

Move to Angerstein

FOR the 1913-14 season, the club took a three-year lease on the Angerstein Athletic Ground in Horn Lane, which they shared with Southern Suburban League rivals, Deptford Invicta, charging threepence admission per game. The Angerstein ground was on the edge of the Greenwich Marshes, about a quarter of a mile from the Thames, and was said to hold 4,000 spectators. The land can still be seen next to the approaches to the Blackwall Tunnel.

Charlton's first game at the ground was a Southern Suburban match against Army Ordnance on 5 September 1913, won 3-1 before a crowd of 500. In their first season in the London League, Charlton were narrowly pipped for the championship — the handsome Dewar Shield — on goal-average by West London Old Boys. On the last day of the season, they went to play Barking Reserves, needing a 3-0 victory to win the title on goal-average. They got three and then Barking scored, spoiling the goal-average calculations. Charlton then scored four more, running out 7-1 winners, but still not enough to overtake the Old Boys.

In the Kent Senior Cup, they went out 1-0 at Gravesend after a hard close-fought game. The London Senior Cup saw their exit, 5-2, at Old Kingstonians after they had to play the last three-quarters of the game with ten men because of injury. The Eastern Section was again won in the 1913-14 season, the club taking 32 points out of a possible 40. But this time they went down to defeat in the play-off, 2-0 against Old Kingstonians again.

At the club's annual dinner, at the White Horse on Woolwich Road on 9 May 1914, the secretary of the London League, Mr E.Eden, prophetically described the club's rapid progress: "During Charlton's nine years existence in junior football, they have won 20 trophies and over 300 medals. I hope

Charlton Athletic in 1913-14. Back row (left to right): F.Hunt, F.Cross, A.Hunt, A.Hampton, S.Owen, H.Gritton, A.Watt, E.Chapman. Second row: W.Budden, F.Chick, J.Gritton, J.Farlie, H.Saywood, S.Mew, G.Farrer, J.Merryweather, J.Scrivner. Seated: J.Wotten, W.Blagrove, A.Kingsley, E.Marshall, A.Mills, H.Franklin, J.Mitchell, H.Hughes, E.Heath. On ground: E.Hornsey, A.Mitchell. Trophies are (left to right): Woolwich League Shield, Woolwich Cup and Southern Suburban League Shield.

I shall be able to look upon the time when Charlton Athletic will be a great club''.

The 'Addicks

IN these pre-war days, Charlton had developed a nickname, the 'Addicks. The name sounds like a version of Athletic but it derives from the South London slang for the haddock fish. Versions differ slightly on the exact derivation. One has it that the players simply liked boiled haddock, another that the players invited opponents for post-match haddock and chips meals. The fishmonger who supplied them was reputedly a Mr Arthur Bryan. Joe Merryweather, the son of the member of the club's first committee, recalls his father telling him that the name did derive from the suppers laid on for opponents.

In the summer before the 1914-15 season, Charlton spent 'all their spare money' on improving the ground and stand. The new season was marked by another historic step in the club's history — Charlton's first entry in the FA Cup. But the occasion was marred by controversy.

The club were drawn at home against Dartford but opted to lose ground advantage because Dartford had a higher admission charge and guaranteed Charlton Athletic £4 from the match. The club's supporters were now fairly numerous and strong protests greeted the decision. The tie was drawn 0-0 but the replay, at Dartford again, saw Charlton go out of the competition, 2-1.

The 1914-15 season started normally, despite the outbreak of war, but attendances slumped as fans either enlisted in the armed forces or worked long hours in local factories. For the same reason, the teams put out by Charlton were also weakened and sometimes not even 11 players could be fielded.

Besides the FA Cup, Charlton competed in the FA Amateur Cup for the first time. Their first qualifying-round tie against Burberry's was a walkover because their opponents could not field a side. Curiously, Burberry's agreed to a friendly the previous week because they knew in advance they could not play.

Charlton beat their next opponents, City of Westminster, 6-1 at home, before going out in the first-round proper, 4-1 at Grays Athletic. Maybe they were distracted by the fact that their dressing-room at the Angerstein ground had been burgled during the week.

In March 1915, the Charlton club decided to close down because of lack of players and dwindling support. The last match played was on 17 April, a friendly against a Charlton Charity Cup XI. Charlton won 4-1, but only 56 people attended and less than 14 shillings (70p) was collected. In the words of the 1927-8 handbook, 'the majority of the boys' left 'to take part in the Greater Game Overseas'.

But, as the war dragged on, so the club reappeared, staging games to raise money for local hospitals and to provide comforts for wounded sailors and soldiers. Some £800 was raised during the war and the club did not take one penny for themselves. A small band of devotees got Charlton on their feet again after the war, including Ted Pritchard who audited the books of the reformed club and showed that Charlton had a credit balance of just fivepence. Regular Tuesday meetings were held at the Mission Hall, Troughton Road, to plan the post-war future.

The Angerstein ground had been taken over as a petrol dump during the war and was not available when post-war football started up. In the immediate period after the war, Charlton played friendlies on Charlton Park or Rectory Field.

The earliest known photograph of a match in progress at The Valley, a ground carved out of a chalk pit.

Valley Discovered

ONCE again, the hunt was on for a new home and this time the club found one that was to last it for 66 years — The Valley. The site in the centre of Charlton Village was discovered by the club's assistant secretary and initially made over on a five-year lease from a local landowner. The ground came into use in August 1919.

The site was a derelict sand and chalk pit, containing a well and known as Charlton Sand Pits, colloquially called 'The Swamp'. It was a natural bowl but not big enough to accommodate a minimum-sized football pitch. An army of volunteers, plus some hired labour, helped to dig the pit into shape, forming the immense banking which was to dominate the ground on two sides. Large quantities of chalk from the northern end were deposited in the marshy area on the southern side. Some of the extra gravel and earth brought on to the site came from a nearby hospital excavation and was said to have been full of old bones.

A letter dated 18 January 1919, from the club to the local council, was found in the files of the London Borough of Greenwich many years later. It stated that the club was 'engaged in laying out a sports ground at Floyd Road, Charlton, and in preparing the football pitch the services of a (steam) roller will be most necessary'. The letter, in very clear longhand, went on to request the hire of such a roller.

Charlton Athletic had just 2s 3d (11p) in the kitty when they made the move and the MP for Greenwich and club president, Sir Ion Hamilton Benn, promised to act as guarantor for a sum of £700 out of the £1,000 it was reckoned would be needed to carry out the conversion. But the enthusiasm of all those connected with the club was such that the money was raised independently. This was a considerable feat as many of the Charlton streets were areas of real poverty at the time and the more affluent Victorian villas tended to be rugby strongholds because of the close proximity of the Blackheath club.

The nature of the site made the name The Valley an obvious one, although it was some time before the title came into use. At first the ground was simply called the 'Charlton enclosure'. In the beginning, there were virtually no facilities and just a roped-off pitch. Even the fencing was not ready for the opening game so once again in the club's history, the collecting-box came into use.

At first the Charlton players changed in a house in Ransom Road, taking their meals in a local pub. Joe Merryweather was a notable sight in the early days of The Valley, carrying a banner with a large haddock emblazoned on it.

For some time the newly created chalk-pit stadium of the 'Addicks remained as basic as its derivation suggests. The great manager of Charlton's First Division years from 1936 to 1957, Jimmy Seed, played there just a year after it was constructed and recalled in later years 'how dreary' The Valley was.

He played there for Tottenham Hotspur's reserve team in a friendly against Charlton. "After a cold, wet and thoroughly miserable day, we were unable to take a bath or shower, but had to stroll to a nearby

Charlton line-up in 1918-19, soon after the end of World War One. Back row (left to right): W.Reed, E.Heath (honorary general secretary), A.Burney, S.Payne, W.Chenery, A.Watt (financial secretary), G.Pleasant, F.Lee, H.Gritton (assistant financial secretary), H.Farnall, F.Madeley, A.Madeley, H.Barned, F.Barned (honorary secretary). Middle: A.White, A.Seccombe, F.Jewhurst, A.Sheppard, T.Keen, G.Ambler. Front: S.Payne, F.Jamieson, A.Kingsley (captain), E.Bass.

hut so that we could change into our dry clothes''. The 'hut' was presumably one of a number of little corrugated huts near the Harvey Gardens end. The first match at The Valley was an 'A' team fixture in the Southern Suburban League on 13 September 1919, against Summerstown, Charlton winning 2-0.

This first post-war season of 1919-20 saw the club pursue their growing ambition by winning election to the Kent League which contained a number of part-time professional sides.

The Isthmian Turning Point

HOWEVER, the Kent League was not Charlton's first choice in the search to step up status. In May 1919 they had applied to join the powerful Isthmian League but were turned down as the Isthmians decided to retain their pre-war membership. Ironically, had Charlton been accepted by the Isthmian League, they would almost certainly never have become a professional club and so never have made the breakthrough to the Football League.

They were elected to the Kent League on 7 June 1919 and shortly afterwards received an invitation to join the Spartan League, but it came too late. Their first home game in the Kent League came against Chatham on Saturday, 25 October. The *Kentish Independent* reported:

'Mr J.Jennings's renowned brass band will be in attendance and will render popular selections before and after the match and during the interval. The charges for admission will be 6d, including tax, and 4d for boys, and it is hoped supporters will attend in force and show their appreciation for the club's efforts on behalf of sport in general in the district'.

But The Valley's first senior game was marred by controversy. Charlton went one up in the second half, through Beldham, but Chatham equalized with five minutes to go. Then, with three minutes left, Sheppard scored for Charlton from a Kingsley centre. The Chatham players protested that the ball had gone through the side netting and refused to start the game. The referee waited until full time and then blew the final whistle for the result to stand.

This was the Charlton first team's first and last season in the Kent League and they finished fourth with 29 points from 24 matches. The performance of the amateur team in the partly professional league had been a highly creditable one. Charlton also competed again in the London League, coming second with 20 points from 14 matches. An 'A' team played in the Second Division of the London League and in the First Division of the Southern Suburban League. The first team also won the Woolwich Memorial Cup that season, beating the Royal Army Service Corps 7-0 in the Final. Charlton also played what was to prove their last game in the FA Amateur Cup, a 2-1 defeat at The Valley in January 1920, at the hands of Oxford City, watched by almost 4,000 spectators.

The Kent League was not big enough to contain Charlton's growing ambitions, which were nurtured by Sir Ion Hamilton Benn. If they could compete with part-time professionals, why could they not go one better and compete professionally themselves in a higher sphere? At the time, the professional game was continually growing in popularity across the country. But the issue of professionalism was to cause a deep split among the club's members.

Professionalism Voted In

WHAT had particularly spurred the club's ambitions was the friendly against Spurs' Reserves, in which Jimmy Seed had played, on 6 March 1920. The game was abandoned midway through the second half because of heavy rain with Spurs leading 3-0, the first goal coming from Seed. His recollection seems a little too gloomy because he was reported as 'contributing songs' at tea with the Charlton players afterwards when 'an all to short hour was spent in song and story,' according to the *Kentish Independent* report.

But a month later, in April, the *Independent* was to report more momentous news — that Charlton had decided to run a professional team for the following season. The report said this was a direct outcome of the Spurs match, but the major surprise was that 'The Spurs directorate will provide the money for the directorate of the club and, although Charlton will direct its own affairs, the Spurs will have a representative to advise with regard to players'.

Both the issues of professionalism and a Spurs 'takeover' obviously produced ructions in the club, since a week later the paper reported that Charlton still regarded professionalism as an 'open question'. The club also stated firmly that it would remain under its 'own management and control next season'.

Events then moved on to a club meeting in June at The Antigallican in Church Lane, when the momentous decision to go professional was taken. The post-war auditor, Ted Pritchard, moved the motion but the decision was far from unanimous. It upset a number of the club's founder members, whose ambitions to make Charlton one of the greatest amateur clubs in the country were blown sky-high. Among those founders opposing was Eddie Marshall, the club's centre-half, who had dearly wished to join the Isthmian League.

The first plan of action as a professional club was to go into the Football Combination, but Charlton instead decided to apply to join the Southern League and were accepted. The Southern League had been, up to then, second only to the Football League in power and influence. Walter Rayner, a former Luton and Norwich player, was recruited, as the first full-time secretary-manager from the Spurs staff.

But the Southern League which Charlton were joining was a reconstituted one as the Football League had made a momentous decision to form a Third Division and the Southern League was losing 20 out of its 21 members to the new division. Nine of the departing clubs decided to keep reserve teams in the Southern League and four others, including Charlton, made the total strength up to 13.

Charlton Athletic made their professional debut on 28 August 1920, in an away game against Norwich City Reserves, winning 2-1. The first professional match at The Valley was against Brighton & Hove Albion Reserves. The first teams of both Norwich and Brighton had just started playing in the new Third Division of the Football League.

The season saw the club successfully consolidate their new status, finishing eighth in the league of 13 teams, with 24 points from 24 games. The champions were Brighton Reserves, followed by Portsmouth Reserves and Millwall Reserves.

Charlton also kept up a strong presence in other leagues, the first team finishing sixth out of eight in the South-Eastern League, with nine points from 13 games, and the Reserves winning the Kent League with 49 points from 32 games. But Charlton Athletic's stay in the Southern League was to be as short as in the other leagues in their short and meteoric career. Now the Football League itself beckoned.

League of Struggle, Cup of Fame

IN less than a year from their first appearance as a professional club, Charlton Athletic were elected to the Football League. The new Third Division of 1920-21 had been the interim step to a four-division league. It was almost entirely composed of clubs from the Southern League and with the foundation of Division Three North, a year later, the former Division Three became the Southern section.

It was decided to make this section up to 22 clubs, so Brentford and Gillingham, the two clubs who would have had to apply for re-election, kept their places automatically and an election was held for two new members. The clubs voted in at the meeting of the Football League on 30 May 1921, were the Welsh side, Aberdare Athletic, with 38 votes and Charlton Athletic with 30 votes. They were elected by a comfortable margin. The third club in the voting order, Bath City, received only 12 votes. A few days later, Charlton's reserve team was elected to the London Combination.

Out of the division went Crystal Palace, promoted as champions to Division Two, and Grimsby Town, the odd club out in the 1920-21 Division Three as the sole Northern representatives. Grimsby had been relegated from Division Two in the 1919-20 season and were logically switched to the new Third Division North in 1921-2.

The commitment for a side like Charlton Athletic, so new from minor league football, was an immense one. Charlton had planned for their application by deciding, in January 1921, to form a limited company with a capital of £10,000 which enabled them to buy The Valley. The first chairman was Douglas Oliver. They also furthered their claim for membership by signing some experienced players, notably goalkeeper Joe Hughes from Bolton and three from West Ham — Dan Bailey, Frank Burton and Harry Lane.

The Valley was still a very basic ground and without even a stand when the club was elected to the League, although one factor believed to have influenced the vote in favour of Charlton was an article in the influential *Athletic News* which extolled the virtues of The Valley as a future national 'home' for the Football Association and as a venue for Cup Finals and international matches. This was before the building of Wembley Stadium. Charlton entered into a contract with Messers Humphreys Ltd, an engineering firm, for £14,000 to build a grandstand with dressing-rooms on the flat, west side of the ground and install terracing and turnstiles.

The sum of £14,000 was a huge commitment in those days, with no certainty that there would be enough fans to justify the outlay. The final bill came to £21,314, nearly £20,000 of which was for the grandstand alone. But Charlton were forced to begin their League career without the grandstand being ready, as difficulties beset the project from the start. Humphreys could not start as soon as they had hoped and the work was not finished until well into the following year, 1922.

The stand was only 60 yards long, but it was tall and distinctive and its multi-span roof was a feature of The Valley until 1979, when it was replaced with a flat modern cover. It was almost an exact copy of the main East Stand at Highbury, built in 1913, although much shorter at only four spans. The Highbury East Stand was demolished in 1936. There were similar multi-span roofs at Wolverhampton Wanderers' Molineux ground, built in 1932 and demolished in 1978, and at Clapton Orient's Homerton ground.

To add to the building difficulties, Charlton's attendances fell short of expectations. By March, the club's expenditure exceeded its income by about £100. In fact, some fans were seeing the games for nothing. Above the south-west side of the ground was a line of allotments — and a lot of people were found to be working on them on a Saturday afternoon.

A large part of the vast East Terrace was still virtually a chalk cliff, offering a fine view but a potential risk to the spectator's safety. But The Valley was clearly a stadium with a magnificent location and, even then, it looked worthy of the higher things suggested by the *Athletic News* — as, indeed, it did throughout its lifetime.

The club's problems off the pitch were compounded on it because the team could not play in the FA Cup. Their election to the League was confirmed after the exemptions for the Cup had been announced — and there was no space in the League programme for them to play through the first four qualifying rounds.

The First League Game

CHARLTON'S first game in the Football League was on 27 August 1921, against Exeter City at The Valley. They won 1-0 through a 33rd-minute goal by Tommy Dowling, who scored with a fine, low ground shot from the edge of the penalty area. It was the only goal Dowling ever scored at senior level. His League career with Charlton spanned 17 games that season and only four games in the following two seasons.

The Charlton team that day was: Hughes; Mitchell,

Goodman, Dowling, Hampson, Dunn, Castle, Bailey, Halse, Green, Wilson. The attendance was 15,000.

Harold Halse, from Chelsea, was a distinguished new signing for the debut season — an international forward, now 35 and originally from Leytonstone. He had appeared in the Cup Final teams of three clubs — Manchester United, Aston Villa and Chelsea — finishing on the winning side with the first two. He also gained a League Championship medal with United in 1911.

In those days, it was the Football League's practice for teams to play each other home and away on successive Saturdays and Charlton met Exeter at St James' Park the following Saturday, the sequence being broken by a 2-0 midweek defeat at Gillingham. This time Exeter reversed the scores, winning by 1-0. The 'twinning' of fixtures was to last another two seasons.

Charlton collected a satisfactory 28 points from their first 26 games, but then fell away, winning only two of their last 16 games to finish the season in 16th place with 37 points. The Reserves, playing the second teams of other southern-based League clubs in the London Combination, had a similarly satisfactory season, collecting 34 points from 40 games. A reserve team also played in the Southern League, averaging a point per game.

The club's secretary-manager since professionalism had been adopted, Walter Rayner, had to call on a very large number of players as he tried to settle on a side that would meet the requirements of League football. No fewer than 36 players made first-team appearances. Of the old stalwarts besides the Mitchell brothers, Mosky Mills appeared twice that season. Scotty Kingsley played 20 games before reluctantly being transferred to Fulham in January 1922, for £1,500.

The Black Prince

APART from Halse, two other notable recruits in that historic first League season were Arthur Whalley, a player also in his mid-30s and described as a 'prince among centre-backs', and Bobby Thomson, a centre-forward also from Chelsea, who had lost an eye in

Dan Bailey was one of three players signed from West Ham United. Bailey scored 13 goals in 55 Southern League games for the Hammers and nine in 35 Football League games, so he was a relatively experienced forward. For Charlton he was to score eight goals in 33 League games.

a childhood firework accident but who seemed not in the slightest bit bothered by his disability.

Whalley may have been a 'prince' on the playing field, but he had a notorious past to live down. He had been understudy at Manchester United to one of the greatest players of the time, Charlie Roberts. He then established himself in his own right in the

Walker Hampson (right) and Bert Dunn (left) both played in Charlton's first-ever Football League match.

The start of Charlton's League career as reported in the *Athletic News* of 29 August 1921.

CHARLTON START WELL.

Exeter Beaten by the Only Goal of the Match

Charlton Athletic..1   Exeter City.......0

A VERY promising start was made by Charlton Athletic, who defeated Exeter City by the only goal of the game.

Fifteen thousand spectators were attracted to "The Valley" for this game, and they made their presence felt when DOWLING scored the only goal after thirty-three minutes' play. He had secured a return from a visiting defender, and after directing the ball between the Exeter backs, he ran forward and secured again, leaving Fryer helpless with a well-placed low shot.

The game was always interesting, in spite of the hard ground and summerlike weather that prevailed.

Charlton were represented by practically a new team, and were naturally at some disadvantage, although Exeter City had a pretty big spring clean after last season.

Charlton owe their victory mainly to a fine display at half-back of Dowling, Hampson, and Dunn. Hampson, who last season played for South Shields, was an outstanding success of the game. His tackling was always sure, and he seldom wasted a ball. Dowling is better at placing the ball, but Dunn is a most difficult man to pass.

WEAKNESS IN FRONT.

Mitchell, the diminutive back, and Goodman both showed up to advantage, while Hughes in goal always inspired confidence.

The attack never really enjoyed much sustained effort, and this was mainly due to Halse failing to produce his form as leader. He was seldom in the limelight, and the best work came from Bailey and Castle. They combined with excellent effect, and generally had the opposing defenders guessing.

Fryer kept a good goal for Exeter, and M'Kechnie was the better of two fairly strong backs. Brown kept Halse in subjection, while Mitton also did well, being generally too good for Wilson, the home left wing man. Exeter possess two strong wing men in attack, for both Edge and Dockray are clever and fast, but Crompton was the only inside forward who was at all responsive.

Charlton Athletic.—Hughes; Mitchell, Goodman; Dowling, Hampson, Dunn; Castle, Bailey, Halse, Green, and Wilson.

Exeter City.—Fryer; M'Kechnie, Stewart; Mitton, Brown, Green (A.); Edge, Crompton, Bullock, Green (J.), and Dockray.

Referee: E. Small, Bristol.

Full-back Bert Goodman made 38 appearances in Charlton's first League season, equal highest with Arthur Whalley. Goodman had made 16 appearances for Spurs when they won the Second Division championship in 1919-20.

United first team from 1912 and was a contemporary of Halse at United.

Whalley's claim to notoriety was that he had been one of the group of United and Liverpool players who 'fixed' a key League game in 1915. The game was played on Good Friday at Old Trafford, although Whalley was not in the United team that day. United were third from bottom of Division One, whilst Liverpool were in the comparatively safe position of 14th out of 20 teams in the division.

Not only did the group of players conspire to fix the match to help save United from relegation, they also arranged the scoreline at 2-0 to benefit from the betting allowed at the time on single-match results. The fixing was, in fact, so obvious that the crowd booed and jeered and the United secretary-manager, John Robson, left in disgust before the final whistle.

On 23 December 1915 an FA Commission found Whalley, along with two other United players and four Liverpool players, guilty of conspiring to pre-arrange the result 'for the purpose of betting and winning money thereby'.

The players were 'permanently suspended from taking part in football or football management' and forbidden to enter any football ground in future. Whalley survived the war after serving as a soldier and being wounded at Passchendaele and was allowed to play again. He moved briefly to Southend, before joining Charlton in 1921. Despite his role in the conspiracy, he was a player of inspirational character on the field.

The episode was the biggest scandal in the history of League football until the revelations of match fixings in the 1960s by the Sunday newspaper, *The People*. Then the fixing ring was ironically led by another player with Charlton connections, Jimmy Gauld, who briefly succeeded Eddie Firmani in the Charlton forward line in 1955.

Thomson, a scheming forward with a distinguishing quiff of hair, had played with Halse for Chelsea in the 1915 FA Cup Final at Old Trafford, the so-called 'Khaki Final' when thousands of uniformed soldiers were in the crowd. It was Chelsea who had been the prime victim of the United-Liverpool fix, having finished in the second relegation spot in the 1914-15 season with 29 points, with United one point ahead.

The aftermath was that in January, 1916, the League announced that the United-Liverpool result would stand, the reasoning being that the match could not be replayed as the players were now scattered around the country, in and out of uniform. But Chelsea's place in Division One was saved with the expansion of the League to 22 clubs after the war.

Before joining Chelsea, Thomson had played for Dartford and Croydon Common. Once asked by the Chelsea manager how he managed when the ball was crossed from his blind side, he replied: "I shut my good eye and bundle into the nearest back."

Another player with a distinctive background in Charlton's first League season was the former West Ham full-back Frank Burton. He stood 6ft 1½ins tall, was born in Mexico and known as 'Bronco'. He was a formidable defender, who had also played for Queen's Park Rangers and had a distinguished war record. He was wounded six times and received several decorations. Among them was the Croix de Guerre.

Distinctive too, in both name and performance, was Baden Herod who made just two appearances in this initial season but went on to become a pillar of the new League side. His full name was Edwin Redvers Baden Herod. He came from Ilford and was a popular man, who obviously enjoyed his football and later formed a strong full-back partnership with another stalwart, Norman Smith, that was a feature of Charlton sides in the 1920s.

Right-half Albert Purdy, a survivor of the Battle of the Somme, had come from Spurs for the Southern League season. He doubled up playing with ground duties. These included the unofficial role of rat-catcher, at which he became very skilled around the rodent-infested sandpits near the pitch. He later become Fulham's groundsman and lived in the famous Craven Cottage for more than 30 years.

Schoolboy international Bill 'Moggy' Cox was signed from Watford after serving in North Africa. At 5ft 7ins, he played at outside-right or as a diminutive centre-forward.

Inside-right or wing-half Alex Steele was a Belfast man and an amateur international. He was signed from Glenavon and was to go on to win four full caps for Ireland, two with Charlton against Wales and Scotland in 1926 and then two with Fulham. Also from Glenavon, via Hull City, was outside-left Harry Wilson, later to win an Irish cap with Linfield.

The player who equalled Whalley with the highest number of appearances that season — 38 — was Bert Goodman, full name Albert Abraham Goodman but known affectionately as 'Kosher'. He played for Tottenham in their Second Division promotion year in 1919-20. He was a utility player, capable of appearing in most positions. Syd Castle, a speedy winger, made up a trio of former Spurs players in the Charlton team

But in this first season of League football, the club seriously overstretched themselves with an army of creditors awaiting and they were forced to make their first major sale of a player. The hapless victim was Scotty Kingsley, who did not agree to the move to Fulham until the state of Charlton's finances had been explained to him.

Such was the state of things that on 19 September 1922, Arthur Brandon, Charlton Athletic's first salaried secretary, tendered his resignation to the board in this letter:

'I beg to tender my resignation as secretary of the company, owing to the position, as far as I am concerned, becoming untenable. The position is that, from time to time, I, upon your behalf, arrange for certain services to be rendered to the company by various tradesmen, but can hardly ever succeed in inducing the chairman to meet these liabilities.

I regret therefore that I am unable to serve under these conditions any longer, and ask to be released at your earliest convenience. As you are aware, there are certain monies due to me which I have advanced to the company from time to time, and I ask that an arrangement may be made for the settlement of these amounts as the fact of them not being repaid is causing me financial embarrassment.'

The unfortunate Brandon still kept an interest in the club, serving on the Supporters' Club committee for the next decade. Amongst those army of creditors were other clubs. Chelsea were busy pursuing Charlton for the money owed on the Halse and Thomson transfers and the Irish club, Glenavon, on the Steele transfer.

The Great Cup Run

IT was Charlton's second League season — 1922-3 — that saw them shoot to fame — not in the League, but in the FA Cup which they had been forced to miss in the first year. For the first time, enthusiasts all over the country had to look at their maps to find the location of this London village of Charlton.

The Cup success began early that year — in the

Arthur Whalley, the man described as the 'prince among centre-backs', who gained notoriety as one of the Manchester United players who helped 'fix' a game against Liverpool in 1915.

Outside-left Harry Wilson also played in Charlton's first-ever Football League game. He was signed from Hull.

Early problems. Secretary Arthur Brandon's letter of resignation. Charlton's first salaried secretary was unhappy that the club was not meeting its obligation to local tradesmen.

Opposite: Darlington's goalkeeper punches clear during the FA Cup sixth-round qualifying tie at The Valley in 1922.

Nearly all the players pictured here are wearing Darlington shirts, but that did not prevent Charlton taking the lead with this goal.

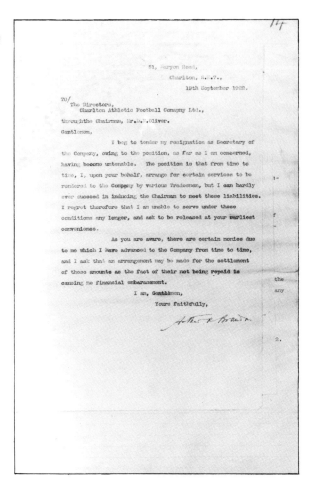

London Challenge Cup, then a first-team competition. Charlton won that trophy by beating Crystal Palace 2-1 in the Final at New Cross.

In the FA Cup, the club was exempted until the fifth qualifying round. In the fifth, they beat Northampton Town at home, 2-0. Another home tie followed in the sixth qualifying round — against Darlington — Charlton winning 2-1 and Darlington missing a penalty near the end of the game when Charlton goalkeeper Freddy Wood threw himself to the left to turn away a well-hit shot which was going just inside the post. It was to prove a momentous save.

In the first round proper, where the big clubs came into the hat for the first time, Charlton drew a 'plum'

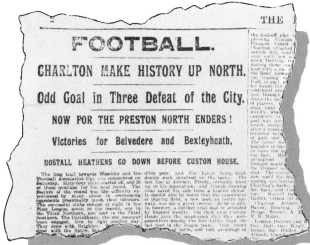

FOOTBALL.

CHARLTON MAKE HISTORY UP NORTH.

Odd Goal in Three Defeat of the City.

NOW FOR THE PRESTON NORTH ENDERS !

Victories for Belvedere and Bexleyheath.

BOSTALL HEATHENS GO DOWN BEFORE CUSTOM HOUSE.

match — away to Manchester City at the Hyde Road ground. The Charlton team for the game was: Wood; Burton, Herod, Purdy, Whalley, Plum, Castle, Steele, Goodman, Thomson and Smith. The same team was to stay unchanged through the marvellous Cup run that was to follow. Freddy Wood, Seth Plum and Steve Smith were new players to the team in its second year of League football.

Wood, the goalkeeper, played for Crystal Palace and Millwall before joining Charlton in the summer of 1922. He was to play in all 42 League games that season. Plum, at left-half, was a former Royal Navy man. He was an amateur who was later that season to play in the full England international side that beat France 4-1 in Paris in May — Charlton's first international player. It was his one and only appearance in the full side.

Many years later, in 1963, a Charlton fan, going into a garage for petrol near Tottenham's White Hart Lane ground, made a surprise discovery — the pump attendant was Seth Plum. It was a sad commentary on how the club had lost contact with its first-ever international player and how even the greatest players of that era found themselves rapidly returned to the humdrum existence of everyday life, once their days of stardom were ended. Steve Smith, a winger, was the son of the Aston Villa and England player of the same name.

These were the dying days of the Hyde Road ground and its famed labyrinth of corridors. A major fire had gutted the stand and the lease of the ground was running out. Charlton were given no chance as Manchester City were almost invincible at home in those days. Sportingly, the crowd of almost 29,000 gave Charlton a hand of applause as they took the field, little dreaming of what was in store. But soon the City players and crowd began to realize that here was no walkover. The Charlton defence mastered City comfortably and 40 minutes passed before Wood in the Charlton goal was called upon to save a worthwhile shot.

This fine performance by Charlton was despite the handicap of losing Whalley after 17 minutes for a brief period when a cut to the head, which he had received the week before at Watford, opened up and he had to go off to have it bandaged.

Three minutes before half-time, City's

apprehension turned into dreadful reality. Smith, on Charlton's left wing, got by the City back, Sammy Cookson, and centred perfectly for Goodman to head into the net past City's goalkeeper, J.F.Mitchell. Mitchell was a noted amateur of his day who played in horn-rimmed spectacles, kept in place by a band around the back of his head.

City got back into contention in the second half and equalized when Murphy centred for Johnson to score. But now the bandaged Whalley became the game's dominant and heroic figure. Seven minutes from time, City's Irish international centre-half, Micky Hamill, was pressured into giving away a corner. Castle floated it over for Whalley's bandaged head to force it home.

The Charlton team had turned into giantkillers, winning 2-1. The City flag was immediately lowered to half-mast and Charlton returned home to find a jubilant crowd welcoming them at Euston Station.

Even greater glory was to follow. The famous Preston North End came to The Valley in the second round. The year before, the 'Invincibles' had been beaten by Huddersfield in the last of three Finals to be played at Stamford Bridge and the first Final to be decided by a penalty. The Preston goalkeeper that day was J.F.Mitchell, who was transferred to Manchester City shortly afterwards.

Preston were the first Division One side to play at The Valley. Their team had cost £15,000 to put together, about the same sum as Charlton had invested in making The Valley fit for League football.

Charlton were unchanged for the match, but at first it seemed as if their good fortune had deserted them. Preston dominated them in the first ten minutes and the difference in class between the two sides looked obvious. But then Charlton began to get into the game, with Purdy and Plum starting to exert their influence in midfield. Goodman, Steele and Castle all missed chances. Within two minutes of the start of the second half, Preston found themselves a goal down. Roberts, their centre-forward, was given offside and Burton sent the free-kick to Goodman, who drove it into the Preston net from 20 yards out. It was a magnificent Cup goal.

Preston were stung into all-out attack for an equalizer, but the Charlton defence were playing marvellously. Fourteen minutes later, Whalley passed to Steele, who gave the ball to Smith. He shot and the ball crashed against the underneath of the crossbar into the goal. Charlton were 2-0 up. Preston now attacked desperately and in one incident, the referee penalized Herod for pushing in the penalty area. But it was just not Preston's day. Their outside-right, Rawlings, took the penalty and sent it yards wide.

As the final whistle went, the delirious crowd invaded the pitch to try to congratulate their heroes. Only Syd Castle was caught and he was carried shoulder-high. Sportingly, Preston's veteran centre-half and captain, the former England international, Joe McCall, rushed across the pitch to congratulate the Charlton skipper, Arthur Whalley.

The crowd then gathered in front of the stand and shouted for the players to appear. Goodman came out, waved and said a few words that were lost in the din. The crowd shouted: "We want Whalley," — not knowing that he was feeling unwell after giving his all during the match. The Preston captain, McCall, who had a fine game, continued his good sportsmanship. He also came out to talk to the crowd and his message was heard loud and clear: "Your team surprised ours today and I hope you'll win the Cup."

The call for the Charlton players continued and at last Whalley came out. He punched the club's message home to the fans. The team would continue 'to give good, clean football' but in return, the public would have to support them in still greater numbers. The crowd cheered again and then broke up. The attendance was the biggest in The Valley's short history. Some 22,490 spectators had paid £1,402.

In the third-round draw, Charlton drew another home tie against First Division opposition, this time West Bromwich Albion. Applications for tickets, especially the 2,400 stand seats at 5s 9d each, poured in from all over London and Kent. Charlton decided to make extra terracing available on the East Side slope and there was even optimistic talk of an attendance of more than 50,000.

West Bromwich packed five England internationals into their side — Joe Smith, Tommy Magee, Sid Bowser, Bobby McNeal and Freddy Morris — and two Welsh caps, Ivor Jones and Stan Davies. Jones was the father of Cliff Jones, who played in the legendary Spurs double side of 1960-61 and also appeared in the Welsh national side.

The Valley on Saturday, 24 February 1923, seemed to be the most popular place in London and a couple of hours before the kick-off, roads were blocked with people and traffic. Long rows of fans led to every turnstile and marshalls tried to keep order with

Syd Castle, whom the fans carried shoulder-high after the Cup win over Preston North End.

West Brom goalkeeper Hubert Pearson tips a Charlton shot around the post during the third-round game at The Valley.

megaphones. Pickpockets had a field-day, but some were caught and one old offender was later sentenced to six months' hard labour.

The crowd totalled 31,489. When Whalley led the team out, the cheer that met him 'must be heard down in Brighton', he commented later. He won the toss but, like Preston, Albion got off to a fine start. Whalley again proved a key figure as Charlton once again began to turn a game around against First Division opponents. He began to find Thomson and Steele with his passes. Then the wingers, Castle and Smith, who had been tightly marked, began to find more room at last.

The balance of the game had changed and Charlton's belief in themselves was showing through. Then, early in the second half, came the only goal. Plum got the ball from Goodman, feinted to pass but, instead, went by his opponent and centred. Thomson swung round and shot at goal. The ball cannoned off an Albion back to the surprised goalkeeper, Pearson, who failed to collect it and saw, to his dismay, that Goodman was rushing in to bang the ball into the net.

Hard as Albion tried, they could not retrieve the game. The 'Addicks had completed a hat-trick of Division One victims and, once again, there were jubilant scenes at the final whistle. As the crowd gathered yet again in front of the grandstand, Whalley refused to come out. But goalkeeper Freddy Wood did: 'It's because I'm the goalkeeper,' he shouted. 'I'm the only one left with enough wind to speak.'

The club's exploits had made them the talk of the land. Newspaper headlines spelled out their success — 'Miracle Babes Rout Lancastrians', 'Charlton Makes History' and 'Onward the Reds, Ever Onward'. It was the first time a Third Division side had ever gone this far in the FA Cup. The nickname 'Babes' was to stick through the 1920s, in addition to the 'Addicks and the Reds. The description, 'The Happy Valley' was also coined during these epic Cup exploits.

Charlton were drawn at home in the fourth round on 10 March, against Bolton Wanderers, another First Division side and one boasting eight internationals, including the legendary David Jack at inside-right. Although Charlton fans were now convinced that nothing was beyond them, the newspapers still tipped Bolton to win, but a little cautiously in view of the hat-trick of fallen Division One giants. 'Charlton', wrote one reporter, 'cannot wholly be trusted to remember their station in life'.

The Charlton team went to Freshwater on the Isle of Wight, as guests of the chairman, for special training for the match. A snapshot of the time, taken on the island, showed the Charlton team seated in an old-style charabanc, open at the top and with solid-tyred wheels.

On the day of the match, the gates opened at midday. The club could only guess at what the crowd would be for this momentous occasion. Extra crush barriers had been installed and, by one o'clock, 20,000 people had already amassed inside The Valley. The final crowd was 42,023, bringing in receipts of nearly £2,800. The Preston, West Brom and Bolton attendances were all successive Valley records. Few other clubs can have broken their attendance records three times in just 35 days.

But now the fairy-story ended, Charlton going out to a goal by David Jack ten minutes before half-time. Vizard exchanged passes twice with Joe Smith and their link-up drew the Charlton defence towards them. The ball was clipped inside and found Jack,

Wing-half Tommy Dowling (top) scored Charlton's first-ever League goal.
Baden Herod (below) made only two appearances in Charlton's first League season but went on to become a pillar of the club's defence.

unmarked about 12 yards from goal. He fired in a shot which Freddy Wood could not even get near.

The game had been a hard and even one with furious movement but few goalscoring chances. But the huge crowd was simply too much for the very basic ground which was The Valley. In several incidents, railings at the Station (south) End were broken. The first incident was before the start. The second came early in the game when spectators on the upper terraces pushed forward and then overbalanced. The movement snowballed downwards and the pressure in the front was so great that fences collapsed and many spectators spilled on to the pitch. Fortunately, there were no major injuries. One young fan was carried away in the arms of the Charlton manager, Walter Rayner. Order was quickly restored and play continued while the gaps in the fencing were blocked with stakes and scaffold poles.

But then a much worse incident followed. Just before half-time, the railings gave way again. Men, women and children were thrown forward even more violently, falling into a struggling heap. The referee stopped play and the players themselves went to the rescue, to be joined by police and ambulance workers on the alert after the earlier troubles. Many of the fans at the bottom of the heap were small boys and girls, who had been allowed to stand at the front to get a better view. Several were found unconscious. One little girl, carried by a policeman, was crying for her mother who was lying motionless in the arms of another policeman.

Minor injuries were treated on the pitch, but about two dozen spectators were taken to the club's recreation room, which was converted into a temporary casualty clearing station. The more seriously hurt were then transferred from there to Greenwich Hospital. All were to be released within a day or two.

The experience was a grim one, but at least it partly prepared Bolton Wanderers for the chaos of the first-ever Cup Final at Wembley, when 200,000 people turned up and the amazing crowd scenes were controlled by the famous white police horse. Bolton won the Cup, beating West Ham 2-0.

Although there were meetings after The Valley incidents at which safety questions were raised, the size of the crowd itself seemed at the time a portent of good times to come.

In the League, the club finished in 12th place, averaging a point a game. The club's new prominence was marked in May 1923, by two of its players gaining England caps. Besides Seth Plum's cap against France, Harold Miller played against Sweden in Stockholm on 24 May and scored in a 3-1 win. Miller had not played in the Cup run, coming into the team later. Following his one international appearance, he left for Chelsea without playing another game for Charlton.

Norman Smith, signed from Usworth Colliery Welfare, made his first-team debut in March and was to become the automatic choice at right-back for 12 years as a quick and able defender of high quality.

To Catford and Back

BUT the impact of the Cup run was short-lived. Attendances dropped back again and the directors were massively and understandably disappointed. Despite income from the Cup run, money problems reared their head again. So shaken were the board that, the month following the Cup exit, they made up their minds that The Valley would never yield enough support to make the team viable. Just four years after moving to The Valley, they decided to uproot again to Catford, four miles to the south-west of The Valley.

Yet another large investment was called for, some £17,330, to make the ground, to be called The Mount, on Laleham Road and near the centre of Catford, fit for League football. The ground was the home of Catford Southend FC, an amateur club in the London League, and the two clubs amalgamated their playing activities, Catford dropping out of the London League. It was proposed that Charlton take the Catford Southend name, but the Football League would not permit it, presumably on the grounds that Charlton would be passing their Football League membership on to another club not democratically elected.

In protest at the move, some of the original committee of the pre-League days formed an amateur club called Old Charlton, who applied to join the London League and were accepted in Catford's place.

The money for the move was raised mainly by subscription and work was begun on levelling a big slope at The Mount, machines excavating the top and filling in the bottom. So anxious were the directors to get the work done as quickly as possible, that the work even went on after dark by artificial light. There were complaints about the noise of blasting, and then tragedy, when a workman was killed by a fall of clay. Board meetings were switched to the Dartmouth Hotel, close to the ground, and then to new offices acquired at 25 Bromley Road, Catford.

The ground was not ready for play until nearly half-way through the 1923-4 season. The first game at The Mount was on 22 December 1923, when a goalless draw was played out against Northampton Town before 8,000 spectators. To mark the occasion,

Charlton turned out in the dark and light blue stripes of the Catford club and stated that they were thinking of adopting the colours permanently. Despite the rush, the project was an uncompleted one. There was not time or money for the club to put up adequate accommodation for the spectators. The Heath Robinson-type stand provoked particular mockery. Attendances were even poorer than at The Valley.

Charlton had to seek special permission to stage their second-round FA Cup tie against Wolves in February 1924 at The Valley because of The Mount's inadequate seating accommodation. It is probably the only recorded case in FA Cup history of a club being allowed to switch a home tie to a second home venue. During this time, the Reserves continued to play Kent League games at The Valley, and Millwall were reported to be interested in taking it over. It took just half a season for Charlton Athletic to call it a day and creep back to The Valley, poorer and wiser.

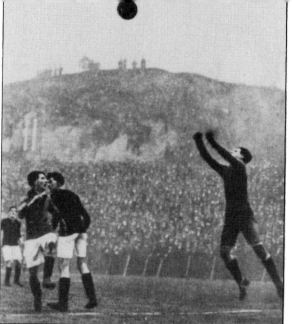

Two photographs showing action from the FA Cup tie against Wolves in February 1924. Charlton, who were then playing at The Mount, had to get FA permission to stage their home game back at The Valley. In the top picture, Freddy Wood punches clear for Charlton. In the bottom one, it is the turn of Wolves' goalkeeper George to tip the ball over the bar.

More action from the Cup tie against Wolves as Charlton press the visitors' goal.

Some Scottish players came south to join MacFarlane, including half-backs, Alex Hardie and Willie Paterson, and a fine scheming inside-forward, Johnnie Rankin, who arrived in September 1925, having played for Hamilton, Doncaster and Dundee. Under MacFarlane, the team moved to the Scottish short passing game.

But the situation of retrenchment to which MacFarlane came could only provide temporary respite. Enormous capital debts still loomed over the club, threatening its whole existence, similar to the threat 60 years later.

Humphreys to the rescue

THE only salvation lay in the tolerance of the builders, Humphreys, who, unpaid for most of their work, agreed not to foreclose but to accept an issue of debentures instead. To safeguard their new financial interest, Humphreys put a member of their own staff, David Clark, on the board in 1925. Clark, who had once been an amateur with Tottenham Hotspur, had supervised the building work at The Valley. He was to serve with distinction on the board for many years through the triumphs that were to follow.

Another personality who was to be a mainstay of the Charlton club for many years until his death in 1958 was Dr John Montgomery, who took up general practice in the Charlton district in 1924 and then became the club's medical officer.

The club's pull back to solvency was accomplished in the 1925-6 season, with income exceeding running expenditure for the first time in the club's professional life. The overall loss for the year was under £1,000, against under £3,000 the year before. But that same season, the club had to seek re-election for the only time in its existence, after finishing second to bottom.

The one event of note was that a third Charlton player became an England international, George Armitage playing against Ireland at centre-half, in Belfast in October 1925. Like Plum and Miller, his international career lasted only one game. He had joined Charlton in 1924 from Wimbledon and was one of the most consistent players in the side from the mid to late 1920s.

The year 1925 also saw the departure of one of the stalwarts of Charlton's first years in the League, Bert Goodman, who left for Gillingham. Besides his playing prowess, he was the organizer around 1924 of a full-scale boxing show at The Valley, held just in front of the stand.

The 1926-7 season saw Charlton climb again to 13th place and for the first time in their League

Edwin Radford now became chairman, although Douglas Oliver remained on the board. Catford Southend re-formed and competed in the Kent League in place of Charlton Reserves.

Although some games had attracted capacity crowds of 10,000, only 1,000 people attended the last game at The Mount in the 1923-4 season. Only 13 League club visitors had made their way to The Mount, but one had to make the journey twice — Exeter City. On their first visit, torrential rain caused the game to be called off after 50 minutes with the score 1-1. Lievesley's goal for Exeter was, in fact, the first Charlton had conceded at The Mount, but it was erased from the records. When the match was replayed, Charlton won 1-0.

Today, the site of The Mount is part of a pleasant park, Mountsfield Park, with the plateau of the playing area still there and traces of mounds that made the terracing. All else has gone, save for some lumps of concrete from the terraces, spread under a long hedge.

The club had lost £17,000 on the venture but had still to pay the £14,000 bill for The Valley itself. The situation was a desperate one with not even enough cash to call players up for training or buy footballs and equipment. Somehow the club struggled into its fourth season in League football, but after three months, were not able to meet the players' wages. The threat loomed of the players appealing to the Football Association.

On the expenditure side, there was retrenchment all round. An inquiry into the club's affairs led to the suspension of manager Rayner. To save money, the jobs of manager and secretary were combined in the person of the former Scottish international, Alexander 'Sandy' MacFarlane, who gave up the managership of Dundee to take over the reins of Charlton.

MacFarlane was an inside-forward who won five caps for Scotland between 1904 and 1911. He began his football career with Baillieston, later joining Airdrie. He was transferred to Newcastle United for £30 in October 1898, returning to Scotland three years later to play for Dundee, winning a Scottish Cup winners medal with them in 1910. In 1913, he went back to England to join Chelsea, but retired as a player the following year. He managed Dundee from 1919 until joining Charlton.

Flat caps on The Valley's East Terrace when 27,000 saw the 1-1 draw against Millwall on 8 October 1927.

Charlton pictured in 1925-6, wearing an unfamiliar strip. The photograph also shows the old standing place in front of the Main Stand, before seats were installed. Team: Back row, left to right: E.J.Godfrey (inset), S.McIntosh, T.H.Wilson, C.D.F.Preedy, J.H.Bailey, H.H.Kirby, G.H.Armitage, T.McCrorie, R.W.Tricker (insets). Middle: C.Hollidge (trainer), W.F.Paterson, A.Steele, J.Semple, H.J.Soundby, F.J.Jones, J.Gibson, G.W.Biswell, F.Currie, E.A.Millard, W.C.Cox, J.E.Mitchell (trainer). Front: J.P.Rankin, D.G.Inglis, H.A.Allen, N.Smith, A.S.Hardie, H.McGinn, A.Hooper, E.R.B.Herod, H.McGuire.

history, they had a consistent goalscorer, Scottish winger, David Sherlaw, who found the net 19 times.

The 1927-8 season was notable for two arrivals from Wales — goalkeeper Albert Lindon from Merthyr Town joined the club as player-manager in place of MacFarlane. He brought the youthful Dai Astley with him from the Merthyr club, who at that time were fellow members of the Third Division South. MacFarlane left in December 1927 to return to Dundee.

Astley proved to be both a talented inside-forward and centre-forward and went on to become a regular Welsh international, although he gained only one cap with Charlton before leaving to join Aston Villa.

The man who took over from Wood as the club's regular goalkeeper from the 1924-5 season until 1927-8, Charlie 'Spider' Preedy, departed for the Wigan Borough club in Division Three North. But Charlie's career was to bloom spectacularly when he returned to London to join Arsenal and play in their winning 1930 FA Cup Final side against Huddersfield.

Promotion at last

IN June 1928, MacFarlane unexpectedly returned from Scotland to take over the managerial seat once again, with Lindon remaining on the playing staff and as his assistant. This time MacFarlane enjoyed quick success. After years around the middle to bottom of Division Three South, Charlton suddenly improved their performance in 1928-9, winning the divisional championship and gaining promotion to Division Two. The success was only achieved by the narrow margin of goal-average over South London rivals, Crystal Palace, and Charlton had to win their last game of the season at Walsall to go up. They managed it by 2-0, Johnnie Rankin scoring in the first half and Jackie Horton after the break.

Fred Whitlow was leading scorer in the League with 23 goals, Wilson Lennox got 18 and Jackie Horton 16. Five of Lennox's goals came in an epic away match at Exeter City on 2 February, 1929, when he scored all the goals in a 5-2 victory, beating the club record for an individual scorer in a League game.

Sammy Langford played in every League game, whilst Alex Hird, Jackie Horton and Johnnie Rankin missed only one each. Jack Pugsley, a very experienced player, who had led Grimsby Town to the championship of Division Three North in 1926, played in 40 games. Norman Smith played 39 games at full-back. Hird, a Scottish half-back, signed from South Shields, was to join the club's coaching staff and stayed with Charlton for over 30 years, ending as trainer to manager Jimmy Trotter in the late 1950s.

Unfortunately success on the field was not accompanied by financial success. Losses started to increase again and, between the years 1927 to 1932, ranged between £2,000 to £6,000. The average

Charlton in 1929, as seen by cartoonist Syd Jordan.

Norman Smith, whose full-back partnership with Baden Herod was a feature of Charlton sides in the 1920s.

attendance of 10,000 was not enough at that time to keep the club viable, as it was in the hands of local interests and people. MacFarlane had performed a minor miracle in getting promotion for Charlton in 1928-9, against a background of rigorous financial restraint.

But the club did one good piece of financial business during this time, securing a 14-year option to buy at £500 a site of one and a half acres adjacent to the ground and later to form the site of its car-park. When the club was eventually able to exercise the option, the value of the land was far above the £500 they paid.

The first-ever Second Division game at The Valley was against Cardiff City on 31 August 1929, Charlton winning 4-1 before 25,000 spectators. The team was: Robertson; Smith, Langford, Hird, Pritchard, Pugsley, Wyper, Astley, Whitlow, Rankin, Horton. Peter Robertson was a new goalkeeper signed from Dundee to strengthen the defence and he made 41 appearances that season.

Charlton went on to finish the first season in Division Two comfortably in mid-table at 13th place with Whitlow netting 27 goals in only 32 games, the finest performance by a Charlton forward up to that date. Pugsley gained a Welsh cap against Ireland in Belfast in February 1930, a game Wales lost 7-0.

One departure at the season's end was Johnnie Rankin, who joined Chelsea in May. Johnnie had been a mainstay of the team over five seasons, making 187 League and 17 FA Cup appearances. His goal tally was 36, including two in the Cup. After four years at Stamford Bridge, he finished his career at Notts County.

In their second season in Division Two, 1930-31, the Charlton club had such a settled team that only one other club called on fewer players, Plymouth Argyle. But, surprisingly, only goalkeeper Peter Robertson played in every game. There was one major signing. In December 1930, Charlton splashed out £1,220 on the Scottish forward, Robert McKay, from Sunderland, formerly of Rangers, and a League Championship winner with Newcastle United. McKay was a player who had tremendous ball-control but who, at 30, was now past his peak. He had one Scottish cap to his credit.

But there was one set of games the Charlton side of those days could well have wanted to forget. They ran up against Everton, then making a stay of just one season in Division Two after being relegated the previous season. Charlton went down by 7-1 at Goodison on 4 October 1930. It was the first-ever meeting between the clubs and in the Everton side were a host of internationals, including the legendary Dixie Dean. Even worse was to follow in the return game at The Valley on 7 February, 1931, when Charlton lost 7-0. Everton scored six times in the first 45 minutes, all their forwards netting within 25 minutes. Everton won the Division Two championship that season and the Division One Championship the next.

At the end of the season, in May, 1931, Charlton Athletic said goodbye to the most prolific goalscorer they had had so far in their short League history. Fred Whitlow, who notched up 64 in 100 League and FA Cup games, moved to Exeter City, where he hit another 62 League goals in only 86 games.

These two seasons were also marked by two epic FA Cup tie marathons. In the fourth round in 1929-30, Charlton drew 1-1 at Middlesbrough, then drew the replay 1-1 at The Valley. The second replay took place in Manchester, Charlton being beaten in extra-time by the only goal of the game.

The third-round tie in 1930-31, against West Bromwich Albion, also went to three games, Charlton drawing 2-2 away, then 1-1 at home before going down 3-1 at Villa Park in the second replay.

That season, West Bromwich won promotion with Everton to Division One. Their last game of the season, at The Hawthorns, was against Charlton, who went down 3-2 in a tremendous struggle.

It was also at this time that the new nickname, 'The Robins', came into use. The Supporters' Club handbook for 1931-2 put forward the name, saying: 'The team is in need of a better name than The Addicks. The Robins would be more applicable, this designation combining the club's acknowledged cheerfulness and the familiar club colours of red and white.'

Charlton held on to their Second Division place for four seasons before dropping back in 1933. The club finished the 1932-3 season with only 31 points and in last place. By then new management had taken over who were to revolutionize the club's future.

The Miracle Years

IN the latter part of the 1930-31 season, David Clark, the director put in by Humphreys, met two wealthy London timber merchants with an interest in football, the Gliksten brothers, Albert and Stanley. It was Clark who had supervised the original building work at The Valley and he had long taken a very active role at the club.

The Glikstens made it clear they were ready to put money into the club and they paid several visits to The Valley to look at the set-up. Then followed a meeting at the Savoy Hotel in London, where balance sheets and accounts were discussed. The serious situation of the club was revealed both to the Glikstens and their accountant.

Clark hid nothing. Indeed, his managing director at Humphreys, George Freeman, was more than frank when he met the Glikstens. Albert Gliksten said that he was 'very pleased to meet you!'. George Freeman replied: "You may be now, but I doubt whether you will be after a year or two in the football game."

At the end of 1931, the brothers decided to make an offer for the club, which was accepted. The old board, chairman Edwin Redford and Douglas Oliver, A.G.Chuter and David Clark, resigned at the start of the next year and, in February, 1932, a new four-man board took over, with Clark the only survivor from the old.

Albert Gliksten assumed the chairmanship and Stanley Gliksten became deputy chairman. Their chief accountant, Arthur Arnott, also became a director. The club's secretary-manager, Alex MacFarlane, was retained.

The Glikstens fixed the issue of debentures to Humphreys at £65,000 and guaranteed the premium on the issue and also the interest on other loans.

On the playing side, the Glikstens spent £25,000 to boost the team, then languishing in the bottom half of the table. Five players were bought — Joe Jobling, a half-back from Norwich City, Gerald Kelly, a right winger from Huddersfield Town, Willie Rankin, a massive Scottish centre-half from Blackburn Rovers, the club with whom he had gained an FA Cup winners' medal in 1928, Wilf James, a Welsh international inside-left from West Ham, and Jimmy Yardley, a centre-forward from Luton Town. Together with ground improvements, the total injection of cash totalled close on £100,000.

The late-season spending seemed to have the desired result. A playing revival, with 20 points from the last 12 games, saw Charlton into the top half of the table by the end and held out high hopes for the following season. Horton finished as top scorer with 13 goals and Yardley managed 11 in only 13 games.

For the new campaign of 1932-3, Cyril Pearce, a prolific goalscoring centre-forward from Swansea Town, was signed. The previous season he had set up a new Second Division record for Swansea by scoring 35 goals. Pearce was to prove one of the few successes in the Charlton team this season, notching 23 goals in 29 games.

Another Welsh signing, Les Boulter, an inside-forward from Ebbw Vale, also made his debut that season and was to prove a fine acquisition.

But what followed in the Glikstens' first full season in control was relegation. Full-back Jimmy Oakes was signed in mid-season, from Port Vale for £2,000, and played 19 games but was unable to halt the slide.

Opposite: Joe Jobling, a half-back signed from Norwich, who went on to make 212 League appearances for Charlton.

Charlton attacking the Bradford City goal at The Valley in November 1932. This Second Division game, played before a crowd of 27,343, ended in a goalless draw.

Like Pugsley before him, he had captained a Third Division North championship side when Vale topped the section in 1930.

Winger Harold Hobbis, formerly an amateur with Bromley, who made his debut the previous season at the age of 19, won a regular place, after which Horton was transferred to Chelsea.

In the middle of this disastrous season, manager MacFarlane resigned. The assistant manager, Albert Lindon, carried on until the end of the season. Attendances dropped to 5,000 and the message was clear to the Gliksens — that new leadership had to be brought in if their investment was to pay off.

The Coming of Jimmy Seed

AFTER bottom-of-the-table Charlton were beaten 5-2 at home in the last match by the other relegated team, Chesterfield, Albert Gliksten turned to Clark and said: "We can't go any lower, can we? Well, let's go up to Town, get something to eat, and have a bloody good cry!"

After wining and dining at the Savoy Hotel, Albert Gliksten began, next day, the search for a manager to retrieve the disaster. The search was an extensive one, but it was almost by chance that Gliksten found his man, Jimmy Seed, the manager of Clapton Orient.

Seed was already well-known to the Gliksens, who had been members of Orient's advisory committee. The committee had been set up during an ill-fated attempt by the legendary Arsenal manager, Herbert Chapman, to turn Orient into Arsenal's nursery team. For several years, Orient, a Third Division South club, had faced a difficult financial struggle to keep their heads above water. Arsenal had a debenture on the club and at the end of the 1931-2 season, Major Swears was put in as Official Receiver.

The advisory committee was formed and the Gliksten brothers invited to serve on it. At the same time, Chapman offered Seed, then a Sheffield Wednesday player, an opening in management as secretary-manager of the club. Chapman had first met Seed in 1925, when Seed played in the England-Scotland match in Glasgow and Chapman, then manager of Huddersfield Town, stayed in the same hotel as the England team.

Chapman thereafter made a point of singling out Seed whenever Huddersfield, or later Arsenal, played against Seed's clubs, first Tottenham and then Sheffield Wednesday. During the close season with Orient, Seed spent a couple of days each week studying and learning the great Chapman's methods, experience that was to stand him in valuable stead later at Charlton.

At this time he also met Jack Phillips, later to be Charlton's secretary, when Phillips was brought in from Major Swears' staff at the Stock Exchange to help in the administration of the Clapton club. But then disaster fell on Herbert Chapman's ambitious scheme. The Football Association ruled that Chapman was out of order in seeking to take over the affairs of another League club.

The idea of a nursery club inside the League was now completely dead, following the FA edict, and Arsenal had to withdraw. The Gliksten brothers quit the committee. Seed was left with a virtually bankrupt club, with no money to sign new players or even meet summer wage bills.

The chance nature of Seed's appointment to Charlton a year later was because of a banquet held by Arsenal to celebrate their winning the League Championship in 1932-3. The arrangement for the table seating was alphabetical, which meant that Seed, representing Clapton Orient, found himself sitting next to Albert Gliksten, who represented Charlton Athletic.

They talked of Orient's problems of the past season and of Charlton's plight after relegation to the Third Division South. The Charlton chairman confided to Seed that his club needed a new manager.

Seed replied: "What about me?", feeling that nothing could possibly be financially worse than being at Orient.

31

Gliksten asked: "Have you been lucky in football?"
"Always", said Seed, humorously.

Not long after that, Seed was sitting in his office hut at Clapton when the telephone rang. It was Albert Gliksten asking him to come to his timber merchants' office at Stratford, just a mile away. Albert and his brother Stanley wanted to 'have a chat' with him.

Seed lost no time in jumping into his car and rushing over. He agreed, there and then in Stratford, to take over at Charlton as secretary-manager, declining a contract 'because I thought it was only fair to them that I should first prove myself capable of taking on the job'.

Thus by a kindly hand of fate, Arsenal, Charlton's spiritual 'sister' club, had given Charlton the manager that was to make First Division football rise again in the Woolwich area.

Jimmy Seed was given a free hand to manage the side as he wanted and the promise of money to buy new players. Seed certainly had the pedigree for success — an English international with vast experience of English football at the highest level. He was also a North-Easterner, from Whitburn in County Durham, a fact that was to strongly influence his first scouting policy at Charlton.

As a boy, he stood on the Roker Park terraces, watching the heroes of that era such as Charlie Buchan. He was signed by Sunderland as an inside-forward at the age of 18 in April 1914, but his career was then halted by the war. Seed served in France for three years, with the Leeds Rifles Battalion of the West Yorkshire Regiment, and he was gassed on two occasions. His health apparently affected by the gassing, he briefly dropped into non-League football after the war, turning out for Mid-Rhondda in the old Southern League Second Division and the Welsh League.

But Seed was to prove another in the line of Spurs connections with Charlton. He bounced back to top-class football after only seven months with the Welsh club, Tottenham Hotspur signing him in February 1920. That same season, he appeared in Spurs' FA Cup triumph when they beat Wolves 1-0 in the Final at Stamford Bridge. He went on to many further honours and was capped five times by England.

In 1928, Seed was transferred to Sheffield Wednesday. Now turned 30, he was yet to enjoy the peak of his playing career. Appointed captain during that season, 1927-8, he helped Wednesday escape relegation in a tremendous fight-back after they were seven points adrift at the bottom with only ten games to play. He found himself playing at half-back and full-back as well as in the forward line. Ironically, his old club Spurs were relegated the same season.

Amongst the players at Wednesday was a strong, go-ahead centre-forward, Jimmy Trotter, the idol of the Owls' fans and destined to be Seed's right-hand man at The Valley. But Trotter lost his regular place soon after Seed's arrival.

The next season, 1928-9, saw Wednesday rise to take the League Championship and to repeat the feat the following season. Seed's Wednesday career came to an end when a long-standing knee injury was eventually diagnosed as permanent.

Indeed, some time before, whilst with Spurs, he had applied unsuccessfully for the managership of Leeds United, when he lost his regular inside-forward place in the Spurs side. And just before signing for Wednesday, he had been offered, and turned down, the managership at Aldershot.

Seed, on his departure for Charlton from the Orient job, was owed £130 salary but cut his losses and accepted £50. Unlike the struggle at Orient, the new Charlton manager now had money to spend, but his dire experience at Orient had given him a cautious, economical approach to management and he rebuilt the Charlton team without big spending. It was, anyway, made clear to him that, although the Gliksten were prepared to spend money to boost the club, there were strict limits on their generosity.

In his autobiography, Seed described his start thus: 'The Gliksten had put plenty of cash into launching the new Charlton, but with costs mounting, it was soon made clear to me that there wouldn't be a cheque-book spree. They quite rightly wanted the cash they had put into the club to be paid back as soon as conveniently possible, and when it was all returned, they did not want to finance the club.'

The record of Seed's spending over his 23 years as manager underlines the point. He spent only £55,000 buying players — and he sold players to the value of £170,000.

At first Seed was not too disturbed by the Gliksten' restrictions. His main aim was to foster team spirit and not a 'star player' philosophy. The accent was to be on youth and the search for talent which could be developed. But some of the Press attention surrounding the Gliksten was obviously ironical in view of what he knew about the brothers' ambitions.

Some reports talked about making The Valley the largest stadium in football, including Wembley. Indeed, when Seed was offered The Valley post, the Gliksten had talked to him about their ambition to make the Charlton ground the finest stadium in Britain. One reporter even forecast a stadium with an eventual 200,000 capacity.

Jimmy Seed's record signing for many years was Don Welsh, bought in February 1935, for £3,250 from Torquay. This sum must be compared with the then record fee of £10,890, paid by Arsenal to Bolton Wanderers for David Jack in 1928.

Seed's philosophy was that the wing-half and inside-forward positions of those days were the key to success. In modern terms, he believed in a strong midfield.

The Rebuilding Begins

JIMMY Seed took up his post in September 1933 and set out to fill the midfield positions with effective players. He made it the first act of his new regime to set up a comprehensive scouting system — something the club had never had before. It was a nationwide scheme, but Seed concentrated resources foremost on the North-East which, he observed, had consistently produced more top-class footballers than any other part of the country.

He put his brother, Antony, in charge of a team of five scouts covering this area. The team reported likely prospects to Antony, who then watched them for himself. If a young player really impressed, then he was taken down to South London and given a month's trial. In Seed's reign at The Valley, some 30 players were signed from the North-East.

Seed also made it a practice during his years of management to keep notes on each match his team played, his comments often frank and damning.

The first Jimmy Seed team had Alex Wright in goal. Wright had come from a small side, Irvine Meadow, for £70. The full-backs were Norman Smith, Jimmy Oakes and Ted Ivill.

Smith was the old stalwart, having played for ten years as a first-team regular until Jimmy Oakes was bought from Port Vale nine months before Seed's

Opposite: Jimmy Seed at his desk at The Valley. Seed's arrival at Charlton heralded the revival which culminated in an astonishing promotion from Third to First Division in consecutive seasons.

arrival. Oakes was a strict character in his attitudes, but was respected by the other players for his inspiration and enthusiasm and scrupulous impartiality. He was to be one of a great line of Seed captains.

Ted Ivill was a very experienced right-back, who had been an ever-present for five seasons in a row with Oldham Athletic.

In the half-back line, Jack Pugsley was another stalwart and in what was to be his last season for the club. Joe Jobling and George Biswell partnered him.

The outside-right, Monty Wilkinson, came from Blackpool for £550 and was an expert of his time in putting over centres from the goal-line. At outside-left was Harold Hobbis.

Seed's first signings were two half-backs — Frank Harris, who cost £450 from Cardiff City and Bert Turner, who came on a free transfer from Brithdir in Wales and had only recently left the Army.

Turner had played as a full-back, but Seed earmarked him for the centre-half spot. Seed wanted Jobling, then holding the position down successfully, to move to wing-half because of his ball-playing skills.

By November, all three were successfully welded together in the half-back line.

Other signings during this first season were Harold Butt, for £160 from Bath City, and George Green, for £250 from Barry. Some of the buys of the recent two seasons were quietly released.

During this rebuilding period, Charlton settled comfortably, but unexcitingly, in the top half of the Third Division South table, finishing fifth. Pearce, who broke a leg in the Easter Holiday game against Norwich City at The Valley, still finished top scorer with 26 goals. Sadly, this marked the end of Pearce's

effective career at Charlton. He did not play a game the following season and appeared in only seven more for the club before he left to rejoin Swansea in 1937.

Attendances went up slightly and the loss on the season was some £9,000 less than the previous season.

Terrace Cover

DURING the 1934 close season, the terracing at the north-east end of The Valley was covered — sadly, the last major change at the ground until near the end of the stadium's existence 50 years later.

The impetus for this development had come in a home game against Bristol Rovers in that previous season. It started to rain 15 minutes from time and the 15,000 crowd began to drift away. The Gliksten brothers took notice and went into an immediate huddle. As a result, they asked David Clark to make the plans for the cover behind the goal.

The Promotion Push

IMPORTANT changes took place in the forward line at the start of what proved to be the epic 1934-5 season. Cyril Pearce was out of action, so Seed put Stan Prior, who had been signed for nothing from Swindon Victoria, at centre-forward. But the position still proved a problem, so Seed signed Ralph Allen for £650 from Brentford. Allen was the brother of Jack Allen, who scored the disputed goal for Newcastle United against Arsenal that won them the FA Cup in 1932.

Allen made his debut against Seed's old club, Clapton Orient, two days after signing and scored both goals in a 2-1 win. He went on to notch a remarkable 32 goals in only 28 League games to become the highest scorer in Charlton's short League history.

Third Division Charlton and Second Division Port Vale battle out their FA Cup third-round tie at The Valley in January 1934. Charlton beat Vale to set up a fourth-round game against First Division Birmingham, who won that game at St Andrew's 1-0. Left to right in defence are Bert Turner, Alex Wright (hands stretched), Norman Smith, Frank Harris and Joe Jobling.

George Stephenson, an England international in the twilight of his career, was signed during the summer, from Preston North End for £660, and completed the forward line with Wilkinson, Hobbis and George Robinson.

Robinson had been bought from Sunderland in 1931, for £650, and put on the transfer list the following year. No club came in for him so he was allowed to play for Burton Town during the 1933-4 season whilst remaining on Charlton's books. Some inquiries did come in for him, but the top offer was one of only £100. He was on the transfer list at twice that figure.

Seed decided to take a look at him playing for Burton — his objective being to see whether he should let him go for the £100 or stick out for the £200. But the manager found himself very impressed and saw some of his own style of play in Robinson. He took him back to The Valley to reinstate him in the first team. Robinson never looked back. He played in all 42 League games that season and, after his playing career was over, was to become assistant manager.

Seed's move was met with astonishment by the chairman, Albert Gliksten, who was at a loss to understand why a discarded player should find himself in such favour again.

Seed's other signing before the season started was wing-half Bill Dodgin from Lincoln City, who was later to become a famous manager with Southampton, Fulham, Brentford and Bristol Rovers.

One playing change was tragically forced on Seed that season. The goalkeeper, Alex Wright, lost his life in a seaside accident in September. Wright was bathing at Torre Abbey Sands, Torquay, with a group of Charlton players on the Thursday morning after a Wednesday game against Torquay United, which Charlton had won 2-1. He dived off a raft into shallow water, sustaining fatal injuries to his spine. Wright, who had played in only four games of the new season, died in the early hours of the following morning in Torbay Hospital. At his funeral in his home town of Kilmarnock, some 15,000 people lined the three-mile route of his cortège.

Sam Bartram Arrives

THE reserve goalkeeper was also called Wright — Harry Wright. His first game after the accident came at Luton, where the opposing goalkeeper was, ironically, former Charlton man Charlie 'Spider' Preedy. Harry Wright appeared for half the season until his place was taken, in January 1935, by a raw young giant from the North-East nursery — the man who was to become a club legend, Sam Bartram.

Still 40 years later, Bartram remains the greatest player in the history of the Charlton Athletic club, although he never gained an international cap. Sam was to become the symbol of Charlton — he was Charlton to the nation at large — a giant of a man with carroty red hair, the rock-like foundation behind the club's leap into the First Division, not only in goalkeeping ability but also in morale. He was a complete 100-per-cent dedicated enthusiast, a man who inspired love and respect. When his First Division career finally ended in 1956, the end of Charlton's First Division days was only a short distance behind.

How Sam Bartram became a goalkeeper was a chapter of errors. In fact, he had been a goalkeeper for only a few games in minor league football when the chance fell for him to join Charlton. Rarely can

George Robinson, the former Sunderland player who was with Burton Town in the Midland League when Jimmy Seed rescued his career.

Charlton Athletic 1934-5. Back row: Green, Logan, Raikes, Gee, Thomas, Robinson. Third row: Tann, Arthur Arnott (director), J.Trevor Smith, Butt, Boulter, Wilkinson, Jack Phillips (assistant secretary), Doherty. Second row: Alex Hird (assistant trainer), Johnson, Turner, David Clark (director), Harry Wright, Alex Wright, Stanley Gliksten (director), Harris, Jobling, Jimmy Trotter (trainer). Seated: Stephenson, Norman Smith, Pulling, Jimmy Seed (manager), Jimmy Oakes (captain), Albert Gliksten (chairman), Ivill, Forster, Rist. Front: Brown, Dodgin, Hobbis, Prior.

a top-class goalkeeper have risen so suddenly from so little experience.

Sam came from Antony Seed's patch, the North-East nursery, and was a Durham man like Jimmy Seed. He was born in Simonside on 22 January 1914, the youngest of three boys in a family of six. His father, a miner at Boldon Colliery, had played in his youth at outside-right for the Scottish League club, King's Park, the Stirling outfit which folded during the war to be succeeded by the new Stirling Albion club. But, badly gassed during World War One, he died when Sam was just seven.

Sam's first major representative honour was as a left-half in the Sunderland team which played in the English Schools Shield competition. The captain of the team was one Horatio Carter, a small inside-forward of brilliant promise — and to become better known to the football world as the legendary Raich Carter. Carter's and Bartram's paths were to cross spectacularly again in the first post-war FA Cup Final, when Raich played for the winning Derby County side against Charlton.

As a youngster, Sam spent his Saturdays on the terraces at St James' Park or Roker Park, watching the great sides of those days. After his schooldays, he took the time honoured route to the coal pits.

The young Sam Bartram in his early days at The Valley.

36

Charlton players and directors in 1935-6. Back row (left to right): Tann, Lancelotte, Prior, Bert Chase (groundsman), Diaper, Williams, Wilcox. Third row: Jack Phillips (assistant secretary), Cann, Hunt, Shreeve, Hobbins, Olive, Forster, Boulter, Butt, George Hicks (staff). Third row: Welsh, Pearce, Turner, Dr John Montgomery, Bartram, Allen, Harry Wright, Arthur Arnott (director), Dodgin, Gee, Rist. Seated: Jimmy Trotter (trainer), Wilkinson, Robinson, Smith, David Clark (director), Jimmy Oakes (captain), Jimmy Seed (manager), Albert Gliksten (chairman), Jobling, Stephenson, Hobbis, Alex Hird (assistant trainer). Front row: Thomas, Brown, Harris, Fuller, Davies.

Bartram joined his local team, Boldon Villa, as a left-half. A little later he learned that, by so doing, he had lost the chance of an England Schoolboy cap. He had been selected and then replaced when the selectors learned he had just left school.

From Boldon, Bartram moved to North Shields in the North-Eastern League as a semi-professional, appearing for a time at centre-forward. Gradually,

Jimmy Seed's diary records Sam Bartram's debut against Watford — 'Played very well. Safe, confident.'

though, he found the travelling demands of the semi-professional game too tough, on top of a life down the mines, and returned to Boldon Villa, resuming his regular left-half position.

Then came his first experience of the politicking of football. Rumours began that a League club was watching Bartram. The former England amateur international goalkeeper, Ernie Hoffman, now manager of Jarrow in the North Eastern League, persuaded him to sign for Jarrow, although Bartram was reluctant because of the renewed travelling involved. After a couple of games, Hoffman told him that the club interested in him was Reading and they were prepared to pay £450 for him, if he made the grade after a trial.

Realizing that Hoffman had signed him only in order to get the fee from Reading, Bartram went back to Boldon Villa. A prolonged dispute followed with Jarrow over his contract and Bartram eventually had to appeal to the Durham County FA to get his registration cancelled. He was let off with a caution on the grounds that he had signed in ignorance.

Just a few weeks later, he was approached by the Reading scout directly and accepted the offer of a month's trial. The Reading manager, Joe Smith, the former Bolton Wanderers and England inside-left, tried him out at right-half in the London Combination side, but Bartram failed to make the grade and, after four matches, undertook the long, sad journey back to Durham.

One thing Smith did notice about Bartram was his liking for goalkeeping. When the players went out for shooting practice, Bartram would race into goal, to the anger of Smith who would yell: "Come out of there, you! You're not a goalkeeper!" Years later, when Smith was manager of Blackpool, the two men would joke about the episode.

Back north, Bartram went to Boldon Villa, only to find that they wanted him to play at centre-forward. Convinced he would only gain the attention of a League club at wing-half, he left Boldon Villa 'in a fit of pique' to join Easington Colliery in the Wearside League. In his first game with Easington, he was asked to play centre-forward and scored a hat-trick against Merton Colliery.

Once more, the travelling began to tell and he returned to Boldon, resuming this time at left-half. Then, kindly fate at last took its hand. One day the Villa goalkeeper was injured in a local cup-tie and had to retire. Sam volunteered to help the team by taking his place as a stop-gap because of his enthusiasm in training for keeping goal. His career as a top-class 'keeper was about to be launched.

Seed's brother Antony watched Boldon in the cup final, which took place at South Shields, and was impressed with Bartram's performance in a goalless draw. Also watching the game as a youngster behind Bartram's goal was Stanley Mortensen, later to rise to the top in football as Blackpool and England centre-forward.

Bartram so enjoyed the game that, after it, he told the Boldon committee he would only play for the club the following season if he could be the new regular goalkeeper. The committee disagreed strongly, but Bartram eventually won the argument.

Antony Seed also turned up at the replayed cup final, but this time Bartram had been requested to turn out at his old position of left-half. Boldon won 2-1, but Antony Seed was more impressed by Bartram the goalkeeper than Bartram the left-half.

Antony Seed mentioned Bartram's name during a routine telephone conversation on North-East talent

with Jimmy Seed. At that time, Jimmy Seed did not need a goalkeeper and he let the reference to Bartram pass. The sudden death of Alex Wright was to change all that, however. Seed got on the telephone to his brother to ask the name of the goalkeeper he had mentioned and asked if he was good enough for Third Division football.

When Antony approached Bartram with the offer of a goalkeeping trial, the response was instantaneous. Bartram later recalled: "There had been no work at the pits for a fortnight, and I would probably have agreed to go as a programme seller if I'd been asked."

Jimmy Seed had to go to Scotland to attend Wright's funeral and arranged with Antony to break his return journey at Newcastle, so that Antony could bring young Bartram to see him at the County Hotel. The meeting took place on the same day — Wednesday, 12 September 1934 — that Antony had revealed Charlton's interest to Bartram.

Jimmy Seed told him that he was prepared to offer him a two-month trial with the prospect of a regular job at £5 a week.

At the pits, Bartram had been earning just 17s 6d (87 1/2p) a week. The £5 seemed a fortune.

Seed commented in his autobiography: "As always, I studied the player I was about to sign very carefully and I immediately took a liking to this big, fresh-faced kid with carroty hair. I could see he was as open as a book and as honest as they come."

Bartram arrived at King's Cross Station to start his new life in London in mid-September 1934. Seed's attention to detail was demonstrated to the youngster when a familiar face was waiting to greet him. This was a fellow North-Easterner, Matt Forster, whom Bartram had already met at Reading. Forster, a reserve full-back who had played with Seed at Spurs, took Bartram to digs in Maryon Road, where he was introduced to a trio of Charlton players, Bert Turner, Les Boulter and Harold Hobbis. He was soon to feel even more at home — seven of The Valley playing staff were from the North East and it was turning out to be a home from home.

Bartram's first game was the following Saturday at Luton, for the Reserves. Charlton lost 6-0 — an inauspicious start. But Charlton's assistant trainer, Alex Hird, had seen enough to reassure the anxious youngster that he had played well enough against a side with forwards in tremendous form.

But the three reserve-team matches following the Luton defeat brought problems for Bartram. Seed called him into his office and told him that he would have to improve to stay in first-class soccer. He gave the admonition in a 'friendly, almost fatherly way', Bartram recalled in his autobiography.

Bartram was given intensive training and the initiation of the raw recruit demonstrated the carefulness and methodical nature of the Seed regime, at a time when football management was still very much a basic, unsophisticated art.

Soon Bartram found that this detailed training was producing a physical difference in his reactions. He was speeding up even the most instinctive movements and reaching balls that would have proved impossible to reach a short time previously. Bartram was to develop into one of the most athletic goalkeepers — as well as the Athletic goalkeeper — of his generation.

A quick opportunity came Bartram's way. The first-team goalkeeper, Harry Wright, was unfit and so Bartram made his first-team debut at Watford on 1 December 1934. Charlton lost 2-0, but Bartram had a good game and both players and officials went out of their way to congratulate him.

There followed a short spell in the Reserves, broken by a couple of first-team matches, and then came a run to the end of that championship-winning season as the regular goalkeeper.

From that time on, Sam Bartram was never dropped from the first team. Only twice during that time, did he appear in the Reserves — and each time at his own request.

Once he travelled with the Reserves to Bournemouth because he wanted to visit friends he had made during a wartime stay there. The reserve goalkeeper, Eric Gill, upset a pot of hot tea over his hands, so Sam turned out instead. The other occasion was a reserve match against Chelsea at The Valley. The goalkeeper failed to turn up and when the club heard that Sam had come to watch the match, they quickly enrolled him as a player.

For 21 years, Sam Bartram and Charlton were synonymous. He was an unusual goalkeeper with many unorthodoxies which surprised both crowds and players of those two decades. He was always ready to leave not only the goal area but the penalty area as well if the occasion demanded. Often he would dribble upfield, believing that he could find a man more accurately with a short pass rather than a long kick from the area. He maintained that he never gave a goal away by this practice. But he had some narrow escapes.

During one game at Grimsby, he dashed out to the left wing to beat the winger to the ball but failed. The winger passed to his inside-forward, who hit a fierce point-blank shot. Yet Bartram was there to save it. He had just managed to sprint back in time.

Another trick of Bartram's was to go outside his penalty area and head the ball away. Sometimes he even rushed to the touch-line to take throw-ins. Bartram had one ambition which he nourished during his two decades but never achieved — to continue his upfield dribbles to shooting distance of his opponents' goal and score.

When his long career was over, he claimed that he owed his longevity as a goalkeeper to his learning how to fall properly. He made it a part of his training to practise for hours on end, falling and flexing himself to counteract the jolt.

From the start, Sam was a character and soon became a much-loved one up and down the country. Sadly, this talented goalkeeper was never to appear for his country as a full international. Other goalkeepers of the calibre of Moss, Sagar, Woodley, Swift, Williams, Ditchburn and Merrick were his contemporaries, and the selectors may have looked with doubt on his eccentric foibles, rather than appreciating the sound goalkeeping technique and dedication which underpinned all that Sam Bartram did.

Shortly after Sam's arrival, another player came from Boldon Villa when full-back Jack Shreeve joined Charlton in January 1935. Shreeve was to stay at the club even longer than Bartram, retiring as trainer in 1962.

The Trotter Partnership

SEVERAL important background changes took place at The Valley that season. Jimmy Trotter, Seed's old colleague at Sheffield Wednesday, was appointed trainer. He had played nine seasons for Wednesday, finishing as top scorer in Division One in the 1926-7 season and in Division Two in the 1925-6 promotion season, each time with a total of 37 goals in 41 games.

The two men had lived only two doors away in

Sam Bartram pictured on a card issued by the *Topical Times* in the 1930s.

Trainer Jimmy Trotter (right) shows trainee physiotherapist Charlie Hall a cartilage sample in a bottle.

the same street and had often discussed their futures. Seed had always had ideas of becoming a manager, but Trotter was set on a training career. Seed told him he would keep it in mind if he became settled in a manager's chair.

A keen and conscientious man, Trotter took a postal course in physiotherapy and passed his exams successfully. It was clear to Seed at that time that Trotter had the makings of a first-class trainer.

After Seed had been two years at Hillsborough, Trotter was transferred to Torquay United. He was on his way again after one season — this time to Watford. Watford was journey's end for Trotter as a player. He seriously injured his knee and was forced to retire.

Charlton were playing at Watford — Bartram's debut game — when Trotter took the opportunity to tell Seed about his knee trouble and his intention to now become a trainer.

Seed acted quickly. On the Monday he spoke to the Gliksten brothers and arranged for Trotter to see them at their Stratford offices. Trotter was appointed trainer with immediate effect. So started the partnership of the 'Two Jimmies' that was to last 22 years.

In other background changes, the nearby local amateur side Bexleyheath and Welling became the Charlton nursery side and the directors bought a dozen club houses in the Blackheath area. The club bought extra land on the south side of the ground, which it had coveted for some time.

Up to the Second

BY the turn of the year, Charlton's 1934-5 side were top of the table. They lost the lead for a few weeks and then regained it in February. The only expensive addition to the team at this time was Don Welsh, the Torquay United centre-half, converted by Seed into a forward and then a wing-half and later to follow Oakes as captain. A tall, powerful, balding man, he was to prove a lionheart of a footballer, playing to the limit of endurance and ready to carry on even when in intense pain. He was also to gain three England international peacetime caps besides appearing in wartime internationals — he made his debut in the famous 6-3 defeat of Germany in Berlin on 14 May 1938.

Welsh also had a less fortunate side to the reputation he gained at Charlton — as a giver of penalties. Not a dirty player, he was nevertheless a full-blooded tackler who could not stand off opponents who held on to the ball.

The match which was expected to decide the promotion battle — only one side went up in those days — came on 2 March, when Coventry City, second in the table and just in front of Reading, visited The Valley. The game was watched by 25,000 people, the second-highest attendance in the League that afternoon. It ended in a draw, leaving the promotion issue still open. By this time, Charlton were averaging 15,000 spectators at home — up by a third on the previous season.

Charlton won their next three games and went on

to take the Third Division championship comfortably with 61 points, eight ahead of the second club, Reading. The Jimmy Seed magic had begun.

Charlton Athletic, for the first time in the club's League history, notched a century of League goals, totalling 103. And Jimmy Seed's faith in the side he had built was such that he announced that the promotion team would play unchanged in Division Two.

In his words: "I have always believed team-spirit is the first essential, and I knew we had this plus at Charlton. No manager had a grander bunch of boys fighting for him, and I announced that each and every one of them would be given a chance to prove his worth in the 1935-6 season in the Second Division." Already many experts were forecasting that Charlton would again slip back, as they had done so soon after their previous promotion.

Players Repay Seed's Faith

THE team which began Charlton's return to the Second Division was Harry Wright; Norman Smith, Joe Jobling, Frank Harris, Don Welsh, Bill Dodgin, Monty Wilkinson, George Robinson, Ralph Allen, George Stephenson and Harold Hobbis. The opening game of the season was at The Valley and Burnley were beaten 4-0.

Then the club hit a bad run and Seed's decision not to buy new players during the summer was fiercely criticized. But still no new players were bought. Seed's faith was justified by a revival in playing fortunes and, by the end of October, Charlton were only four points behind the leaders, Tottenham Hotspur, and attendances were averaging a healthy 20,000.

A month later, they beat the new leaders of the Second Division, Leicester City, 1-0 at The Valley in front of 28,000 spectators. A 2-2 draw at The Valley against West Ham a fortnight later attracted 32,000 fans.

At the start of 1936, Charlton were in second place behind Leicester and unbeaten at The Valley. Only one goal had been scored against them at home in the first two months of the season.

Attendances were now averaging 25,000, some 8,000 higher than at the corresponding period of the previous season. The size of the crowds, though, brought problems for a club not used to this consistent size of support. The roads around the ground were muddy and full of potholes, and the situation was not helped by a new housing estate being put up nearby.

Charlton's pattern of play was based on a sound defence, but the team also packed scoring punch with Hobbis at outside-left netting consistently. And the dynamism of Welsh was taking effect. Bartram ousted Harry Wright finally from the goalkeeping position.

The team topped the table for a brief period in January before falling to third place in February. A 6-2 defeat at Blackpool on 22 February dampened hopes of promotion.

Morale was also hit by a rumour that the club was holding back from trying to get promotion because its stadium and administration were not ready for First Division football. But this was given the lie by an important late-season signing by Seed. John Oakes, a centre-half, was bought from Aldershot for £650 to join his namesake, Jimmy Oakes and plug a defensive gap that had emerged after the solid start.

Charlton's form revived but still not consistently. One critic wrote of a home game in March that the display 'was not worth the price of admission'. With six matches to go, they were only just in the running and beset by injury problems.

The Easter Turning Point

EASTER was the turning point. Three games in four days saw Charlton collect five points. On the following Saturday, they won 3-1 at West Ham, but the game was much closer than the scoreline suggests and desperate at times, with Charlton running into two major injury problems.

Bartram had developed a huge abscess high up inside his leg, and the doctor decided against lancing it until the game was over. He was padded and strapped up to prevent chafing and played the game with his mobility badly impaired.

To make matters worse, John Oakes broke his nose in the first half. He was taken to the dressing-room and had cotton-wool plugs inserted into his nostrils so he was able to resume after the half-time break. A mid-air clash with the Hammers' centre-forward, Peter Simpson, saw him land heavily, hitting his face on the ground. Blood pouring, he played on with more swabs and cold sponges applied and plugs refitted.

Charlton had got two goals against the run of play, but West Ham pulled one back and towards the end of the game attacked fiercely, reducing Charlton to desperate clearances from defence. Then Hobbis raced on to the ball, just on the half-way line, and hit it down the field with all the strength he could muster.

During the West Ham onslaught, Herman Conway, the Hammers' goalkeeper had been standing on the edge of the penalty area, arms folded. Sam Bartram described the goal in his autobiography:

'I can see that ball now. Up it went, sailing towards the West Ham goal and seemingly bound for a spot high up on the terraces. Conway watched it almost lazily from the penalty-spot, just as he might have watched a passing aircraft. Then he began to move back, no doubt preparing himself to take a goal-kick; and as the ball floated over his head, it suddenly dipped capriciously and sailed into the back of the empty net.

It was the strangest goal I have ever seen — and it was scored in utter silence, with all the players watching in dumbstruck amazement, and poor Conway looking as though he had taken leave of his senses.'

Charlton now needed just three points from the last two games to gain promotion.

Leicester had dropped out of the race some time back, and Manchester United had soared to the top of the table. Sheffield United were the contenders for the second promotion spot. West Ham, who had earlier led the table, were fourth.

One Game From Division One

ON 25 April, Charlton Athletic beat Bradford 3-1 at The Valley, leaving just one more game — at home to Port Vale, a contest which was to be witnessed by 30,000 spectators.

The game was also a vital one for Port Vale. Defeat or a draw for them meant almost certain relegation, but Charlton were more nervous than their opponents, who obviously intended to make a fight of the match. It was Charlton, though, who went ahead through Hobbis after 20 minutes, when he tapped in a cross from Monty Wilkinson.

Port Vale then piled on the pressure and Bartram had yet another busy game. Five minutes from the end, Vale equalized through their left winger,

Manager Jimmy Seed acknowledges the crowd after the draw with Port Vale that ensured Charlton's promotion to Division One. To his right is stalwart Norman Smith. Behind is Bert Turner and to his left Jimmy Oakes.

Caldwell, to set up a nerve-tingling finish for the players and The Valley faithful.

Sam Bartram also graphically relates the moment when the final whistle blew:

'At last it came. For a moment, there seemed to be a complete silence, and then bedlam broke loose. Over the fences came the crowd, like waves over a breakwater, cheering, shouting, waving and sweeping forward in an ever-thickening mass towards the grandstand, where Jimmy Seed stood with our chairman, Albert Gliksten. Their enthusiasm was so great that I believe I was more bruised by their back-

slapping, thumping and hand-shaking than by all the knocks I had taken in the match. They seemed ready to stay there all night, cheering themselves hoarse.'

The Port Vale players walked silently off the field, relegated to the Third Division.

First Ever to Make the Jump

THE draw was good enough for Charlton and they became the first team ever to rise from Third to First Division in successive seasons, a feat that would not be matched for over 30 years. The feat had been achieved with few alterations to the Third Division team. And not a single match was lost at The Valley.

Hobbis finished as top scorer with 23 goals, playing in every game. His success as a scoring winger brought him England recognition. He was chosen to go on tour and in May played against Austria in Vienna and Belgium in Brussels.

Allen, who suffered injury trouble, still managed 15 goals in just 24 games. Stan Prior finished the season in brilliant style, scoring 11 goals in ten matches. International recognition was to come, too, for Bert Turner, who won the first of his eight Welsh caps in October, against England at Cardiff. The season also marked the retirement of the club's longest-serving player in the League, Norman Smith, who had amassed a total of 449 League and FA Cup appearances, by far the highest of any pre-war player.

The question now was whether this Third Division team would be kept on to play in the First. On the financial side, the season had been remarkable with the club showing a profit for the first time in its history.

The Mystery Saturdays

THE season had also been notable for several sidelines to the main football action. One concern was a vain attempt by the Football League to stop the burgeoning football pools, who used the League's results each Saturday.

Through the League. The 1935-6 Charlton squad that gained promotion to Division One. Back row (left to right): Alex Hird (assistant trainer), Les Boulter, Frank Rist, John Oakes, Sam Bartram, Don Welsh, Bert Turner, George Stephenson, Jimmy Trotter (trainer). Seated: Monty Wilkinson, Jimmy Oakes (captain), Jimmy Seed (manager), Stan Prior, Harold Hobbis. On ground: Norman Smith, Joe Jobling, George Robinson.

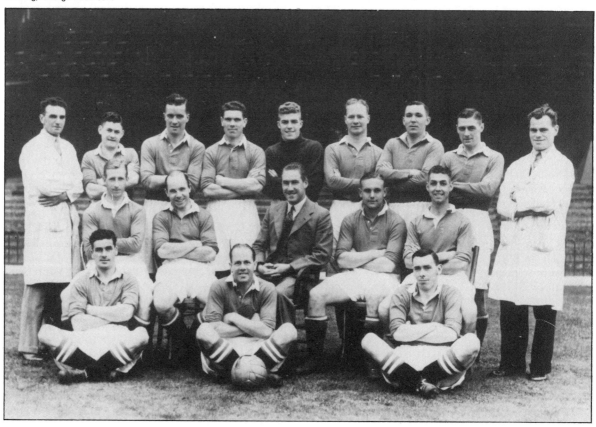

In February 1936, the Football League's management committee, as part of its battle to stop the pools, decided to scrap the season's remaining fixtures, and to inform clubs of their Saturday opponents only on the Friday beforehand — clubs travelling a long distance were to be given the concession of being telegrammed earlier, probably late on the Thursday. The only thing clubs knew was that their home and away sequence of games was to be maintained.

Hardly surprisingly, there were soon protests from many of the clubs, their advertising, ticketing and travelling arrangements completely disrupted. One of the most prominent in opposition was Jimmy Seed.

On the Wednesday before the first mystery Saturday fixture list on 29 February, Charlton informed the League that advanced bookings for Saturday were well down and that some Charlton supporters had threatened to boycott the game, whoever the visitors were and as long as the 'pools war' lasted. The mystery visitors turned out to be Swansea Town, who were beaten 4-1.

This extraordinary scenario lasted for only two Saturdays — Charlton being the mystery visitors to Sheffield United on the second Saturday for a 2-2 draw — before the clubs voted unanimously at a special meeting at the Grand Hotel, Manchester, on Monday, 9 March, to put a stop to it.

Attendances for the mystery fixtures had dropped, but the full effects were not clear because the bad weather at this time of snow, sleet and rain may have played some part. It was not until 1959 that the League came to terms with the reality of the football pools and at last compromised, signing an agreement with the companies to inject royalty payments into football for the use of fixtures.

The Concreting of the East Terrace

ANOTHER sideline to the 1935-6 season was an experiment in goalkeeping headgear by Sam Bartram. The episode arose out of a tragedy when James Thorpe, the Sunderland goalkeeper, died after a game in which he had been bustled and charged. It was later found that he had died from diabetes and not from the result of any football injury, but an enterprising sports manufacturing firm devised a crash-helmet type headgear to protect goalkeepers.

Bartram, who was winning a reputation as a flamboyant goalkeeper and for going in where it hurt, was asked to wear the gear for a trial period. He did not like it and the idea fell out of favour and was dropped.

The close season saw frantic work to meet the demands of First Division football. Sadly, in the work done lay the seeds of The Valley's future demise, although the enthusiasts of the time could never have foreseen this in their wildest nightmares. The sandbank opposite the main stand was concreted into a series of 132 terrace steps at a cost of £5,000. But, fatally, the steps were built over a colossal London County Council sewer. Building it was tricky at the time. Almost 50 years later the difficulties of repairing such a terrace without large-scale spending was a main cause of the closure of The Valley.

A high wooden fence was built in front of allotments on the south side of the ground, finally putting an end to the free spectating that had been going on from the club's first days at The Valley. New turnstiles were built to cope with the even higher crowds expected.

One problem was looked at, but not solved — the Charlton railway station, a small station on the

Winger Harold Hobbis played in every game in the season Charlton won promotion to Division One and was top scorer with 23 goals. His success earned him two England caps in May 1936.

George Tadman, who joined Charlton from Gillingham for £1,000. Right: How the *Kentish Independent* portrayed Charlton's amazing rise.

Southern Railway system and unable to cope quickly and efficiently with the crowds the club's success was generating.

The Southern Railway declined to build a bigger station but did electrify a siding where they could keep half-a-dozen trains standing by at the end of the match. This arrangement gave a three-and-a-half minute service until the crowds were cleared. The Southern Railway also arranged, for the first time, to run special trains for visiting supporters from any part of the country. The Valley, close up to the southern side of the Thames, was never an easy ground to reach for fans from outside the immediate area.

The club drew a lot of its support from North Kent and, even in those days when people travelled largely by public transport, the car was often the only convenient means of access for many Kent people.

Same Again

THE policy on the field was 'same again', as Seed stuck doggedly to his plan of no change of personnel, announcing the moment Charlton were safe in promotion, that the same team was going to play in Division One. He reiterated his confidence in the side at a civic reception given by the Mayor of Greenwich to celebrate the club's success.

The only signings were George Tadman, for £1,000 from Gillingham, and Len Williams from Aldershot and Ronnie Green from Notts County, both for small fees. Another addition to the staff was Welsh international George Green who, after originally joining Charlton in 1934 and suffering from ill health, had left for a one-season spell with the Barcelona club, Español, who were managed by a former Spurs colleague of Seed's. Ralph Allen, a 'great-hearted' forward in Seed's words, dropped out before the season began because Seed thought him unlikely to meet the demands of First Division football. He was sold to Reading for £828.

It was Seed's policy at the start of every season to call the playing staff together for a briefing session. Then, during the season, there were weekly tactical talks in the tea-room under The Valley stand with Seed starting the ball rolling by discussing the previous match, using the blackboard and then talking about the team's next opponents. After Seed had his say, the meeting was thrown open and everyone encouraged to speak. These get-togethers created one of Charlton's most valuable assets in these successful years — the spirit and understanding of the team.

When the team reported for training before the start of their first season in Division One, Seed told the players he was keeping up the policy — 'only more so'. He stressed the pretty severe testing-time ahead, but impressed on the players they had nothing to worry about:

"Simply because a club has a great name and half

a dozen stars on its books doesn't necessarily mean that they are a better team than we are," he said.

"Football's a team game, and the individualist, brilliant though he may be, is of secondary consideration: it's the team as a whole that counts."

On the Saturday before the club's debut in Division One, a practice match was staged at The Valley in aid of charity. Some 9,795 fans attended. Admission charges for the season were set at sixpence (2½p), one shilling (5p) and 2/6d (7½p), and the price of a programme was twopence (less than a new penny).

Top of the First Division

CHARLTON Athletic started their First Division career with an away match at Grimsby on 29 August, which they won 1-0. The first game at The Valley saw no less a personality than Stanley Matthews of Stoke City grace the turf, and 25,000 were there to see him.

By the fourth game, the miracle of the previous season was repeating itself. Charlton, a non-League side only 15 years earlier, were top of the First Division. The team faded slightly after this tremendous start and lost the leadership, but the big event for the Woolwich and Greenwich area came on Saturday, 17 October 1936, when its old team met its new team for the first time in League football.

Some 68,000 people crushed into The Valley to see the mighty Arsenal play Charlton, a game that through the years to come was to attract tremendous crowds — for example, 52,000 in 1938, 58,000 in 1947, 64,000 in 1950 and 66,000 in 1953. The average of the 15 League and Cup games at The Valley during Charlton's first spell in the First Division was 56,198. No other London visitors attracted anywhere near that size of crowd.

The present author remembers as a boy being carried to safety over the railings after being almost

Action from Charlton's First Division game against Liverpool at The Valley in September 1936. Top picture shows Liverpool goal-keeper Alf Hobson clutching the ball as Charlton's Stan Prior threatens. The defenders are Tiny Bradshaw (left) and Tommy Cooper. Bottom two photographs show Sam Bartram first tipping a shot around the post and then punching clear from a Liverpool attack. John Oakes and Jimmy Oakes are to the left and right in the upper picture, and their positions are reversed in the lower picture. The game, watched by 31,000 spectators, ended in a 1-1 draw.

crushed in the 71,767 crowd at the Charlton-Arsenal fifth-round FA Cup tie in February, 1956.

Charlton, Arsenal, Chelsea, and Spurs are the only clubs in the capital to have housed crowds of over 70,000 — a feat achieved by only ten clubs in the country.

Arsenal won that first-ever encounter in the League by 2-0, but Charlton suffered the misfortune early on of losing right-back Sid Cann, who left the field with a knee injury. The Arsenal team that day was Swindin in goal, Male and Hapgood full-backs, Crayston, Roberts and Copping the half-backs, and Kirchen, Davidson, Bowen, Alex James, and Denis Compton the forwards. Bastin was absent, playing for England. The goalscorers were Davidson in the first half and Compton in the second.

The Charlton side was Bartram; Cann, James Oakes; Jobling, John Oakes, Welsh; Tadman, Robinson, Prior, Boulter and Hobbis.

The defeat ended Charlton's unbeaten home run over the past 18 months but it had been a keenly contested and sporting game, and Charlton, a man down, had acquitted themselves well.

Bartram recalled that 'we were, I believe, so thrilled to be playing in such august company that we devoted too much time to watching and admiring their skill, and forgot that we were supposed to be playing ourselves.'

The loss of the unbeaten home record had no effect on the club's momentum in the League. By mid-November, they were only three points behind the leaders.

On 12 December, Charlton beat Everton and went to the top of the League for the second time. After the Christmas and New Year holiday games, they were in fourth place on goal-average only, with 28 points, the same as the clubs above them.

They went up to second place the following week, beating Leeds United. Now they were just a fraction on goal-average behind Arsenal.

By the middle of February, they were back on top for a third time, and the miracle of South-East London went on. Charlton kept their lead in the return game against Arsenal, drawing 1-1 at Highbury before a crowd of 65,000, and then beat Preston North End the next week by 3-1.

Runners-up to the City

THE check came at the end of March, when, at Derby, Charlton crashed 5-0, yielding the leadership to Manchester City who held on to it to win the Championship. Up until Christmas, City had been in the bottom half of the table. Then they hit an inspired streak and went unbeaten for the rest of the season.

One of the Derby goalscorers was their Welsh international centre-forward, Dai Astley, who had been a Charlton player for three seasons before his transfer to Aston Villa in June 1931.

Charlton in fact performed creditably after the Derby disaster, gaining 11 points out of 16 in the last eight games. Their challengers for the runners-up spot were Arsenal and they needed two points from their last game to be sure. The decisive game was at The Valley on 1 May, against Brentford. Charlton won 2-1 with George Robinson getting both goals.

Once again there were tumultuous end of season scenes at the 'Happy Valley'. The team were cheered and escorted from the field by the supporters, who gathered in front of the stand and roared their appreciation. The general chant then developed into an incessant call of "We want Bartram! We want Bartram! We want Bartram!"

The reluctant hero was ushered from the bath with a towel around him to the directors' box. A terrific

Muddy Valley. Players trudge from the field at half-time in the First Division match between Charlton and Preston North End at The Valley in February 1937. Charlton eventually beat that season's FA Cup runners-up, 3-1. Between the Preston pair, the referee and the linesman are Don Welsh, Les Boulter and Harold Hobbis.

cheer went up and then the shout changed to "Speech! Speech! Speech!" All Bartram could say down the microphone was, "Thanks so…thanks very…thanks …it's very nice of you."

The season had been an immense success. With more sharpness in front of goal, the Championship could have been Charlton's. The defence was rocklike, giving away only 49 goals in 42 matches, with five coming in one match, the Derby debacle. The total was the joint lowest in the First Division, Arsenal conceding the same number. This defensive strength meant that no club managed to do the 'double' over Charlton.

But the forwards scored only 58 goals, which was low for the football of those years and more the performance of a lower half of the table team. In fact, that season only four clubs scored less in the First Division and two of those, Manchester United, who had beaten Charlton to the previous year's Second Division championship, and Sheffield Wednesday, were relegated.

The Charlton team had shown a remarkable stability as Seed kept to his word. In defence, Sam Bartram played in all 42 games — the only 'ever-present'. The full-backs, Bert Turner and James Oakes, missed only a handful of games. In the half-back line, Joe Jobling, John Oakes and Don Welsh missed just 15 games between them.

Monty Wilkinson at outside-right, George Robinson at inside-left and Harold Hobbis at outside-right, were also regular performers.

Robinson missed only one game and achieved the distinction of appearing in the side more times than any other player in the three miracle years. He missed only two of the 126 League games played. Boulter and Stephenson shared the inside-left position.

The only regular newcomer was George Tadman, the signing from Gillingham, who finished leading scorer with 11 goals, playing first on the wing and then becoming the regular centre-forward in place of Stan Prior.

The sound defensive performance which underpinned the success was not just due to the defence, but also to the tactical philosophy Seed had developed during his captaincy of Sheffield Wednesday. In modern terms, it would be called 'work-rate'. Seed believed that the inside-forward really worth his salt should be prepared to drop back to pull his weight in defence. He said: "The defence of any successful side starts with the inside-forwards."

One small token of that successful season which remained at The Valley, and in use 40 years later, was a 'Loving Cup' presented to the club to mark the Coronation of King George VI. Only 30 of the

Sam Bartram makes a spectacular leap at the ball during Charlton's 1-0 win over Middlesbrough at The Valley in September 1937. A crowd of 27,782 saw the game. John Oakes is to his right.

intricately-designed and highly-coloured cups were made, at the request of Sir Francis Joseph, the then president of Stoke City, and all 22 First Division clubs received one. The intention was that every club should drink the loyal toast on New Year's Day, or on the date of the match nearest to it. Charlton directors were to drink a toast every year on the appropriate match date with directors of the visiting club. Many of the cups were lost or broken over the years and Charlton's cup was one of the few to remain in use.

Charlton's success on the field was marked by the selection during the season of Joe Jobling and Don Welsh for the England international trial game, and of Welsh as reserve for England in all their representative matches. Bert Turner was capped by Wales for all their international games.

Lasting Success Rebuffs the Critics.

THE success had not been without its difficulties, with some football writers finding it hard to credit the feat of a side almost unchanged from the Third Division South dominating First Division football.

One Press critic slated Charlton as 'the worst team ever to have been at the top of the First Division', although he retracted this cruel remark at the end of the season. Another label stuck on Charlton was that of the 'Old Curiosity Shop of the First Division'.

Seed thought that Charlton were still very much seen as a 'ragamuffin' team suffering by comparison with the success of their Woolwich forebears, Arsenal.

The remaining seasons before the war were to show how shallow the criticism was as the club remained consistently near the top of the League and proved, beyond doubt, that the marvellous, miraculous 1936-7 season was no flash in the pan. A great London club had been born.

The Fleeting Span of Greatness

CHARLTON'S brief reign of greatness really spans the immediate pre-war and post-war years. But even the interruption caused by the war saw the club reach Wembley twice. The tragedy was that those years were not consolidated into lasting greatness through the club's playing success being backed by off-the-pitch endeavour. The basis was there. The club had made a profit on its activities for the second year in succession.

But The Valley was still not the ground of a great First Division club and although improvements were made, they were not of the dramatic kind that should have matched the club's dramatic rise. The standard of dressing-room accommodation was improved, but the stadium stayed largely unaltered.

Soon after Charlton reached the First Division, Seed, according to his autobiography, raised the whole question of The Valley with the Gliksten brothers. He wanted a new stand and he knew that a club could only stay great and gain stature and support by having a stadium to match, even in those days when supporters were prepared to put up with much more basic facilities.

The reply of Albert Gliksten was amazing at the time and tragic and absurd in restrospect. It ultimately destroyed the prospect of Charlton Athletic staying one of the great London clubs and paved the way to the events of nearly 50 years later.

According to Seed, Gliksten's response was: "Will you guarantee to keep us in the First Division for three seasons?"

Seed replied that he thought the team were good enough but that no manager could give the guarantee of success sought unless he was a born gambler.

Gliksten then answered: "Right. There'll be no new stand at The Valley."

Gliksten compounded his error after the outbreak of war. He remarked to Seed: "See what I mean, Jimmy. You wanted us to build a big stand. It would have been disastrous."

In fact, the price of building in the late 1930s compared to the post-war period would have meant that Charlton would have had a profitable money-earning stand in place for the huge attendances the club enjoyed after the war. In Seed's view, in later years, many potential season-ticket holders were deterred through the lack of covered and seated accommodation.

His autobiography contains this passage:

'It is easy to be wise afterwards but Charlton could have become the Arsenal of South-East London if the Glikstens had retained the same enthusiasm as when they took over, although I am the first to appreciate that, having taken one terrific financial gamble with the club, they didn't want to take another chance, even though every penny put into the club had been paid back to them.'

If Charlton had built a second stand and improved the accommodation, not only for fans but also for visiting directors and officials, then The Valley might well have staged international games in London, like Highbury and White Hart Lane. The days of Wembley as the regular home of the international team were still far in the future.

It must be remembered, however, that these were the views of Seed in 1958, after a bitter exit from the club. Whether he was so persistent in them during his managership is open to doubt. In the club's jubilee handbook of 1955, with Charlton still in the First Division, he queried the need for another stand, asserting that 'only on rare occasions are we able to sell all 3,000 seats' in the lone West Stand. Whatever the consistency of Seed's views, however, the policy was one of a club which never foresaw that the world would change about it.

After the remarkable promotion achievements, the Gliksten brothers' policy became one of holding on rather than building up. To use the old adage, they were penny-wise but pound-foolish. In hindsight, it would have been better if, having got their money back from the club, they had left at this stage and passed the club on to more ambitious hands.

Charlton South Africa Bound?

IN fact, after the war, Albert Gliksten, despondent at the tax liability on his income, even seriously considered packing his bags, going to South Africa and taking Charlton with him.

He asked Seed if he would be prepared to pull up his roots, sell his house, and open up the new Charlton in Johannesburg. All players who were interested would be invited to switch to South Africa, and any who did not do so, would be replaced by local South African players.

Amazingly, Seed took the idea seriously and backed it as he liked South Africa. Indeed, in the post-war years he pursued a policy of signing players from the country. But too many difficulties cropped up and the idea, while never relinquished entirely, faded until finally ended by the death of Gliksten. Such a betrayal of supporters would have made the move to Selhurst Park in 1985 seem a mere fleabite by comparison.

Excavation at The Valley

APART from this wider question of The Valley itself, the drainage of the pitch caused concern with the coming of first-class football. The pitch had improved considerably in recent years, but a wet patch persisted awkwardly and obstinately in front of the grandstand. As all efforts at drying it had failed, the club decided to excavate it. The cause of the wetness was found to be two large concrete slabs, the remains of the bases of houses that were never built. The club also had sod samples taken and analysed to determine the correct use of fertilizers.

The club's success in the League in these years had not been matched by success in the Cup. The only performance of note was in 1933-4 when, as a newly-relegated club in the Third Division South, they won through to the fourth round, before going out by the odd goal. Most of the club's Cup history at this time saw them going out in the first game.

In their second season in the First Division, however, their Cup exploits began to reflect their strength in the League. They were exempt until the third round and then had the good fortune of being drawn at home three times. Their first opponents at The Valley were Cardiff City. Charlton won 5-0, with Owens scoring twice, and Robinson and Boulter getting one each. The other was an own-goal.

In the next round, against First Division Leeds United, Charlton were two goals ahead by half-time through outside-right Tadman. Leeds scored in the second half through their centre-forward and captain, Hodgson, but Charlton managed to hang on to win 2-1.

The Highest Attendance

THEIR fifth-round opponents were Aston Villa, who topped the Second Division. The game was historic for it drew The Valley's biggest-ever crowd — 75,031. Charlton failed to live up to the occasion and were one down at half-time. They were reckoned fortunate to equalize in the second half after a generally indifferent performance, Robinson scoring.

Things appeared to improve in the replay at Villa Park with Albert 'Sailor' Brown, deputizing for Boulter, scoring early in the first half. Brown scored again in the second half and with 20 minutes to go, Charlton were still 2-0 ahead. Then Aston Villa got two late goals.

The replay was at Highbury on a Monday evening before a crowd of 64,782 and it proved disastrous. Turner was unfit and could not play, but Charlton went ahead after 28 minutes through Tadman. Then, in just a couple of minutes, the game changed dramatically. John Oakes had to go off and had three stitches put in a cut eye after a collision with Villa's Shell, who also had to leave the field temporarily.

Then Harold Hobbis broke his right leg as he was tackled by Villa's Scottish international right-half, Alex Massie, as he was about to shoot. Charlton held on to their lead through the rest of the first half, but then succumbed.

Two slightly doubtful goals from Broome (58 minutes) and Haycock (84) put Villa in the lead. By the time Broome completed his hat-trick, in the 88th and 89th minutes, to give Villa a 4-1 victory, Charlton were down to nine men with Tadman off the field.

Villa went on both to the semi-final where they were beaten 2-1 by the eventual Cup winners, Preston North End, and to win the Second Division championship.

Hobbis was out of football until the end of the year. Sadly, in Seed's view, he was never to be the same force as before his injury. The consolation in defeat for Charlton was that the three games had drawn a total of 202,343 spectators and a valuable financial windfall for the club from the aggregate receipts of £15,297.

Sam Lost in a Fog

CHARLTON started off the 1937-8 League season with two draws against Leeds United and Grimsby Town, but by the end of September were top again, with the squad of players still largely unchanged. On 2 October, they lost for the first time after a run of 13 unbeaten games, going down 2-0 at Stoke to a team inspired by Stanley Matthews. They won 5-1 at home the next week against Portsmouth, but the old failings of an uninspired forward line let them down and they began to slip.

One of the most humorous incidents the club ever experienced came on Christmas Day against Chelsea at Stamford Bridge. The weather was foggy and the fog got so bad that the referee halted the game. He restarted it, but finally called the game off after an hour. The players went to their dressing-rooms and then someone asked where the goalkeeper, Sam Bartram, was.

Sam was found by a policeman, still standing between his goal-posts, looking into the murk and wondering how the game was going at the other end! He had been on the field by himself for ten minutes. By the time he got to the dressing-room, his teammates were out of the bath and convulsed with laughter.

Another lighthearted recollection of those times comes in the autobiography of Alec Stock who started his professional career with Charlton, and was later to achieve distinction elsewhere as both player and manager. Charlton signed him from the amateur club, Redhill, before the start of the 1936-7 season and he stayed two seasons without breaking into the first team.

Stock recalled how these years were 'happy times' at The Valley and he particularly remembered Bert Turner:

'Bert was an immaculate, big man, over six foot tall and fifteen stone of muscle. His only problem was that every summer he would put on weight and turn up for the first day of training a stone too heavy. Well, at Charlton in those days they had a huge boiler at the back of the dressing-room and that's where

Players from a pools card — the 1937-8 team as shown on a card issued by the pools firm, Sherman's of Cardiff. Back row (left to right): Joe Jobling, Bert Turner, Sam Bartram, John Oakes, Don Welsh, George Green. Front row: George Tadman, George Robinson, James Oakes, Thomas Owens, Les Boulter and Harold Hobbis.

Bert Turner leaping over a Birmingham forward during a game at The Valley in the late 1930s.

Bert always ended up. He was stripped off, had two old red inner tubes fastened to his middle, and was ordered to skip for hours in a track suit, two jumpers and a towel tucked into his neck! 'That'll teach you Bert', Seed would say.'

By the New Year of 1938, Charlton had lost fewer games than any other League club — only four out of 21. But there were too many draws for a credible championship-chasing team. The side was also suffering a succession of injuries, with James Oakes, John Oakes, Green, Welsh, Robinson, Tadman, Boulter, Turner, Brown and Jobling all out more than once.

Charlton ended the season in fourth position behind the champions, Arsenal, runners-up Wolverhampton Wanderers, and Preston North End.

They drew with Preston at The Valley in the last game of the season. The Football League had instituted 'talent money' for the first time, and Charlton just qualified by finishing in fourth place.

Charlton made a gross profit of £14,724 on the season and a net profit of £5,826 after paying interest on debentures etc. Attendances at The Valley had averaged just over 30,000 and gate receipts were £2,000 up on the previous season at £44,000.

During the close season, Albert Lindon, twice acting manager of the club, left to become chief scout at Arsenal. Still the same player policy remained. The team for the next season remained that of the season just past: Bartram; Turner or Shreeve, James Oakes, Green, John Oakes, Welsh; Wilkinson, Robinson, Tadman, Boulter, Hobbis or Brown.

Neville Chamberlain at The Valley

IN the new season of 1938-9, Albert 'Sailor' Brown deputized for the injured Hobbis until December 1938. When Hobbis returned, 'Sailor' Brown, so named because of his rolling gait on the field, kept his place

in the team, replacing Boulter at inside right. Boulter was transferred to Brentford in February for £5,920 and went on to win in the following month his first and only cap for Wales, playing against Ireland in Wrexham.

Charlton suffered a serious blow when Bert Turner broke a shoulder blade against Leeds United on 3 September and did not play again until 14 January.

A draw at The Valley on 1 October 1938, against Birmingham, was notable for two very different reasons. The first was that both teams scored four goals each. The second was that the spectators included the Prime Minister, Neville Chamberlain. The Rector of Charlton led special prayers as a thanks-giving for the Munich agreement on Czechoslovakia.

Charlton's form at this time was uneven and the club was involved in a very unpleasant match at Portsmouth three weeks later on 22 October. They had gone into a two-goal lead when, under mounting Pompey pressure, they conceded a penalty. Bartram, who was having one of his inspired days in goal, saved the kick from outside-right Fred Worrall and then Worrall and James Oakes came to blows. Oakes, who had a record of 15 years unblemished play, and Worrall were ordered off.

Then crowd trouble, reminiscent of modern times, erupted. Two or three fans invaded the field and the Pompey fans behind Bartram's goal began to barrack him. Then Bartram was hit by a half-brick and momentarily stunned. Then fans set fire to the net to complete a disgraceful day. An inquiry followed into the incidents and Oakes was fined £5. But Worrell received stronger punishment, being fined £5 and suspended for a week. The board of Enquiry censured the Portsmouth crowd, ordered Portsmouth to take steps to safeguard visiting teams and made Pompey pay the costs of the inquiry.

November was marked by an episode very much

Tadman (left) scores Charlton's second goal in their 2-1 win over Leeds United in an FA Cup fourth-round game at The Valley in January 1938. A crowd of 50,516 saw Charlton progress to the next round, where they lost to Aston Villa after two replays.

out of character with Charlton's cost conscious policy. Had it succeeded, along with Seed's idea for the development of The Valley, it might have transformed the club.

The Bid for Stanley Matthews

ON 16 November, Seed offered £13,000 to Stoke City for the legendary Stanley Matthews. In those days, that was big money indeed. Just three months earlier, George Allison, the manager of Arsenal, had caused a sensation by paying Wolverhampton Wanderers £14,000 for Bryn Jones, topping the previous record signing of David Jack by Arsenal from Bolton Wanderers.

Seed's offer was made immediately after he watched Matthews play for England against Ireland in

Charlton players stand in silence before their game against Birmingham at The Valley in October 1938. Prime Minister Neville Chamberlain was at the match and prayers were said as a thanksgiving for the Munich agreement on Czechoslovakia. Left to right: George Green, Joe Jobling, Jack Shreeve, 'Sailor' Brown, Jimmy Oakes, George Robinson, Sam Bartram, John Oakes, Les Boulter, Don Welsh, Monty Wilkinson.

Photographs of
Charlton players
training at The
Valley in February
1938. The top
photograph shows
a game of head
tennis. In the
bottom picture,
trainer Jimmy
Trotter (white
coat) watches the
players running
around the cinder
track.

Manchester. England won 7-0 and Matthews had given what Seed called 'one of the finest displays I had ever seen from a wing-forward'.

Willie Hall, the Tottenham inside-forward, had scored five goals, thanks almost entirely to Matthews's tremendous service and mesmerization of the Irish defence. The offer was made to the Stoke City manager, Bob McGrory, after the game. Many clubs had been after Matthews, and Stoke were reluctant to part.

McGrory, a 'dour Scot' in Seed's words, had played at left-back in the Stoke side when Stanley came in during his teens. He was never a Matthews fan, according to Seed, and was willing to do the deal with Charlton. But the decision was up to the directors, and McGrory promised a decision within a couple of days.

Back at Charlton, the response from Albert Gliksten was: "Have you gone mad, Jimmy?"

Seed began to feel uneasy. "Wouldn't I look foolish if Stoke accepted my offer only for the Charlton directors to decide I had acted too impulsively?"

Seed was saved from this embarrassment the next day, when McGrory told him the directors were not interested in selling Matthews at any price.

When war broke out, Seed had to put with up a similar comment from Gliksten to that about his plans for The Valley. "A good job we didn't buy

Chelsea goalkeeper Vic Woodley and defender Arthur Smith are helpless as George Robinson (extreme left) scores for Charlton at The Valley on Good Friday, 1939. Charlton won 2-0 over the lowly Pensioners, in front of 33,000, and three days later, on 10 April, completed an Easter double with a 3-1 victory at Stamford Bridge, where 30,000 saw the game.

Aston Villa goalkeeper Jock Rutherford takes the ball as Charlton's Blott challenges him during the game at The Valley on Easter Saturday 1939. Welsh and Hobbis are to their right. Charlton won 1-0 in front of 17,000 spectators.

Matthews. It would have been £13,000 down the drain.''

Yet more than two and a half decades later, Matthews was still pulling in the crowds. The £13,000 would surely have been paid off with dividends and Charlton would have had the glamour that always eluded the club in their 21-year stay in the First Division.

In the First Division at this time, Charlton's fortunes improved then slipped again, but in February

came a sequence of three remarkable results. Birmingham were beaten away 4-3, and then Leicester were beaten away by 5-1. These two victories were followed by a 7-1 thrashing of Manchester United at The Valley, Tadman getting four, Wilkinson two and Hobbis one.

Charlton were now fourth in the League but the next game saw them going down 4-0 away to Huddersfield Town.

Their form then settled and they took 16 points

Sam Bartram tips a header from Derby County centre-forward Dave McCulloch over the bar at The Valley in November 1938. The game attracted a crowd of 41,816, who saw Charlton win 1-0. John Oakes (left) and Jimmy Oakes look on. Almost in the net is Jack Shreeve. Robinson and Tadman (hidden by the post) are also pictured.

Chelsea's Woodley punches clear from Charlton's Hobbis and Welsh at The Valley on Good Friday, 7 April 1939.

from the next 13 games to finish third with 50 points, nine behind the champions Everton. In fact, they were the only club to bring off the double against the champions.

The club had finished their pre-war seasons in the First Division second, fourth and third. It was a tremendous feat and one achieved with a stable team and little buying.

Had War Not Intervened. . .

THE question will always remain as to what this team could have gone on to achieve had the war not intervened. They had made Charlton great in the span of five seasons.

The success brought all-round recognition for the club and international appearances for Hobbis, Welsh, Turner and Green. Bert Turner, after gaining his first Welsh cap in 1936-7, went on to captain his country the next season, playing regularly for them before the outbreak of war. George Green also won his way into the Welsh team and won four caps, making his debut against Northern Ireland in March 1938. Harold Hobbis totalled the two caps he gained on the 1936 tour and the irrepressible Don Welsh, a reserve many times for England, gained two more peacetime caps after his Berlin debut — against Switzerland in Zurich and Rumania in Bucharest. The Rumanian game on 24 May 1939, was England's last international before war broke out.

Sam Bartram played in an English trial in the autumn of 1937, for the Possibles against the Probables at Goodison Park, and was a reserve against Wales. He also toured South Africa in 1939 in a representative team which included John Oakes and

'Sailor' Brown. Jobling also played in an English trial in 1936.

One notable signing towards the end of the last full peacetime season of 1938-9 was that of Bert Johnson, signed from Spennymoor United in March 1939 for £400, and who was to play such a prominent part in the club's post-war success. He was signed along with Tommy Dawson, a half-back or forward from Spennymoor, through the north-east scouting system.

The Three-game Season

EVEN as the 1938-9 season closed, there was a feeling that the 1939-40 season might never take place. One rumour was that if war started, The Valley would be immediately taken over as an ARP and Decontamination Centre, finishing football there right away.

But during the close season, things had to go on in their normal way. Bartram, Brown, and John Oakes were away touring in South Africa. The authorities announced that it would be compulsory for players to be numbered during the coming season. And Charlton bought an extra car-park for The Valley.

When the players reported back for training, there

George Tadman in action. He scored in Charlton's last game before World War Two saw the League programme suspended for seven seasons.

was an air of unreality everywhere and war was almost the only topic of conversation. The 1939-40 season lasted three games. Charlton lost 4-0 at Stoke in the opening game, with Welsh being so badly injured — he suffered torn ligaments — that it was reckoned he would be out for three months.

The following Wednesday, Charlton beat Leeds United 1-0 at Elland Road, the day before Hitler ordered the invasion of Poland, on the morning of Friday, 1 September 1939.

By Saturday, 2 September, children were already being evacuated from the major urban areas but the League programme went ahead. Only 8,608 spectators turned up for the first — and, as it turned out, last — home game of the season, against Manchester United. The game was a lacklustre affair and, clearly, football was the last priority in the minds of everyone, including the players. Tadman and Dawson scored Charlton's last pre-war goals in a 2-0 win. Next morning, the British ultimatum to Germany passed and war was declared.

The three games played were expunged from the Football League's official records and Charlton's status as a First Division club was maintained for another seven years, without them playing a further League game. Meanwhile, a team at its prime, which had come consistently near to winning the First Division title, was scattered to the winds.

John Oakes, who signed from Aldershot and proved a mainstay of Charlton's defence.

55

Wembley in Wartime

Pre-season
training at The
Valley in August
1939. Three
games into the
season, League
football was
halted. Leading
the way, left to
right, are Don
Welsh, George
Green, Jimmy
Oakes and Bert
Johnson.

AFTER war broke out, all football contracts were cancelled on 15 September, on the instruction of the Football Association. At first the majority of Charlton players went into the Police Reserve, although some found themselves at the Woolwich Arsenal. As the weeks went by, they trickled into the armed forces, some becoming physical training instructors, such as Bartram and Welsh. The immediate impact was the exodus of many players' wives back to the comparative safety of their home towns elsewhere in the country, although some soon returned.

Nobody, of course, was quite sure what the war would entail for football, but the course of events gradually unfolded. By the end of the war, some 62 Charlton players and other members of staff had served in the armed forces — a massive and perhaps surprising number.

Action from the
friendly against
Millwall at The
Den in September
1939. George
Smith gets the
header.

Shortly after the FA edict, the Government placed a ban on all football in the London area. Despite the rumour that The Valley would be taken over

completely for an ARP and Decontamination Centre, only a part of the ground was allocated for the ARP.

The ban on football was relaxed again the following week and Charlton played a friendly game against Millwall at The Den and drew 1-1. For friendlies the players received their expenses and a small retainer, but it was a worrying time for them. A good income of up to £8 per week had dropped to almost the £3 of the average industrial wage and it was going to take a little time before recruiting got into full swing for the services. The Charlton club helped by waiving all rents for players who lived in club houses and for the Christmas of 1939, Albert Gliksten gave them each a turkey.

The club offered season-ticket holders £2.10s (£2.50) back on their £3 payment, deducting ten shillings (50p) for administration expenses, entertainment tax and the one home game played.

At the beginning of October, the future of football in war became a little clearer. A regional competition for London clubs was announced with a starting date of 21 October. The teams taking part were Arsenal, Charlton, Millwall, Tottenham Hotspur, West Ham United, Clapton Orient, Crystal Palace, Norwich, Southend and Watford.

Thirty shillings (£1.50), plus expenses, was to be paid to professional players taking part. Guest players were allowed, and no club was allowed to reclaim any player on contract. In November, Charlton were fined by the Football Association for paying players

Opposite: More aerial action from the Millwall friendly. Charlton goalkeeper Sid Hobbins punches clear from Millwall's Jimmy Richardson with Charlton's George Smith in attendance. Ted Smith opened the scoring for Millwall and Bert Tann equalized for Charlton.

January 1940, when he advertised a training scheme for 16 to 19-year-olds at The Valley. Fifty boys were selected for training under Jimmy Trotter and a series of trial games arranged.

A junior team was formed from the most promising triallists and some friendly matches were played during the latter part of the 1939-40 season. The following season, the juniors played under the name of Charlton Rovers and continued as a local league team in the South-Eastern Combination for the next few years, winning the Combination Cup in 1944.

In the new regional league, attendances sank even lower in the 1939-40 season. Towards the end of the season, Charlton and Fulham shared just £14 8s 8d (£14.43) between them after a game. Only 855 people turned up to see Charlton play Portsmouth, the last peacetime FA Cup winners. Receipts were £35.

On 7 April, Charlton played a game at Chelsea which produced a sensational finish with three penalty-goals in the last five minutes. Charlton were 2-0 up when Charlie Revell was brought down in the area, took the kick himself and scored. Then Chelsea were awarded a penalty which Joe Payne converted. Revell scored again from the spot with the last kick of the match, after Hobbis was fouled.

Revell had not played in Charlton's pre-war League sides, but he was to establish himself as a powerful League player at forward and half-back in the post-war years. He had previously played for Northfleet.

Of the pre-war side, Bartram, John Oakes, Green, Welsh, Turner, Robinson, Brown and Hobbis played from time to time, and Wilkinson and Tadman made a few appearances. The Army took Cann, Green, Shreeve, Tadman, Welsh and Wright. The RAF claimed Bartram, Brown, Hobbis, Lancelotte, John Oakes, Rist, Robinson, Turner and Wilkinson.

At the outbreak of war, Bartram enrolled in the Police Reserve and, after a few months, joined the RAF to train as a physical training instructor, in due course becoming a sergeant-instructor.

When he reported for the training course at Uxbridge in January 1940, he found himself in good company. There also were the Arsenal players Ted Drake, Jack Crayston, George Marks, Alf Kirchen and Laurie Scott, and Vic Buckingham of Spurs and Albert Glidden of Reading. Also on the course were the Surrey cricketers, Bob Gregory, Stan Squires, Jack Parker and Tom Barling.

Bartram was first posted to Derby and guested for Notts County, his first game of football since joining up. He was posted again to Padgate and then to West Kirby, where he guested regularly for Liverpool. Moving again, this time to Bournemouth, he found it possible to play occasional games for Charlton whilst guesting for the Bournemouth club. His next posting took him to Harrogate and a three-season guest spell with York City, the club he was later to manage. Two other Charlton players, 'Sailor' Brown and Tommy Dawson, also ended up in the York team. Brown, despite his nickname, was in the RAF.

Travelling to matches whilst a wartime guest player was not always easy. Bartram thumbed his way to play for York at Hartlepool in a snowstorm. A fire-engine, on a call, picked him up. The icy road made this strange journey hazardous and Sam arrived late to find the game had started and a replacement was in goal. He had to be a reluctant spectator and, to cap the day, York lost.

Don Welsh was one of a group of 19 players whom the FA had initially recommended to the Army for physical education training. Whilst in the Army, he guested regularly with Liverpool, the club he was

more than the 30 shillings. This was later rescinded as other clubs were found to have overpaid in error. But early in 1940, there were reports that some clubs were paying players £3 a game.

The conditions of wartime meant that players flitted from club to club, playing whenever they could and usually getting a game near to where they were doing their duty in the services or in war industry.

The difficulty in getting together regular sides produced some strange results. On 21 October, Charlton played Arsenal at White Hart Lane — a Gunners' 'home' game — in their first match in the competition and lost 8-4. The next week, they beat Southend 8-1 and then defeated Clapton Orient by the same score in the next game.

But the artificiality of the football, allied to the stress of wartime, and population losses through evacuation, meant that the games did not draw many spectators. The last game of 1939, played in fog against Arsenal, drew only 2,000 people. By the time the competition was cancelled in February, the Charlton average home attendance was just 1,600.

In February, the authorities reorganized the whole competition to try to lessen the disparity of the teams taking part. But still wartime football had no appeal, even when guest stars like Tommy Lawton and Frank Swift appeared in the Charlton team.

Charlton Rovers

THE task of the club was to prepare young players for the uncertain time when League football would resume. The first step taken by Jimmy Seed was in later to manage. Another Liverpool guest with Welsh was the Wolves centre-half, Stan Cullis. Welsh had been in the Navy in pre-war days before signing for Torquay, but he became a CSMI in the Army. He was appointed a physical training instructor and coach to the Canadian Army. Later in the war, he was in charge of troop transports.

In 1941-2, his service commitments caused supporters to be concerned that he was attempting to play too much football. They thought he looked jaded. Proof of Welsh's determination to play wartime football had come in the New Year of 1940. He was on leave from his regiment and travelled by road to play for Charlton at Southend. The car skidded and was completely wrecked, although neither he nor his wife were injured. On arrival at Southend, he still wanted to play, but Seed successfully persuaded him otherwise.

Later in the war, Charlton's Welsh international, Bert Turner, was to guest for the Welsh club, Lovell's in the League West section. Lovell's were one of three non-League clubs allowed to join the section and play against League clubs. The other clubs were Bath and Aberaman, a tiny Welsh club from the mid-Glamorgan mining area, for whom another Charlton player, George Tadman, guested in 1943-4. John Oakes became a special traffic policeman before joining the Army.

One of the incoming guests was a familiar face, the former Charlton player, Dai Astley, then with Blackpool. He arrived in London in November 1939, to stay with Bert Turner, his brother-in-law and fellow Welshman. Astley had Blackpool's permission to play for whomever he wanted.

A player from the Scottish League, Third Lanark's Jim Mason, who was serving in the Middlesex Regiment, also guested, although Third Lanark insisted he was heavily insured. From Scotland, too, came another player who was to be a legend in Charlton's history, Chris Duffy, a true all-round Briton. He was born in Fife, married an Irish girl and served in the Royal Welch Fusiliers.

Football with a Battle Overhead

THE opening game of the 1940-41 season at The Valley took place during the Battle of Britain and was a minor classic as an example of the difficulty of wartime conditions. The date was 7 September 1940 and the opponents were Millwall, who were leading 4-2 before a 2,000 crowd with a minute left for play.

Then the air-raid siren sounded and it certainly was no false warning. The raid was a heavy one and shrapnel fell on the stadium. Amazingly, the game was resumed when the all-clear sounded and the last 60 seconds played out.

The subsequent crowds soon dwindled to hundreds. There were frequent air-raid warnings during games, which acted as a deterrent to the keenest fan. And this was not helped by a Home Office ruling that play must stop whenever an alert was sounded. The Home Office would not agree to a proposed 'Spotter' system which would give warning only when danger was imminent.

Play was often interrupted for up to an hour and on one occasion, when the second half had just started, the game was stopped for over an hour. This was too much. Some players simply went home and the referee found other players still in the bath when the 'all-clear' sounded. If a game could not be continued, the score at the interruption went down as the official result.

Why Go On?

TOWARDS the end of the year, the club decided to give up wartime football. They were losing £60 a week. Average attendances were just 400. A lot of these were servicemen and children, who were let in for half-price, and average takings were just £12.

On 7 December, the club were allowed to use a spotter for the first time in the 5-0 win over Arsenal and play continued during an air-raid alert. The attendance was 1,000. Jimmy Seed commented on the situation: "The public don't want football, the directors don't want football — so why go on?"

The ground had suffered several times. Four bombs hit the terraces, two fell on the pitch, one landing on a penalty-spot, and there was a direct hit on the ambulance hut.

The closedown came on 28 December 1940, when Charlton played their final match, losing 3-1 at Portsmouth. But the junior side, Charlton Rovers, were kept going.

The few regular players left, those who had jobs in the area, were absorbed by other London clubs as guest players. Hobbis and Green played for West Ham, Jobling for Clapton Orient and Revell and Robinson for Fulham.

By the following season, daytime bombing had virtually stopped and people were becoming more adjusted to the exigencies of war, often sleeping in shelters at night and coming out by day for normal workaday life.

Breakaway from the League

IN 1941, Charlton decided to resume activities, but not before being involved along with other southern clubs in a massive row with the Football League, who sensationally expelled them and 13 others — fellow full League members Arsenal, Chelsea, Brentford, Fulham, Millwall, Tottenham Hotspur and West Ham, together with associate members, Aldershot, Clapton Orient, Crystal Palace, Queen's Park Rangers, Reading and Crewe Alexandra.

At a meeting in Nottingham on 9 June 1941, the League decided to regularize the structure of wartime football by bringing in a League Championship competition in two sections, north and south. The rebel clubs were opposed to a southern programme which called upon them to travel to coastal areas such as Southend, Southampton, Bournemouth and Swansea, as well as distances to places like Luton and Norwich. Crewe were involved because they had been placed in the southern section to balance numbers.

After a Football League Management Committee meeting at Preston on 5 August, the League secretary announced that the shares in the League of Charlton and the other full-member clubs had been cancelled.

The rebels appealed against their expulsion and the League agreed to let them proceed with their own competition without prejudice to their case. The League could have formally taken over the registrations of the rebels' players and prevented them from playing, but in the difficult conditions of wartime, this would have been too controversial a step and probably impossible to enforce.

Neither was any attempt made by the League to stop rebel club players guesting for League sides or vice versa. The rebels, joined by Watford, Brighton and Portsmouth, now numbered 16 and decided to act in unison. If the affair lasted until the end of the war, then all would stay out of the League if any was refused admission back.

Under the leadership of Arsenal manager, George Allison, who was elected chairman of clubs in the south in the early days of the war, they argued that the League could not be properly constituted during wartime conditions and so had virtually no authority to impose peacetime legislation on clubs. Their line also seemed in accord with Government thinking which was against unnecessary excessive travel in wartime.

Meetings in mid-August failed to reach a settlement and the Football Association decided to sanction the rebels' London League. The long rift was finally ended in April 1942, when the rebels agreed to send letters of regret, withdraw appeals and each pay a £10 fine to be reinstated. Crewe were welcomed back at the same time.

At the start of the 1941-2 London League season, Charlton promoted four or five of their continuing Rovers team to the first team. Some 7,000 spectators turned up at The Valley to see Charlton win their first game, 2-1 against Chelsea. The start was put back to 6pm to allow war workers to attend.

On 1 November, while on the way to Brighton, the Charlton team 'bus hit a telegraph pole. Most of the players were badly shaken but Charlton went on to win the match 5-3.

The opening crowd of 7,000 at The Valley was about the size of crowd which continued to turn up for the competition. The visit of Arsenal in the New Year sparked the traditional interest, with The Valley car-park filled to capacity with both military vehicles and civilian cars, and young autograph hunters clustered around the players' entrance.

The London League Cup created extra interest and Charlton did far better in this than in the wartime League where their form was indifferent. The Cup was organized on a sectional basis. The clubs were divided into four sections of four clubs each. Each club played a home and away game against the other clubs in its section.

The clubs with the best records from these games went forward into the semi-finals, where they played one of the other section winners on a neutral ground. The Final was at Wembley.

Charlton reached the semi-final, losing 1-0 to Portsmouth on 25 April at Stamford Bridge before a crowd of 19,036. Harold Hobbis, the team's outside-left and captain that day, had a double disappointment. He returned home to find his house had been burgled and he had lost his 15 soccer medals.

Over the next two seasons, attendances improved but the admission charge of 1s 6d (7½p) was criticized as too high for the standard of football played. But the fee was laid down for all southern clubs and Charlton had no choice in the matter. And it was

Football school for Canadians, courtesy of Charlton Athletic, at Godalming in 1942. Sergeant-major Don Welsh (seated fourth from left) and Sergeant-major George Green (seated second from right) were assigned to supervise the physical fitness of Canadian troops. Amongst their tasks was laying out a football pitch and teaching the laws of the game.

still costing £60 a week to run the club, despite obviously reduced overheads.

In 1942, came two additions to the board of directors, Dr Montgomery, who had been the club doctor for 15 years, and Robert Law, who replaced Arthur Arnott.

Inevitably, Charlton players on wartime service found themselves involved in dangerous situations. Arthur Turner, an amateur and Charlton Rovers player who made his debut against Arsenal on 27 November 1943, later almost lost his life as a Coastal Command air-gunner when his plane crashed into the Bay of Biscay. He was the only survivor and floated around for hours before being rescued.

Another product of the juniors, goalkeeper Jim Sanders, also experienced the dangers of wartime air-gunning. He completed three flight tours for the RAF, taking part in nearly 200 operational sorties. On his third tour, he was severely wounded in an encounter with an enemy fighter and was invalided out of the service. His soccer career seemed doomed, but he did play again and was transferred to West Bromwich Albion on 14 November 1945, where his career lasted until 1958. Half-back Freddie Ford lost a finger when he was wounded in the Rhine crossing in the later stages of the war.

Millwall Make Home at The Valley

THE wartime conditions continued to produce bizarre results. At the beginning of the 1942-3 season, Charlton lost 6-2 to Arsenal, 7-2 to Aldershot, and 6-1 to Spurs. They then beat Watford 7-0 and Fulham 4-0. For Jimmy Seed, it was a 'headache' to find 11 players to make up a team.

The 1943-4 season saw temporary visitors to The Valley — Charlton's neighbours Millwall. On the last day of the previous season, the main stand at The Den, seating 2,000, was burned to the ground. Millwall moved their first-team games to The Valley and Charlton Reserves went to New Cross. Millwall received permission from the authorities to erect a temporary stand which they hoped to complete by November. It was not ready until March 1944. Charlton's North Stand also suffered a direct hit.

Charlton made a poor start to the 1943-4 season,

but in November 1943, they beat Luton Town 8-2 at The Valley, only to go down the next week, 6-2 again to Arsenal. In the following year, Luton crashed at The Valley by 9-4, Revell scoring six against them.

However difficult those war years proved, they did see Charlton Athletic reach Wembley for the first time. In fact, they appeared in consecutive seasons in the League South Cup, in 1942-3 and 1943-4.

In 1942-3, Charlton won their Cup section and met Reading at White Hart Lane before a crowd of 19,000. A 2-1 victory gave Charlton their first-ever appearance at Wembley. The Final, on 1 May, was against their famous rivals, Arsenal.

The result was a thrashing, Charlton going down 7-1. Reg Lewis, the Arsenal centre-forward scored four goals, Ted Drake, the inside-right, got two and Denis Compton one. George Green scored Charlton's lone goal from a penalty.

It was a disappointment of course, to get to Wembley and then be on the end of such a hammering, but the 75,000 crowd brought the Charlton club a welcome cheque for £2,919 as their share of the proceeds.

The teams were:

Charlton Athletic: Hobbins; Cann, Shreeve, Phipps, John Oakes, Davies; Green, Mason, Welsh, Brown, Revell.

Arsenal: Marks; Scott, L.Compton, Crayston, Joy, Male, Kirchen, Drake, Lewis, Bastin, D.Compton.

Don Welsh (right) and Arsenal's George Male shake hands before their Wembley meeting in the 1943 League South Cup Final.

Charlton's first Wembley Final. The Duke of Gloucester meets the Charlton players before their 7-1 defeat by Arsenal. Arsenal manager George Allison is on the far left. Jimmy Seed is behind Don Welsh (hidden) and the Duke. Charlton players in line (from left to right) are Sid Cann, Charlie Revell, John Oakes, 'Sailor' Brown, Jack Shreeve (shaking hands), Harold Phipps, Jimmy Mason, Cec Davies, George Green and Sid Hobbins.

Eisenhower Cheers the Reds

IN the next season, Charlton won their section again and then beat Tottenham Hotspur 3-0 in the semi-final at Stamford Bridge. They met Chelsea at Wembley on 15 April 1944, before a crowd of 85,000 — the maximum permitted by wartime regulations.

And this time Charlton were victorious, beating Chelsea 3-1 in a game marked by a freak cloudburst. The guest of honour was General Eisenhower, who presented them with the Cup. Hundreds of American servicemen were among the spectators.

The Charlton team was: Bartram; Shreeve, Jobling (who had come out of retirement), Smith, John Oakes, Chilton (guesting from Manchester United), Robinson (Sunderland), Brown, Revell, Welsh (captain) and Duffy (Leith Athletic).

Chelsea lined up: Woodley; Hardwick, Westwood, Russell, Harris, Foss, Ashcroft, Fagan, Payne, Bowie, Mitten.

Chelsea opened the scoring early on through Joe Payne, the legendary Luton forward who scored ten goals in one match in April 1936, against Bristol Rovers.

The Chelsea inside-forward, Bowie, dribbled

Left: This shot from Chelsea's Bowie hit the post and from the rebound, Jobling handled. Payne scored from the resultant penalty. Charlton players are (from left) Shreeve, Oakes and Bartram.

Wembley 1944 and General Eisenhower before he decided to cheer for the Reds. From left: Sam Bartram, Charlie Revell, 'Sailor' Brown, Jack Shreeve, Billy Robinson, Allenby Chilton, Joe Jobling, George Smith. Skipper Don Welsh is obscured by General Eisenhower.

through in the ninth minute and cracked in a shot which Bartram was only able to push out to Payne. Payne's shot hit the post and rebounded on to Jobling's hand. The referee awarded a penalty and Payne took it and scored.

Charlie Revell equalized from an opening by Brown and then Charlton added two more goals before half-time, through Welsh and Revell again. The second half was goalless, although Welsh had a goal disallowed for offside.

Eisenhower reputedly commented on the game: "I started cheering for the Blues, but when I saw the Reds winning, I had to go on cheering for the Reds."

The match-ball was presented to Jobling, who was the longest-serving player in the team. The share of the gate was £3,718 and each member of the Charlton team received, as a memento of victory, a £5 Savings Certificate. Chelsea, as losers, each received a £3 certificate. For one Charlton guest it was the start of a long acquaintance. Chris Duffy, later to take part in the Allied invasion of Europe, was to be permanently transferred by Leith to Charlton, for £330, in September 1945.

Curiously enough, Bartram had predicted the result

to his teammates before the match. He had a 'vivid dream' several days before and dreamed that Charlton won 3-1 after Chelsea had gone ahead from a penalty. As he picked the ball out of the net after the Chelsea penalty, he had yelled to the team: "Now go and get those three goals I told you about."

In these years, the practice was for the winners of the League South Cup to meet the winners of the League North Cup, the victors of this game being unofficially regarded as overall Cup champions.

So the following month, on 20 May, Charlton Athletic played the winners of the Northern Cup, Aston Villa, who had beaten Blackpool on a home and away aggregate basis. The game took place at Stamford Bridge and, although drawn 1-1, it was described as a brilliant display of football. Houghton scored for Villa and Revell a late equalizer for Charlton.

Bartram was to appear at Wembley the following year as well, but not with Charlton. He guested for Millwall in their 2-0 defeat by Chelsea when Millwall's regular 'keeper had been posted overseas. Stationed up north when the Millwall invitation came, Bartram was not playing regularly for Charlton at the time. 'Sailor' Brown also appeared in the Millwall team.

Jimmy Seed Alone

THAT year was the only one in five that Charlton failed to appear at Wembley, for they did not win their section. But peace was now approaching and the club had to think about its post-war future. It had really been kept going by the presence of Jimmy Seed. As timber merchants, the Glikstens had been busy meeting wartime Government orders and had only limited time to give to the club's affairs.

Seed not only ran Charlton practically on his own, but also found time to take part in a lot of local activities. He started a physical training scheme for the public at The Valley and also served in the Observer Corps.

Wartime conditions were so tight in Seed's restricted regime that Charlton players often used to pool their clothing coupons in order to buy new kit, although it must be said that this was a common situation at other clubs, too.

Of other club personnel, Dr Montgomery became a medical officer in the Home Guard and reached the rank of major. Jack Phillips joined the RAF and went to India, becoming a flying-officer. Jimmy Trotter helped in the physical training scheme, did ambulance work and was eventually commissioned in the Home Guard. Alex Hird was also in the local ambulance unit until he was called into the Pioneer Corps, despite his qualifications as a trained masseur.

Wartime Internationals

FROM 1940, important representative games began to be played, including unofficial international matches, in which Charlton players figured prominently. These unofficial internationals continued to the end of the 1945-6 season.

Sam Bartram was in goal when Wales made their first-ever appearance at Wembley, on 13 April 1940 before a crowd of 40,000. The Welsh won with a long-range shot from Bryn Jones, which spun out of Bartram's hands and into the net.

The following month, when England went to Hampden to play the Scots on 11 May, Sam suffered the disappointment of being selected and then having to miss the match. The RAF refused him leave and Vic Woodley was asked to catch the night sleeper

Allenby Chilton (left), the Manchester United player guesting for Charlton, and Chelsea's Fagan in a tussle at Wembley.

Charlie Revell, who scored a late equalizer for Charlton against the Northern Cup winners, Aston Villa, at Stamford Bridge.

Charlton's Dawson (left), John Oakes (right) and Johnson get in some heading practice.

from London to take his place. Also on that train steaming into Glasgow was Don Welsh, who had got Army leave to play.

At that time, the war situation was so desperate that it seemed the game might not take place at all. Rumours to that effect swept Glasgow and 6,000 ticket holders failed to appear, although the crowd was a respectable 75,000. German radio propaganda even forecast that the *Luftwaffe* would carry out an air-raid on the ground in the second half. But Don Welsh and the team escaped the *Luftwaffe's* attentions and the game ended in an uninspiring 1-1 draw.

Both Welsh and Bartram played in the next international game, after a long interval, against Scotland at Newcastle on 8 February 1941. England went down 3-2 before a 25,000 crowd.

It was during this game that Bartram, unknowingly, chipped a bone in a finger. He played on normally after that game and when the damage was discovered, it was too late to reset the bone in its normal position. As the years of goalkeeping knarled and twisted his hands, the injury gradually became unnoticeable.

Don Welsh's most memorable wartime international was undoubtedly the game against the Welsh on 26 April 1941, at the City Ground, Nottingham. He scored all four goals in the 4-1 win and was on form a week later, when England went up to Hampden and won 3-1, Welsh scoring twice.

The list of unofficial international appearances was: Bartram (England v Wales 1940, 1941, v Scotland 1942), Brown (England v Scotland twice, v Wales, France, Switzerland 1945, v Belgium 1946); Green (Wales v England 1940, 1942); Johnson (England v France 1946, v Switzerland 1946); John Oakes (England v Wales 1940); Turner (Wales v England 1940, 1941 twice, 1942 twice); Welsh (England v Scotland 1940, 1941 1942 twice, v Wales 1941 twice, 1942, 1944, 1945).

The Pent-up Demand

THE war had been a difficult time for all clubs, but

Seed's continuing presence at The Valley had laid the basis for a quick post-war revival. Chaotic as wartime football was, it had its merits. Games were often high scoring and played in a spirit of sportsmanship. The practice of players shaking hands with an opponent after a match, rare before the war, became the norm during it and endured afterwards.

When the war ended, there was an enormous pent-up demand for the joys of leisure and relaxation in a world without fear. The game of football was to be one of the main beneficiaries.

Wembley in Peacetime

THE first peacetime season, 1945-6, was a very unusual one. The League management committee sought to restore the pre-war programme, minus promotion and relegation, for this one season, but the clubs narrowly outvoted this proposal because of the continuing aftermath of war with players scattered and stadiums still not in order. But the FA Cup was reinstituted with a significant alteration to the traditional sudden-death system. For the first and only time, it was played on a two-legged, home and away, basis. The system operated up to the semi-finals. The result was decided on the team scoring the most goals over the two legs.

Instead of the management committee proposal, the Football League was divided into a League North and a League South comprising the 44 First and Second Division clubs of the pre-war period. The two leagues featured a 42-match programme, home and away, as a prelude to the League proper resuming in 1946-7. The two Third Divisions were further sub-divided into two localized sections each, to avoid travelling problems and costs.

The damage from the bombs which had fallen on The Valley was repaired and the stadium was given a general clean-up. The administration of the club was back to normal except for Jack Phillips, who was still in India with the RAF and did not return until 1946.

Of the first-team players from the pre-war days, Bartram, Shreeve, Bert Turner, John Oakes, Jobling, Welsh, Rist, George Robinson, Hobbis, Brown and George Tadman all reappeared. For others such as Jimmy Oakes and Monty Wilkinson, who saw service in Burma, the war signalled the end of their playing careers. Newcomers included Chris Duffy at outside-left.

Charlie Revell, who had played to such effect during the war, now had a chance to show his talents in peacetime. The immediate pre-war signings, Bert Johnson and Tommy Dawson, were signed up again by the club in peacetime.

Maurice Tadman, a brother of George and a centre-forward who was to make over 250 League and Cup appearances for Plymouth, played occasionally in the first team and Harold Phipps took over later in the season at centre-half from John Oakes. Phipps had played for Dartford and then gone into the Army. Charlton Rovers players who made it, or who were to make it, included Arthur Turner, who scored 34 goals (including seven in the FA Cup) in that first peacetime season but never played in a Football

Outside-left Chris Duffy, a newcomer to Charlton as peacetime football began to unfold.

Centre-half John Oakes liked to get forward to worry opposing goalkeepers, quite an unusual event considering the stereotyped positions of the time. Here it is Chelsea 'keeper Bill Robertson who is coming under pressure from Charlton's burly 41-year-old defender.

League game. There was also Peter Croker, Cyril 'Squib' Hammond, Eddie Marsh and Malcolm Allison, the latter destined to make only two appearances for Charlton Athletic before making his name with West Ham.

A later recruit was Gordon Hurst, who went on to become the regular outside-right. At the outbreak of war he was on Oldham Athletic's books as an amateur. He enlisted in the Royal Marines and was based at Sandwich as a physical training instructor when he was recommended to Jimmy Seed. Hurst was signed on amateur forms and then offered a professional contract in May 1946.

Regional Leaders

THE 1945-6 season is best remembered for Charlton's first appearance in an FA Cup Final, but this famous exploit was matched by their form in the peacetime regional League. They led the League South for five months and, until a few weeks before the end of the season, it looked as if they would be champions. Instead, the title went to restyled Birmingham, who had added 'City' to their title in 1945. They finished ahead of Aston Villa on goal-average. Charlton finished in third place, one point behind Villa. Their Cup Final opponents, Derby County, were fourth, five points adrift of Charlton.

Had an unusual penalty-kick gone in against Birmingham at St Andrew's in February, the ending might have been different. Before a crowd of 56,615, Birmingham were leading 1-0 through a Charlie Jones goal, when Charlton were awarded a last-minute penalty. What was unusual was that Sam Bartram took it. It was Charlton's captain, Don Welsh, who called on the goalkeeper to do so. This was because Bartram had taken three penalties while guesting for York City and had scored each time. So this time, he ran the whole length of the field to take the kick. But his luck at York did not hold out with Charlton. He hit the bar. He then had to make a dash to get back on his own line, but managed it before Birmingham could put the ball between the posts.

Charlton had, in fact, lost only one of their first 24 matches — to Newport County, who finished next to bottom of the table. One of the reasons for the fall away in their League form was almost certainly the congestion of games at the end of the season through the heavy demands of the Cup run. Sometimes the club were playing three times a week and Charlton were also unfortunate in having to meet three of the division's top clubs in the last four games of the season, gaining only three points.

Defeated but Through

IN the unusual format of the FA Cup, Charlton suffered what was to be a unique record in the annals of the competition — they lost a Cup game, yet went on to reach the Final. Although they beat Fulham 3-1 at home in the first game, they went down 2-1 at Craven Cottage. In the fourth round, they beat Wolves 5-2 at home and drew 1-1 away. In the fifth round, Preston were thrashed 6-0 at The Valley after Charlton drew the away game 1-1. The last two-legged round saw Charlton beat Brentford 6-3 at home and 3-1 away. Of the 26 goals scored by Charlton in reaching the semi-final, eight were netted by outside-left Duffy, including a hat-trick against Preston.

In the semi-final, against Bolton Wanderers at Villa Park, Duffy was in form again, scoring the only two goals of the game. Up until that time Duffy had made no impact nationally, either with the Press or with the fans, but in that match he made his name with a sensational goal.

Charlton were leading 1-0 through a Duffy goal, scored ten minutes before half-time. They were struggling when, after five minutes of the second half, Duffy, in his own half, pounced on a Don Welsh lob. He then began an amazing crooked dribble, going 30 yards and surviving five tackles. He skipped Murphy, then beat Hamlett with a flick to the left. Then another flick, this time to the right, beat Hubbick. Hamlett came on him a second time and Duffy passed him on the right. Then Threlfall came across from the right with a last desperate tackle. Duffy flicked again to the left, jumped over Threlfall's legs and shot past goalkeeper Hanson.

What made the feat more remarkable was that Duffy had had a cartilage removed from his right knee and all the time was trying to get the ball on his left foot to shoot. So unknown was Duffy that when the sports reporters gathered at the dressing-room afterwards, none of them even knew his first name. Seed filled in the details for them — how Chris had been discharged from his regiment following shock after D-Day and how Charlton had paid just £330 for him. Other points emerged in the questioning. Didn't Duffy have only one sound leg? Wasn't he accused of being a greedy player? All the next day's headlines were about Duffy, the man who had sent Charlton to Wembley for their first FA Cup Final.

Allied to Duffy's goals, was the fine form of Don Welsh and 'Sailor' Brown, all of which had swept Charlton through to the Cup Final. Welsh had lost

Opposite: Skipper Don Welsh heads the ball for the benefit of a photographer who was taking pictures of the Charlton players before the 1946 FA Cup Final.

a lot of pace during the war but he was still an inspiring, powerful player.

The attendance at Villa Park was 70,819 and the receipts of £18,011 17s 6d were a record for any game outside London or Glasgow.

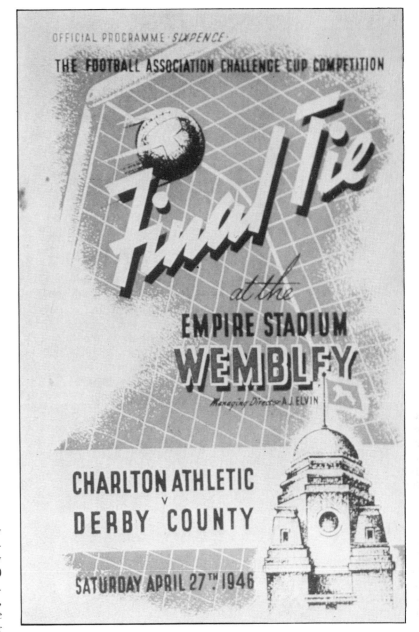

The First Post-war Cup Final

CHARLTON'S opponents in the Final, Derby County, were famed for their two brilliant inside-forwards, Peter Doherty and Raich Carter. Doherty had been transferred from Manchester City for £7,000 just before he was demobilized from the RAF in 1945. Carter was signed from Sunderland for £6,500, immediately before the deadline for eligibility for the third round. Both had already appeared as guests for Derby and knew each other's play.

Derby lost 2-1 to Charlton at The Valley in a League match a week before their clash at Wembley, although both Doherty and Carter were missing from that game.

The Rams went through a ritual before the Final of having a gipsy curse on the team removed. It had apparently been laid when they moved on a family of gipsies in 1895, when they took over the Baseball Ground. The curse had apparently stopped them winning the Cup or the League title and, indeed, they had played in three Finals and lost them all, the last one in 1903 by a record 6-0 scoreline at the hands of Bury. It was an enterprising Fleet Street journalist, with an eye for a story, who took Derby skipper Jack Nicholas to a gipsy camp a few days before the Cup Final. A palm was crossed with silver and the curse duly lifted.

Yet there might well have been no 1946 FA Cup Final. The Derby players were incensed that their wives had been given cheaper stand tickets than the wives of the directors and would have to sit out in the open. Led by Raich Carter, they told the board: "No decent tickets, no game." The Derby directors relented, but Carter is still adamant to this day that, had they not backed down, then there would have been no Cup Final. The question is whether Charlton

Athletic would have made history by gaining a 'walk-over' in an FA Cup Final.

This first peacetime Final, though, was already a momentous day in the annals of British football. The weather fitted the occasion. It was a gloriously sunny day and the King, Queen and Princess Elizabeth were there in the Royal Box. A crowd of 98,215 packed the stadium.

The Charlton team was: Bartram; Phipps, Shreeve, Bert Turner, John Oakes, Johnson, Fell, Brown, Arthur Turner, Welsh and Duffy. Among the players left out were full-back Peter Croker, who had broken a leg shortly before, and Charlie Revell, who was also injured. Revell, incidentally, would make 22 League appearances for Derby after joining them in March 1951.

Derby County lined up: Woodley; Nicholas, Howe, Bullions, Leuty, Musson, Harrison, Carter, Stamps, Doherty, Duncan.

The game was a splendid affair, one of the best Cup Finals that Wembley had witnessed. From the opening whistle, Derby moved into top gear and could have been three goals up at half-time, but for missed chances. Charlton had their fair share of the play, but made no real openings in the first half. Duffy's corner-kicks were particularly disappointing. He put three of them behind the goal.

Two programmes for games against Derby County. The far one is for the League South game between the clubs at The Valley just seven days before the FA Cup, the programme for which is pictured adjacent.

67

Top: Derby's Vic Woodley gathers the ball as the Rams centre-half, Leon Leuty, checks the progress of 'Sailor' Brown.

Middle: Bert Turner (on ground) has just turned the ball into his own net to give Derby the lead, much to the joy of centre-forward Jack Stamps. Jack Shreeve (left of post) and John Oakes look on in dismay.

Bottom: Sam Bartram punches clear as Derby's Peter Doherty waits for a mis-cue.

In the first part of the second half, the tide of the game turned and it was the Charlton forwards who began to make their impact, but they, too, could not take their chances. Don Welsh worked a couple of openings, but Duffy could not take advantage. Leon Leuty, the Derby centre-half, gave an outstanding display to snuff out the Charlton menace.

The score stood at 0-0 until eight minutes from full-time. Then, in the space of 30 seconds, Bert Turner, Charlton's right-half, achieved the remarkable feat of scoring not only twice, but also for both sides. He put the ball into his own net by deflecting a Dally Duncan drive whilst trying to clear. Then he turned despair to jubilation by scoring at the other end after Charlton were given a free-kick, when 'Sailor' Brown was brought down just outside the Derby penalty area. Turner struck a long shot which hit Doherty's hip to leave Woodley on the wrong foot as the ball rolled slowly over the line.

Over 40 years later, Peter Doherty says that it was an own-goal by him that levelled the scores: "Vic Woodley would have got to the ball easily, had it not hit me. But the Press were anxious for an 'angle' and it made a better story to say that Bert scored for both sides."

In the closing minutes, there was yet another remarkable surprise. Jack Stamps, the burly Derby centre-forward, fired in a hard shot which Bartram braced himself to receive. But the ball lost its flight and floated gently towards Bartram, who caught it and found it deflating in his hands. Sam realized the ball had burst completely and was anxious to avoid a bounce-up on his goal-line with a new ball. He hurled the almost shapeless piece of leather as hard as he could towards the touchline. The referee then picked the ball up and saw the burst. When the new ball came, the bounce-up was on the touchline, to Bartram's relief. His ruse had worked. Stamps said later: "It was the quickest piece of thinking that I have ever seen on a football field."

Strangely enough, the chances of a ball bursting in a Cup Final had been discussed in a BBC radio broadcast shortly before the game and the referee, E.D.Smith of Cumberland, had remarked that the chance of this happening was a million to one. The ball was also to burst when Derby and Charlton met yet again in a League match at Derby five days after the Wembley game. And it burst again when Charlton appeared at Wembley the following year. Why this rare event should happen so repeatedly in a short space of time can only now be conjecture. But these games were soon after the war when materials were scarce and of poor quality. Even the numbers on the Derby shirts looked rough and hand cut. Perhaps the ball leather just simply was not good enough. Perhaps footballs burst in other matches, but no one bothered to record it. Again, it made a good story if it surrounded a Wembley Cup Final.

For Charlton, the new ball and extra-time signalled the end of their luck. Derby scored three times to win 4-1, as Doherty and Carter found their finest form. Doherty cracked in the first goal of extra-time inside 90 seconds after Stamps burst through and centred. The Irish international almost knocked Dally Duncan, Derby's left winger, out of the way to slam the ball into the net. Nine minutes later, Stamps — who had been comparatively subdued in normal time — gathered a pass from Doherty to score the second. Stamps had been wounded at Dunkirk and told that he might never play again, so this was a particularly magic moment for him.

It was a repeat performance by the two players at the beginning of the second-half of extra-time, when Stamps was put through once more by Doherty and scored with an unstoppable shot. But it was Raich Carter, in particular, who played havoc with Charlton and the team was overrun and demoralized. The first 90 minutes had been an equal contest. Extra-time was one-way as Derby found inspiration. As those supreme artists, Carter and Doherty wove their magic in the goal area, Charlton's players seemed unable to get near them.

On the credit side of the 120 minutes, 'Sailor' Brown showed his dribbling skills at their best and Welsh gave a typically heroic performance, but there was no doubt that the better side won. One view at the time was that a last-minute tactical talk helped cost Charlton the game. It was decided that the two Berts, Turner and Johnson, would shadow Doherty and Carter wherever they went. It was partially successful, but meant that they were unable to properly service their own inside-forwards, according to this viewpoint. And it failed completely in extra-time when Charlton were overrun.

But Wembley was now in Charlton's blood and the following season was to see the club reach their fourth Cup Final there in five years. In the dressing-room after the defeat, Seed heard someone say: "Never mind, lads, we'll be back at Wembley next year." Seed joined in: "That's right, boys, and next year we'll go one better and win the Cup!" Seed, in his autobiography, quotes Bartram as making the remark, but Sam, in his book, claimed it was another player, although he could not remember which one. As Seed admitted in his story, about his own remark: "It was one of those things that we say without sincerity, just in an effort to cheer up our comrades."

The gross receipts for the 1946 Final were £43,378, far higher than in pre-war days because of higher admission prices. But the ravages of the Entertainment Tax, taking £19,840, meant that the net receipts of £23,538 were lower by £725 than the best pre-war figure.

The Charlton players received two medals each for their efforts. Gold was scarce in those immediate post-war days, so the players were presented with bronze medals. Some months afterwards, the gold ones were at last made and given to the players.

Top: Charlton Athletic's team in 1946. Back row (left to right): Jimmy Trotter (trainer), Alex Hird (assistant trainer), George Robinson, Peter Croker, Sam Bartram, Jack Shreeve, Harold Hobbis, Billy Robinson, Bert Johnson. Front: Maurice Tadman, Charlie Revell, Arthur Turner, 'Sailor' Brown, Chris Duffy, Harold Phipps.

Middle: Arthur Turner, Cup Finalist who never played a League game for Charlton.

Bottom: London banquet for Charlton after the Cup Final defeat by Derby County. Heading the tables (from the foot of the picture) are Dr John Montgomery, Jimmy Seed, Stanley Gliksten, Don Welsh, David Clark and Robert Law. Standing at the top table in the background is Albert Gliksten and seated two places to his left is FA secretary Stanley Rous. On the nearest table (third and fourth places from the left) are Peter and Ted Croker.

A Normal Cup Again

IN the second post-war season, the FA Cup competition was restored to its normal knockout basis. First and Second Division clubs joined in the third round and Charlton beat Rochdale, from the Third Division North, 3-1 at The Valley in the third round. The team were just beginning to find their form — Chris Duffy in particular — after a lacklustre season until then.

West Bromwich Albion were beaten 2-1 away in the fourth round, in a very good performance. Then Charlton were drawn at home to Blackburn Rovers. This match was distinctive because it was broadcast live on television. It was the first time that a Cup tie had been broadcast live, other than the Final itself. The date was 8 February, 1947. But the match was a disappointment for the small audience of those early days of television. With snow and ice on the ground, the pitch was hard and frozen in parts and a quagmire in others. With both teams trying to keep their feet, there was little good football, although Charlton dominated throughout. Only the last attack of the match produced a goal. From a Gordon Hurst corner, Tommy Dawson rose amid a crowd of players to flick the ball into the net with his head and end a frustrating afternoon. As soon as Blackburn kicked-off, the referee blew for time.

The cold, icy weather persisted for the visit of Preston North End to The Valley in the sixth round. The 2-1 victory was marred by some scrapping on the pitch and Revell received a nasty injury. The semi-final against Newcastle United at Elland Road, Leeds, produced problems of a different kind.

Semi-final Crisis

JIMMY Seed took the team to Harrogate for special training and a general tune-up. Everything went fine until the night before the match itself when the team began to go down with food poisoning. The cause was thought to have been salmon sandwiches, which the players had eaten during a visit to a clothing factory that afternoon. Several players were up half

Bert Johnson, one of only five survivors of the 1946 Cup Final side to play at Wembley again 12 months later.

the night and the news was broken to Seed at breakfast by Dr Montgomery and Jimmy Trotter. Dr Montgomery prescribed some medicine, but five players were unable to eat any breakfast and by midday some were still sick. At one time, it looked as if a special plane would have to be chartered to fly in reinforcements.

Seed tried to keep the story from the Press. Newcastle were already hot favourites and the news could help spur their confidence on even more. But the *London Evening Standard* found out and printed the news. The players were allowed only milk pudding for lunch, but the medicine seemed to work and nearly all the team reported themselves 50 per cent better by kick-off time, although a couple said they still felt weak and groggy.

However, all the players got out on to the pitch before a crowd dominated by the black and white favours of Newcastle, with the Charlton supporters easily outnumbered. But then came the shock as the supposedly stricken Charlton side proceeded to produce some of the best football they had played all season. They were 3-0 up at half-time, sending the Charlton fans into an ecstasy of delight and surprise. Newcastle were finally beaten 4-0, Welsh scoring twice, and Hurst and Dawson getting the others.

Sam Bartram had a hot poultice slapped on his stomach after he doubled up when about to take a goal-kick. It helped ease the pain considerably and Bartram had a very good game. But the most remarkable case was that of Don Welsh. He folded up in the dressing-room afterwards and lost consciousness, but had played throughout without giving a clue of the pain he was in. It was the key match in the Cup run as the exhausted players realized in the dressing-room afterwards.

The team that day was: Bartram; Peter Croker, Shreeve, Johnson, Phipps, Revell, Hurst, Dawson, Bill Robinson, Welsh and Duffy.

From Yorkshire, the celebrating Charlton fans brought home countless black and white favours left behind in dejection by the Newcastle hordes. More celebrations were to come. At the next home match on Good Friday, the fans displayed the souvenirs and staged a mock funeral procession around The Valley pitch, carrying a coffin draped in black, preceded by a banner with the inscription: 'Here lies the body of Newcastle United'.

It was an epic victory indeed, achieved against all the odds and all the forecasts. Although Charlton had reached the Final for a second year in succession, the Wembley team contained only five of the men who had played against Derby: Sam Bartram, Jack Shreeve, Bert Johnson, Don Welsh and Chris Duffy. For Bartram, it was, amazingly, his fourth Wembley Final in consecutive years.

A Struggle in the League

THE success had been achieved against a background of struggle in the League, the first time Charlton had known such a situation in their First Division history. From January, they had been locked in a fight to avoid relegation. On the eve of the semi-final, they had a battle for vital League points with Brentford. The 3-0 win at The Valley put them fourth from bottom.

In April, a draw with Arsenal made them virtually safe. The end of the season was marked by a queue of games since no afternoon matches were allowed in the middle of the week — the authorities did not want factory workers taking time off to watch football

— and clubs had to wait until the lighter evenings to play off games. The last match of the season saw Charlton lift their spirits with a 3-1 win at Bramall Lane.

In that historic season, the defence had become settled after the transitory first peacetime season, with Bartram still a permanency in goal, Peter Croker and Shreeve at full-back, Phipps at centre-half and Johnson and Revell sharing the half-back positions. But the forward line suffered many changes and only Duffy made the full 42 League appearances. Bill Robinson, who had come from Sunderland, played at centre-forward or outside-right. Welsh shared the inside-left position with Benny Fenton, transferred from Millwall in January 1947 and to be his successor as captain. Hurst was the other outside-right.

Eight different players were tried in the inside-right

It was Newcastle Who Had the Pains!

SYD JORDAN took his sketch-book to Leeds, with this result.

Cartoonist Syd Jordan's view of Charlton's semi-final victory over Newcastle United at Elland Road.

position and Eric Lancelotte was the most regular. Dawson, who played half his games at inside-right, appeared in five other positions as well. Besides Robinson, six other players were tried at centre-forward. Fenton (£5,000) and Bill Robinson cost £6,000, the first sizeable spending since Welsh joined. Charlie Purves, another forward, was signed from Spennymoor United for £1,150, through Antony Seed. But the money was more than recouped through the transfer of 'Sailor' Brown to Nottingham Forest in May 1946, for £6,650, and by the transfers of Freddie Ford to Millwall, George Smith to Brentford and Jim Sanders to West Bromwich Albion for a total of £6,650.

The fees represented part of a considerable inflation of transfer prices in the post-war period. Fees continued to rise rapidly and Charlton went on to pay £7,650 for Alex McCrae, from Hearts in the summer of 1947, and £8,500 for Tommy Brown, from Millwall in October 1948.

The Cup Final Opponents

FOR the Cup Final, there was one change from the team which appeared against Newcastle in the semi-final, Bill Whittaker replacing Charlie Revell. Revell had twisted his right knee and failed a test, so missing a second Wembley Final through injury. Whittaker, a schoolboy star who never quite lived up to his promise, had made only six appearances in the League side, but Seed decided to take the gamble on him at left-half. He had toyed with the idea of switching Welsh from attack to the position and bringing in the veteran George Robinson at inside-left. Two of Seed's squad were Cup-tied and so could not be considered — Benny Fenton with Millwall and Charlie Vaughan with Sutton United.

Opposite: Winger Gordon Hurst, who was at the beginning of a career which would yield 369 League appearances for Charlton.

71

THE FOOTBALL ASSOCIATION CHALLENGE CUP COMPETITION

BURNLEY v CHARLTON ATHLETIC

FINAL TIE

AT THE EMPIRE STADIUM

WEMBLEY

Managing Director : SIR ARTHUR J. ELVIN M.B.E.

SATURDAY, APRIL 26TH 1947. KICK OFF 3 PM

OFFICIAL PROGRAMME SIXPENCE

Above:
Programme for
the 1947 FA Cup
Final. Opposite:
Don Welsh shakes
hands with
Burnley skipper
Alan Brown at
Wembley.

booklets which were put on sale at one shilling (5p) each. But the pool policy was taken to extremes, much to Seed's discomfort. The players refused to let Press photographers take their pictures without first paying a fee. This aggressive approach led to several major rows with the newspapers, who refused to pay. Seed disassociated himself from the policy, but could do little more. He had team spirit to keep up before the all-important match.

The team went down to Brighton for special training, a move really designed to get them away from home and from the pressure and clamour of fans asking for tickets. They left Brighton for the Empire Stadium on the morning of the match. The last stage of the journey to Wembley was by coach with a motor-cycle escort. As the coach approached the first set of traffic lights, which were showing red, the escort waved on the driver to ignore them. Dr Montgomery, who was accompanying the team, did not notice and looked worried when Don Welsh remarked that the coach had jumped the lights. One or two members of the party then jokingly forecast that the coach was going to cross against all the red lights between central London and Wembley. Dr Montgomery said: "I bet we don't," and the challenge was accepted. It was decided that he would pay £1 into the kitty every time the coach crossed a red light and the rest would pay a similar amount every time it crossed a green. At every crossing the lights were red and Dr Montgomery was obliged to pay out about £10. "With luck like that, you can't go wrong today. I think the Cup's ours without doubt", he said. Dr Montgomery had produced a shrewd piece of psychological reasoning, for his little guessing game had kept the players laughing and relaxed instead of being tensed up before the big game.

Final of Defences

THE crowd at the stadium was again officially put at 98,215. They saw a dour match with the defences of both sides dominating. The major excitement came when the ball burst for the second consecutive time in a Final.

After 30 minutes, Bert Johnson picked it up for a throw-in to find it deflated. Seed was sitting on the touchline with a new ball in his hand. It was though he 'sensed' the incident of the previous final might repeat itself, he recalled later in his autobiography. He immediately threw the new ball to Johnson for play to resume. The deflated ball was taken away by an FA official at the end for a post-mortem with the manufacturers the following Monday. Seed never did hear the result.

The game went once again into extra-time. A curious feature of those days was that other fixtures were played on Cup Final day. These days the whole squad of a Cup Final team come to cheer on the team at Wembley, but Burnley Reserves were playing that day at Turf Moor. The Clarets' reserve defender, Horace Rudman, later recalled that nerve-wracking day at Turf Moor as extra-time was reached. The Burnley reserve players looked constantly at the scoreboard to see how the first team were doing. "No score . . .15 minutes. No score . . .30 minutes. No score . . .full-time. As our match ended we tore off the field to find out what was happening. 'Extra-time at Wembley' — came the message. Quickly we changed, then dashed to the recreation room to listen to the broadcast." Finally the deadlock between the two clubs was broken six minutes from the end by what still remains the most memorable goal in Charlton's history.

Charlton's opponents, Burnley, lined up: Strong; Woodruff, Mather, Attwell, Brown, Bray, Chew, Morris, Harrison, Potts, Kippax. They were a promising young Second Division side, who gained promotion as runners-up that season and went on to finish third in Division One the following season. This was their first season under the managership of Cliff Britton and their success was based on a cast-iron defence revolving around their centre-half and captain, Alan Brown. They had conceded only 29 goals in the League that season.

The weeks before the Final had been marked with the well-worn occurrence of a player revolt over payments. The Charlton team, led by skipper Don Welsh, were not happy with their share of the profits from an anticipated £50,000 of Wembley gate receipts. So they started up their own pool. The most they could otherwise earn, apart from their maximum wage of £11 a week, was £275 which the FA allowed to be shared by 14 players of each team, plus £12 for each member of the winning side. Including the Final itself, the Charlton team made six Cup appearances. A player turning out in every match could collect just over £60 in bonuses if the team won the Final — a poor reward, even in those days.

Welsh worked on a plan to produce 10,000 Cup

Charlton's Billy Robinson tangles with Burnley defender Harry Mather during the Cup Final. Mather had played as a guest for Charlton during the war.

The Duffy Epic

JOHNSON sent centre-forward Bill Robinson away. Robinson dribbled to the right wing, beat Mather and put a centre across the goalmouth which Welsh glanced with his head to Duffy on the far side. Duffy was some 14 yards from goal and hit a half-volley with tremendous power, first-time into the net. The goalkeeper, Jim Strong, did not see the ball until he picked it out of the back of the net.

His arms above his head, little Duffy raced down the pitch in joy, his teammates trying to catch up with him to shower their congratulations. The run took him over the half-way line before Shreeve seized him and lifted him aloft. Duffy's exuberant reaction was notable in an age when goals were greeted with much more restraint than they are now, and it left an indelible memory in the minds of the spectators.

The closing minutes were agonizing. Charlton inside-right Tommy Dawson, collected the ball about 15 yards inside his own half and began to dribble up the field. Seed shouted: "Hit it, Tommy," but Dawson kept on the ball and was then dispossessed. Play quickly swung to the Charlton goalmouth and a Burnley shot struck the crossbar.

Two views of Chris Duffy's Wembley winner. Opposite: Newspaper photograph showing the players' positions. Below: Duffy (far right) raises his arms in triumph as his half-volley hits the back of the Burnley net.

SYD JORDAN "LINES UP" THE CHARLTON CUP FINAL TEAM.

DON WELSH. SAM BARTRAM. PETER CROKER. JACK SHREEVE. BERT JOHNSON. HAROLD PHIPPS. CHARLIE REVELL. GORDON HURST. TOMMY DAWSON. BILL ROBINSON. CHRIS DUFFY.

The "Mercury" cartoonist, who will be at the match to-morrow, contributes this special drawing of those who were expected to compose the Charlton team at Wembley.

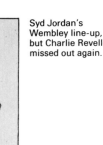

Syd Jordan's Wembley line-up, but Charlie Revell missed out again.

The tackle left Dawson limping badly and he started to come off the pitch for treatment from the trainer. There were only three minutes left and Seed jumped up and ran to meet him, shouting: "Get back on the field. Go out and fight, there's only three minutes to go!" Dawson obeyed and went back.

Don Welsh collected the Cup from the Duke of Gloucester, then Sam Bartram led the rest of the players for their winners' medals from the Duchess of Gloucester. Charlton Athletic had won their first, and only, major trophy.

Welsh was interviewed on the pitch before the British Movietone News cameras, an interview remembered for the nervous laugh with which he closed it. Said Welsh: "We're all very pleased to have won the Cup after such a disappointing year last year when we lost. We're very tired. We've all got cramp. But it's a wonderful feeling. Thanks."

After a night of celebration, Seed awoke next day to find a case of Scotch in the front porch of his home 'with the complements of Mr Walter Head'. Seed telephoned Head, a Charlton season-ticket holder, to inquire about the gift and was told: "Oh, that's OK, Jimmy. I won £1,200 backing Charlton for the Cup. I didn't tell you beforehand. Thought you might worry!"

Burnley's goalkeeper Jim Strong watches the ball fly up over his penalty area at Wembley.

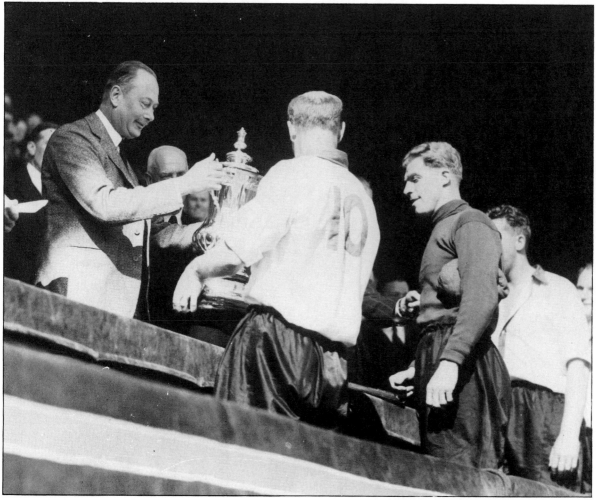

The Duke of Gloucester presents the FA Cup to Charlton skipper Don Welsh. Goalkeeper Sam Bartram looks on expectantly. Behind him is Jack Shreeve.

The Broken Cup

THE eventful aftermath of the FA Cup was not over for Seed yet. Charlton went off to a 'welcome home' celebration given by the Mayor of Greenwich at the Town Hall, and Seed found himself in an embarrassing incident — he dropped and broke the Cup. The players had left The Valley by coach for the Town Hall and Seed was planning to follow by car with the trophy. But while opening the door of his car and balancing the Cup, he dropped the lid and broke the top off.

He solved the emergency by calling at a garage and explaining what had happened. The mechanics set to work to repair the Cup with their soldering irons. Seed arrived a few minutes late at the reception and no one knew about the incident. Next day, he arranged for a silversmith to take the Cup away and do a first-class job on it so that it was as good as new when eventually returned to the FA at Lancaster Gate. The FA Cup is insured by the club that holds it. The FA then valued it at £100 and that was the sum Charlton would have had to pay had it been lost or destroyed. But Seed took no chances and insured it for £250.

Even then, the eventful trip to Greenwich Town Hall was not the end of Seed's adventures with the Cup. He later took it to Sheffield for a charity show at a theatre. On his way back, he decided to stop in Mansfield to see an old friend, Frank Pattison, who had played at outside-right in the same Mid-Rhondda team as Seed.

Frank was the landlord of Mansfield's Railway Hotel and was still in bed when Seed arrived in the afternoon. His wife asked Jimmy to wait while she woke him, so Seed decided to surprise him by putting the Cup on his sideboard. Ten minutes later, Frank came down to surprised delight and suggested they call on his son-in-law who had a pub nearby. Seed was going to take the Cup with him but Pattison replied: "Don't worry, Jimmy, it'll be safe here. We won't be gone more than 15 minutes anyway."

The men did not return until much later, at around 7.30pm, and Seed went into the sitting room to be met with the sight of a bare sideboard. For a few seconds, Seed panicked and ran to tell Frank the news. He was worried, too, but then he glanced into the public bar and laughed. The Cup was there full of beer and the locals were passing it round. Seed had drunk wine from it at Wembley. Now he joined the locals in drinking ale from it in a Mansfield pub. The locals cheered him, but Seed was anxious to get the trophy back as soon as possible. The risk of breaking it twice was simply too much to bear. Great times and great days for Charlton in a post-war Britain where the thirst for football was at its height.

Charlton's glory. Don Welsh holds aloft the FA Cup as Charlton players go on a lap of honour around Wembley. Holding him high are Sam Bartram and Peter Croker. Chris Duffy (second from right) and Jack Shreeve (right) look happily on. Next to the policeman is Bill Robinson.

Boom and Decline

THE 1947 Cup Final represented the peak of Charlton Athletic's fortunes, although another decade of First Division football was to follow. Not until 40 years later, did Charlton return to Wembley and then in the much humbler circumstances of the Full Members' Cup. The succeeding seasons, 1947-8 and 1948-9, rather than being ones of consolidating success, saw more changes in playing staff, in part due to the war which had taken years off the first-class soccer lifespan of the players.

Of the pre-war players, many left — mostly for managerial and training jobs. John Oakes went to Plymouth Argyle as assistant trainer and played a season for the side. Bert Turner went to play for Dartford. George Green went as trainer to Millwall. Sid Cann became manager of Southampton and Don Welsh went to manage Brighton, moving on to manage Liverpool and then Bournemouth, where his career in football management ended in 1961.

Harold Hobbis helped the newly-formed Tonbridge club and later, for many years, was landlord of the Valley pub. Bob Wright became manager of Bristol City after a spell as assistant manager at The Valley — he had appeared briefly at wing-half either side of the war. Seed admitted that it took him a couple of seasons after the war 'to weigh up my assets and liabilities at The Valley'.

The main difficulty in 1947-8 lay with the wing-half and inside-forward positions. Benny Fenton became a firm favourite at half-back but otherwise players were tried in a succession of permutations, including Charlton's record signing up to that date, Alec McCrae from Hearts. McCrae played at outside-left for most of the season but failed to fit in. He was sold to Middlesbrough for £10,000 in October the following season and Charlton's profit of £2,350 was very much a testimony to Seed's financial acumen.

In goal, Bartram was as regular and dependable as ever. Phipps played regularly at centre-half, Duffy at outside-left and Hurst at outside-right. Charlie Vaughan took over the centre-forward position from Bill Robinson and Frank Lock was the regular left-back. Lock had represented the Army and came straight to Charlton on his release. Right-back was shared by Shreeve and Jimmy 'Jock' Campbell, another player who came straight to the club from the Army.

The 1947-8 season was marked by the goalscoring exploits of Charlie Vaughan, a centre-forward of ball-playing skill, who had made his League debut the previous season and now became a first-team regular. He scored 15 goals out of the League total of 57 that season and 19 out of 63 the next. A fulsome tribute to Vaughan was paid in later years by Joe Mercer, an Arsenal player at the time of Vaughan's exploits. Looking back on great forwards he had known, Mercer recalled in Tony Pawson's book, *The Goalscorers*: 'The best of them all, fortunately, was

Middle right: Charlton defenders fail to stop this Aston Villa goal at Villa Park in 1947.

Bottom right: Charlton's Charlie Vaughan gets in a shot, despite the close attention of Arsenal's Ray Daniels.

Charlton began the era in the best possible way, in possession of the FA Cup. Back row (left to right): Robinson, Peter Croker, Bartram, Shreeve, Phipps. Middle: Alex Hird (reserve-team trainer), Hurst, Dawson, Robinson, Whittaker, Jack Phillips (assistant secretary). Seated: Revell, Jimmy Seed (manager), Dr John Montgomery (director), Jimmy Trotter (trainer), Welsh. On ground: Johnson, Duffy.

on my side. I have never seen anyone to better Bill Dean as a goalscorer. But the ones that worry you are not always the best players. Charlie Vaughan of Charlton was not a great centre-forward in anyone's book. But he gave me the shivers. I had a bad game against him to start with and that gave him confidence and undermined mine. After that, he could usually

do what he liked with me. I worried for a time. Then I thought there is always someone who plays in a way that probes your particular weakness. Everyone has his Achilles' heel and you have to recognise that some player is going to find it. The important thing is not to be disturbed and to recognise that this is just one game of many. And to be honest about it and warn the others they may have a bit more covering to do for you in that game.'

To try to solve the inside-forward dilemma in the 1948-9 season, Seed paid another £8,500 to neighbours Millwall, on 1 October, 1948, for Tommy Brown. Like the McCrae deal, the Brown transfer was unsuccessful. Brown had been chosen for the Scottish team whilst a 17-year-old with Hearts, but he lost form and was given a free transfer to Millwall. Brown arrived at Charlton in the same month that McCrae left. He was a fine ball-player and there was no question over his ability. But he failed to fit in and scored only one goal in 14 appearances at inside-left and six at left-half. He was transferred to Leyton Orient at the end of the following season, on another free transfer, and at Brisbane Road he at last enjoyed success.

Despite the changes in personnel, Charlton finished a comfortable 13th and 9th in those two seasons — 1947-8 and 1948-9. But they could not keep their hands on the Cup. In the 1947-8 season, they got to the fifth round, beating Newcastle United at home 2-1, and Stockport County, also at The Valley, 3-0.

Sam Bartram's Greatest Game

THEN followed an epic away tie against Manchester United. Charlton lost 2-0, but the match was notable, not only for marking the exit of the Cup holders but also for what Sam Bartram regarded as the pinnacle perfomance of his goalkeeping career. That may be considered remarkable as Charlton were defeated but Bartram, in his autobiography, described it as the 'one match, and one moment, that stood out from all the others and remained carved in my memory'.

Opposite (top): German prisoners of war clearing snow from The Valley during the bitter winter of 1946-7. (Bottom): Don Welsh challenges Arsenal goalkeeper George Swindin.

Bartram had to perform well because Charlton, quite simply, were overrun and outclassed by what was to prove the first of United's post-war teams and one that established Matt Busby's reputation as a manager. This first Busby team were now approaching the height of their brilliance. At that time, Old Trafford was still out of action because of war damage, so United were still sharing Maine Road with their keen rivals, Manchester City, the most sustained spell of groundsharing until Charlton's venture with Crystal Palace in 1985. City had also been drawn at home, and in those days there was no Sunday football to remove the problem when both teams landed a home cup-tie. So the venue had to be outside Manchester. Charlton tactlessly suggested Stamford Bridge or Highbury, but Manchester United were not going to hand them this London advantage. United considered Villa Park but this was already booked by Villa for a friendly against Newcastle.

United's final choice took them across the Roses boundary to Huddersfield Town's Leeds Road ground — which in those days boasted a capacity of nearly 70,000 and had a Cup pedigree as a staging ground for semi-finals. It was a terrible day with continuous rain reducing the pitch to a quagmire. The game kicked-off a few minutes before 2pm because Charlton wanted to catch a train from Wakefield to London after the match. The train was being specially stopped for them and a police escort laid on to escort their coach to the station.

Charlton's record against Manchester United that season was already poor. United had beaten them 2-1 the month before at The Valley and by 6-2 early in the season at Maine Road. In the United team was a well-known face to Charlton — Allenby Chilton, who had guested for them in the Football League South Cup Final against Chelsea in 1944.

The attendance was just 33,000, although the police had fixed a limit of 55,000. Three factors were blamed — the weather, the police crowd limit which probably made many would-be spectators fear they might have difficulty getting in; and last, but not least, the fact that down the road the Huddersfield were playing Bradford Northern in the Rugby League Challenge Cup.

United soon slipped into top gear with United forward Johnny Morris at his best and forcing several fine saves from Bartram in the opening minutes. For nearly half an hour, Charlton managed to keep United at bay. Then, with Bartram still in the thick of the action, bad luck intervened. The United right-half, Jack Warner, collected the ball and shot powerfully but Bartram had the ball covered. At the last moment it struck the leg of Roy Bicknell, who had come into the side at the last minute. The ball deflected past Bartram's reach into the net and Charlton were on their way out of the Cup.

From then on, the Charlton defence was under constant pressure. Shots poured into Bartram's goal at all angles. 'No Aunt Sally at a fairground ever underwent so prolonged and furious a peppering', Bartram was later to recall.

The wind and rain were against Charlton in the second half and they seemed unable to find the impetus to reach United's penalty area. They created only one serious chance, when Charlie Vaughan slipped the ball to McCrae who shot hurriedly wide.

Those shots that Bartram did not catch, he managed to push over the bar or around the post. Never before or since, he recalled, had he taken so many goal-kicks in a match. As soon as he kicked the ball upfield, it seemed to come straight back again on the toes of United's famous forward line. Diving to save a swerving shot from United outside-right, Jimmy Delaney, Bartram crashed into a post and was so unsteady on his feet towards the end of the game, tottering shakily at one particular goal-kick, that the referee had to inquire about his condition.

Five minutes from time, the second goal went in — a header from the United outside-left, Charlie Mitten, into the top left had corner of the net from a perfect centre by Delaney. Mitten recalled later: "We seemed to be shooting in at Sam all the match. Near the end of the game, he was so tired his goal-kicks were hardly getting out of the penalty area, some going 'plop' just outside the box. When this happened, I shouted jokingly, 'Oh, well kicked Sam lad', and he shouted back 'I'm knackered Charlie'. So I said, 'So that's why you let that header of mine go past you!' You know he was so tired he could hardly put his hands over his head! Sam was a great player and a terrific sportsman."

The United left-back, John Aston, was to remark: "It could have been double-figures if it hadn't been for Sam, who played out of his skin." The crowd realized just how magnificent a feat in the annals of the goalkeeping art Bartram's performance had been. He was carried shoulder-high from the field,

Opposite: Durham-born Bert Johnson, one of the most consistent half-backs in the League.

80

and most of those carrying him were neither United nor Charlton supporters. Players from both sides came to congratulate him including his opposite number in the United goal, Jack Crompton, who went the length of the field to reach him. Thus delayed, Sam had to finish dressing in the coach so it could reach Wakefield Station in time.

During the journey back to London, Dr Montgomery told Bartram he thought nobody had left the ground until the final whistle. Everyone in the stand had stood to cheer him off the field.

Fittingly, the Cup holders lost to the Cup holders-elect. United continued playing their splendid football all the way to Wembley, where they beat Blackpool 4-2 in one of the most entertaining Cup Finals in memory.

For Charlton, the game itself was an embarrassment, as the right-half and captain that day, Bert Johnson, was to recall as late as the 1980s: "However, I have only unqualified praise for that pre-Babes United side. Statistically Charlton were the Cup side they all had to beat at the time. We had no quarrel with our defeat at Leeds Road, nor was it a surprise that United went all the way and took the Cup. We were not as formidable on the day as our reputation made out, though that does United less than justice, and probably we were only as good as we were allowed to be. All I am prepared to say is that we all seemed willingly to accept the amount of defending we had to do that day and it remained a sore point among our players for some time."

Jimmy Seed's notes on the game read: "If the forwards had been as good as the defence, we would have stood a chance, but they were woefully weak. Manchester United were a really good side without a weakness and a forward line that always spelt danger."

In 1948-9, Charlton's departure from the Cup was more mundane. They tumbled out in the third round, going down 2-1 to Burnley, their beaten opponents in the 1947 Final.

Free From Debt

THESE post-war years were years of boom financially both on and off the field. Attendances averaged a massive 40,000 in 1948-9 and the club was free from all debt as the Gliksten brothers reclaimed all their money and did not reinvest it in the club. Seed now turned his attention away from the 'happy, hunting ground' of the North-East which had provided him with so many youngsters in the 1930s. The aftermath of the war and the shortage of 'young and ambitious' players had left the area as 'barren soil' to Seed. His North-East scouting staff numbered only two. And the actual signing of players was becoming more and more difficult. Transfer fees were rocketing and illegal payments were on the increase in those days of the maximum wage with players looking for a nice tax-free piece of what they called 'security'. The new source of recruitment to which Seed turned could hardly have been a greater contrast to his native North-East.

South African Venture

IN 1929, when Seed had captained the English touring team that toured South Africa, he had made a good friend of George Brunton, the South African right-back and captain. Seed's thoughts began to turn in this post-war period to South Africa, where he remembered talented players. So began one of the most colourful episodes in Seed's managerial career and the history of the club itself.

At this time, another friend he had met in Rhodesia on the 1929 tour, Frank Bonniwell, visited Seed's home in Bromley, Kent, before going on his annual visit to South Africa, where business would bring him in contact with Brunton. Seed said to Bonniwell: "Ask George if he knows of any good young footballers out there. Believe me, we're short of them in Britain."

The first fruits of the South African venture came with Syd O'Linn, a Cape Town inside-forward, agreeing to come to London for a trial. O'Linn also asked if Charlton would give a chance to his friend, Dudley Forbes, a wing-half, and on 6 December, 1947, both men arrived together in England. Others were to follow — all for just the price of a boat fare. Seed found them willing to train, well-disciplined and well-behaved on and off the field.

If left out of the team one week, they never came in asking to be transferred. Some failed to make the grade and were simply content to return to South Africa. O'Linn was an inside-forward of skill and forcefulness and his career with the club was to last nine seasons.

The South African connection was to underpin Charlton's position in Division One until the mid-1950s and to bring to the club several of its greatest players. In fact, one of this wave of South Africans went on to achieve the distinction of becoming Charlton's most capped player — not for South Africa but for Scotland. This was John Hewie, who made his debut for Charlton in August 1951 and immediately established himself as a first-team regular. He went on to gain 19 caps between 1956 and 1960.

Another of the intake, Eddie Firmani, went on to gain similar distinction with the Italian national team after he left Charlton to play in the Italian League. Not all signings were, of course, so successful. The next signing after O'Linn was the goalkeeper, Albert Uytenbogaardt, from the Cape Town team, Tramways. His nickname became 'Humphrey' at Charlton, as his awkward surname

Albert Uyten-bogaardt, the South African-born goalkeeper who was unable to displace Sam Bartram in the Charlton team.

Jimmy Trotter chats to three South African imports to The Valley. From left: Stuart Leary, John Hewie and Syd O'Linn.

seemed to approximate to that of the famous film star. But he could not displace Sam Bartram and after only six League games in five seasons, he returned home, becoming the established goalkeeper for the South African national team. His most spectacular feat for Charlton, seen by a handful of spectators at a reserve game, was to score with a clearance from his own penalty area. The ball, helped on by the wind, bounced over the opposing goalkeeper as he came out. To complete the bizarre episode, another South African, Firmani, crashed into the net as he followed up and brought the crossbar down.

In 1948-9, Seed decided to visit South Africa himself again. His immediate target was an outside-left, as Chris Duffy was beginning to lose form, and one player he looked at was Bill Perry of Rangers of Johannesburg. Blackpool beat Seed to Perry's signature, but he did recruit a left-back called Norman Nielson. Nielson failed to make the grade at Charlton but made nearly 200 League appearances as a centre-half for Derby County, Bury and Hull City.

Seed's visit aroused a lot of comment in the South African Press and the South African FA was getting worried at what it referred to as the poaching of South African players by British clubs.

On a second visit in September 1949, still pursuing the abortive Perry deal, Seed also planned to watch a 15-year-old schoolboy forward from Cape Town called Stuart Leary, whom O'Linn had brought to Seed's notice. The trip, on which Stanley Gliksten accompanied Seed, was supposed to be a secret. The 'secret' did not last a day. Next morning it was reported on the front page of the *Daily Express*. Seed and Gliksten were in ignorance of this when they arrived in Johannesburg. But Reuters, the international news agency, had cabled the story to South Africa and they were met at the airport by South African sports journalists.

Freddie Fell, the president of the South African FA, had made a statement in the local papers saying that Seed's visit was the worst possible news for South African football and its future international

commitments. One of the journalists showed Seed the statement. It contained these words: "At the moment we are powerless to stop South African footballers being taken away, but we are determined to fight tooth and nail against this latest threat.

With Perry now opting for Blackpool, Seed could not have the left winger he wanted. Instead, he looked at a full-back called John Hewie, who played in Pretoria. In contrast to the drawn-out Perry chase, the Hewie signing was one of the quickest Seed ever made. He and Gliksten hired a car and met Hewie in a restaurant in the town. The tea room was empty and the forms produced promptly for the signing. The signing was quick but the transfer somewhat slower.

As Hewie was signing the last form, Seed looked up at a mirror facing him and saw a head peeping round a door directly behind him. He did not take a lot of notice at the time, but Hewie told him that the restauranteur was an official of his club. Next morning the South African newspapers came out with the announcement that South African players could not be signed unless seven days notice was given to the South African FA. The sanction was applied that any player breaking the ruling and then failing to make the grade as a professional, would not be allowed to play football in South Africa again. Seed and Gliksten argued that the signing was made before the ruling was announced. Therefore the ruling did not apply. Hewie was worried at first but then decided to take his chance of English football. He told Seed: "Ah, well, if I am a failure at soccer, I can always turn my hand to rugby."

In fact, Hewie's handling prowess was such that in the later years of his career he was to keep goal for Charlton during an injury crisis. That was just one of many positions this versatile player turned out in for Charlton, although he played at left-back for his adopted country. Jimmy Seed preferred him at right-half, but played him specially at left-back when he heard Scotland were looking out for a player in that position, and invited a member of the Scottish FA selection committee down to see him. When John travelled to Hampden Park for his international debut it was the first time in his life he had seen Scotland! He qualified because his father was Scottish by birth. Seed had discovered this earlier when checking Hewie's papers after the England manager, Walter Winterbottom, had shown interest.

Before he joined Charlton, Hewie had already seen Sam Bartram play — when Sam toured South Africa with the FA team in 1939. The game was in Durban and Hewie was just seven years old at the time. Unable to afford the entrance money, he climbed into the ground through a lavatory window. His coat caught on a hook and he was left dangling in mid-air until he managed to tear himself free and sneak unobserved into the crowd.

Leary and Firmani

AFTER the signing of Hewie, the viewing of Leary was the next task for Seed in South Africa. The boy was appearing for the Clyde team at inside-right and partnering him in the match against Liesbeck Park was a player called Eddie Firmani. Clyde ran out 7-2 winners, Firmani scoring five and Leary two. Seed decided to go after both boys and went to visit their parents. The boys were firm friends and knew each other before becoming teammates in the Clyde team. Both had very contrasting styles even then. Firmani was a hard hitter of the ball, Leary in Firmani's own words 'a born artist with a football' and a player with a 'delicate style'.

Firmani commented in his autobiography: "Even at kick-about games, I realized that in him I had found the perfect partner." Firmani idolized Leary and in turn Leary idolized Syd O'Linn. Firmani first played at left-half before switching to inside-left.

The fine, well-cared for grounds of South Africa had given both players, early on as youngsters, the chance to develop ball skills without being clogged down by the mud of an English winter.

When the boys arrived in England the following season, they were still some months short of their 17th birthdays. Firmani even wanted to continue his studies and had arranged to do so in England. They trained hard together on the long voyage to Southampton, getting up at five in the morning for a run around the deck and a fierce session of PT.

Firmani remembers shivering for the first time in his life when they were off Madeira and the weather began to change. The boys lost each other at the station at Southampton, Firmani arriving at Waterloo two hours ahead of Leary, to be greeted by O'Linn and assistant manager George Robinson.

The boys made their debuts for the third team against Sutton United. Firmani played at centre-forward and Leary at inside-left. Hewie played at half-back. Firmani scored the only goal of the match with a long shot, but found the heavy ground sapping his strength, as he recalled later.

On the boys' arrival, Seed faced a problem, unbeknown to them. He had not realized just how young they were. He would be breaking the rules of the Football League if he signed them at under 17. But if he didn't sign them, he would be breaking his promise to their parents that they would be signed on at £7 a week. Seed took the risk and signed them. The age gap was not discovered at first. It came to official notice when the Football League asked for their birth certificates for the League Benevolent Scheme. But all the League did was to write disapproving of Seed's impulsive action. The signings

Eddie Firmani, who found the perfect partner in Stuart Leary.

were not contested. Both went on to become two of the finest players ever to wear the Charlton colours.

In all, Seed signed 14 Springboks for Charlton Athletic: Karl Blom, Kenneth Chamberlain, Eddie Firmani, Peter Firmani, Dudley Forbes, Leslie Fourie, Henry Griesel, John Hewie, Kenneth Kirsten, Stuart Leary, Norman Nielson, Syd O'Linn, Ronald Oosthuizen, Albert Uytenbogaardt.

Trotter for England

IN October 1948, came an England honour for the club. Jimmy Trotter was given the job of looking after the training of all England's international sides. He had trained England in 1947, for their game against Belgium, and later toured the Continent as England trainer. It was after training England in September, 1948, for the game against Denmark that he was given the position permanently.

It was Seed who originally suggested the idea to Albert Gliksten, who was a personal friend of Stanley Rous, the secretary of the Football Association. Besides helping Trotter, Seed saw the move as a little extra way of giving Charlton more national prominence. Besides his training ability, Trotter had

Derek Ufton
(opposite)
dislocated his
shoulder but was
back on the field
in five minutes.

Billy Kiernan
(opposite, below)
refused to ask for
a trial because he
thought he was
not good enough,
but Jimmy Seed
thought
otherwise.

also built a considerable reputation as one of the leading experts of his day on the physical fitness of footballers. Eddie Firmani in his 1960 autobiography paid him this tribute: "I have never met a masseur who could cure a twisted ankle or pulled muscle so quickly. He would work on a freshly twisted ankle with the lightness and daintiness of a woman but, when circumstances demanded, Jimmy revealed a tremendous power in those same hands. I remember to this day the first time Derek Ufton dislocated his shoulder. He was in great pain, but Jimmy gave one good clean pull and it slipped back before Derek had even realised it. He was strapped up and back on the field in five minutes. Jimmy Trotter always seemed to be one step ahead of everyone else."

Sadly no Charlton player ever had a run in the England team to compare with Trotter's. Charlie Vaughan was chosen to go on an FA tour of North America in 1950 and Charlton contributed three players to the FA party which toured Australia in 1951, winning all 21 games. Those players were Sam Bartram, Frank Lock and Gordon Hurst. Vaughan gained one further honour, an England 'B' cap against Holland in 1952.

Worst Yet in the First

SEASONS 1949-50 and 1950-51 were grim ones for Charlton Athletic with relegation only narrowly

Top: Blackpool's
George Farm
smothers a shot
from Charlton's
Charlie Vaughan
during a Cup tie
between the clubs
in 1951 at The
Valley. Charlton
lost after a replay
and Blackpool
went on to
Wembley.
Middle: Blackpool
score one of their
two goals in the
2-2 draw at The
Valley. Charlton
defenders are:
Forbes (6),
Bartram, Phipps
(5), Peter Croker
(2).
Bottom: Forbes,
Phipps and Revell
cannot prevent
Tottenham's Les
Bennett getting in
a shot.

being staved off. It was the goals of Charlie Vaughan that came to the rescue in the grim struggle of 1949-50. He scored 19 out of 53, the club's lowest total for 24 years. Charlton would almost certainly have been relegated but for Vaughan whose two goals against Birmingham on 22 April 1950 gave the team a reprieve and doomed the losers to go down with Manchester City.

Charlton lost 23 games, the highest in the division, but 15 were by the odd goal. They finished third from bottom with 32 points, their worst season so far in Division One. In contrast, the Reserves won the Football Combination title.

Chris Duffy, the Cup Final hero of 1947, lost his form, playing only two games that season, but the consolation was that a new goalscoring winger was ready — Billy Kiernan. Seed had signed him in July 1949, when he was playing for the Army while with the Royal Ulster Rifles in Hong Kong. Seed failed to realize at the time that Kiernan had already been on his books once before. The previous time, Kiernan was a 15-year-old amateur but the club lost trace of him. When Seed arranged for Kiernan to come from Hong Kong with his family and sign as professional, he did not realize that the 15-year-old W.Kiernan was the same player.

While playing in Hong Kong, Kiernan had repeatedly refused to write to Football League clubs asking for a trial because he did not consider he had enough ability. His career at Charlton, which saw him gain an England 'B' cap against Germany in 1955, was to prove otherwise.

The 1949-50 season also saw the debut of Derek Ufton, one of Charlton's two post-war England internationals. He had signed professional forms in 1948, and earlier played a season for the amateur club, Dulwich Hamlet. Ufton, who played at wing-half before settling down to the centre-half berth in 1951, was fast and swift in the turn. As a big man, he was a match for many of the physical centre-forwards of his day. He knew the centre-forward position well, because that was where he had played for Dulwich Hamlet. The following season saw the debut of wing-half Cyril 'Squib' Hammond, a tireless worker whose career, like Ufton's, was to span the rest of these First Division years of the 1950s, and of John Evans, an inside-forward from Tilbury Bata, who was to become noted for his powerful heading ability.

With the 1950-51 season as bad as the previous season, Seed was again desperately in need of goals. He always reckoned himself a 'lucky' manager and it was a stroke of good fortune that helped him in 1951 to avoid the dreaded drop. Charlton were struggling badly around Christmas 1950. At a board meeting, it was agreed that the club would not get out of trouble unless a new forward was brought in to add goalscoring punch. But they and Seed were unwilling to pay what they regarded as the sky-high transfer fees of the time for top players — £20,000 or more. Then came a brief, but amusing, piece of salvation — in the unlikely shape of a Swedish amateur forward.

Hans Jeppson

OUT of the blue came a letter from an old foreign friend of Seed's — Sigge Anderson, secretary of the Swedish club, Norrkoping, whom Seed had first met when Charlton made a tour of Sweden in 1938. In that letter, Anderson referred to a Swedish international player who was coming over from Sweden to London for three months to study business methods on behalf of his firm, which manufactured office equipment. The player's name was Hans Jeppson and he had led the Swedish attack in the World Cup in Brazil that year.

Jeppson wanted to play League football whilst in London — he had Arsenal in mind — and was going to start off his plan by visiting the Football Association headquarters at Lancaster Gate in London. Seed found out the time of his appointment and decided to be there at the same time. At 11am on the morning of 5 January 1951, he arrived to find Jeppson there in the waiting room. Seed's coup succeeded far better than he could have anticipated because Stanley Rous was unable to keep the

Charlton Athletic, 1949-50. Back row (left to right): Jimmy Trotter (trainer), Charlie Revell, Jock Campbell, Tommy Brown, Sam Bartram, Frank Lock, Harold Phipps, Bert Johnson, Jimmy Seed (manager). Front: Syd O'Lynn, Gordon Hurst, Tommy Lumley, Charlie Vaughan, Charlie Purves, Chris Duffy, Benny Fenton.

appointment, leaving Jeppson in his hands. Seed's quick brain sized up the situation and the need to get Jeppson to see Charlton before he could enter the more glamorous marble halls of Highbury. The result was that Jeppson became a Charlton player.

Charlton soon found out what the Swedish international could do. The Jeppson miracle started on 13 January against Sheffield Wednesday at The Valley. Charlton were then fourth from bottom of Division One. In just 11 League games for the club, Jeppson was to transform totally the club's season. Wednesday were the first victims of his skills, the Swede scoring the winner in a 2-1 Charlton victory.

Top: Stan Pearson (extreme left) and John Aston (next to him) draw Phipps and Bartram (on ground) whilst Cliff Birkett scores for Manchester United, who won 2-1 at The Valley in January 1951.

Bottom: Charlie Vaughan gets in a fine header against Liverpool. Charlton won this home game, also played in January 1951, 1-0.

Hans Jeppson, Charlton's Swedish star who moved into the Italian League — a player with 'amazing' confidence.

Although the next match saw Charlton go down at home to Manchester United, there then followed eight games without defeat. The week after the Manchester United defeat, Jeppson scored the only goal of the match against Liverpool at The Valley. Then he hit two at Wolverhampton as Charlton gained a precious 3-2 away victory. In a friendly match, at West Ham, he netted four in a 5-1 victory. Then, on 24 February at Highbury in the League, he scored a hat-trick in a 5-2 victory. In March, Charlton beat Chelsea 3-2 at Stamford Bridge with Jeppson getting the winning goal. But by the end of March, the brief but meteoric Charlton career of the Swedish international was over. He had scored nine goals in his 11 League appearances, not counting the four against West Ham. And those 11 games brought Charlton 17 vital points.

Charlton were safe and a delighted Stanley Gliksten tried to arrange for a helicopter to land on The Valley pitch after the match against Portsmouth so that Jeppson could catch the Saturday afternoon boat from Tilbury to Sweden. Failing to get hold of a helicopter, he did the next best thing by arranging for a fast launch to race Jeppson from Greenwich to Tilbury.

Jeppson was made captain for the game but could not score on his last appearance, Portsmouth winning 1-0. With Jeppson gone, Charlton could win only one of the five matches remaining, slipping to finish 17th.

A handsome, articulate man, Jeppson was outstanding as an individual and a player. He stood 6ft tall and weighed 12st 2lbs. According to Seed, he had 'an amazing confidence' in himself, and at tactical talks was always ready with ideas which he expressed in perfect English. Seed said of Jeppson: "He placed special emphasis on the fact that the ball should be kept on the ground, and some of our players must have felt humble to hear this foreign player passing on advice which every youngster in Britain should know and follow."

Jeppson was really ahead of his time in the British game. Seed observed that he was agile to a far greater degree than British players and his game was entirely based on skill and ball-playing, eschewing the physical style of British football at that time. "But, unlike most Continental players then, he possessed a deadly shot."

Jeppson played for Charlton as an amateur but his Charlton fame led to far more reward than he could ever have expected as a Charlton player in those days of the maximum wage. The Italians, having seen what he could do in English football, moved in for him. In August 1951, he was signed by the First Division club, Atalanta. His personal fee was £18,000, a massive sum for those days. In June 1952, he was on the move again, to Naples, who paid £55,000 for his services. Out of that fee, Jeppson was reported to have received another £18,000. But Naples was not quite so happy a place as The Valley. After quarrelling with the club, he returned to Sweden, only to come back again to Naples. He eventually left on a free transfer, having at that time made more money out of football than any player in the world. He kept in touch with Charlton through his enthusiasm for tennis. Each year he would return for the fortnight of the Wimbledon championships and make a point of calling on Seed and Stanley Gliksten.

The Jeppson episode in Charlton's history was not without controversy. Some clubs complained to the Football League at what they saw as the unfair advantage gained by Charlton. Although their protests came too late to stop the magic Jeppson wove at the club, they did have their effect on the Football League administrators. The League took steps to stop foreign stars coming over in similar circumstances and then cashing in overseas on their success.

One reason why Jeppson's goals were so valuable was that Charlie Vaughan was off his normal goalscoring form, netting only seven. But the following season, he was back to his best, scoring 22 goals out of the club's 68, as Charlton put aside the difficulties of the previous season and rose to tenth in the table. The season was marked by the fine displays of Kiernan on the left wing. He netted 11 goals that season and was top scorer the next with 14.

The Death of Albert Gliksten

ON 22 December 1951 came an event which not only saddened Seed but was also to have long-term consequences for his own future at Charlton. Albert Gliksten, whom he described as 'a real friend', died suddenly of a heart attack in British Honduras. Seed's relationship with Gliksten's brother, Stanley, was never as warm and friendly. Albert Gliksten had already warned him that all was not well. Seed traced his own disquiet back a little earlier. He recorded

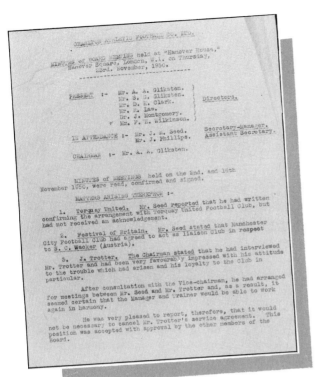

that the Cup-winning season of 1946-7 was one of the last seasons that he was 'really happy' with the club.

In the years before his death, Albert Gliksten spent more and more time abroad — in South Africa, British Honduras, Jamaica and the United States. But he kept in close touch with Seed by letter and Seed recounted touchingly in his autobiography: "I still treasure some of his last letters." Before he left to make his last trip from England, Albert Gliksten gave Seed a hint of the shape of things to come. He begged Seed not to resign or take any drastic steps until he returned to England. According to Seed: "I knew exactly what he was getting at, but with Albert dead I was never given the opportunity to resign."

The Happy Valley that had seen the club rise so triumphantly through the divisions of the Football League was clearly happy no more. That unhappiness was also reflected in a deteriorating relationship between Seed and Trotter, who had spent a large part of their careers together at Sheffield Wednesday and Charlton. The two men had entirely contrasting temperaments. Trotter was 'dour, determined, forthright, and a man of few words' with a singleness of purpose and determination to reach the top, according to Seed. He was also less of a worrier than Seed and less sensitive to criticism. But Trotter's reserved personality could wrongly give out the impression of unfriendliness among those who did not know him well.

Although there were sometimes clashes early on with Seed and his more open personality, these were not serious and only to be expected from two men working so closely together. But for some seasons before Seed's dismissal in 1956, the two Jimmies were not 100 per cent in accord and players and directors were aware of the atmosphere between them. Seed commented in his autobiography: "I am sure in the last few seasons the lack of co-operation between us caused the directors embarrassment."

The deterioration was very much in personal relationships. The two men rarely differed on tactics and playing policy. In the dressing-room, Trotter had a completely free hand and Seed did not interfere with his method. Towards the end of Seed's managership, Seed's worrying became more intense

and the job began to fray him. He admitted that, even sometimes near the end of a game, he stood at the top of the stairs leading from the stand to the offices and would slip down before the end, scuttling back when he heard the roar of "Goal!" Despite this, he was still able to exude an air of calmness after a game, misleading many around him as to his almost neurotic state of nerves.

One person who had witnessed his state of nerves was the journalist and broadcaster, Ivan Sharpe, who some years later was to write: 'I remember broadcasting an Everton match at Charlton in a snowstorm from a box near the touch-line. Michael Standing of the BBC did the window-cleaning while I tried to do the talking, and bobbing up-and-down behind the box was a huddled figure who could only muster nerve to watch the battle at intervals . . .Manager Seed!'

An Amateur Episode

THE more daring side of Seed's managership was shown in a remarkable game at Spurs on Boxing Day, 1951, when he did what would now be unthinkable in modern football. Into the side he called an England amateur winger in his 30s, who had not even been blooded in the Reserves. But it proved an inspired act on Seed's part. The amateur scored the winning goal. That player was Tony Pawson — one of the foremost amateur players of an era when amateur football drew big attendances — and later to become a distinguished journalist.

The event is recalled in his book *The Goalscorers*. Charlton at that time used to spend one training day each season on the Aylesford Paper Mills Ground near Maidstone. The attraction was a sauna which had been left to the company by the Finnish Olympic team, who brought it with them to the 1948 Games in London. Charlton did a light training session followed by the sauna to make a break from their normal routine. The connection with the Paper Mills came through the Gliksten brothers and their timber interests.

Pawson worked at Aylesford and was asked to look after Charlton on their visit. At that time he was a 31-year-old greying player with the famous Oxbridge side, Pegasus. He was a Winchester and Oxford man. The day turned out to be a surprise indeed for Pawson, for over lunch, Jimmy Seed asked him to sign for the club. Pawson did not take the offer too seriously, thinking Seed wanted him for the occasional reserve game. He said he played for Pegasus on Saturdays and was not free midweek. He added: "However, I

Opposite: Extract from the Charlton Minute Book recording the attempt to patch up the differences between manager Jimmy Seed and his assistant, Jimmy Trotter.

Charlton Athletic 1951-2. Back row (left to right): John Hewie, Derek Ufton, Sam Bartram, Frank Lock, Bert Johnson, Chris Duffy. Front: Gordon Hurst, John Evans, Charlie Vaughan, Billy Kiernan.

Boxing Day 1952. White Hart Lane. My first game in the First Division. As the powerful Spurs team hustle us Charlton are two goals down before I've touched the ball.

But before half-time we level the scores and it is still 2–2 minutes from the end. Alf Ramsey heads out from under the Tottenham bar with goalkeeper Ditchburn beaten. The ball comes straight to my feet where I have cut in from the wing. An instant shot sails into the net to win the match.

It is a story book ending to my first game with the stars. The lessons? Keep trying and anything can happen. An instinct for goals is more important for a forward than keeping to fixed positions.

will be glad to sign if you give me a free ticket to watch your home game with Spurs at Christmas.''

Pawson watched Spurs, the then League Champions, beat Charlton 3-0 at The Valley on Christmas Day. After that game, Seed said: "Now you can play at White Hart Lane on Boxing Day. We meet Tottenham again and you might change our luck.'' So Pawson gave up his Christmas dinner and did some training near his home, running twice up the steep Tovil Hill just outside Maidstone.

According to Pawson's account of his big day: 'Arriving early at White Hart Lane, I waited expectantly for detailed tactical instruction that I presumed separated the professionals from the amateurs. Perhaps I missed the team briefing. My own was simple enough. "What I want you to do", said the captain Benny Fenton, "is kick your corners to the far post." "And what I advise you", said the club doctor, "is to have a tot of whisky for your nerves." The second instruction was easy enough to carry out. There seemed no point in mentioning, however, that I found it hard to hit corners as far as the middle of the goal even on a dry ground, let alone on the muddy quagmire that the Tottenham pitch used to become when it rained, as it did on this day.

'As we went out, my Kent cricketing colleague and inside partner for the day, Syd O'Linn, said, "Seed has never seen you play and the scout who

recommended you after one of your Amateur Cup games is in a bit of a state. He's told Kiernan and me to make sure you have a good game or Seed will have his head."

'At least, it was comforting to know one's inside was out to make life easy. For a quarter of an hour, there was nothing remotely easy about it. Never had I run so far, or so fast — and yet made no contact with a ball that was forever spirited away from me. We were already two goals down and I felt out of breath and out of my depth. Then came the dreaded moment — a corner to take. The run-up was short and confined and in the extra effort to reach the far post, my left foot slid away and my right sliced the ball diagonally backwards along the ground. It was not the type of corner to which Division One players were accustomed and 20 of them stared at it in contemptuous amazement. The 21st, Kiernan, ran on to the ball and swept it low inside the far post before anyone moved. I was in the game.''

Then just before half-time, he centred for Kiernan to head home and make the score 2-2. But even better was to come. In the final minutes with the game still tied at 2-2, Alf Ramsey, the Spurs full-back, was on the goal-line to head out a shot, but put the ball straight to Pawson. From 12 yards out, Pawson hit it back over Ramsey's head into the roof of the net. It was the winner.

After the game, Seed invited Pawson back to Charlton for drinks and then asked his expenses. "Ten shillings and sixpence," was the answer. Seed and assistant secretary Jack Phillips took him over to the safe, and Seed said: "I am very pleased with the way you played today. Here is ten guineas." Pawson was acutely conscious of his amateur status and refused the money. Recalls Pawson: 'That led to a heated argument with Jack Phillips taking the money out and then putting it back, as one or other held the floor. Finally Seed laughed and gave me another drink instead.'

In later seasons, when Pawson went back to Charlton, he was to be introduced in the manner of a character in a Bateman cartoon as 'the amateur who asked for ten shillings expenditure.' But Pawson remembered that goal as the one it gave him most pleasure to score in his career. But it was not the start of a long acquaintance with Charlton. He played only one more game, and that was the following season.

The 1952-3 season saw Seed's South African imports really begin to make their mark. Firmani and Leary did so well that Seed was able to release Charlie Vaughan to Portsmouth for a sizeable fee.

Charlton's inspiring post-war skipper, Benny Fenton. Behind him is Jimmy Campbell.

Firmani's Struggle

FIRMANI, despite his later goalscoring feats, had problems establishing himself as a forward. He made his debut the previous season as a left-back against Derby County in a 3-3 draw at The Valley. He had tried the position in the Reserves and third team at the suggestion of Jimmy Seed. The debut match was his sole game in the 1951-2 season — in contrast to Stuart Leary, who also made his debut that season and played in five games. He broke into the side again in the 1952-3 season at left-back, but with the confidence coming into his football, decided to try again at being a forward. He asked Alex Hird, the reserve-team trainer, if he could have a run out in the Reserves at inside-left — and made his point by scoring two goals in a midweek game against Coventry City. So impressive had been his display that he found himself in the first team at inside-left the following Saturday, against Manchester City at Maine Road on 15 November. The side went down 5-1 — their second biggest defeat that season. On 27 September, they had also been thrashed in Lancashire, by 8-4 at Blackpool, the Bloomfield Road club's biggest-ever League win.

But Seed kept faith with the side that had played at Maine Road. He put it out unchanged for the next match, against Stoke City at The Valley. Firmani scored a hat-trick in a 5-1 victory and the Firmani legend was born. The patient coaching and attention of George Robinson, who paid him particular attention, and Jimmy Seed, had borne fruit. And Seed had shrewdly seen that Firmani's experience as a defender would give him the knowledge as a forward of how to beat the tight marking of defenders and escape into precious open space.

After this, Firmani was kept at inside-left with Leary at centre-forward. The play of Leary and Firmani began to blend just as it had done in South Africa and Charlton rose to fifth place in the League,

Stuart Leary (pictured) and Eddie Firmani did so well in 1952-3 that Seed was able to release Charlie Vaughan to Portsmouth for a large fee.

their best placing since the war. The following season, 1953-4, the team slipped to ninth, but recorded the highest League victory in the club's history. Middlesbrough were beaten 8-1 at The Valley on 12 September, 1953, with Firmani scoring a hat-trick.

Eddie Firmani in action against Huddersfield Town during a First Division game at The Valley in 1953.

89

The other scorers were Gordon Hurst (2), Syd O'Linn (2) and Stuart Leary.

That season Leary set a post-war scoring record for Charlton with 26 League and Cup goals. His partner, Firmani, was to equal that the next. Firmani's shooting was now becoming more and more powerful and, every Monday and Tuesday, the wingers, Billy Kiernan and Gordon Hurst, spent long periods of training putting over crosses for Firmani to hit on the half-volley. "Never stop the ball — hit it first time", was the advice given to Firmani by George Robinson. And by constant practice hitting a ball against a low wall and striking it on the rebound with either left or right foot, whatever the angle or speed it came at, Firmani built up the same shooting power in his left foot as in his right.

He scored hat-tricks on successive Saturdays, against Sheffield United and Sheffield Wednesday in November and December 1954, and then followed this up on 5 February 1955, by hitting five against Aston Villa in a 6-1 victory — a memorable weekend for Firmani since on the Sunday, his wife, Pat, George Robinson's daughter, gave birth to their son, Paul. They had married in March 1954.

Sam Bartram gets ready for another day's training. Opposite: Bartram in a mid-air duel with Portsmouth's Len Phillips.

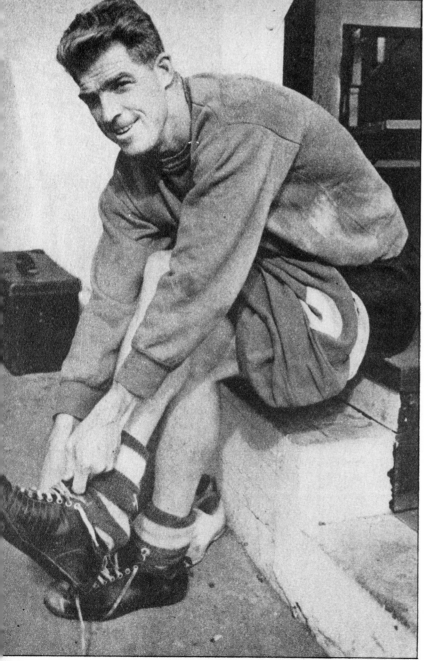

The Bartram Records

AS the young Firmani and Leary rose to stardom, one of the stalwarts of Seed's reign, Sam Bartram, was now nearing the end of his career. In the final match of the 1952-3 season, he passed the record of games played by any player in League Football — 467 by the England and Everton goalkeeper, Ted Sagar — and this despite the missing years of war. From then on, each game he played set a new record. He was also the longest-serving player with one club in the history of the game. The highlight came on 6 March, 1954, when Bartram played his 500th League game. Fittingly, it was at The Valley. The opponents were Portsmouth. Counting Cup ties, friendlies and wartime games, it was Bartram's 701st appearance for the club.

Bartram owned a small sports shop just outside The Valley and on the morning of the Portsmouth match, it was crowded by well-wishers wanting to shake his hand. His mother made the all-night journey down from the North-East to see the memorable game.

Before the match, he was presented with a silver tea-service from the club, and then the Portsmouth club sportingly came into the act. First, one of the Pompey directors, Harry Wain, handed Bartram an inscribed silver salver. Then the Pompey skipper Jimmy Dickinson took Bartram into the treatment room, where stood a cake shaped in the form of a football pitch with models of 22 players in the colours of Charlton and Portsmouth.

Then it was out on to the field for photographs with Jimmy Dickinson and after the match, Bartram faced the television cameras. Bartram, who by habit normally came second out of the tunnel, led the Charlton team out on to the field as captain for the day and a roar of appreciation broke out from the heights of the crowded Valley — "A roar that warmed my heart and made me glow with pride," he recounted in his autobiography. It was a magical day — one of the happiest in the club's history, of which Bartram formed so massive a part. Even the result went the

right way. The game itself was a scrambling affair but Charlton won 3-1.

Derek Ufton's First and Last International.

THE 1953-4 season was also notable for a first and only England cap for Derek Ufton, against the Rest of Europe at Wembley in October. A player beset by recurring shoulder trouble through his career, Ufton's debut could not have been a more unlucky one. So unlucky that it was his first and last appearance for England.

Bartram's 500th League appearance: Left: Cutting the 'birthday' cake with another veteran, Pompey's Jimmy Dickinson. Right: Skipper for the day, Bartram leads out the team. Bottom: Cheers! A toast from Jimmy Seed.

back. The defence tightened up and England managed a 4-4 draw.

Although not foreseen at the time, the game was the forerunner of the Hungarian disaster, when the same England defence, minus Ufton, conceded six goals.

Had Winterbottom had his way, Ufton would have been in the team again. After the match, he praised the Charlton player for his self-sacrificing performance and promised him another game. But selection in those days was not in the hands of the manager, but of an FA selection committee. They did not pick Ufton again and Harry Johnston of Blackpool took the number-five shirt again to meet his nemesis against another deep-lying centre-forward, Hidegkuti of Hungary. It was to be Johnston's last match for England, too.

Under-23 Caps

OTHER international honours that season went to Stuart Leary and full-back Syd Ellis, who played for England's Under-23 team against Italy, in the first international staged at that level. But Leary's international career was blighted when the nationality qualifications were tightened up and he became ineligible for England teams. The blow deflated Leary and Charlton. He was widely regarded as the best footballing centre-forward of his day and the problem was compounded by the fact that Leary was English enough to do two years' National Service in the RAF — but not to play for the country. Syd Ellis could not keep up his good form and, like Leary,

Derek Ufton (above) was capped for England in the game against the Rest of Europe and faced the deep-lying centre-forward, Gunnar Nordahl. Syd Ellis (opposite) played for the Under-23 side against Italy in the first international staged at that level.

The match was held to mark the 90th anniversary of the Football Association and was against a team chosen by FIFA from Europe's best, excluding the Hungarians who, a month later, were to inflict an historic 6-3 defeat on England at Wembley. Before the Hungarian defeat, English football was still caught in its post-war time-warp of arrogance. The FIFA team was regarded as a scratch one, ready for the taking by England. It was into this woeful scenario that the hapless Ufton was thrust. In reality, the team was up against Europe's best and deadliest players. And Ufton was called on to face a deep-lying centre-forward, the Swede Gunar Nordahl, a tactic then unknown in England but just emerging on the Continent. Ufton stayed with Nordahl but the defensive gap was not properly covered. With England trailing 3-2, manager, Walter Winterbottom, changed tactics at half-time and kept Ufton

Bobby Ayre (right), a forward from Berwick, now became a Charlton regular. Frank Lock (left) moved to Liverpool with John Evans. Don Townsend (bottom) had to wait more than four years for his League debut.

went on to play three League games in the first team that season and then went on to establish himself as a scheming inside-forward in the last years of the club's First Division days.

A player who took somewhat longer to make his debut was Don Townsend, signed as an inside-left from Trowbridge in 1950. He did not make the Division One team until August 1954 and then as a full-back, first taking over on the left while Jock Campbell recovered from injury and then becoming a regular fixture. A Swindon man, he was a railway signalman before going to London. Strangely enough, the man who took over Townsend's job in the signal box, was England Youth international footballer Roy Jennings, who went on to sign as a professional with Brighton, also playing at left-back.

The 1954-5 season also saw the debut of Scottish inside-forward John Ryan, who became known as 'Buck'. He was a consistent scorer but, like White, went in and out of the team.

In March 1955, Gordon Jago made his debut, in The Valley clash against Arsenal. An England Youth captain, he signed as an amateur for Charlton in

his first Under-23 cap was his only one. Christmas 1953 saw the departure of John Evans and Frank Lock to Liverpool, a double signing by Don Welsh, the Merseyside club's manager. Bobby Ayre, an inside or outside-right from Berwick, now became a regular in the team and went on to win England Under-23 caps in 1955, against Scotland and Italy.

Ronnie White, who signed for Charlton in March 1954 from local Sunday league football, remarkably

Derek Pace and Colin Gibson of Aston Villa rejoice, but the effort was disallowed.

Action from the mid-1950s. Eddie Firmani (far left) scores against Sunderland.

February 1950. He had also captained London Boys while a schoolboy at Erith. When he signed professional forms, Jago found himself as one of eight centre-halves on the club's books. Not content with just playing the game, he became a qualified FA coach and taught hundreds of schoolboys in the Woolwich and North Kent districts, experience which paved the way for his English and North American managerial career in years to come.

Charlton's form in the FA Cup during these years was abysmal. In the four years from 1951 to 1954, they went out at the first hurdle, in the third round. But in 1955, they managed to reach the fifth round and a game against the League leaders, Wolves, at Molineux. Wolves won easily, 4-1.

The Cup defeat heralded a slide down Division One, the side failing to win in their 14 remaining League games of the 1954-5 season. They finished 15th.

The average attendance that season fell to 24,005, a healthy figure to modern eyes, but the lowest in Division One that season and compared to an overall

First Division average of 32,656. At the end of the season, one of Charlton's original South Africans, Syd O'Linn, called it a day and decided to return to South Africa. O'Linn was one of the many footballer-cricketers of his day and one problem of his departure was that he was committed to a summer professional contract with Whitburn in the Durham Senior League. The problem was solved when Fred Lucas, the reserve wing-half, agreed to take over the contract. Lucas had also been with Kent County Cricket Club up to the previous year and played in several county matches. He was both a batsman and useful change bowler.

The Charlton club had particularly close links with Kent. Derek Ufton was a regular in the county side and was reserve wicket-keeper to the great Godfrey Evans. Stuart Leary, doing his National Service in the RAF, made the occasional appearance for Kent. And with such cricket talent in the side, summer games of cricket were frequent for the Charlton team of those days, including the annual outing to Aylesford Paper Mills. O'Linn continued his cricketing career back home, becoming a Test cricketer at a time when South Africa was still a part of the international sporting scene.

Sampdoria Swoop

FIRMANI'S fame had now spread abroad, to countries other than South Africa and the summer of 1955 saw one of the most famous transfer deals of the 1950s, with the Italian club, Sampdoria, swooping for him.

The deal was initiated by the Italian agent, Gigi Peronace, who told Seed that he represented an Italian First Division club who wanted to buy Firmani, although he did not disclose the name of the club. At that time, Peronace was not the well-known figure in English football he later became. He asked the price and Seed boldly quoted what was an extremely high figure for the time — £35,000. Peronace asked if he could have first refusal at that price and said he would return to Italy for talks with the directors of the club, which Seed thought was Milan.

Firmani also met Peronace, with the agent saying he intended to contact leading Italian clubs on Firmani's behalf. Later, Firmani heard from him that Torino were interested and were prepared to pay a signing-on fee of £7,000. In the meantime, the story broke in the newspapers both at home and in Italy. And then Seed received several telephone calls directly from Milan, who said they were also interested. Clearly, they were not after all the first inquirers, but their approach was not in the form of a definite offer. This was followed by a telephone call from a Jack Hooper, who was an Englishman in the

shipping business and an agent for a firm in Genoa. The head of the firm was also the president of Sampdoria FC, Signor Ravano. Hooper said that Ravano was ready to meet Seed's valuation of the player. This was the signal for negotiations which led to Sampdoria paying Seed's full price.

Firmani received what in those days was a massive signing-on fee of £5,000, to be spread over two years with an initial £2,500 to be lodged in a London bank. His weekly wage was to be £18 plus bonuses.

Left: Brian Pilkington of Burnley gets past Charlton's John Hewie. Right: Wolves goalkeeper Bert Williams grabs at the ball during a Cup tie against Charlton. Below: Billy Kiernan (11) races in to score against Birmingham City.

Charlton Athletic in 1954-5. Back row (left to right): Fenton, Campbell, Bartram, Ufton, Hewie, Hammond. Front: Hurst, O'Linn, Leary, Firmani, Kiernan.

Left: August
1955. Eddie
Firmani is bound
for Italy and says
a temporary
farewell to his
wife, Pat and son,
Paul. Right:
Jimmy Gauld,
who was later
disgraced in a
bribes and betting
scandal.

But the deal was not to be as simple as that and plenty of complications followed. His departure was delayed three times through technicalities. The problem was that Italian officials could not find the birth certificate of Firmani's grandfather, Pietro Cleito Firmani, a fisherman from Ortona-Mare on the Adriatic Coast. Without the legal evidence of Firmani's Italian ancestry, the deal was in jeopardy. This was because the Italian FA permitted each club only one foreigner on their books and Sampdoria already had an Argentinian.

Ortona-Mare had been badly knocked about during the war and many records destroyed. The confused situation was eventually resolved by the Italian embassy in London and Firmani, after laying on a champagne celebration for his Charlton teammates and directors, left to start a career that would see him become an Italian international footballer.

As an interesting sidelight on the very different life of English professional footballers in those days, the £2,500 in the London bank meant that Firmani had a cheque book for the first time in his life. He took his boots, officially owned by Charlton Athletic, with him with the club's permission. He soon dispensed with them. As he commented later: "It did not take me long to appreciate that the light-weight boots — and gear in general — worn by the Italians were superior to the London kit." Most facilities for players in Italy at that time were years ahead of anything in England, as Firmani soon found to his delight.

His move was the start of the early English transfer trail to Italy and the famous John Charles was soon to follow from Leeds United.

There remained a Firmani on Charlton's books, his younger brother, Peter, who came over from Cape Town in 1953 and made his debut in the year after his brother's departure, at right-back against Cardiff City on 21 April, 1956, at The Valley. But he was a lesser player than his brother and played in only 31 League games for the club.

Jimmy Gauld

EDDIE Firmani's replacement for the 1955-6 season was Jimmy Gauld, who had been signed in April 1955, from the League of Ireland club, Waterford, where he had broken the League goalscoring record for a season. Gauld was a Scotsman and a player who was tremendously quick off the mark. He had a creditable first season, finishing second-highest scorer behind Stuart Leary, with 17 goals, as Charlton finished in 14th position.

While Firmani sailed on to Italian glory, Gauld was to go on to make headlines of a more unsavoury sort and become part of the blacker history of the game, when he was jailed in 1964 after being accused of 'fixing' games as a Mansfield Town player.

But in that happier season, he had both a special soccer series of articles in the Sunday newspaper, the *Empire News*, and had a full-length portrait of himself in *Charles Buchan's Football Monthly*. In view of what was to come, the Charlton programme of 28 January 1956, struck a rich vein of irony when it reported Jimmy Gauld going to jail in Dublin, barely 24 hours after leaving the field at Everton on Saturday, 14 January. 'But don't get alarmed — Jimmy's visit was quite voluntary,'' the programme added. He had gone across from Liverpool to the Republic to attend the big annual charity carnival at Dalymount Park, Dublin.

'After taking part in the frolics at Dalymount, which included a comic football match — The Inkpots versus the The Crackpots — Jimmy Gauld who has a lovely tenor voice (you should hear him in the bath at The Valley) accompanied a concert party to Mountjoy Prison to entertain the inmates. Jimmy told us afterwards that he didn't wish to cause another breach of the peace within the prison walls, so he didn't sing.'

The programme showed a more serious note of foresight earlier that season, in September, 1955, when it looked at the 'missing millions' of soccer, a familiar phenomenon in the years to come. It commented in words which sound just as apt today on the modern surfeit of football and football competitions:

'One hears a lot about the 'missing millions' in soccer. It is true that League attendances are down,

but we should not overlook the increased number of special matches — internationals, floodlit friendlies, representative games, etc. Overall it is our opinion that more millions watch football than ever before, but the trouble is that League games are being overshadowed by the more glamorous international matches.

'Moreover, at the start of a season, League clubs are called upon to play eight matches in the first four weeks, and in these days of high prices it is asking a lot to expect supporters to turn out to all these matches. To the average fan, midweek games become an embarrassment, both from the financial and inconvenience points of view. Fans are being asked to contribute too much to the sport. In our view, football is as popular as ever, the only difference compared with the old days being that the supporters have a wider choice.'

And that was before the days of the League Cup, Full Members Cup and so on.

In the FA Cup that season, Charlton again managed to get to the fifth round. In the third round, before a 29,610 crowd at The Valley, they ran up their record Cup win, defeating the Birmingham League side, Burton Albion, 7-0. Burton had caused a shock by eliminating Third Division North side, Halifax Town, in the second round, but they were no match for First Division Charlton. Jack Stamps, the man who had scored twice for Derby County against Charlton in the 1946 Cup Final, would have played for Burton that day, had he not been nursing an injury sustained in an earlier round. Stuart Leary scored a hat-trick and Billy Kiernan twice. The other scorers were Jimmy Gauld and Gordon Hurst. It was 23 years since Charlton had last played a non-League side in the FA Cup, when they beat Bath City 3-1 in a first-round replay.

In the fourth round, Charlton had another home tie and beat Swindon 2-1. The end when it came in the fifth round was spectacular — a tie against Arsenal at The Valley on Saturday, 18 February, bringing record receipts of £8,163 and a crowd of 71,767. Charlton were beaten 2-0. On the following Wednesday came a curious contrast. An afternoon League match against Chelsea at Stamford Bridge on a snow-covered pitch drew only 8,473 fans. Charlton lost 3-1.

End of the Bartram Era.

ON Saturday, 10 March, Arsenal were again the opponents at The Valley, this time in the League before a crowd of 39,533. This second encounter was also a momentous occasion, for it was Sam Bartram's last game for Charlton. Bartram had a private informal agreement with Seed that he would end his career at the top. When Seed thought he was no longer good enough, that would be the signal for his retirement. He would never be dropped. In fact,

Left: Everton's O'Neill breaks up a raid by Jimmy Gauld. Right: Don Townsend (3) in a tussle with Dulin of Spurs. Below: Gauld scores a goal past Portsmouth's Norman Uprichard.

Sam Bartram, whose great era was about to come to an end.

the situation never arose. The game was his last because he had been appointed manager of York City on the Friday. He was made captain for the day as Charlton won 2-0 to complete a first-ever League double over the historic foe and gain some consolation for their Cup exit. Jimmy Gauld scored both goals.

At the end of the game, the crowd surged on to the pitch, shouting, "We want Sam". Then to the strains of *Auld Lang Syne* echoing over the loudspeakers, the hero appeared in the directors' box, a towel draped over his perspiring shoulders. Again words failed him as they had before and he could only manage a few of words of farewell to the idolizing crowd. In the dressing-room, Sam was toasted in champagne by fellow players and staff. *The Times* report of the match read: 'Fittingly he kept his goal intact in his usual inimitable style, making several splendid saves which belied his 42 years. His play was such to emphasize that football was losing one of its great goalkeepers. It was small wonder that at the end of the game the crowd rose to him in a final tribute to a loyal and distinguished player.'

Jimmy Seed's notes after the game read: 'His last match for us. Kept brilliantly.' It was the end of an historic career, for Bartram had advanced the art of goalkeeping itself, bringing it into the modern era. Goalkeepers now dominated the whole of the penalty area and not just their goal-line. It was Bartram who showed that goalkeeping was more than just the art of fine saves, but also the cutting out of through-passes and deep centres. He was desperately unlucky never to have won an England cap.

Despite the war years, Sam had chalked up a massive total of 579 League games and played in 44 FA Cup matches — still a club record of appearances. And he had been an ever-present in five seasons, again a continuing record.

Into his place for the remaining games of the season came young Frank Reed, who had made his debut against West Bromwich Albion at The Valley on 11 February 1956. Reed looked like a young clone of Bartram's, hailing too from the North-East, from Seaham Harbour. He was 6ft. 3½ ins tall and Charlton had signed him in August 1954 after seeing him play in the Murton Colliery team. He worked as a blacksmith's striker. Although he had an initial run of promising games, he failed to progress and he was

reduced in the following seasons to a 'bit player' on the Charlton scene.

Neither Bartram nor the club realized it at the time, but Bartram's departure was to herald the club's parting from Division One. The strains of *Auld Lang Syne* also marked farewell to Charlton as a great club. Without Bartram, some of the spirit seemed to drain from The Valley and Charlton lasted just one season more in the top flight. In his autobiography, he described the end movingly and in words that were, alas, to prove prophetic indeed.

'Perhaps you can imagine my feelings as I walked down to the ground for the last time. It just did not seem possible that this was the end of almost a lifetime with Charlton.

'All the old familiar features took on a new look as I realized that everything I did, and which I had been doing for more than 22 years, was for the last time. I am afraid my thoughts were far away as I changed and hung my clothes on the number-one peg; I looked round the dressing-room and saw again all the faces of the men who had been colleagues through the years, and it seemed impossible that now I too was to become a ghost.'

To anyone who remembered Sam and walked around the deserted overgrown Valley, the memory, the presence, the 'ghost' of Sam was surely there amidst that scene of desolation.

Gordon Hurst of Charlton and Bill Shorthouse of Wolves battle for the ball during Charlton's 3-2 win at The Valley in September 1950.

Relegation and a Near Return

WHEN the 1956-7 season opened, it seemed yet another normal season of challenge for an established First Division club. Of the 22 teams in the division, only six — Arsenal, Bolton, Chelsea, Portsmouth, Sunderland and Wolves — could boast a better unbroken run than Charlton's 13 seasons. During that time, only once, in 1949-50, had Charlton finished as low as 20th, the last non-relegation place. With the exception of the retired Sam Bartram, the side that started the 1956-7 campaign was virtually the same one that had finished 14th the previous season.

But the storm clouds of a season of a disaster came in the very first game, at Villa Park on 18 August. Aston Villa had only just escaped relegation the previous season with a superior goal-average over

Jimmy Gauld is foiled by Blackpool's George Farm.

relegated Huddersfield, but they beat Charlton 3-1. Although Villa took a two-goal lead, Charlton were still in with a chance when Bobby Ayre scored in the 83rd minute. A minute later, however, Syd O'Linn conceded an own-goal.

But the truth was that Charlton had played badly, disturbingly badly, and Jimmy Seed recognized just how badly. In his match notes, he wrote: 'A very poor show against very poor opposition.' But his words had a much harsher tone than this. He also wrote: 'No anticipation. No spirit or fight. No team work.' He ended with ominous, dramatic words: 'The Red is Shining.'

It was the story of the season already. The team failed to win a single point in the first five games. The Villa Park defeat was followed by a home defeat, 2-1 against Leeds United. All that could be said of that demoralizing start at The Valley was that it left at least one good memory in the minds of Charlton fans, that of the sportsmanship of the great John Charles. Early on, Derek Ufton suffered yet another of his series of shoulder dislocations and Charles sportingly kicked the ball out of play so Ufton could get immediate attention.

This was followed by another 2-1 defeat at The Valley, against Luton Town, and then a 4-0 defeat in the return match against Leeds at Elland Road. Then came the ultimate debacle — an 8-1 mauling at Roker Park. This disastrous opening run spelled the end of Seed's 23-year reign as manager. On Monday, 3 September 1956, Seed was dismissed in circumstances degrading to the club and a betrayal of all the values which Seed, one of the great managers in football history, had built at Charlton. The trigger of this shameful episode was the 8-1 hammering by Sunderland. Ironically, Seed's professional soccer career, which began at Roker Park, was to end there too.

Seed knew there would be a serious inquest later but simply did not contemplate that his career as manager was about to end. In the Roker boardroom after the defeat, he managed to hide his depression. One of the Sunderland directors, Laurie Evans, came over and sympathized with him on the defeat. Seed chuckled and replied: "Never mind, Mr Evans, I'll find a nice little cottage by the sea at Whitburn in which to spend my old age."

On the Monday, Seed received a telephone call from Bob Law, the vice-chairman, asking him to go to meet the chairman, Stanley Gliksten, at his office, Hanover House in Hanover Square, London, at 4pm. Seed knew it must be the expected inquest over the 8-1 defeat but did not realize at first the seriousness of the meeting. He thought it was to be one of Gliksten's 'pep talks'. He told Jimmy Trotter about it and Trotter asked if he could go along too. It was when Seed put this request to Law that the true intent of the meeting began to dawn on him. He was told Trotter could come one hour later.

His disquiet at what 'Mr Stanley' — as Seed always addressed him — intended was further heightened when he arrived and Law told him to wait outside until Gliksten was free. Such treatment had never happened to him before. He was then called in and asked to sit down. Gliksten fingered his tie nervously and Seed could see he was upset. According to Seed's later account he told Seed: "Y'know, Jimmy, we've had a bad start, and naturally we are all worried about it. We've got to do something about it. Mr Law and I have had a chat and we think the time has come for us to part." He then continued at a faster tempo: "We've known each other for over 25 years, Jimmy, and you are getting old. You aren't well, and we think in your interests, as well as those of the club, we should get a younger man to take your place."

Seed sat in his chair and words wouldn't come. The chairman, his voice filled with emotion, went on: "I'm going to see that you're looked after, Jimmy. You've been a great servant to Charlton and I will personally see to it that you'll be equally well rewarded." Seed was heartbroken but his concern was to avoid unpleasant recriminations. He broke the uneasy silence that followed with these words: "Can I say something, Mr Stanley?"

"Yes, Jimmy, please do."

"First of all, let me thank you for putting the position clearly, but most of all let me say how much I appreciate your generosity and your friendship, not only for what you have just done, but the way you have treated me during all the time I have been with Charlton."

Gliksten now beamed with obvious relief and in all the years Seed had known him, he had never seen him so grateful. The worst over, they now got down to the cold business of fixing the details. A solicitor was sent for and a resolution was recorded for the club minutes. A Press statement was prepared and typed out: 'After nearly 23 years' loyal service as manager of Charlton, Mr J.Seed has retired.'

Seed records that it was all 'very clinical.' At the time, he was 61 and had 14 months of his contract still to run. He had already been making plans for his retirement at 65, which would have seen him complete over a quarter of a century with the club. The time had now reached 5pm and Jimmy Trotter arrived to hear the news. Seed never gave it a thought at the time that Trotter could possibly be his successor. Next the two other directors, Dr Montgomery and F.H.Wilkinson were told. Both had been helped to join the board by Seed and he counted both as personal friends. Yet while both were directors, neither had been called into the discussions between Gliksten and Law — an insight into the autocracy of 'Mr Stanley'. Seed asked to leave before the two directors were informed and left with Trotter.

It was now the rush hour and the two men could not get a taxi. So they took a bus to Charing Cross station. On the slow journey in the crowded traffic, Trotter did not say much. Seed drove him to his home from Charlton station and then went back to the ground to pick up a few personal belongings. He stayed in his office for three hours, sadly reliving the memorable moments of his life and football career. "I felt old and tired." His reverie was only broken by a telephone call from his wife, now under siege from reporters. Outside, an autumn mist descended on the deserted night-time scene of The Valley as he left his office for the last time.

He went home to give the reporters their story and to undergo half an hour of flashing cameras. He did not see fit at the time to tell them he had been sacked. He went along with Gliksten's retirement version of his parting from the club. The sacking had health repercussions for the 61-year-old Seed. He broke out in a rash all over his face and body. He had swellings on his legs and face, and Dr Montgomery came to see him and order him to bed. For three days and nights he was a sick man, unable to do little but perspire and sleep. Seed also claimed later that it was the shock of reading about his departure from

Jimmy Seed pictured towards the end of his days at Charlton.

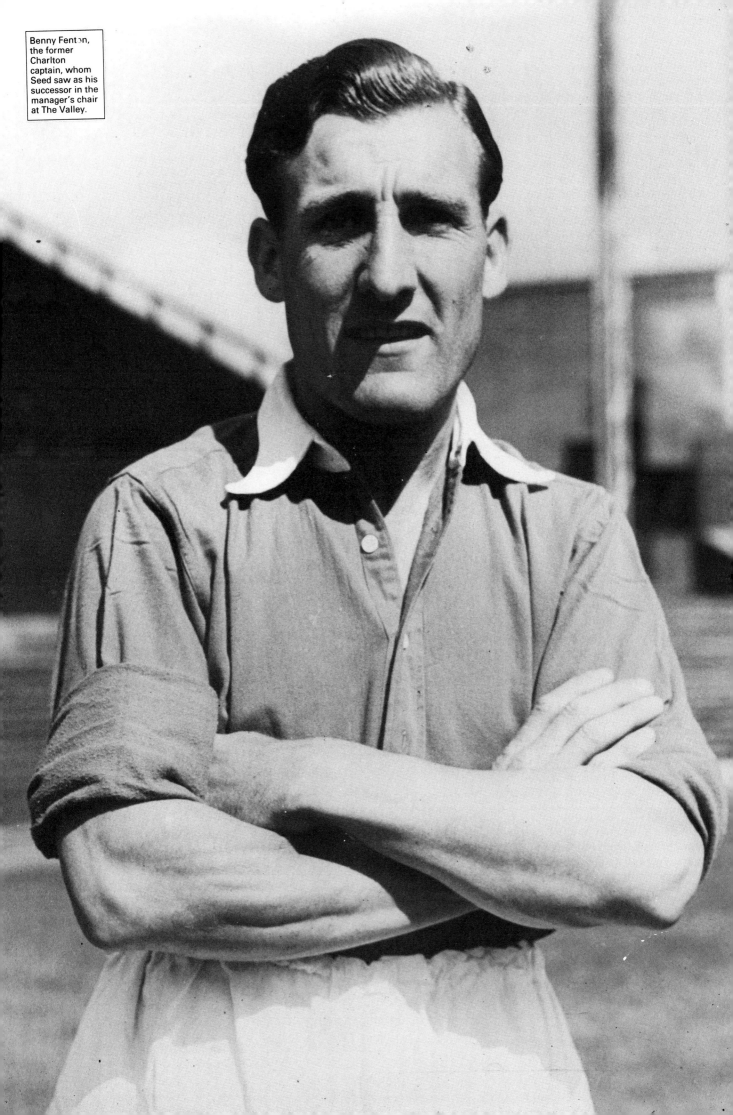

Benny Fenton, the former Charlton captain, whom Seed saw as his successor in the manager's chair at The Valley.

Charlton that caused his daughter, Gladys, to give birth to his first grandson, James Peter Dutton, three weeks prematurely.

'Mr Stanley' was anxious he should finish off a job he had started — the signing as a professional of Mike Stewart, the Surrey batsman and inside-forward with Corinthian Casuals. From his sick bed, Seed 'phoned Stewart and asked him to come and see him. Seed moved for Stewart in the summer but the deal had been delayed because Stewart, an England Amateur international, hoped to go to the Melbourne Olympics of that year with Britain's soccer team. In the event, Stewart didn't make the trip because his status as a professional cricketer led to his amateur football status being queried in some Olympic quarters.

The conditions of the signing were agreed in Seed's bedroom. Seed telephoned his former chairman to tell him that Stewart would definitely be signing in a couple of weeks. An emotional Gliksten expressed his gratitude and then Seed felt almost embarrassed as Gliksten began to discuss his successor. One name in Seed's mind was Benny Fenton, the former club captain signed for £5,000 from Millwall and a success as player-manager with Colchester United. He suggested this to Gliksten, who seemed impressed.

"I think, Jimmy, you have rung a bell.' But what was hurtful to Seed was the emerging fact that Gliksten had sacked Seed without even lining up a successor. Seed confessed he would have been more flattered had the board nominated a younger manager and then told him the time had come for a parting of the ways. It would, of course, have made even more sense to groom a young man as Seed's assistant, seeing that Seed was coming to an end of his career anyway. No such commonsense idea ever seems to have crossed the mind of Stanley Gliksten, even though Seed publicly touted Benny Fenton, then with Colchester, in the *Kentish Mercury* as his successor.

Trotter chosen

THE Charlton directors spent a whole day discussing the appointment and then came up with the bizarre choice of Jimmy Trotter as team manager. Jack Phillips, the assistant secretary, was promoted to secretary. It was some time before the whole ugly truth came out about Seed's sacking. Many of his friends and acquaintances genuinely thought he had resigned, including the president of the South African Football Association, one of his old adversaries, Freddie Fell. In a touching tribute to Seed, he wrote a letter on 12 November, which is quoted in full in Seed's autobiography:

Dear Jimmy,
It came as a terrible shock when I heard of your retirement as manager of Charlton Athletic.

I have purposely delayed writing as I had every hope that saneness would prevail and that the directors would persuade you in some way to withdraw your resignation.

The club will never be the same without you, Jimmy; no one could have done as much for any club as you have done; you brought them from obscurity to the highest peak.

I did not always see eye to eye with you over the question of South Africans taking up professional football, but I must confess that in all your actions you have been most honourable and we all owe you a tremendous debt of gratitude for what you have done for the players from my country.

Every player who has served under you cannot speak too highly of your treatment of them, and it is you, and you alone, who have made many of our players bring honour to the country of their birth, South Africa. It is also you who have built up that great colony of South Africans who are playing football in Britain today. Only Jimmy Seed could have selected a South African born team who gave Scotland's full international team such a great game.

The least I can say is 'Thank you Jimmy' and I sincerely trust you will be spared for many years to enjoy this evening of your life, and that I shall have the privilege of your company should I visit England or you should decide to come to South Africa again.

Trusting you are in the best of health and with all good wishes.
Freddie Fell.

In the programme for the Chelsea versus Charlton game at Stamford Bridge exactly a month later, on Saturday, 3 November, Chelsea's manager, the former Arsenal and England international, Ted Drake, laboured under the same delusion when he wrote in tribute to Seed: 'It was a sad thing when Mr Jimmy Seed, after so many years in management of this famous club had to resign for health reasons. . . .' The myth of Seed's retirement persisted for some considerable time.

The Truth Comes Out

IT was only with the publication of Seed's autobiography in 1958, that the truth was finally revealed. The greatness of Seed, his supreme ability in man-management, was summed up in the following passage from Eddie Firmani's autobiography:

' 'Headmaster' of Charlton Athletic was Jimmy Seed, silver-haired, softly-spoken, kind-hearted and one of the most human men it has ever been my pleasure to work under. For all his understanding and sympathetic approach to people, Jimmy Seed was certainly a man's man. There was never any doubt that he was 'the Boss'. As a man-at-the-helm, Jimmy knew the course he was going to take. He mapped out a plan for all the young players serving under him, and I do not think anyone could fail to benefit from his astute handling of their soccer destiny.

'Faith in Jimmy Seed was something we all had, from the directors to the players, during my spell at The Valley. I shall always recall with affection the talks he had with me, and the wisdom which prevailed whenever he sat down with us to discuss tactics.

'Unlike some folk, who get a kick out of telling footballers how to play the game, Jimmy Seed never made this approach. He made everyone feel, from the moment he entered the dressing-room, that he was dealing with adults who were specialists in their particular job. After all, we were professional footballers, and Mr Seed never overlooked this fact. He usually concentrated on examining carefully the style, strength and weakness of the teams we were to oppose. And during a match, I would often realise just how accurate he was in his sizing up of the team we were playing.'

The cruel and panicked decision of Stanley Gliksten did not even have the justification of the ends justifying the means. The team simply went from bad to worse through the season, losing 7-3 at Wolverhampton in February, and by other big scores,

Jimmy Gauld scores the first goal of Charlton's 4-4 draw with Sheffield Wednesday at The Valley in September 1956. The Wednesday defender is Don McEvoy.

frequently conceding four or five goals. As with all poor teams, the side could not even create its own luck. On 10 November at The Valley, the team hit the Cardiff woodwork no fewer than six times — and Cardiff ran out 2-0 winners.

Early in March, Tom Finney scored the 100th League goal against the club that season, in a 4-3 defeat at Deepdale against Preston North End. It began to look as if Charlton would sink to the ignominy of conceding the most First Division goals ever. Blackpool held that record — 125 goals against in 1930-31. The massive total against stopped mercifully short at 120, although six were conceded in the last game of the season when Charlton, long since doomed to relegation, went down 6-2 to Tottenham at White Hart Lane. Their number of points, only 22, was the lowest since Grimsby's total of 22 in 1947-8 and Leeds United's 18 in the first post-war season the year before.

The team was weak in many places and constant problems with injuries worsened the crisis. Changes followed changes and some 30 players were used — and these were days without substitutes. The total of 30 players used was the second highest in the history of the club, beaten only in the club's first season in League football and equalled only once in 1923-4. Seed eventually turned up in football again as a director of Millwall and his experience and his dignity, the essence of Charlton's success, were lost forever. For Trotter, the pressures of management meant he could no longer continue as England's trainer and he gave up the post in 1957.

Summers and Lawrie

DURING that relegation season, two new forwards were signed to try to halt the decline — Johnny Summers from Millwall and Sam Lawrie from Middlesbrough. Both arrived at The Valley on the same day — 16 November 1956. The combined fee was £7,800. Even in those days, that was a remarkably small price for two players of heart and talent, who played well and with spirit for a new but ailing team their efforts could not save. Summers ended the season as top scorer with 14 goals in only 23 games.

Summers was to become a Charlton legend and one of the game's greatest ever goalscorers, although he joined Charlton comparatively late in his football career. He was born in Shepherds Bush and started his career with Fulham at 16 but was 22 before he made his League debut against Bolton on 12 November 1949. He made only four appearances for Fulham, without scoring, before moving to Norwich in 1950 and Millwall in 1954.

In his four years at Carrow Road, Johnny scored 33 times in 70 League outings and he hit another 40 goals in 92 League games for the Lions. Eddie Marsh, a Scottish-born goalkeeper, started the season in place of Frank Reed and made 20 appearances. Marsh was originally signed from Erith & Belvedere and spent ten years at The Valley, waiting for his chance of a regular place. But neither he nor Reed were the obvious answer to the goalkeeping problem left by Bartram's departure and eventually Trotter solved the dilemma by signing Willie Duff, then doing his National Service in the Army, from Hearts.

The transfer was completed on Duff's 23rd birthday. He made 20 appearances for Charlton that season. Duff had won both Scottish League Cup and FA Cup medals with Hearts, playing alongside the legendary Dave Mackay, who was later to star with the Spurs' double-winning side of 1960-61. Mackay and Duff also played together in the same Edinburgh junior club. Eddie Marsh did not remain much longer at Charlton. He was transferred to Luton in June 1957.

Three players who made their debuts in that troubled season and went on to distinguished careers were Brian Kinsey, John Sewell and Micky Stewart. Kinsey, who was to become a stalwart of the Charlton side through the 1960s at full-back, made his debut as an outside-left against Newcastle at The Valley

'Squib' Hammond (opposite, top) and Jimmy Campbell (opposite, bottom) were both drawing to the end of their careers at The Valley.

Willie Duff was signed from Hearts in a bid to solve Charlton's goalkeeping problem.

on 27 October, 1956. A local boy, born close to The Valley, he had played as a Roan Grammar schoolboy for London Schools against Glasgow Schools. He was on Charlton's books as an amateur for several years before signing professional at 17.

John Sewell was an exceptional all-round sportsman. He was an England Under-15 rugby international whilst at Brockley Grammar School and a former sprinter with Blackheath Harriers. He signed as an amateur for Charlton in 1952 and then went on to what was very much Charlton's nursery club in those days, Bexleyheath & Welling. When he signed professional football forms for Bexleyheath & Welling in 1954, he had to resign from the Blackheath club, according to the rules of the Amateur Athletic Association. He was transferred back to Charlton on 5 January, 1955, the day he joined up for National Service. He made his League debut at right-half against Sheffield Wednesday in January 1957, although it was as a rugged back that he made his mark with the club.

He later recalled of that dreadful season: "I shall never forget those matches. Every one was as tense as a Cup tie." Strangely he did not play for the first team in the following season. It was not until Christmas 1958 that he came back to establish himself as a first-team regular at right-back.

Stewart was the signing Seed had negotiated as he left Charlton. Stewart signed professional forms shortly afterwards the same month, joining Charlton's list of footballer-cricketers. He made his debut at inside-forward against Aston Villa in December 1956, but it was not as a footballer or Charlton player that he found fame. He only made fleeting appearances in the team over the next three years, but he had a long and distinguished career in cricket, as both player and manager with Surrey, and also as both player and manager with the England team.

Another player who made his debut but whose career proved short and meteoric was Trevor Edwards. Edwards won two Welsh caps that season at right-back, the first in April 1957, after only seven first-team matches for Charlton. He was 20 and the nephew of Dai Astley, Charlton's pre-war Welsh star. After leaving Charlton and playing for Aston Villa and Derby, Astley had coached in Sweden and, at the time of his nephew's debut for Charlton and Wales, was landlord of the White Horse public house at Ramsgate. Edwards was one of the Charlton players who, like Sewell, combined National Service life with professional football. He was demobbed from the RAF just a month after his international debut in a 0-0 draw against Ireland in Belfast.

Another Charlton favourite of those years who broke into the team in that relegation season was Fred Lucas. Lucas had made a single appearance in the first team in the previous season, playing at inside-right at Burnley on Easter Monday 1956. He went on to play 13 matches in 1956-7 and then became a regular member of the side, usually at half-back. His entire career right after leaving Crayford Secondary School had been spent at The Valley, first working as an office boy and playing as an amateur and then signing professional forms in 1952. Lucas was also a fine cricketer and one of Charlton's Kent cricketing fraternity.

An indication of just how big a part National Service played in the life of clubs in those days was that of Charlton's playing staff at the start of the season, no fewer than ten were in the forces. They even included Stuart Leary, despite his South African

background, who was doing National Service in the RAF. Goalkeeper Frank Reed was another doing his time in the services.

Some small consolation for the dismal season came for John Hewie, who established himself as a regular in the Scottish team at left-back, despite the poor form of his club side. Ironically, one of Hewie's best games for the club was in the 8-1 defeat at Sunderland. Hewie was always a dogged, determined fighter, not least when his team was up against it. He was the sort of player who would not give up, even in a game like the Sunderland debacle, and towards the end he scored Charlton's only goal.

One notable departure shortly after Trotter took over was the player whom Seed had hoped would be Firmani's successor, Jimmy Gauld. In October, he left for Everton for a fee of £10,500, having scored a useful 21 goals in 47 games. After seven goals in 23 League games for Everton, Gauld moved to Plymouth Argyle. He then moved on to Swindon, St Johnstone and Mansfield Town before scandal broke out in 1964 over his role as ringleader of a player's betting ring fixing matches.

Even Christmas did not go right for Charlton in that dreadful season. After beating Wolves 2-1 at The Valley on Christmas Day morning when Summers scored the winning goal, the Charlton team set off at 7am the next morning for the Boxing Day return. It was snowing heavily when they arrived in Wolverhampton and the game was called off. Further discomfort followed with a wait of several hours for a train home. The game was rearranged for February — and Charlton went down 7-3.

Programme Blandness

THE tally of the 1956-7 season was that Charlton lost 29 League games, 11 at home, and went down in the FA Cup at The Valley in a third-round replay against Second Division Middlesbrough. In the continual struggle against relegation, what was striking throughout the season was just how little the club communicated with its fans. The programmes were models of blandness, hardly indicating the tremendous fall from grace of a once great club.

The game that finally sealed Charlton's fate was against Burnley on Saturday, 13 April 1957, at The Valley, Charlton going down 2-1. But the programme did not even mention the awful significance of this match or deign to look back in anger at what had gone before. The club notes simply started by congratulating Trevor Edwards on winning his first Welsh cap and then welcomed Burnley and described their playing record that season — they were ninth in the table.

The next game, against Spurs on Good Friday, 19 April, was Charlton's last home game in Division One. It ended in a 1-1 draw, John Hewie getting the Charlton goal. Few could have guessed at the time it was the last Division One game The Valley might ever see. And then the club was at last forced to acknowledge to the fans the fact of relegation — in five paragraphs at the start of the club notes. And then the tone was glib rather than angry or despairing. The loyal fan was told that the club had long since 'dried their eyes'. The epitaph read:

'Today sees 'the curtain act' so far as our home League programme is concerned, and when the curtain goes up again next August, Charlton will be a Division Two club. While we share with our supporters the natural disappointment at the loss of Division One status, those guiding the destinies of the club have long since dried their eyes and for some time have been busy with plans to recover what has been lost.

'The task of team re-building was commenced months ago, and recent results give every indication that the policy of giving Charlton's young players their big chance, is the most likely to restore the club to its rightful place.

'It is a policy which should have been pursued at The Valley years ago, when sentiment was allowed to over-ride good judgement. It has been proved time and time again that it is a mistake to constantly play old and established players at the expense of denying experience to youngsters. Far better to give the younger players their chance when the team is doing reasonably well than to wait until things go wrong and the risk is far greater.

'Youth will play a more dominant role at Charlton than ever before, and the search for more youngsters of promise is being intensified. At The Valley in future, once a younger player is ready for his League baptism, he will get it.

'From letters received, and from the great encouragement given to Charlton's players, we are convinced that our supporters fully appreciate what we are trying to accomplish. During the most critical period, Charlton's directors and officials were heartened by the unswerving loyalty and deep concern of the club's supporters. Let us work together to make Charlton Athletic greater than ever before.'

The Missing Chequebook

THE words were, of course, cruelly and desperately unfair on Jimmy Seed, who had always had to develop youngsters of promise. What had gone wrong was that Stanley Gliksten had never handed him the chequebook the Gliksten brothers could well afford. The youth policy did bloom in time — only then the young stars were sold to other clubs as they matured, so destroying the club's hopes of Division One football for almost 30 years.

The draw against Spurs was followed next day by a last visit to Highbury and a 3-1 defeat. The Easter return match against Spurs was on Easter Monday and Charlton's last dismal game in Division One for 29 years. Charlton trailed 1-0 at half-time but then an avalanche of goals resulted in a cruel end to their First Division life, with Spurs romping home 6-2. Part of the impetus behind Spurs' performance was because they needed to win to claim the runners-up spot in the League behind Manchester United. Fred Lucas and Stuart Leary were the Charlton scorers.

The Missing Razzamataz

LOOKING back over what proved to be the long-lasting tragedy of relegation, it is clear to see why Charlton Athletic never grasped the opportunity of greatness. The club had spirit and loyalty, but it lacked owners with foresight, who were determined to keep the club at the top. And it lacked the razzamataz so necessary in the entertainment business, the need to have star names.

What star names were there to attract the crowds? Sam Bartram certainly, Eddie Firmani certainly, Hans Jeppson during his brief exciting stay, Don Welsh, Charlie Vaughan probably, Stuart Leary and John Hewie probably. But after that the list declines. If only Seed had bought Stanley Matthews. If only he had had a kinder board with a bigger chequebook.

It is remarkable that, despite a stay of 21 years in Division One, Charlton produced so few international players and no regular player for England. Only three players had been capped in the post-war period — John Hewie for Scotland, Trevor Edwards for Wales and Derek Ufton for England. At the time of relegation, Charlton thought they could bounce back quickly. They were wrong, but only by a whisker. The weak, struggling team of the season before was transformed into strong promotion challengers with the defence much tighter and Johnny Summers

John Hewie, one of the few Charlton star names.

in brilliant form as a high-scoring forward, aided by Stuart Leary and Bobby Ayre, a devastating trio.

The Gliksten Dynasty

IT was during 1957 that Stanley Gliksten was joined on the board by his two sons, David and Michael, so continuing the Gliksten dynasty. Michael Gliksten, appointed on 29 August 1957, the day of Charlton's first Division Two game at The Valley for 21 years, was just 18 at the time — his 19th birthday being a few days away on 5 September. It was an amazingly young age for a football director. His brother, David, was just two years older. Wheras Michael, a tall red-haired man of charm and obvious drive, was keen to continue the family tradition, David appeared to have little natural enthusiasm for football. And so it was to prove.

The Second Division team began with a 3-3 away draw at Huddersfield, a portent of the goalscoring feats to come. The first home game, a midweek game at The Valley against Sheffield United, saw Charlton win 3-1 before a crowd of 17,699, with goals from Stuart Leary, Bobby Ayre and Johnny Summers. This was the first of three wins in a row — twice against Sheffield United and once against Grimsby — giving a marvellous start to the season. Not until 19 September was the team beaten, going down 3-2 at Leyton Orient.

Charlton's Most Remarkable Game Ever

ALTHOUGH October proved a set-back, with the team losing three games in a row, including a 3-0 home defeat against West Ham, Charlton were still in a strong position as Christmas and the New Year neared. During the game at Middlesbrough on 20 October, Sam Lawrie, playing against his old side, aggravated an old knee injury so badly that he had to undergo an operation in hospital later and could not play League football again until the following Easter.

Just four days before Christmas, there occurred the most remarkable game in Charlton's history — and probably the most remarkable game ever in the history of League football. The match itself looked ordinary enough. It was a routine game against another faded giant of yesteryear, Huddersfield Town. The date was 21 December 1957 but it was to prove a Summers day in winter. Charlton were reduced to ten men after 16 minutes, when Derek Ufton dislocated a shoulder and was taken to hospital. In those days, substitutes were not allowed. The Huddersfield goals piled in and with 28 minutes left, Charlton were losing 5-1, their lone scorer being Johnny Summers. John 'Buck'

Ryan scored to make it 5-2. Then Johnny Summers burst forth in a blaze of goalscoring unique in the annals of the game. He had been switched from the left wing to attack down the centre. After 64 minutes, he netted his second goal. He had changed his boots at half-time and now magic appeared to be working in the new pair. In the space of eight minutes, he scored three more times to make it 6-5 in Charlton's favour with nine minutes left. The Valley crowd were now roaring the team on to victory when John Hewie, playing an outstanding game as an attacking centre-

Johnny Summers (opposite) scored five goals in one of the most remarkable Football League games ever played.

Stuart Leary gets in a header during the remarkable 7-6 win over Huddersfield Town. Summers looks on.

half in Ufton's place, had the misfortune to score an own-goal. But Charlton surged back again and in the final seconds, Lucas gave the ball to Ryan, who smashed it home to make the score 7-6. Thus, Huddersfield Town became the first and only team to score six goals in a League game and finish up losers.

The epic made Johnny Summers, now 30 years old, a legend in Charlton history. Unusually, he scored all five with his right foot, although he was a naturally left-footed player. His equalizing goal was the best of the lot, a tremendous shot, whipped in on the turn. And this wonderful display came after a period when he had been losing form and his place was in doubt. Following Wilson Lennox and Eddie Firmani, he became the third player in Charlton's history to score five goals in a match.

The crowd could hardly contain themselves. As the game ended, the players were submerged and had to struggle back to the dressing-room as supporters slapped them on their backs. Even the journalists in the press box rose and cheered, for they had been watching history in the making. The crowd gathered in front of the stand, chanting Summers' name: "We want Summers — we want Johnny." With the rest of the team he appeared in the directors' box to acknowledge the fans. Then he was whisked to a BBC television studio in London to tell the nation: "I still can't believe it," and then unselfishly praised his colleagues.

For the record, the goal timings were: Charlton — Summers 47 minutes, 64, 73, 78, 81; Ryan 63, 89. Huddersfield: Massie 27; Bain 35, 49; McGarry (penalty) 51; Ledger 62, Hewie own-goal (later credited to Howard) 86.

Jimmy Trotter commented: "Things had not been coming off for Summers. So I moved him from inside-left to centre-forward. As a last resort, I switched him to outside-left, his last chance to make good. How well he took it!" *The News of the World* described the game as 'the most fantastic match of the century'.

The FA Cup draw paired the two teams together again just a month after the epic clash. The first tie at Huddersfield ended in a 2-2 draw. The leading soccer writers of Fleet Street, having missed the 7-6 encounter, now descended on The Valley to see if lightning could strike twice. It didn't and Charlton won by a disputed goal before losing at home to Fulham in the next round.

Another illustration of the modest lifestyle of professional football players of that time concerned Stuart Leary. He passed his driving test and took delivery of his first car, and this was some six years after his Football League debut. Professional players in those days used public transport like the fans. The author remembers a game against Leyton Orient in 1959, when Charlton fans on a tube train were joined by Johnny Summers and Fred Lucas on their way home.

On the playing side, one feature of this eventful 1957-8 season was the conversion of Billy Kiernan to left-half, where he played a key part in strengthening the team's defence. Another was the club's farewell to the last of its 1947 Cup Final heroes still on the playing staff, Gordon Hurst, who took over as player-manager at the Kent League club, Tunbridge Wells. He played only two games in the Charlton first team before departing towards the end of the season. He later left the Kent club to become player-manager of Llandudno in the Welsh League and eventually went on to become secretary of Bury.

Billy Kiernan was converted to wing-half and played a key role in strengthening Charlton's defence.

Gordon Hurst took over as player-manager of Tunbridge Wells FC after a great career at The Valley.

Seed at Bristol

ONE of the most poignant games was against Bristol City at Ashton Gate on 18 January 1958. For who else should be leading the Bristol City team as caretaker manager, but Jimmy Seed. After seeing Atyeo give his new side a 34th-minute lead, he must have had very mixed feelings as Charlton hit back to win through a Johnny Summers goal and an own-goal. This eventful season, for all its drama and interest, was, alas, to end in heartbreak.

For the last half of the season, Charlton were firmly in second position, chasing on the tails of London rivals, West Ham. A set-back at The Valley on 29 March against Bristol Rovers when Charlton lost 3-2, was followed by a string of good results — a 4-0 win at home against Rotherham, a 0-0 draw away against the leaders West Ham, a 5-1 away win at Rotherham, followed by two successive 4-1 wins, against Notts County at home and Ipswich away. The West Ham game was played on a waterlogged pitch before a crowd of 30,000. It was an exciting keenly-fought tussle with Charlton's defence mastering the West Ham forwards, who were also scoring freely that season. Johnny Summers actually had the ball in the net, only for the referee to rule that the Charlton move started from an offside position. Charlton also had to survive the last 20 minutes without their forward, John 'Buck' Ryan, who was sent off.

That game and both Rotherham games were played over the Easter holiday, giving Charlton a vital five points out of six. The Notts County game saw Charlton notch up a century of League goals. Ryan suffered more misfortune in the Ipswich game, the penultimate match of the season, being injured early on and playing as little more than a passenger on the left wing for most of the game. The fact that Charlton were again playing with really only ten men made the 4-1 win even more impressive. The many Charlton supporters who made the trip to East Anglia let off red and white balloons before the match and kept up their cheering throughout, making it a memorable day.

John Ryan, sent off in one game and injured in the next.

But promotion challengers, Blackburn Rovers, were also on a winning run and even the string of very good Charlton results was not enough to lift the team to the safety of promotion. When the last game arrived on 26 April 1958, Charlton needed just one point to return to Division One at the first attempt. They were lying second to West Ham but their visitors to The Valley in that last game were Blackburn Rovers, now lying third and needing to win to go up. The scene was set for a dramatic confrontation.

Charlton took the lead after only four minutes when Fred Lucas fired in a brilliant header, but then Stuart Leary missed a sitter and it was to prove a turning point in the game. Blackburn, inspired by their England international forward Bryan Douglas, hit back to go into a 4-1 lead with goals from Peter Dobing (2), Roy Vernon and Douglas himself. Then Charlton produced a late two-goal rally, Peter Firmani and John Hewie scoring, Hewie from a penalty. But Rovers held on to clinch promotion with a 4-3 victory. The only consolation amidst the disaster was that the attendance was a record for Division Two at The Valley — 56,535. Charlton won 24 games that season, more than any other team in the division. But their failure to win vital points against promotion rivals cost them dear. They took only five points from the eight games against West Ham, Blackburn, Liverpool and Fulham.

The Charlton fans were inconsolable after the game, despite kind commiserations from the Blackburn supporters, for these were the days when opposing fans mixed freely on the terraces. No Charlton Athletic supporter — even in his darkest nightmares — could imagine how lastingly tragic that defeat was to prove in the history of the club.

Back to Division Two. Charlton Athletic in 1957-8. Back row (left to right): Alex Hird (trainer), Hammond, Ellis, Campbell, White, Summers, Reed, Jago, Hurst, Lucas, Kiernan, Jack Shreeve (coach). Front: Sewell, Ayre, Lawrie, Jimmy Trotter (manager), Hewie, Edwards, Cox.

Goals Galore

ALTHOUGH the failure to gain promotion caused a great wave of depression over Charlton Athletic, those opening post-war seasons in Division Two were notable for the highest-scoring era in the club's history. After the 'promotion miss' season of 1957-8, in which they scored a massive 107 League goals, Charlton hit 92 the following season, 90 the next and 97 the season after that. The legendary Johnny Summers, in particular, ran into inspired form. Unfortunately, the goals-conceded total almost matched the goals-scored total during these entertaining seasons, ruining the club's chances of promotion.

The fans were certainly being entertained but they were not seeing their dreams come true of First Division football again at The Valley. The reality of soccer at that level was only a couple of signings away, but the club under Stanley Gliksten's leadership was lacking foresight and inspiration. The 1958-9 season saw the average attendance drop to 16,800. Despite the goals, the crowds continued to dwindle. Early in 1960-61, the 'gate' touched a low of 7,698 and several other games attracted less than five figures.

The programme for the opening game of 1958-9 pointed clearly to the financial panic beginning to affect Stanley Gliksten. As the club pursued short-sighted financial cost-cutting policies, it was also cutting away its hopes of ever returning to Division One. The front cover of the programme carried a message which started as follows:

In extending a cordial 'Welcome Back!' to all Charlton supporters at The Valley on this, our opening match of the season, we take this opportunity of putting across a message of great urgency — a message of vital importance to all concerned with the future of Charlton Athletic Football Club.

Despite one of our best seasons ever from a playing stand-point, with goalscoring records broken both at home and away and promotion back to Division One missed only by a single goal, Charlton finished last season with a loss considerably over £10,000. The position is particularly worrying having arisen in spite of the very careful management of the club and of the fact that home 'gates' improved by an average of nearly 2,000 per match last season.

With wages and other costs on the increase, the management needs and needs urgently the co-operation and help of the backbone of every football club — THE SUPPORTERS.

The supporters, by banding themselves together in great numbers and taking an interest in the working of the club, can help Charlton Athletic to continue as a first-class club.

At the end of last season, the Charlton F.C. directors and management decided that the club's supporters should be taken more into their confidence. The supporters can, and we hope will, assist in shaping the future destiny of Charlton.

The appeal went on to refer to 'a very successful public meeting' at Woolwich Town Hall and to further discussions between the Charlton management and the supporters' club. But it was hardly likely that the old management could change its spots and the club continued to have, as with most League clubs, an unenlightened attitude to the disclosure of any but the barest information to supporters.

The appeal also referred to the need for a supporters' club with its own headquarters. A development fund was set up which did go on to raise substantial sums, organized by men who were later to join the board, Bill Jenner and Bill Wheeler. The supporters' headquarters idea eventually did come to some sort of reality with the opening of The Valley Club in 1969.

The programme also referred to the passing of one of the well-known figures in Charlton's rise to Division One, the director and medical officer, Dr John Montgomery, who died on 17 July 1958. In a tribute in the *Kentish Independent*, his colleague of many years, David Clark, wrote:

'We have lost a staunch friend as well as a most capable medical officer and director. Dr Montgomery was extremely well versed in football, and his wisdom was such that he will be missed tremendously.'

In May 1958, Bobby Ayre was transferred to Reading. He had made 20 appearances the previous season. His career, which had once promised so much after his England Under-23 selection, had not long to go. He moved on from Reading to Weymouth in the Southern League and was then forced to quit the game, through injury, in the 1960-61 season.

Storm Floods Valley

DURING the 1958 close season, the club had installed new drainage sumps around The Valley in an attempt to solve flood-water problems at the Harvey Gardens end of the ground. The improved drainage was put to the test just before the opening of the season, when a torrent of water was satisfactorily absorbed. But then disaster struck just before the Grimsby Town game on 6 September, in which the programme ironically described the new drainage improvements.

A tremendous storm caused the worst flooding in The Valley's entire history. Only four hours before the game was due to begin, the Harvey Gardens end was under water up to six inches deep. The offices, dressing-rooms and boardroom were flooded and, as the water subsided, it left behind a two-inch depth of foul-smelling black mud. When the groundstaff arrived, the position looked hopeless. But Jimmy

one-sided affair it looked and that Charlton were 'the equals of their victors' in footballing ability although 'Barnsley had the pull in being able to accept their chances.' This looked like a rather trite explanation of a terrible result but perhaps the writer was right, for Charlton ran out winners of the return by 4-0.

It turned out to be that sort of season with helter-skelter results in abundance. Besides the Rotherham win, Charlton ran up 5-1 victories over Ipswich at home and over Grimsby away. But the Barnsley away débâcle was not the last. Charlton went down 6-1 at Leyton Orient and 5-0 at Sheffield United. Ironically, Barnsley were relegated that season.

The flood was not the last of the misfortunes to hit The Valley itself. Three weeks later at the stadium on Saturday, 27 September, after a Colts game against Luton, a fire was spotted in the main stand. Stanley Gliksten and other directors present, the assistant groundsman, Albert Werge, father of the player Eddie Werge, and Peter Croker, the former full-back, fought the fire with extinguishers until the fire-brigade arrived. Damage was not extensive, but the main stand was a wooden structure and the result could have been more horrific. The club believed that a cigarette-end was responsible and, at the next League game at The Valley, appealed to spectators to stub out cigarette butts before they were discarded.

In those days, The Valley itself was still used for the club's regular training sessions. And when the weather was bad, the club had to fend for itself as best it could in a way that looks very unprofessional to the modern eye. Around the New Year period, conditions were so bad that the pitch could not be used. On one occasion, Charlton were indebted to Harvey's Sports Club for the use of a pitch, giving the players their first chance of a thorough workout for days — hardly ideal preparation for a club hoping to reclaim its Division One status.

The helter-skelter results did not endear themselves to all supporters. At the beginning of 1959, there were a number of letters in the local Press, criticizing various aspects of the club. In one of the letters, the writer hinted that the Charlton players were not training hard enough to last a hard 90-minute match. The club responded strongly in the programme:

We hasten to point out that no club could possess a more wholehearted or enthusiastic playing staff than Charlton. In every aspect of their training our players give absolute satisfaction. They co-operate to the fullest possible extent and show in unmistakable terms that they enjoy their preparation.

In the training and coaching of footballers, the psychological and mental approach is the most important, and the best results are attained by those coaches and trainers who fully understand the various temperaments of those under their care. That is what this particular writer fails to appreciate. You can't train footballers like race-horses.

'Charlton's coaching and training staff are men of long and varied experience and there is implicit trust in trainer and player alike. No, like most clubs, we have our shortcomings, but lack of proper training is not one of them. Rest assured on that point.

But the fact remained that the defence was shipping-in large numbers of goals, conceding one of the highest totals in the division, and the forwards were having to race to keep the club in the top half of the table.

Sam Lawrie had a fine spell from early December

Trotter, groundsman Jack Myton and his staff borrowed a motor pump from a local firm and the London Salvage Corps sent two pumps from Islington. The work proved slow and laborious and at midday the prospects of saving the game looked small. Although one o'clock came without much hope, by now people were drifting into the ground and helping. By two o'clock, the pitch was cleared and the referee decided to let the game go ahead. Charlton were rewarded for their enterprise by a 2-1 victory.

So far the season had been an anti-climax after the previous season's near return to Division One. An opening 1-1 draw at The Valley had been followed by a 4-3 defeat at Rotherham and a 2-2 draw at Brighton. Then came a welcome 5-2 victory over Rotherham at The Valley, before the Grimsby success.

Then, however, Charlton's hopes of staging another promotion fight were jolted by a 7-1 defeat at Barnsley. Charlton actually took the lead after six minutes' play, through Eddie Werge, before the avalanche hit them, Barnsley inside-left Malcolm Graham scoring four and right winger Jack Lunn hitting two penalties past Willie Duff. Charlton, incidentally, missed a penalty.

The game was a midweek one, on Wednesday, 10 September, to be followed by a midweek return match on Thursday, 18 September, kicking-off at 5.35pm as Charlton had no floodlights. The programme claimed that the game at Oakwell had not been the

Sam Lawrie enjoyed a good spell from early December. Opposite: Charlton trio (from left) Jimmy Fryatt, John Hewie and Trevor Edwards on their way to Cup-tie training at the seaside.

A 6-4 defeat at Plymouth at the start of October did not seem too bad, but six weeks later came disaster.

Massacre at Villa Park

THE fateful match was at Villa Park, where Charlton went down to the club's biggest-ever League defeat, 11-1 against the Second Division leaders. The result could not be passed away as anything but a humiliation, but there were some extenuating circumstances. Early on, Stuart Leary pulled a thigh muscle when the score was 2-1, Villa having taken the lead before Dennis Edwards equalized in the 22nd minute. Leary became a virtual passenger in a time when substitutes were not allowed. Charlton's forwards stuttered to a standstill and horrendous holes appeared in the defence.

With the score mounting to 6-1 after an hour's play, Willie Duff dislocated a finger going down for the ball. After going off the field for attention by a doctor, Duff resumed at outside-left. His replacement in goal was Don Townsend, who was beaten three times. Then Stuart Leary took over until the end of the game and he was beaten twice more. An ironic footnote to the débâcle was that John Hewie's rugby handling prowess was not available that day. He was also missing through injury.

Strangely enough, at The Valley that day, almost the reverse was happening, the Reserves thrashing Nottingham Forest Reserves 7-0 in the Football Combination. Jim Fryatt, later to become a football wanderer around clubs and to score the fastest goal in League football, netted four. Forest Reserves also had extenuating circumstances — they were short of a goalkeeper and had to put in coach Joe Mallett, a Charlton player over 20 years previously. Fryatt, who came from the Southampton district, played in five first-team games that season and eventually left the club in June 1961 to join Southend United. His record goal was for Bradford in just four seconds against Tranmere Rovers at Park Avenue on 25 April 1964.

The pattern of attacking strength marred by defensive weakness continued in that season of 1959-60. Charlton lost 5-1 at Cardiff in January, 5-2 at Swansea in February and 5-3 at Lincoln in April. The 6-4 defeat at Plymouth in October was balanced by a 5-2 home win in February. The thrashing at Villa Park was avenged on 2 April at The Valley, when Charlton beat Aston Villa 2-0.

to the middle of March, scoring 16 times in 17 League and Cup games. The year 1958 marked the last time that Charlton played a match on Christmas Day and the Charlton pairing with faraway Huddersfield for the holiday games on 25 and 27 December showed just how hectic life could be in management — and by then Jimmy Trotter was hardly a man in his prime. He travelled with the team on Christmas Eve to stay in Leeds, ready for the game at Huddersfield the following day. After the match, a 1-0 defeat, it was back to London with the team, arriving home just before midnight. On Boxing Day morning, he had to go down to The Valley on club business, including selection for the game on Saturday, 27 December. Then he went over to Fulham to watch the match against Brighton in the afternoon.

Bumper Crowds at Goodison

THE season was marked by an epic pair of FA Cup games against Everton in the fourth round. The first game, at The Valley, was drawn 2-2, with Charlton goalkeeper, Willie Duff, being sent off in the last minute. The replay, at a fog-bound Goodison Park, drew the highest crowd to attend a floodlit FA Cup tie — 74,482. The match went to extra-time, but Everton emerged winners by 4-1.

On 6 March 1959, John 'Buck' Ryan was transferred to Newcastle United in exchange for another centre-forward, Reg Evans, who failed to make an impact on the side. Another arrival at The Valley, in February 1959, was the Wycombe Wanderers forward, Dennis Edwards, an England amateur international.

Despite their 92 goals, Charlton could manage only eighth place in the League in the 1958-9 season — and even that flattered them as the points total was only 43 from the 42 games played.

The 1959-60 season saw Charlton continue on the same high-scoring note. A 3-3 draw in the opening game at Rotherham was followed in September by a 4-0 win at Hull, a 4-2 victory over Bristol City at The Valley and then a 6-1 victory at home against Derby. But yet again, heavy defeats were to come.

114

The last two home games at The Valley ended that season on the same note of extravagant scoring, Scunthorpe being despatched 5-2 and Portsmouth 6-1. The season finished with Charlton being joint top scorers of the division with three other teams — runners-up Cardiff City, Liverpool and Middlesbrough. But only two teams — Plymouth Argyle and relegated Bristol City — conceded more goals than Charlton's 87. The club were never in serious contention for promotion and finished in seventh place.

The Missing Derbies

ONE factor that particularly hit the club financially that season was the lack of south-eastern clubs in Division Two. With Fulham having been promoted, Charlton's only London counterparts were Leyton Orient. Brighton and Portsmouth were the only other southern teams and the only other near-neighbours were Ipswich. The lack of derby fixtures had its effect on attendances, whereas only three years previously The Valley had swelled to visits from Arsenal, Chelsea and Tottenham.

That season the club decided to incorporate the arms of Greenwich Borough as its badge, putting the emblem in blue and silver on its blazers with the club title above in silver lettering. It was certainly a more attractive badge than the sword later to be adopted.

The season also marked the last Scottish appearance of Charlton's most capped player, John Hewie, who gained his 19th cap against Poland at Hampden Park in May, the Scots going down 3-2.

Charlton Athletic in 1958-9. Back row (left to right): Cox, Hinton, Laraman, Duff, Reed, Sanders, Ord, Sewell, West. Second row: Alex Hird (trainer), Jack Myton (groundsman), Titcombe, Tucker, Summers, Peter Firmani, Jago, Hewie, Townsend, Stone, Edwards, Kiernan, Jack Shreeve (coach), Charlie Hall (assistant trainer). Seated: George Robinson (staff), Jack Phillips (secretary), David Gliksten (director), F.H.Wilkinson (director), David Clark (director), Stanley Gliksten (chairman), Robert Law (vice-chairman), F.W.Edmonds (director), Michael Gliksten (director), Jimmy Trotter (manager), V.France (staff). On ground: Bailey, Werge, Lucas, Ryan, Ufton, Leary, Lawrie, White, Rolph.

Willie Duff dislocated his finger against Aston Villa and returned at outside-left as Charlton crashed to their worst-ever defeat.

Hewie's Departure and Return

IT also looked like marking the end of John Hewie's career with Charlton, for he left during the summer of 1960 to return to South Africa and join the Arcadia

115

John Hewie returned from South Africa.

was eventually to emigrate to Sydney, where he played for the Hakoah club.

Another great Charlton personality also said farewell at the same time as Hewie. But this was a lasting farewell — from Derek Ufton, who, after a fine career often spent facing severe injury problems, finally hung up his boots. But in another set of boots, his cricket ones, he went on playing with distinction as Kent's wicket-keeper alongside Stuart Leary, who had the honour of being the county's highest-scoring batsman in 1960.

For Charlton, there followed an incredible fourth consecutive season of prolific scoring. The 1960-61 campaign saw a bounty of high-scoring games. Over the Christmas period, two games against Plymouth saw both sides blasting goals against each other, Charlton winning 6-4 at home on Boxing Day and going down by the same score at Home Park the following day. Charlton scored seven at The Valley against Portsmouth to win 7-4, with Summers notching five in a match for the second time. Charlton made further history in an epic 6-6 home draw against Middlesbrough, which equalled the record-highest draw in the League's history. Charlton's Dennis Edwards and Middlesbrough's Brian Clough both scored hat-tricks. In other big-scoring games, Swansea

club of Pretoria, the side he had left 11 years before to come to The Valley. Peter Firmani and defender Keith Cox, neither retained by Charlton, also went to South Africa, Firmani to the Highlands Park club and Cox to the Johannesburg club, Marist Bros. But Hewie was back by the New Year, unable to settle with his family in the Union. He was to play another six seasons for Charlton.

Hewie's erstwhile companion at full-back, Trevor Edwards, also departed in the close season of 1960, to Cardiff City. Hewie, on his return, moved into the house vacated by Edwards in Blackheath. Edwards

Full-back Trevor Edwards (left) was transferred to Cardiff City, whilst his namesake Dennis Edwards (right) scored a hat-trick in the record-equalling 6-6 draw against Middlesbrough at The Valley.

were beaten 6-2 at home and Brighton 5-3 away. But Stoke beat Charlton 5-3 at the Victoria Ground in what proved rather a strange game.

The team travelled up by train on the day the match was due to take place — Saturday 14 January — only to find Stoke was enveloped in fog. Jimmy Trotter left the team at the station and went to the ground to find that play was out of the question. The game was rearranged for the following Monday and Charlton travelled back again to find further misfortune. The Victoria Ground offices and dressing-rooms were plunged into darkness through an electrical failure. One floodlight pylon was put out of action and part of another affected. The Charlton players changed by candlelight and the game started a quarter of an hour late with the lights still dimmed. Things were not put right until half-time, and by then Charlton were 4-2 down.

Early on in the season, in September, a familiar face had come back to The Valley — Sam Bartram with the Luton team. He had become manager in the close season after his spell at York. It was not a happy return for Sam — Luton were despatched 4-1.

In the FA Cup, the third round brought a memorable game at White Hart Lane against the famous Tottenham team, who that season were to become the first club to carry off the League and Cup double this century. Charlton lost 3-2 but at one stage they had been 3-0 down. Leary pulled a goal back just before the interval and a magnificent second-half performance, which saw Lawrie net a second for Charlton, left Danny Blanchflower's team hanging on desperately for victory.

Eddie Werge, seen here flying through the air during Charlton's promotion battle against Blackburn Rovers in 1958, left The Valley in May 1961 after scoring 19 goals in 44 League games for the club.

The season also marked Charlton's entry into the new Football League Cup. They played on the opening day of the competition, Monday, 26 September 1960, and lost 3-1 at West Ham.

The epic games of this season were the last the fans were to see of Charlton's high-scoring antics in these frantic few years at The Valley, a strong contrast to the solidly defensive teams that had brought Charlton success in the 1930s and 40s. No Charlton team was to score 80 League goals again in a season, let alone 90 or 100. When the team finished fourth in 1963-4, the total goals scored was 76 and when Charlton came third in 1968-9, the total was only 61. In the 1969-70 season, when Charlton escaped relegation by just one place, they scored a meagre 35 goals.

So now, a much greyer epoch was on hand and hope of a return to the First Division remained just that, not a reality — just hope.

Tottenham goalkeeper Bill Brown dives bravely at the feet of Charlton's Stuart Leary during the third-round FA Cup game at White Hart Lane.

A Second Division Club for Ever and a Day

CHARLTON were to stay a Second Division club for 15 long seasons. And when they finally left, it was in the wrong direction — to Division Three, which they had left so gloriously 38 years before.

When they were relegated in season 1971-2, no club at that time had spent a longer period as a Second Division club. All the teams in Charlton Athletic's first post-war Second Division season of 1957-8 had either been promoted or relegated. Only Charlton had stayed. Too many of those seasons were marked by a grim struggle against relegation. Only rarely did Charlton look like regaining Division One status after that epic season of 1957-8.

Decline was rapid. In 1965, in his book *Football in London*, David Prole recorded that a visit to The Valley was usually a depressing experience, no matter what the match was like. The bustle of a big club's ground was largely absent and the crowd seemingly lacking in urgency. Eric Nicholls of the *Kentish Mercury* was a persistent and acute critic of the club's apparent lack of ambition. With what now seems ominous foresight, he commented: "The weed-strewn wide-open spaces on the terraces where fans once stood and the barn-like grandstand that brings back memories of the past, combine to give The Valley an air of impending doom." Charlton were on their way to making the transition from big club to small club.

The goal spree of those early years back in Division Two was not enough to keep Jimmy Trotter in his job. The last of the epic seasons, 1960-61, when Charlton scored 97 goals but conceded 91, had seen the club slump to tenth place, their worst since going down.

The 1961-2 season started disastrously. With nine games lost out of the first 12, and only one victory, the start was as poor as the beginning of the last season in Division One. And managerial retribution was just as swift. In October 1961, Trotter and Charlton parted company. Six weeks later, Frank Hill, a former Scottish international wing-half whose clubs had included Aberdeen, Blackpool, Arsenal (where he had gained three League Championship medals) and Southampton, took over. He was very experienced, but already 55 when he arrived after a managerial career spanning Crewe, Burnley, Preston and Notts County, his most recent job. Charlton did not believe in going for younger managers.

Although after 18 games, Charlton had still only

Frank Hill, a former Scottish international wing-half, took over as manager at The Valley.

118

three wins and nine points to their credit, the revival under Hill was swift. Of the remaining 24 matches, 12 were won and only six lost. The club climbed to 15th place and 39 points. The close of the season was remarkable for one particular team change. With relegation still very much a possibility, the versatile John Hewie was called on to take over the goalkeeping position. This was because Willie Duff badly injured knee ligaments in a match at Southampton and the reserve goalkeeper, Frank Reed, was also out with injury.

Hewie's first game between the posts was against Plymouth at The Valley on Saturday, 7 April, with Charlton fifth from bottom of Division Two, only two points ahead of the club second from bottom, Leeds United. He played exceptionally well in a 3-1 victory. It was the first time Hewie had ever played in goal in his career and his success was a tribute to his natural all-round athletic ability. He remained in goal for the following three matches — all away games — and none were lost. A 2-2 draw at Brighton was followed by a 2-0 victory at Huddersfield and a 2-2 draw at Bristol Rovers. Duff had not much longer to go in his Charlton career, being transferred to Peterborough just before the season closed.

Mike Bailey Emerges

ONE of the redeeming features of this difficult season was the emergence of an effective half-back line in the South African-born Brian Tocknell, Marvin Hinton, who won three England Under-23 caps in 1962 and 1963, and Mike Bailey, who went on to gain two England caps in 1964 — Charlton's last England international.

Bailey, born in Wisbech, had been recommended to the club by former Charlton player, Joe Jobling, and joined the groundstaff in May 1958 from Gorleston Juniors, signing professional forms in March 1959. He made his debut at left-half at Plymouth the previous season, on 27 December 1960, and played four games before establishing himself in the 1961-2 season.

In later years, Bailey was to recount what being a young player was like in the late 1950s. At 16, he earned £8 a week for duties which included cleaning boots and dressing-rooms and replacing divots on The Valley pitch. When he signed as a professional at 17, he got £1 a week more. He paid £2 15s (£2.75p) for digs and sent his laundry home to his mother in Norfolk. And like many Charlton players of earlier eras, he had fond memories of the Charlton boiler-room where the players drank their mugs of tea. "In those days, football was my religion. I trained until I dropped with tiredness and at holiday times, I'd watch Millwall in the morning, Fulham in the afternoon and Spurs at night. Fabulous. . . ."

The Death of Johnny Summers

WHAT illustrated the club's decline most in the 1961-2 season was the goals-for total. It dropped by almost a third. Johnny Summers, who had played 39 games the previous season, was missing through illness. In fact, he had played his last game for Charlton. Tragically, the illness was to prove more serious than anyone could have imagined. The news of his condition through the season gave little hint of the tragedy to come. Early on, the news seemed almost hopeful. At the end of September 1961, he was reported up and about in hospital after an operation, 'very cheerful' and looking forward to getting back to The Valley.

At the home match against Huddersfield on 25

Willie Duff takes the ball off the feet of Derby County centre-forward Bill Curry. John Sewell looks on.

Mike Bailey proudly displays his England cap. He is the last Charlton player to play in a full international for England.

November, Summers, on weekend leave from hospital, popped his head round the dressing-room door to say hello and then went to the Huddersfield dressing-room to chat with former Millwall colleague, Pat Saward, the wing-half. 'The boys were delighted to see him looking so well,' the programme recorded.

Alas, Johnny Summers died on 2 June 1962, from cancer, greatly mourned by Charlton fans and their neighbours at Millwall, who had also watched the career of this fine, buccaneering forward who, with

119

Gordon Jago's
League career at
Charlton had
spanned seven
years but was
now at an end.

Marvin Hinton
made 131 League
appearances for
Charlton before
going on to
greater things
with Chelsea.

trade, young John trained twice a week at The Valley. His position was full-back but, sadly, he never made the grade. But for all Charlton fans of that era, the memory of the great Johnny Summers is enough — the memory of a tank-like player of immense courage, who simply went unstoppably through defences to score impossible goals.

Floodlit Valley

THE 1961-2 season saw, at long last, the coming of floodlights at The Valley. It was in January 1961, that the club announced they were going to put up floodlights. The installation was due to be completed for the first match of the season on Tuesday, 22 August, against Stoke City. But delays in delivery of materials put the contractors behind schedule. So with the lights unfinished, the Stoke game kicked off at 6.30pm.

In those days, the players still did their regular training on The Valley pitch, and they had to cut out most of their pre-season training there to let the construction work go on, as well as helping groundsman Jack Myton prepare the pitch for the new season. The training was switched to the J.Stone and Company sports ground.

The lights were finally switched on for the match against Rotherham United on Wednesday, 20 September 1961, kick-off 7.30pm. Charlton were relatively late amongst League clubs in installing lights — floodlights were first used in League games in 1956 — but the programme announced the news as 'this big and bold step forward'. Their installation gave a little insight into the financial state of the club in these later years under Stanley Gliksten. He committed himself to 'advancing' the £20,000 needed, but this was to be paid back by the Charlton Athletic Supporters' Development Club 'over a period'. The supporters had already raised £7,500 by the switch-on.

Having no lights had already led to some oddities. Charlton regularly entered the Southern Professional Floodlit Challenge Cup, but they had to play all their matches away. The advent of lights for League clubs had not only added to the number of midweek matches possible, but also led to the end of the three-game rush at Christmas and Easter. From a complete League programme on Christmas Day, the number of games fell away rapidly so that, by 1963, there were no games at all on 25 December. Charlton's last Christmas Day game had been the 1-0 defeat at Huddersfield Town in 1958.

The four steel towers that sprouted at The Valley in 1961 were 120ft high and carried 24 floodlight units, each having a 1,500-watt lamp. The incoming electricity supply was 11,000 volts and one mile of power cable was used in the installation, besides minor cables for sub-circuits and controls. The standard of illumination was considered good, for the time, the result of the first floodlight encounter less so, Charlton going down 3-2.

The Changing Structure

THE structure of football itself was now moving against the smaller club — and the unenterprising club, that is to say the sort of club Charlton had now so obviously become. In 1961, the maximum wage was abolished, overturning a League rule which had stood since 1901. The campaign against it had gathered momentum since Jimmy Hill, then a bearded forward with Fulham, had taken over as chairman of the Professional Footballers' Association in 1957. But the young Michael Gliksten did show

only a little more first-time ball control, might have been one of the all-time greats. He was just 34.

In his five vintage years at The Valley, he scored 100 goals in 171 League games and four goals in 11 FA Cup games. He remains one of three Charlton players to share the club's individual scoring record of five goals in a match, but is the only one to achieve the feat twice — in the epic 7-6 and 7-4 victories over Huddersfield and Portsmouth. He also had eight hat-tricks.

There were fond nostalgic hopes that another Johnny Summers might one day play for Charlton in the shape of his son. Aged 15 and in the printing foresight, coming to the notice of his League elders as a vocal supporter of the PFA's case.

This was the same year that the notorious entertainment tax was abolished, which had been a burden on football clubs since World War One and especially since World War Two, when it rose to cover one-fifth of all gate receipts. So an extra flood of cash was released into the game, with little of it going into the pockets of the players.

Two years after the ending of the maximum wage, the 'retain and transfer' system itself was ruled illegal after England international inside-forward, George Eastham, took Newcastle United to the High Court over the issue.

23-year-old chairman

IN February 1962, Stanley Gliksten died at his home at Furnham Common, Buckinghamshire, and Michael Gliksten took over as chairman. He was just 23 and the youngest-ever League chairman. Youth should have provided impetus to the club but Charlton's lack of progress of previous years, both on and off the field, was to prove a mounting burden, particularly as the national economic problems of the decade made life difficult for all but the most successful of clubs.

These times of change in the wider football world coincided with the first of Charlton's real crisis struggles against relegation to Division Three, in 1962-3 when a succession of heavy defeats piled up — 5-0 away and 4-1 at home by Chelsea, 6-1 by Plymouth away (reversed into a 6-3 win in the return game) and 6-3 by Stoke away. The backlog of fixtures caused by the severe winter, when Charlton completed only one League game in January and February, did not help.

The departure of the fine attackers of yesteryear — Summers, Leary, Kiernan and Lawrie — was now complete and the forward line was short of experience and class.

Above: Smiles all round. Colin Cowdrey (second left) in conversation with Frank Hill (far right). Stuart Leary (second right) and Bill Jenner (left) look on. Below: Fund-raising. Chairman Stanley Gliksten (right) receives a cheque from Bill Jenner. Opposite: Michael Gliksten, at 23 the youngest chairman in the Football League.

Leary's Goodbye

STUART Leary's attempt to combine careers in football and cricket sadly took him away from The Valley in December 1962 to waste his talents in a lower division. At the end of season upon season at Charlton, he had switched from football to cricket without a break and a bitter dispute over the need for a holiday led to him quitting the club and signing for Queen's Park Rangers, then in Division Three, for £17,000. In 376 League games for Charlton, he had scored 153 goals, a record which still stands, and added another ten in 27 Cup matches. He played another 94 League games for QPR, scoring 28 goals, and another three goals in the FA Cup, before retiring from football in 1966.

Leary's successful cricket career continued and in 1970 he was a member of the Kent team that won the County Championship for the first time since 1913. He also continued to play an active part in the Charlton Athletic Supporters' Club before eventually making his home again in South Africa. He was to die tragically in August 1988, found dead on the slopes of Table Mountain in Cape Town after he had been missing for several days. The subsequent verdict was suicide.

The only bright notes of the 1962-3 season were the debuts of two young forwards, Len Glover and Keith Peacock, the improving scoring form of inside-forward Roy Matthews, and the impact of Mike Kenning, a quick and effective winger, signed in November 1962 from Shrewsbury. Four years later he was transferred to Norwich City, then to Wolves, before rejoining Charlton for a second time. Glover and Peacock had come through the junior ranks, signing professional forms in the summer of 1962. Slough-born Matthews signed as a 17-year-old in 1957, from Arbroath Victoria.

Keith Peacock was one of two young forwards to make their debuts in the 1962-3 season. Peacock later made history as the first-ever substitute in a League game. He is pictured here wearing Charlton's new strip of white shirt and red shoulder flash.

The really memorable game of the season was Stanley Matthews' last appearance on The Valley turf, at the age of 47, on 18 September 1962. The result was a 3-0 defeat by Stoke but the match was watched by the second-highest attendance of the season, 17,821. Matthews' first match at The Valley had been almost 30 years previously — in April 1933, when Stoke were beaten 1-0.

Stan Matthews had always been a popular attraction at The Valley. The attendance of 56,664 when he came with Blackpool to The Valley in the 1953-4 season was the highest-ever to watch a match between the two clubs, home or away. Significantly, in the previous season, 1952-3, and the succeeding season, 1954-5, only 15,913 and 16,354 respectively turned up to see Blackpool at The Valley. Matthews was missing on both occasions. When he appeared again in 1955-6, the crowd went up to 30,134.

A small indication of Charlton's decline came in that season of 1962-3 with London Transport's decision, because of lack of support, to cut out the special bus laid on from the Dulwich area, starting at Goose Green. The service was an indication of just how wide an area Charlton had served as a club in South London generally, apart from its Greenwich, Woolwich and wide Kent support. As far back as February 1961, London Transport had advised that the service was in danger.

A Desperate Finish

THE finish to the 1962-3 season was absolutely desperate. The last home game was against Southampton at The Valley, a replay of the original fixture in January, which was called off in the 58th minute — with Charlton winning 1-0 — because of a howling snow blizzard. Anything short of victory would mean Charlton going down to Division Three. All went well in the first-half, with Charlton leading 1-0 through a Jim Ryan goal. Then early in the second-half, Terry Paine put the Saints level. The minutes ticked away until, with barely a minute left for play, the situation looked hopeless. Then Cliff Durandt got possession of a ball from the right and with his right foot sent it skidding into the goal past 'keeper Ron Reynolds to make the final score 2-1. This meant Charlton had to win at Walsall in the very last game on 21 May to avoid going down with the Saddlers, who were in the same desperate plight. They needed a point to stay up.

The game was goalless when a torrential storm flooded the pitch at half-time and the match was abandoned. Four days later Charlton returned to the Midlands and won 2-1 with Walsall reduced to nine men and losing their goalkeeper with a fractured cheekbone. The goals came from Keith Peacock and Mike Kenning and the result meant Charlton just pipped Walsall on the goal-average formula of those days.

Among the close-season departures were Marvin Hinton, who had grown into a defender of tremendous timing and anticipation before signing for Chelsea, and goalkeeper Frank Reed, who although displaced by Willie Duff, had actually managed to survive one season longer than Duff at The Valley. He went to Gravesend & Northfleet as player-coach. His replacement was Michael Rose, a 20-year-old from Isthmian League club, St Albans City, who signed professional in July.

Rose went on to establish himself as first-team goalkeeper in 1963-4, ahead of Peter Wakeham, who had been signed from Sunderland in July 1962. But Rose's debut was one of the most disastrous of any

Charlton goalkeeper. In the opening match of the 1963-4 season, at The Dell, Southampton put six goals past him. But Rose was blamed for none of them and hung on to his place, appearing in 34 League games that season.

Perhaps only one other goalkeeping debut matches that of Rose's for misfortune — that of the young Les Surman, at Portsmouth more than two years later in a Christmas-week game on Tuesday, 28 December 1965, at a snowbound Fratton Park. After only 18 seconds, he let a back-pass from Billy Bonds roll past him. Charlton went on to lose 3-1 and Surman never played for the first team again. Surman, born in the same house at Tamworth in which famous England goalkeeper, Harry Hibbs, once lived, went on to join Rotherham United and then played a few games for Southern League Burton Albion before dying tragically young, in his early 30s from a terminal illness.

The 1963-4 season was marked by a major change in the club's colours. The shirts changed to white with red shoulder 'flashes'. Charlton were to retain these colours for three seasons. The club also acquired the fourth nickname in their history. After a competition amongst supporters, the official tag became 'The Valiants', but although still official to this day, it has never caught on in the way the 'Addicks, the Robins and the mundane Reds had. The now familiar sword emblem was introduced as part of the relabelling.

Although the 1963-4 season started badly with three defeats in a row, the team began to pick up and brighter times seemed to be around the corner when one of Charlton's legends, Eddie Firmani, returned in October to the club from his eight-year Italian adventure. A hint of his impending return was given in the programme of 30 March 1963, which reported that Frank Hill and Michael Gliksten had gone to see Firmani play for Genoa at Venice, but that the match was cancelled because of severe weather. It also reported that Firmani was over from Italy the previous week and had 'looked in at The Valley for a couple of training sessions with the boys'.

The item was tucked well away and made no mention of any Charlton interest in signing him. There were protracted difficulties over his signing, but Firmani's emotional and domestic ties with Charlton were strong. He was, of course, married to George Robinson's daughter.

Firmani scored two goals in his first game and his signing sparked a revival which saw Charlton rise up the League. They were never in real contention with champions Leeds and runners-up Sunderland, but still finished fourth, despite getting only eight points from their last 12 games.

It was during this season that Mike Bailey was to bloom on the international scene, his robust all-action wing-half play bringing him to the attention of the selectors. He won five England Under-23 caps before going on to play for the full England team in the 10-0 thrashing of the USA in May 1964 and in the 2-1 win over Wales in November the same year. These up-and-down years in Division Two were not matched in the FA Cup, when Charlton managed to get past the fourth round only once, when they lost 2-1 at Villa Park in 1962. The record continued equally dismally until their relegation.

The year of 1964 also saw Michael Gliksten elected to the Football League management committee, setting yet another record of youthfulness. At 25, he was the youngest man ever to sit on the League's ruling body. He remained until 1975, when the

regionalization of representatives eliminated his place.

The Nemesis of Jimmy Gauld

IN the autumn of 1964, the career of the former

Top: Mike Kenning. Bottom: Eddie Firmani, on his return to The Valley, pictured with manager Frank Hill.

Charlton forward, Jimmy Gauld, as a 'fixer' of matches for fixed-odds betting reached its nemesis when he was jailed for four years at Mansfield Magistrates Court and ordered to pay £5,000 costs. Gauld had begun his activities at Swindon and continued them at Mansfield, where he broke his leg on Boxing Day, 1960, after only three games for the Stags. His enforced rest only led him to step up his fixing and betting.

Following a series of exposures by *The People*, he first appeared in court at Rochdale in 1963 and was fined a token £60 for offering bribes to footballers. By that time, his career in football was already finished by his injury and the FA did not impose a playing ban. It was not until May 1964, after Gauld had co-operated with *The People* in further revelations, that the FA banned him permanently from football and football management.

Sentenced with him at Mansfield were nine other players, including two England internationals, Peter Swan of Sheffield Wednesday and Tony Kay of Everton. Swan had never even seen or spoken to Gauld until they were together at the court. Both he and Kay were jailed for four months and then banned from football by the FA within days of leaving prison.

Although the plight of Swan and Kay attracted much attention over the years, Gauld slipped from the public limelight and was not seen again by his nine companions. He never appealed against the lifetime ban from football. It was a far cry from the days when he was the expectant hero waiting to step into Eddie Firmani's scoring boots.

The 1964-5 season was marked by the debut of a player who became an instant favourite with the Charlton fans, full-back Billy Bonds. His first game was on 20 February 1965, at The Valley against Northampton Town. Aged 18, Bonds was born in Woolwich and captained Woolwich Boys and Kent Boys. A bow-legged, strutting, aggressive player, he imposed himself on the field, despite his tender years.

But still the club searched for an effective team combination. Between 1965 and 1968, Charlton Athletic used no fewer than 44 players.

Older players were signed but were obviously well past their peak — Ian King and Colin Appleton from Leicester City, Cliff Holton from Watford. They made little impact and soon departed. The exception was Ron Saunders, signed from Watford, who netted 24 goals in two seasons before retiring from League football in 1967. Between the 1964-5 and 1967-8 seasons, the club stayed in the bottom half of Division Two, often perilously close to relegation.

These years of failure brought more managerial changes in a club previously famed for the stability of its management. In August 1965, Frank Hill left, to be replaced by the Bury manager, Bob Stokoe, the former Newcastle United centre-half. Stokoe stayed for two years before being replaced, in turn, by Eddie Firmani in September 1967. Firmani had left the club again in June 1965 to play for Southend United and it was Stokoe who enticed Firmani, then aged 33, back in March 1967, for a third playing spell at The Valley to help the club in the struggle against relegation. Stokoe was very bitter about his dismissal and relationships long remained strained. But he was to show his ability by leading Sunderland to victory in the 1973 FA Cup Final.

First-ever League Substitute

THE strange ability of the Charlton club to set football 'firsts' continued in one of the major developments in League football when substitutes were allowed from the 1965-6 season onwards. On the first day of the season, 21 August 1965, Charlton's Keith Peacock passed into the history books by becoming the first-ever substitute to play in a League game.

The match was against Bolton Wanderers at Burnden Park and after just 13 minutes, goalkeeper Mike Rose was injured and had to leave the field. So it fell to manager Bob Stokoe to make the first-ever substitution, bringing on Peacock with John Hewie taking over in goal. Charlton lost 4-2.

That same match saw the League debut of Scottish midfield player, Alan Campbell, who started his career with Charlton as a colt in 1964, scoring four goals in his first game, away against Watford. He went on to win four Scottish Youth caps in 1966.

Alan Campbell, who scored four goals in his first colts game for Charlton.

In December 1965, Charlie Hall was appointed trainer to the club in succession to Jock Basford, who went to Exeter City. Charlie had already been at The Valley for 20 years, first as a player and from 1949 as physiotherapist and assistant trainer.

In other changes behind the scenes, the historically close ties between Charlton and Kent County Cricket Club were reinforced when the Kent and England cricketer, Colin Cowdrey, became a director of the club in 1966. He remained on the board until 1973.

The year 1966 also saw the retirement of secretary Jack Phillips in the summer after 25 years. After the match against Blackburn on 30 August at The Valley, Phillips was presented by the directors with a gold wristlet watch and by the players with a table-lighter. Shortly before, he had been made the club's first honorary life member. His successor was Kenneth Calver, who took over the post in July 1966, the first

Charlton Athletic in 1965-6. Back row (left to right): Hawley, Scullion, Jenkins, Myers, Keeley, Campbell, Glover, Kenning, Matthews, J.Keirs, Bailey, Elliott, Kinsey, Kennedy, Peacock, Baber. Second row: Jock Basford (trainer), Surman, Causer, Harford, Bonds, Jones, Hewie, Snedden, Rose, Tocknell, Haydock, Grimwood, Morgan, Charlie Hall (trainer). Seated: Peter Croker (chief representative), David Clark (director), Michael Gliksten (chairman), Jack Phillips (secretary), Jack Myton (groundsman). Front: Reeves, Thompson, Curtis, Fagan, Booth, A.Keirs, Bingham, Stenson, Halom.

of a succession of secretaries. None were to match Phillips' 25-year record of service. Calver was a lifelong supporter and former business executive in the old Gold Coast, now Ghana, and had played football for Catford Wanderers.

But the saddest event of the year was the death of the man who was 'Mr Charlton' for so many years, Jimmy Seed, who passed away at Farnborough Hospital in Kent on 16 July, at the age of 71. At the time of his death he was still a director of Millwall, a distinction he was never to enjoy with the club

Left: Frank Haydock, signed in August 1963 from Manchester United to replace Marvin Hinton. Right: Roy Matthews who totalled 181 appearances.

From left: Brian Kinsey, Brian Tocknell and John Hewie. Three stalwarts noted for their spirit and commitment. Like Hewie, Tocknell came from South Africa.

he had created as a force in football and to whom he devoted so many years of his life. Just a fortnight later, Jack Shreeve, a member of Seed's 1947 FA Cup-winning team, also died after collapsing in his shop at Greenwich. After ending his playing career in 1951, Shreeve had stayed on Charlton's staff until May 1962, retiring from the post of trainer he had held for three years.

Mike Bailey Departs

THE club's parting with realistic First Division ambitions was again brought home to fans when Charlton lost their last England international and a player with the driving force the club would need

if ever it were to return to football at the highest level — Mike Bailey.

In February 1966, he was sold for £40,000 to Wolverhampton Wanderers. The Wolves gained a player who would be their back-bone on the field for years to come and for over 400 games. Their gain was the loss of Charlton's hope. But strangely, as a First Division player, Bailey was never to gain another cap. And so he played in the England record books as purely a Charlton player.

Bailey's departure was illustrative of the club's decline. The state to which the club had fallen was seen around the turn of the year in 1966-7. The club were so short of players for reserve games that they

had to fall back on the manager, Bob Stokoe, at centre-half, assistant trainer Peter Angell at wing-half and the club coach, Malcolm Musgrove, at inside or outside-left.

And this was despite the fact that Charlton had left the main reserve league in the South, the Football Combination, at the end of the 1965-6 season and had been the instigators of a new League, the Midweek League, which should have made it easier to staff reserve teams.

In March 1967, goalkeeper Mike Rose left to join Notts County after 84 appearances, including nine Cup games, in four years at The Valley. He added another 109 League outings with County, before ending his League career at Mansfield. Charlie Wright, a Scotsman signed from Grimsby Town the previous year, had replaced him as the regular Valley keeper.

Goodbye to Billy

THEN came yet another blow to the fans' hopes of ever seeing First Division football at The Valley. Billy Bonds departed on 13 May, the day after the last game of the season, a 1-0 victory over Birmingham. His buyers were the club just over the Thames, who had taken over Charlton's First Division mantle, West Ham United. The fee was £49,500.

At least Bailey had given good service to the club over six seasons. But Bonds had made only 95 League appearances for the club — and he was to give even longer distinguished service to his new club than Bailey. He was to play on for another 21 years.

Bonds was the club's only ever-present that season. Another departure was the veteran forward Ron Saunders, who after just two seasons with Charlton, joined Yeovil Town as general manager in that same month — the start of an eventful managerial career.

The blow of losing Bonds was compounded in November 1967, when another of Charlton's outstanding young players, the forward Len Glover, was sold to Leicester City for £80,000, then the biggest ever fee paid by City for a player. Like Hinton, Bailey and Bonds, he was to give long and distinguished service in the cause of his new club.

Belated Revival

IN 1968-9 came a belated revival with Charlton finishing third — but in those days only two clubs went up. They were the champions, Derby County, and Crystal Palace. Charlton were leaders for a brief spell in September 1968, before slipping back.

Behind the revival lay a number of new signings, seen by supporters as belated recognition of how the club had sold away its home-grown talent. England Youth and Schoolboy international, Paul Went, a wing-half or defender, was signed from Leyton Orient in June 1967, for a record fee for a 17-year-old of £24,500. Just before, in May, Welsh international Graham Moore, a forward or midfield player, had been signed from Northampton Town. Republic of Ireland international forward, Ray Treacy, came from West Bromwich Albion in February 1968.

Again, some good home-grown players were also

Welsh international Graham Moore (right) signed from Cardiff City. England Youth international Peter Reeves (far right) was one of the younger players coming through the ranks. Ray Crawford (bottom right), the veteran striker, joined Charlton from Ipswich Town.

coming through, such as full-back Bob Curtis, and defender Peter Reeves, a colleague of Went's in the England Youth team. Alan Campbell, the Scottish inside-forward and former colt, also had an effective season operating from wing-half. He and Peter Reeves were the two ever-present players. Campbell, in addition to his Scottish Youth caps in 1966, went on to gain one Under-23 cap with Charlton in 1970 — against Wales.

Charlie Wright, who had started his career with Glasgow Rangers and gone on to Workington and then Grimsby, established himself as a crowd favourite through his comic antics and sense of fun.

Towards the end of the season, in March 1969, Charlton signed the veteran former England centre-forward Ray Crawford, from Ipswich Town. Former

Far left: Alan Campbell gained Scottish Under-23 honours. Left: Eddie Firmani departed The Valley and eventually settled on a career in the NASL. Below left: Keith Peacock challenges Mike Ferguson of QPR.

winger, Mike Kenning, came back from Wolves, to try to boost the scoring rate, but they could only finish with a tally of 61 goals.

Back to the Bottom

BUT the season's revival was woefully shortlived. The very next season, 1969-70, the club plunged to third from bottom, just missing relegation as they had

missed promotion. Another managerial sacrifice ensued, Eddie Firmani losing his job, following a 5-0 thrashing at The Valley by Leicester City on Easter Saturday, 28 March 1970.

In goal for Leicester that day was the young Peter Shilton, who made his England debut later that year. He did not have a busy time. Before the game, Charlton were third from bottom with 27 points from 37 games, above Preston with 26 points from 36 games and Aston Villa with 22 points from 36 games. The programme contained these words: 'Manager Eddie Firmani and the players are determined not to go down. They know they have to win their remaining matches, no one else can help them to stay up.'

One aspect of the match which caused some surprise was Firmani's strange decision to play winger Mike Kenning at full-back, a move which badly misfired. Ironically, among the Leicester goalscorers was former Charlton winger, Len Glover.

The determination of Eddie Firmani became no longer applicable and, on Easter Monday morning, his long association with the club was terminated. It was a sharp and painful break. Firmani was very close to Michael Gliksten and a dedicated man with a strong sense of moral purpose. But he was also a worrier and seemed to have let the job overcome him. The Kenning switch was one of a number of unpopular team selections. Firmani was out of football for two years until given the opportunity of becoming a manager in the North American Soccer League. He spent the intervening period selling insurance.

His successor at Charlton was Theo Foley, who had joined the club from Northampton Town and made only six appearances in 1967-8. Charlton just

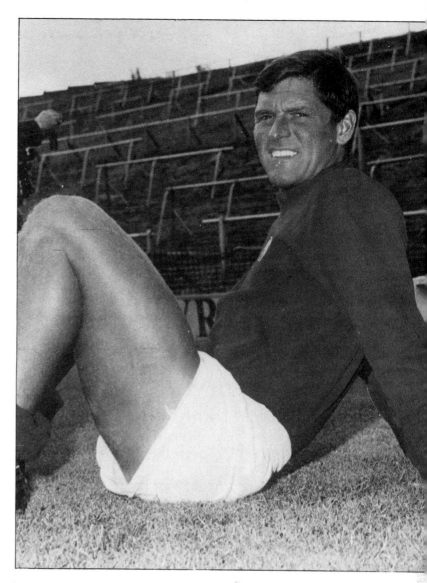

scraped to safety, winning one, drawing two and losing one in their last four games. The last match was against middle-of-the-table Bristol City at The Valley and only victory would assure the team of safety. A gutsy performance before a 15,972 crowd brought about a 2-1 victory, with goals from Alan Campbell and Ray Treacy, Charlton's Graham Moore scoring an own-goal for City. The result sent two famous teams down to the Third Division in Charlton's place — Aston Villa and Preston North End.

At the end of the season, Brian Kinsey retired, having notched up 371 League games, 20 League Cup and 18 FA Cup games. He was later to sign for the South African club Cape Town. In 1979, his son, Mark, was to follow him on to Charlton's books but he never made the first team. Of Brian Kinsey, Theo Foley remarked: "If I had to choose the type of player to build a team around, Kinsey would always be first choice. Loyalty, a good trainer, a good timekeeper, even temperament and dedicated." One brief signing that season was Maurice Setters, the former Coventry City, Manchester United and West Brom wing-half, whose Charlton career lasted only eight games.

Relegation again threatened the following season with the club consistently in difficulty, but at least one dubious record was lost on Saturday, 28 November 1970, when Charlton won 4-1 against Queen's Park Rangers at Loftus Road. This ended a club record of 35 away games without a win. The last away victory had been at Norwich City on 15 March 1969 — by 1-0.

There were many comings and goings at The Valley as Theo Foley, an Irishman of considerable charm, sought to arrest an abysmal start to the season which saw nine games without a win before Swindon were beaten 2-1 at The Valley on 3 October. Amongst the departures was Alan Campbell, the Scottish Under-23 cap, who was sold to Birmingham City for £70,000, and forward Harry Gregory, who moved to Aston Villa. Gregory had amassed a total of 149 League appearances for Charlton after signing from Orient in 1966. With the Campbell and Gregory deals and the sale to Orient of Gordon Riddick, a striker converted to centre-half, Charlton had netted some £87,000.

All three deals were completed on the same day in October 1970, and Foley reinvested £15,000 in Coventry City's German-born defender Dietmar Bruck. Then he paid £25,000 for Tottenham's midfield player, Dennis Bond. Another new recruit was Gillingham's goalkeeper Derek Bellotti, who played his first game in November. In February 1971, £20,000 was invested in centre-forward Barry Endean from Watford.

The Valley Club

IN October 1970, Tony Pocock, sales manager of the Oxford University Press and a member of the Hampshire County Cricket Club committee, became a director of the club. This followed his initiation for the club of a further education scheme for

apprentices and young players, the first such scheme to be implemented by any League club.

In 1969, The Valley sprouted a new social club. A large single-storey building was constructed facing Harvey Gardens, behind the covered end of the ground. It was called The Valley club and included a restaurant, which provided lunches every weekday and cabaret, music and dancing at night. In November, local public figures and supporters turned up for an official opening by Michael Gliksten. The restaurant was managed by Ron Kett, a man whose previous experience had included Maxims Restaurant in Paris and Claridges Hotel in London — all a rather far cry from The Valley. The club remains today, although purely as a social club used for events.

Charlie Wright's national recognition as Charlton's most distinctive goalkeeper since Sam Bartram came in the November 1969 edition of the *Football League Review*. A picture of him appeared on the front cover with the words: 'If someone made an award for the Second Division's most popular player, there's a fair chance, the title would go to Charlton Athletic's goalkeeper Charlie Wright....His sporting approach and sense of humour have made him a firm favourite with the fans.'

It was at this time that John Cartwright began to compile the Radio Valiant programme of requests at matches. John was later to go on to greater fame as Labour, then SDP Member of Parliament for Woolwich.

In July, 1971, the club lost one of its most famous

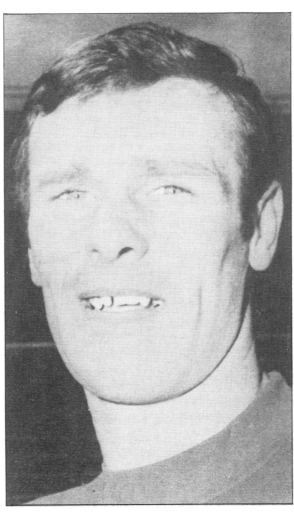

personalities, David Clark, who had saved Charlton from extinction those long years ago when his firm Messrs Humphreys did not foreclose on the debts from the development of the Valley as a League ground. At the time of his death, he was the club's president. He was cremated at the London Crematorium on 19 July. Those attending the funeral service included the chairman and directors, the manager Theo Foley and two players, on behalf of the playing staff, whose combined appearances totalled some 500 games — Mike Kenning and Keith Peacock.

Golden Jubilee

DAVID Clark's death came just a few weeks before the Golden Jubilee of the club's League membership, which fell in the 1971-2 season. Charlton's jubilee celebration match came against Watford on 28 August, almost 50 years to the day since the first League match at The Valley. The Mayor of Greenwich joined the festivities, along with the band of the Royal Artillery. Charlton won 2-0 before a crowd of 11,966.

For the golden jubilee season, the club produced a special handbook. In his foreword, Michael Gliksten gushed forth eloquently on Charlton's tradition and spirit:

'These traditions and standards, however, must be made to serve as an incentive to future success, not just glorious memories, and, in the years to come, we must all be resolute in doing justice to the personalities whose names grace this book, by striving unceasingly to regain our First Division status.'

That season Charlton were relegated to the Third Division they had left 36 years previously.

The season was an unusual one in that the normal Charlton pattern to a season was to start badly and then stage a late revival. This time the season started well and Charlton slipped into serious trouble only in the later stages.

As the bright start faded, Theo Foley was forced to ring the changes. John Dunne, a close-season signing from Aston Villa and a former Chelsea player, took over from Derek Bellotti in goal. Local discovery David Shipperley was given his chance and settled into the central defence. Barry Endean was sold to Blackburn in a deal which took Republic of Ireland international Eamonn Rogers to The Valley. Another departure was Mike Kenning, who went to Watford. Phil Warman, a former winger and England Youth international, now established himself at left-back.

In November, the young Welsh midfield player, Cyril Davies, won his first and only full Welsh cap when he came on as substitute against Rumania in Bucharest. The Welsh went down 2-0. Davies gained four Under-23 caps in that year and in 1972.

Mike Flanagan Signed

A young forward who came briefly into the side was Mike Flanagan, signed early in August from Tottenham. He had been a member of the Spurs team which won the FA Youth Cup and had also played three times for the England Amateur team. Mike, who had been with Spurs since he was 11, was not offered professional forms and went to work in the Civil Service.

It was the eagle eye of the then Charlton chief scout, Les Gore, which brought Flanagan into professional

133

football with Charlton. He played only a few games that season — his impact on the side was still to come.

For a time the side revived and then seemed safe in mid-table, but they flattered only to deceive. Some of the most difficult weather conditions Charlton have ever had to face came on 4 March at Oxford United. The cold was so intense that at the same time, a game at nearby Abingdon was abandoned after six players collapsed through extreme cold and exhaustion.

The Oxford game showed the tricks the English climate can play. The kick-off was in sunshine on a firm pitch. But at half-time the playing surface was under water, buffeted by sleet and snow. In conditions that verged at times on the near-impossible, the sides managed to complete the game, Oxford winning 2-1.

The programme notes had a peculiarly inane quality that season which grated as the playing performance fell away, and nowhere more so than in their almost constant reference to the growing youth of the Charlton team.

On New Years' Day, 1972, the notes referred to how the average age of the team had been reduced from 28 to 24 years. By March, the average had dropped to 23. The notes saw this as a sign of progress to come — 'all soundly based successful teams have gone through a period of at least two years of 'growing up together'.

Relegation by the Seaside

BUT whereas Charlton had previously invariably avoided relegation in their long spell in the Second Division by their desperate end-of-the-season revivals, they finally went down after a season which, though poor, had seen them clear of the relegation area until April.

Perhaps it was that the young players in the team simply lacked the experience and determination to fight back as the results began to go against them. This notion did not seem to have ever occurred to the hapless writer of the programme notes, although it must be added that long-lasting injuries to Peter Reeves and Bob Curtis also affected the team's strength and consistency.

It was two matches at home over Easter 1972, lost 2-1 to Orient and 2-0 to Norwich City, that began the plunge into trouble and then disaster with seven more games left. When the last match arrived, just two more points from two draws had been gained. Charlton had to win to make sure of staying up and condemn one of their rivals in danger — Fulham or Cardiff. Watford were already down.

The crucial match was at Blackpool, ironically managed by the former Charlton manager, Bob Stokoe. Charlton's chance of survival was to quickly disappear. The author remembers well the look of fear and concern in the players' eyes as they left the coach on arrival at Bloomfield Road. It was reflected in their play, the result a disastrous 5-0 defeat, with full-back Phil Warman conceding an own-goal.

As it turned out, had Charlton managed a draw, they would have been safe and Fulham relegated with an inferior goal-average. The wheel had turned full-circle and now Charlton Athletic were back in the lower level of the League they had left so gloriously 37 long years before.

Back to the Third and Back Again

THE first season back in the Third Division since the 1930s was reflected in the attendances, down by over half compared to the start of the previous season — 5,300 for the first home match, a 2-1 defeat against Shrewsbury Town, followed by only 4,283 for the second Valley match, a 6-0 thrashing of Swansea City. They were to pick up later, but then fall away to as low as 3,015 for the home match against Halifax in March 1973 as the team failed to make an impact in the Third Division. The average attendance dropped to 5,658 against 10,430 the previous season.

The first two seasons in the Division saw the club finish in unexciting mid-table positions — 11th and 14th — and they might have stayed in the Third Division for much longer, but for a rule change in the summer following their first season back.

In June 1973, the Football League annual general meeting changed the promotion and relegation system. It agreed to bring in three-up and three-down between the First, Second and Third Divisions and four-up and four-down between the Third and the Fourth.

The move obviously made the Third Division a much more competitive place with seven teams going out of it each season. It also opened up a little more hope of a famous club such as Charlton escaping from their predicament of lower division football.

During the close season of 1972, Paul Went left to play for Fulham, on a career trail that would take him on to Portsmouth, Cardiff and back to Orient. Ray Treacy joined Swindon Town and Arthur Horsfield made the return journey from Swindon, signing for Charlton. Amongst the five new apprentice professionals joining the club that season was 16-year-old Nigerian-born Benjie Odeje, the first coloured boy to play for England Schoolboys. Sadly, he failed to make the League grade.

Although the season held out no promise of a quick return, one bright note of the disappointing campaign was the form of the young Mike Flanagan, who settled into the side and was selected to join the Republic of Ireland squad preparing for the 1974 World Cup, as both his parents were Irish. But in a bitter personal disappointment, he could not take up his selection as he had already played for the England Youth team.

In January 1973, Charlton signed a promising winger from non-League Barnet — Colin Powell — who made the jump in grade effortlessly and became a mainstay of the team for eight years.

Sadly, the first signs of football hooliganism were making themselves felt, even at a peaceful club such as Charlton. The programme for the Grimsby game on 10 March 1973, at The Valley, issued a warning to 'Behave or stay away' to 'a group of so-called Charlton fans, whom we have reason to believe are not regular supporters' who created trouble at the Brentford and Plymouth away games.

The programme stated: 'We hope all genuine supporters of the club will help us stop this hooligan element from causing trouble in the future as we do not want this type of people connected in any way with the club, however remotely.'

During that summer of 1973, the club were to make a remarkable signing although it was not realized at the time. Forward Derek Hales joined Charlton from Luton Town, initially on a three-month loan period. He was very much an unknown quantity, having played only five full games for Luton and two as substitute since his League debut in February 1973, but he was to prove probably the biggest bargain in the club's history.

He made an immediate impact for Charlton in his debut game, against Blackburn Rovers at The Valley on 11 September, scoring in a 4-3 victory. Charlton fans breathed a sigh of relief when Hales was permanently signed in October, for a fee of only £5,000, as it was already clear that he was a striker of great potential, a view strongly shared by the man who played alongside him, Arthur Horsfield. Hales went on to score nine goals that season, although he was out of the side through injury for a time.

The opening game of the season, a 4-2 defeat on 24 August at The Valley against York City, saw a new entry in the club record books when Mark Penfold became the youngest player ever to appear in the Charlton first team, at the age of 16 years 258 days.

One player who did not make the start of the season was Cyril Davies, whose career at 24 was ended by a torn cruciate ligament in his knee — the ligament that keeps the knee stable — which had stretched beyond the point where it could be repaired.

And out with injury again after the opening game was Peter Reeves, who had to go into hospital for an operation following the discovery of a piece of floating bone in his knee. This was to be his last season with the club as he failed to recover completely. His retirement at the age of 25 was a tragedy, for he was a player who genuinely loved Charlton Athletic.

In charge of the youth team that season was a new

Derek Hales, initially came on loan from Luton Town and went on to prove himself probably the best bargain in Charlton's history.

136

coach, the former Reading forward Peter Shreeve, later to go on to greater things and manage Tottenham Hotspur.

The Non-stop Train

ON 15 September 1973, for the game at Brighton, Charlton Athletic made use of the League's new *Leagueliner* train, which had made its inaugural run earlier that year from Burnley to London, carrying Burnley supporters to the Second Division match at Queen's Park Rangers.

The League's idea was to keep fans happy and occupied and out of trouble during away journeys and the train was equipped with a discotheque coach, a four-screen 42-seat cinema compartment and two music carriages.

The Burnley fans were reported to have been delighted. So were Charlton's, although the venture was not well supported, but they had a rather unexpected return from Brighton. Instead of stopping at Charlton station, the *Leagueliner* sailed on to Woolwich, and the club had to make an official complaint to British Rail.

The club also experimented briefly with Friday night football, general manager, Rodney Stone, making the bizarre comment: "The players get upset at the large gaps on the terraces and under the floodlights they won't notice them so much."

On 3 February 1974, Charlton staged the first-ever Sunday match at The Valley, drawing 3-3 with Shrewsbury Town.

The two very average seasons in the Third Division now spelt the end of yet another manager's reign and in April, Theo Foley left the club. His personality had charmed many but the verdict on him seemed to be that he was a better coach than manager, as was to be proved by his success as coach over a decade later, under George Graham at Highbury.

Nelson Takes Over

HE was replaced by a personality who was steeled to what life was like in the lower divisions. The former Ipswich player, Andy Nelson, who had steered Gillingham to promotion from the Fourth Division in 1973-4, as runners-up with the League's highest goal-tally of 90, now took over.

Nelson was a hard, demanding taskmaster and, at first, his firm touch worked at Charlton, too. He took the club to third place the following season and promotion as the second-highest scorers in the Third Division.

One of his key signings came in August 1974 — David Young from Sunderland, a member of Sunderland's FA Cup winning squad in 1973. He lined up in central defence alongside Arthur Horsfield, who was switched from the forward line to centre-half for part of the season. Another signing in October 1974 was of the 33-year-old Millwall veteran defender, Harry Cripps, one of The Den's most revered personalities and a close friend of Nelson.

The gradual increase in violence at football matches as the 1970s wore on was shown at the game against

Right: David Young — key signing from Sunderland. Far right: Andy Nelson, who had made his name as a manager in the Fourth Division with Gillingham, and had been centre-half in Alf Ramsey's Ipswich League Championship side.

Crystal Palace at Selhurst Park on Saturday, 30 November 1974. A 15-year-old supporter and season-ticket holder, Drew Robertson from Sidcup, was assaulted by a group of 20 youths after the match and stabbed in the back. He was taken to Mayday Hospital, Croydon, where, thankfully, he recovered from his injuries.

With promotion looking a strong possibility, Nelson won the Bells Whisky Third Division Manager of the Month award for March. His prize was a gallon bottle of whisky, presented at the home game on Saturday, 19 April, against Bury whose secretary was appropriately the former Charlton winger, Gordon Hurst. Charlton's success was marked by a rise in attendances to over 10,000.

Promotion Clincher

THE game which clinched promotion was the last of the season, on Tuesday, 29 April 1975, against Preston North End, before a crowd of more than 24,000 at The Valley. Charlton won 3-1 to take the third promotion place.

Two marvellous goals from Derek Hales, following an equalizer from defender Bobby Goldthorpe after Preston had gone ahead, were the highlights in a great all-round team effort. Blackburn were champions, followed by Plymouth Argyle. Charlton had good reason to bless the change in the promotion rules.

Would the lessons of the spell in Division Three now be learned and would the club now seriously aim at regaining its First Division status? For a time, the future looked more promising as the club settled into a position in the first half of the Second Division.

The Third Division years had been graced by Arthur Horsfield, who had won by his wholehearted play the admiration of the Charlton fans. But he was one of the early departures of the new Second Division years. After only two games in the number-nine shirt, he was sold by Nelson to Watford in September.

In defence, the club now blooded a tall young defender, who was to be a defensive mainstay over the next decade. In October 1976, 6ft 2in tall Les Berry made his debut in an away game at Bristol City.

Now loomed one of the saddest tragedies in the club's history — a serious injury to young goalkeeper Graham Tutt, who had made his first-team debut as a 17-year-old in March 1974 at Shrewsbury and had taken over the regular spot in November that year, shortly after the departure of John Dunn on a free transfer.

During a League game at Roker Park in February 1976, a Sunderland forward kicked his head as they both went for the ball. Tutt was badly hurt in the

Harry Cripps, a friend of Nelson's, joined Charlton from Millwall.

John Cartwright MP (left) and Councillor Dick Neve, two Charlton stalwarts pictured at the microphone in October 1974.

Left: Les Berry, the tall defender who made his Charlton debut at Ashton Gate and proved a great asset over the next decade. Far left: Pop mega-stars The Who in concert at The Valley. Two big pop concerts were staged in 1972 and 1974.

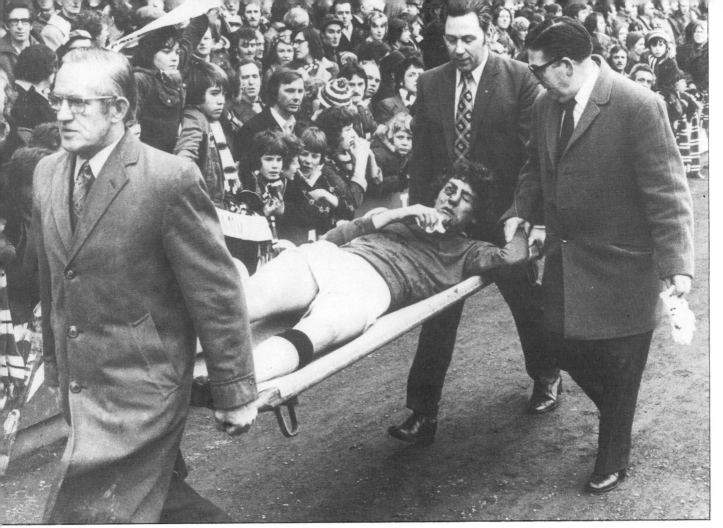

Graham Tutt is carried off at Roker Park after sustaining the serious eye injury which ended his career.

face, suffering an horrendous eye injury which affected his vision. The incident was to finish his League career, although he later made a forlorn and brave attempt at playing again.

He recovered sufficiently to appear in pre-season friendlies before the 1976-7 season, but it was soon clear that his vision would not allow him to play on. Towards the end of the season, a testimonial match was held for him, with Sunderland providing the opposition. Charlton won 3-2, with England and Arsenal striker Malcolm Macdonald guesting for them and scoring twice.

In Tutt's place came Jeff Wood, who had started the season in the much lower environment of the old Athenian League with Harlow Town. Wood was to remain an ever-present for almost three years before being displaced by Nicky Johns.

The following season, 1976-7, a young defender, David Campbell, became the first associated schoolboy under a new scheme for schoolboy registration, to appear in the Charlton team. He was still at Roan School and on leaving the school, became a contract player in June 1977, going on to play in the first team while still a student at London University.

With the Nelson regime having apparently strongly stabilized the club's position in the Second Division, Harry Cripps now combined his playing role in the Reserves with coaching and was appointed later that season as assistant manager to Nelson.

Goodbye to Hales

Opposite: Third Division goalscoring partnership. Derek Hales and Arthur Horsfield (left) celebrate a Charlton victory.

A large part of the club's success in the Second Division had been due to Hales repeating his goalscoring form from the Third Division. At the higher level, this commanded much more attention and he was even tipped as a potential England

international. Inevitably, First Division clubs came to look at him and in December 1976, one took the bait, Derby County.

Hales was sold for £300,000. His Charlton goalscoring record was 73 in 129 League games, but it was a rate he could not maintain with Derby, a

Charlton Athletic in 1976-7. Back row (left to right): Richie Bowman, Kim Connett, Les Berry, Jeff Wood, Graham Tutt, Jim Giles, Mike Flanagan, Mark Penfold. Middle row: Andy Nelson (manager), Harry Cripps, Phil Warman, Colin Powell, George Hope, David Campbell, Geoff Hammond, Peter Shearing (coach), Charlie Hall (physiotherapist). Front row: Johnny Harrison, Keith Peacock, Derek Hales, David Young, Peter Hunt, Tony Young.

club troubled by internal dissension. He was to make 22 appearances for Derby, scoring seven goals, before moving to West Ham, for £110,000 in September 1977, where he also played only briefly, making 23 appearances and scoring ten goals.

Mike Flanagan celebrates a goal against Blackburn Rovers at The Valley in December 1976.

Peter Bonetti stops a blaster from Derek Hales at Stamford Bridge in November 1976.

Fury as coach and with the later demise of the NASL, went into an American garage business and then coached in the Middle East.

International in the Snow

THE form of Mike Flanagan at last brought international recognition in February 1978 when he was selected to play for the England 'B' team in West Germany. The England side won 2-1 at the Rosenau Stadium, Augsburg, in sub-zero temperatures on a pitch covered with two inches of snow.

Flanagan made one bad miss in the first half and then a hamstring injury removed him half-way through the second. He suffered the injury when turning in the snow. But he was reckoned to have given a competent, industrious performance. The 'B' team manager was Bobby Robson. The effects of the injury were to bring a halt to Flanagan's early season goalscoring form with severe consequences.

February was an eventful month on a wider front. Freedom of contract for players was agreed by club chairmen at a meeting in London on Thursday, 13 April.

And Charlton announced that same month a surprising agreement that was to have controversial repercussions later that season. They agreed a tie-up with the New England Teamen of the North American Soccer League. Amongst players earmarked to play for the Teamen that summer was Mike Flanagan.

The money Charlton gained from the deal saw them indulge in a bout of transfer activity. Another former Tottenham apprentice forward, Martin Robinson, signed for Charlton for £15,000. Dave Shipperley, the giant defender, was re-signed from Gillingham after a four-year absence, and the forward, Terry Brisley, was signed from Millwall. Total spending was £80,000. The month saw the departure of full-back Bob Curtis to his home-town club, Mansfield, after a 12-year career at The Valley in which he had made

With part of the money, Nelson went out and bought Dick Tydeman, a midfield player from Gillingham, and Hugh McAuley, a winger from Plymouth, for a total of £77,000.

At that time, Charlton were only four points off the leading three promotion positions. They were to end the 1976-7 season in a respectable seventh place, still four points off the promotion places, but a two-place improvement on the previous season. They lost only four out of the last 25 games and it seemed that the departure of Hales was successfully weathered. The team still continued to play good attacking football, finishing fifth-highest scorers with 71 goals.

But there was a wretched incident before the end of the season. On Monday, 11 April 1977, The Valley for the first time caught the full force of the vandalism afflicting the game. The catalyst was a 4-0 defeat of Chelsea.

The rampage started when Charlton were 3-0 ahead. The Chelsea fans chanted: "We're worse than Manchester United," and hundreds of them invaded the pitch, trying to get the game stopped. A bonfire was lit behind the goal, using planks and litter containers. The game was finished, but not the havoc. The social club had its windows smashed, four houses had their windows broken, a shop front was smashed and three parked cars were damaged. A lump of concrete was found embedded in a wall of a ladies lavatory.

Despite the beating, Chelsea went on to promotion in second place behind Wolves. Nottingham Forest were third and with Brian Clough at the helm, were to take the First Division Championship next season. Mike Flanagan had now reached his prime and become a player of considerable distinction, scoring 23 League goals that season. The next season he continued in the same impressive form. On 15 October 1977, he scored a hat-trick against his old club, Tottenham Hotspur, in a 4-1 Charlton victory at The Valley. The season marked the start of the career of a quite remarkable player, Steve Gritt, a midfield signing from Bournemouth, who was to demonstrate an amazing ability to play in any position in the years ahead.

Across the Atlantic, Eddie Firmani was now making a big impact as a coach and manager, first with Tampa Bay Rowdies and then with the New York Cosmos, whom he helped to the North American Soccer League title in 1977, with players under him such as Pelé, Franz Beckenbauer and the former Brazilian captain, Carlos Alberto. In December 1977, another former Charlton favourite, Gordon Jago, took on the Tampa Bay job, quitting his post as Millwall manager. Firmani later joined Philadelphia

Martin Robinson, another former Tottenham apprentice, joined Charlton for £15,000 and went on to score 58 goals in 228 League appearances.

358 League and Cup appearances, and won admiration for his consistently determined and wholehearted performances.

One part of the American deal was that if the Teamen reached the NASL play-offs, the Charlton players would miss the start of the following season. But equally significantly the deal also meant their missing the end of the current season.

That sparked off controversy in the Second Division because of the implications of Charlton fielding what was, in effect, a weakened team. Besides Flanagan, it was also made known that another of the club's strongest players, Colin Powell, was to accompany Flanagan. A third player was also to go — Laurie Abrahams.

At the time, Charlton looked safe from relegation but other threatened clubs, who feared a distortion of the end-of-season results, protested vehemently. The Millwall manager, George Petchey, spoke out against the move and Cardiff City took their case to the Football League without success. The players departed in the first week of April.

But it was on the club itself that the move rebounded terribly. In November, they had been on the fringe of the promotion race, but they slid to a disastrous end to the 1977-8 season.

They managed to win only one of their final six matches and only a goalless draw at Orient in their final game kept them clear of the drop. The midweek game was a replay of an earlier game abandoned because of torrential rain. Orient, FA Cup semi-finalists that season, were in desperate relegation trouble too, but went on to save themselves as well.

Whilst Flanagan and Powell played in North America, with Powell actually transferring to the Teamen for a short while, Charlton moved in July to buy back Derek Hales. He was signed from West Ham for £75,000, after a stay at Upton Park of just nine months.

In the States, Flanagan was proving a sensation. He scored 30 goals for the Teamen, becoming the second highest scorer in the North American Soccer League, and was named 'Most Valuable Player' in a poll of players in the NASL, following in the illustrious footsteps of stars such as Pelé and Beckenbauer. Second behind him came the Birmingham and England star, Trevor Francis, who was with Detroit Express, and joint third were Beckenbauer and Carlos Alberto. Flanagan's prize was a Toyota car.

Whereas previously, he had been the junior partner to the highscoring Hales, he now teamed up with him as an England 'B' international and as an American soccer star. It looked to be a powerful combination, but it was aborted soon into the new season when Hales suffered a groin injury in September which put him out for 17 games.

The start to the 1978-9 season was a good one. The team were fifth after 14 games. In November, Flanagan's good form brought him another England 'B' honour when he was picked for the side to face Czechoslovakia in Prague. Defenders Lawrie Madden and Peter Shaw, signed the previous season, now became regulars. Madden, a Manchester University graduate, was a former Arsenal junior and Shaw came from Staines Town.

Success on the pitch was marred by problems off it. The ugly face of soccer hooliganism once again showed itself in pitch encroachments in the Football League Cup game against Stoke at The Valley on 7 November.

The club endured the humiliation of being warned

by the Football Association about future crowd behaviour. In the programme, Michael Gliksten called it 'a sad blow to our proud record of having one of the best behaved crowds in the country.'

Another international tie-up now took place — and much happier than the American one had been. A friendship burgeoned between Charlton and the Danish club, Hvidovre, and in December 1978, the chairman of Hvidovre, Niels Erik Madsen, joined the Charlton board.

Just previously, some of the Hvidovre players had trained at The Valley for a few days. This hospitality

Steve Gritt, who signed for Charlton from Bournemouth in October 1975 and stayed to see Charlton become a First Division side again.

143

Keith Peacock in action against Fulham at The Valley in November 1978 during his final season.

Colin Powell trying to weave his way past Alan Devonshire and Billy Bonds of West Ham at The Valley in April 1979.

was returned in the preparations for the following season, when Charlton players went to Copenhagen for a week. And in the 1978-9 and 1979-80 seasons, two friendlies were played against Hvidovre at The Valley. At that time, the Hvidovre club was taking on its first full professionals.

Just after the Danish tie-up, at the end of December, a loan deal brought goalkeeper Nicky Johns from Sheffield United, for what was initially intended as a three-month stay. Johns, too, had North American experience. He had been Millwall's goalkeeper before joining Tampa Bay Rowdies for £150,000 in June 1978. He had joined Sheffield United on loan at the start of the English season. Johns was signed permanently by Charlton from Tampa Bay for £100,000 in August, 1979.

The Flanagan-Hales Incident

IN January 1979 came what was the most disgraceful on-the-field incident in Charlton's history and one that was to have continuing repercussions on the club — on dressing-room morale, on the authority of the board and, ultimately, on the standing and future of the manager himself.

The occasion was an innocent-looking FA Cup third-round tie against a non-League club, Maidstone United, on Tuesday, 9 January. The game had originally been scheduled for Saturday, 6 January, but was postponed because of severe weather conditions.

Five minutes from the end of what proved a tough, difficult game, with the score 1-1, there was a scuffle. The Charlton fans were bewildered. They could not see an amber Maidstone shirt involved. Then, to their absolute amazement, two Charlton players were sent off the pitch — their star striking partners, Derek Hales and Mike Flanagan.

Hales had failed to reach a through-ball from Flanagan and the two players appeared to blame each other for the wasted chance. In the words of the referee, Brian Martin of Nottingham: "I ran back past the two players and heard one player saying something to the other. I turned round and saw them exchanging blows.

'I couldn't believe my eyes. In 20 years of refereeing, I've never seen anything like it. I had to consult a linesman to confirm what I had seen — then had no alternative but to send them both off."

The Maidstone players looked on in bewilderment as the other Charlton players realized what was happening and rushed in from all sides to separate their fighting teammates. Ironically, only eight minutes earlier the two players had been shaking hands as Flanagan equalized a 13th minute goal from Maidstone's Glenn Coupland, a former Charlton player who had played briefly in the Reserves.

Manager Andy Nelson described the incident as 'the most serious breach of discipline in the club's history'. That same evening a special meeting of the Charlton board took place. Charlton players were banned from discussing the incident in public on penalty of a fine of two weeks' wages. Needless to say, the fight made national headlines.

On Friday, 12 January the board announced they would terminate the contract of Hales on 26 January without prejudice to Charlton's right to a compensation fee'. Flanagan's role was viewed less seriously. He was fined £250. Both were due to miss the next game automatically, a League match at Wrexham the next day. But that game also fell a victim of the weather conditions and so both Flanagan and Hales were missing when Charlton travelled to

Mike Flanagan (above) and Derek Hales (below) were involved in one of the most astonishing incidents ever seen on a Football League ground.

Maidstone for the replay staged on Monday, 15 January.

Charlton won 2-1 with goals from David Campbell and Martin Robinson. Nicky Johns made his debut for the club, displacing Jeff Wood, who had been an ever-present over the past 134 games since his debut in 1976.

But when Glenn Coupland pulled one back for Maidstone with four minutes to go, Charlton had longer than the four minutes to hang on. Two minutes from time, the floodlights failed after overheating. After a lengthy delay, they were repaired and the remaining two minutes played.

The Flanagan-Hales affair was, however, by no means over. On Wednesday, 24 January, Hales appealed to the Football League management committee over the Charlton board's decision to end his contract but retain his registration. The case was adjourned until 14 February, with Charlton agreeing to still pay his wages.

Then there came repercussions on the Flanagan side. Flanagan, now rated the more financially valuable of the two at around £400,000 in Press estimates, was smarting from the fine and on Friday, 2 February, put in a written transfer request, although he had two years of a three-year contract to run. The board now faced losing both their star strikers. Two clubs, Southend United and Cardiff City, had made inquiries for Hales.

On Monday, 5 February, Charlton went out of the FA Cup, 1-0 at Bristol Rovers in a fourth-round tie already postponed three times. On Friday, 9 February, Hales was reinstated at the club after both the League and the Professional Footballers' Association had asked the board to modify their hardline stance. Hales was fined two weeks wages instead.

On 14 February, Gordon Jago, the manager of Tampa Bay Rowdies, who was in London, was reported as putting in a £700,000 bid for Flanagan

in talks with Michael Gliksten. Things now started to go badly wrong indeed in Flanagan's relations with the club. On Tuesday, 20 February, he failed to turn up for training. Meanwhile, his wife was quoted in the Press, saying he would not go back to the club until 'a transfer is sorted out that suits him'. Flanagan was also reported as favouring rejoining his American team, the New England Teamen instead of Tampa Bay.

There was a heavy touch of irony when Hales replaced the absent Flanagan in the team for the match against Leicester City at The Valley on Saturday, 24 February. It was his first game since his dismissal against Maidstone.

There then followed weeks of confusion over Flanagan's future. The Teamen had first option in the NASL on Flanagan because he had played for them. Their president, Derek Carrol, arrived in London on 3 March to talk to Flanagan and an SOS had to be sent by Charlton through the Press to contact the missing player.

On Friday, 2 March, Andy Nelson was quoted on the saga: "I personally delivered yesterday letters about the negotiations to Flanagan's house, which was in darkness, to his mother and father, and to his in-laws.

"I spoke to his mother and father-in-law. Neither knew where he was, and they must be the most uncommunicative family in the world."

A week later on Thursday, 8 March, Flanagan revealed in the Press that he had been on holiday in the Caribbean. He said: "Charlton have been saying that I walked out because the move to Tampa Bay had fallen through. That is not the case. I left because the club had reinstated Derek Hales. That was the only reason. I have been at Charlton seven years and in that time I have been a loyal servant to the club.

"I don't want people to get the impression that I'm a troublemaker because I am not. What's brought

Nicky Johns in action for Charlton after joining the club from the North American Soccer League.

146

ll this about is the club's handling of the Hales situation."

Meanwhile, the saga wreaked havoc on team morale and form. Before the Maidstone incident, Charlton were tenth in the League, seven points off the leaders, Crystal Palace and Stoke. From 3 March until up to the last game of the season, at The Valley against Oldham on 5 May, they did not win a single game.

Charlton were now in desperate trouble and needing to win to stand a chance of staying in the Second Division. They had 33 points from 41 games. Below them were Sheffield United with 33 points from 39 games, Millwall with 26 points from 36 games and Blackburn with 24 points from 39 games.

Andy Nelson had become increasingly bitter in his public utterances. On 20 April, before the team drew 0-0 at home to West Ham, he was quoted as saying: 'We're clearly in trouble and if we go down, that boy's got a lot to answer for.'

For the Oldham game, Nelson used the programme itself to vent his feelings: "The Mike Flanagan issue has also had a profound effect on the club and despite working hard we were unable to finalise the situation before the transfer deadline which would have enabled us to strengthen the team.

"Charlton Athletic has acted honorably throughout this matter contrary to some reports in the newspapers, and have nothing to be ashamed of.

"We believe that at the end of the day our handling of the situation will reflect credit on the club."

He continued: "We are aware that we could go down and the chairman and myself have discussed the situation at some length. Our ambition will in no way be diminished if this happens and it will still be our aim to produce an excellent team in an excellent stadium."

Charlton defeated Oldham 2-0, but even that victory left them in the hands of others and their survival ultimately depended on the failure of clubs around them with games to play.

With the issue of Flanagan's future unresolved between the two American clubs, Flanagan spent his long months of inactivity working for his father's industrial painting and decorating business. At last an English club stepped in to try to break the American impasse. On Wednesday, 16 May, Manchester City made a bid of £750,000. But the saga continued. Flanagan turned the offer down because he wanted to stay in the London area. At the same time, it was reported that Crystal Palace, the Second Division champions that season, were interested, but at a lower figure.

On Wednesday, 1 August, the saga, which had dragged on for seven months, finally ended with Palace agreeing to pay £650,000 for Flanagan. The player was in Cork at the time for the birthday celebrations of his 100-year-old grandfather. He broke off the stay for a day, to travel to London. Amongst the Palace officials waiting to meet him was Arnie Warren, later to become Charlton general manager.

There was another future Charlton connection too. Palace had already paid £450,000 to Queen's Park Rangers for Gerry Francis to prepare for the First Division, and they raised part of the Flanagan money by selling teenager Steve Mackenzie to Malcolm Allison's Manchester City for £300,000. Mackenzie, who had not even appeared in the Palace first team, was later to become a key First Division player with Charlton.

Part of the cash Charlton received went to signing Nicky Johns permanently from Tampa Bay Rowdies for £100,000. Colin Powell was bought back from the New England Teamen for £30,000, and the Millwall midfield player, Phil Walker, was signed for £120,000.

The saga may have been over but its after-effects lingered on. Nelson's managership never again reached its previous pinnacles and the club failed to shake off the disastrous form it had run into. Morale is a delicate thing in any team game, hard to create and even harder to restore, as the club was to find to their cost.

The Changing Valley

THE aim of 'an excellent team' in Nelson's programme notes was now a long way off, but the club was at last turning The Valley into the sort of stadium it should have been decades previously. But necessity had been the cause.

In 1977 had come into force an act that was to have ominous consequences for many clubs — and for no club more so than Charlton Athletic.

It was the Safety of Sports Ground Act, and the capacity of the once mighty Valley dropped more than for any other League ground. Down went the maximum attendance figure from 66,000 to only 20,000. In January 1981, it fell even lower to the ludicrously low level of 13,000, thanks to an edict from the Greater London Council which had to license the club under the Act.

The Act was an extreme one. In no way would a crowd of 20,000 plus been dangerous in such a large stadium with such space. But it revealed only too starkly the years of physical decline at The Valley.

The real problem was the vast decaying terraces. The lack of entrances close to the mighty East Terrace was another problem in this more safety-conscious era. The directors were forced to take action and the solution was a smaller stadium with more seats. Between 1978 and 1981, there were three major projects undertaken with the eventual aim of an all-seater stadium. The distinctive roof of the West Stand

Andy Nelson, whose managership of Charlton never again reached its previous pinnacle following the Hales-Flanagan incident.

147

Colin Powell
made over 300
League appear-
ances for Charl-
ton in two spells
either side of
playing for the
New England
Teamen in the
NASL.

with its four gables was replaced in 1979 with modern but characterless cover. The club had considered the expensive option of replacing the West Stand but, after being advised that the structure of the old stand was basically sound, they decided to go ahead with the new roof instead. In another project, seats were put in the covered terrace area of the North Stand. The terrace was closed for a time early in 1981 while the seating was installed.

The most dramatic development of all was a new stand which was erected on the South Bank, covering the old terrace area with modern concrete. It was officially opened on 18 August 1981, as an all-seater stand. It was named the Jimmy Seed Stand, in a belated tribute to the great man. The new Jimmy Seed Stand was alas to prove, not a sign of better things to come but a death knell.

The Jimmy Seed Stand had a capacity of 8,000 and the total improvements gave The Valley a total of 10,000 seats. Unfortunately, at the same time a periphery fence was built around three sides of the ground with only the West Stand excepted. This was in line with modern safety requirements, but it wrecked many viewpoints of the ground and made The Valley, hitherto a basic but friendly ground, much colder in atmosphere and even a little sinister.

A new training ground was also acquired at Eltham with the laudable hope of producing more young talent for the club. The idea at the time was also to use it as a sports and leisure centre for supporters and the local community.

A new public-address system was put in and the total bill came to about £450,000. The safety work required by the GLC after the cutdown of capacity in January 1981 would have totalled another £500,000. The safety work would have restored the capacity to a respectable 44,000. Some of the funding would have been from the Football Grounds Improvement Trust, but first the club had to find the money upfront — a difficult task.

There were other plans for further improvements. According to director Bill Jenner, writing in the club's 75th anniversary handbook: 'Exciting though these developments are, however, they are merely the start.'

One project was for wings to be added on both sides of the West Stand. The plans were actually drawn up and the building was to be in two stages. The first on the south side of the West Stand was for a wing comprising new dressing-rooms, a medical room, laundry and players' lounge on the ground floor and 'sophisticated' spectator facilities on the first floor.

This would then have released space in the main West Stand for a major overhaul, so that all the club's administration could be concentrated on the ground floor and an executive club and restaurant installed on the first floor.

It was also proposed to rebuild the Valley Grove turnstiles in a new position adjoining the new wing of the West Stand. A new wall would also be erected on the north side of the West Stand to make the stadium more compact and create a wide concourse with more parking space.

This first stage also envisaged an assault on the problems of the East Terrace under the new ground safety regulations. The rear terraces would be removed to make a wide walk-way with more spectator facilities. There would also be improved access at the Bartram Gate, the main entrance to the club.

The second stage would be the building of a north wing on the West Stand which would accommodate a souvenir shop and first-aid and police rooms on the ground floor. The existing West Stand would then be refaced to match the new wings.

There was even a third stage, described as 'still in embryo' in this grand scheme of things. That was to convert the old North Stand into a double-decker with seating on the upper tier and a roof matching the West and South Stands.

This was, alas, the proverbial 'stuff of which dreams are made'. At the end of the 1979-80 season, Charlton Athletic dropped once again into the Third Division with the joint lowest points total in their history — 22pts — equalled only in the disastrous last season in the First Division. Although the club was to regain its Second Division status in only 12 months, it was hardly an auspicious start for the dream of a new Valley. And the plans simply melted away in the club's new financial troubles.

The 1979-80 season set another low as well. The team won only six League matches all season, one fewer than the previous low. There were no away victories and only four points gained from away trips. Every other statistic about the season was also depressing. The six wins at The Valley were the lowest number of victories there for 34 years. And the away haul of four points was only one point better than the previous worst season.

Although Flanagan had scored 16 goals the previous season, Martin Robinson had scored 19, and it was hoped that Robinson and Hales would strike up a partnership along with Walker. But Hales's early absence through injury frustrated this plan.

The season started off disastrously with Charlton being knocked out of the League Cup on aggregate by Fourth Division Peterborough. Then came the first home League match of the season and a 3-0 defeat by Preston North End.

Not until the seventh League game of the season did the team win a game. Shrewsbury were beaten by 2-1, a match which saw the debut of Tony Hazell, an experienced defender signed for £15,000 from Crystal Palace. In the week before the game, the poor start to the season claimed its first casualty with assistant manager, Harry Cripps, leaving the club he had first joined as a player in 1974.

Nelson commented on the club's plight: "It is absolutely up to me now to go out each day with the players and knock them into the sort of team to pull us up the table. I've got to get hold of what's left and shake it together. We haven't won a match yet, and that run has got to stop. We've had a bloody awful 18 months, and, in fact, it is nearly two years since we did anything."

For Nelson, the decision to part with Cripps must have been particularly painful. They had been friends for over 20 years and lived in the same road.

Shortly after Cripps's departure, there was one small bright note to the season, with the signing, on 1 October on a three-year contract, of the 17-year-old Paul Walsh. Walsh had joined the club in April that year and made his debut as a substitute against Shrewsbury at The Valley on 22 September, in the 2-1 win.

A New Saga — of Managerial Control

OCTOBER saw the return to The Valley of Charlton's last England international, Mike Bailey, who was appointed chief coach. In effect, he appeared to be the new manager, replacing Andy Nelson, as he was given 'complete control of the training, coaching and selection of the playing staff.'

Nelson was now to devote 'more time to the club's

Andy Nelson (left) and Mike Bailey.

Opposite: Johnny Ostergaard and Vigo Jacobsen with the Danish flag.

financial and business interests'. It seemed obvious that Nelson's tenure on the title of 'manager' could not last long, although he stated in the programme that Bailey 'was my choice as the club's new chief coach'.

Unfortunately, the board had created confusion at the club, unsettling things even more after the Flanagan-Hales incident and its long aftermath.

Bailey, now 37, had spent 15 months as player-manager of Hereford United in the Fourth Division. He had previously been assistant manager and coach with the Minnesota Kicks in the United States, where he went after leaving Wolves. The Kicks manager was the former Birmingham City boss, Freddie Goodwin.

There was a brief flourish under the new coach, with home wins against Cardiff and Oldham and a draw at Preston, before the club slipped back into losing ways.

At the time of Bailey's arrival, the club turned to the contacts it had made in Denmark, perhaps hoping for a Scandinavian boost similar to that given by the amazing Hans Jeppson many years earlier. Charlton signed two Danes — a burly striker, Johnny Ostergaard (24) in October from Ikast, where he had scored 22 goals the previous season, and a midfielder, Vigo Jacobsen (25) from the Kastrup club in November. The versatile Ostergaard was also a Danish ice-hockey international.

The signings were the result of a six-week tour of Scandinavia by Benny Fenton, now styled as the club's European scout. Both players were put on contract until June 1982.

Jacobsen made his debut in the home game against West Ham on 1 December with Ostergaard as substitute. Charlton were then one off the bottom place in Division Two.

Danish flags flew on the floodlight pylons and they heralded what was probably Charlton's best game of the season. The Hammers were beaten 1-0, but in the following matches, the team's performances again tailed away and both Danes failed to match up to the demands of English League football. Jacobsen was to make only nine full appearances that season and Ostergaard seven.

The only other result to compare with the West Ham one was just before Christmas, when Leicester City, the eventual division champions, were beaten 2-0.

Charlton's appalling League season was reflected with a vengeance in the FA Cup. In the opening game of the competition, in the third round at fellow Second Division side Wrexham, on 5 January 1980, Charlton suffered the worst Cup defeat in the club's history, going down by 6-0. Coach Mike Bailey blamed his own tactics:

"The heavy defeat was in many ways my own fault and on reflection I probably made the wrong tactical decisions at half-time.

"I demanded that we kept attacking and get forward and felt that we had a chance of nicking a goal, but this style of play left us open at the back and Wrexham took full advantage of the gaps we left."

Even the third-round draw had gone wrong for Charlton in an amazing mistake when the teams were drawn out of the hat on Monday, 16 December. The teams from the First and Second Divisions were as usual numbers 1 to 44 in the draw in alphabetical order. Or they should have been. But Wolves and Wrexham were mistakenly transposed. Instead of being number 43, Wolves were numbered 44. Wrexham were 43 instead of 44. The draw was Notts County versus Wrexham and Wolves versus Charlton. But then the mistake was found and the draw amended to read Notts County versus Wolves and Wrexham versus Charlton. So Bailey missed the chance to go back to his old club.

The Wrexham debacle was to have an amazing repercussion and bring to a head the management confusion at the club. On Tuesday, 14 January, Bailey was told that Nelson was again being given the responsibility of selecting the side. Naturally there were problems with Bailey debating whether to quit Charlton. He was in the difficult position of buying a house after moving his family from the Midlands.

On Thursday, 17 January, came two more developments in this latest unhappy saga. The players were reported in the Press to be unhappy at Nelson taking on team selection again. And a meeting of the board passed a vote of confidence in Nelson, confirming that Bailey 'was appointed ten weeks ago as chief coach — not team manager — with responsibilities to the manager, Mr Andy Nelson.' But the board stated they hoped Bailey would stay with the club.

Bailey decided to make a decision after the League match at Wrexham on the following Saturday, where he joined the team from his home in the Midlands and talked over the situation with Nelson.

Although Bailey agreed to stay, it was obvious even to the board that the confused situation they had created was too demoralizing to Bailey and the players to continue.

So it was Nelson who proved the managerial casualty. The parting of the ways came on 25 March, with only eight League games to go, bringing to an end Nelson's six-and-a-half-year reign as manager. Mike Bailey, who had a three-year contract as coach, took over the official managerial reins, although only on a 'temporary' basis at first.

Nelson blamed his demise on his lack of influence over the players. "I have probably stayed too long with the club," he said.

"I just didn't have the same influence over the players in the last year that I had in the first few years."

Ironically the ending of Nelson's reign coincided that week with the second occasion on which a former Charlton goalkeeper lost the managership of York City. Charlie Wright followed the way of his predecessor, Sam Bartram.

On Friday, 28 March, Bailey was officially named as manager. But the ending of the confusion at the top came too late to halt the decline. The dismal season continued unabated and the final 12 games failed to produce a single win.

There were few things to remember with satisfaction that season but one was the consistency of defender Les Berry, who had switched the previous season from full-back to the centre-half role. He was the only player to appear in all 42 League games and was deservedly voted as Player of the Year by the supporters. At the end-of-season dance, Les made sure everyone could celebrate by taking the trophy round Woolwich Town Hall and asking everyone to have a drink from it — the only cup of cheer that season for Charlton's demoralized supporters.

But success and failure are all part of the football coin and the end of the season saw the departure on a free transfer of defender David Campbell, for whom the same bright future had been predicted as was already being forecast for Paul Walsh.

Sadly, down with Charlton went Burnley, their opponents in the 1947 FA Cup Final. They finished second to bottom with Fulham, the third club to be relegated.

As in times past, the voice of the club as expressed in the programme seemed to accept relegation with almost complacency, again simply holding out future hope.

To many Charlton fans, the real problem was that the club seemed content with Second Division and not First Division football for which the end logic of such apparent complacency was relegation from the Second.

It was left to club statistican, Colin Cameron, to strike a more accurate and franker note in a more obscure part of the programme:

'Third Division football is not good enough fare to offer this district with its vast potential, and in these dark days our aims, and our ambitions, must be rekindled! If with respect, clubs such as Carlisle, Orient, Brighton and Crystal Palace can reach the First Division, it should not be beyond Charlton who, after all, spent half of their first 30 seasons as one of the elite 22.

'So if you are not only sad, but angry, at the sight of our club being relegated, I am particularly pleased because if you are not angry it only indicates resigned acceptance of the situation, and this must never happen.'

But after just one season, the club was back in the Second Division and Mike Bailey looked to be on his way as a permanently successful manager of Charlton.

Paul Walsh in action against Watford in 1980.

151

Same Again for Promotion

SURPRISINGLY, Bailey announced to the Press at the start of the 1980-81 season that he would stick by his playing staff 'and make better players of them'. For a team that had so abysmally failed the previous season, that seemed a rash act of loyalty. But promotion was achieved with virtually the same set of players whose performance had seen the club relegated.

The shining difference was the inclusion of the young star Paul Walsh, who had featured in the team towards the end of the previous season and in the 1980-81 season began to demonstrate fully his precocious potential.

On the debit side, the Danes faded out with Jacobsen playing no further part in the first team and Ostergaard only starting one game.

The impact of Paul Walsh was seen in the opening League Cup games against Brentford. He scored in the 3-1 defeat at Griffin Park and then got a hat-trick in the second leg at The Valley, Charlton running out winners by 5-0. Derek Hales scored the other two.

Unusually, Brentford were the opponents in all three opening games of the season, being Charlton's first opponents in the League after the Cup games. They were beaten 3-1 at The Valley.

The next game, a 2-1 victory away at Newport, ended a dismal sequence of two years and 34 away games without a win. The last win had been at Oldham in December, 1978. Incredibly, the last time Charlton had opened a season with two League wins was as far back as 1953-4.

A 1-1 draw away at Plymouth was followed by four more victories — two in the League and two in the League Cup — before a 2-0 defeat at Millwall. But Charlton fans were intolerant of their team's demise into Third Division football whatever the success on the field. Attendances in this opening spell hovered around the 4,000 and 5,000 levels and, after a fall away in the early season form with four successive defeats including a League Cup defeat against West Ham, they dropped to just 3,359 for the visit of Walsall in a midweek game on 7 October. But by then, the team was on the start of a remarkable run.

The last of the successive defeats had been by 4-3 at Exeter at the end of September. Nicky Johns now displaced Jeff Woods in goal for the following game at Barnsley — a 0-0 draw. The result heralded a revival in form which was to see Charlton go 15 League games without defeat, with 28 points gained out of 30. The 2-0 win over Walsall followed the Barnsley game.

The run, a record one in the club's history, continued until 31 December when the team, by now firmly established as leaders of the table, went down 1-0 at Oxford. The previous League record had been 13 games in 1927. A second record of seven successive League wins was also set during the run with a 1-0 victory at Huddersfield on 1 November.

The form of the young Walsh inevitably attracted the attention of a number of First Division clubs and already Bailey was having to issue 'hands off' statements.

The month of October saw Bailey win the Bells Whisky Third Division Manager of the Month award and Walsh accept the *London Evening Standard* Footballer of the Month award. Bailey was to win the Bells award again in January, yet another 'double' month for the club with Nicky Johns taking the *London Evening Standard* award. Walsh was to

establish himself as a regular in the England Youth team during the season.

In November, Bailey made his first signing — the Spurs defender Terry Naylor, aged 31, on a free transfer after 11 years at White Hart Lane.

Off the field came a surprising piece of news in December. Following Fulham's apparently successful attempt at launching a Rugby League team, Charlton were reported to be interested in joining the Rugby League. Crystal Palace had already applied to join.

Charlton secretary, Bill Stevens, said the club's inquiry was of a 'tentative' nature. "We have just been looking into how a rugby club is organized and financed," he said. The closing date for applications for the following season was 31 March.

In January, Charlton announced their first-ever sponsorship deal. It was with the Orpington-based FADS company, one of the largest paint and wallpaper firms in the country.

The firm's chief executive, Malcolm Stanley, was

a lifelong supporter and the firm already supported the club extensively by ground and programme advertising. The deal was launched with a champagne party at The Valley on Tuesday, 13 January, and the FADS logo was worn for the first time in the game against Plymouth at The Valley on 31 January.

The deal was for two and a half years and Charlton were to get £4,000 by the end of the season and a total of £40,000 if they were promoted. The deal could be worth up to £70,000 if they reached the First Division.

It was also during January that the club officially confirmed plans for an all-seater stadium and announced that seats were to be installed behind both goals.

Charlton also hoped to boost their finances by holding a regular open-market in the car-park on Thursdays. A similar scheme had been tried three years previously but failed. This time, the club brought in an outside firm, Countrywide Markets,

to run it. The market was officially opened by the comedy actress Barbara Windsor on 19 March.

On the field, the team were also going well in the FA Cup, reaching the fifth round for the first time since 1976. They were drawn to play Ipswich Town at Portman Road on 19 February. Some 5,000 fans travelled to East Anglia to see the team go down 2-0 to an Ipswich team who headed the First Division at the time.

There was a peculiar episode on Saturday, 14 March, when Charlton turned out at Sheffield United's ground at Bramall Lane, wearing a Sheffield Wednesday strip. It resulted from the new world of shirt sponsorship which brought problems no one had quite envisaged. Water swamped the ground after heavy rainfall in South Yorkshire. The game was allowed to go but not the fixture at nearby Millmoor, the home of promotion rivals Rotherham United, where the pitch was declared waterlogged. Yorkshire Television had been due to cover the Millmoor game but switched instead to Bramall Lane.

Eltham smiles. Charlton players during a training session before the FA Cup game against Ipswich Town in February 1981. From left: Lawrie Madden, Derek Hales, Colin Powell, Les Berry and Dick Tydeman.

Terry Naylor was Mike Bailey's first signing as Charlton manager.

Nicky Johns, named in the PFA's Third Division team.

inspired United, against what looked like their historic rivals, rather than Charlton, who went down by 3-2.

The following day in London, Derek Hales and Nicky Johns had the honour of being named in the Third Division award team at the Professional Footballers' Association annual dinner.

Charlton were looking certainties for promotion after two successive away victories at the end of March, against Blackpool and Reading, put them on the 54-point mark. Then they began to flounder, with four defeats in a row, the first of which — 2-1 to Huddersfield at The Valley — saw them lose the leadership to Rotherham. That game was followed by a 3-0 defeat at Millmoor.

A 0-0 draw at home against Oxford left Charlton needing to win in the penultimate game at Carlisle on Saturday, 25 April, to clinch promotion.

A large amount of snow had fallen around Carlisle that April weekend, but the Brunton Park pitch was in perfect condition. Some 400 Charlton fans made the journey by rail and road for the game. At half-time, Charlton were 2-0 up, Walsh scoring after 18 minutes from a Colin Powell pass, and then Martin Robinson netting in the 40th minute from a Powell free-kick.

But the game was still not over and, after Carlisle, with a strong wind at their backs, got one back 14 minutes from time, there were some anxious moments.

The Carlisle side included a young Peter Beardsley, the future England international, playing his last game before going to America. He hit a free-kick against the bar in the second half.

The 2-1 victory was Charlton's 11th away victory of the season, the club's highest total in League football. Carlisle had also been beaten twice in the League Cup and at The Valley in the League, making them the first League opponents Charlton had beaten four times in a season.

One strange aside to the victory was that it was Charlton's first win in FADS shirts. They had either lost or drawn in them previously — or else they had appeared on television, as they did several times, and had been prevented from wearing the shirts.

In fact, Malcolm Stanley in desperation even offered to let them wear plain shirts for the Carlisle game, an offer that was refused.

Stanley often travelled to away matches in his own executive plane and one of his passengers to Carlisle was Michael Gliksten, who, with promotion assured, then departed on a three-week business trip to Australia.

For the team, train travel was the means of transport in those days and they were given a boisterous, happy reception when they arrived back at Carlisle Station. They had to almost fight their way on to the platform through the delighted supporters. The manager made a point of kissing all the women supporters who had made the journey. On the train, the celebrations continued with the team sharing champagne with the supporters. The celebrations were boisterous and spirited but good-natured in the Charlton tradition, the police congratulating everyone on their excellent behaviour.

Victory in the last match, 2-1 at home to Gillingham, saw Charlton finish with 59 points, being pipped for second place by Barnsley on goal-difference. Rotherham were champions with 61 points.

The game, action-packed and full of goalmouth incident, was a fitting climax to the season with the

At that time, the commercial television companies and the BBC were adamantly against sponsored shirts appearing on the nation's television screens, yet all Charlton had with them was their FADS crested change strip — Sheffield United also wore red. And Yorkshire Television would not tolerate the situation.

The problem was solved by the television company going to Hillsborough and getting a strip from Wednesday for Charlton to wear. The strip evidently

Gillingham team sportingly providing a guard of honour as Charlton went on to the pitch. Although the club had not gone up as champions, as seemed certain at one time, that did not abate the enthusiasm on the pitch after the game. The players threw their shirts into the crowd and then gathered in the directors' box with Mike Bailey to acknowledge the cheers of the fans.

On top of the long unbeaten run and the seven successive games without defeat, the season had also set yet another record. The Charlton goals-against column in the 46 League games was only 44, beating the club's previous League low of 45 for the 42 matches played in 1923-4.

There was still doubt over whether the team could prosper in the Second Division so quickly after the disastrous showing of the season before. But, as always with Charlton, fate was never simple and upset was at hand before the club resumed its career in the Second Division.

Celebrations after promotion at Carlisle in April 1981. Back left: Terry Naylor, Lawrie Madden, Dick Tydeman, Colin Powell (obscured). Front (left to right): Nicky Johns, Paul Walsh, Martin Robinson (obscured), physiotherapist Charlie Hall (hand clenched), coach John Collins, Kevin Smith (with bottle), Paul Elliott (in tie), Steve Gritt (with bottle), Phil Warman, assistant manager Benny Fenton and Leroy Ambrose.

Left: Phil Warman. Right: Lawrie Madden.

155

The Crisis Years

TOWARDS the end of the promotion season Michael Gliksten had given the *Kentish Independent* some estimate of just what it was costing him to run Charlton Athletic. Despite the season's success, attendances were almost the same as they had been in the dismal relegation season — an average of 7,206 against 7,175 — and rarely exceeding the 10,000 mark and often far below.

Gliksten stated that the general expenses of the club came to £180,000 a year. These expenses covered repairs, pitch maintenance, team travelling expenses, medical and sports equipment, ticket costs, administration, electricity, Value Added Tax and police.

Gate money brought in £305,000 a year and sponsorship and other income provided an extra £80,000. A figure for wages was not given, but Gliksten said that the club was running at a £140,000 yearly deficit, which he was covering.

Gliksten pursued the idea of making the market in the club grounds a Sunday market, as part of a plan to raise a further £320,000 of finance for ground improvements. The immediate purpose of the hoped-for-money from the market venture was to replace The Valley turf — a surface long regarded as one of the best in the League — with an all-weather pitch to expand the commercial and sporting use of the stadium.

It was in May that the club announced they were exploring the 'exciting possibilities' of such a pitch. This was the period in which Queen's Park Rangers were preparing for the installation of their artificial pitch at Loftus Road, the first-ever in the Football League, a move that was the talk of the football world and of great controversy.

But with Charlton, it remained purely an idea. The Sunday market failed, to Gliksten's bitter regret, to get approval from the council and the consequence was that the plan for the artificial pitch was abandoned.

Gliksten's plans also saw the return of Andy Nelson, who had been out of a job since leaving the club. He was appointed commercial manager at the Valley Leisure training ground in Eltham. There were two full-sized pitches and five-a-side pitches at Eltham and the facilities were to be open to the public with new amenities planned. It was stressed that Nelson would have no role in the club's playing side. On to the board came Richard Collins, a chartered surveyor, whom Gliksten had asked to oversee the Valley Leisure operation.

Sam Bartram Dies

WITHIN two months, in the summer of 1981, Charlton suffered the deaths of two of their most famous servants. In June, Bert Turner died at Margate. He had retired the previous year as landlord of the Jolly Farmers pub at Manston, after the death of his wife.

His death was followed, in July, by that of Sam Bartram at the age of 67 — one of football's greatest characters and still lovingly remembered. Sam had been present at the promotion celebrations against Gillingham — the last time he had seen Charlton play.

He died on Friday, 17 July, just a month before the official opening of the stand named after his manager and colleague, Jimmy Seed, on Tuesday, 18 August. Sam's funeral took place at Harpenden in Hertfordshire on Monday, 27 July.

As the Charlton stars of yesteryear gathered for the opening of the new stand, along with such great personalities as Sir Stanley Rous and Sir Matt Busby, it was impossible not to feel the absence of Sam Bartram. Don Welsh, Peter Croker, George Green, Harold Hobbis, Frank Lock, Frank Rist, John Evans and Maurice Tadman were among those attending, as well as players of later eras. The opening ceremony was performed by Jimmy Seed's daughter, Gladys Sutton, and among the guests were Seed's grandson, Jamie, and former secretary George Hicks and his son, Marshall, who was named after Seed's middle name. On that happy day, no one could have foreseen how shortlived was to be the life of the stand, far shorter indeed than the career of the legend after whom it was named.

On the playing side, an earthquake in the club's affairs came in June with the departure of the promotion hero, Mike Bailey, who became manager of First Division Brighton. It was entirely unexpected and it seemed from Bailey's comments as if the tangle over responsibilities with Nelson at the start had created insecurity and a rift that had never quite healed.

He stated that he had 'always felt I was on trial at The Valley' and was disappointed, after obtaining promotion, not to be rewarded with a three-year contract in place of the ten months to run on his

Michael Gliksten
and Alan Mullery
toast success on
Mullery's
appointment in
July 1981.

existing agreement. Michael Gliksten's response was that Bailey had not asked for a contract replacement and Charlton had offered him an unsolicited increase in salary and an offer of re-negotiation of his contract when it expired.

Whatever the rights and wrongs, the blow was a grievous one as Bailey had set a style and sense of direction for the club. And for him personally, the move to Brighton was to signal the quick end of a managerial career that might have lasted longer had he stayed at The Valley.

The Brighton vacancy had come about through a row between chairman Mike Bamber and manager Alan Mullery, who walked out of the club and was tipped to take over the managership of West Bromwich Albion. But the outcome turned out to be a straight swop between the clubs, with Mullery joining Charlton in July.

He was interviewed by both Charlton and First Division West Bromwich Albion, but West Brom kept him hanging on whilst the board made up their minds. The Charlton job was on immediate offer so he took it. The Charlton approach was made, ironically, through the former manager, Andy Nelson.

Mullery was a distinguished former England international and Spurs and Fulham player and, like Bailey, his stay with the club was to be a brief one. The strange events of his brief year's stay with the club are recalled in an autobiography he wrote in 1985.

Mullery recalled how he had arranged to meet Gliksten — 'an Old Etonian and a lovely man' — at a Chelsea restaurant. Gliksten had actually gone to Marlborough, but the impression was undoubtedly public school.

Mullery used these words in his autobiography: 'Gliksten charmed me with his style and delighted me with his enthusiasm for the club and football. Most importantly of all, he seemed desperate for me to have the job.'

While West Bromwich delayed, Gliksten rang Mullery at home and asked for an answer within 24 hours. Mullery sat down with his former Brighton assistant manager, Ken Craggs, and their wives and debated the question.

The next morning, he contacted the former Charlton director, Bill Smith, to seek his advice.

Smith's answer was this. If he took over at Charlton and made a hash of the job, there would be no pressure on him. "No one will expect miracles at The Valley", he said, although he added that he regarded the club as a 'sleeping giant'.

Mullery had had two years in the First Division with Brighton when he took the Second Division Charlton job. Gliksten was delighted and the Press conference to announce the appointment was 'full of champagne corks, ambitions and back-slapping', to use Mullery's own description.

Gliksten acted generously, matching Mullery's Brighton salary and gave him a three-year contract and a company car.

Mullery recalled: 'As I walked into Charlton for the first time, I knew I was happy with Michael Gliksten. He was my type of person. I trusted him and he was confident that we were going to be good for each other. "We are a good partnership," he said. "Let's get going."

Gliksten had told him that the club did not have much money to operate in the transfer market. Bill Stevens, the secretary, whom Mullery had known as assistant secretary at Tottenham, confirmed that the club were struggling financially and had to cut back wherever possible.

Ken Craggs, also a former Fulham player and who had been with Mullery at Brighton, was appointed assistant manager.

Stevens, meanwhile, left to take a job outside football and in his place came John Stacey, who at 54 gave up his job as Metropolitan Police chief superintendent and head of Bexley Police Division — the first police officer to join the administrative staff of a Football League club.

The Coming of Hulyer

BUT it was on his first full day at The Valley that Mullery had an eventful and fateful meeting — with a young man called Mark Hulyer. Mullery was on the telephone in his office checking out the availability of certain players when an XJS Jaguar pulled up on the forecourt and a smart young man, dressed in an expensive coat, got out and walked into the reception area.

He asked who was in charge, and as the chairman was away on business, Mullery said he supposed he was. According to Mullery's description of the event in his autobiography, Hulyer handed him a cheque for £50,000 made out to Charlton Athletic Football Club and said it was a gift.

Mullery asked him why and Hulyer told him he had supported Charlton since he was 11.

Mullery relates that Hulyer told him: 'The only thing I require in exchange is five years advertising for my company across the face of the Main Stand.'

Mullery checked the money out with Hulyer's bank, telephoned Gliksten and the deal was done. The Hulyer presence, so dramatically started, was to grow and grow.

Across the face of the Main Stand duly appeared a sign advertising the Hulyer company, Marman. Meanwhile, Mullery immediately set about making playing changes at the club, despite the club's promotion success. He signed six players in three weeks — Don McAllister from Spurs, Steve Harrison from Watford, Leighton Phillips from Swansea, John Phillips from Brighton, Billy Lansdowne from West Ham, and Phil Ferns from Bournemouth.

McAllister was a highly experienced defender who had become a free agent as a result of a Spurs contract error. Harrison was Watford's captain and left-back. Leighton Phillips was a Welsh international defender. His namesake, goalkeeper John Phillips, from Brighton, had also been with Chelsea for eight years. Lansdowne was a midfielder and Ferns a left-back. Departures were Phil Warman to Millwall and Dick Tydeman and Colin Powell

From left: Don McAllister, Billy Lansdowne and Phil Ferns.

to Gillingham, where Keith Peacock had taken over as manager.

On Tuesday, 25 August, the new public facilities at the Eltham training ground were officially opened by the chairman of the Sports Council, Dickie Jeeps. They comprised an all-weather playing surface, three five-a-side pitches and two netball courts. The all-weather pitch cost £90,000, of which £70,000 came from a Sports Council grant. Appointed as recreational director at the complex from the end of the year was a former Austrian international player, Danish national manager and Hvidovre club manager, Ernst Netuka.

In July, Charlton had also announced further plans for The Valley, a set of ten executive boxes to be installed at the rear of the Main Stand with an estimated annual revenue of almost £30,000.

With this intensity of activity off the field as well as on, it looked as if Charlton were taking on new life and that Michael Gliksten was energetically

Leighton Phillips (left) and John Phillips (right).

forging a new future for the club. No one foresaw, or imagined in their wildest dreams, the tragedies to come in such a short space of time.

Charlton lost their first game of 1981-2, 3-0 at Luton, but the first home game of the season saw a 2-0 win over Blackburn and the team's play steadily improved. Paul Walsh and Derek Hales began to combine well and both scored goals. The 17-year-old Paul Elliott, who captained England to victory in the European Youth Championships in Yugoslavia in September, established himself in the side and put on some fine performances in the central defence.

Regular videos of Charlton home matches were now made for the first time, shot by the Finches Leisure Sports concern of Forest Hill. And a luxury coach, used by the England team, now took the place of the train for away travel.

It was around Christmas that things started to go really well. In 15 matches from 28 December, Charlton lost only once and moved up to sixth place. Mullery and Craggs could sense a Brighton-type 'miracle' again. Craggs told Mullery: "We are going to get promoted. It is a miracle but if we keep going like this, we'll do it."

Meanwhile, the presence of Hulyer troubled Mullery more and more. According to Mullery, he was not only in the boardroom after matches, but was also on the coach with the players, becoming 'one of the lads'.

Mullery commented in his autobiography: 'He threw his money around and I couldn't understand why a 28-year-old man (*sic*) of substance should behave like an excited fan. He was younger than some of the players and although they seemed to get on with him, deep down I had my doubts about this man who had arrived from nowhere and in a few months had become part of the furniture.' But it was with Michael Gliksten that Mullery claimed he ran into difficulties as he sought to buy two players to boost the club's gallop up the table and push for promotion, one of the players being Scottish international, Archie Gemmill, of Derby County and Nottingham Forest fame.

According to Mullery, Gliksten apologized to him and said that had he had the money, he would have backed him all the way.

Mullery recalls: 'And how could I feel bitter? Here was a man who loved Charlton and had kept the club afloat for years with large chunks of his own money. But Gliksten had put his hand in his pocket for the last time.'

In fact, one player was signed at the start of 1982, and that was the former Millwall midfielder, Dave Mehmet, from the NASL club, Tampa Bay Rowdies, for £80,000.

Mullery broke the news of the rejection to Craggs, whose reaction was that they should look for another job.

The despondency of the two men seemed to rub off on the players. During the next 11 games, Charlton won only once and dropped to finish the season in 13th place.

End of the Dynasty

CLOSE on these events followed the end of Gliksten's direct involvement with Charlton and the end of the Gliksten dynasty.

Gliksten contacted Mullery to tell him that Hulyer had bought all his shares in the club and he was going to resign. The sell-out in June 1982 was actually to the Marman company, of which Hulyer was

Dave Mehmet.

Mark Hulyer takes over, pictured here with fellow directors (from left) Bill Jenner, Peter Crystal, Richard Collins, Hulyer, Malcolm Stanley, Michael Gliksten.

Mark Hulyer — a tempestuous reign as chairman.

managing director. But what Gliksten had not sold was The Valley itself. Thus the ownership of ground and club was split for the first time in The Valley's history and thus were the first seeds of the crisis sown.

The development plans Gliksten had been promoting at the season's start had seemed full of optimism and hope. But the season itself had been a very disillusioning one in attendances, part of a general steep fall throughout the League in the early 1980s.

The club's normal attendances were now down to just over 5,000 and an ominous and prophetic headline appeared in the *News of the World* on Sunday, 28 February 1982, after the 1-0 win over Shrewsbury Town, which attracted only 4,575 spectators. It was 'Death Valley' accompanied by a picture of the sparse terraces.

On Saturday, 6 February, just 9,972 had watched

Terry Naylor (top) and Leroy Ambrose (bottom) were two of the five players who refused to re-sign after being refused a rise on their basic salaries.

the derby at The Valley against Crystal Palace, which Charlton won 2-1. For the equivalent fixture on 15 September 1964, the crowd had been 31,498. In April came the lowest League gate since the war — 3,379 for the game against Bolton.

The only small consolation was that at least the dwindling number of Charlton fans kept up their long-standing reputation for good behaviour. They were given an award from the M1 Blue Boar service station company for being the best behaved supporters in the land.

The financial straits in which the club found itself was reflected in five players whose contracts had come to end being offered no increase in their basic wage. The five — Terry Naylor, Steve Gritt, Leroy Ambrose, Martin Robinson and Les Berry — all refused to sign.

This was the grim background leading up to the Gliksten resignation, but Gliksten's leaving was a shock nevertheless. And the accession of the virtually unknown Hulyer was an equal surprise. Just nine months before, he had been a terraces spectator, having supported the club since he was a youngster in Eltham. He was 32, not 28 as Mullery had recollected, but he became the youngest chairman in the Football League, as Gliksten himself had once been.

Hulyer publicly pledged to get Charlton into the First Division almost immediately. "As far as I am concerned, it is all or bust to get to the First Division next season." Yet another sadly prophetic statement, but not in the way Hulyer intended.

Gliksten told the Press he had lost some of his enthusiasm and as a 'realist' had decided to hand over control of the club to Hulyer, who had as great a love for the club as he had.

One of the undoubted factors which swayed Gliksten was the farming enterprise he had started in New South Wales in Australia, which was claiming increasing amounts of his time and took him both physically and psychologically away from the day-to-day business of running a struggling football club, which ate away continuously at his assets.

Hulyer's company, Marman, was described as an international trading firm in commodities, including projects in grains and other major food items in South East Asia. It was also involved in power-boat racing sponsorship.

The upshot of these events was Mullery's departure from the club, but the resignation was a messy affair. Comments by Mullery about Charlton angered fans. He was quoted as saying: "I want to manage a First Division club again or a club with the potential to achieve that aim. I don't feel Charlton can provide this. If you look at Charlton's gate, there is not enough interest to achieve very much." The comments were perhaps accurate at the time, but best left unsaid by someone who was departing the club and had spoken such words of hope on his arrival only the length of a season before.

A Bitter Split

THE biggest blow to Mullery was that he had expected his friend and long-term confidante, Ken Craggs, to resign with him and partner him in his next managerial venture — Crystal Palace was to prove the destination. Instead Craggs became manager, unwilling to embark on the next Mullery adventure. Thus ended a seven-year partnership with Mullery which had begun when they were players at Fulham.

The two men shook hands and parted before the managerial offer was made to Craggs. But Mullery was bitter and told Craggs he would never return for him again. He did not speak to him again for a year. The men had known each other for 25 years. It was the wives of the two men who brought them back into contact in the summer of 1983, but they did not work together again in football.

Appointed as player-coach to Craggs was the team captain, Leighton Phillips. Ernst Netuka was given charge of the youth team. Craggs had played for Fulham, then managed Hounslow Town and returned to Fulham as youth-team coach and then first-team coach. He had then gone to Brighton to assist Mullery.

In another appointment, Hulyer installed as managing director Richard Collins, who was given control of the day-to-day running of the club. Besides ownership of The Valley, Gliksten also retained ownership of the Eltham Valley Leisure concern.

Collins, a lifelong supporter, was a 40-year-old chartered surveyor, who had previously lived in Lansdowne Road just behind The Valley. He was senior partner of the Lewisham-based chartered building surveyors, Kennedy and Partners.

New appointments to the board were Peter Crystal, a solicitor whose firm acted for Charlton and Malcolm Stanley, the chairman of shirt sponsors, Fads.

Gliksten remained on the board along with Bill Jenner. Four directors stepped down — Bill Wheeler, Bill Whitehead, George Neighbour and the Dane, Neils Madsen, thus severing Charlton's formal connection with Danish football. The Marman company formed a new subsidiary, Marman Sports, to oversee Charlton and their power-boat activities.

Charlton, who had won the London Midweek League the previous season, now rejoined the Football Combination with Tuesday evening selected for their reserve games.

The new era also saw Paul Elliott, Nicky Johns, David Mehmet and Phil Walker all sign three-year contracts, a positive start indeed for Hulyer. But there was more to come. Welsh international forward Carl

Harris was signed from Leeds United in July for £180,000, followed by midfielder Terry Bullivant from Aston Villa for £100,000. Bullivant was a former Fulham player.

But the fans rising hopes were then subdued in the same month by the sale of Paul Walsh, just 19, to Luton Town in a £500,000 deal. The deal was partly an exchange, with Luton forward Steve White moving to Charlton, with a £250,000 valuation, and Luton paying the £250,000 balance on Walsh's valuation.

Craggs stated that Walsh had wanted to play First Division football, but it was a lasting disappointment to the Charlton faithful that a player of such startling promise should have departed at such a young age.

Walsh had signed a three-year contract at the start of the previous season and had scored 13 goals during

Richard Collins, installed as managing director at The Valley — the start of a fight for the club's survival.

Terry Bullivant (left) and Carl Harris (right) were both six-figure signings as Charlton embarked on a new era.

the season. Steve White had scored 19 Second Division goals and been an ever-present in the Luton side when they won promotion to the First Division, but he was to prove a short-lived replacement for Walsh.

The Arrival of Lawrence

MEANWHILE, the club announced yet another staff appointment which attracted only minor interest at the time, but which was to prove the one worthwhile legacy left to the club from these eventful days. A former Blackheath schoolteacher, Lennie Lawrence, was appointed as reserve-team coach.

Lawrence was coach of Third Division Lincoln City and had previously been Malcolm Allison's assistant at Plymouth Argyle. His appointment followed the departure of the previous reserve-team coach, Ian Salter, to Crystal Palace with Alan Mullery. Lawrence had spontaneously applied for the post after reading of Salter's departure.

During August, the club suffered its final defeat in the battle for a Sunday market at The Valley. It had appealed the previous month at a public inquiry against Greenwich Council's refusal to give permission. The Thursday market was a financial success but the club had also fallen foul of Greenwich Council over a market it started in Eltham, which was closed down under powers granted to the council under a 40-year charter. The charter gave the council powers to close down any market within the borough within seven miles of the market at Beresford Square.

The inspector gave his verdict in August on the Sunday application and turned it down on the grounds of nuisance to local residents. At the inquiry, Richard Collins had given further financial figures about the club. He told the inspector that the club's annual spending was £951,000 against income of £623,000.

Meanwhile, Hulyer was beginning to show signs of his appetite for a big signing with an attempt to recruit the England international Kevin Keegan from Southampton. In company with Craggs and Collins, he flew to Holland where Southampton were on a club tour and had talks with Saints' manager Lawrie McMenemy. Hulyer was quoted as saying he was 'prepared to pay Southampton whatever they wanted'. Keegan was not with the Southampton party and the initiative was to prove too late. As events transpired, he had already been approached by Newcastle United and made up his mind to join them.

The new era heralded a boom in ticket sales and on Sunday, 21 August 1982, six days before the start of the season, the new Hulyer management team met some 4,000 fans at an open day at The Valley. Executive boxes had been installed at the back of the stand and the car-park had been tarmacked. On display was a new away-game coach from Thamesmead Coaches, painted in red and white with the Charlton name and crest on the side. Hulyer confirmed that the idea of Rugby League at The Valley was now dead.

The club also went in for advertising to try to boost support. There was advertising on Friday evening on the two London commercial radio stations, Capital and LBC, and on milk bottles.

The season opened with a 2-1 win at Leicester. It seemed a good augury. It was the first time Charlton had won an away match on the opening day for 46 years. The last time had been in 1936 — a 1-0 victory at Grimsby. The scorer of both goals at Filbert Street was Phil Walker, making his return to League football after a year out following a pelvic operation.

But the good opening was to prove a delusion. Four defeats followed, including a 5-0 thrashing against Wolves at Molineux and a 3-0 defeat at home by Sheffield Wednesday. The fourth defeat, a 1-0 loss at home against Grimsby, was watched by only 4,361 people, the lowest crowd that day in the Second Division. Quite clearly, things were far from what Mark Hulyer had hoped for and his response was an amazing one.

Allan Simonsen

THE club had stabilized a little with a 2-2 draw at Oldham and a 3-0 home win against Fulham. Then it was announced that Charlton were trying to sign Allan Simonsen, the legendary Danish forward who had twice been European Footballer of the Year, from Barcelona. The fee Barcelona were asking was £300,000.

Hulyer, Craggs and Collins flew to Copenhagen to meet Simonsen to discuss personal terms. The connection with Simonsen had come about because of the club's ties with Danish football. Simonsen was friendly with the Charlton youth-team manager, Ernst Netuka, who was manager of Simonsen's home-town club, Veyle, when Simonsen joined them as a 12-year-old. He also managed the Danish national side when Simonsen played.

A fortnight later, on Friday, 15 October, Simonsen signed a two-year contract at a Press conference dramatically staged by Hulyer at a London hotel, with Simonsen smuggled in via a back door so that his entrance at the conference would surprise the waiting reporters and cameramen.

He had just arrived from Spain by plane to Heathrow with Hulyer and Collins. On the Saturday, he was off in the air again, this time with Hulyer by a private aircraft from Biggin Hill in Kent to see Charlton play at the League's furthermost outpost, Carlisle. He could not have been impressed with what he saw as Charlton slumped to a 4-1 defeat.

Simonsen signs, watched by Mark Hulyer (left) and Ken Craggs.

Barcelona's price of £300,000 represented a club record fee for Charlton Athletic. Simonsen, who had first come into prominence in the West German Bundesliga with Borussia Mönchengladbach, was just two months short of his 30th birthday.

Although he had scored the goal which gave Barcelona victory in the European Cup-winners' Cup Final against Standard Liège in May, he had not played a game for Barcelona in the new season because of the club's signing of Diego Maradona from Argentina.

Spanish League rules permitted only two foreign players a club and their names had to be announced at the start of the season. Barcelona's other foreign import was the West German, Bernd Schuster, so Simonsen's career with Barcelona had been effectively ended.

But from a club with attendances of 100,000, Simonsen was going to one with an average gate of only 6,000. It was a signing of high risk, as Hulyer's own comments made clear. He said the club would have to double their attendances to break even, but he was confident of getting more support once Simonsen's influence was felt.

"I will be heartbroken if people do not come and support the team now we have signed Allan.

"We could not have done any more to show our ambition and get back to the First Division."

Hulyer also revealed the fragile nature of the deal. It was only possible because Barcelona were prepared to accept delayed payment of the fee over three years. This contrasted with the Football League's edict to clubs for domestic buys of 50 per cent down and the rest within 12 months. But what Hulyer did not disclose were the personal terms to which Simonsen had agreed and were to prove absolutely beyond Charlton's means.

Despite the signing, Simonsen had yet to receive international clearance and Barcelona had yet to check the bank guarantees Hulyer was depositing, so the expected home debut against Burnley did not take place. Instead Simonsen was introduced to the home fans by Mark Hulyer in language remarkable for a club chairman in the number of expletives used. Charlton won 2-1 and Simonsen saw Derek Hales sent off a minute from time for retaliation, the fourth dismissal Hales had suffered in his Charlton career.

It was not until Tuesday, 9 November 1982, that Simonsen finally appeared on the field in a Charlton shirt — against Swansea Reserves in a Football Combination fixture. And even then, although six weeks had passed, it was a rushed affair. An English

freelance journalist in Spain, Graham Turner, was asked to bring the international clearance papers from the Spanish FA in Madrid. He arrived from Madrid at The Valley just five minutes before kick-off and Simonsen came on as a substitute for 40 minutes. Hulyer and Simonsen made it from Barcelona with just 45 minutes to spare. Some 2,000 fans, instead of the normal 400 for reserve fixtures, watched the game which Charlton won 4-1.

Hitherto, many Charlton fans had assumed the Simonsen signing was a publicity myth and not reality. Now, on the following Saturday, a crowd of 10,807 turned up to see the Dane make his debut against a Middlesbrough side managed by the former Charlton player, Malcolm Allison. Simonsen wore the number-seven shirt and played down both wings, but he was not match fit and still to reach any kind of understanding with his colleagues. Charlton were three down with eight minutes to go when Derek Hales pulled one back. Then with five minutes left, Simonsen scored with a free-kick that went in off the 'Boro defensive wall.

Commented Ken Craggs: "Now all the razzamatazz is over, I want to settle down to just playing football and climbing up the Second Division table." He was doomed to disappointment in a club where events were now moving fast indeed and storing up more and more trouble.

Beside the entry of Allan Simonsen, there were other changes in the club's personnel. At the start of November, defender Mark Aizlewood was signed from Luton Town. Andy Nelson left his commercial post, so finally severing his connection with the club. Then Bill Jenner resigned from the board after 14 years. Into his place stepped the mysterious figure of Chief Francis Nzeribe, an international trader from Nigeria and described as chairman of a company called Fanz International in Mayfair. Despite his international trading background, he had no previous connections with Hulyer or his Marman business as was supposed at the time.

Craggs Sacked

SIMONSEN now missed the next two matches with a hamstring injury but by the time he took the field again, Ken Craggs had gone. Craggs had managed him for one game and had a managerial career lasting just 173 days at Charlton.

The sacking was a classic, even by the strange standards of football. The game following the Middlesbrough match was another home fixture, against Rotherham United, and the Simonsen-less Charlton were thrashed 5-1. They were down 2-1 just before half-time when Steve White was sent off, having first been booked for dissent and then dismissed for elbowing a Rotherham defender in the face. Rotherham went on to dominate the second half and forward Ronnie Moore got a hat-trick, helped by the former Millwall winger, Tony Towner.

Simonsen watched the débâcle from the directors' box. The attendance figure had slumped to 6,761. The defeat left Charlton fifth from bottom of the table and Craggs confided to Peter Burrowes, the *Kentish Independent* sports editor, that he felt his job was on the line. But that Saturday night, it did not appear to be. Hulyer took him out to dinner and, according to Craggs, he was given assurances about his future at the club. Indeed, Hulyer broke off half-way through the dinner to tell a national newspaper that Craggs was staying. Craggs was quoted the next day as saying: "The chairman has assured me that my job is safe."

On the Monday morning, a board statement was

a parting blast at the club, including the ending of the sponsorship deal with his company, the decorating retailers, FADS.

Stanley, managing director of FADS, commented: "We are pulling out because FADS is an upright and clean company. That is something which can no longer be said about soccer. It is a sick sport. We would rather sponsor netball."

It was the departure of Michael Gliksten that was to herald the enormous rift the club was about to undergo. Stanley's words, meanwhile, were a portent of the bitter times ahead.

Several names were now mentioned in the Press as managerial candidates including the former Wolves boss, Ian Greaves, and the Arsenal veteran and former Chelsea defender, John Hollins. In another twist of irony, Mike Bailey was sacked as manager of Brighton shortly after Craggs's dismissal. But there was 'no chance' of his coming back, stated Hulyer.

Lawrence Appointed

BUT the speculation died as Lawrence was handed the managerial job until the end of the season with four of his trial games gone. His managerial qualities began to show through strongly as the team steadied itself and began to pick up points. Simonsen scored four times in his first four games. Lawrence described his appointment as the 'biggest moment' in his life.

"I am delighted and honoured to be manager of a club as big and ambitious as Charlton, and I assure supporters that I will do my best to bring them success," he said.

Few supporters knew him at the time. Even the name seemed almost to have a music-hall feel about it. His first name was actually Robin. But a successor was in the making at last, after so many years, to the great Jimmy Seed. And no manager in English football history could ever have endured the tribulations Lawrence was about to endure and to overcome so triumphantly.

His first problem was Simonsen. Simonsen was

issued, saying the club was parting company with Craggs. Hulyer explained his actions thus: "It was not a straightforward matter. I would never undermine anyone who is employed by the club, and when I had dinner with Ken Craggs on Saturday, he was still part of Charlton.

"It would have been very unfair to tell the media anything other than that he was still the manager.

"But there has been concern about the inconsistent team performances and the 5-1 defeat on Saturday did not help."

Hulyer appointed, as 'caretaker manager' for seven matches, the reserve-team coach Lennie Lawrence. The club's affairs were now causing obvious concern. In December, two more directors left the board — Michael Gliksten and Malcolm Stanley, who fired

Lennie Lawrence takes charge — his first team picture as manager in December 1982. Back row (left to right): Dave Mehmet, Don McAllister, Steve White, Paul Curtis. Middle row: Charlie Hall (physiotherapist), Lennie Lawrence (manager), Geoff Scott, Mark Aizlewood, Billy Lansdowne, Nicky Johns, Paul Elliott, Les Berry, Terry Naylor, Leighton Phillips (player-coach), Bill Gallagher (assistant physiotherapist). Front row: Carl Harris, Kevin Smith, Allan Simonsen, Terry Bullivant, Derek Hales, Steve Gritt, Martin Robinson.

Paul Elliott (top) was another Charlton youngster to make outstanding progress, but he also moved to Luton Town in the footsteps of Paul Walsh (bottom).

undoubtedly a star. The 2-0 defeat of Newcastle at The Valley was watched by an estimated 60 per cent of the Danish population on television, even though United's Kevin Keegan was absent from the anticipated clash of two European Footballers of the Year.

But the attendance for the home game against Barnsley on the dreaded last Saturday shopping day before Christmas fell to just 4,942. There could be no long-term future for a player on Simonsen's personal terms on attendances like that.

By now the financial storm clouds were well and truly gathering. A crowd of 17,000 for a third-round FA Cup tie at The Valley against Ipswich, lost 3-2, briefly stirred hopes, only for them to be dashed the following week when only 6,000 saw the 2-1 victory over Leicester City.

Hulyer said that Charlton were facing the same economic and financial problems as every other club. In this, of course, he was wrong in that few other clubs had taken the kind of speculative gamble on Simonsen that his regime had witnessed. But it was undoubtedly true that, against a background of national economic troubles, these were grim times for football, with attendances plunging.

But now Hulyer began to hint of the troubles ahead and to shed his buoyant image. He commented: "Our supporters should not be lulled into thinking that Charlton can't go out of business. I am disappointed with the public's response and worried about the situation."

Hulyer, who had now lost most of his board of directors, also appealed forlornly for three new directors to come on to the board and make a substantial cash input.

On the playing side, there was the first departure under Lennie Lawrence's management with Leighton Phillips, the player-coach, leaving the club after continuing injury problems failed to clear up.

There followed a disastrous 7-1 defeat at Burnley, when Charlton, reduced to nine men after Hales and Aizlewood were sent off, conceded five goals in the last 13 minutes.

Then, in the week after the defeat, on Wednesday, 3 March 1983, a more stunning departure was announced. The young defender, Paul Elliott, followed Paul Walsh to Luton for £150,000. Both youngsters had been outstanding prospects and their quick departures whilst still teenagers, ripped out the hopes of many Charlton supporters. And to add insult, they had gone for fees which looked far too low.

And now it was hinted that Simonsen could be on his way. But it hardly needed a genius to see that, not as a possibility but almost a dead certainty. However, the emerging management talents of Lennie Lawrence were recognized — despite the club's lowly 17th place in the table — with the offer of a contract until the end of the following season.

Open Conflict

IN the same week as Elliott's departure, the simmering discontent between the old and the new owner broke out completely into the open and Charlton fans had the reality of the club's situation forcibly brought home to them. Hulyer had apparently failed to meet the financial terms Gliksten agreed with him. Gliksten now threatened legal action over a sum of £420,000 he claimed he was owed. Hulyer contested the sum, claiming it should be just £54,000, but he admitted he was behind with a payment owed to Gliksten.

Gliksten won a summary judgement in the High Court for the money and then lodged a bankruptcy notice on Hulyer at the Medway High Court Division. Hulyer was given seven days to pay or produce a defence to set aside the judgement. In the event, Gliksten decided to hold off for the time being until the club's future looked clearer.

The precise details of the deal the two men had struck when the club changed hands now emerged. In addition to a £110,000 a year rental payment by the club on The Valley under a 30-year lease, a further financial deal had been agreed. Gliksten had sold his shares to Hulyer for £1,000 and then loaned the club £300,000 to be paid back over four years in quarterly instalments at a fixed rate of interest.

Gliksten claimed that he did not want to hurt Charlton but his grievance was with Hulyer, who had acted as a personal guarantor in the deal. The deal contained a clause which allowed him to take legal action in default of payment.

Hulyer said the deal was signed only in November and the first instalment of rent had been paid. The second instalment was missed and the third was not yet due.

"In view of the extremely restricted cash flow in the past few months, we put alternative proposals to Mr Gliksten which he was not prepared to discuss."

He said there was a £600,000 overdraft when he took over the club. Gliksten paid off half of it and gave the club the loan for the other half which was to wipe out the balance.

He added: "The club had no benefit whatsoever from the loan because it had to wipe out the other advance which was there before I took over."

Hulyer also disclosed that he had been attempting to buy the ground through an independent party because he felt the rental payment was far too high.

In the next week, the toll of financial disaster mounted with the revelation that Charlton had failed to meet payments due on the transfer fees of Carl Harris from Leeds and Terry Bullivant from Aston Villa.

Simonsen Departs

THERE was no respite from the bad news and in the following week the expected came with the announcement that the club were releasing Simonsen, who, ironically, had just played his finest game for Charlton in the 5-2 thrashing of Chelsea at The Valley, when the Dane scored twice.

He was now going back to his home-town club of Veyle on a free transfer, a condition of his original agreement with Hulyer if Charlton could not guarantee to keep him after June 1983. Charlton still owed a large part of his transfer fee to Barcelona. Hulyer told a Press conference that it would have cost the club £250,000 to keep Simonsen on for another season, clearly a figure that was now completely unviable.

The Dane's farewell game was against Leeds at The Valley on Saturday, 19 March 1983. He never got into a game which Charlton lost 1-0.

In happier times, Simonsen might have led Charlton out of the years of failure, but he was not only playing in a struggling team — which reduced a great player to merely a good one — he was also playing against a background of continuing crisis.

His career had lasted just 130 days, 17 matches and nine goals. As he left the field, the crowd applauded him for they had come to appreciate fully the skill he possessed and he gave them a last wave in return.

Because of their failure to honour transfer

Danish star Allan Simonsen — going home as the full financial implications of his signing came to light.

payments, Charlton had a transfer embargo placed on them by the League. So without Simonsen, they now had to struggle on as best they could.

A new twist in the fate of The Valley came in news that an 80-year-old millionaire Kent property developer, Ron Billings, wanted to buy the ground and turn it into a leisure centre.

Billings was a distinctive man, who founded and ran an entirely amateur club, Corinthian, at his private sports complex at Fawkham in rural Kent. But he made it clear he had no ambition to take over the Charlton Athletic club itself. "I am not interested in professional football," he said.

Billings was willing to pay around £750,000 in a total package which would include the training area at the Valley Leisure Centre in Eltham. And he said he would probably halve the rental the club had contracted to pay Michael Gliksten.

His plans included squash courts, a gymnasium, seven-a-side football pitch, sauna and even an artificial full-size playing surface.

The Billings initiative at last offered a ray of hope but it was short-lived. Talks with Michael Gliksten broke down over the question of the loan debt owed to Gliksten. Billings said he thought agreement could have been reached over the freehold price, but he was not prepared to clear up the debt from the deal between Hulyer and Gliksten.

Gliksten made it clear that he still intended to press for the bankruptcy order against Hulyer. "When I serve the order, it will be a matter for me to decide."

On 14 April, a 2-1 defeat at Craven Cottage saw Charlton drop into the bottom three for the first time that season. But the standing of Lennie Lawrence remained high and he was now given a contract to keep him at The Valley for the next two years.

Bolton Decider

WHEN the last game of the season arrived, Charlton were fourth from bottom with 45 points, just above Bolton with 44 points and a goal-difference of minus 16. Their opponents on the last Saturday of the season, 14 May, were . . .Bolton. It was also their last game, but even a draw might not be enough to save Charlton from relegation, for the second-to-bottom team, Rotherham, had 44 points, a goal-difference of minus 23, and a game to play. The bottom team, Burnley, had 43 points, a goal-difference of minus 9 but with two games to play. It was a tight situation indeed.

With an hour of the game gone, Charlton were a goal down. Steve Gritt came on as substitute for Kevin Smith and seemed to bring the team both luck and good fortune. Charlton scored four goals in 12 minutes to make the issue safe. Derek Hales, suffering from a knee injury which needed an injection before the match, scored twice, one from a penalty. The other goals came from Steve Gritt and Carl Harris.

Said Lennie Lawrence afterwards: "I have got to make sure we are not in a similar position again. People have got to have pride in wearing a Charlton shirt. We have made some progress in the last few months. Now we have got to march on and do much better."

Lawrence had sensed just how crucial that game was in Charlton's history. With finances fading fast, Charlton might have found it difficult to ever return from the Third Division. For Bolton, another club who, likewise, had seen much better days, the same equation held true. They finished bottom of the Division and, at the time of writing, have not returned from the Third Division.

The season was over but the financial saga could not end so simply. Hulyer now attempted a firm bid for The Valley. He offered £700,000 plus repayment of the £300,000 loan. The obvious question raised was where Hulyer, who had failed to keep up payments to Gliksten, who had failed to settle transfer fees and who had failed to retain Simonsen, was going to find that kind of money.

He refused to give details except to say that it would be raised through business deals and outside sources. He described the £110,000 current payment a year to Gliksten as 'a crippling amount of money to pay.' He added: "If we can purchase the ground, it will solve many of our problems."

His plans for The Valley were very similar to Billings' — a sports complex including a seven-a-side pitch, squash courts, sauna and possibly a restaurant. This was hardly surprising since, three weeks later, Billings was revealed as Hulyer's backer in the offer.

But there was one move that would prove significant for the club's future. He said he was looking to involve the local authority, Greenwich Council, in community activity and support.

The purchase offer was not immediately taken up by Gliksten. Shortly afterwards, Hulyer hinted that he might be prepared to stand down as chairman, although still being closely involved with the club. Whether this was a hint that other interests were thinking of coming in was at this stage still unclear.

Leeds and the Inland Revenue Act

THE humiliating financial position of the club plunged to even further depths when, in July 1983, Leeds United sought a winding-up order against Charlton, the first case in League history where one club had taken such action against another.

The League, mindful of their reputation, had tried to stop the move but Leeds had simply run out of patience with the failure to pay them the money owed on the Carl Harris deal. Some £35,000 was still outstanding.

There was still no end to the hectic scenario of the Hulyer regime and now it was confirmed that negotiations were going on behind the scenes for a consortium to take over the club.

The Leeds hearing took place at the Chancery Division of Leeds County Court on Friday, 8 July. Ominously, a third opponent to Hulyer, in addition to Leeds United and Gliksten, now moved into play. The Inland Revenue joined the Leeds action. The court gave Charlton until 25 July to pay a tax bill of £145,000 and the £35,000 owed to Leeds for Carl Harris. The possible closure of the club now loomed as a credible, awful reality

It was now that Billings' identity was revealed as the backer for Hulyer's Valley offer. So, too, was the identity of the consortium revealed and it was not a comforting one.

The Rotherham United chairman, Anton Johnson, was the leader of the five-man consortium and the figure they were prepared to invest was £600,000. Johnson was a former Charlton season-ticket holder and his regard for the club could not be doubted, but he was already known in football circles as a 'broker' or less favourably a 'wheeler dealer' in the affairs of a number of League clubs.

He had talks with Gliksten, but stated he thought the club might have to go into receivership before the consortium could move in. Once more the Billings offer to buy The Valley was withdrawn. Billings said of the situation: "Mr Gliksten lent Mr Hulyer a loan of £300,000 but now wants £420,000. The extra £120,000 is the interest over four years and I am not prepared to pay the extra cash."

Gliksten responded that he was fed up with the whole affair. "This is not the first time I have been let down by these people.

"I reluctantly came to a deal because things had dragged on for too long. Then Mr Billings dropped out and we are back to square one."

Hulyer said he was still hopeful of persuading Billings to go ahead and that his company, Marman, was prepared to make up the difference in the sums. But Billings had now withdrawn for the last time.

On Monday, 25 July 1983, came yet another of the

series of financial dramas that had become part of the life of Charlton Athletic. The club now brushed close to the ultimate catastrophe of closure but was reprieved, if only for a few months.

In the resumed hearing at Leeds High Court, the Inland Revenue agreed to the adjournment of the winding up order until 7 October on condition the debt of £145,000 was paid. It meant that Charlton could now look on the future 1983-4 season as reality.

But Judge Blackett-Ord warned that proceedings might be started against the club in the meantime if the tax bill was not paid. The Inland Revenue wanted £25,000 immediately and further payments totalling £43,000 by 19 September. The rest of the money was to be paid by the time of the hearing.

The Marman company paid the wages of the players during the summer of 1983 but things were now so bad that the players met part of the cost themselves of a few days break at a country club in Cornwall and bought their own food. On the wider front, another devastating blow was dealt to the average smaller size clubs by the Football League's decision to allow home club's to keep all their match receipts, rather than share them with their visitors. The path to financial solvency was now even longer for Charlton.

The 1983-4 season started surprisingly well, despite the financial threat hanging over the future. By the end of September, Charlton were third in the table and unbeaten. The transfer embargo had been lifted and the forward, Ronnie Moore, signed from Rotherham for £30,000.

But October was to bring a rude awakening both on and off the pitch. The first game of the month — on 1 October — saw Charlton crash to one of the heaviest defeats in the club's history, 7-0 away to Brighton, with former Liverpool player Jimmy Case scoring a hat-trick. Charlton then began to slip down the table.

On Friday, 7 October, Hulyer solved his problems with the Inland Revenue by coming to an agreement with them, but this was abruptly followed up by Michael Gliksten seeking the winding-up order instead. His application was now due to be heard in Leeds on Monday, 17 October 1983. Gliksten, claiming he was owed a total of £573,000, had a bankruptcy claim down against Mark Hulyer the following day, Tuesday, 18 October, at Medway County Court.

Gliksten's Statement

GLIKSTEN did not comment directly on his actions but issued a statement through a public relations firm hired on behalf of his company, Adelong, which owned The Valley.

The statement recounted the history of Gliksten's relationship with Hulyer. It related how Hulyer approached Gliksten with an offer to take over the club and claimed he was advised against the move because the club's overdraft was more than £600,000, but persisted.

Gliksten accordingly agreed to sell his shares for a nominal amount. An agreement had been signed in June 1982 with Gliksten paying £420,000 for The Valley and lending Charlton £300,000 to clear the overdraft. A 35-year lease was negotiated for The Valley and the club's training ground.

The first month's rent was paid in October 1982, according to the statement, but apart from the money for the shares, this was the only money Gliksten received, it alleged.

The statement went on to say that in January 1983,

a writ was issued against Charlton for alleged rent arrears and another against Hulyer, Marman and the club for the return of the money lent, plus the interest under the original agreement.

It claimed that up until 7 October 1983, Hulyer kept putting off paying any money and produced different propositions but never any money to substantiate them.

It said Gliksten had always intimated that if Hulyer came up with the £250,000 total so far due, he would be happy to discontinue his actions. A more positive solution would be for someone to buy him out and take over the liabilities, but this would cost in the region of £1 million.

It seemed highly unlikely that Hulyer could meet these terms and there seemed little chance, at this time, of a consortium riding into view to save the club. Hulyer said he would be making an offer to Gliksten but if it was not accepted then 'we do not have a hope in hell's chance of surviving.'

He added: "I am astonished he is attacking the club. He has the opportunity to make me bankrupt so why does he want to ruin the club as well?"

'Last-ever' Games

IT was against this sombre background that the fans filed into The Valley for the match against Manchester City on Saturday, 15 October 1983, fearing it could be the last time ever they would see their team play. It was to be first of several such 'last-ever' games over the coming months, a gruesome, drawn-out scenario that no other set of fans in the history of football had ever had to undergo.

Yet still the team continued to show a heart and a spirit that belied the truly desperate situation the club were in. Manchester City, second in the division and with five successive victories to their credit, were beaten 1-0 in a hard, keenly-contested game played in driving rain, with skipper Derek Hales scoring in the second half. Some 7,639 fans attended the 'death-bed' game, the best attendance of the season so far but an indication of just how the core support had shrunk.

The loyalist supporters roared passionately for the team and gave the players a standing ovation at the end. Charlton were unbeaten at home and now sixth in the table. Were they to go out of business, they would enjoy the grim distinction of being the highest-placed team in the League ever to disappear.

But it was not the last game. All the players were given the Monday off to await the unfolding drama in Leeds. Manager Lennie Lawrence kept vigil in his office waiting for the telephone call that would tell him whether the team would ever play again.

The wait was an agonizing one. The hearing should have started at 11am, but did not get under way until three hours later. Then, with the agreement of Gliksten, the High Court writ for the winding up of the club was adjourned to give further time for the club's affairs to be sorted out.

The club was given until 7 November to put a survival package together. On that day, another court date was to be fixed to decide the club's future, with 20 November the expected day.

Mr James Allen, representing Gliksten's company, Adelong, said Charlton owed it more than £500,000 and that with other debts and interest charges, the club was more than £1 million in the red.

After the hearing, Gliksten commented that he was horrified to discover that there were 14 other creditors involved and further debts of more than £300,000.

"It all adds up to the fact that the club is in a

disastrous situation. Perhaps the adjournment will give the opportunity for people who do not want to see the club fail to come up with a rescue plan, even at this late stage."

The following day, the bankruptcy case against Hulyer, at Medway County Court, was also adjourned to a date to be fixed the following month.

Meanwhile, any residual hope that Greenwich Council might step in faded away. The council leader, John Austin-Walker, had met Mark Hulyer and Richard Collins the previous week and amongst the solutions discussed was the council taking over the freehold of The Valley. But a meeting of the ruling Labour group on the same Monday as the Leeds hearing ruled out any idea of the council putting money into the club and this was confirmed at a full council meeting on the Wednesday, although the council added that it might reconsider if the club was financially reconstituted.

The following Saturday, after a 2-2 draw at The Valley against Swansea City, Hulyer resigned as chairman in the hope this would help settle matters with Gliksten but the stepdown was to prove only temporary. Hulyer remained as a director and Richard Collins became chairman as well as managing director.

Hulyer stated he was prepared to sell his shares for a nominal sum to any party who was willing and financially able to run the club and satisfy the winding up petitions. He stated that he had put £300,000 into Charlton but there was 'a limit to the amount of money any one person can find.'

Collins now set about trying to find someone who could save the club. He disclosed that four possible consortia and a number of individuals had contacted him about the possibility of saving the club. Collins went into a series of discussions with them, working 14-hour days and cancelling a holiday in Spain.

But the club's debt situation and entanglement with Michael Gliksten was to defeat him. The new date for the winding up order was now fixed for Thursday, 24 November 1983.

Meanwhile what of the 'poor, bloody infantry', the supporters who watched haplessly as the court battle raged. Their first tangible response came with the launch of a 'Save Charlton' campaign at the Swansea game and the distribution of leaflets. This was followed by the formation of an action group as a sub-committee of the supporters' club.

But their attempts to meet with Gliksten to avert the winding-up order failed. Gliksten departed on a business trip to Australia and left a message with his public relations firm saying it was too late in the day for such a meeting to be of any value.

The Days Tick Away

IN a magnanimous gesture, Chelsea agreed to bring forward their match at The Valley from Saturday, 18 February, the next year, to Tuesday, 15 November, to try to help Charlton over the immediate cash crisis. It was a much appreciated gesture from the Chelsea chairman, Ken Bates.

As the days ticked away to the new hearing date, another attempt to buy The Valley from Gliksten failed. This time it came from a group headed by a West End textile businessman, Leslie Wise, who admitted to being an Arsenal supporter.

His interest was in buying the ground and offering it to the club on a 60-year lease, not in running the club. He offered £850,000 with £500,000 to be paid immediately as a sign of goodwill but Gliksten was

said by Richard Collins to be seeking £1.25 million as the price.

This apparently consisted of about £700,000 for the ground, the rest covering rent arrears, loan repayments and interest charges. Collins described himself as bitterly disappointed at the rejection of the offer.

The first hint of a ground move as a way out of the club's troubles came with an offer from the Millwall chairman, Alan Thorne, of facilities at The Den if Charlton ever needed them.

The supporters made clear their feelings at the game against Blackburn on Saturday, 5 November, carrying banners proclaiming that 'Charlton must not die.' But the attendance was just 4,563, although the 2-0 victory lifted the club back into sixth place.

Further bad news came on the following Tuesday with Greenwich Council again turning down the club's renewed application for a Sunday market. Objections were received from 40 residents, saying

the proposal would generate extra traffic, parking problems, noise, rubbish and general disturbance.

The blow was a double one because a businessman had said he was prepared to inject £250,000 into the club if the plans went through.

The legal battle now took a dramatic change of direction as the club decided to sue Michael Gliksten. A writ was taken out over certain aspects of the sale of The Valley, seeking the ground transaction nullified over alleged breaches of the Companies Act, 1981. The writ was due to be heard in Coventry early in December 1983. This action now meant that the hearing in Leeds on 24 November was likely to be adjourned while the new situation was looked at.

The midweek Chelsea match went ahead with a total of 14,393 fans watching a 1-1 draw and the club banking welcome receipts of some £40,000.

The supporters' club now raised a new issue — the grants paid to the club by the Football Grounds Improvement Trust in February 1982 and by the

Sports Council in August 1981. The trust had paid £228,626 and the council £70,000. The supporters' club argued that some account should be taken of this money in the settlement of the dispute between the club and Gliksten, but it did not emerge as an issue in the hearings.

The supporters' club also said it was looking into the possibility of forming a company to be called Charlton Athletic Supporters' Company Limited, which would issue shares at £10 each with the aim of raising between £50,000 and £100,000 to buy an equity interest in the football club. But it was an idea that came to nothing. Quite clearly the money

Charlton Athletic, 1983-4. Back row (left to right): Charlie Hall (physiotherapist), Peter Mountford, Shane Westley, Mark Aizlewood, Les Berry, Tommy Taylor, Nicky Johns, Steve White, Geoff Scott, Terry Naylor, Carl Harris, Paul Curtis, Bill Gallagher (assistant physiotherapist). Front row: Steve Gritt, Martin Robinson, Derek Hales, Lennie Lawrence (manager), Eddie May (assistant manager), Kevin Smith, Kevin Dickenson, Barry Little.

stakes were too high for the supporters' club to have a realistic chance of involvement.

The plan was disclosed at a well attended meeting which also discussed part of the reason why attendances were so low. At a time of mounting unemployment, the club had pursued a policy of high admission prices to cover its losses. The £3 terrace admission price, although it gave access to seating behind both goals, was the highest in London. One supporter pointed out that the admission charge to First Division West Ham was almost half the price.

The hearing on 24 November was adjourned as anticipated. No details of the club's finances were given during the 10-minute hearing and Judge Blackett-Ord adjourned the application indefinitely. The matter was now expected to be heard by the High Court in London in the New Year of 1984, with the writ issued by the club against Gliksten's Adelong company also being dealt with.

The following week Richard Collins resigned from the chairmanship and the board, leaving Hulyer not only to take on the post again but also as the only active member of the board. Chief Francis Nzeribe, the only other director, had been out of the country for some time and had not been seen at The Valley for a year.

Collins had been just five weeks in the job and he pointed out the severe difficulties he had faced in trying to find a consortium willing to take on the club's obligations. He had also come to the conclusion that there was no hope for the club whilst Hulyer remained. Once again the humiliating situation arose of Charlton defaulting on transfer fees. They had to face a Football League commission to explain why they had not made the 50 per cent cash downpayment laid down under League rules for the signing of Ronnie Moore from Rotherham. The regulation was a recent one and Charlton had the dubious honour of being the first-ever club to default on it.

Charlton had offered Rotherham £12,500 — money received from the transfer of Steve White to Bristol Rovers — but this had been turned down by the Yorkshire club. The club's bank account had now been frozen and this caused further difficulty in resolving the situation.

The Football League hearing was at the Great Western Hotel at Paddington and Charlton could have been penalized by the deduction of League points. Instead, the club escaped with a fine. Moore remained a Charlton player, and the supporters' club chipped in £8,000 towards the fee.

On the playing field, the team still stayed in the top half of the table and did not lose their unbeaten home record until the turn of the year, going down 2-1 to Huddersfield on 31 December.

Hales Outburst as Flanagan Returns

AND there were signs — false ones as it proved — that the club's desperate financial troubles were lifting. The transfer embargo was lifted, enabling an amazing return to the club of a former star, Mike Flanagan. The wanderer made his return on 12 January 1984, from Queen's Park Rangers for £50,000.

The news of the return had broken before the third round FA Cup tie away to Colchester which Charlton won 0-1, and then trouble broke out with Derek Hales. After an outburst in a national newspaper, he was dropped for the tie, relieved of the club captaincy and put on the transfer list.

As before, Hales survived because of a change of heart by the club. He was back for the next League

match against Cambridge United at The Valley, the game in which Flanagan made his first appearance following his signing. And Hales got the captaincy back.

There seems to have been some sort of reconciliation between the two men. They trained together at The Valley and were seen chatting to each other as they lapped the pitch.

The renewed partnership saw Charlton gain their biggest win of the season, 5-2, against Cambridge United on 21 January, and Hales scored twice, including the opening goal, from a penalty.

From the kick-off, Flanagan took three superb consecutive corners and it was the last which produced the penalty as Cambridge's Tom Finney climbed over Charlton's right-back Paul Curtis. As Hales netted, the first player to go over to shake his hand was Flanagan.

Meanwhile Mark Hulyer seemed apparently content to be the only director. He commented: "I am not worried about new directors. I have a superb management team running the club." With Lennie Lawrence at the helm, he was, of course, right.

And in the same month, he gave a four-and-a-half year contract to Lawrence. Hulyer at least showed his good football judgement, commenting on the contract: "I look forward to him realizing his full potential with Charlton. Lennie is capable of managing a First Division club and I hope he will do that with Charlton."

The false dawn of optimism continued with the fourth-round home FA Cup tie against Watford, a game which almost seemed like old times at The Valley as 22,392 spectators watched. Receipts were a record £70,423, although Charlton lost 2-0.

Crisis Anew

ON Monday, 30 January 1984, the financial crisis broke anew and it was to spell the end of the club in its present form and of the short-lived, but eventful, Hulyer regime.

In the High Court, the Inland Revenue asked for a winding-up order against the club because of tax owing of £108,554. The case was adjourned for two weeks for the club to try to find the money. Besides the taxmen, Gliksten's Adelong company was also represented. It seemed likely that the Inland Revenue would want at least £70,000 before dropping their action.

It was to Greenwich Council that Hulyer once more turned to try to solve the problem. He announced that he was seeking a 'short-term cash loan'. At the same time, the club hoped for long-term plans for the council to become permanently involved with the club.

One report said that a merchant bank were prepared to provide substantial cash for the council to obtain the freehold of The Valley and become the club's new landlords. This could mean The Valley becoming a centre for community sports facilities with the possibility of a synthetic sports pitch. This rumoured initiative came to nothing and so did any further hope of council involvement in any form.

Hulyer kept up an optimistic front, although the crisis was now clearly moving to a head. He was quoted in the *Kentish Independent* as saying: 'Apart from the Revenue, we have no other pressing financial problems and a number of debts to smaller creditors have been met. Apart from the money owed to the taxman, Charlton is not under any serious threat and is far more stable now.'

As the crisis gathered, one of the greatest non-playing stalwarts in the club's history died on 7 February — Dick Neve at his home in Plumstead at the age of 67. He had been the club's announcer for 30 years and a man prominent in the civic life of the area, having served as Mayor of Greenwich. One of his first duties in the early days had been to take the classified results into the dressing-room after a match and read them to the players.

Ironically, just a few days before his death, he was featured in the match-day programme against Brighton when his great nephew, Matthew Neve, was mascot for the day. And perhaps, it may be reflected, fate dealt him a kindly hand in that as a man who truly loved the club he was spared the dreadful days immediately ahead.

Mark Hulyer's hopes of a rescue by the council were short-lived. The council refused his request to act as second guarantor on a loan of £110,000 to meet the tax bill.

The council leader, John Austin-Walker, said there was no indication that any such support would have any long-term benefit for Charlton.

"We are prepared to consider any proposals put by Charlton Athletic which will secure the long-term future of the club, but this can only come about if there is a substantial injection of capital into Charlton."

In the midst of this saga, the club's match against Sheffield Wednesday at Hillsborough on 11 February 1984, was featured on BBC TV's Match of the Day, Charlton going down by 4-1.

On Monday, 13 February, at the resumed hearing in the High Court, the club was given yet another reprieve when the hearing was adjourned a further two weeks. Judge Mervyn Davies was told by the club that a company called Flintgrange was interested in buying it.

Flintgrange was a company associated with Hulyer's erstwhile colleague on the board, the Nigerian Chief Francis Nzeribe. But that initiative fell too as the two men failed to reach agreement.

Hulyer stated that it would not be in the best interests of Charlton for the chief's company to take over the club or have a major financial stake in its affairs, but he refused to elaborate on his statement. He said that debts owed to Chief Nzeribe were being settled.

There the Flintgrange interest ended and it was never ascertained just how firm a proposition it would have been had Hulyer allowed it to progress. He was now entirely on his own. Meanwhile, the total owed to the taxman now officially totalled £159,000.

Unknown Interests

BUT, although Flintgrange had disappeared, it still seemed that there were interests around who might be ready to save the club. But the tactics of these parties seemed to be to have nothing to do with Hulyer.

The aim of these unknown interests, although never stated, seemed to be to let the old company fold so that a new one could emerge free of any Hulyer entanglement. But these were only reports. For the fan, the unbelievable end of the club was looming once again.

It was clearly asking too much of the High Court to allow a fourth reprieve, but Hulyer made one last desperate attempt to stave off the inevitable. At the hearing on Tuesday, 27 February 1984, he offered to pay the outstanding debt in three instalments of £30,000.

The money was to be offered by way of bills of exchange from the Swiss bank account of his company, Marman, through the French bank, Indo Suez.

The Inland Revenue countered this offer by saying that what was, in effect, being offered were three post-dated cheques and that it was not an arrangement that was enticing.

Their case was that the money was coming from a Swiss company on which nothing was known and was the substance of a business deal involving a shipment of rubber from Bangkok.

If correct, it was certainly an exotic way of saving Charlton, but Judge Mervyn Davies was having no more of Hulyer's attempts at payment:

"I have the impression that if I give another adjournment, there would be yet another story of hopes unfulfilled next time we came back to court."

The Dead Company

HE said the club was 'hopelessly insolvent' and that he had no alternative but to agree to the winding-up order.

And so the Charlton company was finally dead. The *South East London Mercury* called the club dead, but 'company' and 'club' were to prove different concepts. But could the 'club' survive the death? Time was running out fast with a League match due at Blackburn on Saturday, 3 March 1984. Failure to meet that fixture now looked certain to spell the absolute end of Charlton Athletic.

Despite the dreadful finality of the judge's comments, still the hapless Hulyer persisted. After the hearing, he held an urgent meeting at The Valley with Lennie Lawrence and secretary Graham Hortop.

He once again tried to get a deal from the Inland Revenue, whom he attacked as 'totally unreasonable and unrealistic', in the hope of getting the winding-up order rescinded. He also said he was considering an appeal.

He stated: "We are dead but not yet buried. There is 72 hours to keep the club going and we are still fighting for our lives. Charlton must survive. That is the only thing that matters."

After the court case, emerged the same day the identity of one of the background interests said to be interested in saving the club. And the white knight proved to be a mighty one indeed — no less than the Beckenham-based Sunley company, one of Britain's biggest property developers, with assets of more than £400 million.

Tuesday, 6 March 1984, and anxious hours at The Valley Club for Lennie Lawrence (right), assistant physiotherapist Bill Gallagher (centre), assistant manager Eddie May (left), chief scout Les Gore (next left) and physiotherpist Charlie Hall (far left).

The Official Receiver takes charge. The padlocked Valley in March 1984.

Two days later on Thursday, 1 March, Hulyer finally quit and gave up any hope of an appeal.

He agreed to write off the £300,000 which his company, Marman, had invested in the club. The consortium meanwhile, its identity revealed, refused to confirm or deny its plans but at last hope loomed for those who were suffering worst of all — the fans who had devoted their lives to supporting the club and who had stuck with it through all the long years of failure — 'the bloody heroes, all of them', as the club's long-serving statistician Colin Cameron was to so eloquently and emotionally describe them.

The Sunley Rescue Plan

BUT it was the club's great past that was saving it. For the managing director of Sunleys was John Fryer, a supporter of the club since his first visit to The Valley at Christmas 1927.

Fryer's interest in a rescue was not spontaneous. It was spurred by a supporter with no connection with the club's management, Michael Norris, a chartered surveyor from Eltham and a major shareholder in a Knightsbridge property company.

As it became obvious towards the end of 1983 that only new ownership could save the club, so Norris, a man who had spent long years on the terraces, decided he had to become involved. Through his business contacts with Fryer, he knew they both shared affections for the club. So he approached Fryer to ask whether he was prepared to consider stepping

in. Fryer's initial desire was simply to acquire The Valley as a benevolent landlord and lease it at a peppercorn rent to a reconstituted club.

Collins, in trying to steer a rescue course for the stricken club, had undergone considerable personal financial risk in staying on while its affairs plunged into disarray. Now freed from an impossible situation, he started the fight afresh.

Up until that time, neither Norris nor Collins had met. Now they were to be the negotiators for Fryer's rescue.

The size of the rescue commitment was put at £2 million including new capital and an estimated £700,000 to clear debt but the consortium waited until the complex situation facing the club was sorted out in the courts.

Perhaps consortium was the wrong word to use since the money was Sunleys' but in personality terms, it was the three-man team of Fryer, Norris and Collins. Malcolm Stanley, the former director, was also involved but dropped out in the later stages.

The consortium had prepared its plans in detail in the months up to March but the rescue was to prove a close run thing indeed.

Gliksten himself had been woken at 5am at his farm in Australia to be told the news of the winding-up, and immediately arranged to fly back to London.

He confirmed he had been in negotiations with the consortium over The Valley and added: 'I am delighted that it appears that Charlton are to be saved. I am very impressed with the people wishing to take over and they seem very responsible. The last thing I wanted was to see Charlton fold. There now seems to be some light at the end of the tunnel.'

Sadly, what seemed to be a hopeful relationship between Gliksten and the consortium was not to bear fruit, but only sowed further tragic seeds of crisis.

Meanwhile Lennie Lawrence, facing stoically the pressures that he could hardly ever have envisaged as part of a football manager's job, had the task of telephoning the players, trying to keep them together and arranging training.

Soon after the court winding-up, there was no Valley to go to. The ground was locked up on the orders of the Official Receiver. The only concession was that the club was allowed to take away its kit before the gates were closed. Lennie Lawrence and the staff had to make their temporary headquarters in the Valley Social Club. The staff were now technically sacked and their wages were overdue and unpaid.

The League, in the person of secretary Graham Kelly, set out what Charlton must do to survive. Kelly said the League would look favourably on any consortium coming forward which could guarantee all creditors being paid. Anyone taking over the club would have to pay 60 per cent of debts to normal creditors, 70 per cent to football club creditors and 100 per cent to the Inland Revenue.

If no deal were made, the registration of the players would revert to the Football League. The club's record would be expunged from the Second Division table. This last step would have had quite a serious effect since leading contenders Sheffield Wednesday and Chelsea would have lost four points each.

The 72 hours seen as necessary by Hulyer to save the club turned instead into a chilling nine-day crisis. The consortium had hoped to tie up a deal quickly. A hearing in the High Court took place on Friday,

2 March 1984, before a public gallery packed with supporters, but the Official Receiver asked for more time to study the proposals. He made it clear he was unhappy at the apparent haste and complained that he was 'having a gun pointed at his head'.

This opposition by the Official Receiver meant securing the League's agreement to postpone the game at Blackburn on the Saturday. Otherwise his opposition would mean the end of the club's League membership and its almost certain demise.

The team were due to leave for Lancashire at 2pm on the Friday, but the departure was put off as the High Court hearing began in the afternoon. If the team had left on time, they might have arrived without a Charlton Athletic to play for. It was a weird, macabre situation which had surely never faced a set of professional footballers before.

Lennie Lawrence, the players, and staff waited in the Valley Social Club as the drama unfolded in the High Court — their link through a public call box in the foyer as messages came in from the reporters at the court. Meanwhile, other journalists gathered at the club sitting in an adjoining room to Lawrence and the players.

The team's luxury coach was waiting by the ground and the driver joined the club staff and players as they passed the time playing cards or pool or reading the newspapers.

The then sports editor of the *Kentish Independent*, Peter Burrowes, a man closely associated with the club as programme editor, described the scene thus:

"Black coffee was the order of the day for manager Lennie Lawrence, who was beginning to show the strain. What a baptism of fire he has had since taking over as Charlton's boss.

"Every time the telephone rang, people jumped up in anticipation of good news. But the news they wanted never came."

Blackburn

INDEED, as the telephone calls came into the public call box, it looked as if things were getting worse. Then, just before 5pm, came the news that the match at Blackburn had been postponed and the court hearing adjourned until Monday, 5 March, without prejudicing Charlton's membership of the Football League.

Lawrence sent his emotionally exhausted players home: "I certainly did not fancy a six-hour coach trip to Blackburn on top of what we have been through", he said.

"It has been the worst day of my life. Let's hope it all gets sorted out."

The manager of the Valley Club had had bottles of champagne ready in case of positive news of the consortium's takeover. He put them away, hopefully for another, happier, day. The journalists tucked into sandwiches before leaving for their offices. Charlton were still alive — just.

The League, in agreeing to the postponement of the Blackburn game, had taken a very rare step in their wish to help Charlton. But they also made it clear the situation could not continue.

A deadline was set by the League of 5pm on Thursday, 8 March, for the consortium to obtain the High Court's agreement to the survival package. Failure to meet the deadline would mean the club's expulsion from the League and its almost certain demise.

The game on the following Saturday was against Grimsby Town. Would it ever take place? Would the red shirts ever be seen again against the green of The Valley turf and its stunning backdrop of high terracing? Not only Charlton fans, but the whole football world stood and waited for the events that were to come.

The Monday hearing lasted just one minute and was adjourned again — until the next day. Then on Tuesday, Simon Mortimore, counsel for the consortium, asked for a final adjournment until 3pm on the Thursday, 8 March, just two hours before the League's ultimate deadline.

Mr Michael Crystal, counsel for the Official Receiver, said that neither the Football League nor the Official Receiver was in a position to give approval to any rescue plan and negotiations were still going on.

"It would be premature to say that a successful outcome of this matter is in any way assured," he commented.

The crisis was making daily headlines in the national media. According to Peter Burrowes in the *Kentish Independent*: 'There were enough scribes around to form a football team and somebody suggested the events would be better entertainment than *Match of the Day*.'

The word 'entertainment' was hardly the one the suffering Charlton fans would have used, unless the entertainment comparison was to a late night horror movie.

Some of the reporters spent some of the time walking from the court up to Holborn to the offices of the solicitor for the consortium, Peter Crystal, ironically a cousin of the counsel for the Official Receiver. But his secretary, according to Peter Burrowes, was well-primed to deal with the constant flow of callers.

"No, Mr Crystal is not here", she would say. "No, he is not available. No, the consortium are not meeting here. No, we have no comment."

With the débâcle moving rapidly to a cliff-edge finish, there was small piece of good news on the penultimate day of Wednesday. If there was a Charlton Athletic football club still in existence, then Greenwich Council were prepared to make a £250,000 grant at £50,000 a year over the next five years.

The sum was likely to include shirt sponsorship, and in return the council wanted to be represented on the new board of directors and The Valley open to local people for community use.

The deal, to be ratified by the full council, was dependent on the club's viability being assured and the outstanding rates bill being paid.

The attitude of the Football League tried the patience of at least one member of the consortium, Malcolm Stanley, the managing director of FADS, the former club shirt sponsors. He called the League 'inflexible' and unreasonable in its demands: "They want £500,000 up front before they will register the new club. If we have to find that money immediately, it will rob us of working capital."

He said the League had not given Charlton enough time to sort out its affairs: "Trying to form a new club and transfer the lease of the ground in such a short time is almost impossible," he said.

"It takes a month or more to buy a house, yet we are being given a week to buy a football club".

He also revealed that if the new consortium were successful in buying The Valley from Michael Gliksten, it planned to build a sports complex at the stadium.

Stanley's outburst was a little too strong for the other members of the consortium who were worried about its possible effect on the League, and they dissociated themselves from his remarks, saying he was not speaking on their behalf.

On that final Wednesday evening, it looked as if Charlton might be doomed even before the High Court hearing, for John Fryer was wondering whether it was all worth the candle.

Five sets of lawyers had been battling it out — for the Official Receiver, Michael Gliksten, Mark Hulyer, the consortium and the creditors, of whom literally hundreds had now emerged. At a night-time meeting in the flat of the Sunley chairman and majority shareholder, John Sunley, with Richard Collins and John Sunley, Fryer said he felt that there was no point in going on.

Surprisingly, it was John Sunley, a man known for his love of horse-racing, who persuaded Fryer to keep up the fight. As he had spent money in racing, so he saw no reason why his partner, Fryer, who had the minority shareholding in Sunleys, should not spend money rescuing the football club. And, as Fryer was now in his 60s, it was time for him to devote money to a lifelong love.

And so events moved on to the fateful Thursday, 8 March 1984, in the High Court. And once more Lennie Lawrence, the players and staff endured a long afternoon of agony as they waited for events to unfold across London in the High Court.

Even as the High Court hearing started, the consortium had not reached agreement with Hulyer on the takeover terms. The agreement was signed only 20 minutes after the High Court hearing into it started and a messenger was sent racing to the High Court from Peter Crystal's Holborn offices.

Michael Norris, fan, property man and chartered surveyor, who activated the bid to save Charlton from extinction.

It was a desperately close-run thing. Peter Crystal said of the last minutes before the agreement was reached: "We were ready to walk out at that stage."

But would the High Court agree and would the League? When the three-man consortium, John Fryer, Richard Collins and Michael Norris finally arrived in the courtroom, they had to stand in the aisle because the public gallery was packed with Charlton supporters wearing the club's red and white colours.

As the afternoon wore on, so the details of the old Charlton company's dreadful plight were revealed before Judge Mervyn Davies. The company owed £999,583 and had assets of just £27,900.

The court heard that the club's two former owners had wiped the slate clean in respect of money owed and had dropped the litigation against each other over the leasing of the ground.

To secure the new company's future, Sunley Holdings were prepared to deposit £700,000 with the Football League. Preferential creditors would be paid in full and unsecured creditors 60p in the £ under the terms of the deal.

Saved

THERE were just 35 minutes left until the League's deadline when the package was accepted by Judge Mervyn Davies. But even then, acts still had to be carried out to save the club — it was still too early to celebrate. The consortium now had to go to the City offices of the League's solicitors for their approval.

They made the 5pm deadline but it was another two hours before the League's approval was given.

The Charlton club lived again in the shape of a new company, Charlton Athletic Football Club (1984) Limited. Seventy-nine years of history and one of the country's most famous clubs had been saved — but it had been a truly desperate knife-edge business.

Had Charlton gone under, the shock waves through other clubs in the League would have been immense. No club had had to drop out of the League during a season since Accrington Stanley in March 1962. And no club of Charlton's stature had ever been in this situation before. The only previous comparison with any similarity to the magnitude of Charlton's forfeiture of League status would have been that of Leeds City in 1919. But Leeds City had been expelled for financial irregularity and only after eight games of the 1919-20 season.

Back at The Valley Social Club, the champagne at last flowed and supporters joined in with players and staff in the celebrations. But many were too emotionally drained to be really happy. The crisis had seemed never ending. Now it was over — or was it?

The rush to reach agreement as the High Court hearing started had left gaps in the agreement, as later events were to show.

The details of the agreement were brought by the consortium and Peter Crystal to the celebrations at The Valley Social Club. It was nearly 8pm before they arrived to meet the players, staff, supporters — and the Press.

The most obvious drawback was that the consortium had failed in its intention to buy the Valley. Instead they were to lease it. Peter Crystal said the exact details could not be revealed, but that the agreement that had been reached on the lease was mutually satisfactory to all sides and would ensure football at The Valley in the foreseeable future. Few

saw at that time the consequences this failure to acquire the ground was to have for the club.

Still the fatal split continued between ground ownership and club ownership. Still The Valley remained in Gliksten's hand and the new Sunleys Charlton were just tenants, as Mark Hulyer had been. It materialized later that Sunleys had made an offer of £1.25 million for The Valley without success. Michael Gliksten also retained ownership of Charlton's training ground at New Eltham.

It also materialized later that the consortium's tenancy was at a cost of £70,000 per season on a seven-year lease.

But now the thoughts of players and supporters turned to the game they had doubted would ever take place — the home League match at The Valley on Saturday against Grimsby Town.

On the day of the game, the new three-man board of directors held their first official board meeting. And they confirmed the four-and-a-half year contract given to Lennie Lawrence by Mark Hulyer.

After the meeting, John Fryer said they were totally committed to Charlton and "would stand on their heads" to make the club successful.

"It will be run on business lines and we hope Charlton will become a roaring success", he said. "We are very enthusiastic about the future.

"We have only been in business 48 hours and have not yet formulated any plans for the future, but we will back the team to the full."

Commented Lennie Lawrence in an epic quote on the long drawn-out, courtroom saga: "I've not learned too much about football, but I've become an expert in company law."

Happy Valley Once More

BY the Saturday, the identity of the new owners was taking physical form at The Valley. Across the top of the giant East Terrace ran the sign 'Sunley welcomes you to Charlton Athletic'. Curiously on the façade of the new roof of the West Stand, the old 'Marman Welcome You To Charlton' wording of the Mark Hulyer régime was to remain.

After the trauma of the fight for existence, a joyous happy atmosphere settled over the terraces and stands as the ground began to fill for the Grimsby game. A Happy Valley once more.

The three men who had saved the club from extinction — new chairman John Fryer and fellow directors Richard Collins and Mike Norris — were presented on the pitch to the crowd.

They received a warm heartfelt ovation. Its warmth was such that they then went to the Charlton 'kop' end of the ground, the covered end, for yet another enthusiastic welcome.

John Fryer, once a winger in his younger days with Catford Wanderers, then kicked a ball over the pitch to Derek Hales during the pre-match warm-up. It was a moment the crowd cheered heartily, a moment of magic, unadulterated delight. All was well with the world and the football game was almost incidental.

With the transfer deadline just days away on the following Thursday, there was no hope that the consortium could go and buy players, but that simply did not matter for the rest of the season ahead.

The game looked set to be a celebratory triumph for Charlton when they led 3-2 and were playing injury time. They had gone into a two-goal lead with

Saved! Michael Norris (left), new chairman John Fryer and Richard Collins toast Charlton's survival.

177

Opposite: All's well at The Valley. Chairman John Fryer, once a winger with Catford Wanderers, performs a celebratory kick before the game against Grimsby Town. Above: Lennie Lawrence forgave the players for their display against Grimsby. "They've been through hell," he said.

Derek Hales volleying in a shot off the post in the 28th minute and Robert Lee scoring on his debut, a minute after the start of the second half. Then Grimsby hit back to equalize but Martin Robinson scored what looked like the winner, two minutes from time. Alas, Grimsby scored a last-gasp equalizer to share the points.

Despite the draw, the game was a good one with John Fryer describing it as 'a super game of football'.

Manager Lawrence although disapointed with the defensive performance was nevertheless understanding: "The players have been through a hell of a lot in the last ten days so I don't want to hammer them too much".

Probably the most significant statistic of the game was the crowd figure — at just 7,626, only around a thousand up on the season's average.

The Core Support

WHAT it really meant was that this was Charlton's core support, an awesome decline for a club that had once had average crowds of 40,000. For there could

hardly have been a single keen local Charlton fan who would not have attended this celebration of a game, come hell or high water. Admittedly, the terrace admission price at £3 was the dearest in London but that was hardly a deterrent for a single match of such significance.

On the Valley terraces stood the Greenwich Council leader John Austin-Walker and his deputy Dave Picton. They held a press conference afterwards to give details of the £250,000 the council proposed to inject into Charlton.

Among the proposals was for the club to make its facilities open to the local community and for the players to take on a greater role in the coaching of youngsters. The council hoped to get the Greater London Council to give a grant for an all-weather pitch. And the council also hoped that a sports centre could be eventually built at the ground. In return for its financial backing, the council sought a seat on the board.

But the optimistic hopes of the two councillors were almost dashed the following Monday when, at a special council meeting, their proposals scraped through by just seven votes. Clearly not everyone in the borough supported the council and its community aspirations for Charlton. But the division in the council was not along party lines. So the last part of the financial jigsaw was in place and the club could plan again for its future.

In July, the liquidator's report summed up the final picture of the old company's plight — a total estimated deficiency of £1,516,536. It came to this conclusion: 'In the opinion of the Official Receiver, the company's failure and insolvency are attributable

Three players who helped Charlton battle on. From left: Paul Curtis, ever-present Kevin Dickenson, and debutant Robert Lee.

to the actions of the directors, particularly those in office since June 1982 and more especially Mark Hulyer who appears to have been the dominant director since 1982, in that they caused the company to continue an unprofitable course of trading involving the outlay of substantial wages without the introduction of adequate additional permanent capital to finance the losses incurred.'

But for the new Charlton Athletic, the years of crisis were over — or were they? The separation of a football club from the ownership of its ground invariably spells trouble for the club. Without such ownership, problems arise over finance, adminstration and the upkeep and improvement of a ground. And in the world of the 1980s, football grounds in valuable urban areas faced the increasing risk of property development. The High Court terms had been agreed in a rush. They had to be. And so the tangled skein of events in the courtroom led to still more momentous events for the distinctive, but cursedly unlucky football club that is Charlton Athletic.

Kevin Smith made 36 appearances in all, in what was his last season in the Football League.

Goodbye
to The Valley

THE régime had changed but the playing performance seemed to remain the same. The fare of average-to-poor Second Division football looked set to continue. It was the diet as before — or so the fans felt, even if their club had been saved — but even they had no inkling of the amazing triumph and the amazing tragedy to come.

On the field of play, Charlton lost their last five games and sank into the lower half of the table, finishing in 13th place. The next season, 1984-5, started promisingly, but then performances again fell away. At one time Charlton were again in danger of relegation, but finished in 17th place. The young forward, Robert Lee, a former turnstile operator at The Valley, established himself in the side and the experienced Alan Curbishley, the former West Ham midfielder, was signed from Aston Villa. Otherwise the changes were few. The old warhorse, Derek Hales, played his last game at Shrewsbury on 9 March 1985, still five goals short of Stuart Leary's record total of 153 League goals, but was the record overall scorer with 168. He departed for Gillingham.

Derek Ufton and Bill Strong, a Greenwich councillor, joined the board for the start of the season, to be followed in November by television commentator and former Fulham player, Jimmy Hill. Strong's appointment followed the sponsorship deal with the council. Hill was to bring the club the benefit of his wide contacts in the football world and his publicity skills.

In February 1985, the other half of the 'two Jimmies', Jimmy Trotter, died at the age of 86, so finally closing the chapter of the great Seed era.

With one full season behind them, it was now that the new Sunley management took decisive action and Lawrence was given his head in the signing of players. It was a chance he took brilliantly, demonstrating his ability and shrewdness in the judgement of players.

A complete new defence was signed — full-backs John Humphrey from Wolves and Mark Reid from Celtic and central defenders John Pender, from Wolves, and Steve Thompson, who had been with Lawrence at Lincoln. Midfielder George Shipley also came from Lincoln and forward John Pearson from Sheffield Wednesday. Jim Loveridge was the seventh new player that summer — from Swansea.

Loveridge's career with the club was short-lived but Lawrence's other six signings proved inspired buys. With another young home-bred forward, Mark

Stuart, joining Lee in the side and Mark Aizlewood playing ever better in midfield, the Charlton fans were surprised to find that, at last, they had a team with the potential to end the club's 29-year absence from the top flight.

In another far-sighted move, the club attempted to bridge the gap in the ranks of supporters by the formation of a Junior Reds section, inspired by Michael Norris and Jimmy Hill.

A tremendous start saw Charlton win four and draw one of their five opening games and the optimism of the fans began to rise. But off the field, ominous

Full-back Mark Reid, from Celtic, was one of a completely new defence signed by Charlton for 1984-5.

180

things were happening of which they knew little, marring the hope stirred on the field after so many barren years.

New Drama

THE physical decline of The Valley and the club's loss of ownership of the ground were now to have the most horrendous effects imaginable for the Valley faithful.

That summer, while the new team was being assembled, a new drama began to break over The Valley. It unfolded both through the actions of Michael Gliksten and because of the fire disaster at another Valley, the Valley Parade home of Bradford City, in May 1985.

The controversy following the fire led to repercussions in football stadiums across the country, and nowhere more so than at The Valley. Nemesis came to the historic East Terrace in the shape of the Greater London Council, who, in further action against London League grounds, ordered its complete closure.

At almost the same time, Michael Gliksten decided to claim over two acres of The Valley site, behind the West Stand, an area covering car-parking, toilets and turnstiles. It was a move which would have left the ground without its most important turnstiles and without its car-park.

The Charlton '84 board claimed it would have made the staging of matches difficult to impossible under the new climate of crowd control, as the safety authorities might feel it a sufficient excuse to prevent the whole ground being used. The epitaph on The Valley, according to some cynical pundits, was that it was being sandwiched by the socialism of the Greater London Council on the one hand and the capitalism of property interests on the other. The majority of supporters simply expressed bewilderment.

The East Terrace had been an acknowledged problem for a long time. Not only was the concrete crumbling but the terrace was being supposedly twisted and cracked by movements in the sewer underneath, although this was found later not to be the case.

The sewer ran at an awkward angle under the terracing, making piecemeal development difficult. The total cost of development was estimated at a staggering £2 million. It was almost certainly a sum which Michael Gliksten was unwilling to pay and a sum which the new régime could hardly be expected to pay as they were simply tenants. They had, anyway, already put £2 million into saving the club.

How the GLC could close the whole terrace nevertheless still beggared belief. Its capacity was 20,000, yet Charlton's entire crowd around this time was not much more than 5,000. There would have been no conceivable danger from allowing a few thousand on the terracing.

The aftermath of the Bradford City disaster had caused sheer bureaucratic panic. But the GLC did allege a previous cause of complaint against the club. In 1979, the GLC had sought to limit the East Terrace to 3,000 spectators. But then they agreed a concession that they would allow 10,000 on the understanding that repair work would be done.

The repair work was not carried out, according to the GLC. Their action in 1985 was, in part, a reaction to this. Appeals by Charlton in the courts failed to stop them. On 5 August 1985, the Greater London Council began its offensive. It announced that it was applying for a summons against the club under section 10 of the Safety of Sports Ground Act.

The immediate cause was a pre-season friendly against Liverpool on 7 August.

The summons to stop the use of the East Terrace was taken because the GLC said it had not received an assurance from the club that it would close the terrace itself.

The GLC Public Services and Fire Brigade Committee stated: 'The GLC will not tolerate the use of any part of the football ground where there is a risk to spectators, especially in the light of the Bradford tragedy.'

Perhaps The Valley could have coped as a three-sided ground but Gliksten's action on the other side of the ground led to further confusion and turmoil. Gliksten owned The Valley through his private company, Adelong. The two acres he claimed were not included in the seven-year lease. The new men knew that Gliksten could occupy this land any time he chose but they and the fans were still taken aback.

Gliksten did not go through the stages of applying for planning permission to build on the site. He simply ordered the area to be fenced off. It was reported that he planned to put up houses or a hotel.

Just how far Michael Gliksten was aware of the effects of what the GLC was doing can only be guessed at, but it was deeply demoralizing to see both actions occurring together.

Fryer's Response

JOHN Fryer, the new chairman, was, like Gliksten, a man of powerful character and the dreadful situation he was in prompted him to decisive and tragic action. He decided that a move and a break from the lease was the only way out. The fashionable concept of ground sharing, so touted by the media, was the goal he now pursued.

Charlton approached West Ham United, across the river, but were turned down and an approach was reportedly made to Millwall, although Millwall deny this. Even Arsenal, the former Woolwich team, was considered as a home before a deal was struck with Crystal Palace.

The advantages were that Selhurst Park was a more modern stadium and that the Palace board were holding out welcoming hands since they could use the extra cash generated. Both teams were of roughly equal status so one would not overshadow the other.

But the crowning disadvantage was that Crystal Palace was in a very different geographical area of London. It was away from the river scene of the Thames, from the distinctive and historical Greenwich and Woolwich, from the din of the Blackwall Tunnel. And it was in the Surrey area of London, not the traditional Kentish area from which Charlton drew support.

The distance between the grounds was only seven miles but that disguised one of the most difficult urban drives in London through inadequate, congested roads, blocked to capacity on Saturdays. There was no direct rail connection and a bus needed an hour for the journey.

The way the move was announced left a particularly bitter taste in the mouths of Charlton fans. The first they heard of it was when they turned up for the League game at The Valley on 7 September 1985. Their opponents were — Crystal Palace.

As the fans turned up, they were given, to their shock and horror, a leaflet announcing the move. In these circumstances, the game itself was somewhat of an anti-climax, to say the least. The 3-1 win confirmed Charlton's opening good form — but that seemed almost irrelevant now.

The Valley —
abandoned and
soon overgrown.

Meanwhile, Michael Gliksten was quoted in the Press as saying: "It will be the saddest day for me if Charlton Athletic abandon their traditional home at The Valley." The fans were hostile to both him and John Fryer, angry at both men's actions. The Valley was their home, whoever the owner might be, and whoever owned the team.

Michael Gliksten strongly rejected allegations that he had forced the club to leave, successfully suing London Weekend Television for libel for an undisclosed sum which he donated to charity. He also demanded and received an apology from *Football Monthly* magazine for a similar statement.

As the board prepared for the removal to Selhurst, Gliksten claimed that Charlton owed him the remaining five-and-a-half years' rental of £70,000 a year as agreed in 1984. On 14 September, it was announced that Gliksten was taking legal action in an attempt to stop the move. If Charlton continued with the move, but remained liable for rental, this could have meant another bill of almost £400,000 for Charlton on top of the rental to Palace.

Gliksten was reported as saying: "They (Charlton) rented the ground from me to play football and they cannot just walk away from that. That is why I am taking legal action." John Fryer was reported as calling the threatened legal action 'a joke'.

The lease agreed with Palace was for seven years, with Charlton paying ten per cent of gate receipts.

Greenwich Council's five-year £250,000 sponsorship deal with Charlton was also to become a casualty of the move and was eventually cancelled.

The ground sharing between Palace and Charlton was given the official sanction of the Football League on 12 September 1985, after the Management Committee received assurances that the clubs could fulfil their fixture obligations. The day after, a Friday night, Charlton went down to their first League defeat of the season — 2-1 at Oldham. The one previous defeat had been by Crystal Palace in the League (Milk) Cup.

The Last Game

MEANWHILE the protest of supporters was taking shape with rumours surfacing of demonstrations at the last game at The Valley — on Saturday 21 September 1985, against Stoke City. And the growing bitterness began to take its toll on personalities. Supporters Club chairman, Jack Linsdell, who had previously described the move as a 'disgrace' was now quoted as saying he fully understood the reasons. "After meeting with club officials, we realize that there is no alternative." It was a statement that infuriated many loyalists and particularly a younger generation of intelligent, vociferous fans that was growing up around the club. The official supporters' club seemed, in their eyes, to be playing a mute role at an earth-shattering time in the club's history.

Club secretary, Graham Hortop, was quoted at the same time as saying: "We can all understand the fans' sadness because they are having to change the habits of a lifetime. But we are trying to make it as least inconvenient as possible, because we need them if we are to realize our ambitions to become a First Division club again. We hope they will all come with us. But naturally, there is great sadness and it is shared by all the staff here as well as the supporters."

John Fryer disclosed details to the Press of the new set-up he was aiming for at Selhurst — a joint company to own the ground with each club taking 50 per cent. He put the cost to Charlton at around £1 million.

In the strange sad atmosphere of The Valley's last game, Charlton won 2-0 before a crowd officially put at 8,858. The teams that day were: **Charlton Athletic:** Nicky Johns; John Humphrey, Mark Reid, Jimmy Loveridge, Steve Thompson, Les Berry, Mark Stuart, George Shipley, John Pearson, Mark Aizlewood (Robert Lee), Mike Flanagan. **Stoke City:** Peter Fox; Steve Bould, Mick Mills(Carl Beeston), Steve Parkin, Paul Dyson, George Berry, Neil Adams, Chris Maskery, Keith Bertschin, Carl Saunders, Phil Heath. The referee was Mike James of Horsham.

Teenagers Mark Stuart and Robert Lee scored the second-half goals that put Charlton fifth in the table. Lee's goal was the last scored at The Valley and Lee was perhaps the most fitting player to score it, since he had worked as a turnstile operator at the ground.

Banners were waved in protest, fans laid wreathes and a half-time demonstration on the pitch held up the second half. At the end there were tearful and emotional scenes as fans dug up pieces of their beloved turf to grow in their suburban gardens as a memory. The groundsman, Maurice Banham, found himself without a job.

Large numbers gathered around the main entrance for over an hour after the game, simply unwilling to leave despite a request to do so.

On Monday, 24 September, Charlton issued an announcement about the venue for their reserve games. They chose the ground of the Isthmian League side, Bromley, just over the historic Kent catchment area side of the boundary from the Surrey suburbia of Crystal Palace.

Later that week, Welling United, the Southern League club formed as recently as 1962 from an under-15 parks side, denied reports that they were actively seeking a move to The Valley. Shortly afterwards at the start of October, yet another Southern League club came into the picture. Fisher Athletic, based in a new little stadium in London's docklands near Rotherhithe, launched an advertising campaign on the commercial London radio station, LBC, in the hope of attracting Charlton supporters unhappy with the move to Selhurst. Their commercial manager, Tony Incenzo, commented: "We are especially hopeful of attracting disillusioned Charlton supporters. I went to the last match at The Valley and got the impression that a lot of people won't follow the team to Crystal Palace."

Signs of the obvious rush to leave The Valley now emerged — and the disturbing fact that it was done without the fullest board consultation. Bill Strong, Greenwich Council's representative on the Charlton board, said he had not been involved in the decision to leave The Valley and share Selhurst. He commented: "I was a bit upset not to be involved in that decision." As time went by, it emerged that the decision had been very much the personal initiative of John Fryer.

The last game at The Valley versus Stoke. Top: View from the empty East Terrace. Middle: Young fans protest at half-time. Bottom: Robert Lee scores the last goal at The Valley.

But a tiny beacon of hope emerged during these days of tragedy. Greenwich Council stated it was their aim that The Valley should remain an open space for sport and recreation. The council added they would resist any plans for development. It was a beacon that was to guide the small devoted army of Charlton fans who kept faith with the club in the immediate years ahead.

While The Valley remained, even in decay and growing ruin, hope sprang eternal of a return some day. It sat like a ghost of a stadium, but it was there and remained there, undeveloped, unbuilt on. Could it be all over yet? Could a football stadium simply die like this?

Players of yesteryear before the last match at The Valley on 21 September 1985. Back row (left to right): Harold Hobbis, Charlie Revell, Arthur Horsfield, Peter Croker, Ted Croker, Billy Robinson, Eric Lancelotte, George Green, Derek Ufton. Front row: Paul Went, Cec Davies, 'Sailor' Brown, Charlie Hall (club physiotherapist), Phil Warman, Brian Kinsey, Eddie Marsh, Mike Bailey, Derek Hales.

Selhurst - Triumph and Sadness

AND so to Selhurst — South London still, but a very different South London amid the outskirts of Croydon and one of the longest seven miles ever. London is not one amorphous mass, however much it may seem that at times, and it was very much a different world the Charlton fans were entering. Some — many indeed — from the northwest Kent fringes actually lived nearer to Selhurst, but participating in the first permanent groundsharing in League history was an experiment of which they would rather have not been a part.

The first game at Selhurst was played in a strange atmosphere. On the main Selhurst stand, the black and red roundel of Charlton joined the insignia of Crystal Palace. And the physical presence of Charlton was a portakabin block by the main stand — a symbol of what seemed a transient status.

The first playing presence was the day before the opening game at Selhurst which was to be against Sunderland on Saturday, 5 October. A training session was held on the pitch on the Friday. Through the week the players had trained on a ground in New Eltham.

Said the ever-patient Lennie Lawrence: "It's difficult to say how the players will react, but at least we have five or six newcomers who didn't really have time to develop a sense of identity with The Valley."

Charlton were still going strongly near the top of Division Two, so the real question was the attendance. Free coach rides were laid on from the Greenwich area for the first games. The crowd was 5,552 against the usual crowd figure for the season of around 4,000. And, of course, it included large away support from Sunderland.

There was an atmosphere of resignation in contrast to the bitterness of the previous match, and Charlton ran out 2-1 winners, Mark Stuart scoring the winning goal seven minutes from the end. A Pearson header dropped to Stuart whose shot went in off the far post. Mark Reid had scored the first goal at Selhurst — a penalty to put Charlton in front after 29 minutes. Eric Gates scored Sunderland's equalizer in the 58th minute after a drive from Walker had hit the underside of the bar.

The teams were: **Charlton Athletic:** Nicky Johns; John Humphrey, Mark Reid, Jimmy Loveridge(Mike Flanagan), Steve Thompson, John Pender, George Shipley, Robert Lee, John Pearson, Alan Curbishley,

Mark Stuart. **Sunderland:** Bob Bolder; George Burley, Alan Kennedy, Peter Daniel, Gary Bennett, Shaun Elliott, Frank Gray, Barry Venison, David Swindlehurst(David Hodgson), Eric Gates, Clive Walker. The referee was Jeff Bray of Leicester.

From this good start in playing terms, the miracle, the impossible, one of the momentous achievements in Football League history, began to unfold. Despite the enormity of the club's plight, Lawrence managed to keep his players' minds on promotion. Incredibly to the outside world and indeed to the Charlton fans

Promotion partners John Pearson and Robert Lee.

First game at Selhurst Park. Skipper Steve Thompson leads out the Charlton team against Sunderland on 5 October 1985.

themselves, the promotion challenge grew stronger and yet stronger.

Pearson formed a scoring partnership with Mike Flanagan, Mark Stuart and Robert Lee also hit scoring form. And to boost this incredible challenge, just before the March transfer deadline, Lawrence pulled off a bargain of a signing to give the extra goal power and aggression in attack needed to ensure promotion.

The much-travelled Scottish player, Jim Melrose, was signed for £45,000 from Manchester City and scored on his debut in a 2-2 draw at Millwall. He went on to score five times in 11 games as the promotion push formed into hard reality.

Faraway Carlisle

ONCE again, as before in Charlton's post-war history, faraway Carlisle became the crucial final staging point for promotion. With Portsmouth's challenge fading and Norwich firmly at the top of the table, it looked as if Charlton and Wimbledon were the teams to take the other promotion spots. Charlton needed to win at Brunton Park to make virtually certain of promotion.

For the horde of Charlton fans who made the long journey northwards, there were heartaches galore as the match unfolded. True to the club's tradition, nothing ran to form at the vital moment. For the game was a desperate one for Carlisle, too, as they needed to win to save their own Second Division place. It also bore similarity to the last game in which

Charlton had clinched promotion to the First a half-a-century before when a draw for the opponents that day, Port Vale, doomed them to relegation.

The Carlisle game shaped like a disaster. Charlton found themselves 2-0 down as half-time loomed, but then kindly fate intervened in the form of an absurd own-goal by Carlisle's Jim Tolmie, who shot past his own goalkeeper just before half-time. But the agony continued. It was not until the last 20 minutes, when Charlton scored twice to run out 3-2 winners, that the fans could start to celebrate. The equalizer came from a Mark Stuart header and then captain Mark Aizlewood powered through for a dramatic winner.

Triumph amid sadness. It was the long awaited return to Division One which many thought they would never witness. But it was not to The Valley that First Division football would return. The successors of Bartram and Firmani and Leary and Ufton would not tread the same turf.

A crowd of 13,214 — the largest to watch Charlton at Selhurst so far — saw the last game of the season, appropriately against South London rivals Wimbledon, who had also ensured their promotion place. A goalless draw saw Charlton take the runners-up position and Wimbledon the third place.

First Division Football

HAD the club a strong enough team for Division One? Would the miracle continue? Lawrence — with really little choice — made few signings as the club prepared for life in Division One.

187

Getting ready for life in Division One. Charlton's trio of former Sheffield Wednesday players (from left), Peter Shirtliff, Bob Bolder and John Pearson pictured during training in August 1986.

Meanwhile, Greenwich Council acted to make sure that he could not develop the rest of The Valley. They designated the land for public recreational use.

Whether Gliksten wanted to sell and on what basis — land for housing or simply to the council for recreational use — remained a matter of speculation.

Meanwhile, the ground deteriorated and trees started growing both on the pitch and on the fated East Terrace. And the vandals made the North Stand their target, with at least one fire started in it.

At the back of the North Stand, the Valley Club still functioned under the former international, Mike Bailey, and once he even went on to the pitch to mow one of the goalmouths. Former groundsman, Maurice Banham was more unlucky. He was chased off the ground by guard dogs.

Sadly the magic, the miracle of First Division football surfaced only in the hearts of a few thousand fans. Too many of the old Division One era lay in their graves, not replaced by a new generation, while others refused to make the journey to the alien land of Selhurst. Thus, a crowd of only 8,501 saw the debut match in Division One, against Sheffield Wednesday at Selhurst. Robert Lee scored the opening goal, Charlton's first in Division One for almost three decades. But Wednesday equalized to make the game a 1-1 draw. With only one win from the first eight games — a memorable 1-0 victory at Old Trafford where Mark Stuart was the scorer — it began to look as if Charlton's Division One life would be a short one.

To strengthen the midfield, Lawrence signed Colin Walsh, a former Scottish Under-21 international from Nottingham Forest and Andy Peake, who had gained England Youth and Under-21 honours with Leicester City, from Grimsby Town. They made their debuts in the game against Liverpool at Anfield on 13 September and Walsh soon took the role of midfield creator.

It looked as if Lawrence had done the trick. In October, the club won all six games — four in the League and two in the League Cup, now the Littlewoods Cup. The League victories pushed the team up to mid-table, in 12th place, and it looked as if the club would establish themselves securely in Division One. November saw an exact reversal of this tremendous form with all six games lost — five in the League and one in the Littlewoods Cup. So the club plunged back to the relegation zone, falling to bottom place on Boxing Day, 1986, before a 5-0 victory over Manchester City at Selhurst Park two days later lifted them off again.

The Move for a Return

IN attendances, the move to Selhurst was now finally revealed as disastrous. First Division football was on offer, yet frequently the club failed to achieve a 6,000 attendance. The long-simmering discontent over Selhurst now began to spiral.

In the autumn of 1986, a 10,000-signature petition was gathered, urging a return to The Valley. Matters came to a head at a scheduled annual meeting of the supporters' club on 20 October. It had to be abandoned as a formal meeting as 700 people packed into the Valley Club, still operating by the side of the ghostly Valley. Many more could not get in as a large group of hecklers in front of the stage caused chaos when directors Michael Norris and Derek Ufton attempted to speak. It was an undignified occasion to say the least as fingers were stabbed close to Norris and Ufton. Even Ufton's reputation as one of

One signing proved highly significant — that of defender Peter Shirtliff, a player reared at Sheffield Wednesday and who had helped the Owls battle out of Division Three to regain their First Division status. Another signing was to prove significant but not so immediately — that of the man who had kept goal for Sunderland on Charlton's debut at Selhurst Park, Bob Bolder. Bob had also played for Wednesday in their rise from Third to First Division, although, unlike the Barnsley-born Shirtliff, he was a southerner, a Dover-born man. From Wednesday, he had gone to understudy Bruce Grobbelaar at Liverpool for two seasons without once making a first-team appearance, before arriving at Sunderland.

For the devoted and suffering Charlton fan, the advent of the First Division was a miracle. And it was wonderfully nostalgic for the older fan, who had last seen First Division football 29 long years ago. The regret which united both older and younger fans was that The Valley had not lived to see the day.

If only Charlton's new Division One career could have been there. If only . . .if only.

The actions of Michael Gliksten remained a mystery. A year after the move, neither he nor his company, Adelong, had made any planning application for the two-acre site he had claimed.

Jim Melrose with the match-ball after scoring a hat-trick in the 3-2 defeat of Everton at Selhurst on 11 October 1986.

Charlton's greatest-ever players did not save him from the wrath of young fans, who either did not know his past or did not care.

Captain Mark Aizlewood was forced to try to calm the young fans down. He said: "If there were a practical way to return to The Valley, the players would, I am sure, back the campaign to put it into effect. I can assure them that the chairman, John Fryer, is as big a supporter of Charlton Athletic as anyone else."

Ufton told the meeting how the directors had earlier that year tried to buy The Valley back, but their offer of more than £1 million had been rejected.

In November, little more than a year after the move, Charlton announced their intention to try to return

Mark Stuart challenges Ronnie Whelan for the ball at Anfield in September 1986. Charlton's visit to the League Champions resulted in a 2-0 defeat for the newly-promoted Londoners.

Charlton's first Division One goal for 29 years, scored by Robert Lee, a former Valley turnstile operator. Lee is seen putting Charlton ahead against Sheffield Wednesday at Selhurst on the opening day of the 1986-7 season.

Charlton's first win back in Division One came against Manchester United at Old Trafford on 30 August 1986. Here John Humphrey keeps control of the ball to go past Jesper Olsen.

191

Squad for Charlton's second spell in the top flight, after the signing of Colin Walsh and Andy Peake in September 1986. Back row (left to right): George Shipley, Andy Peake, John Humphrey, Mark Stuart, Jim Melrose, Steve Jacobs. Middle row: Charlie Hall (physiotherapist), Brian Eastick (coach), John Pender, Nicky Johns, John Pearson, Bob Bolder, Peter Shirtliff, Colin Clarke (youth-team coach), Bill Gallagher (assistant physiotherapist). Front row: Robert Lee, Colin Walsh, Steve Gritt, Mark Aizlewood (captain), Lennie Lawrence (manager), Steve Thompson, Alan Curbishley, Mark Reid.

Skipper Mark Aizlewood tried to calm Charlton's angry young fans as a meeting at the Valley Club erupted.

to their home area of Greenwich. The Selhurst move was now quite clearly a failure as attendances for First Division matches at the stadium were demonstrating only too clearly.

After a meeting on 6 November, the directors, local councillors and a group of supporters agreed they would explore the possibility of creating a new ground in Greenwich. Vice-chairman Richard Collins stated: "Now there is an expression of intent to return to the borough, I hope the fans who have been boycotting matches will come and support us at Selhurst Park." But it was still just 'an expression of intent' and still the fans had to wait and hope.

The Low

THE home game with Oxford United in March 1987 drew only 4,205 spectators and briefly held the record for the lowest crowd for any First Division game since World War Two, until Wimbledon took over the dismal honour. The following month, Jimmy Hill resigned from the board to go to another club facing the loss of a famous ground — taking over as chairman of his old club, Fulham, where once again he would be involved in an attempt to share grounds.

The struggle on the field to hold on to First Division status inevitably led to changes in the team. The captain, Mark Aizlewood, and John Pearson both departed for Leeds early in 1987. In the other direction came the experienced Tottenham defender Paul Miller and Dundee United midfield player, Ralph Milne.

Even if automatic relegation was avoided, there now loomed the threat of play-offs for the club finishing fourth from bottom of Division One. They would fight it out with the third, fourth and fifth teams in Division Two, in a new system inaugurated by the League. Part of the League's aim was to reduce the First Division by one club each season for the next two seasons until membership stood at 20 clubs.

But this difficult season had one silver lining — an appearance at Wembley in the second season of the new Full Members' Cup for First and Second Division sides. The final was against Division Two Blackburn Rovers before a crowd of 40,000 on Sunday, 29 March. To see Charlton again at Wembley was certainly a nostalgic occasion if not quite like the real thing of an FA Cup Final. It provided a day-out and a little relief from the League struggle. But the day-out ended with Charlton going down to a late Blackburn goal from Hendry.

In May, Charlton featured in another Final, this time in the FA Youth Cup. It was the first time in the club's history that they had gone this far in the competition and the first leg against Coventry at Selhurst was drawn 1-1. Coventry took the lead in the first half and Ronnie Mauge equalized in the 68th minute, ramming the ball home after a Carl Leaburn shot was blocked. The Coventry team featured two sets of identical twins. The return leg at Highfield Road saw Coventry lift the trophy when they scored the only goal of the game in extra-time.

With time running out in the relegation struggle, Lawrence signed another former Spurs favourite, the experienced striker Garth Crooks from West Bromwich Albion. Crooks had previously played for Stoke.

A fine 3-0 win at St James' Park against Newcastle rekindled hope and then the club managed to gain, if not outright safety, then at least a place in the play-offs in a nerve-racking final game of the season at Selhurst, when they beat Queen's Park Rangers 2-1.

If that had been nerve-racking, the play-offs almost brought heart failure and an emotional experience which fans still quiver with now. Charlton's first opponents, Ipswich Town, were dispatched 2-1 on aggregate. Then in the final games, Leeds were beaten 1-0 at Selhurst, but reversed the scoreline at Elland Road, to send the two teams for a final confrontation at St Andrews in Birmingham. If the scores were level after extra-time, then penalties would decide the issue. In the Leeds side were Mark Aizlewood and John Pearson, the men who had done so much to secure Charlton's Division One place and who now threatened to end it.

After 90 minutes, the score was 0-0. A superb goal from a free-kick in extra-time from John Sheridan of Leeds looked to have doomed Charlton. But Peter Shirtliff played an heroic captain's role by scoring twice in the final minutes to save Charlton's Division One future. Agony and triumph again. And another miracle.

Peter Shirtliff, captain courageous whose stirring play helped keep Charlton in Division One before he returned to his former club, Sheffield Wednesday.

Charlton Athletic and Blackburn Rovers emerge from the Wembley tunnel for the 1987 Full Members' Cup Final.

Steve Gritt, physically and mentally exhausted after Charlton's battle for survival against Leeds.

Far right: From promotion triumph to play-off survival. Lennie Lawrence shouldered high by fans at Carlisle.

Michael Gliksten Resurfaces

Meanwhile, Michael Gliksten resurfaced in another football context in the pages of the *Sunday Times* which reported in March 1986 on his new love — Clapton Football Club, of The Old Spotted Dog in Forest Gate. Clapton, once a top amateur club, now languished in bottom place in Division Two North of the Vauxhall League and Michael Gliksten had become their president, harkening back to the involvement of his father and uncle in another Clapton club, Clapton Orient.

Gliksten, through the *Sunday Times* criticized the professional game of which he had been so much a part, blaming administrators, rather than players, for professional football's insolvency and for erosion of the spirit which made the game fun.

In the close season, John Fryer, now nearing his own professional retirement, stepped down as chairman of Charlton Athletic, becoming joint president with his colleague, John Sunley. Richard Collins again became chairman, but Sunley Holdings retained ownership of the club.

On to the board now came a Lloyds broker and farmer, Roger Alwen, a Charlton supporter since 1949. He had first met the Charlton board when a guest of the late Coventry City chairman, John Poynton, at Highfield Road in February. Alwen made an immediate impact by acquiring, with Michael Norris, for £500,000 the training ground the club were

using since the loss of their New Eltham premises. The ground, the Aries Sports Ground off Sparrows Lane, was totally refurbished with a manager's office, medical room, weight-training room, dressing-rooms, showers, kit room and laundry. It had three pitches and, in effect, became the new headquarters of Charlton Athletic. The 18-acre ground was officially opened on Sunday, 4 October 1987 by the Minister of Sport, Colin Moynihan, a personal friend of Alwen's. For the 1987-8 season it was decided to switch reserve matches from Bromley's ground to that of Welling United.

During the summer of 1987, Lawrence had acted to strengthen his midfield. Former England Youth star, Steve Mackenzie, was signed from West Bromwich Albion for £200,000. For Mackenzie, it was a return to Selhurst Park. A player developed in the apprentice ranks of Crystal Palace, he had been sold by Malcolm Allison as a 17-year-old for £250,000 to Manchester City in 1979, amazingly without even having played a first-team game for Palace.

Charlton's signing of him was one in the mould of many Lawrence signings — players of high talent who had fallen from form, perhaps from a difficult playing or managerial environment so that the man-

management talents and the kindlier atmosphere of Charlton could revive them.

Mackenzie struggled at first as Charlton dashed the hopes raised by the previous end-of-season revival and trailed along at the bottom of the League, losing five and drawing one of their opening six games. The play-offs had taken an emotional and psychological toll of the players which they were finding difficult to shake off.

Melrose, a perpetual mover between clubs, departed

Top: Colin Walsh's free-kick goes in past the Liverpool wall at Anfield in September 1987.

Left: The unlucky Colin Walsh, pictured at home after breaking his leg in the 2-1 defeat at Newcastle in November 1987.

Middle left: Sports Minister The Rt. Hon. Colin Moynihan MP, a declared Charlton supporter, officially opens the new training ground, at Sparrows Lane, New Eltham, on Sunday, 4 October 1987. He is shaking hands with Charlton skipper Peter Shirtliff. Opposite: Club-house at the new training centre, reckoned to be amongst the best-equipped in Division One.

early in the season for Leeds. He had never sold his house in Cheshire and had been a player perpetually in transit between north and south. His departure left Charlton even shorter of fire-power up front.

To try to solve the situation, Lawrence paid £300,000 for the Welsh international Andy Jones of Third Division Port Vale, but although he scored early goals, the team still struggled. But then with Mackenzie beginning to find his true form in midfield, the team began to revive dramatically and hauled themselves off the bottom where they had remained anchored for so long. Not just miracle men, another name began to appear for them — the Houdinis of the First Division.

The group of young and intelligent fans which had emerged since the move from The Valley, now came into their own, campaigning to hasten the hoped-for departure from Selhurst Park. They did so in two dramatic ways — one short-term, one long-term. The short-term move was to call for a fans' boycott of the game at Selhurst on 26 March against Oxford United — a fixture they knew would be one of the weaker attractions of the League programme.

For the long-term they realized that the Supporters' Club newsletter could never be the unfettered voice they wanted, since the club exercised ultimate control over it. Thus, in February 1988, these young, disaffected fans launched their own publication *Voice of the Valley*. It was immediately effective — iconoclastic, hard-hitting, brilliantly written and often very cruel to the club's personalities. It rapidly became accepted as one of the best of the emerging 'fanzine' publications that were springing up around the country.

Soon after, in March 1988, came the tangible breakthrough in the club's plans to return to Greenwich. On 2 March, Mike Norris, the vice-chairman, and Roger Alwen announced that they had acquired, in their personal capacity, the Gliksten company owning The Valley, Adelong, with the help of finance from Laing Homes. The question now was whether The Valley would be redeveloped into a smaller stadium with part of the site used for housing, or whether The Valley would be developed entirely by Laing and the proceeds used to construct a new stadium elsewhere.

No fee for the sale was disclosed at the time but the figure was later revealed as £2.6 million. The future — the new ground or smaller Valley — would depend to a great degree on Greenwich Council which had so resolutely blocked Michael Gliksten on the site.

As a result of the announcement, the proposed boycott of the Oxford United game on 26 March, called for by the independent supporters' group based on *The Voice of The Valley* magazine was called off. For a year, various new sites in Greenwich were inspected and considered, the two serious contenders being a site on the Greenwich peninsular, the Metrogas Sports Ground which was owned by British Gas, and the Thames Polytechnic Sports Ground at Eltham. The Metrogas site had the sentimental attraction that it was close to the site of the old Angerstein ground of Charlton's pre-World War One days.

For a second season running, there was a nerve-racking finish. With one game to play, Charlton were level on points with fellow relegation strugglers Chelsea but with a far better goal difference. And that last game was against Chelsea. Charlton needed to win or draw to avoid the play-offs. Chelsea needed to win.

Behind to a penalty in the 15th minute, Charlton looked set again for the play-offs. Then a courageous and desperate effort in a crowded penalty area by Paul Miller in the 65th minute took a deflection and the ball hit the back of the Chelsea net. Another 25 tense minutes, and Charlton had again saved their Division One life by the skin of their teeth.

Alwen and Norris Takeover

IN June 1988, ownership of the club changed again. Roger Alwen and Michael Norris announced that they had become joint owners, each with 50 per cent. Thus, ownership of The Valley was finally reunited with ownership of the club. With John Fryer having come to the end of his career with Sunleys, the move was a natural one but it meant that the massive financial power of Sunleys was now removed. The deal cost some £3¼ million, including the acqusition of £350,000 shares at par and cleard Sunley's net debts.

John Fryer had not long to live. He died in Florida in June 1989, aged 69, after a long illness. He was still joint president at the time of his death.

News of the move to Greenwich remained in a state of suspense but hopes for the more promising alternative site, Metrogas on the peninsular, began to fade. British Gas wanted the land to go for housing development and a football stadium was not part of the plan.

In this strange quiet, as the directors negotiated and negotiated, Charlton began the 1988-9 season still holding out the prospect of First Division football at The Valley. Could the club hold its place long

Woolwich Town Hall on 23 March 1989. Charlton supporters applaud Roger Alwen's announcement that their club is to return to The Valley.

enough for this to happen or a new stadium to be occupied?

This season, with Division One reduced to 20 teams, there would be no play-offs for Division One clubs. Just three relegation places to avoid.

Meanwhile, the affairs of Mark Hulyer had experienced the full weight of the law of the land. On 25 September, at Southwark Crown Court, he pleaded guilty to fraudulent trading and not properly keeping and preserving accounting books. He was sentenced to two years' imprisonment, suspended for two years, as well as being fined £10,000 and ordered to pay prosecution costs of £7,560. He was also disqualified from being a director of a limited company for five years.

In September, the directors held a public meeting at Greenwich Town Hall to present a progress report to supporters but still there was no definite news. On the field of play, meanwhile, a new saviour was at hand as a goalscorer at last emerged again — the Lawrence-bred talent of Paul Williams, a signing from non-League Woodford Town. With Williams scoring consistently, and the midfield and defence bedding in, the club rose to mid-table in October. That month, Lawrence paid out a club record £430,000 to Chelsea for their central

defender, Colin Pates, tangible proof of the club's ambition. Then Williams was injured in the match at Wimbledon the following month. The goals dried up and the team's form slipped.

Charlton hovered above the three relegation places uneasily but then came significant developments that made the fans turn momentarily away from the dramas of Division One. Roger Alwen, the joint owner of The Valley, became chairman in March 1989, with Richard Collins remaining a director and becoming a president. Shortly after Alwen's accession, a meeting was called for Thursday, 23 March, at Woolwich Town Hall. The fans guessed what the news might be but it leaked out anyway. As Roger Alwen rose to announce the news, the packed hall was ready to hail him. When he reached the words, 'which will enable Charlton Athletic Football Club to once again play football at The Valley', rapturous applause engulfed him — a rare occasion for any Charlton chairman. It was a rare coming together in absolute unity of a club and its followers. The pandemonium of emotion that followed was predictable but marvellously uplifting — applause, cheers, cries and tears. The end of the long night of exile beckoned at last.

Return and Rejection

BUT it is tragedy that ever stalks Charlton Athletic as a club and soon the fans were to experience the heights of wonderful emotion and the depths of bitter despair as the future of The Valley was again shrouded with uncertainty. The announcement of the move back brought first elation, then a sombre reflection — what a cruel irony if the return to The Valley was to Second Division football. That sort of awesome bad luck would have been only too apt in the Charlton tradition of missed opportunities.

The sombre reflection began to turn into grim reality. With three games to go the team, having stayed above the relegation places for most of the 1988-9 season, slumped to the third relegation place, two points behind Sheffield Wednesday. This followed a 5-2 thrashing on the plastic pitch of fellow strugglers, Luton Town. The despair turned into elation and the Luton débâcle faded simply into a bad dream. Successive home wins over Wimbledon and Derby County lifted the team to 14th place — a position of almost comfortable safety which hardly did justice to the dramas of the season.

On Sunday, 2 April came a symbolic return to The Valley. The occasion — an astute piece of foresight and a touchingly sensitive gesture by the board. Their action was simple. They asked the fans to come and clear up The Valley, to remove the debris and clear

Below: Paul Mortimer indulges in a high-kicking routine during the 1-0 victory over Manchester United at Selhurst Park on 22 April 1989. Black armbands were worn after the Hillsborough tragedy. Opposite page: Carl Leaburn celebrates his goal which gave Charlton a 2-1 victory at Villa Park on 25 February 1989. Robert Lee (left) and Paul Williams embrace the goalscorer.

Right: Paul Williams tussles with Liverpool's Scottish international, Gary Gillespie, in the Merseysiders' 2-0 win at Anfield on 1 March 1989. Far right: Paul Williams battling again, this time with Wimbledon's Eric Young in Charlton's crucial 1-0 victory at Selhurst on 6 May 1989. This victory saw Charlton climb out of relegation trouble.

Valley rebel and chairman's wife come together at The Valley clean-up on Sunday, 2 April 1989. Left is Rick Everitt, editor of the *Voice of The Valley* fanzine. Right is Heather Alwen, wife of Charlton chairman Roger Alwen, who, with Michael Norris, led the move.

the vast terraces and the pitch of the overgrowth of trees and bushes. But the occasion was inevitably infinitely more than a cleaning-up. It was deeply symbolic — a reunion of the heart and soul between the club and its supporters. So, on a grey, wet Sunday morning in South London, the fans returned and the great Valley stadium heaved with life again.

Across the terraces, hundreds of people moved like figures in a Lowry painting, shovelling, sweeping, pulling up trees and bushes. In what was once the centre of the pitch, a giant bonfire burned, the leaping flames bringing back colour to what had been a ghost of a ground for three long years and more.

The club was home again, and for all of those present on that Sunday morning — including the author of this history — it was one of the most emotional moments of our lives. As we smiled at old friends and colleagues, there was a tremendous sense of warmth and good fellowship. Our Valley lived in us. That morning was full of memories. There was the fan who tried to find the West Stand seat of his father, a season-ticket holder who had died the previous year. Sadly, it had gone. There were young fans who only knew of Selhurst, who were now seeing The Valley and its giant slopes for the first time. There were fans who had come from long distances, from as far away as Somerset, to show how much they cared.

Lennie Lawrence gave an inpromptu Press conference whilst Steve Gritt, a player who now linked the old and the new Valley eras and surely one of the most loved footballers in the club's history, showed his young children the scene of so many of his playing years. The new chairman walked round carrying an air of nervous embarrassment at being the hero of such an unique and momentous occasion.

On the East Terrace, his wife and son were among the many busy figures cleaning away the debris. Two young girls found a new resident of the East Terrace slopes — a frog — and wondered what to do with him, now his damp, muddy habitat had been swept away. The club's commercial manager, Steve Sutherland, climbed the slopes to look out again from his boyhood viewpoint. Many others did the same.

On a cassette radio, over and over again came the *Red, Red, Robin* song of the club. And from the Valley Club came a stream of welcome hot cups of tea. Perhaps the most symbolic sight of all — a group of young fans playing football once again on The Valley turf.

Somewhere in the heavens above those grey damp skies, some faces must have looked down upon the scene — the great Sam, Jimmy Seed, Chris Duffy, Johnny Summers, Stuart Leary and all — and smiled again.

That wonderful emotional April day lives in the memory of all who took part but it was to lead to even more bitter disappointment than anything that had gone before in the six years of crisis and tragedy.

For as the promised land beckoned, so it disappeared — the dream laid to waste by Greenwich Council. Changes of mind and personnel saw the council begin to shift its position from being protectors of The Valley to opponents.

Shortly after that Sunday morning of emotional return, which was followed by a second clear-up Sunday, came an event that was to shake the football world — the death, on Saturday, 15 April, of 95 Liverpool fans at Hillsborough on FA Cup semi-final day.

Like the Bradford Valley Parade tragedy before it, it was to have implications for The Valley in that the lesson drawn in the bitter aftermath was the need for all-seater grounds.

On Sunday, 20 August 1989, at the club's open-day at New Eltham, plans for a magnificent new stadium were unveiled. A model on display showed the new Valley as it would finally look after all stages of development were completed — an all-seater stadium holding between 22,000 and 25,000 spectators.

Crucially, it was exactly the sort of stadium for which the Government and the football authorities were calling after Hillsborough. And the reality now

Symbolic return to The Valley as Charlton supporters clear the debris and undergrowth of three and a half years of neglect.

The Valley loses its floodlights in 1989— destination Biggleswade Town — as the ground is prepared for the move back.

Model of the new Valley. Only the Jimmy Seed Stand, on the left, would have survived. The West Stand, to the left of the Seed Stand, would have been the first stage of the new development.

loomed near. February 1990 was the targeted date for the move back to The Valley.

A new West Stand would then be ready, a 6,000-seater stand with executive boxes to be built as soon as the plans were approved.

The other immediate development would consist of the refurbishment of the old North Stand and the relaying of the lower half of the vast East Terrace to accommodate 6,000 fans.

It now emerged as fact that it was the lack of proper foundations, not the sewer underneath, that was the

Joint editors of the *Voice of the Valley* magazine and Valley Party campaigners, Steve Dixon (left) and Rick Everitt (right), hand a petition to John Cartwright, Social Democratic MP for Woolwich, outside The Valley in 1989, protesting at the Government's plan for football identity cards. Cartwright strongly backed Charlton's return to The Valley.

cause of the subsidence and decay in that mighty bank of terracing.

Over a five-year development period, two more new stands were to be developed on the north and east sides with executive boxes. Only the Jimmy Seed Stand would remain of the old.

The new North Stand would include a banqueting suite and restaurant and 30,000 square feet of office space. It would entail the demolition of the Valley Club.

Both the West and North stands would be cantilever-roofed and the third and final stage of the development would involve extending the cantilever roof over the East Terrace.

A fortnight later, plans were presented to Greenwich Council in the form of two applications — one for the West Stand and one for the rest of the project, including 24 flats on the land at the top of the East Terrace.

But now the first signs of new disaster beckoned. As the autumn wore on there was a surprising lack of reaction from Greenwich Council. The seeds of doubt began to cloud the minds of the faithful. As time slipped away, February looked to be increasingly unrealistic as a date for the return. Even once planning permission was granted, there would be a 16-week wait for the steel girders needed for construction.

No date emerged for the hearing of the application and then the reason began to emerge. Some residents in The Valley area began to voice their opposition, citing fears of football hooliganism and traffic problems arising both from match-days and the wider restaurant and office use to which the club wanted to put the new Valley.

This paved the way for a council 'consultation' exercise. Three 'consultative' residents' meetings were arranged and the wholesale support which the leaders

of the council had previously given publicly now began to look dubious indeed, for the 'problems' cited by residents were all ones that could have been anticipated much, much earlier.

The meetings took place at the end of October — some eight months after Roger Alwen's announcement of the intended return. What emerged was astounding. It became quite clear that planners and new political leaders were adopting attitudes very different from the public stances adopted by previous leaders.

The planners appeared to question the restaurant and office use and new personalities in the form of the chairman of the planning committee, Councillor Simon Oelman, and the leader of the council, Councillor Quentin Marsh, took a similar stance.

The euphoria which had existed from May to August now turned into despair and depression. Meanwhile, the growing months of delay were once again putting a question mark against the club's whole future.

Some £300,000 had already been invested in clearing up the ground and demolishing the old West Stand. Meanwhile, the worsening financial situation began to affect the club on the field.

After a good start to the season in which the team had been unbeaten in its first four games — a 3-0 victory over Chelsea and three draws — and briefly reached third place, a rot set in and the next five games were all lost to send Charlton down the table.

Of course, the problems of The Valley meant there was now no money to invest in new players. Before the start of the season, yet another club record fee of £600,000 had gone to Chelsea, for Pates' old partner,

Charlton's 1988-9 squad. Back row (left to right): Andy Jones, Mickey Bennett, David Campbell, Darren Pitcher, Steve Gritt, Mark Stuart, Paul Mortimer. Middle: Jimmy Hendry (physiotherapist), Bill Gallacher (kit manager), Steve Mackenzie, Bob Bolder, Carl Leaburn, Jim McDonagh, Paul Miller, Colin Clarke (youth-team manager), Mike Flanagan (coach). Front: Mark Reid, Robert Lee, Colin Walsh, Garth Crooks, Lennie Lawrence (manager), Peter Shirtliff (captain), John Humphrey, Andy Peake, Paul Williams.

Joe McLaughlin, Charlton's record signing from Chelsea.

203

the central defender Joe McLaughlin. And £100,000 was spent on experienced goalkeeper Mick Salmon from Wrexham as cover for Bolder. They were to be the last big-fee signings.

McLaughlin replaced Peter Shirtliff, who for personal reasons had returned 'home' to Sheffield Wednesday to the immense regret of all Charlton supporters, who were sad to lose such a spirited and committed player.

International recognition came to Paul Williams, who gained four England caps in the European Under-21 tournament in France in the summer. Williams scored three goals and Paul Mortimer, who won two caps in the same tournament, netted twice. Williams followed up this success by gaining two England 'B' caps during the season, against Yugoslavia and the Republic of Ireland.

The residents' meetings attracted about 150 people in all, a large proportion being Charlton fans, but no firm conclusions could be drawn except for the attitudes now emerging from Greenwich Council.

The result was a decision by the council not to take any action until a meeting of the planning committee on 31 January — a mammoth ten months after the Alwen announcement.

Charlton fans drew the conclusion from the woefully long drawn-out process that the council had been trying to avoid a commitment either way before the local council elections of May 1990.

But now the pressure of events had led to decision time at the fateful meeting at Woolwich Town Hall. Some 400 fans marched from The Valley and they were joined by many more outside the Town Hall.

But there was only room for 600 inside and the doors were closed three quarters of an hour early. About 1,000 fans gathered outside and hundreds of them steadfastly remained there for three hours on a rainy evening.

The committee voted ten to two against Charlton's application and it was obvious from the proceedings that minds were already made up. The *Eltham Times* commented of the rejection: 'When the council does not listen, when the decision has already been made behind closed doors and when everyone knows it is a pretence, then democracy has been ridiculed in Greenwich.'

The rejection came just two days after the report by Lord Justice Taylor on the Hillsborough disaster, which called for all-seater stadiums. Yet here, incredibly, was just the kind of stadium Taylor called for being thrown out for inexplicable reasons.

Every other First Division ground has non-football uses. It is an accepted part of modern football economics that a modern stadium cannot pay its way just once a fortnight.

Yet Greenwich Council seemed blind to this. They seemed blind to the fact that the club had been at the ground since 1919 and residents had moved to the area knowing perfectly well that there was a football ground there, or at least since 1986 that Charlton were trying to return.

On the criteria adopted by the council, hardly any football ground in the country would be allowed to exist. The great London stadiums of Arsenal and Spurs, for example, are in densely-populated urban areas with little parking.

In fact, The Valley, with the East Side finishing on the edge of a chalk pit, with a railway line and main road near, was a better situated ground than most others in London.

And among the councillors there was simply a devastating lack of awareness of what a football team means in the tradition of an area and the feelings and loyalties it creates.

As one fan remarked with penetrating sarcasm: "They treated Charlton like it was an application from Sainsburys."

Just two days later, a death followed that was poignant and symbolic — that of 78-year-old Don Welsh, the FA Cup-winning captain and the greatest outfield player in the club's history.

Charlton, he said, were 'his only football love' through the years of his life. At his funeral in Luton, the Charlton Athletic Supporters' Club wreath bore these words: 'In memory of Charlton's greatest captain. He who would valiant be. . .' The words of that Bunyan-inspired hymn are so tragically appropriate for every Charlton supporter. They follow on — 'against all disaster'.

Those who had fought for The Valley were now steeled for all disaster and the struggle had bred an amazing tenacity — a spirit that could not be obliterated until and unless The Valley itself was physically obliterated .

In the bitter aftermath of the Greenwich Council refusal, the Charlton fans used an amazing piece of imagination — and one that was to do them great credit. If impending local elections had spelt doom for the new Valley, why shouldn't they, the fans, take part in those elections?

And so true to the unique, eccentric traditions of the club that is Charlton Athletic, another first was created in English football and perhaps the world. Charlton became the first club ever to have its own political party. The Valley Party was formed and contested 60 of the 62 seats in the council elections on Thursday, 3 May 1990. The only seats not fought were those of the two councillors who had voted for the return to The Valley — Bob Callow and Jim Coughlan.

The Valley Party, led by Barry Nugent, were realistic enough to know that they would not win seats on a single issue. From the start, they said it was the size of the vote that mattered.

The secretary of the supporters' club, Roy King, became agent and another fan, Richard Hunt, a director of a London advertising agency, devised a brilliant poster and leaflet campaign which tore into the central issue — what was at stake were feelings of identity, belonging, community.

Around Greenwich arose posters stressing the club's links with the past of the area, stressing the future by depicting a lone young fan and using irony and humour by asking the council how would they like it if they were sent to Croydon.

As the campaign gained in force and brilliance, so sadly was the First Division life ebbing out of Charlton on the field. A 3-1 defeat at Wimbledon

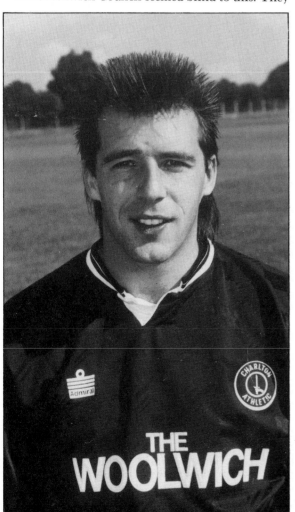

Andy Jones, Welsh international striker.

LET'S SEND THE COUNCIL TO CROYDON AND SEE HOW THEY LIKE IT.

VOTE VALLEY MAY 3RD

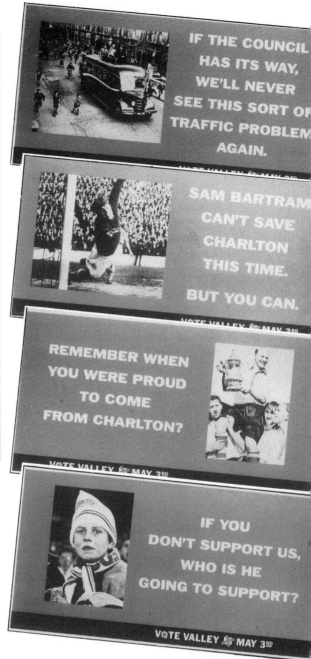

IF THE COUNCIL HAS ITS WAY, WE'LL NEVER SEE THIS SORT OF TRAFFIC PROBLEM AGAIN.

SAM BARTRAM CAN'T SAVE CHARLTON THIS TIME. BUT YOU CAN.

REMEMBER WHEN YOU WERE PROUD TO COME FROM CHARLTON?

IF YOU DON'T SUPPORT US, WHO IS HE GOING TO SUPPORT?

VOTE VALLEY MAY 3RD

The campaign posters — feelings of identity, belonging to the community. Pictured below in Bugsbys Way, Charlton.

on Boxing Day planted them at the bottom of the table, where they stayed for ten weeks before a brief revival saw them lift just one place off, above Millwall.

At the heart of the team's troubles was an appalling goalscoring record. They finished the season with only 31 League goals — the lowest in the club's history — and the lowest-ever average per game of 0.8158.

And for the first time since the return to the First Division, manager Lennie Lawrence was forced to sell players, Mickey Bennett going to Wimbledon for £250,000 and Colin Pates to Arsenal for £500,000. The brief revival ended and the team lost its last six games of the season to finish second from bottom with only 30 points.

In the elections on 3 May, the Valley Party scored a massive 14,838 votes, an astounding total for a single issue party, and managed to unseat the chairman of the planning committee, Councillor Simon Oelman.

The campaign and the vote had shown the true depth of feeling in Greenwich, wanting Charlton back at their rightful home, and just how shallow the council had been to listen to a number of residents who were simply not representative of the views of the people.

Many of those voting for the Valley Party were not even football supporters but knew that Charlton was part of their area and its traditions, and that the fans had fought an honest and just fight.

Three days later, Charlton played their last game in the First Division, at what Bobby Charlton had so elegantly described as the 'theatre of dreams' — Old Trafford.

In a dull game ending in a 1-0 defeat, the emotion was saved for the end when the players went over to their travelling fans and threw their shirts into the crowd. And the day was particularly marked by the generosity of the Manchester United supporters, to fans they recognized as having undergone so much heartbreak. Their remarks and their friendship paralleled the warm feelings towards the club in the rest of the football world.

And as the fans mingled and exchanged scarves,

Tommy Caton rises above Malcolm Allen in the 1-0 defeat by Norwich City at Selhurst Park on 3 March 1990.

shirts and mementoes, it was a small reminder that there still remained many times in the troubled world of football, where fans could get together and acknowledge they were all part of one family – the family of football.

But as the Charlton faithful made the long journey home, all knew that had those First Division years been at The Valley then Charlton might have had a fighting chance of adjusting to the economics of First Division life and have stayed in the top flight.

The 1989-90 squad pictured at the New Eltham training ground. The team coach at the wheel of the team coach is Mike Flanagan! At the door is Carl Leaburn with his arm on Darren Pitcher. Standing (left to right) are: Andy Jones, John Humphrey, Bob Bolder, Colin Pates (captain), Colin Walsh, Mark Reid, Paul Mortimer, Andy Peake, Mike Salmon, Steve Mackenzie, Lennie Lawrence (manager). Front row: Gordon Watson, Paul Williams, Robert Lee, Paul Bacon, Scott Minto, Jason Lee, Jimmy Hendry (physiotherapist).

Left: Andy Peake, a tenacious midfielder. Far left: Colin Pates, from Chelsea to Charlton to Arsenal.

Charlton
Athletic's last
First Division
game at their
adopted home of
Selhurst Park, on
28 April 1990
against Sheffield
Wednesday, who
were to join
Charlton in being
relegated to the
Second Division
at the end of that
season. The
Wednesday
forwards sit it out
as Bob Bolder, a
former Owls'
goalkeeper, grabs
at the ball. Joe
McLaughlin is the
Charlton man
stumbling
forward.

One More Heartbreak

AND so the wheel at Selhurst Park had turned full circle. Charlton were back in the Second Division they had started out in at Selhurst.

And there was little hope of an immediate return to the top flight after the collapse in playing strength of the previous season.

But it turned out that the May council elections had provided the turning point in the club's fortunes.

On the Labour side, the election had brought new people to the helm and in particular Norman Adams to the all-important chairmanship of the planning committee. He was to prove a much more sympathetic voice.

Harder to assess was how the ruling Labour Party regarded the continuing future of the Valley Party. Flushed with the success of the local elections, the Valley Party now threatened to stand not only in the highly-marginal Greenwich Borough Parliamentary seats of Woolwich and Greenwich, held by the SDP, and the outside marginal seat of Eltham, held by the Conservatives, but also in the neighbouring Tory marginals of Lewisham West and Lewisham East.

Even the Valley Party campaigners realised that a General Election was very different from a local election, and that when the future government of the country was at stake, the Valley Party might well be swept aside.

But in an election when Labour needed every last vote and to take all marginal seats to have any hope of forming a government, it seemed a foolish venture indeed to put at risk five possible gains for the sake of a bunch of football supporters.

And even if the Valley Party only secured a small fraction of the vote, the difference could still be crucial.

On the club's side there was also a willingness – born out of desperation – to compromise even though many supporters regarded the original stadium scheme as the only one which offered long term viability.

A fortnight after the elections came the first sign of a drawing together.

Chairman Adams said the planners were ready to talk.

"We recognise the legitimate needs of the club and of its supporters and, if we can have meaningful discussions with Charlton, we would be happy to meet them.

"The only real concern has been the environment of local residents. That is the only issue that separates us. We are not opposed to a return to The Valley. Everyone has made their point and now is the time to sort it out. We want to get over the impasse.'

On Tuesday, June 5, came the resumption of talks between the two sides when Alwen and Norris met with the planners at an 8 a.m. meeting.

Alwen commented afterwards: "We're all talking and it's all very positive."

He added: "There has been a fair amount of compromise on our side and I think that, with luck, we can get something agreed that would suit just about everyone.

That meeting was the first of a series and it soon became apparent just how Charlton were relinquishing the bold ambition of their original plans.

In particular, the large scale office and banqueting development at the back of the North Stand disappeared together with the housing element. A Laings Home option on 4.5 acres behind the old West Stand had already lapsed in February.

The new West Stand was now to house the nub of the club's facilities and community elements such as leisure facilities and a creche were to be incorporated into it.

The removal of the housing element would allow for some 300 to 400 parking spaces. And there was to be no development on the other three sides of the ground.

What was not clear was how the club could possibly fund the development once the commercial elements of the original scheme had been removed.

By the start of July, the police and the borough engineer had signified their assent to the outline scheme being drawn up by Charlton and the planners.

Then in mid July came the answer to the mystery of how Charlton would finance this new plan. The answer was a bowling alley under the new West Stand.

In spite of the economic recession of the time, bowling alleys had proved a big economic success in London, and the seven-day-a-week income from a successful alley was seen as the key to securing The Valley finances.

The stand's seating capacity was 4,500 against the 6,000 of the original scheme.

The East Terrace was to be relaid up to the central gangway at first with complete relaying at a later date. It would be a standing terrace still but raked so as to be able to take seats for the summer of 1994.

This was to meet the requirements of the report by Lord Justice Taylor into the Hillsborough disaster which stipulated the revolutionary change for First and Second Division football clubs of all-seater stadia with the lower divisions falling in line five years later.

With the North and South (Jimmy Seed) Stands being refurbished and seated, the capacity of the stadium was envisaged as 20,000.

It was hoped that the plans would be put to the October meeting of the planning committee with Charlton's return heralded for the start of the 1991-92 season.

On the playing side, the loss of income from the First Division attendances, television payments and other common income meant the club could not hope to hold on to its star players.

Life in the Second Division would mean that the club would be earning only half the income to meet its current running costs and pay packets negotiated in the First Division.

First John Humphrey departed (£450,000 to Crystal Palace), then Paul Williams (£600,000) to Sheffield Wednesday) and Joe McLaughlin (£350,000) to Watford). Garth Crooks was to retire early in the new season.

212

The parting of Humphrey, three times Player of the Year, was particularly bitter for the Charlton faithful. What it partly involved was Charlton clearing off their remaining debts to their landlord, some £70,000. And the price seemed far too low for a player of obvious First Division quality.

Into the club came defenders Simon Webster (£120,000 from Sheffield United), Stuart Balmer (£100,000 from Celtic) and after a loan spell, Alex Dyer (£100,000 from Palace). Alan Curbishley returned as reserve team coach but also as a member of the playing staff.

In August, with groundsman Colin Powell on holiday, Maurice Banham, the groundsman at The Valley for 21 years and now 66, returned to take care of the new grass, another development that brought a lump to the throats of the fans.

But the Valley story had seemed a continual one of

Left: Alex Dyer – signing from landlords Crystal Palace. Began his professional career with Blackpool, transferring to Hull and then Palace.

Right: Simon Webster – signed from Sheffield United and quickly became a firm favourite with fans for his acknowledgement and applause of them at the end of every game, home and away. Later, he took over the captaincy on Andy Peake's departure to Middlesbrough.

hope followed by despair. And new despair was just about to crush the fragile optimism of the club and its supporters.

The blow came from an unlikely and completely unanticipated quarter.

In May what appeared to be a very localised industrial dispute had flared up at Greenwich Council when 200 housing workers walked out in a dispute over payments for the collection of poll tax. There seemed no connection between that item of news and the fate of Charlton Athletic Football Club. But that summer the workers' union, NALGO, began targeting other departments for industrial action to bring pressure on the council.

A walk-out in September by officers of the development control section of the planning department put paid to hopes of October approval for the new Valley.

Just days before the walkout, the club had submitted on September 12, 1990, its formal planning application. Most of the features were now familiar but changes included a function room in place of the banqueting suite, the new Valley Club in the West Stand, and

12 workhouses in Valley Grove with residential space above them.

The most significant new feature was a roadway across the middle of the East Terrace to provide access for emergency vehicles. This eliminated all hope of a completely relaid East Terrace. It cut the immediate capacity of the half-opened terrace to 5,000 with just 3,450 when seats were installed. It meant the total capacity of the restored Valley would be just 17,000.

But the immediate debate over the plans became academic as the NALGO dispute became one of the longest running in the council's history.

The gloom over The Valley was paralleled on the field of play where the demoralisation of the final games in the First Division continued into the Second with the club plunging to the bottom of the table.

All four first games were lost. A 1-1 draw at Oldham on Monday, September 18, lifted the team just one place off the bottom. The first victory did not come until the seventh game, on Saturday, September 29, a 2-1 home victory over Barnsley when the gate dipped for the first time that season below the 5,000 mark at 4,379.

Darren Pitcher – a player of spirit and determination. Seen here going up for the ball with Mick Quinn of Newcastle United in a 1 – 0 victory at Selhurst Park in April, 1991.

Webster after a nervous start was beginning to show heroic qualities.

The turning point came in the game at Middlesbrough on November 10, 1990. The match was a hard physical contest with few quarters given and the Middlesbrough fans in full roar behind their team who after four successive victories were fourth in the table.

Charlton took the lead through Lee after 23 minutes but then with just four minutes to go, Simon Webster was sent off for a trip on Ian Baird in the penalty area.

Baird converted the penalty and it looked as if the most the ten men could expect was to hang on to the draw. But in the last minute, John Hendrie fouled Alex Dyer in the box and Tommy Caton lashed in the penalty at full speed to give Charlton the points.

That started un unbeaten run of four wins and two draws which lifted the club out of the relegation area and paved the way for a slow climb up the table.

Scott Minto received recognition with selection for the England Under 21 team in a 0-0 draw against Wales at Cardiff in December and Sidcup-born Gordon Watson, who had broken into the first team towards the end of the previous season, was also selected for the squad.

By November, with the NALGO dispute still rumbling on, the Charlton Athletic Supporters Club began digging a little more deeply into the issue.

They were spurred on by the fact that the contractors had to be on site by January if the August 1991 date for the Valley return was to be kept.

To their surprise, they found that the council still had the powers to process the Valley application despite the dispute in the planning department.

The Supporters Club Chairman Roy King stated: "We have taken professional advice and have been assured that Greenwich Council could process the application without the strikers if they chose to do so.

"The leader of the council could instruct the senior officers, who are not on strike, to do the work themselves.

"Alternatively, the members could decide to call the application before the full council. It has been drawn up in close consultation with the planning department after all.

"Providing what they were doing was properly advertised in the local press, so that the public could have their say, the members have the power to approve it themselves."

It was now almost two years since Charlton had announced their hope to return home, but the council made no immediate response to King's proposals.

In January 1991, as the dispute staggered into its second year, the club issued an artist's visual of what the revised Valley plan would look like. A 36-lane bowling alley plus 26 executive boxes were now envisaged.

For a second time, the fans had a pretty picture to look at but no Valley in reality.

But in mid January, it began to look at last as if the NALGO dispute might be over and that Charlton's application would receive priority over the 400 applications held up by the dispute.

An agreement was worked out between the council and the NALGO leaders only for the compromise to be rejected by the rank and file.

But it was not back to square one for Charlton. For Roy King had been right. The council did have powers to progress the application itself and this is what the council now did, stating they would bring the application before a special committee by the end of March.

It was galling for Charlton to find that their application could have been heard in October 1990 in the first place. The episode cast doubt on the strength of the new council's original commitment to The Valley.

By the middle of October, the club was bottom again after six defeats in ten games and, for the first time, there was serious debate about the future of Lennie Lawrence and whether he could remotivate the team.

Other names were circulated as potential successors including Mike Bailey, now boss at Fisher Athletic, the docklands club, and Keith Peacock, now managing League newcomers Maidstone United.

Lawrence's authority had been jolted in September by the suspension and then dismissal of coach Mike Flanagan for remarks made on the Sunday evening soccer programme on the local radio station, RTM, in which he seemed to distance himself from Lawrence's team tactics.

In his place, Alan Curbishley stepped up from reserve team duties which were now taken over by Steve Gritt.

At Selhurst Park itself, the close season had seen major building alterations to the main stand, including new dressing rooms at the Holmesdale end which meant the players coming on the field from the corner of the ground. Seats installed at the front of the Arthur Wait stand now made it an allseater.

Despite the poor start, there were several features which pointed to a revival in the club's playing fortunes. Robert Lee was fighting adversity by turning on some of the most spirited performances of his career.

Darren Pitcher at right back was playing with a tenacity and spirit which made fans wonder why no place had been found for him in the team the previous season in the fight against relegation. And Simon

In January, with Tommy Caton out with what was to prove a permanent foot injury requiring three ultimately unsuccessful operations, Alan Kernaghan made his debut on loan from Middlesbrough in a 3-1 home victory against Notts County. He immediately struck up a powerful partnership with Webster. The loan deal saw Colin Walsh depart for a spell with Boro.

January also saw the death at 75 of Les Gore, the club's former chief scout. Les had joined the club from Orient in November 1967 and was still working on a part-time basis up to the previous year.

In February came another bitter blow on the playing side to the fans as the club's financial problems were exposed yet again. On February 14, the enormously promising young striker Gordon Watson departed for £250,000 to Sheffield Wednesday, plus another £100,000 dependent on appearances.

He was just 19 and was highly popular with the fans for being a keen Charlton fan himself which made the loss of such future potential all the harder to bear.

Steve Mackenzie was shortly to follow the steps of Paul Williams and Watson to Hillsborough, first on loan and then as a permanent signing by the Wednesday manager, Ron Atkinson.

But happenings on the field were inevitably overshadowed in this strange season by the happenings off it. At long last came the announcement that the crucial Greenwich Council planning meeting on The Valley would be held on April 2 – exactly two years to the day after the emotional Sunday morning return of the fans to clean up the derelict Valley.

The planning officers' report backed the application but with a number of conditions, with the proposed bowling alley the main focus of attention.

It looked as if the application must pass the committee as the ruling Labour group appeared to be in support, but as the day approached, the fans' nerves rose.

Some 100 tickets were allocated for the meeting at Woolwich Town Hall, shared between the club, supporters' club and residents. Some 500 fans were allowed in the public hall where the proceedings from the

Fans gather outside Woolwich Town Hall. Inside: Anxious fans listen to the debate.

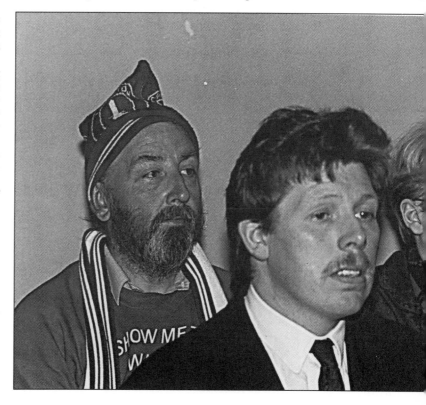

215

Charlton's last
home League
match at
Selhurst
Park – Scott
Minto celebrates
after scoring
Charlton's
equaliser against
West Ham, the
last home goal to
be scored at
Selhurst.

committee room were relayed back to them. Many more gathered outside where the news was passed to them by supporter Andy Lopata on a megaphone.

Inside the committee room, four speakers were allowed from the Charlton supporters and four from those residents opposing the plans. In turn, Rick Everitt, Steve Dixon, Roy King and Richard Hunt put their case for the Valley return.

The residents insisted they were not opposed to football at The Valley but to the effects crowds and extra traffic would have on the area – but their distinction was not a convincing one.

But some of the exaggeration was cruel and absurd, including allegations of frequent urinating in and damage to nearby front gardens in Charlton's past existence at The Valley.

Your author who had never seen one instance of such behaviour in four decades of walking to The Valley simply wondered at the extraordinary lengths of imagination people could go to when they perceived their own interests to be threatened.

At 8.47 p.m., the decision was made. The application was approved by 17 to one, the lone councillor voting against being the Charlton ward councillor Sukhdev Sanghara.

There were emotional scenes inside and out of the Town Hall. The long exile was over. Charlton were returning home at last.

New directors
who were to play
a key role in
securing
Charlton's return
at last to The
Valley. Left,
Martin Simons,
and right,
Richard Murray.

216

But even on this night of emotion, there were doubts and fears. They centred on the conditions the committee set on the hours of the West Stand bowling alley, amending the report of its own planners.

The club had sought opening hours up to 2 a.m. The committee changed that to midnight from Sunday to Thursday. That the club could have lived with. But the committee added the further rider that the opening hours would be for a six month trial. And it was not clear whether the trial period was of the hours or the alley itself.

What this meant was that the club would be set an immense problem trying to find an operator willing to run the alley on such a short-term basis. And without the alley, the viability of the new Valley operation was in serious doubt.

The club hoped work would start in a month's time – at first on the relaying of the East Terrace, but without a seating rake because of the lack of time. The new season would start on Saturday, August 17, and The Valley had to be ready by then.

But The Valley would reopen without the new West Stand where work was anticipated to start in September.

A significant change now took place at board level. Two new members, Martin Simons, a Lloyds underwriter from Blackheath who had previously been in the oil business, and Richard Murray from Reigate, the chairman of television programme and giant screen operating company, AVESCO, were recruited.

Ironically, Murray had been one of the few new supporters attracted by the move to Selhurst – the nearest League ground to Reigate.

By now the financial support of the existing board members was being seriously stretched and Simons and Murray injected desperately needed new finance which was to prove crucial in the club's survival over the next two years.

Last Selhurst game

THE LAST League game at Selhurst was a 1-1 draw against West Ham on Saturday, May 4, 1991, before 16,137 fans.

After the Hammers had gone ahead through Martin Allen after 15 minutes, Scott Minto scored Charlton's last home League goal at Selhurst on the half hour when he struck the net after the ball rebounded off goalkeeper Ludek Miklosko from an Alex Dyer shot.

At the end of the game, a yellow-coated ring of police surrounded the pitch. But it was all unnecessary. The leaving of Selhurst was simply a sad and sombre occasion, a feeling of how so many years had been wasted in a pointless venture.

The club from day one at Selhurst had never intended to set roots down in Croydon and few had grown, save for an important group of youngsters who were now going to a new home they hardly knew.

But for aficionados of this unfortunate chapter in Charlton's history the actual last game came on Thursday, May 9, when Charlton's reserves ran out onto the Selhurst pitch to play Millwall Reserves in a postponed Combination match.

The normal Welling venue was unavailable because of work on the pitch.

Some 108 people entered Selhurst through the Glaziers Club bar to watch the match. Four minutes from time, Rossi Franco notched himself a place in Charlton's history to score the club's last ever home goal at Selhurst. The result was a 3-0 victory, with The Vinh Nguyen and Dean Dye scoring the other goals in the first half.

Before the game started, the dismantling of the Charlton insignia and notices was under way. Within

minutes of it ending, none was left on the stadium and portakabins. And one small boy was seen happily scampering up Holmesdale Road with a Charlton roundel under his arm.

Six long years had symbolically been brushed away in minutes.

Charlton wound up the 1990-91 season with a 2-0 defeat at Plymouth on May 11 to finish 16th.

The actual work on The Valley did not begin until the second week of May as the club had to wait for the granting of a safety certificate.

The first work consisted mainly of removing the ugly old security fences, the faded red railings, the decrepit crush barriers and the foundations of the old floodlights.

Then came the first of a series of terrible blows that were to shatter the plans for a quick return. In June, the main contractors Percy Trentham went into receivership after just a fortnight's work at The Valley.

Work was delayed but they were quickly take over by Beazer Homes, whose subsidiiary Beazer Construction restarted the work.

At the end of May came news of a surprise development, a £100,000 temporary West Stand for the start of the season before work on the permanent stand began. The temporary structure would be so designed as to allow for work to start and progress on the permanent structure.

Safety problems now emerged over the Bartram gate exit to Lansdowne Mews and until they were resolved, the East Terrace's capacity was cut to just 3,000, cutting down total expected capacity to a 10,000 to 12,000 estimate.

Police insistence that the South Stand should be used

Historic moment. The ball enters the net for the last ever home goal at Selhurst – scored by Rosario Franco in the reserve match against Millwall.

Saying goodbye to the welcome – Charlton staff member Paul Pace takes down the Charlton roundels from Selhurst Park after the reserve game against Millwall.

Help Lennie buy this player **WOOLWICH**

THE **WOOLWICH**

for away supporters because of the unavailability of the exit compounded the problem.

The club had planned for two thirds of the stand to be given to home fans with the away fans exiting through Valley Grove.

On the financial side, it was now confirmed that some £800,000 of Football Grounds Improvement Trust money would be given to the club to help meet the cost of refurbishment. The money due to Charlton had lain dormant during the years of exile.

The impending return to The Valley had a dramatic effect on season ticket sales. By the end of May 1991, they had passed the 1,600 total of the previous season and were soon to reach almost 3,000.

That summer saw the death of one of the last of the pre-war legends Harold Hobbis at 78.

It saw too the departure of Mark Reid back to Scotland on a free transfer to St. Mirren.

In the world of football at large, the real prospect of the break-up of the Football League was now near to becoming ugly reality as the FA produced its own plans for the breakaway of the First Division clubs.

Then came a piece of playing news that was to have far more momentous consequences than Charlton fans realised.

Lennie Lawrence was trying to buy Alan Kernaghan from Middlesbrough, after a highly successful loan period totalling 13 appearances. Lawrence was asking the directors to match a bid of £300,000 from Barnsley.

In the last week of June, 1991, the Boro manager Colin Todd resigned. To most Charlton fans, it simply signalled an awkward delay in Lawrence's attempts to sign the player.

Then in just three days in July, it all happened. Lawrence's dealings over Kernaghan had impressed the Boro board and they scrapped their shortlist of six from 100 applicants for the manager's post and went for Lawrence instead.

On Monday, July 8, Boro made their approach known and Lawrence was given permission to talk to them.

On the morning of Tuesday, July 9, Lawrence put his head through the hole in a cardboard mock-up of a Charlton footballer, posing for press photos to boost season ticket sales.

That afternoon, Middlesbrough firmed up their approach and next day Lawrence was on his way to Middlesbrough for the talks.

He never came back as Charlton manager although the Charlton board had wrongly assumed that he would be reporting back to them.

Instead he was paraded on the Ayresome pitch that Wednesday to be introduced to the local press.

And Alan Kernaghan actually arriving back at the ground that day from his honeymoon expecting to sign for Charlton, found Lawrence on the pitch as his new manager.

The first Roger Alwen and Mike Norris heard of the appointment was through the press, although Boro stated they had tried to contact them.

Whatever the misunderstanding between Lawrence and the Charlton board, there was no doubt that Boro had acted discourteously in their rush to parade Lawrence.

Lawrence had only just signed a two-year extension to his contract on on July 1, and although he had a clause allowing him freedom to join a bigger club, contractual wrangles followed the Middlesbrough announcement which marred his going.

But in the modern soccer world of high finance and greatly increased material reward, there was little likelihood of another Jimmy Seed emerging to stay 23 years, and Lawrence was already the third longest serving manager in the League after Brian Clough at Nottingham Forest and Joe Royle at Oldham.

But with The Valley return so apparently imminent,

it seemed a terrible time to depart, a denial of all the striving and endeavour of the past seven years.

But Lawrence had long been frustrated by the never-ending saga of The Valley return and depressed by the lack of money available to him to show his full worth as a manager.

He explained his reasons for going in a long statement to the Mercury: "There has been a pre-occupation with The Valley in the supporters' minds, perhaps even in the owners' minds, and the team has been put second.

"That's not good for me as a manager but I've gone along with it and willingly sold the lifeblood of the club to keep it going. I haven't made it as difficult as possible. I've thrown myself into getting people out the door.

"I got stick for it, nearly lost my job for it, and wouldn't relish the prospect of doing it again, which can't be discounted."

In fact, analysis of the Lawrence period shows that the club was only forced into selling of players as the Valley financial pressures built up in the season the club lost its First Division status.

Lawrence had the frustration in the First Division, of not being able to spend significantly on players, but he did not lose his best players for the first three seasons.

But he was undoubtedly right that relegation plus the financial pressures of The Valley return would mean the selling policy continuing. After so much battling against the odds, it was understandable that pastures new appealed to him.

Yet another shock came in the directors' choice to replace him. A number of top names in the football world were understood to be interested in the post and the fans' choice was the old Charlton stalwart Keith Peacock who had managed with distinction at Gillingham and Maidstone.

Instead the Charlton directors opted for coach Alan Curbishley and reserve team manager Steve Gritt to share the job as joint coaches.

It was an unheard-off scenario in the football world, complicated by the fact of General Manager Arnie Warren being given control over transfer and contracts.

To the fans, it looked like idiocy, a solution borne out of the need to cut costs and save on the wage bill.

But for once it proved a case of the directors being wiser and more farsighted than the fans, as the start of the new season was dramatically to prove.

For they reasoned that the last thing the club needed as this delicate stage in its history was disruption in the dressing room with a new broom sweeping far too clean.

They had been impressed with how Curbishley and Gritt had led and coached the playing staff after Lawrence's departure and wanted to see if they could continue in this way. And to keep the club's posts "in the family", they appointed Peacock as reserve team coach, creating a triumvirate of experience in the running of the club.

The plans for The Valley return had meanwhile undergone further change. In July, the club scrapped its plans for standing on the East Terrace in favour of 3,000 temporary open air seats.

The summer had been a wet and dismal one and the bad weather had left the contractors with insufficient time to renew the concrete.

Valley Club goodbye

THE ANNOUNCEMENT spelt the final end of the East Terrace as the country's biggest standing terrace.

It was also decided to demolish the Valley Club as it was in a worse state than expected, and replace it with a large temporary cabin.

With the demolition of the wall in Harvey Gardens, the ground was in full view of the road through large wire fencing.

Alan Curbishley (left) and Steve Gritt – surprise partnership.

The fans could see with their own eyes the work in progress and although few of them were building experts, the prospect of football actually taking place by August 17 seemed hardly believable.

On Monday, July 15, the board took the decision to postpone the date of the Valley return. The option they took up was with West Ham United and the news was announced a week later.

Rumours had abounded that Charlton might go temporarily to Millwall, Gillingham, or even Welling, but there were difficulties with each of these venues, particularly in relation to the need to seat Charlton's large number of season ticket holders.

Upton Park was a surprise choice although nearby Orient had been mooted. It was much nearer to Charlton than Selhurst but it was across the psychological and awkward divide of the Thames and the Blackwall Tunnel.

The first game back at The Valley was now expected to be on Saturday, September 14, 1991, against Portsmouth.

Last days of the Valley Club.

The temporary stand takes shape in August 1991 – it proved to be more permanent than anyone expected.

On the playing side, Lennie Lawrence's last acts had been to sign the old Chelsea stalwart, midfielder John Bumstead, and sell Paul Mortimer to Aston Villa for £300,000.

Mortimer had wanted away – it was not a sale the club had sought. Bumstead who lived nearby at Mottingham had made over 300 appearances for Chelsea in 14 seasons.

Just before the start of the season, Curbishley went back to his old club Brighton for two more signings, defender Steve Gatting, the brother of test cricketer Mike Gatting, on a free, and forward Garry Nelson.

Gatting had started his career with Arsenal and gone on to make 316 appearances for Brighton. In a roving career, Nelson had also played for Southend, Swindon, and Plymouth. Both were at the veteran stage, Gatting being 32 and Nelson 30.

Roy King – from fan to stadium manager.

Despite the blow of the delayed Valley return, the work continued apace, giving fans no hint that anything was seriously wrong.

At the start of August, the shell was in place for the temporary West Stand and the new modernistic floodlighting pylons had arrived for erection.

Roy King, the Supporters Club Chairman, was appointed Stadium Manager. Roy had a wealth of experience from his own self-employed contracting work which he now gave up to concentrate on The Valley itself.

The opening game, at 'home' against Newcastle United was switched from Saturday, August 21, to Sunday, August 22, because West Ham were at home on the Saturday.

But the start of the 1991-92 season was further delayed for thousands of Charlton fans who had not foreseen the problems the journey through the Blackwall Tunnel would bring.

On the day of the match, these were ironically compounded by Greenwich Council whose workmen inexplicably decided to take up two lanes of the three lane approach road to undertake tree cutting.

A traffic queue several miles long of frustrated fans built up south of the river and many did not reach the game until half time. Robert Lee scored Charlton's first 'home' goal at Upton Park in the 63rd minute to put Charlton one-up.

Nineteen minutes from time, Carl Leaburn made it 2-0 with a header to the wry amusement of the crowd. It was his fifth first team goal for the club and they had all been scored at grounds with Park in the name – Selhurst, St.James's, Villa, Ewood and now Upton.

Franz Carr pulled one back for Newcastle nine minutes from the end.

The change of scene to Upton Park seemed to boost the players. The team had climbed by the end of October to third in the table before being checked by four defeats and a draw in the next games.

But as the playing picture brightened under the new management team, so the problems at The Valley worsened.

Contractors withdraw

THE DATE of the return was again postponed and then came a serious development.

Just two days after the start of the season, on Monday, August 20, 1991, Kier Construction group which had incorporated Beazer Construction, withdrew their plant from The Valley despite reports on an agreement on a £1.8 million total refurbishment cost.

Quite clearly, serious financial problems were beginning to develop and Kier spoke of the return not being possible before January 1.

The club gave an inkling of the underlying problem by stating:- "There is still a considerable amount of work to be done which has largely been caused by extensive safety requirements insisted upon by Greenwich Council."

What was happening was that the council were treating The Valley as a new stadium under the terms of the Taylor report. And the Taylor demands were stringent indeed. The extra cost of meeting these demands was put at £500,000.

The temporary stand was now looking anything but temporary and the club was having considerable difficulty with foundation work in the Valley soil composed as it was of rubbish, chalk and other assorted mixtures.

There was still some activity at the ground with men from another firm installing seats in the West Stand but the main work was at a standstill. The new floodlights,

First home goal at Upton Park, scored by Robert Lee against Newcastle United – Lee was later sold to Newcastle to help offset the losses incurred in the Upton Park sojourn.

weighing nine tonnes apiece and 27 metres high, looked majestically down on a scene of scattered earthworks and partially completed building structures.

And there was silence too on the progress on financing for the permanent main stand and bowling alley. It emerged that the club had tried for £6 million funding from an unnamed German financial concern but without success.

Twenty other different sources of funding were also tried for in the midst of one of the worst post-war depressions.

The weeks passed in almost agonising silence with the fans in deep fear that the Valley saga could be coming to a dismal finale. It was now conceivable that the club might now never return and to never return would mean the end of the club. The nomadic existence could not continue.

Charlton were paying West Ham £10,000 a game to play at Upton Park and although they succeeded in cutting police costs from an initial £9,000 to £6,000 a game, they were making almost nothing on their gate, after allowing for season ticket income already paid and for other running costs such as stewards and turnstile operators.

Then at the end of September 1991 came the bombshell the fans had been expecting – the full dreadful extent of the problem the board had been struggling with was starkly revealed.

Roger Alwen admitted: ''The problem is not time. It is money.''

He estimated that just six to eight weeks work remained to be done. It was a case of so near and yet so far.

But that was not the only damaging news. Vice Chairman Mike Norris departed from the board at the same time as Alwen broke the news.

The split was a bitter one. Norris had been the man overseeing The Valley development and the awesome problem of the escalating safety costs had led to tension between him and the rest of the board.

But worse still, his property business was in severe difficulties, a victim of the prolonged recession the country was now facing.

This was as serious for Charlton as the mounting safety costs as Norris was half owner of the club, half owner of the training ground and controlled Adelong, the company owning The Valley.

It was Adelong which held responsibility for the building work at The Valley, not the club itself. The other interest in Adelong was held by Laing Homes, who had retained a stake following the demise of the housing scheme and had three of their representatives on the board. They still owned The Valley freehold.

So added to all the other uncertainties was the uncertainty as to how the disposal of Norris's assets would affect the club and The Valley itself. This too was at the heart of the rift which saw him leave the board.

It was sad in the extreme that Mike Norris should depart from Charlton in this way. For Charlton would always be in his debt for their very existence after his monumental efforts in saving the club in 1984. He was and remained a genuine fan. Richard Collins now took over the responsibility for the work at The Valley. His firm, the Kennedy Woodward partnership, were already the project's architects.

Safety costs had now soared by £750,000. In Alwen's words: ''The safety plan from day one is unrecognisable from the one we've got now.''

In the middle of October, even the West Stand seating contractors withdrew from the site leaving work at a total standstill and the fans to peer through the open wire fence in Harvey Gardens and not even see one shred of activity.

It was one more heartbreak on the long road back to The Valley.

The Homecoming

EVERYTHING now seemed unreal as the club and its future lay in a state of limbo.

It was the builders Kier who now actively searched for a way out of the deadlock so as not to jeopardise the future of the club while attempting to safeguard their own financial interests – shades of how the builders Humphreys were similarly sucked into the business of the club seven decades ago.

Meanwhile Norris's interests in club and ground were now in the hands of the merchant bank Hill Samuel under a scheme of voluntary administration. His 50% share in the club was diluted by a rights issue which gave Martin Simons and Richard Murray 12.5% each of the club's ownership.

At the end of November, captain Andy Peake left the club to rejoin Lennie Lawrence at Middlesbrough. The fee was £150,000 and in his place Alan Pardew came on a free transfer to the club from Crystal Palace.

The money from the Peake sale was desperately needed as board members were again dipping into their pockets to meet player wages.

In the New Year, the troubles were briefly lightened by one of the most famous performances in the club's history. 3-0 down to Newcastle in 34 minutes at St.James's Park, the team staged the biggest fightback ever in an away game to run out winners by 4-3.

In the 36th minute, the 18-year-old back Anthony Barness, with only nine full appearances to his credit, hit a devastating curling shot which found the net from 25 yards out.

In the 53rd minute, Kim Grant came on as sub and his penetrative runs began to drain the confidence from the United defence. Colin Walsh who had broken a leg at St.James's in 1987, now erased that bitter memory with two goals in three minutes.

First came a low shot into the bottom of the net. Then after United keeper Tommy Wright dropped a cross from John Bumstead under pressure from Alan Pardew, the ball fell to Walsh who hammered it in.

Just a minute from time, Pardew's splendid persistence won the day. A fierce shot was headed out in spectacular fashion by Steve Watson only for the ball to fall at Pardew's feet. Without a moment's hesitation, he powered it in again to see it deflect off Liam O'Brien and into the net.

In February, Charlton recruited another director – a Chicago businessman, Mike Stevens, who was born in Plumstead and had kept up a lifelong interest in the club.

Stevens put £300,000 into the club but it was now estimated that at least £1 million more was needed to complete The Valley's refurbishment, the cost of which had now soared to £3 million.

There was only one place left to turn – the fans. And so following on the Valley Party success, another monumental effort now took place to restore the party to its rightful home.

The idea had been mooted by the fans themselves in the Mercury newspaper, on the local radio station RTM and in the club fanzines.

The club responded by announcing in March a ten-year debenture share offer to fans who could invest between £25 and £3,000.

The object was to raise £1.5 million of the £3 million needed. The remainder would be met by £1 million of Football Trust money and £600,000 in deferred loans from Kier.

There would be discounts on season tickets for debenture holders and the investment would be refunded in ten years under an insurance guarantee scheme.

Voting rights would be in proportion to the debentures held and one person would be elected to the board to represent the interests of the holders. Details of the scheme were mailed to the club's 5,500 members.

The initial response brought in 2,200 pledges of over £1 million but then the scheme was suddenly halted in May three weeks into the close season as the insurers Legal & General found themselves unable to resolve technical problems in guaranteeing the repayment.

The situation looked impossible as Kier had set the date of June 16 for work to begin if the club were to return to The Valley for the start of the 1992/3 season on August 15.

Hope was now failing fast for the club's ambitious development of a new West Stand. The club had changed

Help from the USA – Mike Stevens.

222

its plans to run the bowling alley directly itself but repeated attempts at financing the project came to nothing.

The end of the 1991-92 season had seen the club come tantalisingly close to achieving a play-off position. With three games to go, a magnificent 2-0 win at Upton Park against automatic promotion contenders Leicester City lifted hopes which were then dashed just three days later as Charlton fell 1-0 at Upton Park to Tranmere Rovers in a dismal game.

The last remaining game was at Bristol Rovers' temporary home at Twerton Park, Bath, with Blackburn Rovers challenging for the sixth place and last play-off position. Defeat by 1-0 and a 3-1 win for Blackburn at Plymouth killed the dream of a return to Division 1. But the uncertainty surrounding The Valley would have made life in Division 1 difficult indeed.

At the start of June, it became quite clear that a Valley return for the start of the season was impossible and October 31 was now mooted as the hoped-for date of return.

The club now relaunched their fundraising scheme in the form of the Valley Investment Plan, a straight investment scheme in which fans were asked to give between £50 and £2,000 to the club in return for season ticket discounts and other concessions.

The scheme was announced on June 11 and was aimed at raising £1.2 million from the supporters. The concessions included the offer again of the right to elect a board member. Each subscriber was to receive one vote per £50 investment.

The money raised was to be deposited in a separate account held by the club's solicitors and only released on the club buying the freehold of The Valley or taking a lease and on agreement being reached to complete the remaining building work. If these conditions had not been met by August 31, the money would be refunded.

The club also revived the plan of standing on the lower relaid half of the East Terrace which would cost an extra £500,000.

Alan Pardew – shot twice to force in Charlton's winning goal in their historic comeback at St. James's Park.

Last minute goal – the ball nestles at the back of the Newcastle net to signal Charlton's greatest ever fightback in an away game.

Announcing the Valley Investment Plan are directors Martin Simons and Richard Murray (second and first right), Steve Clarke, Supporters Club Chairman.

Right: August 28, 1992 – Roger Alwen announces the return home.

Garry Nelson scores Charlton's last goal at Upton Park in the 3 – 1 defeat by Newcastle United. Nelson, like Webster, had endeared himself to supporters by his warm acknowledgement of them.

Of the £3.1 million to complete the already planned refurbishment, Kier would receive £2.1 million and other contractors £1 million. This was on top of over £1 million already spent so far. Kier's deferred loan of £600,000 was to be for two years on interest free terms.

Alan Curbishley and Steve Gritt were confirmed by the club in June as joint managers with complete responsibility for all administration on the playing side following the retirement at 64 of general manager Arnie Warren.

The 1992-93 season opened with the club in the new 'First Division', the result of the renaming of the divisions after the FA's formation of the FA Premier League.

The club set a new and odd record when the opening game was at 'home' for an eighth consecutive season. The visitors were Grimsby Town, beaten by 3-1 with goals from Carl Leaburn, Alex Dyer and Garry Nelson.

The team won their first four games – the best start ever to a season. It was also the first time since early in the 1968-69 season that Charlton had led the race to top flight in the 'second' division.

Not until a 0-0 draw at home to Cambridge on September 12 did they lose the lead to Newcastle United. And the unbeaten League run continued until October 10 when the team lost 2-1 away to Bristol City.

By the time of the Grimsby opening game, the Valley Investment Plan total was soaring well past the £900,000 mark. In the latter half of August, it went past the £1 million mark but then the input of funds slowed down, short of the £1.2 million sought.

But with the shortfall so narrow, the directors took on the added financial responsibility of bridging the gap.

On Friday, August 28, 1992, the directors invited the press to the Sparrows Lane Training Ground to announce that The Valley return was to take place against Portsmouth on Saturday, December 5.

The most nomadic club in the history of English football was going home at last.

Uncertainties still remained. The return was still dependent on The Valley freehold being bought and on the necessary safety certificate from Greenwich Council.

The question of the freehold was resolved on August 31 when it was acquired for £1.25 million – the first time the club had owned The Valley since 1982. The deal formed part of the clearing-up of the affairs of the Adelong company and involved a new subsidiary of the football club being set up, Charlton Holdings Ltd., which leased The Valley back to Charlton.

The deal was carried through thanks to a massive loan from director Martin Simons, an ebullient and outgoing man who had become a favourite personality with the supporters.

On Sunday, September 6, volunteers entered The Valley to make it ready for the final building work due to be started by the contractors on Monday, September 21.

The Charlton team return to The Valley for their first training session there for seven years. Left to right: (back) Bob Bolder, Alex Dyer, Garry Nelson, Simon Webster, Alan Pardew, Mike Salmon, Stuart Balmer, Carl Leaburn, John Bumstead; (front) Alan Curbishley, John Robinson, Darren Pitcher, Scott Minto, Paul Gorman, Steve Gritt.

In the next two weeks, Anthony Barness was sold to Chelsea for £350,000 and Robert Lee to Newcastle for £700,000. The money was earmarked to cover the losses incurred at Upton Park, to meet tax, VAT and other claims – and not for The Valley refurbishment.

It was a bitter pill for the fans to take at a time when the team were second in the new First Division. And the loss of Lee was doubly sad. Not only was he a player of huge talent but he was the only direct playing link left with The Valley, if one discounted Steve Gritt, now almost retired on the playing side.

John Robinson, yet another player from Brighton, was signed to replace Lee in the right midfield. The fee of £75,000 was later decided by a transfer tribunal.

And then it became a time of magic for the Charlton fans as the final steps took place in the long and emotional saga of The Valley return.

Just as they had watched in dismay the standstill of building work, so they now watched the hustle and bustle as the eagerly anticipated day in December drew near. So much so, that the club had to warn fans not to cause traffic jams in the locality. It was a rainy autumn turning into winter, causing problems in the laying of concrete and tarmac, but Kier were never more than days behind their schedule.

On October 7, another of Charlton's old stalwarts and a member of the 1947 FA Cup winning side, Bill Robinson, died at 73. His death meant that only three of that side now remained – Peter Croker, Bert Johnson and Harold Phipps.

On October 29, Alwen told supporters at the supporters club AGM what they had long suspected – that the East Terrace would never be a standing one again because of the Taylor requirements.

He confirmed the club was looking at building a new stand on the terrace before doing anything on the west side because it was quicker and cheaper. The achievement of Notts County in rebuilding three sides of their ground in just 17 weeks was quoted.

The club also stood in danger of losing Football Trust funding if the wait for the West Stand went on.

The line-up for the Valley return was that 495 away supporters would be allowed in the temporary West Stand which had a total of 2,368 seats, giving a ground total of 8,337. The South Stand capacity was 3,052, the North 2,877 with 20 places for wheelchair fans and 20 for their helpers.

A huge portakabin complex behind the West Stand would hold 800 people, including a large bar and facilities for directors, press and players.

On Saturday, November 14, came the last game at Upton Park, against leaders Newcastle United. Charlton had now dropped to sixth in the table after going through a bleak October without a win.

The game featured the return of the prodigal son Robert Lee. Garry Nelson netted Charlton's last 'home' goal at Upton Park five minutes into the second half but by then Charlton were already 2-0 down by half-time to

The Covered End lives again – The Valley's North Stand in gleaming new condition.

The Jimmy Seed Stand restored – the South Stand which marks the memory of Charlton's most famous manager.

225

Jubilation, celebration at The Valley homecoming. Top left: the balloons soar into the air over the North Stand. Second top left: Valley Party candidate, Gwen King, one of the many who dressed for the occasion. Above: musical welcome back. Right: Parading the flag. Right, below: Youngsters await their first Valley game.

two goals from Gavin Peacock, the son of Keith Peacock. The final score was 1-3, Steve Howey heading in just after the hour.

But as the fans trailed out into an East End night and one more journey through the Blackwall Tunnel, it was still difficult to believe or know if this would prove the final game at Upton Park.

On November 17, the first of the mighty floodlights was turned on to illuminate the new Valley. The lights were above UEFA standards at 1,300 lux and controlled by computer. Each bulb was directed to illuminate a particular spot and a grid was laid on the pitch to set them up accurately. The letters C and A were depicted in the bulbs.

Across the East Terrace, a long silver scar marked the walkway for home fans to the Jimmy Seed Stand, an elevated scaffolded passageway large enough to take a fire appliance to that corner of the ground as demanded under the Taylor conditions.

The emergency staircase built in the summer of 1991 to the Bartram Gate was abandoned.

Also abandoned was the former main entrance at the junction of Floyd Road and Harvey Gardens, now blocked by new electricity switch room while a new roadway entered the ground in Harvey Gardens.

The total cost of the return had now mounted to £4.4 million, paid for by £1 million of VIP contributions, a £1 million Football Trust grant, a £0.9 million loan from Kier Construction (formerly Beazers) and £1.5 million in directors' loans with directors bridging the £200,000 shortfall on the VIP scheme.

On Tuesday, November 24, the dressing rooms arrived, portable units to be placed at the side of the 'temporary' West Stand. And on this day too, the last

tickets were sold for the Portsmouth game – it was the expected sell-out at a capacity of just 8,337.

On Thursday, November 26, the players trained at the ground for the first time – a symbol indeed that the emotional homecoming was proving to be a reality.

Volunteers and directors took part in the final painting and Roger Alwen and Martin Simons were seen numbering the seats.

On Thursday, December 3, the Mayor of Greenwich, Councillor Brian O'Sullivan came down to The Valley to hand over ceremonially the precious safety certificate which meant at last the return was a certainty.

On Friday, December 4, the supporters held a celebration social at The Meridian Club, Charlton.

But even in these final days, the fans, by now convinced the dream was coming true, had doubts about the December 5 date. The Valley was still a frantic and confusing place.

Then came the day itself. Often long-anticipated events end in anti-climax, somehow never matching up to exaggerated hopes and expectations.

This day was different. It went perfectly, almost like a dream as the club and its fans went back to the future.

In the winter time of December, even the weather was kind and generous to them.

The fans woke to find a day of glorious sunshine from a blue sky.

Some were planning to make a symbolic march of return from General Gordon Place, Woolwich, to The Valley. Others were planning fancy dress or simply to wait the long wait outside The Valley for the gates to open at 12 noon.

And Bromley Borough supporters chartered an open top bedecked bus to make a slow journey through the

borough's towns marking the club's return to a wider public. Three versions of the Red, Red Robin, including the treasured Billy Cotton version, sounded out from loudspeakers amid the bunting and balloons.

Even on the morning itself, the last touches of building work remained to be done with stadium manager Roy King supervising the filling of the remaining holes by Harvey Gardens with tarmac.

Roger Alwen opened the gates on 12 to let the first fans rush in. As the crowds gathered in and outside the ground, it was noticeable that it was a meeting of all generations, the old and the young, a real coming together of a community.

And for many of the young with their faces painted red in Charlton symbols, it was really a visit to a ground they had never known but which had assumed the status of a legend.

But for all the homecoming fans it was really a new Valley they were coming to, devoid of the huge terraces that had made it such a grand and awesome ground.

Grand and spectacular as the Old Valley had been, it had been a basic and stark ground in its amenities. The New Valley gleamed in its shining bright paint, its glistening new tarmac and concrete.

The transformation from building site to bright stadium in just months had been startling.

Crowds of fans lingered outside to take in this new scenery and an impromptu band played in the street.

Inside, the West Kent 14th Boys Brigade Band marched and performed. And a buzz of surprise and excitement filled Floyd Road and Harvey Gardens as the Bromley bus turned the Floyd Road corner, still blasting out its Red, Red Robin themes after two hours of travel.

It was not just the older fans with their memories who felt the emotions of the return.

227

Fans on the Bromley Bus. Below: Warpaint for a young fan. Bottom: the bus turns around the Floyd Road corner. Top right: an embrace for Derek Hales. Bottom right: an old player with his memories – Sailor Brown.

Inside the ground, emotions were stirred as the heroes of yesteryear paraded around the ground, men such as Derek Hales, Sailor Brown, Charlie Revell, Peter Croker, Benny Fenton, Gordon Jago, Arthur Turner, George Green, Charlie Wright, Ray Treacy, Theo Foley, Brian Kinsey, Peter Reeves, Mike Flanagan, Martin Robinson and Phil Warman.

And it is doubtful if at any club an ex-player has experienced such an emotional outburst of warmth as Derek Hales. The stadium erupted with noise, applause and cheering as he marched onto the field with his two sons. It erupted again as a fan ran onto the field to plant a kiss on the old pirate's cheeks.

But the emotion drained the others too as men like Sailor Brown, Charlie Wright and Ray Treacy admitted afterwards.

And then with five minutes to go, 2,632 red and white balloons were released into the sky, each one marking a day of the long exile from The Valley.

The only unpredictable thing about the occasion was the football game itself. Could the Charlton team win to make the day complete?

It was fitting that Portsmouth should be the opponents. It was their 38th League visit to play Charlton – no other club had ever met Charlton so many times.

Then the players came onto the field and for the older

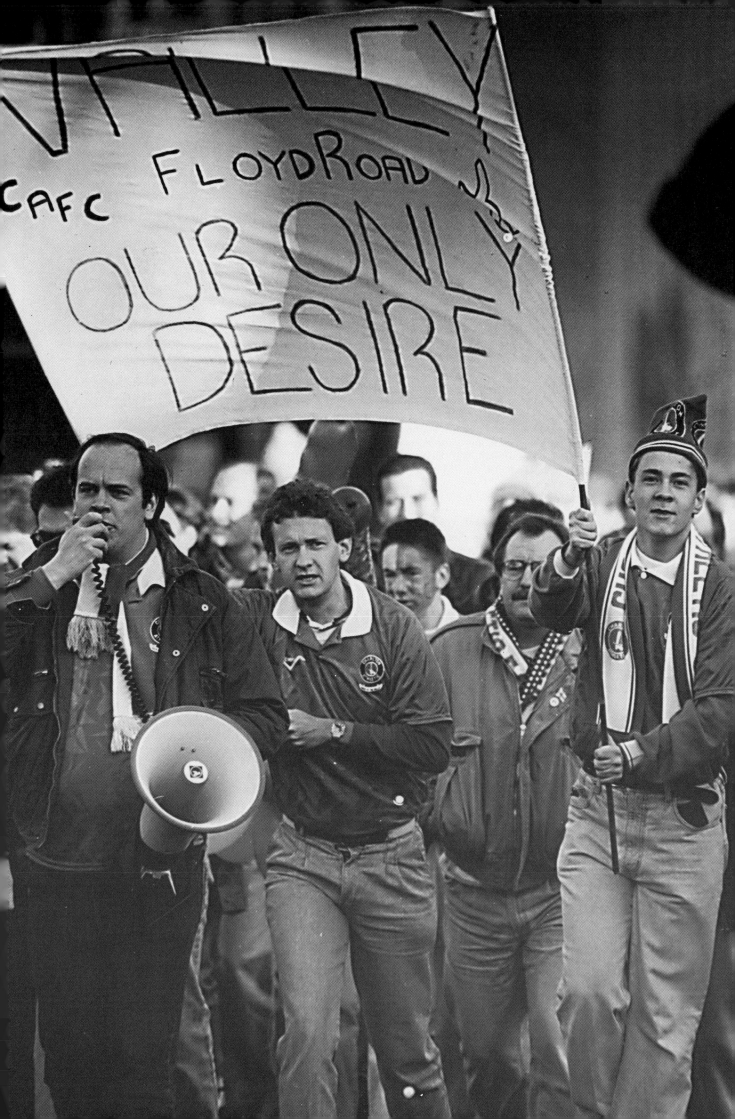

Home at last: the Charlton team come out onto The Valley turf with their Portsmouth opponents.

Right: New plain red shirts were worn for the occasion. And in them could almost be seen the players of yesteryear. Shirt billowing, John Robinson attacks.

Charlton fans, it was like a trip into memory lane as old style plain red shirts were worn again to mark the return.

And as the game started, you could almost see the heroes of yesteryear in those shirts as they billowed in the wind – just as Chris Duffy's shirt seemed to depart from his body as he whistled down the wing.

The team was Bob Bolder, Darren Pitcher, Scott Minto, Steve Gritt, Simon Webster, Stuart Balmer, John Robinson, Lee Power, Carl Leaburn, Garry Nelson, Colin Walsh, with Kim Grant coming on as substitute for Power, a young Lewisham-born striker on loan from Norwich.

The only playing connection with the team that had last trodden The Valley turf was the veteran Steve Gritt, although ironically another favourite of the old Valley came off the Portsmouth bench to appear as a substitute – Paul Walsh.

In the seventh minute came the long-awaited goal that cheered the hearts and calmed the nerves of the Charlton supporters.

Carl Leaburn put a square ball to Darren Pitcher who held off a challenge from Gavin Maguire 20 yards from the 'Covered End' goal to thread the ball to Colin Walsh who placed a low ground shot to to the right of goalkeeper Alan Knight.

Poor Portsmouth. They seemed bemused by the occasion and afraid to wreck the party.

Despite some nerve stopping moments in the second half as the talented Portsmouth side at last came into the game, Charlton held on to hear the whistle of referee Alan Gunn blowing for time.

Charlton as a club had achieved the near impossible – the only instance, in peacetime, of a club returning to a home ground after years of dereliction and exile.

The return could be not be the end of the story – the huge financial and physical problems of transforming The Valley into a modern and viable stadium remained. Even the very existence of the club itself was still not secure.

But the episode was one unlikely to be repeated in the history of English football. So much had happened that would have been unbelievable when John Fryer made his near fatal decision to uproot the club.

The long years of exile had provided a unique lesson not just to the Charlton club but to the wider football world – that a football club is a community with its own precious identity in an increasingly impersonal world.

It is not to be scorned or for rich men to play around with it. It is not to be arrogantly laid aside for the fashionable remedies of the so-called experts who so assiduously promoted the idea of ground sharing and other half-baked remedies to the game's national plight.

During the years of exile, with no ground to mark the club's existence, the fans were the club's identity, its only link between past and future.

And it was this feeling of identity, brought into such sharp and bitter focus by the loss of ground, that propelled the fans into their epic fight to return.

Out of The Valley of Tears had come The Valley of Joy.

Overleaf: Rick Everitt, fan extraordinary, leads the march from General Gordon Place. Everitt (with mike) as Mercury reporter, fanzine editor, and Valley Party campaigner, had had a mighty and unique influence in keeping the Charlton flame alive and galvanising the younger generation of supporters.

Leader of the Charlton attack, Carl Leaburn. Leaburn had become a cult figure with the fans and now the chants of Leaburn, Leaburn, were to ring across The Valley.

Top: View from the defunct East Terrace.
Left: Garry Nelson heads goalwards, Lee Power looks on.
Bottom: Kim Grant discovers the dressing rooms. Far left: Victory for Roger Alwen – Pompey chairman Jim Gregory presents him with a model of the famous ship. Bottom: missing hero. Bert Johnson, 1947 Cup winner, was amazingly too shy to come. But he made his own quiet return from his Leicestershire home for the game against Notts County on Saturday, January 30, 1993. Beside him, the Cup team picture.

Charlton Abroad

IN THESE MODERN days of international football it is hard to recall or appreciate just what an adventure foreign football was for the clubs of yesteryear. With this history now almost over, it is time to look at a more exotic — perhaps quixotic — side of Charlton Athletic's story — the story of Charlton abroad. It really is the story of how English clubs fared before the coming of organized European competition.

Charlton's historic rise through three divisions in successive years in the 1930s, not only took England by storm. The feat also brought the club to international notice in a world where English football was still looked up to as the most advanced in the game. Until then Charlton's excursions abroad had been modest. Their first trip had been in May 1924, when they played two games in Belgium, beating Liège 3-1, with goals from Wilson (two) and Cox, and Ent Standard, at Veritens, 2-0 with goals from Steele and Rees.

In March 1931, Charlton played a Dutch representative team in Rotterdam, drawing 3-3 with goals from Astley, Peters and Kidd.

The first major signs of international acclaim came when it was almost certain Charlton were going to become a First Division club. Suddenly they received offers to tour Spain, North Africa and South Africa. These could not be arranged in time, but they were indicators of things to come.

The next offers came from Czechoslovakia, Russia, Romania, South Africa, Argentina and France. Then, in January 1937, Albert Gliksten went to North America where he arranged a tour of the United States and Canada.

During the 1930s, it had become the practice for countries in Europe to invite the leading British football clubs to play the occasional game abroad during the season and also to make short tours during the summer.

Although the British international teams remained aloof from the World Cup, the rush to get British sides abroad for short tours reached such a pitch that the Football Association ruled that clubs could only be allowed to make tours officially arranged through them. The FA's intention in making this ruling was to make sure that clubs honoured commitments they entered into and to distribute British clubs evenly between various countries.

In the troubled political times before World War Two, the policy saw the FA preventing some clubs touring in countries where they might have faced hostility or been used as propaganda tools to the embarrassment of the Government.

Charlton's first match abroad as a First Division club was in Paris, where they played the French national team on Sunday, 11 April 1937. They came in as late replacements for the Italian national team which had withdrawn. Charlton beat Huddersfield Town at The Valley on the Saturday and at 9pm that night, the party, which included eight of the side which met Huddersfield, left Victoria Station.

In Paris the weather was showery, the ground wet and the team naturally a little short on rest and sleep. In an even first half, both sides scored twice, but Charlton dominated the second half, scoring three more times to run out 5-2 winners.

The team was: Bartram; Turner, Shreeve, Jobling, John Oakes, Ford, Tadman, Robinson, Welsh, Boulter and Hobbis. The goals were scored by Welsh (two), Tadman (two) and Hobbis. The party stayed the Sunday night in Paris and were back in London at 5pm on Monday.

John Oakes (opposite) was a member of the Charlton party which made a brief visit to Paris in April 1937. It was the club's first match abroad as a First Division club.

All set for North America. The 1937 squad pictured at The Valley. Back row (left to right): Jack Shreeve, George Stephenson, Freddy Ford, Bert Turner, Sam Bartram, Bert Tann, John Oakes. Middle row: Don Welsh, Jimmy Trotter, David Clark, Jimmy Seed, Dr John Montgomery, Harold Hobbis, George Tadman. Front row: Sid Cann, George Robinson, Les Boulter, Joe Jobling, George Green, Monty Wilkinson, Les Williams.

North America

THE tour to North America started on 19 May 1937, when the Charlton party left Southampton on the *Empress of Australia*, bound for Quebec. Altogether 17 players made the trip. They were: Bartram, Turner, Shreeve, Cann, Jobling, Tann, Green, John Oakes, Ford, Wilkinson, Robinson, Welsh, Boulter, Hobbis, Williams, Tadman and Stephenson. They were accompanied by Jimmy Seed, Jimmy Trotter, Dr Montgomery and David Clark and his wife.

The secretary of the Canadian Football Association, Sam Davidson, met them at Quebec and stayed with the party to host them throughout the tour. From Quebec, Charlton went by train to New York via Montreal. They were met at New York by Albert Gliksten and welcomed by a crowd of 20,000 New Yorkers.

The first game was at the New York Polo Grounds on Sunday, 30 May, against a USFA XI, before a crowd of 10,500. It was played in intense heat and the ground was very hard and dry. Charlton started well and Welsh put them ahead. Then they tailed off and the Americans equalized through a penalty. The final score was 1-1, with the American goalkeeper, Stan Chesney, putting on a stunning performance in the unusual outfit of baseball trousers, baseball cap and sun-glasses. The Charlton players learned afterwards just why his handling was so good — he was a top basketball player.

Jimmy Seed wrote at the time: 'The Americans are pleased with themselves. We are not.' The highspot of the team's visit to New York was a radio programme from Radio City in which Jimmy Seed played the piano and the players gave the American audience a rendering of songs such as *Nellie Dean* and *Genevieve*.

It was still very hot for the next match against a Pittsburgh representative side. The temperature was 92 degrees Fahrenheit in the shade when the match was played on 2 June. The pitch was hard, dry and bumpy. The game also was quite a novel experience for the Charlton team, since the match kicked off at 8.45pm and was under floodlights. Under local rules, substitutes were allowed and Pittsburgh replaced five of their side in the second half. Nevertheless, Charlton won 2-0.

The next stop was Detroit where Charlton arrived on 5 June. Some of the party went to the local races, but their betting was not as hot as their football. The party lost $40 between them. The attendance for the Detroit game was a disappointing 1,000 and the ground a narrow one. Charlton won 4-1.

From Detroit, Charlton travelled overnight to Chicago and the next day played the Illinois All Stars

On deck of the *Empress of Australia* on the way to America.

On tour in Canada, 1937. Left to right: George Tadman, George Green and Harold Hobbis.

Another group of the 1937 tour. Back row (left to right): Freddy Ford, George Stephenson, Jack Shreeve, Bert Turner, Sam Bartram, Bert Tann, John Oakes. Middle row: Arthur Arnott, Don Welsh, Jimmy Trotter, David Clark, Jimmy Seed, Dr John Montgomery, Harold Hobbis, George Tadman, Stanley Gliksten. Front row: Sid Cann, George Robinson, Les Boulter, Joe Jobling, George Green, Monty Wilkinson and Len Williams.

on a very bad ground with a surface of cinders, and dust blowing down the pitch in gusts from a high wind. Illinois went ahead in the first half, aided by the wind. But Charlton scored four in the second half to win 4-1. The attendance was 3,000.

The programme for the game described Charlton in the following terms: 'Unmatched by the record of any club in the British Isles, cradle of Association Football, or Soccer, the history of Charlton Athletic, one of the most sensational aggregations of the booting game ever to assay an invasion of the United States and Canada, is truly monumental in athletic annals.

'No other team in England ever has won promotion from the Third Division English League to the Second Division and from the Second to First in successive seasons. Not only is that the Kent club's record, but it won the Championship in each League as it moved up — two top clubs in each of the lower Divisions win promotion to the next higher class each season — and in its first year in the big time of the kicking game, it led the pack for a considerable period after a slow start and went down the home stretch trading the lead with Arsenal and Manchester City.

'Owned and operated by millionaire lumber merchants, who make it both their hobby and an important sideline business, the Charlton outfit, that even without expensive outlays in transfers, or the purchase of expensive stars, lost $200,000 in the 1935-6 season alone, but in the past season wrote off in toto its $325,000 debenture bonds, deserves taking apart and seeing what makes it tick.'

The programme also gave a short review of the club's leading personalities.

Throughout the tour, Charlton enjoyed generous local Press coverage, with comments such as 'The co-ordination of Charlton was superb and their adroit passing a revelation', and 'What the crowd came to see was an exhibition of soccer as it should be played — and they were not disappointed.'

From Chicago, Charlton went back into Canada, to Calgary where they won an overwhelming victory against the Alberta Province side by 12-1 before a

crowd of 3,000. They left for Vancouver the next morning. On Saturday, 12 June, they played Vancouver All Stars, who gave them far tougher opposition. Charlton were three goals ahead 20 minutes from the end. Then Vancouver scored from a penalty and immediately scored again. Charlton faced a desperate struggle but just held out to win 3-2

The party then made the short sea trip to Vancouver Island to play Victoria, whom they beat 4-0 on 14 June. They then crossed back to the mainland the next day to set off on a 1,000-mile train journey to Saskatoon. In the evening of 17 June, they thrashed the Saskatchewan provincial side 12-2. The highlight of the game was really afterwards when Jimmy Seed was made a chief by the chief of the local Red Indians. In return, the chief received the match-ball signed by the Charlton players.

In the Saskatchewan team were two Red Indian brothers called Greyeyes, who played at left-back and centre-half. Both men played well and later the Charlton goalkeeper, Sam Bartram, was to meet one of the brothers who came to Britain during the war with the Canadian Army.

The high scoring continued with a 9-1 victory in Winnipeg and a 6-1 victory against the Ontario Selects in Toronto. Then it was back to the United States for a 7-0 victory over Eastern Pennsylvania and a return match against the USFA in New York, won by 4-0. The final game was in Canada, a 4-0 victory over Montreal. Charlton had won 12 of their 13 games and drawn the other, scoring 72 goals against nine conceded. The leading scorers were Welsh (20), Tadman (19) and Hobbis (12).

Charlton embarked for home on the *Empress of Australia* on Friday, 2 July. From the point of view of sportsmanship and goodwill, the tour had been a tremendous success. But attendances were disappointing. Charlton's income was guaranteed in advance but the tour promoters lost £1,200.

Pre-war and Post-war in Sweden

THE following year Charlton had three offers to go abroad at the season's end. The invitations were all European, from France, Germany and Sweden, and it was the Swedish offer that was accepted. Once again, Charlton were asked to fill in for an international match against France, when Austria pulled out. But this time Charlton did not accept as they were advised against going by the Football Association.

Only three matches were played on the Swedish tour. The Charlton party comprised of Jimmy Seed, Jimmy Trotter, Dr Montgomery, and players Bartram, Turner, James Oakes, Shreeve, Jobling, Tann, John Oakes, Green, Wilkinson, Robinson, Blott, Boulter, Brown, Lancelotte and Mallett.

The first game was against a Swedish representative side at Norrköping and ended in a 1-1 draw. The next game, also against a representative side, in Gothenburg, ended 1-1 again and attracted a crowd of 21,000 — a measure of the support football was now attracting throughout Europe. The last match, against AIK Stockholm, ended in a 3-2 victory.

With the onset of war, it was not until Sunday, 19 May 1946 that Charlton played abroad again — with an epic 6-2 victory over Racing Club de Paris at the Colombes Stadium, Paris. Then followed another Swedish tour. Albert Gliksten went with the party which comprised 15 players: Bartram, Bert Turner, Shreeve, Croker, Johnson, Phipps, Revell, Dryden, Tadman, George Robinson, Dawson, Arthur Turner, Bill Robinson, Welsh and Duffy.

The first match was again in Norrköping, against the Norrköping club, who were both Cup holders and League champions. Charlton played poorly but still achieved a 2-2 draw. The second match was also a draw but in very different circumstances. Against AIK in Stockholm on 7 June, Charlton were 4-0 up at half-time after a brilliant display. AIK got one back just after the interval but then Charlton raced into a 7-1 lead with 25 minutes to go. But AIK staged an amazing comeback against a bemused Charlton defence, scoring six times to draw 7-7. For Charlton, Welsh and Billy Robinson each scored a hat-trick, Duffy hitting the other Charlton goal.

Against their next opponents, Jönköping, Charlton also built up a 4-0 lead. Then Jönköping pulled back three goals. But five minutes before the end, Charlton scored again to make it 5-3. The fourth and last game repeated this pattern of Charlton building up a big lead only to see it whittled away. The match was against Malmö on 14 June on a wet day. Charlton led 3-0 at half-time only to see the lead wiped out in the second half through three goals from Malmö. Then, in the last few minutes, Duffy scored to make it 4-3.

The attendances for the matches were 16,000 against Norrköping, 12,000 against AIK, 6,600 against Jönköping and 4,600 against Malmö.

In the autumn, Charlton entertained Norrköping to a return match at The Valley and also played Benfica in Lisbon. They flew to Lisbon on 18 September, and went down 2-1 to the Portuguese club. The Norrköping return match took place in October. Charlton lost 3-2 after conceding an early goal. New Year's Day 1947 saw Charlton in Paris again, playing out a 2-2 draw against Stade Français. On Armistice Day 1947, Charlton were in Belgium to play Liége. On the morning of the match, they walked around World War One cemeteries in pouring rain. It hardly proved ideal preparation. Charlton lost 5-0 in a match played on very heavy ground.

Hotel scene in Stockholm, 1938. Back (left to right) are a member of the hotel staff, John Oakes, Bert Turner and Sam Bartram. Middle row: Bert Tann, hotel staff member, Cyril Blott, Eric Lancelotte, Jack Shreeve, Joe Mallett, hotel receptionist, Jimmy Oakes, Les Boulter, Jimmy Trotter, Joe Jobling, Jimmy Seed and the tour courier. Kneeling: George Robinson, 'Sailor' Brown, Monty Wilkinson, George Green and Dr John Montgomery.

The defeats against Benfica, Norrköping and Liège proved just how fast Continental football was advancing. In May 1948, Charlton travelled to Ireland and played three matches, beating Ballymena, 4-2, Distillery 5-1 and drawing with Drumcondra 3-3 after leading 3-0 at half-time.

On 3 April, 1949, Charlton played against Stade Français again in Paris, drawing 2-2 once more. This

Welcome from the Swedish captain in Norrköping, 1938. Charlton's skipper is Jimmy Oakes. To the left of Oakes is George Green, then left to right are Les Boulter, Bert Tann, John Oakes and Sam Bartram.

was followed on 8 May by an end-of-season game at Saarbrücken in a Germany still occupied by the Allies. Charlton won 1-0 on a poor pitch composed mainly of loose ash. Sam Bartram was captain for the day, and before the kick-off had an unusual experience for an English player. As the teams lined up, he was presented with a bouquet of flowers by an attractive girl and then kissed on both cheeks, to the amusement of his teammates.

Turkish Fright

NEW ground was broken that same month when Charlton went on a tour to Turkey, flying by Skymaster to Istanbul. Jimmy Seed and Dr Montgomery accompanied the 16 players who were: Bartram, Campbell, Lock, Shreeve, Forbes, Allison, Phipps, Brown, Johnson, Hurst, Purves, Davies, Vaughan, Cullum, Duffy and D'Arcy.

The players stayed at a resort a few miles from Istanbul. The visit was very much a contrast to their tours nearer home. They found the weather sticky and oppressive, and the rich, oily food not to their liking.

Their first two opponents were the leading Istanbul sides, Galatasaray and Beşiktaş, who were among the founders of Turkish football in 1905 as members of the first Turkish league competition, the Istanbul Sunday League. Galatasaray had actually been the first Turkish team ever to defeat foreign opposition, beating the Hungarian club, Klozwar, 4-2 in 1911 in Istanbul.

The opening match was against Besiktas at the Istanbul Stadium in fine weather. Charlton won 2-1 but did not play well. Perhaps the firecrackers set off around the stadium indiscriminately throughout the match did not appeal to them. Sam Bartram later recalled the match as 'rather like playing soccer in the middle of a fireworks display'.

The Turkish players did not like the hard English tackling and their appeals to the crowd drew catcalls for Charlton from time to time. The referee was English and apparently less sympathetic to Turkish protests than a local referee would have been. Charlton's second goal came from an indirect free-kick and the Charlton players were surprised to find that the Beşiktaş side seemed to have no idea how to line up to meet the situation or form a defensive wall. Consequently, Charlton scored easily. The ball was tapped to Tommy Brown who slipped it into the net. The Turkish players complained at the goal and drew a chorus of boos and hisses from the crowd.

The pitch was protected by wire-net fencing but as the Charlton players reached the shelter of the dressing-room, bricks started to rain in through the windows. The team had to stay there until a police escort arrived to take them back to their hotel.

Charlton also won 2-1 against Galatasaray, again at the national stadium, in another disappointing display, marred by stones being thrown at both referee and players. When Charlton were awarded a penalty, the game almost degenerated into a riot. The Galatasaray players protested vigorously and their goalkeeper refused to take his place for the kick. Trainers and managers came on to the field to try to restore order and the crowd behind the wire netting looked frightening indeed to the Charlton players. Once again they had to be escorted back after the match to the safety of their hotel.

During the following week, two of the directors, Stanley Gliksten and Robert Law arrived, and the party found time to do a lot of sightseeing.

The third game against Fenerbahçe was played on 28 May. There was an argument over substitutes and Charlton would only agree to goalkeepers being changed. This time they played at the top of their form and won 3-0. According to Sam Bartram in his account of this eventful tour in his autobiography, the Fenerbahçe team featured two players who were serving gaol sentences and had been let out for the match. One had been convicted for stabbing a man to death.

The convicted murderer was playing at outside-left but after only five minutes he ran straight into the Charlton right-back Jimmy Campbell, flew head-first over his shoulder and crashed onto the bone-hard ground. He was carried off on a stretcher and taken unconscious back to prison. His fellow prisoner lasted the 90 minutes.

Dudley Forbes, another South African import for Charlton, who went on the trip to Turkey.

Charlton before their game against Beşiktaş in 1949. Back row (left to right): Chris Duffy, Bert Johnson, Gordon Hurst, Sam Bartram, Bill Robinson, Charlie Revell, Frank Lock. Front row: Tommy Brown, Syd O'Linn, Harold Phipps, Charlie Vaughan, Jack Shreeve, Jimmy Campbell.

The last game, against a combined national team, resulted in an easy 5-0 victory. And this time, the Charlton team had the crowd on their side because of their excellent display

Trapped in South America

IN 1954, Charlton went on the most ambitious tour in their history — to Colombia. The approach to them came from an official of the Bogota club, Millionarios FC, who proposed a tour of six matches. It seemed a good idea at the time and Charlton were promised a planned itinerary, first-class hotels and a good time all-round. Events turned out otherwise. The Charlton party departed in May, 1954, with 18 players. Along with Jimmy Seed, came trainer Alex Hird and directors David Clark and Dr Montgomery.

As soon at the party arrived, they knew they were in trouble. They were dumped in a second-class hotel with no cash to spend or the itinerary promised. The first match was against the Millionarios club on 23 May. It was drawn 2-2. Four days later Charlton played their second match — against Santa Fé — and again drew 2-2. In another three days, they were asked to play Millionarios again. This time the chaos off the field spread on the field. The match ended in a free fight and a 1-0 win for Millionarios, who had ten players from Argentina in their side.

Some of the Argentinians began to kick the Charlton players. Derek Ufton and Don Booker were injured. Then Rossi, a 6ft 3ins Argentinian, kicked Benny Fenton, only 5ft 7ins tall. Words were exchanged and Rossi hit Fenton on the nose. Fenton went in with both fists flying. He could not reach Rossi's face but he got in some body punches. The local crowd broke the netting around the ground on to the pitch. They were met by police and soldiers armed with rifles. The episode ended safely, but the Charlton party's state of mind was even more disturbed.

Charlton met Santa Fé again and the result was another draw — 0-0. Most of the party were now far from well, suffering from heat fatigue, the altitude and the food. Even the doctor in the party, Dr Montgomery, was ill.

Charlton were not as big an attraction as the Millionarios officials had hoped and they began to try to juggle the remaining fixtures, attempting to persuade Charlton to go off to Ecuador and Peru. More arguments followed and Seed demanded a £1,000 guarantee for any extra matches, without success. To make matters worse, the party's passports had been collected on arrival at Bogota. When Seed repeatedly asked for their return, he was always told 'mañana' but tomorrow never seemed to come. And the Millionarios officials held the return air tickets to London. So off the captive Charlton went to Peru, losing 3-1 to the University Club and 5-2 to Alianza. These two fixtures made up the six matches Charlton had agreed to play. But their hosts were not finished with them. They fixed up a last match at Guayaquil in Ecuador. Seed again asked for £1,000 but the money was never seen, although Charlton spent years through FIFA trying to collect it.

The Guayaquil match was against Barcelona and Charlton won their only victory of the tour, by 3-2. The party returned home exhausted in the middle of June.

The only pluses were that Charlton had benefited by a few thousand pounds, even though their claims for extra money were abortive, and that the tour saw the blooding of Don Townsend, who made a big impact at right-back. He went on to make his Football League debut in August. But the tour took its toll at the start of the English season, with the first two matches being lost.

Real Madrid's Laundry

IN April 1955, Charlton played a Sunday game against the famous Real Madrid in Madrid. The team flew to Spain on the evening of a Saturday league game against Everton. When the players arrived in Madrid in the early hours of Sunday morning, they had with them their strips and boots from the previous day's game — still filthy. After breakfast, they were taken to the ground and the kit collected. When they returned later to prepare for the match, the kit was handed back in immaculate condition, cleaned and pressed and the boots cleaned and treated with dubbin.

Real Madrid won the game 5-3 before a crowd of 40,000. Charlton were leading 2-1 at half-time, through goals by Hewie and Leary, when a torrential downpour hit the pitch. After Real equalized, Charlton regained the lead through White, but then the Spaniards struck back three times.

Early in their first post-war season back in Division Two, Charlton hit the European trail again to play an Italian XI in Milan on Wednesday, 20 November 1957. They left Heathrow on a BEA Viscount on Monday, 18 November, returning on the Thursday. The Italian side was really the national team, preparing for a World Cup qualifying match against Northern Ireland, and Charlton did superbly well to draw 1-1. A 65th-minute Bobby Ayre goal was cancelled out by a goal from Nicole.

The Italians used 17 players, including the renowned Boniperti and Schiaffino. Charlton brought on one substitute, Cyril Hammond coming on to replace the injured Gordon Jago. The *Reuter-AP* report summed up the match as follows: 'Charlton outplayed 17 star Italians here today. 'Keeper Bugatti saved Italy. It was Charlton nearly all the way and only their poor shooting and the great goalkeeping of Bugatti saved Italy.'

With European competition now developing — the European Cup had started in 1955-6 — the unfamiliarity of playing abroad and the novelty of new opposition began to evaporate. And so did Charlton's hopes of playing in the new European era with the club's demise as a First Division force. There were occasional tours, but not with the same importance and impact, overshadowed as they were by European competitions. In many cases, these trips were now simply warm-ups for a new season, often against weak opposition.

One close-season tour of note was in 1971, when Charlton visited both Spain and Holland, winning three games, drawing three and losing one. The results in Spain included a 2-2 draw against Palafrugell and a 1-1 draw against CD Sabadell.

In Holland, Charlton beat Blauw-Wit 2-0 in their opening game, the goals coming from Keith Peacock and Barry Endean. This was followed by a 0-0 draw against AZ 67, and then a 2-1 defeat against Haarlem, Peacock scoring. The tour was rounded off with a 1-0 victory against Excelsior, Kenning scoring.

Danish connections of the club towards the end of the 1970s saw consecutive trips to Denmark in 1979, 1980 and 1981, when the principal opposition was Hvidovre, the Danish First Division club whose chairman, Neils Madsen, was a Charlton director. Results against Hvidovre were 1-1, 1-0 and 0-2 respectively.

The 1981 tour was combined with a trip to Sweden, followed by a short visit to that country in 1982, the forerunners of several pre-season tours to Sweden, usually for practice games before a new season.

The problem of hooliganism made Charlton, along with other other clubs, fairly secretive about whether they were making tours at all — despite the almost trouble-free behaviour of Charlton supporters.

The only fixture of the 1980s that could compare with the grander fixtures of the past, was in 1987 when a home and away pair of games were played against the Italian First Division club, Pisa, for whom the former Charlton central defender, Paul Elliott, now played. The first game was in Italy and the kick-off put back to around 9pm to avoid the heat of an Italian summer's day. Pisa won 3-0 but Charlton scored a 3-1 victory in the return at Selhurst Park, when Crooks, Reid (penalty) and Mackenzie scored.

Then in May 1990 the club undertook its longest tour of all — to Australia. The secrecy was continued, even for a trip of this distance, and no announcement was made. This lack of trust deeply annoyed supporters who wanted to tell their relatives in Australia who supported the club, and the few who might have made the long journey.

The matches were played against representative sides. Results, venues and scorers were: Australian Capital Territory (in Canberra) 1-1, Williams; Queensland (in Brisbane) 2-2, Mortimer and Jones; South-East Queensland (in Bundaberg) 1-0 before being abandoned because of rain, Pitcher; Central Queensland (in Rockhampton) 5-1, Flanagan, Minto, Peake, Pitcher, Williams; North Queensland (in Townsville) 4-0, Gritt, Jones, Watson and Williams.

Don Welsh meets Norrköping's great centre-forward, Gunnar Nordahl, before the game at The Valley in October 1946.

Charlton in the Football League

Charlton's 1922-3 side with the London Challenge Cup. Back row (left to right): C.Hollidge (trainer), Syd Castle, T.Sullivan (director), Frank Burton, Freddy Wood, Baden Herod, M.Cadman (director), Steve Smith, F.T.Williams (director). Seated: Bobby Thomson, Bert Goodman, Walter Rayner (manager), Councillor Douglas Oliver (chairman), Albert Whalley (captain), Alec Steele. On ground: Albert Purdy, Seth Plum. Insets: S.Hartgrove, H.Isaacs and S.Dixon (all directors). This was Charlton's second season in the Football League.

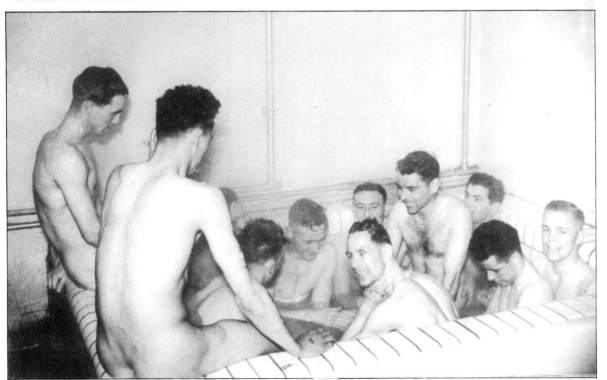

Crowded bathtime at The Valley in 1939. George Green (left) and Harold Gee look from the side. Fourth from left is Tommy Dawson and right of him is 'Sailor' Brown. Opposite him, looking round, is Bert Tann. Sid Cann sits in the middle and on the far right of the picture is Bert Johnson.

239

Division 3 South 1921-22

	P	W	D	L	F	A	W	D	L	F	A	Pts
Southampton	42	14	7	0	50	8	9	8	4	18	13	61
Plymouth A	42	17	4	0	43	4	8	7	6	20	20	61
Portsmouth	42	13	5	3	38	18	5	12	4	24	21	53
Luton T	42	16	2	3	47	9	6	6	9	17	26	52
QPR	42	13	7	1	36	12	5	6	10	17	32	49
Swindon T	42	10	7	4	40	21	6	6	9	32	39	45
Watford	42	9	9	3	34	21	4	9	8	20	27	44
Aberdare A	42	11	6	4	38	18	6	4	11	19	33	44
Brentford	42	15	2	4	41	17	1	9	11	11	26	43
Swansea T	42	11	8	2	40	19	2	7	12	10	28	41
Merthyr T	42	14	2	5	33	15	3	4	14	12	41	40
Millwall A	42	6	13	2	22	10	4	5	12	16	32	38
Reading	42	10	5	6	28	15	4	5	12	12	32	38
Bristol R	42	8	8	5	32	24	6	2	13	20	43	38
Norwich C	42	8	10	3	29	17	4	3	14	21	45	37
CHARLTON A	42	10	6	5	28	19	3	5	13	15	37	37
Northampton T	42	13	3	5	30	17	0	8	13	17	54	37
Gillingham	42	11	4	6	36	20	3	4	14	11	40	36
Brighton & HA	42	9	6	6	33	19	4	3	14	12	32	35
Newport C	42	8	7	6	22	18	3	5	13	22	43	34
Exeter C	42	7	5	9	22	29	4	7	10	16	30	34
Southend U	42	7	5	9	23	23	1	6	14	11	51	27

	Home	Away
Aberdare A	2-1	3-3
Brentford	1-1	2-0
Brighton & HA	1-0	0-2
Bristol R	2-0	0-2
Exeter C	1-0	0-1
Gillingham	0-0	0-2
Luton T	0-1	0-2
Merthyr T	1-0	0-1
Millwall A	2-1	1-0
Newport C	1-1	1-2
Northampton T	2-2	0-1
Norwich C	2-1	0-2
Plymouth A	0-0	0-3
Portsmouth	1-2	0-1
QPR	1-1	1-3
Reading	0-1	2-1
Southampton	1-2	0-6
Southend U	4-0	1-1
Swansea T	1-0	0-0
Swindon T	4-5	0-0
Watford	1-0	2-2

Appearances

Bacon E.F.	3
Bailey D.	33
Barnes E.	21
Briggs A.H.	2
Burton F.J.	25
Castle S.R.	30
Cox W.C.	26
Dadley B.J.	8
Dodd G.F.	1
Dowling T.P.	17
Dunn B.S.	8
Eggleton J.A.	2
Filliston J.W.	5
Goodman A.A.	38
Green A.	17
Halse H.J.	18
Hampson W.	15
Harbidge C.W.	6
Herod E.R.B.	2
Hughes J.	19
Jewhurst F.H.	3
Kingsley A.J.	20
Lane H.W.	3
Mills A.H.	2
Mitchell A.G.	1
Mitchell J.E.	16
Moody A.G.	2
Pleasant G.	2
Purdy A.	18
Smith C.	7
Steele A.	13
Thompson J.W.	2
Thomson R.J.	12
Upex D.	3
Whalley A.	38
Wilson H.	24

Scorers

Bailey D.	8
Cox W.C.	7
Halse G.J.	5
Castle S.R.	4
Whalley A.	4
Steele A.	3
Green A.	3
Kingsley A.J.	2
Filliston J.W.	2
Wilson G.	1
Mitchell A.G.	1
Dowling T.P.	1
Thomson R.J.	1
Own goal	1
Total	43

Division 3 South 1922-23

	P	W	D	L	F	A	W	D	L	F	A	Pts
Bristol C	42	16	4	1	43	13	8	7	6	23	27	59
Plymouth A	42	18	3	0	47	6	5	4	12	14	23	53
Swansea T	42	13	6	2	46	14	9	3	9	32	31	53
Brighton & HA	42	15	3	3	39	13	5	8	8	13	21	51
Luton T	42	14	4	3	47	18	7	3	11	21	31	49
Portsmouth	42	10	5	6	34	20	9	3	9	24	32	46
Millwall A	42	9	10	2	27	13	5	8	8	18	27	46
Northampton T	42	13	6	2	40	17	4	5	12	14	27	45
Swindon T	42	14	4	3	41	17	3	7	11	21	39	45
Watford	42	10	6	5	35	23	7	4	10	22	31	44
QPR	42	10	4	7	34	24	6	6	9	20	25	42
CHARLTON A	42	11	6	4	33	14	3	8	10	22	37	42
Bristol R	42	7	9	5	25	19	6	7	8	10	17	42
Brentford	42	9	4	8	27	23	4	8	9	14	28	38
Southend U	42	10	6	5	35	18	2	7	12	14	36	37
Gillingham	42	13	4	4	38	18	2	3	16	13	41	37
Merthyr T	42	10	4	7	27	17	1	10	10	12	31	36
Norwich C	42	8	7	6	29	26	5	3	13	22	45	36
Reading	42	9	8	4	24	15	1	6	14	12	40	34
Exeter C	42	10	4	7	27	18	3	5	13	20	66	33
Aberdare A	42	8	6	7	25	23	3	3	15	17	47	29
Newport C	42	8	6	7	28	21	0	5	16	12	49	27

	Home	Away
Aberdare A	1-1	1-3
Brentford	1-1	3-0
Brighton & HA	0-1	0-1
Bristol C	1-0	1-3
Bristol R	0-0	1-1
Exeter C	0-0	0-0
Gillingham	3-1	2-2
Luton T	2-1	2-2
Merthyr T	1-0	0-3
Millwall A	0-2	1-1
Newport C	6-0	0-4
Northampton T	2-0	0-0
Norwich C	3-0	3-2
Plymouth A	1-0	0-2
Portsmouth	0-2	0-3
QPR	1-1	2-1
Reading	1-0	1-2
Southend U	5-1	0-0
Swansea T	3-1	2-3
Swindon T	3-1	1-2
Watford	0-0	2-2

Appearances

Ayres G.A.	7
Bacon E.F.	2
Briggs A.H.	3
Burton F.J.	38
Castle S.R.	36
Cox W.C.	10
Dowling T.P.	3
Eggleton J.A.	15
Filliston J.W.	20
Goodman A.A.	30
Halse H.J.	3
Herod E.R.B.	34
Jewhurst F.H.	1
Knight B.H.	3
McKinnon A.	15
Miller H.S.	20
Plum S.L.	26
Purdy A.	24
Rees E.	20
Smith N.	2
Smith S.C.	30
Steele A.	31
Thomson R.J.	19
Whalley A.	28
Wood F.R.	42

Scorers

Steele A.	13
Miller H.S.	11
Goodman A.A.	8
Castle S.R.	6
Filliston J.W.	5
Thomson R.J.	4
Rees E.	3
Smith S.C.	3
Ayres G.A.	1
Whalley A.	1
Total	55

Division 3 South 1923-24

	P	W	D	L	F	A	W	D	L	F	A	Pts
Portsmouth	42	15	3	3	57	11	9	8	4	30	19	59
Plymouth A	42	13	6	2	46	15	10	3	8	24	19	55
Millwall A	42	17	3	1	45	11	5	7	9	19	27	54
Swansea T	42	18	2	1	39	10	4	6	11	21	38	52
Brighton & HA	42	16	4	1	56	12	5	5	11	12	25	51
Swindon T	42	14	5	2	38	11	3	8	10	20	33	47
Luton T	42	11	7	3	35	19	5	7	9	15	25	46
Northampton T	42	14	3	4	40	15	3	8	10	24	32	45
Bristol R	42	11	7	3	34	15	4	6	11	18	31	43
Newport C	42	15	4	2	39	15	2	5	14	17	49	43
Norwich C	42	13	5	3	45	18	3	3	15	15	41	40
Aberdare A	42	9	9	3	35	18	3	5	13	10	40	38
Merthyr T	42	11	8	2	33	19	0	8	13	12	46	38
CHARLTON A	42	8	7	6	26	20	3	8	10	12	25	37
Gillingham	42	11	6	4	27	15	1	7	13	16	43	37
Exeter City	42	14	3	4	33	17	1	4	16	4	35	37
Brentford	42	9	8	4	33	21	5	0	16	21	50	36
Reading	42	12	2	7	35	20	1	7	13	16	37	35
Southend United	42	11	7	3	35	19	1	3	17	18	65	34
Watford	42	8	5	8	35	18	1	7	13	10	36	30
Bournemouth & BA	42	6	8	7	19	19	5	3	13	21	46	33
QPR	42	9	6	6	28	26	2	3	16	9	51	31

	Home	Away
Aberdare A	3-1	1-4
Bournemouth & BA	*1-2	0-1
Brentford	*3-1	0-0
Brighton & HA	*0-2	0-3
Bristol R	*1-3	0-2
Exeter C	*1-0	0-0
Gillingham	*0-0	1-0
Luton T	*1-1	1-0
Merthyr T	1-0	1-2
Millwall A	0-1	0-1
Newport C	2-1	1-0
Northampton T	*0-0	0-1
Norwich C	0-0	2-2
Plymouth A	*0-1	1-1
Portsmouth	*1-1	0-0
QPR	*3-0	0-0
Reading	*0-0	1-3
Southend U	4-1	2-2
Swansea T	1-3	0-1
Swindon T	3-1	1-1
Watford	1-1	0-1

* Games played at The Mount

Appearances

Armitage G.H.	8
Ayres G.A.	26
Berry W.G.	11
Burrill F.	13
Burton F.J.	19
Champion E.F.	2
Chipperfield J.J.	3
Cox W.C.	14
Dowling T.P.	1
Dudley W.E.	2
Eggleton J.A.	9
Filliston J.W.	5
Goodman A.A.	26
Hannaford C.	20
Herod E.R.B.	30
Hutchins A.V.	21
Jewhurst F.H.	5
Plum S.L.	21
Preedy C.J.F.	3
Purdy A.	28
Rees E.	18
Richards A.C.	15
Smith N.	14
Smith S.C.	28
Steele A.	21
Thomson R.J.	24
Walsh W.	9
Whalley A.	22
Williams T.H.	5
Wood F.R.	39

Scorers

Thomson R.J.	9
Goodman A.A.	5
Ayres G.A.	4
Burrill F.	4
Whalley A.	3
Berry W.G.	2
Hannaford C.	2
Richards A.C.	2
Walsh W.	2
Williams T.H.	2
Filliston J.W.	1
Hutchins A.V.	1
Steele A.	1
Total	38

Division 3 South 1924-25

	P	W	D	L	F	A	W	D	L	F	A	Pts
Swansea T	42	17	4	0	51	12	6	7	8	17	23	57
Plymouth A	42	17	3	1	55	12	6	7	8	22	26	56
Bristol C	42	14	5	2	40	10	8	4	9	20	31	53
Swindon T	42	17	2	2	51	13	3	9	9	15	25	51
Millwall A	42	12	5	4	35	14	6	8	7	23	24	49
Newport C	42	13	6	2	35	12	7	3	11	27	30	49
Exeter C	42	13	4	4	37	19	6	5	10	22	29	47
Brighton & HA	42	14	3	4	43	17	5	5	11	16	28	46
Northampton T	42	12	3	6	34	18	8	3	10	17	26	46
Southend U	42	14	1	6	34	18	5	4	12	17	43	43
Watford	42	12	3	6	22	20	5	6	10	16	27	43
Norwich C	42	10	8	3	39	18	4	5	12	14	33	41
Gillingham	42	11	8	2	25	11	2	6	13	10	33	40
CHARLTON A	42	12	6	3	31	13	1	6	14	15	35	38
Reading	42	9	6	6	28	15	4	5	12	9	23	38
Bristol R	42	10	5	6	26	13	2	8	11	16	36	37
Luton T	42	9	10	2	34	15	1	7	13	15	42	37
Aberdare A	42	13	4	4	40	21	1	5	15	14	46	37
QPR	42	10	6	5	28	19	4	2	15	14	44	36
Bournemouth & BA	42	8	6	7	20	17	5	2	14	20	41	34
Brentford	42	8	7	6	28	26	1	0	20	10	65	25
Merthyr T	42	8	3	10	24	27	0	2	19	11	50	21

	Home	Away
Aberdare A	5-1	0-2
Bournemouth & BA	2-2	1-2
Brentford	3-0	0-1
Brighton & HA	1-0	0-1
Bristol C	0-1	1-1
Bristol R	1-1	0-4
Exeter C	1-0	1-2
Gillingham	2-0	0-2
Luton T	2-0	0-1
Merthyr T	3-0	1-2
Millwall A	0-2	0-1
Newport C	1-0	1-2
Northampton T	0-0	1-2
Norwich C	3-2	1-2
Plymouth A	2-1	2-3
QPR	2-0	0-0
Reading	1-2	0-0
Southend U	0-0	3-0
Swansea T	0-0	1-6
Swindon T	1-0	2-2
Watford	1-1	0-0

Appearances

Allen H.A.	23
Armitage G.H.	32
Bowers A.G.W.	5
Briggs A.H.	4
Burton F.J.	15
Cox W.C.	24
Goodman A.A.	32
Groves F.W.	7
Haley W.T.	18
Herod E.R.B.	39
McGinn H.	2
Millard E.A.	16
Preedy C.J.F.	31
Purdy A.	29
Rees E.	25
Richards A.C.	5
Sloan A.S.	1
Smith N.	32
Smith S.C.	32
Steele A.	35
Thomson R.J.	15
Trayler F.C.	6
Turnbull R.	6
Vanner H.J.	2
Wilson T.H.	11
Winter P.	4
Wood F.R.	11

Scorers

Rees E.	11
Haley W.T.	6
Cox W.C.	5
Smith S.C.	5
Wilson T.H.	4
Millard E.A.	3
Steele A.	3
Goodman A.A.	2
Turnbull R.	2
Allen H.A.	1
Armitage G.H.	1
Briggs A.H.	1
Richards A.C.	1
Thomson R.J.	1
Total	46

Division 3 South 1925-26

	P	W	D	L	F	A	W	D	L	F	A	Pts
Reading	42	16	5	0	49	16	7	6	8	28	36	57
Plymouth A	42	16	2	3	71	33	8	6	7	36	34	56
Millwall	42	14	6	1	52	12	7	5	9	21	27	53
Bristol C	42	14	3	4	42	15	7	6	8	30	36	51
Brighton & HA	42	12	4	5	47	33	7	5	9	37	40	47
Swindon T	42	16	2	3	48	22	4	4	13	21	42	46
Luton T	42	16	4	1	60	25	2	3	16	20	50	43
Bournemouth & BA	42	10	5	6	44	30	7	4	10	31	61	43
Aberdare A	42	11	6	4	50	24	6	2	13	24	42	42
Southend U	42	13	2	6	50	26	6	2	13	28	53	42
Gillingham	42	11	4	6	36	19	6	4	11	17	30	42
Northampton T	42	13	5	3	47	26	4	4	13	35	54	41
Crystal P	42	16	1	4	50	21	3	2	16	25	58	41
Merthyr T	42	13	5	3	51	25	1	8	12	18	50	39
Watford	42	12	5	4	47	26	3	4	14	26	63	39
Norwich C	42	11	5	5	35	26	4	4	13	23	47	39
Newport C	42	11	5	5	39	27	3	5	13	25	47	38
Brentford	42	12	4	5	44	32	4	2	15	25	62	38
Bristol R	42	9	4	8	44	28	6	2	13	22	41	36
Exeter C	42	13	2	6	54	25	2	3	16	18	45	35
CHARLTON A	42	9	7	5	32	23	2	6	13	16	45	35
QPR	42	5	7	9	23	32	1	2	18	14	52	21

	Home	Away
Aberdare A	1-0	1-3
Bournemouth & BA	5-0	1-4
Brentford	0-2	0-4
Brighton & HA	1-1	0-1
Bristol C	3-1	0-4
Bristol R	0-1	1-4
Crystal P	1-1	1-4
Exeter C	1-0	3-5
Gillingham	1-0	0-0
Luton T	2-1	0-1
Merthyr T	0-0	1-0
Millwall A	1-4	1-1
Newport C	0-0	0-0
Northampton T	3-3	1-2
Norwich C	3-0	0-3
Plymouth A	0-5	0-1
QPR	1-1	2-2
Reading	1-2	1-1
Southend U	5-0	2-1
Swindon T	2-0	0-3
Watford	1-1	1-1

Appearances

Allen H.A.	15
Armitage G.H.	31
Bailey J.H.	4
Biswell G.W.	13
Cox W.C.	24
Currie F.	7
Gibson J.	4
Godfrey E.J.	12
Hardie A.S.	28
Hawkins T.W	10
Herod E.R.B.	39
Hooper A.	7
Inglis D.G.	2
Jones F.J.	10
Kirby H.H.	7
McCrorie T.	5
McGinn H.	9
McGuire J.	6
Millard E.A.	22
Paterson W.F.	32
Preedy C.J.F.	38
Rankin J.P.	32
Semple J.	2
Smith N.	42
Steele A.	32
Steele H.G.	3
Tricker R.W.	20
Wilson T.H.	4
Winter P.	2

Scorers

Cox W.C.	6
Steele A.	6
Tricker R.W.	6
Rankin J.P.	5
Smith N.	4
Biswell G.W.	3
Gibson J.	3
Godfrey E.J.	3
Hardie A.S.	3
Jones F.J.	2
Millard E.A.	2
Armitage G.H.	1
Currie F.	1
Hawkins T.W.	1
Herod E.R.B.	1
Own goal	1
Total	48

Division 3 South 1926-27

	P	W	D	L	F	A	W	D	L	F	A	Pts
Bristol C	42	19	1	1	71	24	8	7	6	33	30	62
Plymouth A	42	17	4	0	52	14	8	6	7	43	47	60
Millwall	42	16	2	3	55	19	7	8	6	34	32	56
Brighton & HA	42	15	4	2	61	24	6	7	8	18	26	53
Swindon T	42	16	3	2	64	31	5	6	10	36	54	51
Crystal P	42	12	6	3	57	33	6	3	12	27	48	45
Bournemouth & BA	42	13	6	2	49	24	5	3	13	20	42	44
Luton T	42	12	9	0	48	19	3	5	13	20	47	44
Newport C	42	15	4	2	40	20	4	2	15	17	51	44
Bristol R	42	12	4	5	46	28	4	5	12	32	52	41
Brentford	42	10	9	2	46	20	3	5	13	24	41	40
Exeter C	42	14	4	3	46	18	1	6	14	30	55	40
CHARLTON A	42	13	5	3	44	22	3	3	15	16	39	40
QPR	42	9	8	4	41	27	6	1	14	24	44	39
Coventry C	42	11	4	6	44	33	4	3	14	27	53	37
Norwich C	42	10	5	6	41	25	2	6	13	18	46	35
Merthyr T	42	11	5	5	42	25	2	4	15	21	55	35
Northampton T	42	13	4	4	36	23	2	1	18	23	64	35
Southend U	42	12	3	6	44	25	2	3	16	20	52	34
Gillingham	42	10	5	6	36	26	1	5	15	18	46	32
Watford	42	9	6	6	36	27	3	2	16	21	60	32
Aberdare A	42	8	2	11	38	48	1	5	15	24	53	25

	Home	Away
Aberdare A	5-1	0-0
Bournemouth & BA	1-3	3-0
Brentford	1-1	0-2
Brighton & HA	1-0	2-3
Bristol C	0-1	1-4
Bristol R	3-1	1-1
Coventry C	4-2	0-1
Crystal P	1-2	1-2
Exeter C	1-0	0-1
Gillingham	3-0	1-1
Luton T	2-2	0-1
Merthyr T	3-2	0-3
Millwall A	1-1	0-1
Newport C	3-0	1-2
Northampton T	5-2	1-0
Norwich C	2-0	3-2
Plymouth A	1-1	1-3
QPR	2-0	1-2
Southend U	1-0	0-5
Swindon T	2-2	0-2
Watford	2-1	0-1

Appearances

Armitage G.H.	28
Biswell G.W.	28
Cairns J.	7
Collins N.	1
Davies F.P.	11
Davies J.	17
Devine J.	19
Gibson J.	1
Godfrey E.J.	19
Herod E.R.B.	28
Hipkin A.B.	1
Hirst H.	4
Horton J.W.	41
John R.	8
Kirk H.	8
McCracken H.	1
McKee R.	2
Middleton A.	5
Murphy J.	17
Paterson W.F.	37
Preedy C.J.F.	41
Rankin J.P.	41
Scott J.	1
Sherlaw D.D.	41
Smith N.	34
Tricker R.W.	21

Scorers

Sherlaw D.D.	19
Tricker R.W.	11
Rankin J.P.	8
Biswell G.W.	7
Godfrey E.J.	4
Horton J.W.	3
Cairns J.	2
Kirk H.	2
Armitage G.H.	1
Davies F.P.	1
Herod E.R.B.	1
Total	60

Division 3 South 1927-28

	P	W	D	L	F	A	W	D	L	F	A	Pts
Millwall	42	19	2	0	87	15	11	3	7	40	35	65
Northampton T	42	17	3	1	67	23	6	6	9	35	41	55
Plymouth A	42	17	2	2	60	19	6	5	10	25	35	53
Brighton & HA	42	14	4	3	51	24	5	6	10	30	45	48
Crystal P	42	15	3	3	46	23	3	9	9	33	49	48
Swindon T	42	12	6	3	60	26	7	3	11	30	43	47
Southend U	42	14	2	5	48	19	6	4	11	32	45	46
Exeter C	42	11	6	4	49	27	6	6	9	21	33	46
Newport C	42	12	5	4	52	38	6	4	11	29	46	45
QPR	42	8	5	8	37	35	9	4	8	35	36	43
CHARLTON A	42	12	5	4	34	27	3	8	10	26	43	43
Brentford	42	12	4	5	49	30	4	4	13	27	44	40
Luton T	42	13	5	3	56	27	3	2	16	38	60	39
Bournemouth & BA	42	12	6	3	44	24	1	6	14	28	55	38
Watford	42	10	5	6	42	34	4	5	12	26	44	38
Gillingham	42	10	3	8	33	26	3	8	10	29	55	37
Norwich C	42	9	8	4	41	26	1	8	12	25	44	36
Walsall	42	9	6	6	52	35	3	3	15	23	66	33
Bristol R	42	11	3	7	41	36	3	1	17	26	57	32
Coventry C	42	5	8	8	40	36	6	1	14	27	60	31
Merthyr T	42	7	6	8	38	40	2	7	12	15	51	31
Torquay U	42	4	10	7	27	36	4	4	13	26	67	30

	Home	Away
Bournemouth & BA	1-1	1-3
Brentford	3-2	1-1
Brighton & HA	3-0	2-2
Bristol R	2-1	1-2
Coventry C	2-1	3-3
Crystal P	0-4	0-5
Exeter C	0-0	1-2
Gillingham	1-0	1-1
Luton T	4-3	1-2
Merthyr T	0-0	0-0
Millwall A	1-1	0-5
Newport C	3-2	3-4
Northampton T	2-2	1-2
Norwich C	3-2	0-0
Plymouth A	2-0	0-2
QPR	1-0	3-3
Southend U	1-2	2-1
Swindon T	3-1	2-2
Torquay U	1-0	2-1
Walsall	1-3	0-1
Watford	0-2	2-1

Appearances
Armitage G.H.	27
Astley D.J.	1
Bethell R.	2
Biswell G.W.	22
Borland J.T.M.	5
Codd H.	18
Davies F.P.	14
Herod E.R.B.	41
Hird A.	40
Horton J.W.	42
Lennox W.	16
Lindon A.E.	5
McGill T.	5
McKenna T.	19
McKinley C.A.	23
Paterson W.F.	24
Preedy C.J.F.	18
Rankin J.P.	32
Sherlaw D.D.	35
Smith N.	42
Welsh W.	24
Whitlow F.W.J.	3
Wolfe T.H.	4

Scorers
Sherlaw D.D.	13
Biswell G.W.	9
Lennox W.	9
Horton J.W.	8
Rankin J.P.	7
Welsh W.	7
McKinley C.A.	3
Armitage G.H.	1
Borland J.T.M.	1
Hird A.	1
Whitlow F.W.J.	1
Total	60

Division 3 South 1928-29

	P	W	D	L	F	A	W	D	L	F	A	Pts
CHARLTON A	42	14	5	2	51	22	9	3	9	35	38	54
Crystal P	42	14	2	5	40	25	9	6	6	41	42	54
Northampton T	42	14	6	1	68	23	6	6	9	28	34	52
Plymouth A	42	14	6	1	51	13	6	6	9	32	38	52
Fulham	42	14	3	4	60	31	7	7	7	41	40	52
QPR	42	13	7	1	50	22	6	7	8	32	39	52
Luton T	42	16	3	2	64	28	3	8	10	25	45	49
Watford	42	15	3	3	55	31	4	7	10	24	43	48
Bournemouth & BA	42	14	4	3	54	31	5	5	11	30	46	47
Swindon T	42	12	5	4	48	27	3	8	10	27	45	43
Coventry C	42	9	6	6	35	23	5	8	8	27	34	42
Southend U	42	10	7	4	44	27	5	4	12	36	48	41
Brentford	42	11	4	6	34	21	3	6	12	22	39	38
Walsall	42	11	7	3	47	25	2	5	14	26	54	38
Brighton & HA	42	14	2	5	39	28	2	4	15	19	48	38
Newport C	42	8	6	7	37	28	5	3	13	32	58	35
Norwich C	42	12	3	6	49	29	2	3	16	20	52	34
Torquay U	42	10	3	8	46	36	4	3	14	20	48	34
Bristol R	42	9	6	6	39	28	4	1	16	21	51	33
Merthyr T	42	11	6	4	42	28	0	2	19	13	75	30
Exeter C	42	7	6	8	49	40	2	5	14	18	48	29
Gillingham	42	7	8	6	22	24	3	1	17	21	59	29

	Home	Away
Bournemouth & BA	6-2	2-4
Brentford	1-0	0-1
Brighton & HA	3-0	3-2
Bristol R	1-2	0-3
Coventry C	3-1	1-0
Crystal P	1-3	2-0
Exeter C	3-1	5-2
Fulham	0-0	5-2
Gillingham	1-1	0-1
Luton T	4-1	0-3
Merthyr T	2-2	3-2
Newport C	2-2	0-2
Northampton T	3-1	1-4
Norwich C	1-0	1-0
Plymouth A	2-1	2-2
QPR	2-2	2-2
Southend U	3-2	3-1
Swindon T	4-1	1-1
Torquay U	2-0	1-3
Walsall	5-0	2-0
Watford	2-0	1-3

Appearances
Armitage G.H.	30
Astley D.J.	22
Beach C.H.	1
Bethell R.	1
Codd H.	1
Hird A.	41
Horton J.W.	41
Johnson W.F.	10
Langford A.E.	42
Lennox W.	24
Lindon A.E.	28
McWhirr J.	1
Millsom E.D.	4
Pugsley J.	40
Rankin J.P.	41
Searle F.B.	3
Sherlaw D.D.	2
Slack S.	3
Smith N.	39
Thornett C.W.	4
Welsh W.	4
Whitlow F.W.J.	35
Wolfe T.H.	6
Wyper H.T.H.	39

Scorers
Whitlow F.W.J.	23
Lennox W.	18
Horton J.W.	16
Astley D.J.	11
Rankin J.P.	9
Pugsley J.	4
Wyper H.T.H.	4
Langford A.E.	1
Total	86

Division 2 1929-30

	P	W	D	L	F	A	W	D	L	F	A	Pts
Blackpool	42	17	1	3	63	22	10	3	8	35	45	58
Chelsea	42	17	3	1	49	14	5	8	8	25	32	55
Oldham A	42	14	5	2	60	21	7	6	8	30	30	53
Bradford	42	14	5	2	65	28	5	7	9	26	42	50
Bury	42	14	2	5	45	27	8	3	10	33	40	49
West Bromwich A	42	16	1	4	73	31	5	4	12	32	42	47
Southampton	42	14	6	1	46	22	3	5	13	31	54	45
Cardiff C	42	14	4	3	41	16	4	4	13	20	43	44
Wolverhampton W	42	14	3	4	53	24	2	6	13	24	55	41
Nottingham F	42	9	6	6	36	28	4	9	8	19	41	41
Stoke C	42	12	4	5	41	20	4	4	13	33	52	40
Tottenham H	42	11	8	2	43	24	4	1	16	16	37	39
CHARLTON A	42	10	6	5	39	23	4	5	12	20	40	39
Millwall	42	10	7	4	36	26	2	8	11	21	47	39
Swansea T	42	11	5	5	42	23	3	4	14	15	38	37
Preston NE	42	7	7	7	42	36	6	4	11	23	44	37
Barnsley	42	12	7	2	39	22	2	1	18	17	49	36
Bradford C	42	7	7	7	33	30	5	5	11	27	47	36
Reading	42	10	7	4	31	20	2	4	15	23	47	35
Bristol C	42	11	4	6	36	30	2	5	14	25	53	35
Hull C	42	11	3	7	30	24	3	4	14	21	54	35
Notts C	42	8	7	6	33	26	1	8	12	21	44	33

	Home	Away
Barnsley	2-0	0-2
Blackpool	1-4	0-6
Bradford	2-0	0-4
Bradford C	1-3	1-4
Bristol C	3-1	1-1
Bury	1-2	2-2
Cardiff C	4-1	0-1
Chelsea	1-1	1-1
Hull C	4-0	2-0
Millwall	1-1	1-1
Nottingham F	5-0	2-0
Notts C	1-0	0-4
Oldham A	1-1	0-1
Preston NE	1-1	3-0
Reading	0-0	1-3
Southampton	4-1	0-2
Stoke C	4-4	1-2
Swansea T	0-2	0-2
Tottenham H	1-0	0-3
West Bromwich A	0-1	1-1
Wolverhampton W	2-0	4-0

Appearances
Armitage G.H.	9
Astley D.J.	38
Beach C.H.	2
Brown H.	2
Butler C.R.	1
Hird A.	41
Horton J.W.	42
Langford A.E.	42
Legge A.E.	10
Lennox W.	12
Lindon A.E.	1
Millsom E.D.	1
Pritchard T.F.	21
Pugsley J.	40
Rankin J.P.	41
Robertson P.	41
Searle F.B.	15
Smith N.	36
Watson G.S.	14
Whewell W.T.	4
Whitlow F.W.J.	33
Wood A.	1
Wyper H.T.H.	15

Scorers
Whitlow F.W.J.	26
Astley D.J.	6
Lennox W.	5
Rankin J.P.	5
Horton J.W.	4
Wyper H.T.H.	4
Legge A.E.	2
Watson G.S.	2
Butler C.R.	1
Pugsley J.	1
Searle F.B.	1
Own goals	1
Total	59

Division 2 1930-31

	P	W	D	L	F	A	W	D	L	F	A	Pts
Everton	42	18	1	2	76	31	10	4	7	45	35	61
West Bromwich A	42	14	3	4	40	16	8	7	6	43	33	54
Tottenham H	42	15	5	1	64	20	7	2	12	24	35	51
Wolverhampton W	42	15	2	4	56	25	6	3	12	28	42	47
Port Vale	42	15	3	3	39	16	6	2	13	28	45	47
Bradford	42	15	4	2	71	24	3	6	12	26	42	46
Preston NE	42	15	4	2	55	31	5	6	10	28	33	45
Burnley	42	13	5	3	55	30	4	6	11	26	47	45
Southampton	42	13	4	4	46	22	6	2	13	28	40	44
Bradford C	42	12	5	4	39	26	5	5	11	22	37	44
Stoke C	42	11	6	4	34	17	6	4	11	30	54	44
Oldham A	42	13	5	3	45	28	3	5	13	16	44	42
Bury	42	14	3	4	44	20	5	0	16	31	62	41
Millwall	42	12	4	5	47	25	4	3	14	24	55	39
CHARLTON A	42	11	4	6	35	33	4	5	12	24	53	39
Bristol C	42	11	5	5	29	23	4	3	14	25	59	38
Nottingham F	42	12	6	3	54	35	2	3	16	26	50	37
Plymouth A	42	10	3	8	47	33	4	5	12	29	51	36
Barnsley	42	13	3	5	42	23	0	6	15	17	56	35
Swansea T	42	11	5	5	40	29	1	5	15	11	45	34
Reading	42	11	2	8	47	33	1	4	16	25	63	30
Cardiff C	42	7	6	8	32	31	1	3	17	15	56	25

	Home	Away
Barnsley	1-1	0-5
Bradford	3-1	2-3
Bradford C	2-1	2-3
Bristol C	0-0	0-3
Burnley	2-1	1-1
Bury	3-2	1-0
Cardiff C	4-1	2-0
Everton	0-7	1-7
Millwall	2-0	0-6
Nottingham F	1-1	3-4
Oldham A	1-1	3-0
Plymouth A	1-3	3-1
Port Vale	3-1	1-1
Preston NE	1-3	1-4
Reading	2-1	0-2
Southampton	3-1	0-3
Stoke C	1-2	0-0
Swansea T	3-0	1-1
Tottenham H	1-0	0-5
West Bromwich A	0-4	2-3
Wolverhampton W	1-2	1-1

Appearances

Astley D.J.	34
Beach C.H.	11
Hart J.	5
Hird A.	8
Horton J.W.	41
Knox J.P.	1
Langford A.E.	29
Lennox W.	19
McKay R.	21
McLeod T.	3
Millsom E.D.	7
Morgan L.D.	26
Peters F.	14
Pitcairn J.W.	30
Pritchard T.F.	16
Pugsley J.	38
Robertson P.	42
Searle F.B.	14
Smith N.	41
Sweeney E.	9
Whitlow F.W.J.	25
Wyper H.T.H.	28

Scorers

Astley D.J.	11
Whitlow F.W.J.	10
Lennox W.	9
Horton J.W.	6
McKay R.	4
Peters F.	4
Sweeney E.	4
Wyper H.T.H.	4
Beach C.H.	3
Hart J.	1
Pugsley J.	1
Own goals	2
Total	59

Division 2 1931-32

	P	W	D	L	F	A	W	D	L	F	A	Pts
Wolverhampton W	42	17	3	1	71	11	7	5	9	44	38	56
Leeds U	42	12	5	4	36	22	10	5	6	42	32	54
Stoke C	42	14	6	1	47	19	5	8	8	22	29	52
Plymouth A	42	14	4	3	69	29	6	5	10	31	37	49
Bury	42	13	4	4	44	21	8	3	10	26	37	49
Bradford	42	17	2	2	44	18	4	5	12	28	45	49
Bradford C	42	10	7	4	53	26	6	6	9	27	35	45
Tottenham H	42	11	6	4	58	37	5	5	11	29	41	43
Millwall	42	13	5	3	43	21	4	6	11	18	40	43
CHARLTON A	42	11	5	5	38	28	6	4	11	23	38	43
Nottingham F	42	13	4	4	49	27	3	6	12	28	45	42
Manchester U	42	12	3	6	44	31	5	5	11	27	41	42
Preston NE	42	11	6	4	37	25	4	5	12	38	52	42
Southampton	42	10	5	6	39	30	7	2	12	27	47	41
Swansea T	42	12	4	5	45	22	4	3	14	28	53	39
Notts C	42	10	4	7	43	30	3	8	10	32	45	38
Chesterfield	42	11	3	7	43	33	2	8	11	21	53	37
Oldham A	42	10	4	7	41	34	3	6	12	21	50	36
Burnley	42	7	8	6	36	36	6	1	14	23	51	35
Port Vale	42	8	4	9	30	33	5	3	13	28	56	33
Barnsley	42	8	7	6	35	30	4	2	15	17	41	33
Bristol C	42	4	7	10	22	37	2	4	15	17	41	23

	Home	Away
Barnsley	3-1	4-1
Bradford	2-2	0-3
Bradford C	1-0	1-1
Bristol C	2-0	2-1
Burnley	0-1	1-0
Bury	3-0	0-6
Chesterfield	0-0	2-3
Leeds U	0-1	0-2
Manchester U	1-0	2-0
Millwall	1-3	0-1
Nottingham F	3-1	2-3
Notts C	3-1	2-2
Oldham A	2-2	0-1
Plymouth A	2-0	1-1
Port Vale	2-1	1-0
Preston NE	2-1	2-3
Southampton	2-3	1-1
Stoke C	1-1	0-4
Swansea T	3-3	0-2
Tottenham H	2-5	1-0
Wolverhampton W	3-2	1-3

Appearances

Baker J.E.	21
Beach C.H.	15
Biswell G.W.	8
Black J.	23
Edmunds T.	6
Hobbis H.H.F.	6
Horton J.W.	36
James W.	14
Jobling J.	9
Keizer G.P.	17
Kelly G.M.	12
Kidd G.I.	6
Langford A.E.	22
McKay R.	28
McLeod T.	1
Morgan L.D.	14
Nash T.J.	2
Peters F.	15
Pitcairn J.W.	25
Pritchard T.F.	6
Pugsley J.	39
Rankin W.	8
Robertson P.	25
Robinson G.H.	16
Searle F.B.	23
Smith N.	19
Watkins E.T.	15
Wilson T.H.	18
Yardley J.	13

Scorers

Horton J.W.	13
Yardley J.	11
Watkins E.T.	6
Kelly G.M.	5
Edmunds T.	4
McKay R.	4
Black J.	3
Peters F.	3
Biswell G.W.	2
Hobbis H.H.F.	2
James W.	2
Beach C.H.	1
Kidd G.I.	1
Nash T.J.	1
Pugsley J.	1
Robinson G.H.	1
Searle F.B.	1
Total	61

Division 2 1932-33

	P	W	D	L	F	A	W	D	L	F	A	Pts
Stoke C	42	13	3	5	40	15	12	3	6	38	24	56
Tottenham H	42	14	7	0	58	19	6	8	7	38	32	55
Fulham	42	12	5	4	46	31	8	5	8	32	34	50
Bury	42	13	7	1	55	23	7	2	12	29	36	49
Nottingham F	42	9	8	4	37	28	8	7	6	30	31	49
Manchester U	42	11	5	5	40	24	4	8	9	31	44	43
Millwall	42	11	7	3	40	20	5	4	12	19	37	43
Bradford	42	13	4	4	51	27	4	4	13	26	44	42
Preston NE	42	12	2	7	53	36	4	8	9	21	34	42
Swansea T	42	17	0	4	36	12	2	4	15	14	42	42
Bradford C	42	10	6	5	43	24	4	7	10	22	37	41
Southampton	42	15	3	3	48	22	3	2	16	18	44	41
Grimsby T	42	8	10	3	49	34	6	3	12	30	50	41
Plymouth A	42	13	4	4	45	22	3	5	13	18	45	41
Notts C	42	10	4	7	41	31	5	6	10	26	47	40
Oldham A	42	10	4	7	38	31	5	4	12	29	49	38
Port Vale	42	12	3	6	49	27	2	7	12	17	52	38
Lincoln C	42	11	6	4	46	28	1	7	13	26	59	37
Burnley	42	8	9	4	35	20	3	5	13	32	59	36
West Ham U	42	12	6	3	56	31	1	3	17	19	62	35
Chesterfield	42	10	5	6	25	25	2	5	14	25	59	34
CHARLTON A	42	9	3	9	35	35	3	4	14	25	56	31

	Home	Away
Bradford	0-2	0-3
Bradford C	0-0	0-3
Burnley	2-2	1-0
Bury	1-3	1-3
Chesterfield	2-5	3-2
Fulham	1-2	1-3
Grimsby T	2-3	5-5
Lincoln C	4-2	1-1
Manchester U	0-1	1-1
Millwall	1-4	1-2
Nottingham F	3-0	1-0
Notts C	3-3	2-3
Oldham A	1-0	0-0
Plymouth A	4-1	1-6
Port Vale	2-1	1-2
Preston NE	0-1	2-4
Southampton	2-0	0-3
Stoke C	1-0	0-2
Swansea T	3-1	0-2
Tottenham H	0-3	1-4
West Ham U	3-1	3-7

Appearances

Baker J.E.	4
Biswell G.W.	19
Black J.	8
Blackwell J.	27
Boulter L.M.	14
Doherty J.	4
Halkyard C.	1
Harbot J.W.	1
Hobbis H.H.F.	34
Horton J.W.	9
Ivill E.	19
James W.	14
Jobling J.	37
Kelly G.M.	8
Morris S.	12
Nash T.J.	1
Oakes, James	19
Pearce C.	29
Pugsley J.	35
Rankin W.	18
Robertson P.	9
Robinson G.H.	24
Searle F.B.	11
Smith N.	21
Vickers J.	10
Wilkinson J.	12
Wright A.	28
Wright H.E.	5
Yardley J.	29

Scorers

Pearce C.	23
Yardley J.	11
Blackwell J.	5
Boulter L.M.	5
Hobbis H.H.F.	4
Robinson G.H.	4
Horton J.W.	2
Harbot J.W.	1
James W.	1
Kelly G.M.	1
Own goals	3
Total	60

Division 3 South 1933-34

	P	W	D	L	F	A	W	D	L	F	A	Pts
Norwich C	42	16	4	1	55	19	9	7	5	33	30	61
Coventry C	42	16	3	2	70	22	5	9	7	30	32	54
Reading	42	17	4	0	60	13	4	8	9	22	37	54
QPR	42	17	2	2	42	12	7	4	10	28	39	54
CHARLTON A	42	14	5	2	53	27	8	3	10	30	29	52
Luton T	42	14	3	4	55	28	7	7	7	28	33	52
Bristol R	42	14	4	3	49	21	6	7	8	28	26	51
Swindon T	42	13	5	3	42	25	4	6	11	22	43	45
Exeter C	42	12	5	4	43	19	4	6	11	25	38	43
Brighton & HA	42	12	7	2	47	18	3	6	12	21	42	43
Clapton O	42	14	4	3	60	25	2	6	13	15	44	42
Crystal P	42	11	6	4	40	25	5	3	13	31	42	41
Northampton T	42	10	6	5	45	32	4	6	11	26	46	40
Aldershot	42	8	6	7	28	27	5	6	10	24	44	38
Watford	42	12	4	5	43	16	3	3	15	28	47	37
Southend U	42	9	6	6	32	27	3	4	14	19	47	34
Gillingham	42	8	8	5	49	41	3	3	15	26	55	33
Newport C	42	6	9	6	25	23	2	8	11	24	47	33
Bristol C	42	7	8	6	33	22	3	5	13	25	63	33
Torquay U	42	10	4	7	32	28	3	3	15	21	65	33
Bournemouth & BA	42	7	7	7	41	37	2	2	17	19	65	27
Cardiff C	42	6	4	11	32	43	3	2	16	25	62	24

	Home	Away
Aldershot	1-0	2-3
Bournemouth & BA	4-3	2-1
Brighton & HA	4-3	0-1
Bristol C	2-1	1-0
Bristol R	2-1	5-2
Cardiff C	2-0	1-1
Clapton O	1-1	3-1
Coventry C	2-0	2-3
Crystal P	4-2	0-1
Exeter C	4-1	0-2
Gillingham	2-2	1-1
Luton T	2-0	1-2
Newport C	6-1	1-1
Northampton T	1-1	2-1
Norwich C	3-3	0-3
QPR	1-2	1-2
Reading	0-0	0-1
Southend U	1-3	0-1
Swindon T	1-0	3-1
Torquay U	6-0	4-1
Watford	4-3	1-0

Appearances
Biswell G.W.	1
Blackwell J.	8
Boulter L.M.	16
Butt H.H.	21
Doherty J.	4
Forster M.	1
Harris F.	38
Hobbis H.H.F.	41
Ivill E.	15
Jobling J.	40
Kenyon F.	1
Moore G.W.	1
Oakes, James	41
Pearce C.	32
Prior S.J.	15
Pugsley J.	22
Reed A.G.	1
Smith J.T.	19
Smith N.	27
Tann B.J.	7
Turner H.G.	20
Wilkinson J.	40
Wright A.	32
Wright H.E.	10
Yardley J.	9

Scorers
Pearce C.	26
Wilkinson J.	12
Prior S.J.	10
Hobbis H.H.F.	7
Butt H.H.	6
Smith J.T.	6
Yardley J.	4
Blackwell J.	2
Smith N.	2
Tann B.J.	2
Harris F.	1
Jobling J.	1
Moore G.W.	1
Own goals	3
Total	83

Division 3 South 1934-35

	P	W	D	L	F	A	W	D	L	F	A	Pts
CHARLTON A	42	17	2	2	62	20	10	5	6	41	32	61
Reading	42	16	5	0	59	23	5	6	10	30	42	53
Coventry C	42	14	5	2	56	14	7	4	10	30	36	51
Luton T	42	12	7	2	60	23	7	5	9	32	37	50
Crystal P	42	15	3	3	51	14	4	7	10	35	50	48
Watford	42	14	2	5	53	19	5	7	9	23	30	47
Northampton T	42	14	4	3	40	21	5	4	12	25	46	46
Bristol R	42	14	6	1	54	27	3	4	14	19	50	44
Brighton & HA	42	15	4	2	51	16	2	5	14	18	46	43
Torquay U	42	15	2	4	60	22	3	4	14	21	53	42
Exeter C	42	11	5	5	48	29	5	4	12	22	46	41
Millwall	42	11	4	6	33	26	6	3	12	24	36	41
QPR	42	14	6	1	49	22	2	3	16	14	50	41
Clapton O	42	13	5	3	47	21	2	7	12	18	44	40
Bristol C	42	14	3	4	37	18	1	6	14	15	50	39
Swindon T	42	11	7	3	45	22	2	5	14	22	56	38
Bournemouth & BA	42	10	5	6	36	26	5	2	14	18	45	37
Aldershot	42	12	6	3	35	20	1	4	16	15	55	36
Cardiff C	42	11	6	4	42	27	2	3	16	20	55	35
Gillingham	42	10	7	4	36	25	1	6	14	19	50	35
Southend U	42	10	4	7	40	29	1	5	15	25	49	31
Newport C	42	7	4	10	36	40	3	1	17	18	72	25

	Home	Away
Aldershot	4-0	2-3
Bournemouth & BA	0-1	2-2
Brighton & HA	3-1	1-2
Bristol C	4-1	4-1
Bristol R	2-0	0-0
Cardiff C	3-1	1-2
Clapton O	2-1	2-1
Coventry C	3-3	0-4
Crystal P	2-2	2-1
Exeter C	1-0	1-3
Gillingham	2-0	6-3
Luton T	4-2	2-1
Millwall	3-1	3-1
Newport C	6-0	2-0
Northampton T	0-1	1-1
QPR	3-1	3-0
Reading	3-1	2-2
Southend U	3-0	3-0
Swindon T	6-0	2-2
Torquay U	3-2	2-1
Watford	5-2	0-2

Appearances
Allen R.S.L.	28
Bartram S.	18
Boulter L.M.	18
Butt H.H.	7
Dodgin W.	25
Harris F.	40
Hobbis H.H.F.	37
Ivill E.	1
Jobling J.	27
Oakes, James	35
Prior S.J.	11
Rist F.H.	3
Robinson G.H.	42
Smith J.T.	4
Smith N.	41
Stephenson G.T.	22
Turner H.G.	27
Welsh D.	14
Wilkinson J.	38
Wright A.	4
Wright H.E.	20

Scorers
Allen R.S.L.	32
Hobbis H.H.F.	15
Robinson G.H.	12
Wilkinson J.	9
Harris F.	7
Boulter L.M.	6
Smith N.	6
Prior S.H.	5
Stephenson G.T.	5
Butt H.H.	2
Jobling H.	2
Welsh D.	1
Turner H.G.	1
Total	103

Division 2 1935-36

	P	W	D	L	F	A	W	D	L	F	A	Pts
Manchester U	42	16	3	2	55	16	6	9	6	30	27	56
CHARLTON A	42	15	6	0	53	17	7	5	9	32	41	55
Sheffield U	42	15	4	2	51	15	5	8	8	28	35	52
West Ham U	42	13	5	3	51	23	9	3	9	39	45	52
Tottenham H	42	12	6	3	60	25	6	7	8	31	30	49
Leicester C	42	14	5	2	53	19	5	5	11	26	38	48
Plymouth A	42	15	2	4	50	20	5	6	10	21	37	48
Newcastle U	42	13	5	3	56	27	7	1	13	32	52	46
Fulham	42	11	6	4	58	24	4	8	9	18	28	44
Blackpool	42	14	3	4	64	34	4	4	13	29	38	43
Norwich C	42	14	2	5	47	24	3	7	11	25	41	43
Bradford C	42	12	7	2	32	18	3	6	12	23	47	43
Swansea T	42	11	3	7	42	26	4	6	11	25	50	39
Bury	42	10	6	5	41	27	3	6	12	25	57	38
Burnley	42	9	8	4	35	21	3	5	13	15	38	37
Bradford	42	13	6	2	43	26	1	3	17	19	58	37
Southampton	42	11	3	7	32	24	3	6	12	15	41	37
Doncaster R	42	10	7	4	28	17	4	2	15	23	54	37
Nottingham F	42	8	8	5	43	22	4	3	14	26	54	35
Barnsley	42	9	4	8	40	32	3	5	13	14	48	33
Port Vale	42	10	5	6	34	30	2	3	16	22	76	32
Hull City	42	4	7	10	33	45	1	3	17	14	66	20

	Home	Away
Barnsley	3-0	2-1
Blackpool	1-1	2-6
Bradford	3-1	0-3
Bradford C	2-1	1-2
Burnley	4-0	2-0
Bury	5-2	1-1
Doncaster R	3-0	0-2
Fulham	2-1	0-0
Hull C	4-1	4-2
Leicester C	1-0	1-4
Manchester U	0-0	0-3
Newcastle U	4-2	2-1
Norwich C	4-1	1-3
Nottingham F	4-0	0-0
Plymouth A	1-1	2-4
Port Vale	1-1	1-2
Sheffield U	1-1	2-2
Southampton	2-0	5-2
Swansea T	4-1	2-1
Tottenham H	2-1	1-1
West Ham U	2-2	3-1

Appearances
Allen R.S.L.	24
Bartram S.	39
Boulter L.M.	29
Cann S.T.	9
Dodgin W.	5
Harris F.	4
Hobbis H.H.F.	42
Jobling J.	41
Oakes, James	26
Oakes, John	8
Pearce C.	3
Prior S.H.	10
Rist F.H.	31
Robinson G.H.	41
Smith N.	27
Stephenson G.T.	17
Tann B.J.	1
Turner H.G.	26
Welsh D.	37
Wilkinson J.	39
Wright H.E.	3

Scorers
Hobbis H.H.F.	23
Allen R.S.L.	15
Prior S.J.	11
Robinson G.H.	11
Welsh D.	6
Wilkinson J.	6
Stephenson G.T.	5
Smith N.	4
Boulter L.M.	2
Oakes John	1
Rist F.H.	1
Total	85

Division 1 1936-37

	P	W	D	L	F	A	W	D	L	F	A	Pts
Manchester C	42	15	5	1	56	22	7	8	6	51	39	57
CHARLTON A	42	15	5	1	37	13	6	7	8	21	36	54
Arsenal	42	10	10	1	43	20	8	6	7	37	29	52
Derby C	42	13	3	5	58	39	8	4	9	38	51	49
Wolverhampton W	42	16	2	3	63	24	5	3	13	21	43	47
Brentford	42	14	5	2	58	32	4	5	12	24	46	46
Middlesbrough	42	14	6	1	49	22	5	2	14	25	49	46
Sunderland	42	17	2	2	59	24	2	4	15	30	63	44
Portsmouth	42	13	3	5	41	29	4	7	10	21	37	44
Stoke C	42	12	6	3	52	27	3	6	12	20	30	42
Grimsby T	42	13	3	5	60	32	4	4	13	26	49	41
Birmingham	42	9	7	5	36	24	4	8	9	28	36	41
Chelsea	42	11	6	4	36	21	3	7	11	16	34	41
Preston NE	42	10	6	5	35	28	4	7	10	21	39	41
Huddersfield T	42	12	5	4	39	21	0	10	11	23	43	39
West Bromwich A	42	13	3	5	45	32	3	3	15	32	66	38
Everton	42	12	7	2	56	23	2	2	17	25	55	37
Liverpool	42	9	8	4	38	26	3	3	15	24	58	35
Leeds U	42	14	3	4	44	20	1	1	19	16	60	34
Bolton W	42	6	6	9	22	33	4	8	9	21	33	34
Manchester U	42	8	9	4	29	26	2	3	16	26	52	32
Sheffield W	42	8	5	8	32	29	1	7	13	21	40	30

	Home	Away
Arsenal	0-2	1-1
Birmingham	2-2	2-1
Bolton W	1-0	1-2
Brentford	2-1	2-4
Chelsea	1-0	0-3
Derby C	2-0	0-5
Everton	2-0	2-2
Grimsby T	1-0	1-0
Huddersfield T	1-0	2-1
Leeds U	1-0	0-2
Liverpool	1-1	2-1
Manchester C	1-1	1-1
Manchester U	3-0	0-0
Middlesbrough	2-2	1-1
Portsmouth	0-0	1-0
Preston NE	3-1	0-0
Sheffield W	1-0	1-3
Stoke C	2-0	1-1
Sunderland	3-1	0-1
West Bromwich A	4-2	2-1
Wolverhampton W	4-0	1-6

Appearances
Bartram S.	42
Boulter L.M.	34
Ford F.G.L.	8
Green G.H.	5
Green R.C.G.	3
Hobbis H.H.F.	37
Jobling J.	33
Mordey H.V.	6
Oakes, James	31
Oakes, John	39
Pearce C.	4
Prior S.H.	14
Rist F.H.	3
Robinson G.H.	41
Shreeve J.T.T.	6
Stephenson G.T.	11
Tadman G.H.	29
Tann B.J.	4
Turner H.G.	37
Welsh D.	39
Wilkinson J.	30
Williams L.S.	2

Scorers
Tadman G.H.	11
Hobbis H.H.F.	9
Wilkinson H.	8
Boulter L.M.	6
Prior S.J.	6
Welsh D.	5
Robinson G.H.	4
Pearce C.	3
Jobling J.	2
Stephenson G.T.	2
Green R.C.G.	1
Oakes John	1
Total	58

Division 1 1937-38

	P	W	D	L	F	A	W	D	L	F	A	Pts
Arsenal	42	15	4	2	52	16	6	6	9	25	28	52
Wolverhampton W	42	11	8	2	47	21	9	3	9	25	28	51
Preston NE	42	9	9	3	34	21	7	8	6	30	23	49
CHARLTON A	42	14	5	2	43	14	2	9	10	22	37	46
Middlesbrough	42	12	4	5	40	26	7	4	10	32	39	46
Brentford	42	10	6	5	44	27	8	3	10	25	32	45
Bolton W	42	11	6	4	38	22	4	9	8	26	38	45
Sunderland	42	12	6	3	32	18	2	10	9	23	39	44
Leeds U	42	11	6	4	38	26	3	9	9	26	43	43
Chelsea	42	11	6	4	40	22	3	7	11	25	43	41
Liverpool	42	9	5	7	40	30	6	6	9	25	41	41
Blackpool	42	10	5	6	33	26	6	3	12	28	40	40
Derby C	42	10	5	6	52	36	5	5	11	24	51	40
Everton	42	11	3	7	29	24	6	2	13	26	44	39
Huddersfield T	42	11	5	5	54	34	5	2	14	25	41	39
Leicester C	42	9	6	6	31	26	5	5	11	23	49	39
Stoke C	42	10	7	4	42	21	3	5	13	16	38	38
Birmingham	42	7	11	3	34	28	3	7	11	24	34	38
Portsmouth	42	11	6	4	41	22	2	6	13	21	46	38
Grimsby T	42	11	5	5	29	23	2	7	12	22	45	38
Manchester C	42	12	2	7	49	33	2	6	13	31	44	36
West Bromwich A	42	10	5	6	46	36	4	3	14	28	55	36

	Home	Away
Arsenal	0-3	2-2
Birmingham	2-0	1-1
Blackpool	4-1	0-1
Bolton W	1-1	0-1
Brentford	1-0	2-5
Chelsea	3-1	1-1
Derby C	1-2	2-3
Everton	3-1	0-3
Grimsby T	0-0	1-1
Huddersfield T	4-0	1-1
Leeds U	1-1	2-2
Leicester C	2-0	0-1
Liverpool	3-0	2-1
Manchester C	0-0	3-5
Middlesbrough	1-0	1-3
Portsmouth	5-1	1-2
Preston NE	0-0	1-0
Stoke C	3-0	0-2
Sunderland	2-1	1-1
West Bromwich A	3-1	0-0
Wolverhampton W	4-1	1-1

Appearances
Barron W.	3
Bartram S.	41
Blott C.L.C.	6
Boulter L.M.	34
Brown R.A.J.	17
Ford F.H.L.	14
Green G.H.	24
Hobbins S.H.	1
Hobbis H.H.F.	22
Jobling J.	23
Lancelotte E.C.	11
Oakes, James	32
Oakes, John	35
Owens T.L.	11
Rist F.H.	6
Robinson G.H.	37
Shreeve J.T.T.	14
Tadman G.H.	27
Tann B.J.	1
Turner H.G.	38
Welsh D.	39
Wilkinson J.	25
Williams L.S.	1

Scorers
Tadman G.H.	11
Welsh D.	11
Brown R.A.J.	9
Robinson G.H.	7
Boulter L.M.	6
Hobbis H.H.F.	6
Owens T.L.	5
Wilkinson J.	4
Barron W.	2
Turner H.G.	2
Blott C.L.C.	1
Oakes, John	1
Total	65

Division 1 1938-39

	P	W	D	L	F	A	W	D	L	F	A	Pts
Everton	42	17	3	1	60	18	10	2	9	28	34	59
Wolverhampton W	42	14	6	1	55	12	8	5	8	33	27	55
CHARLTON A	42	16	3	2	49	24	6	3	12	26	35	50
Middlesbrough	42	13	6	2	64	27	7	3	11	29	47	49
Arsenal	42	14	3	4	34	14	5	6	10	21	27	47
Derby C	42	12	3	6	39	22	7	5	9	27	33	46
Stoke C	42	13	6	2	50	25	4	6	11	21	43	46
Bolton W	42	10	6	5	39	25	5	9	7	28	33	45
Preston NE	42	13	7	1	44	19	3	5	13	19	40	44
Grimsby T	42	11	6	4	38	26	5	5	11	23	43	43
Liverpool	42	12	6	3	40	24	2	8	11	22	39	42
Aston Villa	42	11	3	7	44	25	5	6	10	27	35	41
Leeds U	42	11	5	5	40	27	5	4	12	19	40	41
Manchester U	42	7	9	5	30	20	4	7	10	27	45	38
Blackpool	42	9	8	4	37	26	3	6	12	19	42	38
Sunderland	42	7	7	7	30	29	6	5	10	24	38	38
Portsmouth	42	10	7	4	25	15	2	6	13	22	55	37
Brentford	42	11	2	8	30	27	3	6	12	23	47	36
Huddersfield T	42	11	4	6	38	18	1	7	13	20	46	35
Chelsea	42	10	5	6	43	29	2	4	15	21	51	33
Birmingham	42	10	5	6	40	27	2	3	16	22	57	32
Leicester C	42	7	6	8	35	35	2	5	14	13	47	29

	Home	Away
Arsenal	1-0	0-2
Aston Villa	1-0	0-2
Birmingham	4-4	4-3
Blackpool	3-1	0-0
Bolton W	2-1	1-2
Brentford	1-1	0-1
Chelsea	2-0	3-1
Derby C	1-0	1-3
Everton	2-1	4-1
Grimsby T	3-1	1-1
Huddersfield T	2-1	0-4
Leeds U	2-0	1-2
Leicester C	1-0	5-1
Liverpool	1-3	0-1
Manchester U	7-1	2-0
Middlesbrough	3-0	0-4
Portsmouth	3-3	2-0
Preston NE	3-1	0-2
Stoke C	4-2	0-1
Sunderland	3-0	1-1
Wolverhampton W	0-4	1-3

Appearances
Bartram S.	42
Blott C.L.C.	10
Boulter L.M.	22
Brown R.A.J.	30
Cann S.T.	2
Dawson T.	1
Drinkwater C.J.	3
Green G.H.	28
Hobbis H.H.F.	20
Jobling J.	1
Lancelotte E.C.	1
Mallett J.	2
Mordey H.V.	4
Oakes, James	37
Oakes, John	40
Owens T.L.	1
Rist F.H.	1
Robinson G.H.	30
Shreeve J.T.T.	32
Smith G.C.	1
Tadman G.H.	31
Tann B.J.	6
Turner H.G.	17
Welsh D.	41
Wilkinson J.	40
Wright R.C.A.	19

Scorers
Tadman G.H.	24
Brown R.A.J.	12
Hobbis H.H.F.	9
Wilkinson J.	9
Welsh D.	8
Blott C.L.C.	3
Boulter L.M.	3
Green G.H.	3
Robinson G.H.	3
Own goal	1
Total	75

Division 1 1939-40

	P	W	D	L	F	A	W	D	L	F	A	Pts
Blackpool	3	2	0	0	4	2	1	0	0	1	0	6
Sheffield U	3	1	0	0	2	1	1	1	0	1	0	5
Arsenal	3	2	0	0	6	2	0	1	0	2	2	5
Liverpool	3	2	0	0	5	1	0	0	1	1	2	4
Everton	3	0	1	0	1	1	1	1	0	4	3	4
Bolton W	3	1	0	0	2	1	1	0	1	4	4	4
Derby C	3	2	0	0	3	0	0	0	1	0	3	4
CHARLTON A	3	1	0	0	2	0	1	0	1	1	4	4
Stoke C	3	1	0	1	5	2	0	1	0	2	2	3
Manchester U	3	1	0	0	4	0	0	1	1	1	3	3
Brentford	3	1	0	0	1	0	0	1	1	2	3	3
Chelsea	3	1	1	0	4	3	0	0	1	0	1	3
Grimsby T	3	1	1	0	2	0	0	0	1	0	4	3
Aston Villa	3	1	0	1	3	2	0	1	0	1	0	2
Sunderland	3	1	0	1	4	2	0	0	1	2	5	2
Wolverhampton W	3	0	1	0	2	2	0	1	1	1	2	2
Huddersfield T	3	0	0	1	0	1	1	1	0	2	2	2
Portsmouth	3	1	0	0	2	1	0	0	2	1	4	2
Preston NE	3	0	2	0	0	0	0	0	1	0	2	2
Blackburn R	3	0	1	0	2	2	0	0	2	1	3	1
Middlesbrough	3	0	1	0	2	2	0	0	2	1	6	1
Leeds U	3	0	0	2	0	2	0	1	0	0	0	1

	Home	Away
Leeds U	—	1-0
Manchester U	2-0	—
Stoke C	—	0-4

Appearances
Bartram S.	3
Brown R.A.J.	3
Dawson T.	2
Green G.H.	3
Hobbis H.H.F.	3
Oakes, James	2
Oakes, John	3
Robinson G.H.	2
Shreeve J.T.T.	1
Tadman G.H.	3
Turner H.G.	3
Welsh D.	1
Wilkinson J.	1
Wright R.C.A.	3

Scorers
Tadman G.H.	2
Dawson T.	1
Total	3

Note: 1939-40 games do not count in League statistics of results, appearances and scorers.

Division 1 1946-47

	P	W	D	L	F	A	W	D	L	F	A	Pts
Liverpool	42	13	3	5	42	24	12	4	5	42	28	57
Manchester U	42	17	3	1	61	19	5	9	7	34	35	56
Wolverhampton W	42	15	1	5	66	31	10	5	6	32	25	56
Stoke C	42	14	5	2	52	21	10	2	9	38	32	55
Blackpool	42	14	1	6	38	32	8	5	8	33	38	50
Sheffield U	42	12	4	5	51	32	9	3	9	38	43	49
Preston NE	42	10	7	4	45	27	8	4	9	31	47	47
Aston Villa	42	9	6	6	39	24	9	3	9	28	29	45
Sunderland	42	11	3	7	33	27	7	5	9	32	39	44
Everton	42	13	5	3	40	24	4	4	13	22	43	43
Middlesbrough	42	11	3	7	46	32	6	5	10	27	36	42
Portsmouth	42	11	3	7	42	27	5	6	10	24	33	41
Arsenal	42	9	5	7	43	33	7	4	10	29	37	41
Derby C	42	13	2	6	44	28	5	3	13	29	51	41
Chelsea	42	9	3	9	33	39	7	4	10	36	45	39
Grimsby T	42	9	6	6	37	35	4	6	11	24	47	38
Blackburn R	42	6	5	10	23	27	8	3	10	22	26	36
Bolton W	42	8	5	8	30	28	5	3	13	27	41	34
CHARLTON A	42	6	6	9	34	32	5	6	10	23	39	34
Huddersfield T	42	11	4	6	34	24	2	3	16	19	55	33
Brentford	42	5	5	11	19	35	4	2	15	26	53	25
Leeds U	42	6	5	10	30	30	0	1	20	15	60	18

	Home	Away
Arsenal	2-2	0-1
Aston Villa	1-1	0-4
Blackburn R	0-2	0-1
Blackpool	0-1	0-0
Bolton W	2-0	1-0
Brentford	3-0	4-1
Chelsea	2-3	2-2
Derby C	2-4	0-1
Everton	4-1	1-1
Grimsby T	0-0	1-3
Huddersfield T	0-3	1-5
Leeds U	5-0	0-2
Liverpool	1-3	1-1
Manchester U	1-3	1-4
Middlesbrough	3-3	2-1
Portsmouth	0-0	0-3
Preston NE	0-0	1-5
Sheffield U	1-2	3-1
Stoke C	1-0	2-2
Sunderland	5-0	1-1
Wolverhampton W	1-4	0-2

Appearances
Burlison R.L.	1
Bartram S.	41
Campbell J.	5
Croker P.H.	29
Dawson T.	22
Duffy C.	42
Fell L.J.	5
Fenton B.R.V.	17
Hobbins S.G.	1
Hobbis H.H.F.	1
Hurst G.	18
Johnson W.H.	39
Lancelotte.E.C.	20
Lock F.W.	7
Oakes, John	8
Phipps H.J.	41
Purves C.R.	7
Revell C.	23
Rist F.H.	3
Robinson G.H.	7
Robinson W.	35
Shreeve J.T.T.	25
Tadman M.R.	3
Turner H.G.	11
Vaughan C.J.	9
Welsh D.	24
Whittaker W.P.	9
Wright R.C.A.	9

Scorers
Robinson W.	13
Welsh D.	11
Duffy C.	10
Lancelotte E.C.	5
Fenton B.R.V.	3
Dawson T.	2
Fell L.J.	2
Hurst G.	2
Revell C.	2
Vaughan C.J.	2
Johnson W.H.	1
Purves C.R.	1
Own goals	3
Total	57

Division 1 1947-48

	P	W	D	L	F	A	W	D	L	F	A	Pts
Arsenal	42	15	3	3	56	15	8	10	3	25	17	59
Manchester U	42	11	7	3	50	27	8	7	6	31	21	52
Burnley	42	12	5	4	31	12	8	7	6	25	31	52
Derby C	42	11	6	4	38	24	8	6	7	39	33	50
Wolverhampton W	42	12	4	5	45	29	7	5	9	38	41	47
Aston Villa	42	13	5	3	42	22	6	4	11	23	35	47
Preston NE	42	13	4	4	43	35	7	3	11	24	33	47
Portsmouth	42	13	5	3	44	17	6	2	13	24	33	45
Blackpool	42	13	4	4	37	14	4	6	11	20	27	44
Manchester C	42	13	3	5	37	22	2	9	10	15	25	42
Liverpool	42	9	8	4	39	23	7	2	12	26	38	42
Sheffield U	42	13	4	4	44	24	3	6	12	21	46	42
CHARLTON A	42	10	2	9	30	26	7	4	10	22	40	40
Everton	42	10	2	9	30	26	7	4	10	22	40	40
Stoke C	42	9	5	7	29	23	5	5	11	12	32	38
Middlesbrough	42	8	7	6	37	27	6	2	13	34	46	37
Bolton W	42	11	2	8	29	25	5	3	13	17	33	37
Chelsea	42	11	6	4	38	27	3	3	15	15	44	37
Huddersfield T	42	7	6	8	25	24	5	6	10	26	36	36
Sunderland	42	11	4	6	33	18	2	6	13	23	49	36
Blackburn R	42	8	5	8	35	30	3	5	13	19	42	32
Grimsby T	42	5	5	11	20	35	3	1	17	25	76	22

	Home	Away
Arsenal	2-4	0-6
Aston Villa	1-1	1-2
Blackburn R	0-1	0-0
Blackpool	2-0	1-3
Bolton W	2-1	0-1
Burnley	1-1	2-0
Chelsea	3-1	0-3
Derby C	1-5	3-0
Everton	2-3	1-0
Grimsby T	2-3	3-1
Huddersfield T	0-0	1-0
Liverpool	2-0	3-2
Manchester C	0-1	0-4
Manchester U	1-2	2-6
Middlesbrough	1-0	2-1
Portsmouth	2-2	1-3
Preston NE	1-2	2-1
Sheffield U	4-0	1-1
Stoke C	0-1	1-0
Sunderland	1-0	1-0
Wolverhampton W	5-1	0-2

Appearances
Bartram S.	41
Bicknell R.	6
Campbell J.	23
Croker P.H.	4
D'Arcy S.D.	4
Duffy C.	35
Fenton B.R.V.	28
Hipkin R.W.	2
Hobbis H.H.F.	8
Hurst G.	36
Johnson W.H.	23
Lancelotte E.C.	8
Lock F.W.	39
McCrae A.	39
O'Linn S.	11
Phipps H.J.	37
Purves C.R.	3
Revell C.	26
Robinson W.	16
Shreeve J.T.T.	18
Vaughan C.J.	38
Welsh D.	5
Whittaker W.P.	11

Scorers
Vaughan C.J.	15
Duffy C.	8
McCrae A.	8
Hurst G.	7
Fenton B.R.V.	5
Revell C.	3
Robinson W.	3
Welsh D.	2
Hobbis H.H.F.	1
Lancelotte E.C.	1
O'Linn S.	1
Own goals	3
Total	57

Division 1 1948-49

	P	W	D	L	F	A	W	D	L	F	A	Pts
Portsmouth	42	18	3	0	52	12	7	5	9	32	30	58
Manchester U	42	11	7	3	40	20	10	4	7	37	24	53
Derby C	42	17	2	2	48	22	5	7	9	26	33	53
Newcastle U	42	12	5	4	35	29	8	7	6	35	27	52
Arsenal	42	13	5	3	51	18	5	8	8	23	26	49
Wolverhampton W	42	13	5	3	48	19	4	7	10	31	47	46
Manchester C	42	10	8	3	28	21	5	7	9	19	30	45
Sunderland	42	8	10	3	27	19	5	7	9	22	39	43
CHARLTON A	42	10	5	6	38	31	5	7	9	25	36	42
Aston Villa	42	10	6	5	40	36	6	4	11	20	40	42
Stoke C	42	14	3	4	43	24	2	6	13	23	44	41
Liverpool	42	5	10	6	25	18	8	4	9	28	25	40
Chelsea	42	10	6	5	43	27	2	8	11	26	41	38
Bolton W	42	10	4	7	43	32	4	6	11	16	36	38
Burnley	42	10	6	5	27	19	2	8	11	16	31	38
Blackpool	42	8	8	5	24	25	3	8	10	30	42	38
Birmingham C	42	9	7	5	19	10	2	8	11	17	28	37
Everton	42	12	5	4	33	25	1	6	14	8	38	37
Middlesbrough	42	10	6	5	37	23	1	6	14	9	34	34
Huddersfield T	42	6	7	8	19	24	6	3	12	21	45	34
Preston NE	42	8	6	7	36	36	3	5	13	26	39	33
Sheffield U	42	8	9	4	32	25	3	2	16	25	53	33

	Home	Away
Arsenal	4-3	0-2
Aston Villa	0-2	3-4
Birmingham C	1-1	0-1
Blackpool	0-0	1-0
Bolton W	1-4	2-2
Burnley	3-1	0-0
Chelsea	1-1	2-2
Derby C	1-5	1-5
Everton	3-1	1-1
Huddersfield T	3-1	2-1
Liverpool	2-1	1-1
Manchester C	3-2	1-0
Manchester U	2-3	1-1
Middlesbrough	2-0	4-2
Newcastle U	0-0	0-2
Portsmouth	0-1	1-3
Preston NE	0-0	3-2
Sheffield U	2-1	0-2
Stoke C	4-1	2-2
Sunderland	4-0	0-1
Wolverhampton W	2-3	0-2

Appearances
Bartram S.	41
Bicknell R.	1
Brown T.L.	20
Campbell J.	28
Duffy C.	37
Fenton B.R.V.	39
Forbes D.D.	1
Hurst G.	41
Johnson W.H.	18
Lock F.W.	40
Lumley I.T.	11
McCrae A.	4
O'Linn S.	31
Phipps H.J.	41
Purves C.R.	17
Revell C.	25
Robinson W.	2
Shreeve J.T.T.	14
Uytenbogaardt A.G.	1
Vaughan C.J.	40
Vitty J.	2
Whittaker W.P.	8

Scorers
Vaughan C.J.	19
Hurst G.	9
O'Linn S.	9
Duffy C.	7
Fenton B.R.V.	7
Lumley I.T.	4
Revell C.	3
Brown T.L.	1
Lock F.W.	1
Phipps H.J.	1
Purves C.R.	1
Own goal	1
Total	63

Division 1 1949-50

	P	W	D	L	F	A	W	D	L	F	A	Pts
Portsmouth	42	12	7	2	44	15	10	2	9	30	23	53
Wolverhampton W	42	11	8	2	47	21	9	5	7	29	28	53
Sunderland	42	14	6	1	50	23	7	4	10	33	39	52
Manchester U	42	11	5	5	42	20	7	9	5	27	24	50
Newcastle U	42	14	4	3	49	23	5	8	8	28	32	50
Arsenal	42	12	4	5	48	24	7	7	7	31	31	49
Blackpool	42	10	8	3	29	14	7	7	7	17	21	49
Liverpool	42	10	7	4	37	23	7	7	7	27	31	48
Middlesbrough	42	14	2	5	37	18	6	5	10	22	30	47
Burnley	42	9	7	5	23	17	7	6	8	17	23	45
Derby C	42	11	5	5	46	26	6	5	10	23	35	44
Aston Villa	42	10	7	4	31	19	5	5	11	30	42	42
Chelsea	42	7	7	7	31	30	5	9	7	27	35	40
West Bromwich A	42	9	7	5	28	16	5	5	11	19	37	40
Huddersfield T	42	11	4	6	34	22	3	5	13	18	51	37
Bolton W	42	10	5	6	34	22	0	9	12	11	17	34
Fulham	42	8	6	7	24	19	2	8	11	17	35	34
Everton	42	6	8	7	24	20	4	6	11	18	46	34
Stoke City	42	10	4	7	27	28	1	8	12	18	47	34
CHARLTON A	42	7	5	9	33	35	6	1	14	20	30	32
Manchester C	42	7	8	6	27	24	1	5	15	9	44	29
Birmingham C	42	6	8	7	19	24	1	6	14	12	43	28

	Home	Away
Arsenal	1-1	3-2
Aston Villa	1-4	1-1
Birmingham C	2-0	0-2
Blackpool	1-2	0-2
Bolton W	0-0	0-3
Burnley	1-1	0-1
Chelsea	1-0	3-1
Derby C	1-3	2-1
Everton	2-0	1-0
Fulham	2-1	2-1
Huddersfield T	2-2	1-2
Liverpool	1-3	0-1
Manchester C	3-1	0-2
Manchester U	1-2	2-3
Middlesbrough	0-3	0-1
Newcastle U	6-3	0-1
Portsmouth	1-2	0-1
Stoke C	2-0	3-0
Sunderland	2-2	1-2
West Bromwich A	1-2	0-1
Wolverhampton W	2-3	1-2

Appearances
Allison M.A.	2
Bartram S.	42
Brown T.L.	14
Campbell J.	22
Croker P.H.	15
Cullum R.G.	6
D'Arcy S.D.	6
Duffy C.	2
Fell L.J.	5
Fenton B.R.V.	16
Forbes D.D.	29
Hurst G.	34
Johnson W.H.	4
Kiernan W.E.	26
Lock F.W.	25
Lumley I.T.	14
Nielsen N.F.	1
O'Linn S.	37
Phipps H.J.	38
Purves C.R.	19
Revell C.	27
Shreeve J.T.T	20
Ufton D.G.	16
Vaughan C.J.	40
Walls J.P.	2

Scorers
Vaughan C.J.	19
O'Linn S.	8
Revell C.	7
Kiernan W.E.	5
Hurst G.	4
Lumley I.T.	4
Purves C.R.	2
D'Arcy S.D.	1
Duffy C.	1
Phipps H.J.	1
Own goal	1
Total	53

Division 1 1950-51

	P	W	D	L	F	A	W	D	L	F	A	Pts
Tottenham H	42	17	2	2	54	21	8	8	5	28	23	60
Manchester U	42	14	4	3	42	16	10	4	7	32	24	56
Blackpool	42	12	6	3	43	19	8	4	9	36	34	50
Newcastle U	42	10	6	5	36	22	8	7	6	26	31	49
Arsenal	42	11	5	5	47	28	8	4	9	26	28	47
Middlesbrough	42	12	7	2	51	25	6	4	11	25	40	47
Portsmouth	42	8	10	3	39	30	8	5	8	32	38	47
Bolton W	42	11	2	8	31	20	8	5	8	33	41	45
Liverpool	42	11	5	5	28	25	5	6	10	25	34	43
Burnley	42	9	7	5	27	16	5	7	9	21	27	42
Derby C	42	10	5	6	53	33	6	3	12	28	42	40
Sunderland	42	8	9	4	30	21	4	7	10	33	52	40
Stoke C	42	10	5	6	28	19	3	9	9	22	40	40
Wolverhampton W	42	9	3	9	44	30	6	5	10	30	31	38
Aston Villa	42	9	6	6	39	29	3	7	11	27	39	37
West Bromwich A	42	7	4	10	30	27	6	7	8	23	34	37
CHARLTON A	42	9	4	8	35	31	5	5	11	28	49	37
Fulham	42	8	5	8	35	37	5	6	10	17	31	37
Huddersfield T	42	8	4	9	40	40	7	2	12	24	52	36
Chelsea	42	9	4	8	31	25	3	4	14	22	40	32
Sheffield W	42	9	6	6	43	32	3	2	16	21	51	32
Everton	42	7	5	9	26	35	5	3	13	22	51	32

	Home	Away
Arsenal	1-3	5-2
Aston Villa	2-2	0-0
Blackpool	2-3	0-0
Bolton W	4-3	0-3
Burnley	0-0	1-5
Chelsea	1-2	3-2
Derby C	1-2	0-5
Everton	2-1	0-0
Fulham	0-0	3-1
Huddersfield T	3-2	1-1
Liverpool	1-0	0-1
Manchester U	1-2	0-3
Middlesbrough	3-0	3-7
Newcastle U	1-3	2-3
Portsmouth	0-1	3-3
Sheffield W	2-1	2-1
Stoke C	2-0	0-2
Sunderland	3-0	2-4
Tottenham H	1-1	0-1
West Bromwich A	2-3	0-3
Wolverhampton W	3-2	3-2

Appearances
Bartram S.	37
Campbell J.	14
Croker E.A.	8
Croker P.H.	11
Cullum R.G.	21
D'Arcy S.D.	3
Duffy C.	5
Evans J.W.	31
Fell L.J.	2
Fenton B.R.V.	41
Forbes D.D.	27
Hammond C.S.	3
Hurst G.	40
Jeppson H.O.	11
Johnson W.H.	17
Kiernan W.E.	37
Lock F.W.	42
Lumley I.T.	9
Marsh E.W.	4
O'Linn S.	6
Phipps H.J.	28
Revell C.	3
Shreeve J.T.T.	16
Uytenbogaardt A.G.	1
Vaughan C.J.	39
Walls J.P.	6

Scorers
Evans J.W.	14
Hurst G.	14
Jeppson H.O.	9
Kiernan W.E.	9
Vaughan C.J.	7
Cullum R.G.	4
Lumley I.T.	2
O'Linn S.	2
Duffy C.	1
Forbes D.D.	1
Total	63

Division 1 1951-52

	P	W	D	L	F	A	W	D	L	F	A	Pts
Manchester U	42	15	3	3	55	21	8	8	5	40	31	57
Tottenham H	42	16	1	4	45	20	6	8	7	31	31	53
Arsenal	42	13	7	1	54	30	8	4	9	26	31	53
Portsmouth	42	13	3	5	42	25	7	5	9	26	33	48
Bolton W	42	11	7	3	35	26	8	3	10	30	35	48
Aston Villa	42	13	3	5	49	28	6	6	9	30	42	47
Preston NE	42	10	5	6	39	22	7	7	7	35	32	46
Newcastle U	42	12	4	5	62	28	6	5	10	36	45	45
Blackpool	42	12	5	4	40	27	6	4	11	24	37	45
CHARLTON A	42	12	5	4	41	24	5	5	11	27	39	44
Liverpool	42	6	11	4	31	25	6	8	7	26	36	43
Sunderland	42	8	6	7	41	28	7	6	8	29	33	42
West Bromwich A	42	8	9	4	38	29	6	4	11	36	48	41
Burnley	42	9	6	6	32	19	6	4	11	24	44	40
Manchester C	42	7	5	9	29	28	6	8	7	29	33	39
Wolverhampton W	42	8	6	7	40	33	4	8	9	33	40	38
Derby C	42	10	4	7	43	37	5	3	13	20	43	37
Middlesbrough	42	12	4	5	37	25	3	2	16	27	63	36
Chelsea	42	10	3	8	31	29	4	5	12	21	43	36
Stoke C	42	8	6	7	34	32	4	1	16	15	56	31
Huddersfield T	42	9	3	9	32	35	1	5	15	17	47	28
Fulham	42	5	7	9	38	31	3	4	14	20	46	27

	Home	Away
Arsenal	1-3	1-2
Aston Villa	0-1	2-0
Blackpool	2-0	2-1
Bolton W	1-0	1-2
Burnley	1-0	0-1
Chelsea	1-1	0-1
Derby C	3-3	3-1
Fulham	3-0	3-3
Huddersfield T	4-0	0-1
Liverpool	2-0	1.1
Manchester C	0-0	2-4
Manchester U	2-2	2-3
Middlesbrough	4-4	1-2
Newcastle U	3-0	0-6
Portsmouth	0-2	0-1
Preston NE	4-2	0-3
Stoke C	4-0	2-1
Sunderland	2-1	1-1
Tottenham H	0-3	3-2
West Bromwich A	3-3	1-1
Wolverhampton W	1-0	2-2

Appearances
Bartram S.	41
Campbell J.	4
Cullum R.G.	4
Duffy C.	32
Evans J.W.	34
Fell L.J.	1
Fenton B.R.V.	40
Firmani E.R.	1
Gill E.N.	1
Hammond C.S.	14
Hewie J.D.	38
Hurst G.	41
Johnson W.H.	38
Kiernan W.E.	41
Leary S.E.	5
Lock F.W.	41
Lumley I.T.	3
O'Linn S.	1
Pawson A.H.	1
Pembery G.D.	1
Ufton D.G.	41
Vaughan C.J.	38
Walls J.P.	1

Scorers
Vaughan C.J.	22
Evans J.W.	12
Kiernan W.E.	11
Hurst G.	9
Duffy C.	5
Cullum R.G.	2
Fenton B.R.V.	2
Lock F.W.	2
Hewie J.D.	1
Pawson A.H.	1
Own goal	1
Total	68

Division 1 1952-53

	P	W	D	L	F	A	W	D	L	F	A	Pts
Arsenal	42	15	3	3	60	30	6	9	6	37	34	54
Preston NE	42	15	3	3	46	25	6	9	6	39	35	54
Wolverhampton W	42	13	5	3	54	27	6	8	7	32	36	51
West Bromwich A	42	13	3	5	35	19	8	5	8	31	41	50
CHARLTON A	42	12	8	1	47	22	7	3	11	30	41	49
Burnley	42	11	6	4	36	20	7	6	8	31	32	48
Blackpool	42	13	5	3	45	22	6	4	11	26	48	47
Manchester U	42	11	5	5	35	30	7	5	9	34	42	46
Sunderland	42	11	9	1	42	27	4	4	13	26	55	43
Tottenham H	42	11	6	4	55	37	4	5	12	23	32	41
Aston Villa	42	9	7	5	36	23	5	6	10	27	38	41
Cardiff C	42	7	8	6	32	17	7	4	10	22	29	40
Middlesbrough	42	12	5	4	46	27	2	6	13	24	50	39
Bolton W	42	9	4	8	39	35	6	5	10	22	34	39
Portsmouth	42	10	6	5	44	34	4	4	13	30	49	38
Newcastle U	42	9	5	7	34	33	5	4	12	25	37	37
Liverpool	42	10	6	5	36	28	4	2	15	25	54	36
Sheffield W	42	8	6	7	35	32	4	5	12	27	40	35
Chelsea	42	10	4	7	35	24	2	7	12	21	42	35
Manchester C	42	12	2	7	45	28	2	5	14	27	59	35
Stoke C	42	10	4	7	35	26	2	6	13	18	40	34
Derby C	42	9	6	6	41	29	2	4	15	18	45	32

	Home	Away
Arsenal	2-2	4-3
Aston Villa	5-1	1-1
Blackpool	2-0	4-8
Bolton W	2-0	2-1
Burnley	0-0	0-2
Cardiff C	3-1	1-0
Chelsea	2-2	1-0
Derby C	3-1	1-1
Liverpool	3-2	2-1
Manchester C	1-2	1-5
Manchester U	2-2	2-3
Middlesbrough	2-0	0-1
Newcastle U	0-0	2-3
Portsmouth	2-2	1-1
Preston NE	2-1	1-2
Sheffield W	3-0	3-0
Stoke C	5-1	0-1
Sunderland	3-1	1-2
Tottenham H	3-2	0-2
West Bromwich A	0-0	1-3
Wolverhampton W	2-2	2-1

Appearances
Ayre R.W.	2
Barry K.A.	3
Bartram S.	38
Campbell J.	28
Chamberlain K.R.	15
Cullum R.G.	1
Duffy C.	9
Evans J.W.	13
Fenton B.R.V.	42
Firmani E.R.	29
Hammond C.S.	42
Hewie J.D.	36
Hurst G.	37
Johnson W.H.	3
Kiernan W.E.	34
Leary S.E.	30
Lock F.W.	22
O'Linn S.	23
Pawson A.H.	1
Pounder A.W.	1
Ufton D.G.	26
Uytenbogaardt A.G.	4
Vaughan C.J.	22
Walls J.P.	1

Scorers
Kiernan W.E.	14
Firmani E.R.	13
Leary S.E.	13
Hurst G.	10
Vaughan C.J.	7
Evans J.W.	5
Lock F.W.	4
O'Linn S.	4
Fenton B.R.V.	2
Ayre R.W.	1
Duffy C.	1
Hewie J.D.	1
Own goal	2
Total	77

Division 1 1953-54

	P	W	D	L	F	A	W	D	L	F	A	Pts
Wolverhampton W	42	16	1	4	61	25	9	6	6	35	31	57
West Bromwich A	42	13	5	3	51	24	9	4	8	35	39	53
Huddersfield T	42	13	6	2	45	24	7	5	9	33	37	51
Manchester U	42	13	5	3	51	23	5	7	9	22	35	48
Bolton W	42	14	6	1	45	20	4	6	11	30	40	48
Blackpool	42	13	6	2	43	19	6	4	11	37	50	48
Burnley	42	16	2	3	51	26	5	2	14	27	44	46
Chelsea	42	12	3	6	45	26	4	9	8	29	42	44
CHARLTON A	42	14	4	3	51	26	5	2	14	24	51	44
Cardiff C	42	12	4	5	32	27	6	4	11	19	41	44
Preston NE	42	12	2	7	43	24	7	3	11	44	34	43
Arsenal	42	8	8	5	42	37	7	5	9	33	36	43
Aston Villa	42	12	5	4	50	28	4	4	13	20	40	41
Portsmouth	42	13	5	3	53	31	1	6	14	28	58	39
Newcastle U	42	9	2	10	43	40	5	8	8	29	37	38
Tottenham H	42	9	3	7	38	33	5	2	14	27	61	37
Manchester C	42	10	4	7	35	31	4	5	12	27	46	37
Sunderland	42	11	4	6	50	37	3	4	14	31	52	36
Sheffield W	42	12	4	5	43	30	3	2	16	27	61	36
Sheffield U	42	9	5	7	43	38	2	6	13	26	52	33
Middlesbrough	42	6	6	9	29	35	4	4	13	31	56	30
Liverpool	42	7	8	6	49	38	2	2	17	19	59	28

	Home	Away
Arsenal	1-5	3-3
Aston Villa	1-1	1-2
Blackpool	4-2	1-3
Bolton W	1-0	1-3
Burnley	3-1	0-2
Cardiff C	3-2	0-5
Chelsea	1-1	1-3
Huddersfield T	2-1	1-4
Liverpool	6-0	3-2
Manchester C	2-1	0-3
Manchester U	1-0	0-2
Middlesbrough	8-1	2-0
Newcastle U	0-0	2-0
Portsmouth	3-1	1-3
Preston NE	2-1	0-2
Sheffield U	3-0	1-1
Sheffield W	4-2	2-1
Sunderland	5-3	1-2
Tottenham H	0-1	1-3
West Bromwich A	1-1	3-2
Wolverhampton W	0-2	0-5

Appearances
Ayre R.W.	21
Bartram S.	40
Campbell J.	31
Chamberlain K.R.	5
Ellis S.C.	26
Evans J.W.	12
Fenton B.R.V.	31
Firmani E.R.	34
Hammond C.S.	40
Hewie J.D.	33
Hurst G.	42
Kiernan W.E.	33
Leary S.E.	29
Lock F..W.	5
Lumley R.	3
Marsh E.W.	2
O'Linn S.	32
Pembery G.D.	1
Terry P.A.	3
Ufton D.G.	36
White R.T.	3

Scorers
Leary S.E.	24
Firmani E.R.	12
Hurst G.	9
Evans J.W.	7
Kiernan W.E.	6
Ayre R.W.	5
O'Linn S.	4
Hewie J.D.	3
Fenton B.R.V.	2
Hammond C.S.	1
Lock F.W.	1
Terry P.A.	1
Total	75

Division 1 1954-55

	P	W	D	L	F	A	W	D	L	F	A	Pts
Chelsea	42	11	5	5	43	29	9	7	5	38	28	52
Wolverhampton W	42	13	5	3	58	30	6	5	10	31	40	48
Portsmouth	42	13	5	3	44	21	5	7	9	30	41	48
Sunderland	42	8	11	2	39	27	7	7	7	25	27	48
Manchester U	42	12	4	5	44	30	8	3	10	40	44	47
Aston Villa	42	11	3	7	38	31	9	4	8	34	42	47
Manchester C	42	11	5	5	45	36	7	5	9	31	33	46
Newcastle U	42	12	5	4	53	27	5	4	12	36	50	43
Arsenal	42	12	3	6	44	25	5	6	10	25	38	43
Burnley	42	11	3	7	29	19	6	6	9	22	29	43
Everton	42	9	6	6	32	24	7	4	10	30	44	42
Huddersfield T	42	10	4	7	28	23	4	9	8	35	45	41
Sheffield U	42	10	3	8	41	34	7	4	10	29	52	41
Preston NE	42	8	5	8	47	33	8	3	10	36	31	40
CHARLTON A	42	8	6	7	43	34	7	4	10	33	41	40
Tottenham H	42	9	4	8	42	35	7	4	10	30	38	40
West Bromwich A	42	11	5	5	44	33	5	3	13	32	63	40
Bolton W	42	11	6	4	45	29	2	7	12	17	40	39
Blackpool	42	8	6	7	33	26	6	4	11	27	38	38
Cardiff C	42	9	4	8	41	38	4	7	10	21	38	37
Leicester C	42	9	6	6	43	32	3	5	13	31	54	35
Sheffield W	42	7	7	7	42	38	1	3	17	21	62	26

	Home	Away
Arsenal	1-1	1-3
Aston Villa	6-1	2-1
Blackpool	3-3	1-1
Bolton W	2-0	2-3
Burnley	3-1	0-3
Cardiff C	4-1	3-4
Chelsea	0-2	2-1
Everton	5-0	2-2
Huddersfield T	2-1	0-0
Leicester C	2-3	1-0
Manchester C	1-1	5-1
Manchester U	1-1	1-3
Newcastle U	1-1	1-3
Portsmouth	2-2	0-2
Preston NE	0-4	2-1
Sheffield U	3-1	0-5
Sheffield W	3-0	2-2
Sunderland	1-3	2-1
Tottenham H	1-2	4-1
West Bromwich A	1-3	1-2
Wolverhampton W	1-3	1-2

Appearances

Ayre R.W.	29
Bartram S.	42
Campbell J.	38
Chamberlain K.R.	8
Ellis S.C.	3
Fenton B.R.V.	10
Firmani E.R.	35
Hammond C.S.	30
Hewie J.D.	26
Hurst G.	37
Jago G.H.	2
Kiernan W.E.	41
Leary S.E.	33
Lumley R.	3
O'Linn S.	17
Pembery G.D.	14
Ryan J.J.	2
Terry P.A.	1
Townsend D.E.	37
Tucker K.	1
Ufton D.G.	39
White R.T	14

Scorers

Firmani E.R.	25
Ayre R.W.	16
Leary S.E.	10
Kiernan W.E.	8
O'Linn S.	4
Hewie J.D.	3
Hurst G.	2
Campbell J.	1
Fenton B.R.V.	1
Hammond C.S.	1
Pembery G.D.	1
White R.T.	1
Own goals	3
Total	76

Division 1 1955-56

	P	W	D	L	F	A	W	D	L	F	A	Pts
Manchester U	42	18	3	0	51	20	7	7	7	32	31	60
Blackpool	42	13	4	4	56	27	7	5	9	30	35	49
Wolverhampton W	42	15	2	4	51	27	5	7	9	38	38	49
Manchester C	42	11	5	5	40	27	7	5	9	42	42	46
Arsenal	42	13	4	4	38	22	5	6	10	22	39	46
Birmingham C	42	12	4	5	51	26	6	5	10	24	31	45
Burnley	42	11	3	7	37	20	7	5	9	27	34	44
Bolton W	42	13	5	3	56	32	5	4	12	21	34	43
Sunderland	42	10	8	3	44	36	7	1	13	36	59	43
Luton T	42	12	4	5	44	27	5	4	12	22	37	42
Newcastle U	42	12	4	5	54	25	5	4	12	31	34	41
Portsmouth	42	9	8	4	46	38	7	1	13	32	47	41
West Bromwich A	42	13	3	5	37	25	5	2	14	21	45	41
CHARLTON A	42	13	2	6	47	26	4	4	13	28	55	40
Everton	42	11	5	5	37	29	4	5	12	18	40	40
Chelsea	42	10	4	7	32	26	4	7	10	32	51	39
Cardiff C	42	11	4	6	36	32	4	5	12	19	37	39
Tottenham H	42	9	4	8	37	33	6	3	12	24	38	37
Preston NE	42	6	5	10	32	36	8	3	10	41	36	36
Aston Villa	42	9	6	6	32	29	2	7	12	20	40	35
Huddersfield T	42	9	4	8	32	30	5	3	13	22	53	35
Sheffield U	42	8	6	7	31	35	4	3	14	32	42	33

	Home	Away
Arsenal	2-0	4-2
Aston Villa	3-1	1-1
Birmingham C	2-0	0-4
Blackpool	1-2	0-5
Bolton W	3-1	3-1
Burnley	2-1	1-2
Cardiff C	0-0	1-3
Chelsea	1-2	1-3
Everton	0-2	2-3
Huddersfield T	4-1	0-4
Luton T	2-2	1-2
Manchester C	5-2	2-0
Manchester U	3-0	1-5
Newcastle U	0-2	1-4
Portsmouth	6-1	0-4
Preston NE	2-1	2-2
Sheffield U	3-2	0-0
Sunderland	2-1	2-3
Tottenham H	1-2	3-2
West Bromwich A	5-1	3-3
Wolverhampton W	0-2	0-2

Appearances

Ayre R.W.	22
Bartram S.	33
Campbell J.	39
Chamberlain K.R.	5
Ellis S.C.	6
Firmani P.W.	1
Gauld J.	34
Hammond C.S.	36
Hewie J.D.	40
Hurst G.	26
Kiernan W.E.	31
Leary S.E.	42
Lucas F.C.	1
O'Linn S.	16
Oosthuizen R.	1
Pembery G.D.	2
Reed F.N.	9
Ryan J.J.	21
Townsend D.E.	33
Ufton D.G.	34
White R.T.	30

Scorers

Leary S.E.	21
Gauld J.	17
Ryan J.J.	12
Ayre R.W.	7
Hurst G.	7
Kiernan W.E.	5
White R.T.	2
Hewie J.D.	1
Own goal	3
Total	75

Division 1 1956-57

	P	W	D	L	F	A	W	D	L	F	A	Pts
Manchester U	42	14	4	3	55	25	14	4	3	48	29	64
Tottenham H	42	15	4	2	70	24	7	8	6	34	32	56
Preston NE	42	15	4	2	50	19	8	6	7	34	37	56
Blackpool	42	14	3	4	55	26	8	6	7	38	39	53
Arsenal	42	12	5	4	45	21	9	3	9	40	48	50
Wolverhampton W	42	17	2	2	70	29	3	6	12	24	41	48
Burnley	42	14	5	2	41	21	4	5	12	15	29	46
Leeds U	42	10	8	3	42	18	5	6	10	30	45	44
Bolton W	42	9	8	4	42	23	5	6	12	23	42	44
Aston Villa	42	10	8	3	45	25	4	7	10	20	30	43
West Bromwich A	42	8	8	5	31	25	6	6	9	28	36	42
Birmingham C	42	12	5	4	52	25	3	4	14	17	44	*39
Chelsea	42	7	8	6	43	36	6	5	10	30	37	*39
Sheffield W	42	14	3	4	55	29	2	3	16	27	59	38
Everton	42	10	5	6	34	28	4	5	12	27	51	38
Luton T	42	10	4	7	32	26	4	5	12	26	50	37
Newcastle U	42	10	5	6	43	31	4	3	14	24	56	36
Manchester C	42	10	2	9	48	42	3	7	11	30	46	35
Portsmouth	42	8	6	7	37	35	2	7	12	25	57	33
Sunderland	42	9	5	7	40	30	3	3	15	27	58	32
Cardiff C	42	7	6	8	35	34	3	3	15	18	54	29
CHARLTON A	42	7	3	11	31	44	2	1	18	31	76	22

*Equal

	Home	Away
Arsenal	1-3	1-3
Aston Villa	0-2	1-3
Birmingham C	1-0	2-4
Blackpool	0-4	2-3
Bolton W	2-1	1-2
Burnley	1-2	1-2
Cardiff C	0-2	3-2
Chelsea	3-1	3-1
Everton	1-2	0-5
Leeds U	1-2	0-4
Luton T	1-2	2-4
Manchester C	1-0	1-5
Manchester U	1-5	2-4
Newcastle U	1-1	1-3
Portsmouth	1-3	0-1
Preston NE	3-4	3-4
Sheffield W	4-4	1-3
Sunderland	3-2	1-8
Tottenham H	1-1	2-6
West Bromwich A	3-2	2-2
Wolverhampton W	2-1	3-7

Appearances

Ayre R.W.	16
Campbell J.	22
Chamberlain K.R.	9
Cox K.	11
Duff W.	20
Edwards L.T.	12
Ellis S.C.	12
Firmani P.W.	3
Gauld J.	13
Hammond C.S.	23
Hewie J.D.	35
Hurst G.	15
Jago G.H.	14
Kiernan W.E.	27
Kinsey B.R.	15
Lawrie S.	23
Leary S.E.	34
Lucas F.C.	13
McCarthy G.	4
Marsh E.W.	20
O'Linn S.	13
Reed F.N.	2
Ryan J.J.	7
Sewell J.D.	12
Stewart M.J.	6
Summers J.H.	23
Townsend D.E.	18
Ufton D.G.	24
White R.T.	15
Worley L.F.	1

Scorers

Summers J.H.	14
Ayre R.W.	8
Leary S.E.	8
Hewie J.D.	5
Kiernan W.E.	5
Gauld J.	4
Lawrie S.	4
Lucas F.C.	3
Ryan J.J.	3
Hurst G.	2
Kinsey B.R.	1
Sewell J.D.	1
Stewart M.J.	1
Own goal	3
Total	62

Division 2 1957-58

	P	W	D	L	F	A	W	D	L	F	A	Pts
West Ham U	42	12	8	1	56	25	11	3	7	45	29	57
Blackburn R	42	13	7	1	50	18	9	5	7	43	39	56
CHARLTON A	42	15	3	3	65	33	9	4	8	42	36	55
Liverpool	42	17	3	1	50	13	5	7	9	29	41	54
Fulham	42	13	5	3	53	24	7	7	4	44	35	52
Sheffield U	42	12	5	4	38	22	9	5	7	37	28	52
Middlesbrough	42	13	3	5	52	29	6	4	11	31	45	45
Ipswich T	42	13	4	4	45	29	3	8	10	23	40	44
Huddersfield T	42	9	8	4	28	24	5	8	8	35	42	44
Bristol R	42	12	5	4	52	31	5	3	13	33	49	42
Stoke C	42	9	4	8	49	36	9	2	10	26	37	42
Leyton O	42	14	2	5	53	27	4	3	14	24	52	41
Grimsby T	42	13	4	4	54	30	4	2	15	32	53	40
Barnsley	42	10	6	5	40	25	4	6	11	30	49	40
Cardiff C	42	10	5	6	44	31	4	4	13	19	46	37
Derby C	42	11	3	7	37	36	3	5	13	23	45	36
Bristol C	42	9	5	7	35	31	4	4	13	28	57	35
Rotherham U	42	8	3	10	38	44	6	2	13	27	57	33
Swansea T	42	8	3	10	48	45	3	6	12	24	54	31
Lincoln C	42	6	6	9	33	35	5	3	13	22	47	31
Notts C	42	9	3	9	24	31	3	3	15	20	49	30
Doncaster R	42	7	5	9	34	40	1	6	14	22	48	27

	Home	Away
Barnsley	4-2	1-4
Blackburn R	3-4	1-1
Bristol C	1-0	2-1
Bristol R	2-3	0-1
Cardiff C	3-1	3-0
Derby C	2-2	3-1
Doncaster R	2-0	2-1
Fulham	2-2	1-3
Grimsby T	2-0	2-4
Huddersfield T	7-6	3-3
Ipswich T	4-1	4-1
Leyton O	3-2	2-3
Lincoln C	4-1	3-2
Liverpool	5-1	1-3
Middlesbrough	6-2	0-2
Notts C	4-1	1-2
Rotherham U	4-0	5-1
Sheffield U	3-1	3-0
Stoke C	3-0	2-2
Swansea T	1-1	3-1
West Ham U	0-3	0-0

Appearances

Allen D.J.	2
Ayre R.W.	20
Campbell J.	1
Duff W.	41
Edwards L.T.	21
Ellis S.C.	1
Firmani P.W.	19
Hammond C.S.	13
Hewie J.D.	41
Hinton M.	1
Hurst G.	2
Jago G.H.	34
Kiernan W.E.	40
Lawrie S.	11
Leary S.E.	41
Lucas F.C.	20
Reed F.N.	1
Ryan J.J.	19
Stewart M.J.	1
Summers J.H.	42
Townsend D.E.	29
Ufton D.G.	28
Werge E.	8
White R.T.	26

Scorers

Summers J.H.	28
Leary S.E.	17
Ayre R.W.	11
Ryan J.J.	10
Kiernan W.E.	8
Hewie J.D.	6
Lucas F.C.	6
Werge E.	6
Firmani P.W.	2
Lawrie S.	2
White R.T.	2
Allen D.J.	1
Jago G.H.	1
Own goals	7
Total	107

Division 2 1958-59

	P	W	D	L	F	A	W	D	L	F	A	Pts
Sheffield W	42	18	2	1	68	13	10	4	7	38	35	62
Fulham	42	18	1	2	65	26	9	5	7	31	35	60
Sheffield U	42	16	2	3	54	15	7	5	9	28	33	53
Liverpool	42	15	3	3	57	25	9	2	10	30	37	53
Stoke C	42	16	2	3	48	19	5	5	11	24	39	49
Bristol R	42	13	5	3	46	23	5	7	9	34	41	48
Derby C	42	15	1	5	46	29	5	7	9	28	42	48
CHARLTON A	42	13	3	5	53	33	5	4	12	39	57	43
Cardiff C	42	12	2	7	37	26	6	5	10	28	39	43
Bristol C	42	11	3	7	43	27	6	4	11	31	43	41
Swansea T	42	12	5	4	52	30	4	4	13	27	51	41
Brighton & HA	42	10	9	2	46	29	5	2	14	28	61	41
Middlesbrough	42	9	7	5	51	26	6	3	12	36	45	40
Huddersfield T	42	12	5	4	39	20	4	5	12	23	35	40
Sunderland	42	13	4	4	42	23	3	4	14	22	52	40
Ipswich T	42	12	4	5	37	27	5	2	14	25	50	40
Leyton O	42	9	4	8	43	30	5	4	12	28	48	36
Scunthorpe U	42	7	6	8	32	37	5	3	13	23	47	33
Lincoln C	42	10	5	6	45	37	1	2	18	18	56	29
Rotherham U	42	9	5	7	32	28	1	4	16	10	54	29
Grimsby T	42	7	7	7	41	36	2	3	16	21	54	28
Barnsley	42	8	4	9	34	34	2	3	16	21	57	27

	Home	Away
Barnsley	4-0	1-7
Brighton & HA	2-3	2-2
Bristol C	4-1	4-2
Bristol R	4-3	1-2
Cardiff C	0-0	2-1
Derby C	1-2	2-3
Fulham	2-1	1-2
Grimsby T	2-1	5-1
Huddersfield T	2-1	0-1
Ipswich T	5-1	1-3
Leyton O	4-1	1-6
Lincoln C	3-2	3-3
Liverpool	2-3	0-3
Middlesbrough	1-0	3-1
Rotherham U	5-2	3-4
Scunthorpe U	2-3	3-3
Sheffield U	1-1	0-5
Sheffield W	3-3	1-4
Stoke C	1-2	1-2
Sunderland	3-2	3-0
Swansea T	2-1	2-2

Appearances

Cox K.	3
Duff W.	33
Edwards D.	3
Edwards L.T.	15
Evans R.	12
Firmani P.W.	8
Hewie J.D.	29
Hinton M.	9
Jago G.H.	35
Kiernan W.E.	39
Kinsey B.R.	6
Laraman P.K.	1
Lawrie S.	38
Leary S.E.	40
Lucas F.C.	40
Reed F.N.	9
Ryan J.J.	12
Sewell J.D.	20
Stewart M.J.	2
Summers J.H.	32
Townsend D.E.	40
Ufton D.G.	3
Werge E.	8
White R.T.	25

Scorers

Summers J.H.	20
Lawrie S.	17
Leary S.E.	12
Lucas F.C.	10
Hewie J.D.	8
Kiernan W.E.	8
Ryan J.J.	7
Stewart M.J.	2
Werge E.	2
Evans R.	1
Laraman P.K.	1
Sewell J.D.	1
White R.T.	1
Own goals	2
Total	92

Division 2 1959-60

	P	W	D	L	F	A	W	D	L	F	A	Pts
Aston Villa	42	17	3	1	62	19	8	6	7	27	24	59
Cardiff C	42	15	2	4	55	36	8	10	3	35	26	58
Liverpool	42	15	3	3	59	28	5	7	9	31	38	50
Sheffield U	42	12	5	4	43	22	7	7	7	25	29	50
Middlesbrough	42	14	5	2	56	21	5	5	11	34	43	48
Huddersfield T	42	13	3	5	44	20	6	6	9	29	32	47
CHARLTON A	42	12	7	2	55	28	5	6	10	35	59	47
Rotherham U	42	9	9	3	31	23	8	4	9	30	37	47
Bristol R	42	12	6	3	42	28	6	5	10	30	50	47
Leyton O	42	12	4	5	47	25	3	10	8	29	36	44
Ipswich T	42	12	5	4	48	24	7	1	13	30	44	44
Swansea T	42	12	6	3	54	32	3	4	14	28	52	40
Lincoln C	42	11	3	7	41	25	5	4	12	34	53	39
Brighton & HA	42	7	8	6	35	32	6	4	11	32	44	38
Scunthorpe U	42	9	7	5	38	26	4	3	14	19	45	36
Sunderland	42	8	6	7	35	29	4	6	11	17	36	36
Stoke C	42	8	3	10	40	38	6	4	11	26	45	35
Derby C	42	9	4	8	31	28	5	3	13	30	49	35
Plymouth A	42	10	6	5	42	36	3	3	15	19	53	35
Portsmouth	42	6	6	9	36	36	4	6	11	23	41	32
Hull C	42	7	6	8	27	30	3	4	14	21	46	30
Bristol C	42	8	3	10	27	31	3	2	16	33	66	27

	Home	Away
Aston Villa	2-0	1-11
Brighton & HA	3-1	1-1
Bristol C	4-2	2-1
Bristol R	2-2	2-2
Cardiff C	2-1	1-5
Derby C	6-1	2-1
Huddersfield T	1-1	0-4
Hull C	3-2	4-0
Ipswich T	1-3	1-1
Leyton O	0-0	0-2
Lincoln C	2-2	3-5
Liverpool	3-0	0-2
Middlesbrough	1-0	0-3
Plymouth A	5-2	4-6
Portsmouth	6-1	2-2
Rotherham U	2-2	3-3
Scunthorpe U	5-2	1-1
Sheffield U	1-1	0-2
Stoke City	1-2	3-1
Sunderland	3-1	3-1
Swansea T	2-2	2-5

Appearances

Duff W.	42
Edwards D.	20
Edwards L.T.	16
Evans R.	2
Fryatt J.E.	5
Hewie J.D.	35
Hinton M.	22
Jago G.H.	27
Kiernan W.E.	27
Kinsey B.R.	1
Laraman P.K.	1
Lawrie S.	42
Leary S.E.	41
Lucas F.C.	39
Matthews R.H.	1
Sewell J.D.	20
Summers J.H.	35
Townsend D.E.	40
Ufton D.G.	16
Werge E.	10
White R.T.	20

Scorers

Lawrie S.	21
Summers J.H.	20
Leary S.E.	14
Kiernan W.E.	9
Edwards D.	6
Hewie J.D.	4
Lucas F.C.	4
Fryatt J.E.	3
Werge E.	3
Hinton M.	2
White R.T.	2
Evans R.	1
Own goal	1
Total	90

Division 2 1960-61

	P	W	D	L	F	A	W	D	L	F	A	Pts
Ipswich T	42	15	3	3	55	24	11	4	6	45	31	59
Sheffield U	42	16	2	3	49	22	10	4	7	32	29	58
Liverpool	42	14	5	2	49	21	7	5	9	38	37	52
Norwich C	42	15	3	3	46	20	5	6	10	24	33	49
Middlesbrough	42	13	6	2	44	20	5	6	10	39	54	48
Sunderland	42	12	5	4	47	24	5	8	8	28	36	47
Swansea T	42	14	4	3	49	26	4	7	10	28	47	47
Southampton	42	12	4	5	57	35	6	4	11	27	46	44
Scunthorpe U	42	9	8	4	39	25	5	7	9	30	39	43
CHARLTON A	42	12	3	6	60	42	4	8	9	37	49	43
Plymouth A	42	13	4	4	52	32	4	4	13	29	50	42
Derby C	42	9	6	6	46	35	6	4	11	34	45	40
Luton T	42	13	5	3	48	27	2	4	15	23	52	39
Leeds U	42	7	7	7	41	38	7	3	11	34	45	38
Rotherham U	42	9	7	5	37	24	3	6	12	28	40	37
Brighton & HA	42	9	6	6	33	26	5	3	13	28	49	37
Bristol R	42	13	4	4	52	35	2	3	16	21	57	37
Stoke C	42	9	6	6	39	26	3	6	12	12	33	36
Leyton O	42	10	5	6	31	29	4	3	14	24	49	36
Huddersfield T	42	7	5	9	33	33	6	4	11	29	38	35
Portsmouth	42	10	6	5	38	27	1	5	15	26	64	33
Lincoln C	42	5	4	12	30	43	3	4	14	18	52	24

	Home	Away
Brighton & HA	3-1	5-3
Bristol R	2-1	1-3
Derby C	3-1	3-2
Huddersfield T	2-3	2-2
Ipswich T	0-2	1-2
Leeds U	2-0	0-1
Leyton O	2-0	1-1
Lincoln C	3-0	2-2
Liverpool	1-3	1-2
Luton T	4-1	1-4
Middlesbrough	6-6	2-2
Norwich C	0-1	0-4
Plymouth A	6-4	4-6
Portsmouth	7-4	1-1
Rotherham U	4-3	3-2
Scunthorpe U	2-3	0-1
Sheffield United	1-1	0-0
Southampton	1-3	2-1
Stoke City	3-1	3-5
Sunderland	2-2	2-2
Swansea T	6-2	3-3

Appearances

Allen D.J.	3
Bailey M.A.	4
Duff W.	39
Edwards D.	37
Godfrey P.R.	1
Hewie J.D.	17
Hinton M.	21
Jago G.H.	23
Kiernan W.E.	2
Kinsey B.R.	5
Lawrie S.	38
Leary S.E.	41
Lucas F.C.	30
Reed F.N.	3
Sewell J.D.	41
Summers J.H.	39
Tocknell B.T.	39
Townsend D.E.	40
Tucker K.	2
Werge E.	18
White R.T.	19

Scorers

Edwards D.	24
Leary S.E.	21
Summers J.H.	18
Lawrie S.	15
Werge E.	8
Tocknell B.T.	3
Hewie J.D.	2
Kiernan W.E.	1
Lucas F.C.	1
Sewell J.D.	1
Townsend D.E.	1
Own goals	2
Total	97

Division 2 1961-62

	P	W	D	L	F	A	W	D	L	F	A	Pts
Liverpool	42	18	3	0	68	19	9	5	7	31	24	62
Leyton O	42	11	5	5	34	17	11	5	5	35	23	54
Sunderland	42	17	3	1	60	16	5	6	10	25	34	53
Scunthorpe U	42	14	4	3	52	26	7	3	11	34	45	49
Plymouth A	42	12	4	5	45	30	7	4	10	30	45	46
Southampton	42	13	3	5	53	28	5	6	10	24	34	45
Huddersfield T	42	11	5	5	39	22	5	7	9	28	37	44
Stoke C	42	13	4	4	34	17	4	4	13	21	40	42
Rotherham U	42	9	6	6	36	30	7	3	11	34	46	41
Preston NE	42	11	4	6	34	23	4	6	11	21	34	40
Newcastle U	42	10	5	6	40	27	5	4	12	24	31	39
Middlesbrough	42	11	3	7	45	29	5	4	12	31	43	39
Luton T	42	12	1	8	44	37	5	4	12	25	34	39
Walsall	42	11	7	3	42	23	3	4	14	28	52	39
CHARLTON A	42	10	5	6	38	30	5	4	12	31	45	39
Derby C	42	10	7	4	42	27	4	4	13	26	48	39
Norwich C	42	10	6	5	36	28	4	5	12	25	42	39
Bury	42	9	4	8	32	36	8	1	12	20	40	39
Leeds U	42	9	6	6	24	19	3	6	12	26	42	36
Swansea T	42	10	5	6	38	30	2	7	12	23	53	36
Bristol R	42	11	3	7	36	31	2	4	15	17	50	33
Brighton & HA	42	7	7	7	24	32	3	4	14	18	54	31

	Home	Away
Brighton & HA	2-3	2-2
Bristol R	2-1	2-2
Bury	1-0	2-1
Derby C	4-0	1-0
Huddersfield T	0-2	2-0
Leeds U	3-1	0-1
Leyton O	1-2	1-2
Liverpool	0-4	1-2
Luton T	0-1	6-1
Middlesbrough	1-0	2-3
Newcastle U	1-1	1-4
Norwich C	2-2	2-2
Plymouth A	3-1	1-2
Preston NE	4-0	0-2
Rotherham U	0-2	2-3
Scunthorpe U	3-3	1-6
Southampton	1-0	2-1
Stoke C	2-2	0-4
Sunderland	2-0	1-4
Swansea T	3-2	0-1
Walsall	3-3	2-2

Appearances

Bailey M.A.	30
Duff W.	38
Edwards D.	42
Hewie J.D.	41
Hinton M.	40
Jago G.H.	2
Kennedy J.	1
Kinsey B.R.	41
Lawrie S.	37
Leary S.E.	40
Lucas F.C.	16
Matthews R.H.	28
Ord B.R.	7
Platt J.S.	2
Sewell J.D.	41
Stocks D.H.	1
Tocknell B.T.	30
Townsend D.E.	12
White R.T.	13

Scorers

Edwards D.	16
Leary S.E.	13
Lawrie S.	11
Kinsey B.R.	10
Bailey M.A.	7
Lucas F.C.	3
Matthews R.H.	3
Tocknell B.T.	3
Hewie J.D.	1
Own goals	2
Total	69

Division 2 1962-63

	P	W	D	L	F	A	W	D	L	F	A	Pts
Stoke C	42	15	3	3	49	20	5	10	6	24	30	53
Chelsea	42	15	3	3	54	16	9	1	11	27	26	52
Sunderland	42	14	5	2	46	13	6	7	8	38	42	52
Middlesbrough	42	12	4	5	48	35	8	5	8	38	50	49
Leeds U	42	15	2	4	56	19	4	8	9	24	34	48
Huddersfield T	42	11	6	4	34	21	6	8	7	29	29	48
Newcastle U	42	11	8	2	48	23	7	3	11	31	36	47
Bury	42	11	6	4	28	20	7	5	9	23	27	47
Scunthorpe U	42	12	7	2	35	18	4	5	12	22	41	44
Cardiff C	42	12	5	4	50	29	6	2	13	33	44	43
Southampton	42	13	3	5	52	23	5	2	14	20	44	42
Plymouth A	42	13	4	4	48	24	2	8	11	28	49	42
Norwich C	42	11	6	4	53	33	6	2	13	27	46	42
Rotherham U	42	11	3	7	34	30	6	3	12	33	44	40
Swansea T	42	13	5	3	33	17	2	4	15	18	55	39
Portsmouth	42	9	5	7	33	27	4	6	11	30	52	37
Preston NE	42	11	6	4	43	30	2	5	14	16	44	37
Derby C	42	10	5	6	40	29	2	7	12	21	43	36
Grimsby T	42	8	6	7	34	26	3	7	11	21	40	35
CHARLTON A	42	8	4	9	33	38	5	1	15	29	56	31
Walsall	42	7	7	7	33	37	4	2	15	20	52	31
Luton T	42	10	4	7	45	40	1	3	17	16	44	29

	Home	Away
Bury	0-0	1-3
Cardiff C	2-4	2-1
Chelsea	1-4	0-5
Derby C	0-0	3-2
Grimsby T	0-3	1-2
Huddersfield T	1-0	0-2
Leeds U	1-3	1-4
Luton T	2-0	1-4
Middlesbrough	3-4	1-2
Newcastle U	1-2	2-3
Norwich C	0-2	4-1
Plymouth A	6-3	1-6
Portsmouth	2-0	3-3
Preston NE	2-1	1-4
Rotherham U	2-3	2-1
Scunthorpe U	1-0	0-2
Southampton	2-1	0-1
Stoke C	0-3	3-6
Sunderland	2-2	0-1
Swansea T	2-2	1-2
Walsall	3-2	2-1

Appearances

Bailey M.A.	23
Durrant C.M.	13
Edwards D.	20
Glover L.	19
Henderson J.	3
Hewie J.D.	34
Hinton M.	37
Kennedy J.	11
Kenning M.J.	26
Kinsey B.R.	34
Lawrie S.	4
Lucas F.C.	24
Matthews R.H.	33
Ord B.R.	6
Peacock K.	26
Reed F.N.	5
Ryan J.P.	13
Saunders J.H.	1
Sewell J.D.	42
Stocks D.H.	11
Tocknell B.T.	40
Wakeham P.F.	37

Scorers

Matthews R.H.	8
Kenning M.J.	7
Peacock K.	7
Kinsey B.R.	6
Tocknell B.T.	6
Ryan J.P.	5
Bailey M.A.	4
Durrant C.M.	3
Edwards D.	3
Glover L.	2
Hewie J.D.	2
Lucas F.C.	2
Henderson J.	1
Kennedy J.	1
Ord B.R.	1
Sewell J.D.	1
Own goals	3
Total	62

Division 2
1963-64

	P	W	D	L	F	A	W	D	L	F	A	Pts
Leeds U	42	12	9	0	35	16	12	6	3	36	18	63
Sunderland	42	16	3	2	47	13	9	8	4	34	24	61
Preston NE	42	13	7	1	37	14	10	3	8	42	40	56
CHARLTON A	42	11	4	6	44	30	8	6	7	32	40	48
Southampton	42	13	3	5	69	32	6	6	9	31	41	47
Manchester C	42	12	4	5	50	27	6	6	9	34	39	46
Rotherham U	42	14	3	4	52	26	5	4	12	38	52	45
Newcastle U	42	14	2	5	49	26	6	3	12	25	43	45
Portsmouth	42	9	7	5	46	34	7	4	10	33	36	43
Middlesbrough	42	14	4	3	47	16	1	7	13	20	36	41
Northampton T	42	10	2	9	35	31	6	7	8	23	29	41
Huddersfield T	42	11	4	6	31	25	4	6	11	26	39	40
Derby C	42	10	6	5	34	27	4	5	12	22	40	39
Swindon T	42	11	5	5	39	24	3	5	13	18	45	38
Cardiff C	42	10	7	4	31	27	4	3	14	25	54	38
Leyton O	42	8	6	7	32	32	5	4	12	22	40	36
Norwich C	42	9	7	5	43	30	2	6	13	21	50	35
Bury	42	8	5	8	35	36	5	4	12	22	37	35
Swansea T	42	11	4	6	44	26	1	5	15	19	48	33
Plymouth A	42	6	8	7	26	32	2	8	11	19	35	32
Grimsby T	42	6	7	8	28	34	3	7	11	19	41	32
Scunthorpe U	42	8	8	5	30	25	2	2	17	22	57	30

	Home	Away
Bury	3-0	2-0
Cardiff C	5-2	1-1
Derby C	2-0	1-1
Grimsby T	2-1	2-0
Huddersfield T	5-2	1-2
Leeds U	0-2	1-1
Leyton O	1-2	3-0
Manchester C	4-3	3-1
Middlesbrough	2-4	3-2
Newcastle U	1-2	0-5
Northampton T	1-1	2-1
Norwich C	3-1	3-1
Plymouth A	1-0	1-1
Portsmouth	0-1	1-4
Preston NE	3-0	1-3
Rotherham U	4-3	0-5
Scunthorpe U	0-1	1-1
Southampton	2-2	1-6
Sunderland	0-0	1-2
Swansea T	3-1	2-1
Swindon T	2-2	2-2

Appearances
Bailey M.A. ...41
Durandt C.M. ...11
Edwards D. ...34
Firmani E.R. ...24
Glover L. ...40
Haydock F. ...37
Hewie J.D. ...34
Hinton M. ...1
Kennedy J. ...9
Kenning M.J. ...39
Kinsey B.R. ...41
Lucas F.C. ...2
Matthews R.H. ...42
Peacock K. ...11
Rose M.J. ...34
Ryan J.P. ...1
Sewell J.D. ...9
Stocks D.H. ...3
Tocknell B.T. ...41
Wakeham P.F. ...8

Scorers
Matthews R.H. ...21
Firmani E.R. ...16
Kenning M.J. ...13
Edwards D. ...8
Glover L. ...6
Peacock K. ...5
Bailey M.A. ...3
Ryan J.P. ...1
Sewell J.D. ...1
Own goals ...2
Total ...76

Division 2
1964-65

	P	W	D	L	F	A	W	D	L	F	A	Pts
Newcastle U	42	16	4	1	50	16	8	5	8	31	29	57
Northampton T	42	14	7	0	37	16	6	9	6	29	34	56
Bolton W	42	13	6	2	46	17	7	4	10	34	41	50
Southampton	42	12	6	3	49	25	5	8	8	34	38	48
Ipswich T	42	11	7	3	48	30	4	10	7	26	37	47
Norwich C	42	15	4	2	47	21	5	3	13	14	36	47
Crystal P	42	11	6	4	37	24	5	7	9	18	27	45
Huddersfield T	42	12	4	5	28	15	5	6	10	25	36	44
Derby C	42	11	5	5	48	35	5	6	10	36	44	43
Coventry C	42	10	5	6	41	29	7	4	10	31	41	43
Manchester C	42	12	3	6	40	24	4	6	11	23	38	41
Preston NE	42	11	8	2	46	29	3	5	13	30	52	41
Cardiff C	42	10	7	4	43	25	3	7	11	21	32	40
Rotherham U	42	10	7	4	39	25	4	5	12	31	44	40
Plymouth A	42	10	7	4	36	28	6	1	14	27	51	40
Bury	42	9	4	8	36	30	5	6	10	24	36	38
Middlesbrough	42	8	5	8	40	31	5	4	12	30	45	35
CHARLTON A	42	8	5	8	35	34	5	4	12	29	41	35
Leyton O	42	10	4	7	36	34	2	7	12	14	38	35
Portsmouth	42	11	4	6	36	22	1	6	14	20	55	34
Swindon T	42	12	3	6	43	30	2	2	17	20	51	33
Swansea T	42	9	7	5	40	29	2	3	16	22	55	32

	Home	Away
Bolton W	1-3	1-1
Bury	1-2	0-2
Cardiff C	2-2	1-2
Coventry C	3-0	0-2
Crystal P	1-2	1-3
Derby C	1-3	4-4
Huddersfield T	0-0	1-0
Ipswich T	4-0	1-1
Leyton O	2-0	2-4
Manchester C	2-1	1-2
Middlesbrough	0-2	2-1
Newcastle U	0-1	1-1
Northampton T	1-1	0-1
Norwich C	2-1	0-2
Plymouth A	3-2	5-1
Portsmouth	3-3	3-2
Preston NE	2-3	1-2
Rotherham U	1-1	2-3
Southampton	2-5	0-4
Swansea T	1-0	3-1
Swindon T	3-2	0-2

Appearances
Bailey M.A. ...26
Bonds W.A. ...13
Durandt C.M. ...12
Edwards D. ...15
Firmani E.R. ...31
Glover L. ...40
Gough C.S. ...4
Haydock F. ...30
Hewie J.D. ...39
Jones K. ...7
Keeley R. ...1
Kennedy J. ...25
Kenning M.J. ...26
Kinsey B.R. ...42
Matthews R.H. ...36
Miller R.E. ...8
Peacock K. ...22
Rose M.J. ...25
Ryan J.P. ...2
Snedden J.D. ...9
Stocks D.H. ...11
Tocknell B.T. ...28
Wakeham P.F. ...10

Scorers
Firmani E.R. ...16
Matthews R.H. ...11
Kennedy J. ...7
Kenning M.J. ...6
Peacock K. ...6
Glover L. ...5
Edwards D. ...4
Haydock F. ...3
Bailey M.A. ...2
Ryan J.P. ...2
Durandt C.M. ...1
Tocknell B.T. ...1
Total ...64

Division 2
1965-66

	P	W	D	L	F	A	W	D	L	F	A	Pts
Manchester C	42	14	7	0	40	14	8	8	5	36	30	59
Southampton	42	13	4	4	51	25	9	6	6	34	31	54
Coventry C	42	14	5	2	54	31	6	8	7	19	22	53
Huddersfield T	42	12	7	2	35	12	7	6	8	27	24	51
Bristol C	42	9	10	2	27	15	8	7	6	36	33	51
Wolverhampton W	42	15	4	2	52	18	5	6	10	35	43	50
Rotherham U	42	12	6	3	48	29	4	8	9	27	45	46
Derby C	42	13	2	6	48	31	3	4	9	23	37	43
Bolton W	42	12	2	7	43	25	4	7	10	19	34	41
Birmingham C	42	10	6	5	41	29	6	3	12	29	46	41
Crystal P	42	11	7	3	29	16	3	6	12	18	36	41
Portsmouth	42	13	3	4	47	26	3	4	14	27	52	40
Norwich C	42	8	7	6	33	27	4	8	9	19	25	39
Carlisle U	42	16	2	3	43	19	1	3	17	17	44	39
Ipswich T	42	12	6	3	38	23	3	3	15	20	43	39
CHARLTON A	42	10	6	5	39	29	2	8	11	22	41	38
Preston NE	42	7	10	4	37	23	4	5	12	25	47	37
Plymouth A	42	7	8	6	37	26	5	5	11	17	37	37
Bury	42	12	5	4	45	25	2	2	17	17	51	35
Cardiff C	42	10	3	8	37	35	2	7	12	34	56	34
Middlesbrough	42	8	5	8	36	28	2	5	14	22	58	33
Leyton O	42	3	9	9	19	36	2	4	15	19	44	23

	Home	Away
Birmingham C	2-1	2-2
Bolton W	0-1	2-4
Bristol C	1-4	0-0
Bury	0-1	0-3
Cardiff C	5-2	1-3
Carlisle U	3-2	1-3
Coventry C	2-0	1-3
Crystal P	1-0	0-2
Derby C	2-2	0-2
Huddersfield T	0-2	1-1
Ipswich T	2-0	4-1
Leyton O	3-0	2-1
Manchester C	2-3	0-0
Middlesbrough	1-0	2-2
Norwich C	2-1	0-2
Plymouth A	1-1	0-3
Portsmouth	2-2	1-3
Preston NE	5-2	3-3
Rotherham U	2-2	0-0
Southampton	2-2	0-1
Wolverhampton W	1-1	2-2

Appearances
Bailey M.A. ...27
Bonds W.A. ...40
Burridge P.J. ...25
Campbell A.J. ...23/1
Dwyer N.M. ...6
Glover L. ...35
Halom V.L. ...5/2
Harford R.T. ...3
Haydock F. ...17
Hewie J.D. ...17
Holton C.C. ...18
Jenkins P.L. ...2
Jones K. ...18
Keirs J. ...1
Kenning M.J. ...40/1
King J.A. ...11
Kinsey B.R. ...33
Matthews R.H. ...18
Myers C.W. ...4/1
Peacock K. ...21/3
Reeves P.J. ...1
Rose M.J. ...8
Saunders R. ...36
Snedden J.D. ...9/2
Surman L. ...1
Tocknell B.T. ...21
Whitehouse B. ...13
Wright C.G. ...9

Rule change allows substitutes. One per match to replace injured player.

Scorers
Saunders R. ...13
Kenning M.J. ...11
Holton C.C. ...7
Peacock K. ...7
Glover L. ...5
Bailey M.A. ...4
Campbell A.J. ...4
Burridge P.J. ...3
Matthews R.H. ...3
Haydock F. ...1
Reeves P.J. ...1
Tocknell B.T. ...1
Whitehouse B. ...1
Total ...61

Division 2 1966-67

	P	W	D	L	F	A	W	D	L	F	A	Pts
Coventry C	42	17	3	1	46	16	6	10	5	28	27	59
Wolverhampton W	42	15	4	2	53	20	10	4	7	35	28	58
Carlisle U	42	15	3	3	42	16	8	3	10	29	38	52
Blackburn R	42	13	6	2	33	11	6	7	8	23	35	51
Ipswich T	42	11	8	2	45	25	6	8	7	25	29	50
Huddersfield T	42	14	3	4	36	17	6	6	9	22	29	49
Crystal P	42	14	4	3	42	23	5	6	10	19	32	48
Millwall	42	14	5	2	33	17	4	4	13	16	41	45
Bolton W	42	10	7	4	36	19	4	7	10	28	39	42
Birmingham C	42	11	5	5	42	23	5	3	13	28	43	40
Norwich C	42	10	7	4	31	21	3	7	11	18	34	40
Hull C	42	11	5	5	46	25	5	2	14	31	47	39
Preston NE	42	14	3	4	44	23	2	4	15	21	44	39
Portsmouth	42	7	5	9	34	37	6	8	7	25	33	39
Bristol C	42	10	8	3	38	22	2	6	13	18	40	38
Plymouth A	42	12	4	5	42	21	2	5	14	17	37	37
Derby C	42	8	6	7	40	32	4	6	11	28	40	36
Rotherham U	42	10	5	6	39	28	3	5	13	22	42	36
CHARLTON A	42	11	4	6	34	16	2	5	14	15	37	35
Cardiff C	42	9	7	5	43	38	3	2	16	18	59	33
Northampton T	42	8	6	7	28	33	4	0	17	19	51	30
Bury	42	9	3	9	31	30	2	3	16	18	53	28

	Home	Away
Birmingham C	1-0	0-4
Blackburn R	0-0	1-2
Bolton W	0-1	1-2
Bristol C	5-0	0-4
Bury	4-1	1-2
Cardiff C	5-0	1-4
Carlisle U	1-0	0-1
Coventry C	1-2	0-1
Crystal P	1-0	0-1
Derby C	3-1	2-0
Huddersfield T	1-2	1-4
Hull C	1-3	2-2
Ipswich T	2-1	0-0
Millwall	0-0	0-0
Northampton T	3-0	1-1
Norwich C	0-0	1-1
Plymouth A	1-0	1-2
Portsmouth	0.2	2.1
Preston NE	2-0	1-0
Rotherham U	2-0	0-2
Wolverhampton W	1-3	0-1

Appearances

Appleton C.H.	28
Bonds W.A.	42
Booth D.	3
Burns L.G.H.	7
Burridge P.J.	17/2
Campbell A.J.	39/1
Curtis R.D.	1
Firmani E.R.	9
Glover L.	33
Green H.R.	3/1
Gregory G.	31
Halom V.L.	3/1
Keirs J.	13
Kenning M.J.	21
King J.A.	34
Kinsey B.R.	36
Matthews R.H.	2
Myers C.W.	12/1
Peacock K.	24/6
Reeves P.J.	25
Rose M.J.	8
Saunders R.	28/1
Tees M.	9
Wright C.G.	34

One substitute per match now allowed for any reason except sending-off.

Scorers

Saunders R.	11
Campbell A.J.	7
Firmani E.R.	6
Kenning M.J.	6
Gregory G.	4
Tees M.	4
Myers C.W.	2
Appleton C.H.	1
Bonds W.A.	1
Burridge P.J.	1
Glover L.	1
Green H.R.	1
Kinsey B.R.	1
Peacock K.	1
Own goals	2
Total	49

Division 2 1967-68

	P	W	D	L	F	A	W	D	L	F	A	Pts
Ipswich T	42	12	7	2	45	20	10	8	3	34	24	59
QPR	42	18	2	1	45	9	7	6	8	22	27	58
Blackpool	42	12	6	3	33	16	12	4	5	38	27	58
Birmingham C	42	12	6	3	54	21	7	8	6	29	30	52
Portsmouth	42	13	6	2	43	18	5	7	9	25	37	49
Middlesbrough	42	10	7	4	39	19	7	5	9	21	35	46
Millwall	42	9	10	2	35	16	5	7	9	27	34	45
Blackburn R	42	13	5	3	34	16	3	6	12	22	33	43
Norwich C	42	12	4	5	40	30	4	7	10	20	35	43
Carlisle U	42	9	9	3	38	22	5	4	12	20	30	41
Crystal P	42	11	4	6	34	19	3	7	11	22	37	39
Bolton W	42	8	6	7	37	28	5	7	9	23	35	39
Cardiff C	42	9	6	6	35	29	4	6	11	25	37	38
Huddersfield T	42	10	6	5	23	19	3	6	12	17	38	38
CHARLTON A	42	10	6	5	43	25	2	7	12	20	43	37
Aston Villa	42	10	3	8	35	30	5	4	12	19	34	37
Hull C	42	6	8	7	25	26	6	5	10	33	50	37
Derby C	42	8	5	8	40	35	5	5	11	31	43	36
Bristol C	42	7	7	7	26	25	6	3	12	22	37	36
Preston NE	42	8	7	6	29	24	4	4	13	14	41	35
Rotherham U	42	7	4	10	22	32	3	7	11	20	44	31
Plymouth A	42	5	4	12	26	36	4	5	12	12	36	27

	Home	Away
Aston Villa	3-0	1-4
Birmingham C	3-1	0-4
Blackburn R	3-0	2-3
Blackpool	0-2	0-2
Bolton W	2-0	0-2
Bristol C	1-2	2-0
Cardiff C	1-1	0-0
Carlisle U	2-2	0-0
Crystal P	0-1	0-3
Derby C	1-2	2-3
Huddersfield T	4-2	1-4
Hull C	5-1	1-1
Ipswich T	0-1	2-3
Middlesbrough	2-2	1-1
Millwall	1-0	0-0
Norwich C	3-3	1-1
Plymouth A	1-0	4-1
Portsmouth	4-1	0-4
Preston NE	0-0	1-4
QPR	3-3	1-2
Rotherham U	4-1	1-1

Appearances

Bolland G.E.	8/2
Booth D.	13/4
Burns L.G.H.	1
Campbell A.J.	40
Curtis R.D.	25
Firmani E.R.	1
Foley T.C.	6
Glover L.	11
Gregory G.	32
Halom V.L.	1
Hince P.F.	17
Keirs J.	15/1
King J.A.	18
Kinsey B.R.	39/1
Moore G.	20
Mullen J.	2
Peacock K.	40
Reeves P.J.	29
Stenson J.A.	3/5
Tees M.	38
Treacy R.C.P.	18
Went P.F.	41
Willis R.I.	1
Woodley D.G.	2/1
Wright C.G.	41

Scorers

Tees M.	13
Campbell A.J.	9
Peacock K.	9
Treacy R.C.P.	9
Gregory G.	7
Went P.F.	4
Curtis R.D.	3
Bolland G.E.	2
Hince P.F.	2
Glover L.	1
Kinsey B.R.	1
Own goals	3
Total	63

Division 2 1968-69

	P	W	D	L	F	A	W	D	L	F	A	Pts
Derby C	42	16	4	1	43	16	10	7	4	22	16	63
Crystal P	42	14	4	3	45	24	8	8	5	25	23	56
CHARLTON A	42	11	8	2	39	21	7	6	8	22	31	50
Middlesbrough	42	13	7	1	36	13	6	4	11	22	36	49
Cardiff C	42	13	5	3	38	19	7	4	10	29	35	47
Huddersfield T	42	13	6	2	37	14	4	6	11	16	32	46
Birmingham C	42	13	3	5	52	24	5	5	11	21	35	44
Blackpool	42	9	8	4	33	20	5	7	9	18	21	43
Sheffield U	42	14	3	4	41	15	2	7	12	20	35	43
Millwall	42	10	5	6	33	23	7	4	10	24	26	43
Hull C	42	10	7	4	38	20	3	9	9	21	32	42
Carlisle U	42	10	5	6	25	17	6	5	10	21	32	42
Norwich C	42	7	6	8	24	25	8	4	9	29	31	40
Preston NE	42	8	8	5	23	19	4	7	10	15	25	39
Portsmouth	42	11	5	5	39	22	1	9	11	19	36	38
Bristol C	42	9	9	3	30	15	2	7	12	16	38	38
Bolton W	42	8	7	6	29	26	4	7	10	26	41	38
Aston Villa	42	10	8	3	22	11	2	6	13	15	37	38
Blackburn R	42	9	6	6	30	24	4	5	12	22	39	37
Oxford U	42	8	5	8	21	23	4	4	13	13	32	33
Bury	42	8	4	9	35	33	3	4	14	16	47	30
Fulham	42	6	7	8	20	28	1	4	16	20	53	25

	Home	Away
Aston Villa	1-1	0-0
Birmingham C	3-1	0-0
Blackburn R	4-0	1-0
Blackpool	0-0	3-2
Bolton W	2-2	0-3
Bristol C	0-0	0-2
Bury	2-2	3-2
Cardiff C	4-1	1-0
Carlisle U	1-1	1-1
Crystal P	1-1	3-3
Derby C	2-0	1-2
Fulham	5-3	1-0
Huddersfield T	1-0	0-0
Hull C	1-1	2-5
Middlesbrough	2-0	0-1
Millwall	3-4	2-3
Norwich C	2-1	1-0
Oxford U	1-0	1-0
Portsmouth	2-1	1-4
Preston NE	0-1	1-1
Sheffield U	2-1	0-2

Appearances

Bolland G.E.	1
Booth D.	18/3
Burkett J.W.	5
Burns A.J.	2
Campbell A.J.	42
Crawford R.	9
Curtis R.D.	40
Gregory G.	42
Hayward K.W.	1
Hince P.F.	6
Keirs J.	19/2
Kenning M.J.	4/1
Kinsey B.R.	39
Moore G.	37
Mullen J.	5
Peacock K.	23
Reeves P.J.	42
Stenson J.A.	0/3
Tees M.	35/1
Treacy R.C.P.	29/1
Went P.F.	24/3
Wright C.G.	39

Scorers

Tees M.	15
Gregory G.	11
Treacy R.C.P.	8
Moore G.	6
Booth D.	5
Campbell A.J.	3
Crawford R.	3
Curtis R.D.	3
Peacock K.	3
Went P.F.	3
Keirs J.	1
Total	61

Division 2 1969-70

	P	W	D	L	F	A	W	D	L	F	A	Pts
Huddersfield T	42	14	6	1	36	10	10	6	5	32	27	60
Blackpool	42	10	9	2	25	16	10	4	7	31	29	53
Leicester C	42	12	6	3	37	22	7	7	7	27	28	51
Middlesbrough	42	15	4	2	36	14	5	6	10	19	31	50
Swindon T	42	13	7	1	35	17	4	9	8	22	30	50
Sheffield U	42	16	2	3	50	10	6	3	12	23	28	49
Cardiff C	42	12	7	2	38	14	6	6	9	23	27	49
Blackburn R	42	15	2	4	42	19	5	5	11	12	31	47
QPR	42	13	5	3	47	24	4	6	11	19	33	45
Millwall	42	14	4	3	38	18	1	10	10	18	38	44
Norwich C	42	13	5	3	37	14	3	6	12	12	32	43
Carlisle U	42	10	6	5	39	28	4	7	10	19	28	41
Hull C	42	11	6	4	43	28	4	5	12	29	42	41
Bristol C	42	11	7	3	37	13	2	6	13	17	37	39
Oxford U	42	9	9	3	23	13	3	6	12	12	29	39
Bolton W	42	9	6	6	31	23	3	6	12	23	38	36
Portsmouth	42	8	4	9	39	35	5	5	11	27	45	35
Birmingham C	42	9	7	5	33	22	2	4	15	18	56	33
Watford	42	6	8	7	26	21	3	5	13	18	36	31
CHARLTON A	42	7	8	6	23	28	0	9	12	12	48	31
Aston Villa	42	7	8	6	23	21	1	5	15	13	41	29
Preston NE	42	7	6	8	31	28	1	6	14	12	35	28

	Home	Away
Aston Villa	1-0	0-1
Birmingham C	0-1	0-3
Blackburn R	0-0	0-3
Blackpool	0-2	0-2
Bolton W	1-1	1-1
Bristol C	2-1	0-6
Cardiff C	0-0	0-1
Carlisle U	2-1	1-1
Huddersfield T	1-2	0-4
Hull C	1-4	1-1
Leicester C	0-5	2-2
Middlesbrough	0-2	0-2
Millwall	2-2	1-1
Norwich C	3-0	1-1
Oxford U	1-0	1-1
Portsmouth	2-2	1-5
Preston NE	2-1	1-4
QPR	1-1	1-1
Sheffield U	3-2	0-2
Swindon T	1-1	0-5
Watford	0-0	1-1

Appearances
Booth D. 27/3
Burkett J.W. 3
Burns A.J. 8
Campbell A.J. 42
Crawford R. 12
Curtis R.D. 30/1
Gilchrist P.A. 5/2
Gregory G. 35/3
Keirs J. 23/1
Kenning M.J. 17/3
Kinsey B.R. 34
Masiello L. 5
Minnock J.J. 0/1
Moore G. 36
Peacock K. 35/1
Reeves P.J. 36
Riddick G.G 19/1
Setters M.E. 8
Stacey S.D. 1
Tees M. 6
Treacy R.C.P. 27/3
Warman P.R. 3/2
Went P.F. 16
Wright C.G. 34

Scorers
Treacy R.C.P. 6
Campbell A.J. 5
Kenning M.J. 5
Peacock K. 5
Crawford R. 4
Riddick G.G. 4
Gregory G. 2
Moore G. 2
Setters M.E. 1
Stacey S.D. 1
Total 35

Division 2 1970-71

	P	W	D	L	F	A	W	D	L	F	A	Pts
Leicester C	42	12	7	2	30	14	11	6	4	27	16	59
Sheffield U	42	14	6	1	49	18	7	8	6	24	21	56
Cardiff C	42	12	7	2	39	16	8	6	7	25	25	53
Carlisle U	42	16	3	2	39	13	4	10	7	26	30	53
Hull C	42	11	5	5	31	16	8	8	5	23	25	51
Luton T	42	12	7	2	40	18	6	6	9	22	25	49
Middlesbrough	42	13	6	2	37	16	4	8	9	23	27	48
Millwall	42	13	5	3	36	12	6	4	11	23	30	47
Birmingham C	42	12	7	2	30	12	5	5	11	28	36	46
Norwich C	42	11	8	2	34	20	4	6	11	20	32	44
QPR	42	11	5	5	39	20	5	6	10	19	31	43
Swindon T	42	12	7	2	38	14	3	5	13	23	37	42
Sunderland	42	11	6	4	34	21	4	6	11	18	33	42
Oxford U	42	8	8	5	23	23	6	6	9	18	25	42
Sheffield W	42	10	7	4	32	27	2	5	14	19	42	36
Portsmouth	42	9	4	8	32	28	1	10	10	14	33	34
Orient	42	5	11	5	16	15	4	5	12	13	36	34
Watford	42	6	7	8	18	22	4	6	11	20	30	33
Bristol C	42	9	6	6	30	28	1	5	15	16	36	31
CHARLTON A	42	7	6	8	28	30	1	8	12	13	35	30
Blackburn R	42	5	8	8	20	28	1	7	13	17	41	27
Bolton W	42	6	5	10	22	31	1	5	15	13	43	24

	Home	Away
Birmingham C	1-1	1-1
Blackburn R	2-4	0-1
Bolton W	4-0	0-4
Bristol C	1-1	2-2
Cardiff C	2-1	1-1
Carlisle U	1-1	1-1
Hull C	0-1	0-2
Leicester C	0-1	0-1
Luton T	1-1	1-1
Middlesbrough	1-0	0-3
Millwall	1-3	0-2
Norwich C	2-1	0-2
Orient	2-0	0-0
Oxford U	2-0	1-2
Portsmouth	2-2	0-2
QPR	0-3	4-1
Sheffield U	0-2	0-3
Sheffield W	2-3	0-1
Sunderland	1-1	0-3
Swindon T	2-1	1-1
Watford	1-2	1-1

Appearances
Bellotti D.C. 4
Bond D.J.T. 22/1
Booth D. 6
Bruck D.J. 31
Campbell A.J. 10
Curtis R.D. 41
Davies C.J. 23/5
Ellis A. 9/4
Endean B. 17
Gregory G. 6
Hunt R.R. 8/1
Johnson N.J. 1
Keirs J. 2/1
Kenning M.J. 28/1
Kinsey B.R. 5/5
Masiello L. 1
Moore G. 17
O'Kane V. 0/1
Peacock K. 36/1
Plumb R.K. 20/5
Reeves P.J. 37/3
Riddick G.G. 7/2
Shipperley D.J. 13/1
Treacy R.C.P. 32/1
Warman P.R. 11
Went P.F. 37
Wright C.G. 38

Scorers
Kenning M.J. 7
Plumb R.K. 7
Treacy R.C.P. 7
Peacock K. 6
Curtis R.D. 5
Bond D.J.T. 2
Went P.F. 2
Davies C. 1
Hunt R.R. 1
Moore G. 1
Riddick G.G 1
Shipperley D.J. 1
Total 41

Division 2 1971-72

	P	W	D	L	F	A	W	D	L	F	A	Pts
Norwich C	42	13	8	0	40	16	8	7	6	20	20	57
Birmingham C	42	15	6	0	46	14	4	12	5	14	17	56
Millwall	42	14	7	0	38	17	5	10	6	26	29	55
QPR	42	16	1	4	39	9	4	10	7	18	19	54
Sunderland	42	11	7	3	42	24	6	9	6	25	33	50
Blackpool	42	12	6	3	43	16	8	1	12	27	34	47
Burnley	42	13	4	4	43	22	7	2	12	27	33	46
Bristol C	42	14	3	4	43	22	4	7	10	18	27	46
Middlesbrough	42	16	4	1	31	11	3	4	14	19	37	46
Carlisle U	42	12	6	3	38	22	5	3	13	23	35	43
Swindon T	42	10	6	5	29	16	5	6	10	18	31	42
Hull C	42	10	6	5	33	21	4	4	13	16	32	38
Luton T	42	7	8	6	25	24	3	10	8	18	24	38
Sheffield W	42	11	7	3	33	22	2	5	14	18	36	38
Oxford U	42	10	8	3	28	17	2	6	13	15	38	38
Portsmouth	42	9	7	5	31	26	3	6	12	28	42	37
Orient	42	12	4	5	32	19	2	5	14	18	42	37
Preston NE	42	11	4	6	32	21	1	8	12	20	37	36
Cardiff C	42	9	7	5	37	25	1	7	13	19	44	34
Fulham	42	10	7	4	29	20	2	3	16	16	48	34
CHARLTON A	42	9	7	5	33	25	3	2	16	22	52	33
Watford	42	5	5	11	15	25	0	4	17	9	50	19

	Home	Away
Birmingham C	1-1	1-4
Blackpool	2-3	0-5
Bristol C	2-0	0-2
Burnley	2-0	1-3
Cardiff C	2-2	1-6
Carlisle U	1-1	2-5
Fulham	2-2	0-1
Hull C	1-0	3-2
Luton T	2-0	2-1
Middlesbrough	0-2	2-2
Millwall	0-2	1-2
Norwich C	0-2	0-3
Orient	1-2	2-3
Oxford U	3-0	1-2
Portsmouth	1-1	0-0
Preston NE	2-1	1-2
QPR	2-1	0-2
Sheffield W	2-2	1-2
Sunderland	2-2	0-3
Swindon T	3-1	1-2
Watford	2-0	3-0

Appearances
Barnard C.L. 0/1
Bellotti D.C. 10
Bond D.J.T. 36/1
Bruck D.J. 31/2
Clarke A.F. 2
Curtis R.D. 8/1
Davies C.J. 40
Dunn J.A. 30
Endean B. 10
Flanagan M.A. 7/11
Hunt R.R. 22/1
Jones M.K. 12/1
Kenning M.J. 11/2
O'Kane V. 5
Partridge M. 1/1
Peacock K. 37
Plumb R.K. 12/6
Reeves P.J. 21
Rogers E. 25/1
Shipperley D.J. 28/4
Treacy R.C.P. 38
Warman P.R. 42
Went P.F. 42

Scorers
Treacy R.C.P. 14
Peacock K. 11
Hunt R.R. 9
Went P.F. 6
Davies C. 3
Plumb R.K. 3
Rogers E. 3
Bond D.J.T. 1
Curtis R.D. 1
Endean B. 1
Shipperley D.J. 1
Own goals 2
Total 55

Division 3 1972-73

	P	W	D	L	F	A	W	D	L	F	A	Pts
Bolton W	46	18	4	1	44	9	7	7	9	29	30	61
Notts C	46	17	4	2	40	12	6	7	10	27	35	57
Blackburn R	46	12	8	3	34	16	8	7	8	23	31	55
Oldham A	46	12	7	4	40	18	7	9	7	32	36	54
Bristol R	46	17	4	2	55	20	3	9	11	22	36	53
Port Vale	46	15	6	2	41	21	6	5	12	15	48	53
AFC Bournemouth	46	14	6	3	44	16	3	10	10	22	28	50
Plymouth A	46	14	3	6	43	26	6	7	10	31	40	50
Grimsby T	46	16	2	5	45	18	4	6	13	22	43	48
Tranmere R	46	12	8	3	38	17	3	8	12	18	35	46
CHARLTON A	46	12	7	4	46	24	5	4	14	23	43	45
Wrexham	46	11	9	3	39	23	3	8	12	16	31	45
Rochdale	46	8	8	7	22	26	6	9	8	26	28	45
Southend U	46	13	6	4	40	14	4	4	15	21	40	44
Shrewsbury T	46	10	10	3	31	21	5	4	14	15	33	44
Chesterfield	46	13	4	6	37	22	4	5	14	20	39	43
Walsall	46	14	3	6	37	26	4	4	15	19	40	43
York C	46	8	10	5	24	14	5	5	13	18	32	41
Watford	46	11	8	4	32	23	1	9	13	11	25	41
Halifax T	46	9	8	6	29	23	4	7	12	14	30	41
Rotherham U	46	12	4	7	34	27	5	3	15	17	38	41
Brentford	46	12	5	6	33	18	3	2	18	18	51	37
Swansea C	46	11	5	7	37	29	3	4	16	14	44	37
Scunthorpe U	46	8	7	8	18	25	2	3	18	15	47	30

	Home	Away
AFC Bournemouth	1-1	1-3
Blackburn R	1-2	1-3
Bolton W	2-3	0-3
Brentford	2-1	0-1
Bristol R	3-3	1-2
Chesterfield	2-2	0-1
Grimsby T	1-1	2-0
Halifax T	1-0	0-3
Notts C	6-1	1-3
Oldham A	4-2	1-0
Plymouth A	3-0	0-5
Port Vale	2-0	1-3
Rochdale	1-0	2-0
Rotherham U	1-2	1-2
Scunthorpe U	2-0	2-0
Shrewsbury T	1-2	2-0
Southend U	0-0	1-1
Swansea C	6-0	1-2
Tranmere R	1-1	0-4
Walsall	1-1	2-3
Watford	2-1	1-1
Wrexham	2-1	2-2
York C	1-0	1-1

Appearances

Arnold J.W.L.	1
Bond D.J.T.	12/3
Bowman R.D.	4
Curtis R.D.	37/4
Davies C.J.	7/1
Davies P.	41/3
Dunn J.A.	37
Ellis A.	0/1
Flanagan M.A.	42
Franklin W.H.	4
Goldthorpe R.J.	10/3
Horsfield A.	46
Hunt P.J.	26/10
Hunt R.R.	4
Jones M.K.	25
Kearns M.	4
O'Kane V.	24/2
Peacock K.	24/4
Powell C.D.	13/2
Reeves P.J.	45
Rogers E.	12/1
Shipperley D.J.	40
Tumbridge R.A.	7
Walker M.S.G.	1
Warman P.R.	39
Wood A.E.	1

Scorers

Horsfield A.	25
Flanagan M.A.	12
Davies P.	7
Peacock K.	7
Shipperley D.J.	4
Curtis R.D.	3
Hunt P.J.	2
Davies C.	1
Goldthorpe R.J.	1
Hunt R.R.	1
O'Kane V.	1
Powell C.D.	1
Reeves P.J.	1
Warman P.R.	1
Own goals	2
Total	69

Division 3 1973-74

	P	W	D	L	F	A	W	D	L	F	A	Pts
Oldham A	46	13	6	4	50	23	12	6	5	33	24	62
Bristol R	46	15	6	2	37	15	7	11	5	28	18	61
York C	46	13	8	2	37	15	8	11	4	30	23	61
Wrexham	46	15	6	2	44	15	7	6	10	19	28	56
Chesterfield	46	14	6	3	31	16	7	8	8	24	26	56
Grimsby T	46	14	6	3	48	21	4	9	10	19	29	51
Watford	46	12	6	5	34	21	7	6	10	30	35	50
Aldershot	46	14	5	4	37	16	3	8	12	19	39	49
Halifax T	46	9	11	3	23	15	5	10	8	25	36	49
Huddersfield T	46	14	5	4	37	16	3	8	12	19	39	47
AFC Bournemouth	46	11	5	7	25	23	5	10	8	29	35	47
Southend U	46	10	7	6	40	30	6	7	10	22	32	46
Blackburn R	46	13	4	6	38	21	5	6	12	24	43	46
CHARLTON A	46	13	5	4	39	29	6	3	14	23	43	46
Walsall	46	11	7	5	37	19	5	6	12	20	29	45
Tranmere R	46	10	8	5	31	15	5	7	11	19	29	45
Plymouth A	46	13	6	4	37	17	4	4	15	22	37	44
Hereford U	46	10	5	8	31	25	4	10	9	22	32	43
Brighton & HA	46	10	3	10	31	31	6	8	9	21	27	43
Port Vale	46	12	6	5	37	23	2	8	13	15	35	42
Cambridge U	46	11	7	5	36	27	2	2	19	12	54	35
Shrewsbury T	46	7	7	9	24	24	3	4	16	17	38	31
Southport	46	4	14	5	19	20	2	2	19	16	62	28
Rochdale	46	1	12	10	24	38	1	5	17	14	56	21

	Home	Away
AFC Bournemouth	0-0	0-1
Aldershot	2-0	1-2
Blackburn R	4-3	1-1
Brighton & HA	0-4	2-1
Bristol R	1-1	1-2
Cambridge U	2-0	0-1
Chesterfield	3-3	1-3
Grimsby T	2-1	0-5
Halifax T	5-2	1-2
Hereford U	2-0	3-2
Huddersfield T	2-1	0-2
Oldham A	4-1	2-0
Plymouth A	2-0	0-1
Port Vale	2-0	1-3
Rochdale	3-0	1-1
Shrewsbury T	3-3	3-3
Southend U	2-1	0-2
Southport	0-1	2-1
Tranmere R	1-0	0-2
Walsall	0-1	0-4
Watford	1-3	3-1
Wrexham	0-0	0-4
York C	2-4	1-0

Appearances

Arnold J.W.L.	0/4
Bowman R.D.	8
Curtis R.D.	35/4
Davies P.	9/2
Dunn J.A.	30
Dunphy E.M.	22/2
Flanagan M.A.	40/2
Forster D.	9
Goldthorpe R.J.	36/1
Hales D.D.	26/3
Horsfield A.	46
Hunt P.J.	11/3
Jones M.K.	21
Peacock K.	36
Penfold M.	13/1
Powell C.D.	42/3
Reeves P.J.	27/2
Shipperley D.J.	11/3
Smart R.W.	30/1
Tumbridge R.A.	30/3
Tutt G.C.	7
Warman P.R.	17

Scorers

Horsfield A.	18
Flanagan M.A.	11
Hales D.D.	9
Peacock K.	6
Powell C.D.	6
Curtis R.D.	4
Davies P.	2
Dunphy E.M.	2
Shipperley D.J.	2
Goldthorpe R.J.	1
Smart R.W.	1
Warman P.R.	1
Own goals	3
Total	66

Division 3 1974-75

	P	W	D	L	F	A	W	D	L	F	A	Pts
Blackburn R	46	15	7	1	40	16	7	9	7	28	29	60
Plymouth A	46	16	5	2	38	19	8	6	9	41	39	59
CHARLTON A	46	15	5	3	51	29	7	6	10	25	32	55
Swindon T	46	18	3	2	43	17	3	8	12	21	41	53
Crystal P	46	14	8	1	48	22	4	7	12	18	35	51
Port Vale	46	15	6	2	37	19	3	9	11	24	35	51
Peterborough U	46	10	9	4	24	17	9	3	11	23	36	50
Walsall	46	15	5	3	43	18	3	8	12	21	39	49
Preston NE	46	16	5	2	42	19	3	6	14	21	37	49
Gillingham	46	14	6	3	43	23	3	8	12	22	37	48
Colchester U	46	13	7	3	45	22	4	6	13	25	41	47
Hereford U	46	14	6	3	42	21	2	8	13	22	45	46
Wrexham	46	10	8	5	41	23	5	7	11	24	32	45
Bury	46	13	6	4	38	17	3	6	14	16	45	44
Chesterfield	46	11	7	5	37	25	5	5	13	25	41	44
Grimsby T	46	12	8	3	35	19	3	5	15	20	45	43
Halifax T	46	11	10	2	33	20	2	7	14	16	45	43
Southend U	46	11	9	3	32	17	2	7	14	14	34	42
Brighton & HA	46	14	7	2	38	21	2	3	18	18	43	42
Aldershot	46	13	5	5	40	21	1	6	16	13	42	*38
AFC Bournemouth	46	9	6	8	27	25	4	6	13	17	33	38
Tranmere R	46	12	4	7	39	21	2	5	16	16	36	37
Watford	46	9	7	7	30	31	1	10	12	22	44	37
Huddersfield T	46	9	6	8	32	29	2	4	17	15	47	32

* Aldershot were deducted one point for playing an ineligible player.

	Home	Away
AFC Bournemouth	2-3	2-1
Aldershot	3-1	0-3
Blackburn R	2-1	1-3
Brighton & HA	2-1	1-1
Bury	0-1	1-2
Chesterfield	3-2	0-2
Colchester U	4-1	0-3
Crystal P	1-0	1-2
Gillingham	2-1	1-0
Grimsby T	1-1	1-1
Halifax T	3-1	2-2
Hereford U	2-0	2-2
Huddersfield T	1-0	3-1
Peterborough U	3-0	1-1
Plymouth A	0-2	1-1
Port Vale	2-2	0-1
Preston NE	3-1	0-2
Southend U	2-1	1-2
Swindon T	3-3	0-2
Tranmere R	3-3	1-0
Walsall	4-2	1-0
Watford	4-1	2-0
Wrexham	1-1	3-0

Appearances

Bowman R.D.	33/1
Cripps H.R.	17/2
Curtis R.D.	43
Davies P.	1/1
Dunn J.A.	7
Dunphy E.M.	17/1
Flanagan M.A.	15
Franklin W.M.	9
Goldthorpe R.J.	20/5
Hales D.D.	44
Hart A.M.	3
Horsfield A.	46
Hunt. P.J.	32/3
Kelly M.L.	10
Peacock K.	34/1
Penfold M.	8/1
Powell C.D.	43
Tumbridge R.A.	6
Tutt G.C.	30
Warman P.R.	33/1
Young D.	44

Scorers

Hales D.D.	20
Horsfield A.	10
Curtis R.D.	8
Powell C.D.	7
Bowman R.D.	4
Cripps H.R.	4
Flanagan M.A.	4
Goldthorpe R.J.	4
Peacock K.	4
Warman P.R.	4
Kelly M.L.	3
Hart A.M.	2
Dunphy E.M.	1
Hunt P.J.	1
Total	76

Division 2 1975-76

	P	W	D	L	F	A	W	D	L	F	A	Pts
Sunderland	42	19	2	0	48	10	5	6	10	19	26	56
Bristol C	42	11	7	3	34	14	8	8	5	25	21	53
West Bromwich A	42	10	9	2	29	12	10	4	7	21	21	53
Bolton W	42	12	5	4	36	14	8	7	6	28	24	52
Notts C	42	11	6	4	33	13	8	5	8	27	28	49
Southampton	42	18	2	1	49	16	3	5	13	17	34	49
Luton T	42	13	6	2	38	15	6	4	11	23	36	48
Nottingham F	42	13	1	7	34	18	4	11	6	21	22	46
CHARLTON A	42	11	5	5	40	34	4	7	10	21	38	42
Blackpool	42	9	9	3	26	22	5	5	11	14	27	42
Chelsea	42	7	9	5	25	20	5	7	9	28	34	40
Fulham	42	9	8	4	27	14	4	6	11	18	33	40
Orient	42	10	6	5	21	12	3	8	10	16	27	40
Hull C	42	9	5	7	29	23	5	6	10	16	26	39
Blackburn R	42	8	6	7	27	22	4	8	9	18	28	38
Plymouth A	42	13	4	4	36	20	0	8	13	12	34	38
Oldham A	42	11	8	2	37	24	2	4	15	20	44	38
Bristol R	42	7	9	5	20	15	4	7	10	18	35	38
Carlisle U	42	9	8	4	29	22	3	5	13	16	37	37
Oxford U	42	7	7	7	23	25	4	4	13	16	34	33
York C	42	8	3	10	28	34	2	5	14	11	37	28
Portsmouth	42	4	6	11	15	23	5	1	15	17	38	25

	Home	Away
Blackburn R	2-1	0-2
Blackpool	1-1	1-2
Bolton W	0-4	0-5
Bristol C	2-2	0-4
Bristol R	3-0	0-0
Carlisle U	4-2	1-1
Chelsea	1-1	3-2
Fulham	3-2	1-1
Hull C	1-0	2-2
Luton T	1-5	1-1
Nottingham F	2-2	2-1
Notts C	1-2	0-2
Oldham A	3-1	0-2
Orient	1-1	1-0
Oxford U	2-1	0-1
Plymouth A	2-0	0-1
Portsmouth	1-3	2-2
Southampton	4-1	2-3
Sunderland	1-2	1-4
West Bromwich A	2-1	1-1
York C	3-2	3-1

Appearances
Berry L.D.	14/1
Bowman R.D.	26/3
Campbell D.A.	1/2
Cripps H.R.	0/1
Curtis R.D.	24/2
Flanagan M.A.	38
Giles J.A.	42
Goldthorpe R.J.	4
Hales D.D.	40
Harrison J.M.	5
Hope G.	12
Horsfield A.	1
Hunt P.J.	36/1
Peacock K.	39
Penfold M.	24
Powell C.D.	37/1
Tutt G.C.	28
Warman P.R.	29
Wood J.R.	14
Young D.	32
Young T.A.	16

Scorers
Hales D.D.	28
Flanagan M.A.	6
Warman P.R.	6
Giles J.A.	3
Hunt P.J.	3
Bowman R.D.	2
Harrison J.M.	2
Hope G.	2
Powell C.D.	2
Berry L.D.	1
Curtis R.D.	1
Peacock K.	1
Young T.A.	1
Own goals	3
Total	61

Division 2 1976-77

	P	W	D	L	F	A	W	D	L	F	A	Pts
Wolverhampton W	42	15	3	3	48	21	7	10	4	36	24	57
Chelsea	42	15	6	0	51	22	6	7	8	22	31	55
Nottingham F	42	14	3	4	53	22	7	7	7	24	21	52
Bolton W	42	15	2	4	46	21	5	9	7	29	33	51
Blackpool	42	11	7	3	29	17	6	10	5	29	25	51
Luton T	42	13	5	3	39	17	8	1	12	28	31	48
CHARLTON A	42	14	5	2	52	27	2	11	8	19	31	48
Notts C	42	11	5	5	29	20	8	5	8	36	40	48
Southampton	42	12	6	3	40	24	5	4	12	32	43	44
Millwall	42	9	6	6	31	22	6	7	8	26	31	43
Sheffield U	42	9	8	4	32	25	5	4	12	22	38	40
Blackburn R	42	12	4	5	31	18	3	5	13	11	36	39
Oldham A	42	11	6	4	37	23	3	4	14	15	41	38
Hull C	42	9	8	4	31	17	1	9	11	14	36	37
Bristol R	42	8	9	4	32	27	4	4	13	21	41	37
Burnley	42	8	9	4	27	20	3	5	13	19	44	36
Fulham	42	9	7	5	39	25	2	6	13	15	36	35
Cardiff C	42	7	6	8	30	30	5	4	12	26	37	34
Orient	42	4	8	9	18	23	5	8	8	19	32	34
Carlisle U	42	7	7	7	31	33	4	5	12	18	42	34
Plymouth A	42	5	9	7	27	25	3	7	11	19	40	32
Hereford U	42	6	9	6	28	30	2	6	13	29	48	31

* Goal difference now used instead of goal average to separate teams on equal points.

	Home	Away
Blackburn R	4-0	0-0
Blackpool	1-2	2-2
Bolton W	1-1	0-1
Bristol R	4-3	1-1
Burnley	5-2	4-4
Cardiff C	0-2	1-1
Carlisle U	1-0	2-4
Chelsea	4-0	1-2
Fulham	1-1	1-1
Hereford U	1-1	2-1
Hull C	3-1	0-0
Luton T	4-3	0-2
Millwall	3-2	1-1
Nottingham F	2-1	1-1
Notts C	1-1	1-0
Oldham A	2-1	1-1
Orient	2-0	0-0
Plymouth A	3-1	0-1
Sheffield U	3-2	0-3
Southampton	6-2	1-2
Wolverhampton W	1-1	0-3

Appearances
Berry L.D.	39
Bowman R.D.	11
Burman A.P.	11
Curtis R.D.	36/1
Flanagan M.A.	42
Giles J.A.	36/1
Hales D.D.	16
Hammond G.	15/1
Hope G.	1
Hunt P.J.	33/3
McAuley H.A.	24
O'Sullivan W.F.	0/1
Peacock K.	39
Penfold M.	9/1
Powell C.D.	42
Tydeman R.	24
Warman P.R.	38
Wood J.R.	42
Young D.	0/1
Young T.A.	4

Scorers
Flanagan M.A.	23
Hales D.D.	16
Curtis R.D.	6
Peacock K.	6
McAuley H.A.	5
Burman A.P.	3
Giles J.A.	3
Berry L.D.	2
Powell C.D.	2
Warman P.R.	2
Bowman R.D.	1
Own goals	2
Total	71

Division 2 1977-78

	P	W	D	L	F	A	W	D	L	F	A	Pts
Bolton W	42	16	4	1	39	14	8	6	7	24	19	58
Southampton	42	15	4	2	44	16	7	9	5	26	23	57
Tottenham H	42	13	7	1	50	19	7	9	5	33	30	56
Brighton & HA	42	15	5	1	43	21	7	7	7	20	17	56
Blackburn R	42	12	4	5	33	16	4	9	8	23	44	45
Sunderland	42	11	6	4	36	17	3	10	8	31	42	44
Stoke C	42	13	5	3	38	16	3	5	13	15	33	42
Oldham A	42	9	10	2	32	20	4	6	11	22	38	42
Crystal P	42	9	7	5	31	20	4	8	9	19	27	41
Fulham	42	9	8	4	32	19	5	5	11	17	30	41
Burnley	42	11	6	4	35	20	4	4	13	21	44	40
Sheffield U	42	13	4	4	38	22	3	4	14	24	51	40
Luton T	42	11	4	6	35	20	3	6	12	19	32	38
Orient	42	8	11	2	30	20	2	7	12	13	29	38
Notts C	42	10	9	2	36	22	1	7	13	18	40	38
Millwall	42	8	8	5	23	20	4	6	11	26	37	38
CHARLTON A	42	11	6	4	38	27	2	6	13	17	41	38
Bristol R	42	10	7	4	40	26	3	5	13	21	51	38
Cardiff C	42	12	6	3	32	23	1	6	14	19	48	38
Blackpool	42	7	8	6	35	25	5	5	11	24	35	37
Mansfield T	42	6	6	9	30	34	4	5	12	19	35	31
Hull C	42	6	6	9	23	25	2	6	13	11	27	28

	Home	Away
Blackburn R	2-2	1-2
Blackpool	3-1	1-5
Bolton W	2-1	1-2
Brighton & HA	4-3	0-1
Bristol R	3-1	2-2
Burnley	3-2	0-1
Cardiff C	0-0	0-1
Crystal P	1-0	1-1
Fulham	0-1	1-1
Hull C	0-1	2-0
Luton T	0-0	1-7
Mansfield T	2-2	3-0
Millwall	0-2	1-1
Notts C	0-0	0-2
Oldham A	2-2	1-1
Orient	2-1	0-0
Sheffield U	3-0	0-1
Southampton	1-3	1-4
Stoke C	3-2	0-4
Sunderland	3-2	0-3
Tottenham H	4-1	1-2

Appearances
Abrahams L.A.M.	12/4
Berry L.D.	40/1
Brisley T.W.	15/1
Burman A.P.	5/3
Campbell D.A.	13/3
Curtis R.D.	4
Dugdale A.	30
Flanagan M.A.	32
Giles J.A.	14
Gritt S.J.	28/6
Madden L.D.	3/1
McAuley H.A.	31
O'Sullivan W.F.	1
Peacock K.	40
Penfold M.	7
Powell C.D.	32/1
Robinson M.J.	16
Shaw P.K.	6/1
Shipperley D.J.	16
Smith L.J.	1
Tydeman R.	37
Warman P.R.	37
Wood J.R.	42

Scorers
Flanagan M.A.	16
Robinson M.J.	7
Peacock K.	6
McAuley H.A.	4
Gritt S.J.	3
Powell C.D.	3
Shipperley D.J.	3
Abrahams L.A.M.	2
Berry L.D.	2
Brisley T.W.	2
Tydeman R.	2
Warman P.R.	2
Campbell D.A	1
Own goals	2
Total	55

Division 2 1978-79

	P	W	D	L	F	A	W	D	L	F	A	Pts
Crystal P	42	12	7	2	30	11	7	12	2	21	13	57
Brighton & HA	42	16	3	2	44	11	7	7	7	28	28	56
Stoke C	42	11	7	3	35	15	9	9	3	23	16	56
Sunderland	42	13	3	5	39	19	9	8	4	31	25	55
West Ham U	42	12	7	2	46	15	6	7	8	24	24	50
Notts C	42	8	10	3	23	15	6	6	9	25	45	44
Preston NE	42	7	11	3	36	23	5	7	9	23	34	42
Newcastle U	42	13	3	5	35	23	4	5	12	16	31	42
Cardiff C	42	12	5	4	34	23	4	5	12	22	47	42
Fulham	42	10	7	4	35	19	3	8	10	15	28	41
Orient	42	11	5	5	32	18	4	5	12	19	33	40
Cambridge U	42	7	10	4	22	15	6	5	10	22	37	40
Burnley	42	11	6	4	31	22	3	6	12	20	40	40
Oldham A	42	10	7	4	36	23	3	6	12	16	38	39
Wrexham	42	10	6	5	31	16	2	8	11	14	26	38
Bristol R	42	10	6	5	34	23	4	4	13	14	37	38
Leicester C	42	7	8	6	28	23	3	9	9	15	29	37
Luton T	42	11	5	5	46	24	2	5	14	14	33	36
CHARLTON A	42	6	8	7	28	28	5	5	11	32	41	35
Sheffield U	42	9	6	6	34	24	2	6	13	18	45	34
Millwall	42	7	4	10	22	29	4	6	11	20	32	32
Blackburn R	42	5	8	8	24	29	5	2	14	17	43	30

	Home	Away
Blackburn R	2-0	2-1
Brighton & HA	0-3	0-2
Bristol R	3-0	5-5
Burnley	1-1	1-2
Cambridge U	2-3	1-1
Cardiff C	1-1	4-1
Crystal P	1-1	0-1
Fulham	0-0	1-3
Leicester C	1-0	3-0
Luton T	1-2	0-3
Millwall	2-4	2-0
Newcastle U	4-1	3-5
Notts C	1-1	1-1
Oldham A	2-0	3-0
Orient	0-2	1-2
Preston NE	1-1	1-6
Sheffield U	3-1	1-2
Stoke C	1-4	2-2
Sunderland	1-2	0-1
West Ham U	0-0	0-2
Wrexham	1-1	1-1

Appearances
Berry L.D. 36/2
Booth A.J. 0/2
Brisley T.W. 29/3
Campbell D.A. 39
Churchouse G. 9
Dugdale A. 4
Flanagan M.A. 25
Gritt S.J. 38/1
Hales D.D. 20
Johns N.P. 10
Madden L.D. 37/1
Peacock K. 25/5
Penfold M. 4/2
Powell C.D. 21/7
Robinson M.J. 35
Shaw P.K. 33/1
Shipperley D.J. 33
Tydeman R. 21
Warman P.R. 11
Wood J.R. 32

Scorers
Robinson M.J. 15
Flanagan M.A. 13
Hales D.D. 8
Brisley T.W. 3
Gritt S.J. 3
Madden L.D. 3
Shipperley D.J. 3
Campbell D.A. 2
Peacock K. 2
Tydeman R. 2
Warman P.R. 2
Berry L.D. 1
Powell C.D. 1
Shaw P.K. 1
Own goal 1
Total 60

Division 2 1979-80

	P	W	D	L	F	A	W	D	L	F	A	Pts
Leicester C	42	12	5	4	32	19	9	8	4	26	19	55
Sunderland	42	16	5	0	47	13	5	7	9	22	29	54
Birmingham C	42	14	5	2	37	16	7	6	8	21	22	53
Chelsea	42	14	3	4	34	16	9	4	8	32	36	53
QPR	42	10	9	2	46	25	8	4	9	29	28	49
Luton T	42	9	10	2	36	17	7	7	7	30	28	49
West Ham U	42	13	2	6	37	21	7	5	9	17	22	47
Cambridge U	42	11	6	4	40	23	3	10	8	21	30	44
Newcastle U	42	13	6	2	35	19	2	8	11	18	30	44
Preston NE	42	8	10	3	30	23	4	9	8	26	29	43
Oldham A	42	12	5	4	30	21	4	6	11	19	32	43
Swansea C	42	13	1	7	31	20	4	8	9	17	33	43
Shrewsbury T	42	12	3	6	41	23	6	2	13	19	30	41
Orient	42	7	9	5	29	31	5	8	8	19	23	41
Cardiff C	42	11	4	6	21	16	5	4	12	20	32	40
Wrexham	42	13	2	6	26	15	3	4	14	14	34	38
Notts C	42	4	11	6	24	22	7	4	10	27	30	37
Watford	42	9	6	6	27	18	3	7	11	12	28	37
Bristol R	42	9	8	4	33	23	2	5	14	17	41	35
Fulham	42	6	4	11	19	28	5	3	13	23	46	29
Burnley	42	5	9	7	19	23	1	6	14	20	50	27
CHARLTON A	42	6	6	9	25	31	0	4	17	14	47	22

	Home	Away
Birmingham C	0-1	0-1
Bristol R	4-0	0-3
Burnley	3-3	1-1
Cambridge U	1-1	0-1
Cardiff C	3-2	1-3
Chelsea	1-2	1-3
Fulham	0-1	0-1
Leicester C	2-0	1-2
Luton T	1-4	0-3
Newcastle U	1-1	0-2
Notts C	0-0	0-0
Oldham A	2-1	3-1
Orient	0-1	1-1
Preston NE	0-3	1-1
QPR	2-2	0-4
Shrewsbury T	2-1	1-3
Sunderland	0-4	0-4
Swansea C	1-2	0-1
Watford	0-0	1-2
West Ham U	1-0	1-4
Wrexham	1-2	2-3

Appearances
Ambrose A.L. 8/1
Berry L.D. 42
Booth A.J. 2/4
Campbell D.A. 18
Churchouse G. 4/5
Dickenson K.J. 1
Gritt S.J. 31
Hales D.D. 23
Hazell A.P. 33
Jacobsen V.L. 9
Johns N.P. 34
Madden L.D. 36
Ostergaard J.B 7/1
Powell C.D. 25/6
Robinson M.J. 31/2
Shaw P.K. 25/3
Shipperley D.J. 4
Smith K.P. 4/1
Tydeman R. 33
Walker P.L. 38
Walsh P.A. 7/2
Warman P.R. 23
Wilson R. 16/1
Wood J.R. 8

Scorers
Hales D.D. 8
Gritt S.J. 7
Robinson M.J. 7
Walker P.L. 4
Shaw P.K. 3
Berry L.D. 2
Powell C.D. 2
Tydeman R. 2
Madden L.D. 1
Ostergaard J.B. 1
Smith K.P. 1
Wilson R. 1
Total 39

Division 3 1980-81

	P	W	D	L	F	A	W	D	L	F	A	Pts
Rotherham U	46	17	6	0	43	8	7	7	9	19	24	61
Barnsley	46	15	5	3	46	19	6	12	5	26	26	59
CHARLTON A	46	14	6	3	36	17	11	3	9	27	27	59
Huddersfield T	46	14	6	3	40	11	7	8	8	31	29	56
Chesterfield	46	17	4	2	42	16	6	6	11	30	32	56
Portsmouth	46	14	5	4	35	19	8	4	11	20	28	53
Plymouth A	46	14	5	4	35	18	5	9	9	21	26	52
Burnley	46	13	5	5	37	21	5	9	9	23	27	50
Brentford	46	7	9	7	30	25	7	10	6	22	24	47
Reading	46	13	5	5	39	22	5	5	13	23	40	46
Exeter C	46	9	9	5	36	30	7	4	12	26	36	45
Newport C	46	11	6	6	38	22	4	7	12	26	39	43
Fulham	46	8	7	8	28	29	7	6	10	29	35	43
Oxford U	46	7	8	8	20	24	6	9	8	19	23	43
Gillingham	46	9	8	6	23	19	3	10	10	25	39	42
Millwall	46	10	9	4	30	21	4	5	14	13	39	42
Swindon T	46	10	6	7	35	27	3	9	11	16	29	41
Chester	46	11	5	7	25	17	4	6	13	13	31	41
Carlisle U	46	8	9	6	32	29	6	4	13	24	41	41
Walsall	46	8	9	6	43	43	5	6	12	16	31	41
Sheffield U	46	12	6	5	38	20	2	6	15	27	43	40
Colchester U	46	12	7	4	35	22	2	4	17	10	43	39
Blackpool	46	5	9	9	19	28	4	5	14	26	47	32
Hull C	46	7	8	8	23	22	1	8	14	17	49	32

	Home	Away
Barnsley	1-1	0-0
Blackpool	2-1	2-0
Brentford	3-1	1-0
Burnley	2-0	1-0
Carlisle U	2-1	2-1
Chester	1-0	0-4
Chesterfield	1-0	1-0
Colchester U	1-2	0-2
Exeter C	1-0	3-4
Fulham	1-1	0-1
Gillingham	2-1	1-0
Huddersfield T	1-2	1-0
Hull C	3-2	2-0
Millwall	0-0	0-2
Newport C	3-0	2-1
Oxford U	0-0	0-1
Plymouth A	1-1	1-1
Portsmouth	1-2	0-1
Reading	4-2	3-1
Rotherham U	2-0	0-3
Sheffield U	2-0	2-3
Swindon T	0-0	3-0
Walsall	2-0	2-2

Appearances
Ambrose A.L. 2
Berry L.D. 44
Gritt S.J. 33/7
Hales D.D. 39/1
Hazell A.P. 4
Johns N.P. 37
Lazarus P. 2
Madden L.D. 27/1
Naylor T.M.P. 21/4
Ostergaard J.B. 1/3
Powell C.D. 46
Robinson M.J. 39/1
Shaw P.K. 36
Smith K.P. 24/7
Tydeman R. 43
Walker P.L. 29/8
Walsh P.A. 40
Warman P.R. 30
Wood J.R. 9

Scorers
Hales D.D. 17
Walsh P.A. 11
Robinson M.J. 10
Walker P.L. 8
Powell C.D. 6
Smith K.P. 3
Berry L.D. 2
Lazarus P. 1
Madden L.D. 1
Shaw P.K. 1
Tydeman R. 1
Warman P.R. 1
Own goal 1
Total 63

Division 2 1981-82

	P	W	D	L	F	A	W	D	L	F	A	Pts
Luton T	42	16	3	2	48	19	9	10	2	38	27	88
Watford	42	13	6	2	46	16	10	5	6	30	26	80
Norwich C	42	14	3	4	41	19	8	2	11	23	31	71
Sheffield W	42	10	8	3	31	23	10	2	9	24	28	70
QPR	42	15	4	2	40	9	6	2	13	25	34	69
Barnsley	42	13	4	4	33	14	6	6	9	26	27	67
Rotherham U	42	13	5	3	42	19	7	2	12	24	35	67
Leicester C	42	12	5	4	31	19	6	7	8	25	28	66
Newcastle U	42	14	4	3	30	14	4	4	13	22	36	62
Blackburn R	42	12	3	6	29	15	4	8	9	18	28	59
Oldham A	42	9	10	2	28	20	6	4	11	22	31	59
Chelsea	42	10	5	6	37	30	5	7	9	23	30	57
CHARLTON A	42	11	5	5	32	22	2	7	12	17	43	51
Cambridge U	42	11	4	6	31	19	2	5	14	17	34	48
Crystal P	42	9	2	10	25	26	4	7	10	9	19	48
Derby C	42	9	8	4	32	23	3	4	14	21	45	48
Grimsby T	42	5	8	8	29	30	6	5	10	24	35	46
Shrewsbury T	42	10	6	5	26	19	1	7	13	11	38	46
Bolton W	42	10	4	7	28	24	3	3	15	11	37	46
Cardiff C	42	9	2	10	28	32	3	6	12	17	29	44
Wrexham	42	9	4	8	22	22	2	7	12	18	34	44
Orient	42	6	8	7	23	24	4	1	16	13	37	39

Points system changed to three points for a win.

	Home	Away
Barnsley	2-1	0-1
Blackburn R	2-0	2-0
Bolton W	1-0	0-2
Cambridge U	0-0	0-4
Cardiff C	2-2	1-0
Chelsea	3-4	2-2
Crystal P	2-1	0-2
Derby C	2-1	1-1
Grimsby T	2-0	3-3
Leicester C	1-4	1-3
Luton T	0-0	0-3
Newcastle U	0-1	1-4
Norwich C	0-0	0-5
Oldham A	3-1	0-1
Orient	5-2	1-1
QPR	1-2	0-4
Rotherham U	1-2	1-2
Sheffield W	3-0	1-1
Shrewsbury T	1-0	1-1
Watford	1-1	2-2
Wrexham	1-0	0-1

Appearances
Ambrose A.L.	18/4
Berry L.D.	24/1
Browne S.L.	0/1
Dickenson K.J.	5/2
Elliott P.M.	36/2
Ferns P.D.	26/2
Gritt S.J.	33/1
Hales D.D.	35
Harrison S.J.	3
Johns N.P.	40
Lansdowne W.	24/3
Madden L.D.	6/1
McAllister D.	26
Mehmet D.	16
Naylor T.M.P.	42
Phillips J.T.S.	2
Phillips L.	42
Robinson M.J.	37/2
Smith K.P.	6/4
Walker P.L.	3
Walsh P.A.	38

Scorers
Walsh P.A.	13
Hales D.D.	11
Robinson M.J.	5
Lansdowne W.	4
McAllister D.	4
Gritt S.J.	3
Madden L.D.	2
Smith K.P.	2
Ambrose A.L.	1
Elliott P.M.	1
Mehmet D.	1
Phillips L.	1
Own goals	2
Total	50

Division 2 1982-83

	P	W	D	L	F	A	W	D	L	F	A	Pts
QPR	42	16	3	2	51	16	10	4	7	26	20	85
Wolverhampton W	42	14	5	2	42	16	6	10	5	26	28	75
Leicester C	42	11	4	6	36	15	9	6	6	36	29	70
Fulham	42	13	5	3	36	20	7	4	10	28	27	69
Newcastle U	42	13	6	2	43	21	5	7	9	32	32	67
Sheffield W	42	9	8	4	33	23	7	7	7	27	24	63
Oldham A	42	8	10	3	38	24	6	9	6	26	23	61
Leeds U	42	7	11	3	28	22	6	10	5	23	24	60
Shrewsbury T	42	8	9	4	20	15	7	5	9	28	33	59
Barnsley	42	9	8	4	37	28	5	7	9	20	27	57
Blackburn R	42	11	7	3	38	21	4	5	12	20	37	57
Cambridge U	42	11	7	3	26	17	2	5	14	16	43	51
Derby C	42	7	10	4	27	24	3	9	9	22	34	49
Carlisle U	42	10	6	5	44	28	2	6	13	24	42	48
Crystal P	42	11	7	3	31	17	1	5	15	12	35	48
Middlesbrough	42	8	7	6	27	29	3	8	10	19	38	48
CHARLTON A	42	11	3	7	40	31	2	6	13	23	55	48
Chelsea	42	8	8	5	31	22	3	6	12	20	39	47
Grimsby T	42	9	7	5	32	26	3	4	14	13	44	47
Rotherham U	42	6	7	8	22	29	4	8	9	23	39	45
Burnley	42	10	4	7	38	24	2	4	15	18	42	44
Bolton W	42	10	2	9	30	26	1	9	11	12	35	44

	Home	Away
Barnsley	3-2	0-0
Blackburn R	3-0	0-2
Bolton W	4-1	1-4
Burnley	2-1	1-7
Cambridge U	2-1	2-3
Carlisle U	0-0	1-4
Chelsea	5-2	1-3
Crystal P	2-1	1-1
Derby C	1-1	1-1
Fulham	3-0	1-2
Grimsby T	0-1	1-1
Leeds U	0-1	2-1
Leicester C	2-1	2-1
Middlesbrough	2-3	0-3
Newcastle U	2-0	2-4
Oldham A	4-1	2-2
QPR	1-3	1-5
Rotherham U	1-5	0-1
Sheffield W	0-3	4-5
Shrewsbury T	0-1	0-0
Wolverhampton W	3-3	0-5

Appearances
Aizlewood M.	22
Berry L.D.	39
Bullivant T.P.	30
Curtis P.A.E.	19/1
Dickenson K.J.	11/1
Elliott P.M.	25
Ferns P.D.	9/1
Gray N.R.	3
Gritt S.J.	23/4
Hales D.D.	30
Harris C.S.	42
Johns N.P.	42
Lansdowne W.	4/1
Little B.B.	2
McAllister D.	29
McDonald A.	9
Mehmet D.	13
O'Sullivan P.A.	5
Phillips L.	3
Robinson M.J.	30/2
Scott G.	2
Simonsen A.	16
Smith K.P.	15/7
Walker P.L.	10/1
White S.J.	29

Scorers
Hales D.D.	14
White S.J.	12
Simonsen A.	9
Harris C.S.	6
Robinson M.J.	4
Bullivant T.P.	3
Walker P.L.	3
McAllister D.	2
Smith K.P.	2
Aizlewood M.	1
Berry L.D.	1
Curtis P.A.E.	1
Ferns P.D.	1
Gritt S.J.	1
Little B.B.	1
Mehmet D.	1
Own goal	1
Total	63

Division 2 1983-84

	P	W	D	L	F	A	W	D	L	F	A	Pts
Chelsea	42	15	4	2	55	17	10	9	2	35	23	88
Sheffield W	42	16	4	1	47	16	10	6	5	25	28	88
Newcastle U	42	16	2	3	51	18	8	6	7	34	35	80
Manchester C	42	13	3	5	43	21	7	7	7	23	27	70
Grimsby T	42	13	6	2	36	15	6	7	8	24	32	70
Blackburn R	42	9	11	1	35	19	8	5	8	22	27	67
Carlisle U	42	10	9	2	29	13	6	7	8	19	28	64
Shrewsbury T	42	13	5	3	34	18	4	5	12	15	35	61
Brighton & HA	42	11	6	4	42	17	6	3	12	27	43	60
Leeds U	42	13	4	4	33	16	3	8	10	22	40	60
Fulham	42	9	6	6	35	24	6	6	9	25	29	57
Huddersfield T	42	8	6	7	27	20	6	9	6	29	29	57
CHARLTON A	42	13	4	4	40	26	3	5	13	13	38	57
Barnsley	42	9	6	6	33	23	6	1	14	24	30	52
Cardiff C	42	11	3	7	32	27	4	3	14	21	39	51
Portsmouth	42	8	3	10	46	32	6	4	11	27	32	49
Middlesbrough	42	9	8	4	26	18	3	5	13	15	29	49
Crystal P	42	8	5	8	18	18	4	6	11	24	34	47
Oldham A	42	10	6	5	33	27	3	2	16	14	46	47
Derby C	42	9	5	7	26	26	2	4	15	10	46	42
Swansea C	42	7	4	10	20	28	0	4	17	16	57	29
Cambridge U	42	4	7	10	20	33	0	5	16	8	44	24

	Home	Away
Barnsley	3-2	0-2
Blackburn R	2-0	1-1
Brighton & HA	2-0	0-7
Cambridge U	5-2	2-2
Cardiff C	2-0	1-2
Carlisle U	1-0	0-3
Chelsea	1-1	2-3
Crystal P	1-0	0-2
Derby C	1-0	1-0
Fulham	3-4	1-0
Grimsby T	3-3	1-2
Huddersfield T	1-2	0-0
Leeds U	2-0	0-1
Manchester C	1-0	1-0
Middlesbrough	2-0	0-1
Newcastle U	1-3	1-2
Oldham A	2-1	0-0
Portsmouth	2-1	0-4
Sheffield W	1-1	1-4
Shrewsbury T	2-4	1-1
Swansea C	2-2	0-1

Appearances
Aizlewood M.	31
Anderson D.I.	1
Berry L.D.	42
Curtis P.A.E.	23/1
Dickenson K.J.	42
Dowman S.J.	35
Flanagan M.A.	18
Gritt S.J.	33
Hales D.D.	27/2
Harris C.S.	24
Jones C.H.	17/6
Johns N.P.	36
Lange A.S.	6
Lee R.M.	10
Moore R.D.	27/1
Mountford P.	10/1
Naylor T.M.P.	6
O'Shea D.E.	9
Paye M.C.	2
Robinson M.J.	25/2
Smith K.P.	30/6
Westley S.L.M.	8

Scorers
Hales D.D.	10
Moore R.D.	8
Robinson M.J.	8
Smith K.P.	6
Lee R.M.	4
Curtis P.A.E.	3
Dowman S.J.	3
Flanagan M.A.	2
Harris C.S.	2
Jones C.H.	2
Aizlewood M.	1
Dickenson K.J.	1
Gritt S.J.	1
Mountford P.	1
Own goal	1
Total	53

Division 2
1984-85

	P	W	D	L	F	A	W	D	L	F	A	Pts
Oxford U	42	18	2	1	62	15	7	7	7	22	21	84
Birmingham C	42	12	6	3	30	15	13	1	7	29	18	82
Manchester C	42	14	4	3	42	16	7	7	7	24	24	74
Portsmouth	42	11	6	4	39	25	9	8	4	30	25	74
Blackburn R	42	14	3	4	38	15	7	7	7	28	26	73
Brighton & HA	42	13	6	2	31	11	7	6	8	23	23	72
Leeds U	42	12	7	2	37	11	7	5	9	29	32	69
Shrewsbury T	42	12	6	3	45	22	6	5	10	21	31	65
Fulham	42	13	3	5	35	26	6	5	10	33	38	65
Grimsby T	42	13	1	7	47	32	5	7	9	25	32	62
Barnsley	42	11	7	3	27	12	3	9	9	15	30	58
Wimbledon	42	9	8	4	40	29	7	2	12	31	46	58
Huddersfield T	42	9	5	7	28	29	6	5	10	24	35	55
Oldham A	42	10	4	7	27	23	5	4	12	22	44	53
Crystal P	42	8	7	6	25	27	4	5	12	21	38	48
Carlisle U	42	8	5	8	27	23	5	3	13	23	44	47
CHARLTON A	42	8	7	6	34	30	3	5	13	17	33	45
Sheffield U	42	7	6	8	31	28	3	8	10	23	38	44
Middlesbrough	42	6	8	7	22	26	4	2	15	19	31	40
Notts C	42	6	5	10	25	32	4	2	15	20	41	37
Cardiff C	42	5	5	13	24	42	4	5	12	23	37	35
Wolverhampton W	42	5	4	12	18	32	3	5	13	19	47	33

	Home	Away
Barnsley	5-3	0-1
Birmingham C	2-1	1-2
Blackburn R	1-0	0-3
Brighton & HA	0-1	1-2
Cardiff C	1-4	3-0
Carlisle U	1-1	1-1
Crystal P	1-1	1-2
Fulham	1-2	0-0
Grimsby T	4-1	1-2
Huddersfield T	2-2	1-2
Leeds U	2-3	0-1
Manchester C	1-3	1-5
Middlesbrough	1-0	0-1
Notts C	3-0	0-0
Oldham A	2-1	1-2
Oxford U	3-3	0-5
Portsmouth	2-2	1-0
Sheffield U	0-0	1-1
Shrewsbury T	1-1	1-1
Wimbledon	0-1	3-1
Wolverhampton W	1-0	0-1

Appearances

Aizlewood M.	38
Anderson D.I.	9
Berry L.D.	25/1
Curbishley L.C.	23
Curtis P.A.E.	27/1
Dickenson K.J.	13
Dowman S.J.	25/1
Duffield M.J.	1
Flanagan M.A.	38
Friar J.P.	32
Gritt S.J.	32/3
Hales D.D.	12/2
Harmsworth L.A.	3
Harris C.S.	7/3
Hodson S.P.	5
Horton D.	1
Johns N.P.	36
Kimble A.F.	6
Kimble G.L.	7/2
Lange A.S.	8
Lee R.M.	36/3
Madden D.J.	19/1
Moore R.D.	33/1
Robinson M.J.	5/1
Stannard J.D.	1
Stuart M.R.	4/2
Towner A.J.	22/4
Vaughan J.	6

Scorers

Flanagan M.A.	11
Lee R.M.	10
Hales D.D.	8
Moore R.D.	5
Aizlewood M.	3
Curbishley L.C.	2
Dowman S.J.	2
Robinson M.J.	2
Towner A.J.	2
Anderson D.I.	1
Curtis P.A.E.	1
Gritt S.J.	1
Kimble A.F.	1
Madden D.J.	1
Stuart M.R.	1
Total	51

Division 2
1985-86

	P	W	D	L	F	A	W	D	L	F	A	Pts
Norwich C	42	16	4	1	51	15	9	5	7	33	22	84
CHARLTON A	42	14	5	2	44	15	8	6	7	34	30	77
Wimbledon	42	13	6	2	38	16	8	7	6	20	21	76
Portsmouth	42	13	4	4	43	17	9	3	9	20	24	73
Crystal P	42	12	3	6	29	22	7	6	8	28	30	66
Hull C	42	11	7	3	39	19	6	6	9	26	36	64
Sheffield U	42	10	7	4	35	24	7	4	10	28	39	62
Oldham A	42	13	4	4	40	28	4	5	12	22	33	60
Millwall	42	12	3	6	39	24	5	5	11	25	41	59
Stoke C	42	8	11	2	29	16	6	4	11	19	34	57
Brighton & HA	42	10	5	6	42	30	6	3	12	22	34	56
Barnsley	42	9	6	6	29	26	5	8	8	18	24	56
Bradford C	42	14	1	6	36	24	2	5	14	15	39	54
Leeds U	42	9	7	5	37	30	5	2	14	19	26	53
Grimsby T	42	11	4	6	35	24	3	6	12	23	38	52
Huddersfield T	42	10	6	5	30	23	4	4	13	21	44	52
Shrewsbury T	42	11	5	5	29	20	3	4	14	23	44	51
Sunderland	42	10	5	6	33	29	3	6	12	14	32	50
Blackburn R	42	10	4	7	30	20	2	9	10	23	42	49
Carlisle U	42	10	2	9	30	28	3	5	13	17	43	46
Middlesbrough	42	8	6	7	26	23	3	3	14	18	30	45
Fulham	42	8	3	10	29	32	2	3	16	16	37	36

	Home	Away
Barnsley	*2-1	1-2
Blackburn R	3-0	0-0
Bradford C	1-1	2-1
Brighton & HA	2-2	5-3
Carlisle U	3-0	3-2
Crystal P	*3-1	1-2
Fulham	2-0	3-0
Grimsby T	2-0	2-2
Huddersfield T	3-0	2-0
Hull C	1-2	1-1
Leeds U	4-0	2-1
Middlesbrough	*2-0	3-1
Millwall	3-3	2-2
Norwich C	1-0	1-3
Oldham A	1-1	1-2
Portsmouth	1-2	0-1
Sheffield U	2-0	1-1
Shrewsbury T	4-1	1-2
Stoke C	*2-0	0-0
Sunderland	2-1	2-1
Wimbledon	0-0	1-3

* Games played at The Valley. Remainder played at Selhurst Park.

Appearances

Aizlewood M.	35
Berry L.D.	7
Curbishley L.C.	30
Davies A.	1
Flanagan M.A.	33/4
Friar J.P.	4
Gritt S.J.	11
Humphrey J.	39
Johns N.P.	38
Lange A.S.	4
Lee R. M.	26/9
Loveridge J.C.	5/1
Melrose J.M.	11
Pearson J.S.	42
Pender J.P.	38
Reid M.	42
Shipley G.M.	37
Stuart M.R.	21/9
Thompson S.P.	38
Towner A.J.	0/1

Scorers

Pearson J.S.	14
Stuart M.R.	12
Flanagan M.A.	11
Lee R.M.	8
Reid M.	8
Melrose J.M.	5
Curbishley L.C.	4
Shipley G.M.	4
Aizlewood M.	3
Gritt S.J.	2
Humphrey J.	2
Own goals	5
Total	78

Division 1
1986-87

	P	W	D	L	F	A	W	D	L	F	A	Pts
Everton	42	16	4	1	49	11	10	4	7	27	20	86
Liverpool	42	15	3	3	43	16	8	5	8	29	26	77
Tottenham H	42	14	3	4	40	14	7	5	9	28	29	71
Arsenal	42	12	5	4	31	12	8	5	8	27	23	70
Norwich C	42	9	10	2	27	20	8	7	6	26	31	68
Wimbledon	42	11	5	5	32	22	8	4	9	25	28	66
Luton T	42	14	5	2	29	13	4	7	10	18	32	66
Nottingham F	42	12	8	1	36	14	6	3	12	28	37	65
Watford	42	12	5	4	38	20	6	4	11	29	34	63
Coventry C	42	14	4	3	35	17	3	8	10	15	28	63
Manchester U	42	13	3	5	38	18	1	11	9	14	27	56
Southampton	42	11	5	5	44	24	3	5	13	25	44	52
Sheffield W	42	9	7	5	39	24	4	6	11	19	35	52
Chelsea	42	8	6	7	30	30	5	7	9	23	34	52
West Ham U	42	10	4	7	33	28	4	6	11	19	39	52
QPR	42	9	7	5	31	27	4	4	13	17	37	50
Newcastle U	42	10	4	7	33	29	2	7	12	14	36	47
Oxford U	42	8	8	5	30	25	3	5	13	14	44	46
CHARLTON A	42	7	7	7	26	22	4	4	13	19	33	44
Leicester C	42	9	7	5	39	24	2	2	17	15	52	42
Manchester C	42	8	6	7	28	24	0	9	12	8	33	39
Aston Villa	42	7	7	7	25	25	1	5	15	20	54	36

Charlton Athletic retained First Division place after play-offs.

	Home	Away
Arsenal	0-2	1-2
Aston Villa	3-0	0-2
Chelsea	0-0	1-0
Coventry C	1-1	1-2
Everton	3-2	1-2
Leicester C	2-0	0-1
Liverpool	0-0	0-2
Luton T	0-1	0-1
Manchester C	5-0	1-2
Manchester U	1-1	3-0
Newcastle U	1-1	3-0
Norwich C	1-2	1-1
Nottingham F	0-1	0-4
Oxford U	0-0	2-3
QPR	2-1	0-0
Sheffield W	1-1	1-1
Southampton	1-3	2-2
Tottenham H	0-2	0-1
Watford	4-3	1-4
West Ham U	2-1	3-1
Wimbledon	0-1	0-2

Play-offs
Semi-final
Ipswich T   (a) 0-0 (h) 2-1
Final
Leeds U   (h) 1-0 (a) 0-1
Replay   (*) 2-1
* At St Andrew's, Birmingham.

Appearances

Agboola R.O.F.	1
Aizlewood M.	26
Bennett M.R.	2
Bolder R.J.	26
Crooks G.A.	5/2
Curbishley L.C.	9/1
Gritt S.J.	14
Humphrey J.	39
Johns N.P.	16
Leaburn C.W.	1/2
Lee R.M.	29/4
MacDonald J.	2
Melrose J.M.	30/2
Miller P.R.	14
Milne R.	10/2
Peake A.M.	29
Pearson J.S.	10/9
Pender J.P.	1
Reid M.	42
Shipley G.M.	24
Shirtliff P.A.	33
Stuart M.R.	33/3
Thompson S.P.	34
Walsh C.D.	32/1

Scorers

Melrose J.M.	14
Stuart M.R.	9
Walsh C.D.	6
Lee R.M.	3
Shirtliff P.A.	3
Crooks G.A.	2
Shipley G.M.	2
Aizlewood M.	1
Gritt S.J.	1
Leaburn C.W.	1
Miller P.R.	1
Pearson J.S.	1
Own goal	1
Total	45

Division 1 1987-88

	P	W	D	L	F	A	W	D	L	F	A	Pts
Liverpool	40	15	5	0	49	9	11	7	2	38	15	90
Manchester U	40	14	5	1	41	17	9	7	4	30	21	81
Nottingham F	40	11	7	2	40	17	9	6	5	27	22	73
Everton	40	14	4	2	34	11	5	9	6	19	16	70
QPR	40	12	4	4	30	14	7	6	7	18	24	67
Arsenal	40	11	4	5	35	16	7	8	5	23	23	66
Wimbledon	40	8	9	3	32	20	6	6	8	26	27	57
Newcastle U	40	9	6	5	32	23	5	8	7	23	30	56
Luton T	40	11	6	3	40	21	3	5	12	17	37	53
Coventry C	40	6	8	6	23	25	7	6	7	23	28	53
Sheffield W	40	10	2	8	27	30	5	6	9	25	36	53
Southampton	40	6	8	6	27	26	6	6	8	22	27	50
Tottenham H	40	9	5	6	26	23	3	6	11	12	25	47
Norwich C	40	7	5	8	26	26	5	4	11	14	26	45
Derby C	40	6	7	7	18	17	4	6	10	17	28	43
West Ham U	40	6	9	5	23	21	3	6	11	17	31	42
CHARLTON A	40	7	7	6	23	21	2	8	10	15	31	42
Chelsea	40	7	11	2	24	17	2	4	14	26	51	42
Portsmouth	40	4	8	8	21	27	3	6	11	15	39	35
Watford	40	4	5	11	15	24	3	6	11	12	27	32
Oxford U	40	5	7	8	24	34	1	6	13	20	46	31

Chelsea also relegated after play-offs.

	Home	Away
Arsenal	0-3	0-4
Chelsea	2-2	1-1
Coventry C	2-2	0-0
Derby C	0-1	1-1
Everton	0-0	1-1
Liverpool	0-2	2-3
Luton T	1-0	0-1
Manchester U	1-3	0-0
Newcastle U	2-0	1-2
Norwich C	2-0	0-2
Nottingham F	1-2	2-2
Oxford U	0-0	1-2
Portsmouth	2-1	1-1
QPR	0-1	0-2
Sheffield W	3-1	0-2
Southampton	1-1	1-0
Tottenham H	1-1	1-0
Watford	1-0	1-2
West Ham U	3-0	1-1
Wimbledon	1-1	1-4

Appearances
Bennett M.R.	9/7
Bolder R.J.	35
Campbell D.A.	21
Crooks G.A.	24/4
Gritt S.J.	22/5
Humphrey J.	40
Johns N.P.	5
Jones A.M.	21/4
Leaburn C.W.	10/2
Lee R.M.	22/1
Mackenzie S.	30/1
Melrose J.M.	3
Miller P.R.	21/2
Milne R.	9/1
Mortimer P.H.	11/1
Peake A.M.	14/1
Pender J.P.	3
Reid M.	37
Shirtliff P.A.	36
Stuart M.R.	27/4
Thompson S.P.	23
Walsh C.D.	11
Williams P.A.	6/6

Two substitutes a match now allowed.

Scorers
Crooks G.A.	10
Jones A.M.	6
Stuart M.R.	6
Reid M.	4
Walsh C.D.	3
Lee R.M.	2
Mackenzie S.	2
Shirtliff P.A.	2
Bennett M.R.	1
Campbell D.A.	1
Miller P.R.	1
Total	38

Division 1 1988-89

	P	W	D	L	F	A	W	D	L	F	A	Pts
Arsenal	38	10	6	3	35	19	12	4	3	38	17	76
Liverpool	38	11	5	3	33	11	11	5	3	32	17	76
Nottingham F	38	8	7	4	31	16	9	6	4	33	27	64
Norwich C	38	8	7	4	23	20	9	4	6	25	25	62
Derby C	38	9	3	7	23	18	8	4	7	17	20	58
Tottenham H	38	8	6	5	31	24	7	6	6	29	22	57
Coventry C	38	9	4	6	28	23	5	9	5	19	19	55
Everton	38	10	7	2	33	18	4	5	10	17	27	54
QPR	38	9	5	5	23	16	5	6	8	20	21	53
Millwall	38	10	3	6	27	21	4	8	7	20	31	53
Manchester U	38	10	5	4	27	13	3	7	9	18	22	51
Wimbledon	38	10	3	6	30	19	4	6	9	20	27	51
Southampton	38	6	7	6	25	26	4	8	7	27	40	45
CHARLTON A	38	6	7	6	25	24	4	5	10	19	34	42
Sheffield W	38	6	6	7	21	25	4	6	9	13	26	42
Luton T	38	8	6	5	32	21	2	5	12	10	31	41
Aston Villa	38	7	6	6	25	22	2	7	10	20	34	40
Middlesbrough	38	6	7	6	28	30	3	5	11	16	31	39
West Ham U	38	3	6	10	19	30	7	2	10	18	32	38
Newcastle U	38	3	6	10	19	28	4	4	11	13	35	31

	Home	Away
Arsenal	2-3	2-2
Aston Villa	2-2	2-1
Coventry C	0-0	0-3
Derby C	3-0	0-0
Everton	1-2	2-3
Liverpool	0-3	0-2
Luton T	3-0	2-5
Manchester U	1-0	0-3
Middlesbrough	2-0	0-0
Millwall	0-3	0-1
Newcastle U	2-2	2-0
Norwich C	1-2	3-1
Nottingham F	0-2	0-4
QPR	1-1	0-1
Sheffield W	2-1	1-3
Southampton	2-2	0-2
Tottenham H	2-2	1-1
West Ham U	0-0	3-1
Wimbledon	1-0	1-1

Appearances
Bennett M.R.	11
Bolder R.J.	38
Campbell D.A.	5/8
Caton T.	13/1
Crooks G.A.	10/9
Gritt S.J.	22/3
Humphrey J.	38
Jones A.M.	2/10
Leaburn C.W.	29/6
Lee R.M.	25/6
Mackenzie S.	35/2
Miller P.R.	5
Minto S.C.	1/2
Mortimer P.H.	30/4
Pates C.G.	20/1
Peake A.M.	29/4
Reid M.	36/1
Shirtliff P.A.	33/1
Stuart M.R.	4/2
Walsh C.D.	2/8
Williams P.A.	30/3

Scorers
Williams P.A.	13
Lee R.M.	5
Mortimer P.H.	5
Jones A.M.	4
Mackenzie S.	3
Crooks G.A.	2
Gritt S.J.	2
Leaburn C.W.	2
Shirtliff P.A.	2
Caton T.	1
Humphrey J.	1
Peake A.M.	1
Reid M.	1
Own goals	2
Total	44

Division 1 1989-90

	P	W	D	L	F	A	W	D	L	F	A	Pts
Liverpool	38	13	5	1	38	15	10	5	4	40	22	79
Aston Villa	38	13	3	3	36	20	8	4	7	21	18	70
Tottenham H	38	12	1	6	35	24	7	5	7	24	23	63
Arsenal	38	14	3	2	38	11	4	5	10	16	27	62
Chelsea	38	8	7	4	31	24	8	5	6	27	26	60
Everton	38	14	3	2	40	16	3	5	11	17	30	59
Southampton	38	10	5	4	40	27	5	5	9	31	36	55
Wimbledon	38	5	8	6	22	23	8	8	3	25	17	55
Nottingham F	38	9	4	6	31	21	6	5	8	24	26	54
Norwich C	38	7	10	2	24	14	6	4	9	20	28	53
QPR	38	9	4	6	27	22	4	7	8	18	22	50
Coventry C	38	11	2	6	24	25	3	5	11	15	34	49
Manchester U	38	8	6	5	26	14	5	3	11	20	33	48
Manchester C	38	9	4	6	26	21	3	8	8	17	31	48
Crystal Palace	38	8	7	4	27	23	5	2	12	15	43	48
Derby C	38	9	1	9	29	21	4	6	9	14	19	46
Luton T	38	8	8	3	24	18	2	5	12	19	39	43
Sheffield W	38	8	6	5	21	17	3	4	12	14	34	43
CHARLTON A	38	4	6	9	18	25	3	3	13	13	32	30
Millwall	38	4	6	9	23	25	1	5	13	16	40	26

	Home	Away
Arsenal	0-0	0-1
Aston Villa	0-2	1-1
Chelsea	3-0	1-3
Coventry C	1-1	2-1
Crystal P	1-2	0-2
Derby Co	0-0	0-2
Everton	0-1	1-2
Liverpool	0-4	0-1
Luton Town	2-0	0-1
Manchester C	1-1	2-1
Manchester U	2-0	0-1
Millwall	1-1	2-2
Norwich C	0-1	0-0
Nottingham F	1-1	0-2
QPR	1-0	1-0
Sheffield W	1-2	0-3
Southampton	2-4	2-3
Tottenham H	1-3	0-3
Wimbledon	1-2	1-3

Appearances
Achampong K.	2/8
Bennett M.R.	2/4
Bolder R.J.	38
Caton T.	23/1
Ferguson I.J.H.	1
Gritt S.J.	2
Humphrey J.	38
Jones A.M.	23/2
Leaburn C.W.	8/5
Lee J.	0/1
Lee R.M.	37
Mackenzie S.	11/6
McLaughlin J.	31
Minto S.C.	20/3
Mortimer P.H.	35/1
Pates C.G.	17
Peake A.M.	36
Reid M.	30/1
Walsh C.D.	24/3
Watson G.W.G.	2/7
Williams P.A.	38

Scorers
Williams P.A.	10
Jones A.M.	6
Mortimer P.H.	5
Minto S.C.	2
Walsh C.D.	2
Bennett M.R.	1
Caton T.	1
Lee R.M.	1
Mackenzie S.	1
Own goal	2
Total	31

Division 2 1990-91

	P	W	D	L	F	A	W	D	L	F	A	Pts
Oldham A	46	17	5	1	55	21	8	8	7	28	32	88
West Ham U	46	15	6	2	41	18	9	9	5	19	16	87
Sheffield W	46	12	10	1	43	23	10	6	7	37	28	82
Notts C	46	14	4	5	45	28	9	7	7	31	27	80
Millwall	46	11	6	6	43	28	9	7	7	27	23	73
Brighton & HA	46	12	4	7	37	31	9	3	11	26	28	70
Middlesbrough	46	12	4	7	36	17	8	5	10	30	30	69
Barnsley	46	13	7	3	39	16	6	5	12	24	32	69
Bristol C	46	14	5	4	44	28	6	2	15	24	43	67
Oxford U	46	10	9	4	41	29	4	10	9	28	37	61
Newcastle U	46	8	10	5	24	22	6	7	10	25	34	59
Wolverhampton W	46	11	6	6	45	35	2	13	8	18	28	58
Bristol R	46	11	7	5	29	20	4	6	13	27	39	58
Ipswich T	46	9	8	6	32	28	4	10	9	28	40	57
Port Vale	46	10	4	9	32	24	5	8	10	24	40	57
CHARLTON A	46	8	7	8	27	25	5	10	8	30	36	56
Portsmouth	46	10	6	7	34	27	4	5	14	24	43	53
Plymouth A	46	10	10	3	36	20	2	7	14	18	48	53
Blackburn R	46	8	6	9	26	27	6	4	13	25	39	52
Watford	46	5	8	10	24	32	7	7	9	21	27	51
Swindon T	46	8	6	9	31	30	4	8	11	34	43	50
Leicester C	46	12	4	7	41	33	2	4	17	19	50	50
West Bromwich A	46	7	11	5	26	21	3	7	13	26	40	48
Hull C	46	6	10	7	35	32	4	5	14	22	53	45

Notts County also promoted with top three after play-offs

	Home	Away
Barnsley	2-1	1-1
Blackburn R	0-0	2-2
Brighton & HA	1-2	2-3
Bristol C	2-1	1-0
Bristol R	2-2	1-2
Hull C	2-1	2-2
Ipswich T	1-1	4-4
Leicester C	1-2	2-1
Middlesbrough	0-1	2-1
Millwall	0-0	1-3
Newcastle U	1-0	3-1
Notts County	3-1	2-2
Oldham A	1-1	1-1
Oxford U	3-3	1-1
Plymouth A	0-1	0-2
Port Vale	2-1	1-0
Portsmouth	2-1	1-0
Sheffield W	0-1	0-0
Swindon T	1-2	1-1
Watford	1-2	1-2
West Bromwich A	2-0	0-1
West Ham U	1-1	1-2
Wolverhampton W	1-0	0-3

Appearances
Bacon P.D.	0/1
Balmer S.M.	19/5
Bolder R.J.	39
Caton T.S.	20
Crooks G.A.	2/5
Curbishley L.C.	20/5
Dyer A.C.	34/1
Gorman P.M.	2/6
Grant K.T.	11/1
Gritt S.J.	5/5
Jones A.M.	5/2
Kernaghan A.N.	13
Leaburn C.W.	11/9
Lee R.M.	43
Mackenzie S.	15
Minto S.C.	42/1
Mortimer P.H.	32
Peake A.M.	45
Pitcher D.E.J.	42/2
Reid M.	23/1
Salako A.O.	1
Salmon M.B.	7
Walsh C.D.	10/3
Watson G.W.G.	18/4
Webster S.P.	40
Wilder C.J.	1
Wilson D.G.	6/1

Scorers
Lee R.M.	13
Dyer A.C.	7
Mortimer P.H.	7
Watson G.W.G.	7
Peake A.M.	4
Caton T.S.	3
Pitcher D.E.J.	3
Gorman P.M.	2
Grant K.T.	2
Reid M.	2
Wilson D.G.	2
Crooks G.A.	1
Leaburn C.W.	1
Mackenzie S.	1
Minto S.C.	1
Own goal	1
Total	57

Division 2 1991-92

	P	W	D	L	F	A	W	D	L	F	A	Pts
Ipswich T	46	16	3	4	42	22	8	9	6	28	28	84
Middlesbrough	46	16	5	2	37	13	8	5	10	21	28	80
Derby C	46	11	4	8	35	24	12	5	6	34	27	78
Leicester C	46	14	4	5	41	24	9	4	10	21	31	77
Cambridge U	46	10	9	4	34	19	9	8	6	31	28	74
Blackburn R	46	14	5	4	41	21	7	6	10	29	32	74
CHARLTON A	46	9	7	7	25	23	11	4	8	29	25	71
Swindon T	46	15	3	5	38	22	3	12	8	31	33	69
Portsmouth	46	15	6	2	41	12	4	6	13	24	39	69
Watford	46	9	5	9	25	23	9	6	8	26	25	65
Wolverhampton W	46	11	6	6	36	24	7	4	12	25	30	64
Southend U	46	11	5	7	37	26	6	6	11	26	37	62
Bristol R	46	11	9	3	43	29	5	5	13	17	34	62
Tranmere R	46	9	9	5	37	32	5	10	8	19	24	61
Millwall	46	10	4	9	32	32	7	6	10	32	39	61
Barnsley	46	11	4	8	27	25	5	7	11	19	32	59
Bristol C	46	10	8	5	30	24	3	7	13	25	47	54
Sunderland	46	10	8	5	36	23	4	3	16	25	42	53
Grimsby T	46	7	5	11	25	28	7	6	10	22	34	53
Newcastle U	46	8	6	9	38	30	4	5	14	28	54	52
Oxford U	46	10	6	7	39	30	3	5	15	27	43	50
Plymouth A	46	11	5	7	26	26	2	4	17	16	38	48
Brighton & HA	46	9	7	7	36	37	5	4	14	20	40	47
Port Vale	46	7	8	8	23	25	3	7	13	19	34	45

Blackburn Rovers also promoted with top two after play-offs

	Home	Away
Barnsley	1-1	0-1
Blackburn R	0-2	2-0
Brighton & HA	2-0	2-1
Bristol C	2-1	2-0
Bristol R	1-0	0-1
Cambridge U	1-2	0-1
Derby C	0-2	2-1
Grimsby T	1-3	0-1
Ipswich T	1-1	0-2
Leicester C	2-0	2-0
Middlesbrough	0-0	0-2
Millwall	1-0	0-1
Newcastle U	2-1	4-3
Oxford U	2-2	2-1
Plymouth A	0-0	2-0
Port Vale	2-0	1-1
Portsmouth	3-0	2-1
Southend U	2-0	1-1
Sunderland	1-4	2-1
Swindon T	0-0	2-1
Tranmere R	0-1	2-2
Watford	1-1	0-2
Wolverhampton W	0-2	1-1

Appearances
Bacon P.D.	11/3
Balmer	16/2
Barness A.	16/6
Bolder R.J.	46
Brown S.B.	0/1
Bumstead J.	36
Curbishley L.C.	1
Darlington J.C.M.	1/1
Dyer A.C.	3/10
Gatting S.P.	30/2
Gorman P.M.	5/3
Grant K.T.	0/4
Gritt S.J.	4/10
Hendry J.	1/4
Leaburn C.W.	37/2
Lee R.M.	39
Minto S.C.	32/1
Nelson G.P.	41
Pardew A.S.	23/1
Peake A.M.	20
Pitcher D.E.J.	46
Rosenior L.D.G.	3
Tivey M.	0/1
Walsh C.D.	42
Webster S.P.	44
Whyte D.A.	7/1
Wilder C.J.	2

Scorers
Lee R.M.	12
Leaburn C.W.	11
Nelson G.P.	6
Webster S.P.	5
Walsh C.D.	4
Gorman P.M.	3
Pardew A.S.	3
Pitcher D.E.J.	2
Whyte D.A.	2
Barness A.	1
Dyer A.C.	1
Gatting S.P.	1
Gritt S.J.	1
Hendry J.	1
Minto S.C.	1
Total	54

Division 1* 1992-93

	P	W	D	L	F	A	W	D	L	F	A	Pts
Newcastle U	46	16	6	1	58	15	13	3	7	34	23	96
West Ham U	46	16	5	2	50	17	10	5	8	31	24	88
Portsmouth	46	19	2	2	48	9	7	8	8	32	37	88
Tranmere R	46	15	4	4	48	24	8	6	9	24	32	79
Swindon T	46	15	5	3	41	23	6	8	9	33	36	76
Leicester C	46	14	5	4	43	24	8	5	10	28	40	76
Millwall	46	14	6	3	46	21	4	10	9	19	32	70
Derby C	46	11	2	10	40	33	8	7	8	28	24	66
Grimsby T	46	12	6	5	33	25	7	1	15	25	32	64
Peterborough U	46	7	11	5	30	26	9	3	11	25	37	62
Wolverhampton W	46	11	6	6	37	26	5	7	11	20	30	61
CHARLTON A	46	10	8	5	28	19	6	5	12	21	27	61
Barnsley	46	12	4	7	29	19	5	5	13	27	41	60
Oxford U	46	8	7	8	29	21	6	7	10	24	35	56
Bristol C	46	10	7	6	29	25	4	7	12	20	42	56
Watford	46	8	7	8	27	30	6	6	11	30	41	55
Notts C	46	10	6	7	33	21	2	9	12	22	49	52
Southend U	46	9	8	6	33	22	4	5	14	21	42	52
Birmingham C	46	10	4	9	30	32	3	8	12	20	40	51
Luton T	46	6	13	4	26	26	4	8	11	22	36	51
Sunderland	46	9	6	8	34	28	4	5	14	16	35	50
Brentford	46	7	6	10	28	30	6	4	13	24	41	49
Cambridge U	46	8	6	9	29	32	3	10	10	19	37	49
Bristol R	46	6	6	11	30	42	4	5	14	26	45	41

Swindon Town also promoted with top two after play-offs

*Renamed on formation of FA Premier League

	Home	Away
Barnsley	*0-0	0-1
Birmingham C	0-0	0-1
Brentford	*1-0	0-2
Bristol C	*2-1	1-2
Bristol R	4-1	2-0
Cambridge U	0-0	1-0
Derby C	*2-1	3-4
Grimsby T	3-1	0-1
Leicester C	2-0	1-3
Luton T	0-0	0-1
Millwall	0-2	0-1
Newcastle U	1-3	2-2
Notts C	*2-1	0-2
Oxford U	*1-1	1-0
Peterborough U	*0-1	1-1
Portsmouth	*1-0	0-1
Southend U	1-1	2-0
Sunderland	*0-1	2-0
Swindon T	2-0	2-2
Tranmere R	*2-2	0-0
Watford	*3-1	1-1
West Ham U	*1-1	1-0
Wolverhampton W	*0-1	1-2

*Games played back at The Valley

Appearances
Bacon P.D.	14/4
Balmer S.M.	42/3
Barness A.	5
Bolder R.J.	27
Bumstead J.	18/2
Curbishley L.C.	1
Dyer A.C.	23/7
Garland P.J.	10/3
Gatting S.P.	31/1
Gorman P.M.	5/5
Grant K.T.	11/10
Gritt S.J.	4/3
Houghton S.A.	6
Leaburn C.W.	28/11
Lee R.M.	7
Linger P.H.	0/2
Minto S.C.	34/2
Nelson G.P.	39/5
Newton S.O.	2
Pardew A.S.	29/1
Pitcher D.E.J.	40/1
Power L.M.	5
Primus L.S.	4
Robinson J.	15
Salmon M.B.	19
Sturgess P.C.	1/3
Walsh C.D.	42
Warden D.	1/2
Webster S.P.	43

Scorers
Pardew A.S.	9
Nelson G.P.	7
Dyer A.C.	6
Leaburn C.W.	5
Bumstead J.	3
Balmer S.M.	2
Gatting S.P.	2
Gorman P.M.	2
Grant K.T.	2
Pitcher D.E.J.	2
Robinson J.	2
Webster S.P.	2
Garland P.J.	1
Lee R.M.	1
Minto S.C.	1
Walsh C.D.	1
Own goal	1
Total	49

Charlton in the FA Cup

1914-15
1st Qualifying Round
Dartford (h) 0-0
Charlton forfeited home venue in first game.
Replay
Dartford (a) 1-2
A.Mitchell

1919-20
Preliminary Round
Sittingbourne (a) 2-7
Sheppard, A.Mitchell

1920-21
Preliminary Round
Catford Southend (h) 6-0
Bowen, Upex (3), C.Smith (2 - 1 penalty)
1st Qualifying Round
Margate (a) 0-0
Replay
Margate (h) 3-1
Upex, Kingsley, A.Mitchell
2nd Qualifying Round
Maidstone (h) 1-1
C.Smith
Replay
Maidstone (a) 0-2

1921-22
Charlton withdrew after election to Football League

1922-23
5th Qualifying Round
Northampton Town (h) 2-0
Thomson, Goodman
6th Qualifying Round
Darlington (h) 2-1
Cox, Goodman
Round 1
Manchester City (a) 2-1
Goodman, Whalley
Round 2
Preston North End (h) 2-0
Goodman, S.Smith
Round 3
West Bromwich Albion (h) 1-0
Goodman
Round 4
Bolton Wanderers (h) 0-1

1923-24
Round 1
Accrington Stanley (a) 0-0
Replay
Accrington Stanley (h) 1-0
Hannaford
Round 2
Wolverhampton Wanderers (h) 0-0
Replay
Wolverhampton Wanderers (a) 0-1

1924-25
5th Qualifying Round
Dulwich Hamlet (h) 4-0
Haley (2), Turnbull, S.Smith
6th Qualifying Round
Queen's Park Rangers (a) 1-1
Turnbull
Replay
Queen's Park Rangers (h) 1-2
Haley

1925-26
Round 1
Windsor & Eton (h) 4-2
Millard (3), McCrorie
Round 2
Queen's Park Rangers (a) 1-1
Own goal
Replay
Queen's Park Rangers (h) 1-0
McGinn
Round 3
Huddersfield Town (h) 0-1

1926-27
Round 1
Woking (a) 3-1
J.Rankin, Cairns, Tricker
Round 2
Bristol Rovers (a) 1-4
J.Rankin

1927-28
Round 1
Merthyr Town (a) 0-0
Replay
Merthyr Town (h) 2-1
Sherlaw, J.Horton
Round 2
Kettering Town (h) 1-1
J.Horton
Replay
Kettering (a) 2-1
Biswell (2)
Round 3
Bury (h) 1-1
Biswell
Replay
Bury (a) 3-4
W.Welsh (2), Biswell

1928-29
Round 1
Peterborough & Fletton Utd (a) 2-0
Whitlow (2)
Round 2
Northfleet United (a) 5-1
Astley (2), Whitlow (2), Own goal
Round 3
Portsmouth (a) 1-2
J.Rankin

1929-30
Round 3
Queen's Park Rangers (h) 1-1
Astley
Replay
Queen's Park Rangers (a) 3-0
Lennox, J.Horton, Astley
Round 4
Middlesbrough (a) 1-1
Pugsley
Replay
Middlesbrough (h) 1-1
Lennox
2nd Replay
Middlesbrough (at Maine Road) 0-1

1930-31
Round 3
West Bromwich Albion (a) 2-2
Wyper, Astley
Replay
West Bromwich Albion (h) 1-1
Astley

2nd Replay
West Bromwich Albion (at Villa Park) 1-3
Lennox

1931-32
Round 3
West Ham United (h) 1-2
J.Horton

1932-33
Round 3
Bolton Wanderers (h) 1-5
G.Robinson

1933-34
Round 1
Bath City (a) 0-0
Replay
Bath City (h) 3-1
Pearce, Hobbis, J.T.Smith
Round 2
Gillingham (h) 1-0
Pearce
Round 3
Port Vale (h) 2-0
Pearce, Hobbis
Round 4
Birmingham (a) 0-1

1934-35
Round 1
Exeter City (h) 2-2
Wilkinson, R.Allen
Replay
Exeter City (a) 2-5
Wilkinson, R.Allen

1935-36
Round 3
Clapton Orient (a) 0-3

1936-37
Round 3
Coventry City (a) 0-2

1937-38
Round 3
Cardiff City (h) 5-0
Boulter, T.Owens (2), G.Robinson, Own goal
Round 4
Leeds United (h) 2-1
G.Tadman (2)
5th Round
Aston Villa (h) 1-1
G.Robinson
Replay
Aston Villa (a) 2-2
R.Brown (2)
2nd Replay
Aston Villa (at Highbury) 1-4
G.Tadman

1938-39
Round 3
Cardiff City (a) 0-1

1945-46
Round 3 (1st leg)
Fulham (h) 3-1
Duffy, Fell, D.Welsh
Round 3 (2nd leg)
Fulham (a) 1-2
M.Tadman

Round 4 (1st leg)
Wolverhampton Wanderers (h) 5-2
Duffy (2), A.Turner, G.Robinson, Fell
Round 4 (2nd leg)
Wolverhampton Wanderers (a) 1-1
Own goal
Round 5 (1st leg)
Preston North End (a) 1-1
A.Turner
Round 5 (2nd leg)
Preston North End (h) 6-0
Duffy (3), A.Turner (2), Fell
Round 6 (1st leg)
Brentford (h) 6-3
R.A.J.Brown, Duffy, A.Turner (2), D.Welsh (2)
Round 6 (2nd leg)
Brentford (a) 3-1
Duffy, D.Welsh, A.Turner
Semi-final
Bolton Wanderers (at Villa Park) 2-0
Duffy (2)
Final
Derby County (at Wembley) 1-4 aet
H.Turner

1946-47
Round 3
Rochdale (h) 3-1
Lancelotte, Duffy (2)
Round 4
West Bromwich Albion (a) 2-1
Duffy, W.Robinson
Round 5
Blackburn Rovers (h) 1-0
Dawson
Round 6
Preston North End (h) 2-1
Duffy, Hurst
Semi-final
Newcastle United (at Elland Road) 4-0
Dawson, D.Welsh (2), Hurst
Final
Burnley (at Wembley) 1-0 aet
Duffy

1947-48
Round 3
Newcastle United (h) 2-1
W.Robinson, Revell
Round 4
Stockport County (h) 3-0
Revell (pen), C.Vaughan, Own goal
Round 5
Manchester United (at Leeds Road, Huddersfield) 0-2

1948-49
Round 3
Burnley (a) 1-2
O'Linn

1949-50
Round 3
Fulham (h) 2-2
Hurst (2)
Replay
Fulham (a) 2-1
D'Arcy, C.Vaughan
Round 4
Cardiff City (h) 1-1
C.Vaughan
Replay
Cardiff City (a) 0-2

1950-51
Round 3
Blackpool (h) 2-2
Revell (pen), P.Croker
Replay
Blackpool (a) 0-3

1951-52
Round 3
Luton Town (a) 0-1

1952-53
Round 3
Hull City (a) 1-3
Leary

1953-54
Round 3
Portsmouth (a) 3-3
Leary, Ayre (2)
Replay
Portsmouth (h) 2-3
Leary, Kiernan

Billy Kiernan (1949-50 to 1960-61) (above) and Bobby Ayre (1952-5 to 1957-8) (below).

1954-55
Round 3
Rochdale (a) 3-1
Kiernan, C.Hammond, Hurst

Eddie Firmani (1951-2 to 1954-5; 1963-4 to 1964-5; 1966-7 to 1967-8)

Round 4
West Bromwich Albion (a) 4-2
E.Firmani (pen), Ayre (2)
Round 5
Wolverhampton Wanderers (a) 1-4
Hewie

1955-56
Round 3
Burton Albion (h) 7-0
Leary (3), Gauld, Hurst, Kiernan (2)
Round 4
Swindon Town (h) 2-1
C.Hammond, Own goal
Round 5
Arsenal (h) 0-2

263

1956-57
Round 3
Middlesbrough (a) 1-1
J.J.Ryan
Replay
Middlesbrough (h) 2-3
Leary, Own goal

1957-58
Round 3
Huddersfield Town (a) 2-2
Summers, J.J.Ryan
Replay
Huddersfield Town (h) 1-0
J.J.Ryan
Round 4
Fulham (a) 1-1
J.J.Ryan
Replay
Fulham (h) 0-2

1958-59
Round 3
Bristol Rovers (a) 4-0
Lawrie (2), R.White, Summers

Johnny Summers (1956-7 to 1960-61. Died 1962)

Round 4
Everton (h) 2-2
Lawrie, Summers
Replay
Everton (a) 1-4 aet
Lawrie

1959-60
Round 3
Bristol City (a) 3-2
Lawrie (3)
Round 4
Wolverhampton Wanderers (a) 1-2
Summers

1960-61
Round 3
Tottenham Hotspur (a) 2-3
Leary, Lawrie

1961-62
Round 3
Scunthorpe United (h) 1-0
Kinsey
Round 4
Derby County (h) 2-1
Matthews, Kinsey
Round 5
Aston Villa (a) 1-2
Kinsey

1962-63
Round 3
Cardiff City (h) 1-0
Glover
Round 4
Chelsea (h) 0-3

1963-64
Round 3
West Ham United (a) 0-3

1964-65
Round 3
Cardiff City (a) 2-1
Haydock, M.Bailey

Mike Bailey (1960-61 to 1965-6)

Round 4
Middlesbrough (h) 1-1
Kenning
Replay
Middlesbrough (a) 1-2
Matthews

1965-66
Round 3
Preston North End (h) 2-3
Tocknell, Own goal

1966-67
Round 3
Sheffield United (h) 0-1

1967-68
Round 3
Coventry City (a) 0-3

1968-69
Round 3
Crystal Palace (h) 0-0
Replay
Crystal Palace (a) 2-0
Treacy (2)
Round 4
Arsenal (a) 0-2

1969-70
Round 3
Aston Villa (a) 1-1
Treacy
Replay
Aston Villa (h) 1-0
Gregory
Round 4
Queen's Park Rangers (h) 2-3
Riddick, Gregory

1970-71
Round 3
Hull City (a) 0-3

1971-72
Round 3
Tranmere Rovers (h) 0-0
Replay
Tranmere Rovers (a) 2-4
Treacy (2)

1972-73
Round 1
Tonbridge (a) 5-0
Flanagan, Horsfield, Peacock (2), Own goal

Keith Peacock (1962-3 to 1978-9)

Round 2
Walsall (a) 2-1
P.Davies, Horsfield
Round 3
Bolton Wanderers (a) 0-4

1973-74
Round 1
AFC Bournemouth (a) 0-1

1974-75
Round 1
Chelmsford City (a) 1-0
Horsfield
Round 2
Peterborough United (a) 0-3

1975-76
Round 3
Sheffield Wednesday (h) 2-1
Peacock, Warman
Round 4
Portsmouth (h) 1-1
R.Curtis (pen)
Replay
Portsmouth (a) 3-0
Powell, Flanagan, Hope
Round 5
Wolverhampton Wanderers (a) 0-3

Bob Curtis (1966-7 to 1977-8)

1976-77
Round 3
Blackburn Rovers (h) 1-1
Burman
Replay
Blackburn Rovers (a) 0-2

1977-78
Round 3
Notts County (h) 0-2

1978-79
Round 3
Maidstone United (h) 1-1
Flanagan
Replay
Maidstone United (a) 2-1
D.A.Campbell, M.Robinson
Round 4
Bristol Rovers (a) 0-1

1979-80
Round 3
Wrexham (a) 0-6

1980-81
Round 1
Harlow Town (a) 2-0
M.Robinson, Hales

David Campbell (1975-6 to 1979-80)

Peter Shaw (1977-8 to 1980-81)

Round 2
AFC Bournemouth (h) 2-1
P.Walsh, Hales
Round 3
Plymouth Argyle (a) 2-1
Powell, Hales
Round 4
Fulham (a) 2-1
Shaw, Hales
Round 5
Ipswich Town (a) 0-2

1981-82
Round 3
Orient (a) 0-1

1982-83
Round 3
Ipswich Town (a) 2-3
M.Robinson, Hales

1983-84
Round 3
Colchester United (a) 1-0
Own goal
Round 4
Watford (h) 0-2

1984-85
Round 3
Tottenham Hotspur (a) 1-1
Aizlewood
Replay
Tottenham Hotspur (h) 1-2
R.Moore (pen)

1985-86
Round 3
West Ham United (h) 0-1
Note: Charlton's first FA Cup tie played at Selhurst Park

1986-87
Round 3
Walsall (h) 1-2
Stuart

1987-88
Round 3
West Ham United (a) 0-2

1988-89
Round 3
Oldham Athletic (h) 2-1
Crooks, P.Williams
Round 4
Kettering Town (h) 2-1
P.Williams, R.Lee
Round 5
West Ham United (h) 0-1

1989-90
Round 3
Bradford City (h) 1-1
A.Jones
Replay
Bradford City (a) 3-0
R.Lee, P.Williams, A.Jones
Round 4
West Bromwich Albion (a) 0-1

1990-91
Round 3
Everton (h) 1-2
Dyer

1991-92
Round 3
Barnet (h) 3-1
Gatting, Leaburn, Grant
Note: Charlton's first FA Cup tie played at Upton Park
Round 4
Sheffield United (h) 0-0
Replay
Sheffield United (a) 1-3
Gatting

1992-93
Round 3
Leeds United (a) 1-1
Nelson
Replay
Leeds United (h) 1-3
Pitcher (pen)
Note: Charlton's first FA Cup tie back at The Valley .

Charlton in the Football League Cup

Variously known as Milk, Littlewoods, Rumbelows, Coca-Cola Cup

1960-61
Round 1
West Ham United (a) 1-3
Leary

1961-62
Round 1
Oldham Athletic (a) 4-1
Kinsey (2), Edwards, Leary
Round 2
Stoke City (h) 4-1
Edwards (3), Lucas
Round 3
Rochdale (a) 0-1

1962-63
Round 2
Leicester City (a) 4-4
Peacock (2), Kinsey, Lucas
Replay
Leicester City (h) 2-1
Matthews, Glover
Round 3
Bradford (a) 2-2
Kinsey, Glover
Replay
Bradford (h) 1-0
Peacock
Round 4
Leyton Orient (a) 2-3
Matthews, Peacock

1963-64
Round 2
Blackpool (a) 1-7
Kennedy

1964-65
Round 2
Middlesbrough (h) 2-1
Matthews, M.Bailey
Round 3
Leyton Orient (h) 2-1
Edwards, Own goal
Round 4
Bradford City (h) 0-1

1965-66
Round 2
Carlisle United (h) 4-1
Saunders (2), Kenning, Glover
Round 3
Peterborough United (a) 3-4
Kenning, Saunders, Matthews

1966-67
Round 2
Chelsea (a) 2-5
Saunders, Kenning

1967-68
Round 1
Luton Town (a) 1-1
A.Campbell
Replay
Luton Town (h) 1-2 aet
Tees

1968-69
Round 2
Leeds United (a) 0-1

1969-70
Round 2
Wrexham (h) 0-2

1970-71
Round 1
Southend United (h) 3-0
C.Davies, Treacy, Riddick
Round 2
West Bromwich Albion (a) 1-3
Masiello

1971-72
Round 1
Peterborough United (h) 5-1
Treacy (2), C.Davies, Endean, Bond
Round 2
Leicester City (h) 3-1
Peacock (2), Went
Round 3
Bristol Rovers (a) 1-2
Treacy

1972-73
Round 1
Northampton Town (a) 3-0
Flanagan, Horsfield, Peacock
Round 2
Mansfield Town (h) 4-3
Horsfield, R.Hunt, Flanagan, O'Kane
Round 3
Sheffield United (a) 0-0
Replay
Sheffield United (h) 2-2 aet
P.Davies, Bond
2nd Replay
Sheffield United (a) 0-1 aet

1973-74
Round 1
Brighton & Hove Albion (a) 2-1
Powell, Horsfield
Round 2
Southampton (a) 0-3

1974-75
Round 1
Peterborough United (h) 4-0
Hales, Horsfield, P.Hunt, R.Curtis (pen)

Peter Hunt (1972-3 to 1976-7)

Round 2
Manchester United (a) 1-5
P.Hunt

1975-76
Round 1 (1st leg)
Cambridge United (a) 1-1
Bowman
Round 1 (2nd leg)
Cambridge United (h) 3-0
Hope, Peacock, Giles
Round 2
Oxford United (h) 3-3
Flanagan (2), Peacock
Replay
Oxford United (a) 1-1 aet
Hales
2nd Replay
Oxford United (a) 3-2 aet
Hales (2), Bowman

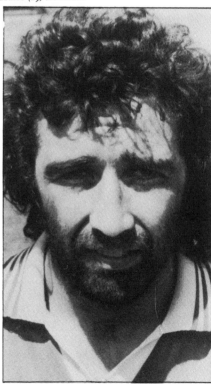
Derek Hales (1973-4 to 1976-7; 1978-9 to 1984-5)

Round 3
Queen's Park Rangers (a) 1-1
Powell
Replay
Queen's Park Rangers (h) 0-3

1976-77
Round 2
Southampton (a) 1-1
Hales
Replay
Southampton (h) 2-1
Hales, Giles
Round 3
West Ham United (h) 0-1

1977-78
Round 2
Wrexham (h) 1-2
Flanagan

1978-79
Round 1 (1st leg)
Colchester United (a) 3-2
Brisley, Hales, M.Robinson
Round 1 (2nd leg)
Colchester United (h) 0-0
Round 2
Walsall (a) 2-1
Flanagan, Peacock
Round 3
Chesterfield (a) 5-4
M.Robinson (2), Peacock (2), Flanagan
Round 4
Stoke City (h) 2-3
Shipperley (2)

1979-80
Round 1 (1st leg)
Peterborough United (a) 1-3
Walker
Round 1 (2nd leg)
Peterborough United (h) 1-1
Hales

1980-81
Round 1 (1st leg)
Brentford (a) 1-3
P.Walsh
Round 1 (2nd leg)
Brentford (h) 5-0
P.Walsh (3), Hales (2)
Round 2 (1st leg)
Carlisle United (a) 2-1
Walker, M.Robinson
Round 2 (2nd leg)
Carlisle United (h) 2-1
Walsh (2)
Round 3
West Ham United (h) 1-2
M.Robinson

1981-82
Round 1 (1st leg)
Reading (a) 2-2
Hales, Lansdowne
Round 1 (2nd leg)
Reading (h) 3-1 aet
Elliott, Hales, M.Robinson
Round 2 (1st leg)
Norwich City (a) 0-1
Round 2 (2nd leg)
Norwich City (h) 0-1

1982-83
Round 2 (1st leg)
Luton Town (a) 0-3
Round 2 (2nd leg)
Luton Town (h) 2-0
Hales (2)

1983-84
Round 1 (1st leg)
Brentford (a) 0-3
Round 1 (2nd leg)
Brentford (h) 2-1
C.Jones, Aizlewood

1984-85
Round 2 (1st leg)
Notts County (h) 0-1
Round 2 (2nd leg)
Notts County (a) 0-2

1985-86
Round 1 (1st leg)
Crystal Palace (h) 1-2
Stuart
Round 1 (2nd leg)
Crystal Palace (a) 1-1
Flanagan

1986-87
Round 2 (1st leg)
Lincoln City (h) 3-1

Stuart, Reid (pen), C.Walsh
Note: Charlton's First League Cup tie played at Selhurst Park.
Round 2 (2nd leg)
Lincoln City (a) 1-0
R.Lee
Round 3
Queen's Park Rangers (h) 1-0
Thompson
Round 4
Arsenal (a) 0-2

1987-88
Round 2 (1st leg)
Walsall (h) 3-0
Crooks (2), C.Walsh
Round 2 (2nd leg)
Walsall (a) 0-2
Round 3
Bradford City (h) 0-1

1988-89
Round 2 (1st leg)
Northampton Town (a) 1-1
P.Williams
Round 2 (2nd leg)
Northampton Town (h) 2-1
Reid (pen), A.Jones
Round 3
Queen's Park Rangers (a) 1-2
P.Williams

1989-90
Round 2 (1st leg)
Hereford United (h) 3-1
A.Jones (2), C.Walsh
Round 2 (2nd leg)
Hereford United (a) 1-0
P.Williams
Round 3
Southampton (a) 0-1

1990-91
Round 2 (1st leg)
Leyton Orient (h) 2-2
Watson, Minto
Round 2 (2nd leg)
Leyton Orient (a) 0-1

1991-92
Round 2 (1st leg)
Norwich City (h) 0-2
Note: Charlton's first League Cup tie played at Upton Park
Round 2 (2nd leg)
Norwich City (a) 0-3

1992-93
Round 2 (1st leg)
Bury (a) 0-0
Round 2 (2nd leg)
Bury (h) 0-1

Charlton in the FA Amateur Cup

1914-15
3rd Qualifying Round
Burberry's walk-over
Opponents scratched
4th Qualifying Round
City of Westminster (h) 6-0
Mills (3), Mitchell (2), Moore
Round 1
Grays Athletic (h) 1-4
Kingsley

1919-20
Round 1
Oxford City (h) 1-2
Sheppard

Charlton in the Full Members Cup

Variously known as Simod Cup and from 1989-90 as Zenith Data Systems Cup.

1985-86
Southern Group
Portsmouth (a) 1-4
Pender
Southern Group
Chelsea (h) 1-3
Pearson

1986-87
Round 2
Birmingham City (h) 3-2
Gritt, Beggs, R.Lee
Round 3
Bradford City (h) 2-0
R.Lee, C.Walsh
Round 4
Everton (a) 2-2 aet
R.Lee, P.Miller
Charlton won 6-5 on penalties
Semi-final
Norwich City (h) 2-1 aet
C.Walsh, Own goal
Final
Blackburn Rovers (at Wembley) 0-1

1987-88
Round 1
Hull City (h) 1-1 aet
C.Walsh
Charlton won 5-4 on penalties
Round 2
Leicester City (h) 1-2 aet
Own goal

1988-89
Round 1
Sunderland (h) 0-1

1989-90
Round 2
Leicester City (h) 2-1
Humphrey, Minto
Round 3
Crystal Palace (a) 0-2

1990-91
Round 2
Brighton & Hove Albion (a) 1-3
Walsh

1991-92
Round 1 Southern Section
Cambridge United (a) 1-1 aet
Gorman
Cambridge United won 4-2 on penalties

Charlton in the Anglo-Italian Cup

1992-93
Round 1
Millwall (a) 2-1
Pardew, Barness
Portsmouth (h) 1-3
Leaburn

Charlton Athletic Career Records
1921-2 to 1992-93

Below are the career records of every first-team player to have played in the three major domestic competitions for Charlton Athletic since the club joined the Football League. The dates given are the first and last seasons in which the player appeared for Charlton. Figures after 'slash' denote additional substitute appearances. Commonly-used first name is followed by the player's initials in brackets. The position is the player's normally recognized playing role and is abbreviated thus: G = Goalkeeper, HB = Half-back, CD = Central defender, S = Striker, M = Midfielder, etc. *Indicates that the player was known to have played in pre-Football League games; †indicates that the player's career was interrupted by World War Two. Games in the aborted 1939-40 season have not been included.

PLAYER	SEASONS	Posn	LEAGUE App	LEAGUE Gls	FA CUP App	FA CUP Gls	FL CUP App	FL CUP Gls
Abrahams, Lawrie (L.A.M.)	1977-8	S	12/4	2	1	0	1	0
Achampong, Kenny (K.)	1989-90	S	2/8	0	0	0	0/1	0
Agboola, Reuben (R.O.F.)	1986-7	RB	1	0	0	0	0	0
Aizlewood, Mark (M.)	1982-3 to 1986-7	M/CD	152	9	6	1	10	0
Allen, Dennis (D.J.)	1957-8 to 1960-61	CF	5	1	0	0	0	0
Allen, Henry (H.A.)	1924-5 to 1925-6	OR	38	1	5	0	0	0
Allen, Ralph (R.S.L.)	1934-5 to 1935-6	CF	52	47	2	2	0	0
Allison, Malcolm (M.A.)	1949-50	CH	2	0	0	0	0	0
Ambrose, Leroy (A.L.)	1979-80 to 1981-82	OL	28/5	1	0	0	1	0
Anderson, Darren (D.I.)	1983-4 to 1984-5	CD	10	1	0	0	0	0
Appleton, Colin (C.H.)	1966-7	LH	28	1	1	0	0	0
Armitage, George (G.H.)	1923-4 to 1929-30	CH	165	4	17	0	0	0
Arnold, John (J.W.L.)	1972-3 to 1973-4	OR	1/4	0	0/1	0	0	0
Astley, Dai (D.J.)	1927-8 to 1930-31	IR/CF	95	28	9	5	0	0
Ayre, Bobby (R.W.)	1952-3 to 1957-8	CF	109	48	6	6	0	0
Ayres, George (G.A.)	1922-3 to 1923-4	IL	33	5	3	0	0	0
Bacon, Ernest (E.F.)	1921-2	RB	5	0	0	0	0	0
Bacon, Paul (P.D.)	1990-91 to 1992-3	M	25/8	0	1	0	3	0
Bailey, Dan (D.)	1921-2	IF	33	8	0	0	0	0
Bailey, John (J.H.)	1925-6	G	4	0	0	0	0	0
Bailey, Mike (M.A.)	1960-61 to 1965-6	RH	151	20	10	1	8	1
Baker, James (J.E.)	1931-2 to 1932-3	FB	25	0	1	0	0	0
Balmer, Stuart (S.M.)	1990-1 on	CD/RB	77/10	2	2	0	2	0
Barnard, Chris (C.L.)	1971-2	M	0/1	0	0	0	0	0
Barnes, Edward (E.)	1921-2	G	21	0	0	0	0	0
Barness, Anthony (A.)	1991-2 to 1992-3	LB	21/6	1	3	0	2	0
Barron, William (W.)	1937-8	OL	3	2	0	0	0	0
Barry, Kevin (K.A.)	1952-3	OL/IL	3	0	1	0	0	0
Bartram, Sam (S.)	1934-5 to 1955-6†	G	579	0	44	0	0	0
Beach, Cyril (C.H.)	1928-9 to 1931-2	RH	29	4	2	1	0	0
Bellotti, Derek (D.C.)	1970-71 to 1971-2	G	14	0	0	0	2	0
Bennett, Mickey (M.R.)	1986-7 to 1989-90	M	24/11	2	1	0	4	0
Berry, Les (L.D.)	1975-6 to 1985-6	CD	352/6	11	17	0	19/1	0
Berry, William (W.G.)	1923-24	OL	11	2	0	0	0	0
Bethell, Roy (R.)	1927-8 to 1928-9	IL	3	0	0	0	0	0
Bicknell, Roy (R.)	1947-8 to 1948-9	CH	7	0	1	0	0	0
Biswell, George (G.W.)	1925-6 to 1933-4	IR	91	21	9	4	0	0
Black, James (J.)	1931-2 to 1932-3	IR	31	3	1	0	0	0
Blackwell, James (J.)	1932-3 to 1933-4	IR	35	7	4	1	0	0
Blott, Cyril (C.L.C.)	1937-8 to 1938-9	CF	16	4	0	0	0	0
Bolder, Bob (R.J.)	1986-7 on	G	249	0	13	0	14	0
Bolland, Gordon (G.E.)	1967-8 to 1968-9	IF	9/2	2	1	0	0	0
Bond, Dennis (D.J.T.)	1970-71 to 1972-3	M	70/5	3	5	0	6	2
Bonds, Billy (W.A.)	1964-5 to 1966-7	RB	95	1	2	0	3	0
Booth, Anthony (A.J.)	1978-9 to 1979-80	OL	2/6	0	0	0	0	0
Booth, Dennis (D.)	1966-7 to 1970-71	M	67/10	5	4	0	1	0
Borland, John (J.T.M.)	1927-8	OL	5	1	2	0	0	0
Boulter, Les (L.M.)	1932-3 to 1938-9	IL	167	28	8	1	0	0
Bowers, Alfred (A.G.W.)	1924-5	HB	5	0	0	0	0	0
Bowman, Richie (R.D.)	1972-3 to 1976-7	M	93/3	7	3	0	10/1	2
Briggs, Arthur (A.H.)	1921-2 to 1924-5	OL	9	1	0	0	0	0
Brisley, Terry (T.W.)	1977-8 to 1978-9	M	44/4	5	3	0	5	1
Brown, Henry (H.)	1929-30	OR	2	0	4	0	0	0
Brown, Robert 'Sailor' (R.A.J.)	1937-8 to 1949-50†	IR	47	21	13	3	0	0
Brown, Steve (S.B.)	1991-2 on	CD	0/1	0	0	0	0	0
Brown, Tommy (T.L.)	1948-9 to 1949-50	LH/IL	34	1	2	0	0	0
Browne, Steve (S.L.)	1981-2	OR	0/1	0	0	0	0	0
Bruck, Dietmar (D.J.)	1970-71 to 1971-2	LB	54/2	0	3	0	3	0
Bullivant, Terry (T.P.)	1982-3	M	30	3	1	0	2	0
Bumstead, John (J.)	1991-2 to 1992-3	M	54/2	3	4	0	2	0
Burkett, Jack (J.W.)	1968-9 to 1969-70	LB	8	0	0	0	0	0
Burlison, Bobby (R.L.)	1946-7	OL	1	0	0	0	0	0
Burman, Tony (A.P.)	1976-7 to 1977-8	S	16/3	3	2	1	0	0
Burns, Tony (A.J.)	1968-9 to 1969-70	CH	10	0	1	0	0	0
Burns, Les (L.G.H.)	1966-7 to 1967-8	CH	8	0	0	0	0	0
Burridge, Peter (P.J.)	1965-6 to 1966-7	HB	42/2	4	2	0	1	0
Burrill, Francis (F.)	1923-4	IR	13	4	2	0	0	0
Burton, Frank (F.J.)	1921-2 to 1924-5	RB	97	0	10	0	0	0
Butler, Charles (C.R.)	1929-30	IR	1	1	0	0	0	0
Butt, Harold (H.H.)	1933-4 to 1934-5	IL	28	8	0	0	0	0
Cairns, John (J.)	1926-7	IF	7	2	1	1	0	0
Campbell, Alan (A.J.)	1965-6 to 1970-71	M	196/2	28	8	0	8	1
Campbell, David (D.A.)	1975-6 to 1979-80	CD	71/5	3	4	1	7	0
Campbell, David (D.A.)	1987-8 to 1988-9	M	26/4	1	1/1	0	3	0
Campbell, Jimmy (J.)	1946-7 to 1957-8	RB	255	1	21	0	0	0
Cann, Syd (S.T.)	1935-6 to 1938-9	RB	15	0	0	0	0	0
Castle, Sid (S.R.)	1921-2 to 1922-3	OR	66	10	5	0	0	0
Caton, Tommy (T.)	1988-9 to 1990-1	CD	56/1	5	4	0	2	0
Chamberlain, Ken (K.R.)	1952-3 to 1956-7	CH	42	0	2	0	0	0
Champion, Ernest (E.F.)	1923-4	FB	2	0	0	0	0	0
Chipperfield, John (J.J.)	1923-4	OL/IL	3	0	0	0	0	0
Churchouse, Gary (G.)	1978-9 to 1979-80	M	13/5	0	0	0	1/1	0
Clarke, Alan (A.F.)	1971-2	G	2	0	0	0	1	0
Codd, Henry (H.)	1927-8 to 1928-9	HB	19	0	2	0	0	0
Collins, Nicholas (N.)	1926-7	OL	1	0	0	0	0	0
Cox, Keith (K.)	1956-7 to 1958-9	HB	14	0	2	0	0	0
Cox, Bill 'Moggy' (W.C.)	1921-2 to 1925-6*	CF/OR	98	18	4	1	0	0
Crawford, Ray (R.)	1968-9 to 1969-70	CF	21	7	0	0	1	0
Cripps, Harry (H.R.)	1974-5 to 1975-6	LB	17/3	4	2	0	0	0
Croker, Ted (E.A.)	1950-51	CH	8	0	0	0	0	0
Croker, Peter (P.H.)	1945-6 to 1950-51	RB	59	0	15	1	0	0
Crooks, Garth (G.A.)	1986-7 to 1990-1	S	41/15	15	3/1	1	3/1	2
Cullum, Riley (R.G.)	1949-50 to 1952-3	IR	32	6	1	0	0	0
Curbishley, Alan (L.C.)	1984-5 to 1986-7 1990-1 on	M	84/6	6	4	0	1	0
Currie, Ford (F.)	1925-6	HB	7	1	0	0	0	0
Curtis, Paul (P.A.E.)	1982-3 to 1984-5	RB	69/3	5	4	0	3/1	0
Curtis, Bob (R.D.)	1966-7 to 1977-8	RB	324/13	34	17	2	17/1	1
Dadley, Benjamin (B.J.)	1921-2*	CH	8	0	0	0	0	0
D'Arcy, James (S.D.)	1947-8 to 1950-51	CF	13	1	3	1	0	0
Darlington, Jermaine (J.C.M.)	1991-92	M	1/1	0	0	0	0	0
Davies, Alan (A.)	1985-6	M	1	0	0	0	0	0
Davies, Cyril (C.)	1970-71 to 1972-3	M	70/6	6	3	0	5	2
Davies, Frank (F.P.)	1926-7 to 1927-8	CH	25	1	6	0	0	0
Davies, James (J.)	1926-7	IL	17	0	0	0	0	0
Davies, Paul (P.)	1972-3 to 1974-5	S	51/6	9	4	1	6	1
Dawson, Tommy (T.)	1938-9 to 1946-7†	IF	23	2	6	2	0	0
Devine, John (J.)	1926-7	LB	19	0	1	0	0	0
Dickenson, Kevin (K.J.)	1979-80 to 1984-5	LB	72/3	1	2	0	5	0
Dodd, George (G.F.)	1921-2	LH	1	0	0	0	0	0
Dodgin, Bill (W.)	1934-5 to 1935-6	RH	29	0	3	0	0	0
Doherty, John (J.)	1932-3 to 1933-4	IL	8	0	0	0	0	0
Dowling, Tommy (T.P.)	1921-2 to 1923-4	RH	21	1	0	0	0	0
Dowman, Steve (S.J.)	1983-4 to 1984-5	CD	60/1	5	2/1	0	1	0
Drinkwater, Charles (C.J.)	1938-9	OL	3	0	0	0	0	0
Dudley, William (W.E.)	1923-4	CH	2	0	0	0	0	0
Duff, Willie (W.)	1956-7 to 1961-2	G	213	0	14	0	4	0
Duffield, Martin (M.J.)	1984-5	RB	1	0	0	0	0	0
Duffy, Chris (C.)	1945-6 to 1952-3	OL	162	33	21	15	0	0
Dugdale, Alan (A.)	1977-8 to 1978-9	CD	34	0	1	0	3	0
Dunn, Bertram (B.S.)	1921-2	LH	8	0	0	0	0	0
Dunn, John (J.A.)	1971-2 to 1974-5	G	104	0	7	0	7	0
Dunphy, Eamon (E.M.)	1973-4 to 1974-5	M	39/3	3	2	0	2	0
Durandt, Cliff (C.M.)	1962-3 to 1964-5	OL	36	4	0	0	0	0
Dwyer, Noel (N.M.)	1965-6	G	6	0	1	0	0	0
Dyer, Alex (A.C.)	1990-1 to 1992-3	S	60/18	14	1	1	2/1	0
Edmunds, Trevor (T.)	1931-2	CF	6	4	0	0	0	0
Edwards, Dennis (D.)	1957-8 to 1964-5	CF/IF	171	61	7	0	9	5

PLAYER	SEASONS	Posn	LEAGUE App	LEAGUE Gls	FA CUP App	FA CUP Gls	FL CUP App	FL CUP Gls
Edwards, Trevor (L.T.)	1956-7 to 1959-60	LB	64	0	2	0	0	0
Eggleton, James (J.A.)	1921-2 to 1923-4	FB/CH	26	0	2	0	0	0
Elliott, Paul (P.M.)	1981-2 to 1982-3	CD	61/2	1	1/1	0	5	1
Elliott, Matt (M.)	1988-9	CD	0	0	0	0	1	0
Ellis, Alan (A.)	1970-71 to 1972-3	M	9/5	0	0	0	0	0
Ellis, Syd (S.C.)	1953-4 to 1957-8	LB	48	0	2	0	0	0
Endean, Barry (B.)	1970-71 to 1971-2	CF	27	1	0	0	2	1
Evans, John (J.W.)	1950-51 to 1953-4	IF	90	38	1	0	0	0
Evans, Reg (R.)	1958-9 to 1959-60	CF/OL	14	2	0	0	0	0
Fell, Les (L.J.)	1945-6 to 1951-2	OR	13	2	10	3	0	0
Fenton, Benny (B.R.V.)	1946-7 to 1954-5	RH	264	22	11	0	0	0
Ferguson, Iain (I.J.H.)	1989-90	S	1	0	0	0	0	0
Ferns, Phil (P.D.)	1981-2 to 1982-3	LB	35/3	1	1	0	3/1	0
Filliston, Joe (J.W.)	1921-2 to 1923-4	CF	30	8	0	0	0	0
Firmani, Eddie (E.R.)	1951-2 to 1954-5 / 1963-4 to 1964-5 / 1966-7 to 1967-8	CF/IF	165	88	9	1	3	0
Firmani, Peter (P.W.)	1955-6 to 1958-9	RB	31	2	4	0	0	0
Flanagan, Mike (M.A.)	1971-2 to 1978-9 / 1983-4 to 1985-6	S	330/17	109	20/1	3	27	8
Foley, Theo (T.C.)	1967-8	RB	6	0	0	0	0	0
Forbes, Dudley (D.D.)	1948-9 to 1950-51	LH	57	1	3	0	0	0
Ford, Fred (F.G.L.)	1936-7 to 1937-8	HB	22	0	0	0	0	0
Forster, Derek (D.)	1973-4	G	9	0	0	0	2	0
Forster, Matt (M.)	1933-4	RB	1	0	0	0	0	0
Franklin, Mike (W.M.)	1972-3 to 1974-5	G	13	0	0	0	0	0
Friar, Paul (J.P.)	1984-5 to 1985-86	RB	36	0	2	0	3	0
Fryatt, Jim (J.E.)	1959-60	CF	5	3	0	0	0	0
Garland, Peter (P.J.)	1992-3 on	M	10/3	1	2	0	0	0
Gatting, Steve (S.P.)	1991-2 to 1992-3	CD	61/3	3	4	2	2	0
Gauld, Jimmy (J)	1955-6 to 1956-7	IL	47	21	2	1	0	0
Gibson, James (J)	1925-6 to 1926-7	CF	5	3	0	0	0	0
Gilchrist, Paul (P.A.)	1969-70	LR	5/2	0	0	0	0	0
Giles, Jimmy (J.A.)	1975-6 to 1977-8	CD	92/1	6	6	0	10	2
Gill, Eric (E.N.)	1951-2	G	1	0	0	0	0	0
Glover, Len (L.)	1962-3 to 1967-8	OL	178	20	7	1	12	3
Godfrey, Ted (E.J.)	1925-6 to 1926-7	OR	31	7	1	0	0	0
Godfrey, Peter (P.R.)	1960-61	OR	1	0	0	0	0	0
Goldthorpe, Bobby (R.J.)	1972-3 to 1975-6	CD	70/8	6	5	0	1	0
Goodman, Bert 'Kosher' (A.A.)	1921-2 to 1924-5	CF/LB	126	15	7	4	0	0
Gorman, Paul (P.M.)	1990-1 on	S	12/14	7	0/1	0	0/1	0
Gough, Charlie (C.S.)	1964-5	LH	4	0	0	0	2	0
Grant, Kim (K.T.)	1990-1 on	S	22/15	4	0/4	1	1/2	0
Gray, Nigel (N.R.)	1982-3	CD	3	0	0	0	0	0
Green, Albert (A.)	1921-2	OR	17	3	0	0	0	0
Green, George (G.H.)	1936-7 to 1938-9	LH	57	3	6	0	0	0
Green, Rodney (H.R.)	1966-7	OL	3/1	1	0	0	0	0
Green, Ronald (R.C.G.)	1936-7	OL	3	1	0	0	0	0
Gregory, Harry (G.)	1966-7 to 1970-71	OR/CF	146/3	24	8	2	3	0
Gritt, Steve (S.J.)	1977-8 to 1988-9 / 1989-90 on	M/D	335/45	25	16/2	0	22/1	0
Groves, Fred (F.W.)	1924-5	IR/OR	7	0	0	0	0	0
Hales, Derek (D.D.)	1973-4 to 1976-7 / 1978-9 to 1984-5	S	312/8	148	17	5	31	15
Haley, Bill (W.T.)	1924-5	IR	18	6	3	3	0	0
Halkyard, Cecil (C.)	1932-3	IF	1	0	0	0	0	0
Halom, Vic (V.L.)	1965-6 to 1967-8	LH	9/3	0	0	0	1	0
Halse, Harold (H.J.)	1921-2 to 1922-3	IR	21	5	0	0	0	0
Hammond, Cyril 'Squib' (C.S.)	1950-51 to 1957-8	LH	201	2	7	2	0	0
Hammond, Geoff (G.)	1976-7	LB	15/1	0	1	0	2	0
Hampson, Walker (W.)	1921-2	CH	15	0	0	0	0	0
Hannaford, Charlie (C.)	1923-4	IF	20	2	4	1	0	0
Harbidge, Charles (C.W.)	1921-2	LH	6	0	0	0	0	0
Harbot, James (J.W.)	1932-3	CF	1	1	0	0	0	0
Hardie, Alex (A.S.)	1925-6	LH	28	3	4	0	0	0
Harford, Ray (R.T.)	1965-6	FB	3	0	0	0	0	0
Harmsworth, Lee (L.A.)	1984-5	G	3	0	0	0	0	0
Harris, Carl (C.S.)	1982-3 to 1984-5	OR	73/3	8	3	0	3	0
Harris, Frank (F.)	1933-4	RH	82	8	5	0	0	0
Harrison, John (J.M.)	1975-6	OR	5	2	0	0	1	0
Harrison, Steve (S.J.)	1981-2	LB	3	0	0	0	2	0
Hart, Alan (A.M.)	1974-5	M	3	2	0	0	0	0
Hart, James (J.)	1930-31	CF	5	1	0	0	0	0
Hawkins, Thomas (T.W.)	1925-6	OL	10	1	0	0	0	0
Haydock, Frank (F.)	1963-4 to 1965-6	CH	84	4	4	1	2	0
Hayward, Keith (K.W.)	1968-9	G	1	0	0	0	0	0
Hazell, Tony (A.P.)	1979-80 to 1980-81	RB	37	0	2/1	0	0	0
Henderson, John (J.)	1962-3	CF	3	1	0	0	0	0
Hendry, John (J.)	1991-2	S	1/4	1	0	0	0	0
Herod, Baden (E.R.B.)	1921-2 to 1927	LB	213	2	23	0	0	0
Hewie, John (J.D.)	1951-2 to 1959-60 / 1960-61 to 1965-6	HB	495	37	24	1	11	0
Hince, Paul (P.F.)	1967-8 to 1968-9	OR	23	2	0	0	1	0
Hinton, Marvin (M.)	1957-8 to 1963-4	CH	131	2	5	0	9	0
Hipkin, Augustus (A.B.)	1926-7	G	1	0	0	0	0	0
Hipkin, Reg (R.W.)	1947-8	LH	2	0	0	0	0	0
Hird, Alex (A.)	1927-8 to 1930-31	RH	130	1	14	0	0	0
Hirst, Henry (H.)	1926-7	HB	4	0	0	0	0	0
Hobbins, Syd (S.G.)	1937-8 to 1946-7†	G	2	0	0	0	0	0
Hobbis, Harold (H.H.F.)	1931-2 to 1947-8†	OL	248	76	18	2	0	0
Hodson, Simeon (S.P.)	1984-5	RB	5	0	0	0	0	0
Holton, Cliff (C.C.)	1965-6	CF	18	7	0	0	0	0
Hooper, Alex (A.)	1925-6	RB	7	0	2	0	0	0
Hope, George (G.)	1975-6 to 1976-7	S	13	2	3	1	1/1	1
Horsfield, Arthur (A.)	1972-3 to 1975-6	S	139	54	7	3	10	4
Horton, Duncan (D.)	1984-5	M	1	0	0	0	0	0
Horton, Jackie (J.W.)	1926-7 to 1932-3	OL	252	53	20	4	0	0
Houghton, Scott (S.A.)	1992-93	M	6	0	0	0	0	0
Hughes, Joe (J.)	1921-2	G	19	0	0	0	0	0
Humphrey, John (J.)	1985-6 to 1989-90	RB	194	3	9	0	13	0
Hunt, Peter (P.J.)	1972-3 to 1976-7	M	138/20	6	8	0	15	2
Hunt, Bobby (R.R.)	1970-71 to 1972-3	S	34/2	11	2	0	1	1
Hurst, Gordon (G.)	1946-7 to 1957-8	OR	369	75	24	6	0	0
Hutchins, Arthur (A.V.)	1923-4	LB	21	1	0	0	0	0
Inglis, Douglas (D.G.)	1925-6	OL	2	0	0	0	0	0
Ivill, Ted (E.)	1932-3 to 1934-5	RB	35	0	2	0	0	0
Jacobs, Steve (S.D.)	1986-7	RB	0	0	0	0	1	0
Jacobsen, Viggo (V.L.)	1979-80	M	9	0	0	0	0	0
Jago, Gordon (G.H.)	1954-5 to 1961-2	CH	137	1	10	0	0	0
James, Wilf (W.)	1931-2 to 1932-3	IL	28	3	1	0	0	0
Jenkins, Peter (P.L.)	1965-6	LB	2	0	0	0	0	0
Jeppson, Hans (H.O.)	1950-51	CF	11	9	0	0	0	0
Jewhurst, Fred (F.H.)	1921-2 to 1923-4	CH	9	0	0	0	0	0
Jobling, Joe (J.)	1931-2 to 1945-6†	RH	212	5	11	0	0	0
John, Reg (R.)	1926-7	LH	8	0	0	0	0	0
Johns, Nicky (N.P.)	1978-9 to 1987-8	G	288	0	14	0	18	0
Johnson, Neil (N.J.)	1970-71	OR	1	0	0	0	0	0
Johnson, William (W.F.)	1928-9	G	10	0	1	0	0	0
Johnson, Bert (W.H.)	1945-6 to 1952-3	LH	142	1	20	0	0	0
Jones, Andy (A.M.)	1987-8 to 1990-1	S	51/15	16	4	2	4/3	3
Jones, Chris (C.H.)	1983-4	S	17/6	2	1/1	0	2	1
Jones, Fred (F.J.)	1925-6	IF	10	2	0	0	0	0
Jones, Ken (K.)	1964-5 to 1965-6	G	25	0	0	0	2	0
Jones, Mick (M.K.)	1971-2 to 1973-4	RB	58/1	0	1/1	0	7	0
Kearns, Mick (M.)	1972-3	G	4	0	0	0	0	0
Keeley Ray (R.)	1964-5	IF	1	0	0	0	1	0
Keirs, John (J.)	1965-6 to 1970-71	CH	73/5	1	3	0	4	0
Keizer, Piet (G.P.)	1931-2	G	17	0	0	0	0	0
Kelly, Gerald (G.M.)	1931-2 to 1932-3	OR	20	6	0	0	0	0
Kelly, Mike (M.L.)	1974-5	M	10	3	0	0	0	0
Kennedy, Jack (J.)	1961-2 to 1964-5	OR	46	8	3	0	5	1
Kenning, Mike (M.J.)	1962-3 to 1966-7 / 1968-9 to 1971-2	OR	212/8	55	9/1	1	8	3
Kenyon, Frank (F.)	1933-4	OR	1	0	0	0	0	0
Kernaghan, Alan (A.N.)	1990-1	CD	13	0	0	0	0	0
Kidd, George (G.I.)	1931-2	WH/CF	6	1	0	0	0	0
Kiernan, Billy (W.E.)	1949-50 to 1960-61	OL	378	89	23	4	0	0
Kimble, Alan (A.F.)	1984-5	LB	5	0	0	0	0	0
Kimble, Garry (G.L.)	1984-5	M	7/2	0	0	0	0	0
King, Ian (J.A.)	1965-6 to 1967-8	CH	63	0	1	0	3	0
Kingsley, Alf 'Scotty' (A.J.)	1921-2*	OR	20	2	0	0	0	0
Kinsey, Brian (B.R.)	1956-7 to 1970-71	LB	371/6	19	20	3	20/1	4
Kirby, Herbert (H.H.)	1925-6	IF	7	0	0	0	0	0
Kirk, Henry (H.)	1926-7	IF	8	2	0	0	0	0
Knight, Bertram (B.H.)	1922-3	OL	1	0	0	0	0	0
Knox, James (J.P.)	1930-31	IR/OR	1	0	0	0	0	0
Lancelotte, Eric (E.C.)	1937-8 to 1947-8†	IR	40	6	1	1	0	0
Lane, Harry (H.W.)	1921-2	RH	3	0	0	0	0	0
Lange, Tony (A.S.)	1983-4 to 1985-6	G	12	0	0	0	0	0
Langford, Sammy (A.E.)	1928-9 to 1931-2	LB	135	1	12	0	0	0
Lansdowne, Billy (W.)	1981-2 to 1982-3	M	28/4	4	1	0	5	1
Laraman, Peter (P.K.)	1958-9 to 1959-60	IL	3	0	0	0	0	0
Lawrie, Sam (S.)	1956-7 to 1962-3	OR	193	70	10	8	5	0
Lazarus, Paul (P.)	1980-81	S	2	1	0	0	0	0

PLAYER	SEASONS	Posn	LEAGUE App	Gls	FA CUP App	Gls	FL CUP App	Gls
Leaburn, Carl (C.W.)	1986-7 on	S	124/13	20	6/2	1	7	0
Leary, Stuart (S.E.)	1951-2 to 1961-2	CF	376	153	24	8	3	2
Lee, Jason (J.)	1989-90	M	0/1	0	0	0	0	0
Lee, Robert (R.M.)	1983-4 to 1992-3	M/S	274/24	59	14	2	14/3	1
Legge, Albert (A.F.)	1929-30	IR/CF	10	2	0	0	0	0
Lennox, Wilson (W.)	1927-8 to 1930-31	CF	71	41	7	3	0	0
Lindon, Albert (A.E.)	1927-8 to 1929-30	G	34	0	2	0	0	0
Linger, Paul (P.H.)	1992-3 on	M	0/2	0	0	0	0	0
Little, Barry (B.)	1982-3	M	2	1	0	0	0	0
Lock, Frank (F.W.)	1946-7 to 1953-4	LB	221	8	8	0	0	0
Loveridge, Jimmy (J.C.)	1985-6	M	5/1	0	0	0	1	0
Lucas, Fred (F.C.)	1955-6 to 1963-4	LH	185	29	9	0	4	2
Lumley, Tommy (I.T.)	1948-9 to 1951-2	IR	37	10	1	0	0	0
Lumley, Bobby (R.)	1953-4 to 1954-5	IF	6	0	0	0	0	0
McAllister, Don (D.)	1981-2 to 1982-3	CD	55	6	2	0	4	0
McAuley, Hugh (H.A.)	1976-7 to 1977-8	OL	55	9	3	0	1	0
McCarthy, Gerry (G.)	1956-7	CH	4	0	0	0	0	0
McCracken, Henry (H.)	1926-7	IR	1	0	0	0	0	0
McCrae Alex (A.)	1947-8 to 1948-9	IL	43	8	3	0	0	0
McCrorie Thomas (T.)	1925-6	IR	5	0	3	1	0	0
McDonald, Alan (A.)	1982-3	CD	9	0	0	0	0	0
MacDonald, John (J.)	1986-7	S	2	0	0	0	1	0
McGill, Thomas (T.)	1927-8	IR	5	0	0	0	0	0
McGinn, Hugh (H.)	1924-5 to 1925-6	CF	11	0	2	1	0	0
McGuire, John (J.)	1925-6	IF	6	0	1	0	0	0
McKay, Bobby (R.)	1930-31 to 1931-2	IF	49	8	3	0	0	0
McKee, Reg (R.)	1926-7	IF	2	0	0	0	0	0
McKenna, Tom (T.)	1927-8	G	19	0	6	0	0	0
Mackenzie, Steve (S.)	1987-8 to 1990-1	M	92	7	6/1	0	8	0
McKinley, Charles (C.A.)	1927-8	OR	23	3	4	0	0	0
McKinnon, Angus (A.)	1922-3	LH	15	0	0	0	0	0
McLaughlin, Joe (J.)	1989-90	CD	31	0	3	0	3	0
McLeod, Thomas (T.)	1930-31 to 1931-2	HB/IF	4	0	0	0	0	0
McWhirr, James (J.)	1928-9	IR/W	1	0	0	0	0	0
Madden, David (D.J.)	1984-5	M	19/1	1	2	0	2	0
Madden, Lawrie (L.D.)	1977-8 to 1981-2	CD	109/4	7	8	0	4/2	0
Mallett, Joe (J.)	1938-9	IF/HB	2	0	0	0	0	0
Marsh, Eddie (W.E.)	1950-51 to 1956-7	G	26	0	0	0	0	0
Masiello, Luciano (L.)	1969-70 to 1970-71	OL	6	0	1	0	1	1
Matthews, Roy (R.H.)	1959-60 to 1966-7	IR	160	46	8	2	13	4
Melrose, Jim (J.M.)	1985-6 to 1987-8	S	44/4	19	1	0	4	0
Mehmet, Dave (D.)	1981-2 to 1982-3	M	29	2	0	0	1	0
Middleton, Alex (A.)	1926-7	LH	5	0	1	0	0	0
Millard, Bert (E.A.)	1924-5 to 1925-6	CF/IL	38	5	4	3	0	0
Miller, Harold (H.S.)	1922-3	IL	20	11	0	0	0	0
Miller, Paul (P.R.)	1986-7 to 1988-9	CD	40/2	2	0	0	3	0
Miller, Ralph (R.E.)	1964-5	RB	8	0	0	0	3	0
Mills, Albert 'Mosky' (A.H.)	1921-2*	OL	2	0	0	0	0	0
Millsom, Ernest (E.D.)	1928-9 to 1930-31	CH	12	0	3	0	0	0
Milne, Ralph (R.)	1986-7 to 1987-8	M	19/3	0	0	0	2	0
Minnock, John (J.J.)	1969-70	W	0/1	0	0	0	0	0
Minto, Scott (S.C.)	1988-9 on	M/LB	129/9	5	2/2	0	4	1
Mitchell, Albert (A.G.)	1921-2*	IR	1	1	0	0	0	0
Mitchell, Johnny (J.E.)	1921-2*	RB	16	0	0	0	0	0
Moody, Alf (A.G.)	1921-2	OL	2	0	0	0	0	0
Moore, Graham (G.)	1967-8 to 1970-71	M	110	1	6	0	4	0
Moore, George (G.W.)	1933-4	OL	1	1	0	0	0	0
Moore, Ronnie (R.D.)	1983-4 to 1984-5	S	60/2	13	4	1	2	0
Mordey, Harold (H.V.)	1936-7 to 1938-9	LB	10	0	1	0	0	0
Morgan, Llew (L.D.)	1930-31 to 1931-2	CH	40	0	4	0	0	0
Morris, Sam (S.)	1932-3	HB	12	0	0	0	0	0
Mortimer, Paul (P.H.)	1987-8 to 1990-1	M	108/5	17	8	0	4/1	0
Mountford, Peter (P.)	1983-84	M	10/1	1	0	0	0/1	0
Mullen, Jimmy (J.)	1967-8 to 1968-9	OL	7	0	1	0	0	0
Murphy James (J.)	1926-7	LH	17	0	0	0	0	0
Myers Cliff (C.W.)	1965-6 to 1966-7	M	16/1	2	1	0	0	0
Nash Leonard (L.T.J.)	1931-2 to 1932-3	IF	3	1	0	0	0	0
Naylor, Terry (T.)	1980-81 to 1983-4	RB	69/4	0	4	0	5	0
Nelson, Garry (G.P.)	1991-2 on	S	80/5	13	5	1	3	0
Newton, Shaun (S.O.)	1992-3 on	M	2	0	0	0	0	0
Nielson, Norman (N.F.)	1949-50	LB	1	0	0	0	0	0
Oakes, James (J.)	1932-3 to 1938-9	LB	220	0	14	0	0	0
Oakes, John (J.)	1935-6 to 1946-7†	CH	130	3	15	0	0	0
O'Kane, Vince (V.)	1970-71 to 1972-3	M	29/3	1	2/1	0	3	1
O'Linn, Syd (S.)	1947-8 to 1956-7	IR/RH	187	32	7	1	0	0
Oosthuizen, Ronnie (R.)	1955-6	OL	1	0	0	0	0	0
Ord, Brian (B.R.)	1961-2 to 1962-3	LB	13	1	0	0	4	0
O'Shea, Danny (D.E.)	1983-4	RB	9	0	0	0	0	0
Ostergaard, Johnny (J.B.)	1979-80 to 1980-81	S	8/4	1	0/2	0	0	0
O'Sullivan, Peter (P.A.)	1982-3	M	5	0	0	0	1	0
O'Sullivan, Willie (W.F.)	1976-7 to 1977-8	M	1/1	0	1	0	0	0
Owens, Clifford (C.L.)	1934-5	G	0	0	2	0	0	0
Owens, Thomas (T.L.)	1937-8 to 1938-9	CF	12	5	3	2	0	0
Pardew, Alan (A.S.)	1991-2 on	M	52/2	12	3	0	2	0
Partridge, Malcolm (M.)	1971-2	S	1/1	0	0	0	0	0
Paterson, William (W.F.)	1925-6 to 1927-8	RH	93	0	9	0	0	0
Pates, Colin (C.G.)	1988-9 to 1989-90	CD	37/1	0	3	0	3	0
Pawson, Tony (H.A.)	1951-2 to 1952-3	OR	2	1	0	0	0	0
Paye, Micky (M.C.)	1983-4	RB	2	0	0	0	0	0
Peacock, Keith (K.)	1962-3 to 1978-9	OL	512/21	92	23/1	3	32/2	12
Peake, Andy (A.M.)	1986-7 to 1991-2	M	174/3	5	8	0	10	0
Pearce, Cyril (C.)	1932-3 to 1936-7	CF	68	52	7	3	0	0
Pearson, John (J.S.)	1985-6 to 1986-7	S	52/9	15	1	0	3/3	0
Pembury, Gordon (G.D.)	1951-2 to 1955-6	LH	18	1	4	0	0	0
Pender, John (J.P.)	1985-6 to 1987-8	CD	41	0	1	0	1/1	0
Penfold, Mark (M.)	1973-4 to 1978-9	RB	65/5	0	3	0	7	0
Peters, Frank (F.)	1930-31 to 1931-2	OR	29	0	0	0	0	0
Phillips, John (J.T.S.)	1981-2	G	2	0	0	0	0	0
Phillips, Leighton (L.)	1981-2 to 1982-3	CD	45	1	1	0	4	0
Phipps, Harold (H.J.)	1945-6 to 1950-51	CH	185	2	16	0	0	0
Pitcairn, Johnny (J.W.)	1930-31 to 1931-2	RH	55	0	0	0	0	0
Pitcher, Darren (D.E.J.)	1988-9 on	RB/M	128/3	7	6	1	6	0
Platt, John (J.S.)	1961-2	OR	2	0	0	0	0	0
Pleasant, George (G.)	1921-2*	G	2	0	0	0	0	0
Plum, Seth (S.L.)	1922-3 to 1923-4	LH	47	0	10	0	0	0
Plumb, Dick (R.K.)	1970-71 to 1971-2	CF	32/12	10	1/1	0	1	0
Pounder, Albert (A.W.)	1952-3	OR	1	0	0	0	0	0
Powell, Colin (C.D.)	1972-3 to 1978-9 / 1979-80 to 1980-81	OR	301/20	30	19	2	18	2
Power, Lee (L.M.)	1992-3	S	5	0	0	0	0	0
Preedy, Charlie 'Spider' (C.J.F.)	1923-4 to 1927-8	G	131	0	9	0	0	0
Primus, Linvoy (L.S.)	1992-3 on	CD	4	0	0	0	1	0
Prior, Stan (S.J.)	1933-4 to 1936-7	CF	50	32	1	0	0	0
Pritchard, Thomas (T.F.)	1929-30 to 1931-2	CH	43	0	1	0	0	0
Pugsley, Jack (J.)	1928-9 to 1933-4	LH	214	7	10	1	0	0
Purdy, Albert (A.)	1921-2 to 1924-5*	RH	99	0	11	0	0	0
Purves, Charlie (C.R.)	1946-7 to 1949-50	IF	46	4	2	0	0	0
Rankin, Johnnie (J.P.)	1925-6 to 1929-30	IL	187	34	17	2	0	0
Rankin, Willie (W.)	1931-2 to 1932-3	CH	26	0	0	0	0	0
Reed, Alfred (A.G.)	1933-4	CH	1	0	0	0	0	0
Reed, Frank (F.N.)	1955-6 to 1962-3	G	29	0	1	0	0	0
Rees, Edwin (E.)	1922-3 to 1924-5	IF	63	14	1	0	0	0
Reeves, Peter (P.J.)	1965-6 to 1973-4	LH	263/5	2	12/1	0	13	0
Reid, Mark (M.)	1985-6 to 1990-1	LB	209/2	15	6	0	16	2
Revell, Charlie (C.)	1945-6 to 1950-51	HB/CF	104	15	13	3	0	0
Richards, Albert (A.C.)	1923-4 to 1924-5	IL/OR	20	3	0	0	0	0
Riddick, Gordon (G.G.)	1969-70 to 1970-71	CF	26/3	5	3	1	2	1
Rist, Frank (F.H.)	1934-5 to 1946-7†	CH	47	1	2	0	0	0
Robertson, Peter (P.)	1929-30 to 1932-3	G	117	0	9	0	0	0
Robinson, George (G.H.)	1931-2 to 1946-7†	IR	238	42	16	3	0	0
Robinson, John (J.)	1992-3 on	M	15	2	2	0	0	0
Robinson, Martin (M.J.)	1977-8 to 1984-5	S	218/10	58	8/1	3	16/3	6
Robinson, Bill (W.)	1946-7 to 1948-9	CF	53	16	8	2	0	0
Rogers, Eamonn (E.)	1971-2 to 1972-3	M	37/2	3	2	0	1/1	0
Rose, Mick (M.J.)	1963-4 to 1966-7	G	75	0	4	0	5	0
Rosenior, Leroy (L.D.G.)	1991-2	S	3	0	0	0	0	0
Ryan, John 'Buck' (J.J.)	1954-5 to 1958-9	CF	61	32	7	4	0	0
Ryan, Jim (J.P.)	1962-3 to 1964-5	CF	16	8	0	0	1	0
Salako, Andy (A.O.)	1990-1	RB	1	0	0	0	1	0
Salmon, Mike (M.B.)	1989-90 on	G	26	0	1	0	1	0
Saunders, Fred (J.H.)	1962-3	OR	1	0	0	0	0	0
Saunders, Ron (R.)	1965-6 to 1966-7	CF	64/1	24	1/1	0	3	4
Scott, Geoff (G.)	1982-3	CD	2	0	0	0	0	0
Scott, James (J.)	1926-7	LB	1	0	0	0	0	0
Searle, Frank (F.B.)	1928-9 to 1932-3	RH	66	2	4	0	0	0
Semple, John (J.)	1925-6	LB	2	0	0	0	0	0
Setters, Maurice (M.E.)	1969-70	CD	8	1	0	0	0	0
Sewell, John (J.D.)	1956-7 to 1963-4	RB	185	5	9	0	10	0
Shaw, Peter (P.K.)	1977-8 to 1980-81	CD	100/5	5	8	1	9	0
Sherlaw, David (D.D.)	1926-7 to 1928-9	W/CF	78	32	7	1	0	0
Shipley, George (G.M.)	1985-6 to 1986-7	M	61	6	1	0	4	0
Shipperley, David (D.J.)	1970-71 to 1973-4 / 1977-8 to 1979-80	CD	145/8	14	10	0	11/1	0
Shirtliff, Peter (P.A.)	1986-7 to 1988-9	CD	102/1	7	5	0	10	0

PLAYER	SEASONS	Posn	LEAGUE App	LEAGUE Gls	FA CUP App	FA CUP Gls	FL CUP App	FL CUP Gls
Shreeve, Jack (J.T.T.)	1936-7 to 1950-51†	RB	145	0	20	0	0	0
Simonsen, Allan (A.)	1982-3	M	16	9	1	0	0	0
Slack, Sam (S.)	1928-9	LB	3	0	0	0	0	0
Sloan, Andrew (A.S.)	1924-5	CF	1	0	0	0	0	0
Smart, Roger (R.W.)	1973-4	M	30/1	1	1	0	2	0
Smith, Cyril (C.)	1921-2*	IL	7	0	0	0	0	0
Smith, George (G.C.)	1938-9	CF	1	0	0	0	0	0
Smith, Trevor (J.T.)	1933-4 to 1934-5	OR/IR	23	6	4	1	0	0
Smith, Kevin (K.P.)	1979-80 to 1983-4	M	79/25	14	2/1	0	7	0
Smith, Lindsay (L.J.)	1977-8	CD	1	0	0	0	1	0
Smith, Norman (N.)	1922-3 to 1935-6	RB	417	16	32	0	0	0
Smith, Steve (S.C.)	1922-3 to 1924-5	OL	90	8	12	2	0	0
Snedden, John (J.D.)	1964-5 to 1965-6	RH	18/2	0	0	0	1	0
Stacey, Steve (S.D.)	1969-70	CD	1	1	0	0	0	0
Stannard, Jim (J.D.)	1984-5	G	1	0	0	0	0	0
Steele, Alex (A.)	1921-2 to 1925-6	LH/IL	132	26	14	0	0	0
Steele, Herbert (H.G.)	1925-6	OL	3	0	0	0	0	0
Stenson, John (J.A.)	1967-8 to 1968-9	M	3/8	0	0	0	0	0
Stephenson, George (G.T.)	1934-5 to 1936-7	IF	50	12	2	0	0	0
Stewart, Mickey (M.J.)	1956-7 to 1958-9	IF	9	3	2	0	0	0
Stocks, David (D.H.)	1961-2 to 1964-5	LB	26	0	2	0	2	0
Stuart, Mark (M.R.)	1984-5 to 1988-9	M	89/18	28	1	1	7/3	2
Sturgess, Paul (P.C.)	1992-3 on	LB	1/3	0	0	0	0	0
Summers, Johnny (J.H.)	1956-7 to 1960-61	CF/OL	171	100	10	4	1	0
Surman, Les (L.)	1965-6	G	1	0	0	0	0	0
Sweeney, Edwin (E.)	1930-31	IL	9	4	0	0	0	0
Tadman, George (G.H.)	1936-7 to 1938-9	CF	87	46	6	3	0	0
Tadman, Maurice (M.R.)	1945-6 to 1946-7	CF	3	0	1	1	0	0
Tann, Bert (B.J.)	1933-4 to 1938-9	HB	19	2	0	0	0	0
Tees, Matt (M.)	1966-7 to 1969-70	CF	88/1	32	4	0	2	1
Terry, Pat (P.A.)	1953-4 to 1954-5	CF	4	1	0	0	0	0
Thompson, Jimmy (J.W.)	1921-2	CF	2	0	0	0	0	0
Thompson, Steve (S.P.)	1985-6 to 1987-8	CD	95	0	3	0	6	1
Thomson, Bobbie (R.J.)	1921-2 to 1924-5	CF	70	15	12	2	0	0
Thornett, Charles (C.W.)	1928-9	G	4	0	0	0	0	0
Tivey, Mark (M.)	1991-2	S	0/1	0	0	0	0	0
Tocknell, Brian (B.T.)	1960-61 to 1965-6	CH/LH	199	14	11	1	10	0
Towner, Tony (A.J.)	1984-5 to 1985-6	OR	22/5	2	1	0	2	0
Townsend, Don (D.E.)	1954-5 to 1961-2	LB	249	1	17	0	2	0
Trayler, Fred (F.C.)	1924-5	IF	6	0	0	0	0	0
Treacy, Ray (R.C.P.)	1967-8 to 1971-2	IR	144/5	43	7/1	5	7	4
Tricker, Reg (R.W.)	1925-6 to 1926-7	CF	41	17	2	1	0	0
Tucker, Keith (K.)	1954-5 to 1960-61	LB	3	0	0	0	0	0
Tumbridge, Ray (R.A.)	1972-3 to 1974-5	LB	43/3	0	1	0	1	0
Turnbull, Bobby (R.)	1924-5	CF	6	2	3	2	0	0
Turner, Arthur (A.A.)	1945-6	CF	0	0	9	7	0	0
Turner, Bert (H.G.)	1933-4 to 1946-7†	RB	176	3	20	1	0	0
Tutt, Graham (G.C.)	1973-4 to 1975-6	G	65	0	6	0	7	0
Tydeman, Dick (R.)	1976-7 to 1980-81	M	158	7	7	0	13	0
Ufton, Derek (D.G.)	1949-50 to 1959-60	CH	263	0	14	0	0	0
Upex, Dick (D.)	1921-2*	CF	3	0	0	0	0	0
Uytenbogaardt, Albert (A.G.)	1948-9 to 1952-3	G	6	0	0	0	0	0
Vanner, Harry (H.J.)	1924-5	OR	2	0	0	0	0	0
Vaughan, Charlie (C.J.)	1946-7 to 1952-3	CF	226	91	11	3	0	0
Vaughan, John (J.)	1984-5	G	6	0	0	0	0	0
Vickers, John (J.)	1932-3	FB	10	0	0	0	0	0
Vitty, Jack (J.)	1948-9	LB	2	0	0	0	0	0
Wakeham, Peter (P.F.)	1962-3 to 1964-5	G	55	0	2	0	5	0
Walker Mike, (M.S.G.)	1972-3	G	1	0	0	0	0	0
Walker, Phil (P.L.)	1979-80 to 1982-3	M	80/9	15	6	0	5/2	2
Walls, Jimmy (J.P.)	1949-50 to 1952-3	CH	10	0	1	0	0	0
Walsh, Colin (C.D.)	1986-7 on	M	163/10	16	9	0	11	3
Walsh, Paul (P.A.)	1979-80 to 1981-2	S	85/2	24	4	1	9	6
Walsh, William (W.)	1923-4	IF	9	2	0	0	0	0
Warden, Danny (D.)	1992-3	M	1/2	0	0	0	1	0
Warman, Phil (P.R.)	1969-70 to 1980-81	LB	313/3	19	16/1	1	31	0
Watkins, Ted (E.T.)	1931-2	CF	15	6	1	0	0	0
Watson, George (G.S.)	1929-30	OR	14	2	1	0	0	0
Watson, Gordon (G.W.G.)	1989-90 to 1990-1	S	20/11	7	0/1	0	2	1
Webster, Simon (S.P.)	1990-1 to 1992-3	CD	127	7	6	0	6	0
Welsh, Don (D.)	1934-5 to 1947-8†	LH/IF	199	44	17	7	0	0
Welsh, Billy (W.)	1927-8 to 1928-9	IF	28	7	1	2	0	0
Went, Paul (P.F.)	1967-8 to 1971-2	CH	160/3	15	7	0	7/1	0
Werge, Eddie (E.)	1957-8 to 1960-61	OL	44	19	0	0	1	0
Westley, Shane (S.L.M.)	1983-4	CD	8	0	1	0	0	0
Whalley, Arthur (A.)	1921-2 to 1923-4	CH	88	8	10	1	0	0
Whewell, William (W.T.)	1929-30	CH	4	0	0	0	0	0
White, Ronnie (R.T.)	1953-4 to 1961-2	IL	165	8	14	1	2	0
White, Steve (S.J.)	1982-3	S	29	12	0	0	2	0
Whitehouse, Brian (B.)	1965-6	HB	13	1	0	0	0	0
Whitlow, Fred (F.W.J.)	1927-8 to 1930-31	CF/IR	96	60	5	4	0	0
Whittaker, Billy (W.P.)	1946-7 to 1948-9	LH	28	0	1	0	0	0
Whyte, David (D.A.)	1991-2	S	7/1	2	0	0	0	0
Wilder, Chris (C.J.)	1990-1 to 1991-2	RB	3	0	0	0	0	0
Wilkinson, Monty (J.M.)	1932-3 to 1938-9	OR	224	48	11	2	0	0
Williams, Leonard (L.S.)	1936-7 to 1937-8	OL	3	0	0	0	0	0
Williams, Paul (P.A.)	1987-8 to 1989-90	S	74/8	23	6/1	3	6	3
Williams, Tommy (T.H.)	1923-4	IF	5	2	0	0	0	0
Willis, Ron (R.I)	1967-8	G	1	0	0	0	0	0
Wilson, David (D.G.)	1990-1	M	6/1	2	0	0	0	0
Wilson, Harry (H.)	1921-2	OL/IF	24	1	0	0	0	0
Wilson, Richard (R.)	1979-80	S	16/1	1	0	0	0	0
Wilson, Tommy (T.H.)	1924-5 to 1925-6 1931-2	RH	33	4	1	0	0	0
Winter, Percy (P.)	1924-5 to 1925-6	OR	6	0	0	0	0	0
Wolfe, Tom (T.H.)	1927-8 to 1928-9	HB	10	0	2	0	0	0
Wood, Alex (A.)	1929-30	IL	1	0	0	0	0	0
Wood, Alan (A.E.)	1972-3	CD	1	0	0	0	0	0
Wood, Freddy (F.R.)	1922-3 to 1924-5	G	92	0	10	0	0	0
Wood, Jeff (J.G.)	1975-6 to 1980-81	G	147	0	5	0	14	0
Woodley, Derek (D.G.)	1967-8	OR	2/1	0	0	0	1	0
Worley, Len (L.F.)	1956-7	OL	1	0	0	0	0	0
Wright, Alex (A.)	1932-3 to 1934-5	G	64	0	2	0	0	0
Wright, Charlie (C.G.)	1965-6 to 1970-71	G	195	0	8	0	6	0
Wright, Harry (H.E.)	1932-3 to 1935-6	G	38	0	4	0	0	0
Wright, Bob (R.C.A.)	1938-9 to 1946-7†	HB	28	0	0	0	0	0
Wyper, Harry (H.T.H.)	1928-9 to 1930-31	W	82	12	6	1	0	0
Yardley, Jimmy (J.)	1931-2 to 1933-4	CF	51	26	1	0	0	0
Young, David (D.)	1974-5 to 1976-7	CD	76/1	0	3	0	7	0
Young, Tony (T.A.)	1975-6 to 1976-7	M	20	1	0/1	0	2	0
Opponents' own-goals				89		9		1

1987 First/Second Division Play-Offs

Bob Bolder 5, Garth Crooks 5, Steve Gritt 5, John Humphrey 4, Carl Leaburn 0/1, Robert Lee 2, Jim Melrose 5 (gls 3), Paul Miller 5, Ralph Milne 0/2, Andy Peake 5, Mark Reid 5, Steve Thompson 3, George Shipley 1, Peter Shirtliff 2 (gls 2), Mark Stuart 3/1, Colin Walsh 5.

Full Members (SIMOD/ZDS) Cup 1985-86 to 1991-92

Kenny Achampong 2, Mark Aizlewood 2, Paul Bacon 2, Stuart Balmer 1, Anthony Barness 1, Billy Beggs 1 (gl 1), Mickey Bennett 6/1, Les Berry 1, Bob Bolder 11, John Bumstead 1, David Campbell 2, Tommy Caton 1, Garth Crooks 2, Alan Curbishley 2, Alex Dyer 2, Mike Flanagan 1, Paul Friar 0/1, Steve Gatting, Paul Gorman 1 (gl 1), Kim Grant 0/1, Steve Gritt 6/1 (gl 1), John Humphrey 11 (gl 1), Andy Jones 2, Nicky Johns 2, Tony Lange 1, Carl Leaburn 1/2, Jason Lee 0/2, Robert Lee 7/2 (gls 3), Jimmy Loveridge 1, John MacDonald 0/1, Steve Mackenzie 2, Ronnie Mauge 0/1, Jim Melrose 3/1, Paul Miller 4 (gl 1), Ralph Milne 2, Scott Minto 4 (gl 1), Paul Mortimer 3/1, Garry Nelson 1, Andy Peake 9/1, John Pearson 4 (gl 1), John Pender 2 (gl 1), Darren Pitcher 2, Mark Reid 12, Andy Salako 0/1, George Shipley 7, Peter Shirtliff 5, Marcus Smart 1, Mark Stuart 6/1, Steve Thompson 5, Tony Towner 2, Colin Walsh 8 (gls 3), Gordon Watson 1/1, Simon Webster 2. (Own goals 2)

Anglo-Italian Cup 1992-93

Paul Bacon 1, Stuart Balmer 2, Anthony Barness 0/1 (gl 1), Bob Bolder 2, John Bumstead 1, Alex Dyer 1/1, Steve Gatting 2, Carl Leaburn 1/1 (gl 1), Robert Lee 1, Scott Minto 2, Garry Nelson 2, Alan Pardew 2 (gl 1), Darren Pitcher 1, John Robinson 1, Colin Walsh 2, Simon Webster 1.

Bibliography

Charlton Athletic, by Anthony Bristowe, Convoy Publications, 1949

The Jimmy Seed Story, Sportsmans Book Club, 1958

Soccer from the Inside, by Jimmy Seed, Thorsons Publishers, 1947

Sam Bartram, Burke Publishing Company, 1956

Football with the Millionaires, by Eddie Firmani, The Sportsmans Book Club, 1960

Football in London, by David Prole, Sportsman's Book Club, 1965

Let's talk about Charlton Athletic, by Tom Morgan, Sentinel Publications, 1946

The Giant Killers, by Bryon Butler, 1982, Pelham Books

Charlton Athletic 75th Anniversary Handbook, Season 1980-81

Charlton Athletic League Golden Jubilee Handbook 1921-1971

Charlton Athletic Jubilee Handbook 1905-1955

History of Charlton Athletic FC, 1903-1937, by Charltonian, 1937

History and High Lights of Charlton Athletic FC (1903-46), by Chas. Cooper, 1946

Charlton Athletic Handbook (1927-28, 1930-31, 1931-32, 1932-33, 1949-50, 1951-52, 1952-53, 1953-54, 1954-55, 1967-68)

Victory was the Goal, Soccer's contribution to the war of 1939-45, Football Association, 1945

Soccer at War, 1939-45, by Jack Rollin, Queen Anne Press, Macdonald 1985

The Datasport Book of Wartime Football 1939-46, by Gordon Andrews, Gardenia Books, 1989

The Goalscorers, by Tony Pawson, Cassell, 1978

Football Grounds of England and Wales, by Simon Inglis, Willow Books, Collins, 1983 (later revised as Football Grounds of Great Britain)

Winners and Champions, The Story of Manchester United's 1948 FA Cup and 1952 Championship winning teams, Alec Shorrocks, 1985, Arthur Barker Ltd.

Alan Mullery, An Autobiography, Pelham Books, 1985

The People's Game, by James Walvin, Allen Lane, 1975.

A Little Thing Called Pride, by Alec Stock, Pelham Books, 1982

The Book of Football Quotations, by Peter Ball and Phil Shaw, Stanley Paul, 1984

The First Voice You Will Hear is..., by Ted Croker, Willow Books, Collins, 1987

The Encyclopedia of Association Football, by Maurice Golesworthy; Robert Hale, London, 1976

Soccer in the Dock, by Simon Inglis, Willow Books, Collins, 1985

League Football and the men who made it, The Official Centenary History of the Football League, by Simon Inglis, Willow Books, Collins, 1988

The Football League 1888-1988, The Official Illustrated History, by Bryon Butler, Queen Anne Press, Macdonald, 1987

Bonzo, An Autobiography, by Billy Bonds, Arthur Barker/Weidenfeld, 1988.

The Valiant 500, written and published by Colin Cameron, 1991.

Battle for The Valley, by Rick Everitt, Voice of The Valley, 1991.

Home & Away with Charlton Athletic 1920-1992, written and published by Colin Cameron, 1992.